Maxim Litvinov
a biography

John Holroyd-Doveton

New Generation Publishing

CONTENTS

1: FROM BELOSTOCK TO LONDON 1

2: A BOLSHEVIK AMBASSADOR 17

3: THE OSTRACISED STATE 38

4: ACCEPTANCE OF BOLSHEVIK RUSSIA 61

5: CHICHERIN AND TROTSKY 81

6: DISARMAMENT 139

7: CHINA AND JAPAN 140

8: LITVINOV'S SUCCESSES WITH FRANCE, POLAND AND GERMANY 166

9: LITVINOV, COMINTERN AND BRITAIN 195

PHOTOGRAPHS 231

10: THE DEPRESSION AND LITVINOV THE ECONOMIST 237

11: THE USA 257

12: THE LEAGUE OF NATIONS 276

13 LITVINOV'S EFFORTS TO PREVENT A SECOND WORLD WAR.............. 305

14: THE FALL 351

15: SOVIET ALLIES, SPAIN AND CHINA 351

16: INTERNAL POLICY 405

17: WAR 427

18: RETIREMENT AT LAST 460

19: CONCLUSION 472

EXPLANATIONS 508

PRIMARY SOURCES 509

SECONDARY SOURCES 511

INDEX 522

This book is dedicated to the whole Litvinov family who under a dictatorship of the most vicious kind kept alive the breath of freedom.

Note for Second edition

The first edition was prepared in haste in order to be ready for a trip to be taken by the author to Russia.

The second edition has provided the opportunity to make a number of improvements   and corrections.

1: FROM BELOSTOCK TO LONDON

Maxim Wallach was born on 17th July 1876 in Belostock in Russia, near the pre-1914 Prussian border, to Jewish parents.[1] His father Moses Wallach was a produce merchant, but had become bankrupt after the business failed. He was then employed by the local bank. Moses Wallach's views were liberal and he sometimes allowed political 'undesirables' to hide in their home. When Maxim was five years old, his father was arrested by the secret police, who ransacked the home. After being kept in prison for six weeks, Moses Wallach was released, as the charges were without foundation. Maxim visited his father in prison and Pope claims the experience made a lasting impression on Maxim.[2]

When Maxim was seventeen he enlisted in the army.[3] He saw this as the best route to higher education which, as a Jew, was denied to him.[4] While in the army Maxim refused to fire on workers, when strikers had clashed with the police and the army was ordered to intervene. Maxim was sent back to barracks. However, Maxim's immediate superior Slugov, who was opposed to the idea of shooting workers, was sympathetic to Maxim and never reported his disobedience to the colonel, but instead obtained Maxim's discharge for breach of some petty regulation.[5]

Maxim's ambition was illustrated by his rapid progress in civilian life. Initially Maxim worked as a clerk, but very soon, after changes of employment and when still only about 23, he became manager of the local sugar factory owned by a wealthy Russian, Baron Ginsburg.[6]

In 1899 Maxim moved to Kiev, where he became involved with the Russian Social Democratic Party and set up a printing press, which was used to distribute revolutionary material. He actually paid for the printing press himself from his earnings.[7] Like Molotov, Maxim Litvinov was betrayed. Like most Bolsheviks Wallach took pseudonyms such as Dotiarsk, Finklestein and Harrison. By the time he became a Bolshvik diplomat he took the name of Litvinov. According to Pope, the name of the person who betrayed Litvinov was Pudken. Litvinov was sentenced to two years' imprisonment. While in prison, the

---

[1] Pope, Arthur: *Maxim Litvinov*, p.32
[2] Ibid. p.33
[3] Ibid. p.36
[4] Tanya
[5] Pope, Arthur: *Maxim Litvinov*, p.38
[6] Ibid. p.38
[7] Phillips, Hugh: *Between the Revolution and the West*, p.3

ambitious Litvinov used his time profitably by improving his English as well as reading the newly established revolutionary paper *Iskra*, just started by a Russian émigré in Geneva, and there he read an article by Lenin.[8]

Carswell gives the fullest account of the escape from prison in 1902 which Litvinov successfully planned with fellow prisoners. The plan was that the supervising guards were invited to a cell on the pretext of a birthday drink. Their drinks had been laced with smuggled sleeping pills. These guards were left stupefied on the floor. The sole armed sentry left in the exercise yard was then overwhelmed, disarmed by the four men, and tied up. Seven others formed a pyramid against the wall, fastened a grapnel (smuggled in from outside) to the top and, with the aid of a rope ladder on top of it, disappeared one after another over the top of the wall, followed by the four who had overpowered the guard. The officer on the watch had been temporarily diverted to another part of the building by the false story of a prisoner being taken ill. The whole operation only took five minutes and, according to Carswell, Litvinov was always proud of this elaborate plan.[9]

Litvinov, as he was being hunted in Russia as an escaped prisoner, decided to leave Russia. He boarded a train to Vilnius where he crossed the border into Germany. He then travelled to Switzerland, where there was a small community of Russians.[10]

In 1901 Lenin had established the League of Russian Revolutionary Socialist Democracy Abroad.[11] This was to supervise the distribution of the movement's magazines. The movement also trained leaders for the Russian revolutionary working class movement. In the summer of 1902 Lenin, who apparently had not yet met Litvinov, appointed him the distribution manager of *Iskra*.[12]

In 1903 it had been originally planned to hold the Second Russian Socialist Congress in Brussels, but due to the fear of police prosecution, the venue had been changed to London. It was during July and August 1903, when Lenin was attending the Second Russian Socialist Congress, that Litvinov first met Lenin in the British Library reading room.[13] Lenin and Litvinov went to Hyde Park to hear some of the speeches,[14] and continued to remain in touch during this pre-revolutionary period. The most important business before the conference was the adoption of the party constitution. It was apparent during the course of the conference that the Russian revolutionary movement was deeply split between one faction led by Lenin, who wanted a centralised and disciplined party as an instrument of

---

[8] Pope, Arthur: *Maxim Litvinov*, p.39; Sheinis, Zinovy: *Maxim Litvinov*, p.20
[9] Carswell, John: *The Exile*, p.51; Sheinis, Zinovy: *Maxim Litvinov*, p.23
[10] Carswell, John: *The Exile*, p.52; Pope, Arthur: *Maxim Litvinov*, pp.51-52
[11] Sheinis, Zinovy: *Maxim Litvinov*, p.25
[12] Ibid. p.26
[13] Carswell, John: *The Exile*, p.52; Pope, Arthur: *Maxim Litvinov*, p.51
[14] Pope, Arthur: *Maxim Litvinov*, p.51

revolution with no concessions to expediency, and the other faction, which, although not yet named, would become the Mensheviks, who were more flexible. Lenin's wording for the constitution was rejected by 28 votes to 22 votes. Lenin did not take kindly to his ideas being rejected and this was the start of the split between the two factions of revolutionaries, although the split was not formalised until 1912. What was daft was that the difference between the two factions over the wording was minute. Lenin wanted membership defined as 'a member of the party is one who accepts its programme and supports it both materially and by personal participation in one of its organisations.' The wording that was approved was: 'A member of the Russian Democratic Social Workers Party is a person who accepts its programme and supports it both materially and by regular co-operation under the leadership of one of its organisations'[15] No wonder Litvinov would become frustrated.

However, Sheinis quotes from a report by V. D. Bonch-Bruyevich and Pavel Andriyevich, who came to see Litvinov. Blumenfeld, a Menshevik, was in charge of the newspaper, and, following a heated argument with Litvinov, Blumenfeld locked Litvinov together with V. D. Bonch-Bruyevich and Pavel Andriyevich in a room. The three were only able to regain their freedom when a compositor threw a screwdriver through the window to enable them to unscrew a lock on one of the doors.[16] Then Litvinov left *Iskra*. Before the end of 1903 Lenin had also resigned from the editorial board.[17]

In view of Lenin's defeat, he called a meeting of 22 Bolsheviks, which met at Geneva in August 1904. As a result, another newspaper, *Vpered* ('Forward'), was founded.[18] Litvinov was in charge of importing that newspaper into Russia. Lenin wrote in 1904: 'There will always be transport as long as we have "Papasha" Litvinov.'[19] After two years abroad, Litvinov was determined to continue his revolutionary work in Russia, so in March 1904 he returned to Russia. By now Litvinov was of sufficient prominence as a revolutionary leader that a coded message was sent to all border guards that Maxim Wallach, who had left Berlin, was wanted and planned to enter Russia. 'Redouble your vigilance.'[20]

On 9 January 1905 a massacre took place in St Petersburg after a huge demonstration. Tens of thousands went on to the streets, and the gendarmes opened fire. It was never known how many people were killed, although Figes thinks it was probably 200. [21] The Mensheviks and Bolsheviks were arguing abroad among themselves and accordingly were in an enfeebled state, so they gave little help when the revolution finally erupted. The impact of these foreign revolutionaries in 1905 was slight and undistinguished.[22]

---

[15] Carr, Edward: *Bolshevik Revolution*, vol.1, p.29

[16] Sheinis, Zinovy: *Maxim Litvinov*, p.29

[17] Carr, Edward: *Bolshevik Revolution*, vol.1, p.32; Pope, Arthur: *Maxim Litvinov*, p.52

[18] Carr, Edward: *Bolshevik Revolution*, vol.1, p.36

[19] Carswell, John: *The Exile*, p.53;

[20] Sheinis, Zinovy: *Maxim Litvinov*, p.31

[21] Sheinis, Zinovy: *Maxim Litvinov*, p.34; Figes, Orlando: *People's Tragedy*, p.178

[22] Carr, Edward: *Bolshevik Revolution*, vol.1, p.45

To add to the Tsar's problem, Russia's defeat in the Russo-Japanese war in 1905 which, like the Finnish war in 1939, advertised the weakness of the Russian army.

Litvinov took a considerable part in assembling an exclusively Bolshevik conference, which came to be known as the Third Party Conference, in the summer of 1905 in Copenhagen, but after pressure from Imperial Russia the authorities demanded that the revolutionaries leave the city.

The same scenario unfolded when they tried to hold the conference in Malmo. However, the Bolsheviks were more successful in London. The Third Congress acknowledged that the aim of the proletariat was for a direct struggle against the autocracy by means of an armed uprising.[23] Litvinov and Krassin were among the delegates. Many of the outstanding leaders had either gone over to the Mensheviks whole-heartedly like Martov or Potresov or half-heartedly like Plekhanov and Trotsky.[24]

On 7 October 1905 a general strike commenced in Russia and on 17 October the Tsar attempted to regain the initiative by conceding freedom of speech, assembly and association, among other demands.[25] In view of the change, Litvinov was appointed manager of a new revolutionary newspaper, *Novaya Zhizn*, which it was decided to publish openly. Its initial publication was on 27 October 1905, but it was short-lived as it was suppressed on 17 December 1905.[26]

Litvinov asked the Central Committee for a new task and it was suggested he might accompany Gorky to the USA on a lecture tour, but Litvinov turned down the offer in order to organise, at the personal request of Lenin, the transportation of arms to the revolutionary movement in Russia.[27] Litvinov's respectable appearance and knowledge of foreign languages assisted him in gaining access to arms producers.

Therefore he could obtain arms, pretending to represent a number of legitimate companies.[28] On one occasion, after alleging he was representing a Belgian company, he went to Karlsruhe to order munitions. When he arrived the salesmen asked Litvinov whether he wished to watch a demonstration of arms with some Russian officers. Litvinov agreed. The arms manufacturer thought the arms were being bought for Belgium and never suspected Litvinov was a revolutionary. The arms manufacturer gave Litvinov advice on which were, in his opinion, the best guns.[29] Litvinov was characteristically so successful at

---

[23] Sheinis, Zinovy: *Maxim Litvinov*, p.36
[24] Carr, Edward: *Bolshevik Revolution*, vol.1, p.45
[25] Pope, Arthur: *Maxim Litvinov*, p.70
[26] Pope, Arthur: *Maxim Litvinov*, p.72; Sheinis, Zinovy: *Maxim Litvinov*, p.42
[27] Sheinis, Zinovy: *Maxim Litvinov*, p.43; Possony, Stefan: *Lenin the Compulsive Revolutionary*, p.109
[28] Sheinis, Zinovy: *Maxim Litvinov*, p.45
[29] Pope, Arthur: *Maxim Litvinov*, p.86

this venture that between July and September 1905 he imported into Russia 15,000 rifles, 3,000 revolvers and several tons of dynamite.[30]

Litvinov returned to St Petersburg but was hunted by the Tsarist police. Whereas Sheinis stated that he vanished into thin air,[31] Phillips stated that Litvinov eluded capture and fled to Bulgaria.[32] Later, Sheinis confirms Phillips' account. According to Sheinis, a spy reported on 27 December 1906 that Litvinov was seen in Varna, Bulgaria, where he was arranging shipment of arms for Russian revolutionaries.[33]

In May 1907 Litvinov met Stalin for the first time at the Fifth Congress in London. Five organised groups attended the conference: Bolsheviks, Mensheviks, Bundists, as well as Latvian and Polish Social Democrats.[34] Figures given for the strength of each group vary. However, all including Trotsky seem agreed that the Bolsheviks were the largest group, but the Mensheviks had only slightly less delegates than the Bolsheviks.[35]

Stalin was present as an alleged delegate of the Transcaucasian Social Democrats. However, as there were hardly any Bolsheviks in Georgia, Stalin was unable to muster the five hundred votes needed for him to attend as a delegate.[36]

According to Trotsky, Lenin proposed that Stalin, together with three other delegates, had the right to participate but not vote. Although Martov challenged the four delegates' right to participate, Lenin's resolution was passed. Trotsky raises the question as to why, if Stalin was there, he did not speak. However, many delegates who go to conferences do not speak. The only record of Stalin making any contribution to the conference is that his name appears on two small statements by Caucasian delegates about their local conflict with Mensheviks.[37]

Stalin evidently lodged at 77 Jubilee Street while attending the conference, although in a guarded comment, Montefiore states that legend has it that Stalin 'spent the first night with Litvinov in the Tower House hostel in Fieldgate Street, Stepney.' The fact that Montefiore uses the word 'legend' indicates doubt as to its authenticity. Arthur Bacon, a Russian-speaking cobbler, remembers Stalin with affection.[38] Arthur Bacon had every reason to so remember Stalin. Bacon used to take messages from Stalin to other delegates, for which

---

[30] Possony, Stefan: *Lenin the Compulsive Revolutionary*, p.112

[31] Sheinis, Zinovy: *Maxim Litvinov*, p.52

[32] Phillips, Hugh: *Between the Revolution and the West*, p.10

[33] Sheinis, Zinovy: *Maxim Litvinov*, p.54;

[34] Payne, Robert: *Life and Death of Lenin*, p.213

[35] Trotsky, Leon: *Stalin*, p.88

[36] Ibid. p.90

[37] Trotsky, Leon: *Stalin*, p.91

[38] Montefiore, Simon: *Young Stalin*, p.146

service Stalin paid him two shillings, 48 times the halfpenny Arthur Bacon normally received.[39] Litvinov was not a delegate but acted as an observer from the public gallery.[40] However, there is a claim that Stalin was attacked by angry dockers and Litvinov defended Stalin. Medvedev refers to this story, but gives no authority for it and casts doubt on it.[41] The incident is not mentioned by either Pope, who had direct access to Litvinov, or Sheinis, who had direct access to the Litvinov family; or Carswell, whose mother had direct access to Ivy Litvinov. However, both Pope and Sheinis are silent on this London conference. There is no known reason why Stalin and Litvinov should have associated with each other.

Foreshadowing characteristics of the Soviet Communist regime, Lenin and the other leaders did not lodge in the East End but stayed in middle-class Bloomsbury,[42] and I wonder whether Litvinov would not have lodged near Lenin in Bloomsbury, as the two men knew each other well.

The *Labour Leader* reported:

> It is significant of the benighted conditions of Russia that the Russian revolutionaries, who are holding a conference at the Brotherhood Church in Islington since the beginning of the previous week, should have been compelled to hold it *in camera* as well as to utter a protest against publication of photographs of delegates in the press. "We would call the attention of the press", so runs a paragraph of the statement, made through Reuter's agency, "to the fact in Russia those belonging to a Socialist organisation one [*sic*] is liable for penal servitude and we hope in view of this the English Press will not play the part of allies of Russian police spies." In spite of all precautions the Russian delegates are marked men. According to Central St Petersburg news message a list of delegates with their description have been sent to all frontier stations accompanied by police instructions to detain, search and telegraph St Petersburg.[43]

The MPs Messrs Thorne, Cremer and Crooks, who sympathised with anti-Tsarist movements, asked a barrage of questions in the House of Commons on whether the British police were in any way co-operating with the Russian police and were assured they were not. However, these MPs wanted an assurance that the Home Office Minister did not and could not give them - that the conference was not being shadowed by private detectives employed by the Tsar, as there was nothing illegal to prevent foreign governments instructing private detectives to obtain information.[44]

---

[39] Service, Robert: *Stalin*, p.65 Montefiore, Simon: *Young Stalin*, p.146; Daily Express 5 January 1950 p.3
[40] Payne, Robert: *Life and Death of Lenin*, p.213
[41] Medvedev, Roy: *Let History Judge*, p.309; Montefiore, Simon: *Young Stalin*, p.321
[42] Service, Robert: *Lenin*, p.65
[43] *Daily News*, 18 May 1907, p.8; *Labour Leader*, 24 May 1907, p.838
[44] *Hansard 1907*, Vol.174, 27 May 1907, 1319

On 31 May 1907 a meeting for sympathisers of the Russian revolutionary movement was held at Holborn Town Hall. According to the *Labour Leader*,

> An observer stated that one could not listen to the speakers without being filled with enthusiasm and at the same time horror and the overwhelming difficulties of the fight. A Mrs Balabanoff spoke in English [and] thrilled us with her intense excitement in her appeals to us to stand by our comrades in their task.[45]

In August 1907 Litvinov attended the 12th International Socialist Conference when he proposed that the movement in the event of war do everthing possible presumably by strikes to sabotage the war effort. Phillips stated that Litvinov maintained good relations with the Mensheviks, despite his personal devotion to Lenin.

However, Pope tells us that Litvinov was disillusioned that the delegates were not radical enough. This was especially true of the German Socialists, who were acting more like Germans than Socialists. Litvinov stated that Lenin was right not to compromise.[46]

In January 1908, on the instigation of the Tsarist police, Litvinov was again arrested in Paris, at the Gare du Nord, carrying bank notes bearing the numbers of notes stolen in a bank robbery at Tiflis in Russia. *Le Figaro* reported that Mr Fabro, the Procurator General, attended a long meeting on the subject of the arrest of Russian terrorists. It was claimed that the arrest, at the instigation of the Russian police, was arbitrary. 'Yesterday afternoon Madam Willm, an advocate, visited her client Dothiarsk in Santo Prison.' Litvinov was then using the name Dothiarsk and he claimed:

> He could not have participated in the robbery at Tiflis because at the time of the robbery he was in France. Dothiarsk had received a packet of securities from the Russian Revolutionary fund but had not concerned himself with the source. He claims he was going to England to sell the securities and that Freda Yampolska was accompanying him as a friend and knew nothing of this matter.

As Litvinov was able to prove that he had been in Paris at the time of the robbery, the Minister of the Interior ordered Litvinov's release, as, in his opinion, French law did not justify his detention. By English law Litvinov would have no doubt been charged with receiving stolen property. Whether it is correct that he could not have been charged with such an offence by French law is unknown. However, he was deported as an undesirable alien.[47]

---

[45] *Labour Leader*, 31 May 1907, p.854
[46] Pope, Arthur: *Maxim Litvinov*, p.93; Phillips, Hugh: *Between the Revolution and the West*, p.12
[47] *Le Figaro*, 19 January 1908, p.5; 22 January, p.4; 23 January, p.4

Litvinov arrived in England in January 1908 for a 10-year stay. In London, Litvinov, helped by an introduction from Gorky, obtained a job with publishing firm Williams & Norgate.[48] However, in 1913 Litvinov then travelled to Switzerland to meet Lenin, who had gone there on account of the ill health of his wife.[49]

At the request of Lenin, Litvinov attended a two-day meeting of the International Socialist Bureau, which started in London on 13 December 1913, and which concerned socialist unity.[50] The conference discussed for one and a half days the question of unifying the Fabian Society, the Independent Labour Party and the British Socialist Party. At 5pm on 14 December the Bureau started to discuss Russia. Kautsky proposed that the Bureau offer their good services to facilitate 'an exchange of opinion' between the various factions in order to promote unity among the Left-wing Russian parties. Rosa Luxemburg proposed an amendment that a special conference should be called which should establish conditions for the re-establishment of a unified party. Litvinov objected to Lenin's reformist allies and also wanted to object to the conference itself, when the Chairman stated time was up. Apart from one further speech by Social Revolutionary Social Democrat Rubanovich, it was stated that the meeting unanimously passed Kautsky's original resolution. Litvinov complained to Lenin of the complete indifference of the Western European delegates, who remained silent and spent most of their time looking at their watches. Litvinov felt the delegates would have voted for any resolution that mentioned the word 'unity.' However, were not the Western Europeans right to regard the arguments between the various Revolutionary factions as ridiculous, as I have commented on what occurred at the Second Russian Socialist Conference?[51] No doubt Litvinov was carrying out the instructions of Lenin. However, in so doing he showed Lenin as being an autocrat and Litvinov should have realised that under Lenin's leadership a democratic system was unlikely to be established. Litvinov told Lenin that his criticism of Rosa Luxemburg, who had proposed the unification of the Mensheviks and Bolsheviks, was a bit too harsh.[52] It was a rare example of Litvinov having the courage to criticise Lenin. On the other hand, although Litvinov received much criticism from people unsympathetic to Bolshevism, I believe the German socialist Rosa Luxemburg was the only person ever to say that Litvinov was 'a complete idiot.'[53]

When war broke out in 1914 the Tsar requested that all Russian émigrés who were in England and liable for Russian military service be returned to fight in the Russian army. However Litvinov did not return as he was able to convince the English officer who interviewed him that if he returned to Russia he would be tried rather than fight in the army.[54]

---

[48] Sheinis, Zinovy: *Maxim Litvinov*, p.65
[49] Ibid. p.66
[50] Ibid. p.69
[51] See No 15 *ante*
[52] Sheinis, Zinovy: *Maxim Litvinov*, p.69; *Russian Review*, 1990, vol.1, p.35
[53] Ettinger, Elzabieta: *Comrade & Lover: Rosa Luxemburg's Letters to Leo Jogiches*, p.182
[54] Sheinis, Zinovy: *Maxim Litvinov*, p.79

In 1914 Litvinov lost his job with Williams & Norgate when that firm ceased publishing translated books. As with his spell in business in Russia, he had been successful with his new firm, his salary rising from one pound fifty pence a week to three pounds ten shillings and, according to Pope, Litvinov's responsibilities expanded so that from time to time he participated in important conferences regarding the entire policy of the firm.

Litvinov was not a man who remained idle. Litvinov next took a temporary job taking a group of Russian tourists around Europe, but the visit was curtailed when the First World War broke out and Litvinov needed his diplomatic skills to successfully negotiate with Swedish officialdom for the tourist party to be allowed to cross Sweden so they could return to Russia.[55]

Litvinov's brief excursion into the tourist trade was therefore abruptly ended with the outbreak of war, but Litvinov soon obtained other employment selling agricultural machinery.[56] All the indications are that had Litvinov been a national of a capitalist country he would have been successful in business.

However, Litvinov refused Lenin's request that Litvinov attend the Second International Conference in Vienna in 1914. Litvinov gave as his reason that he could not be away for three weeks and stated that only Lenin could exercise influence at the meeting.[57]

The war caused a growth in the Russian community, as Russian émigrés living in Belgium and the war-affected areas of France came to England. One of those whom Litvinov met was his future boss Chicherin. The International Socialist Bureau had been suspended after the outbreak of war in 1914 because the French Socialists would not participate in any conference at which German Socialists attended as long as any part of France was occupied.[58]

The *Labour Leader* in 1915, lamenting the suspension of the International, stated:

> It was one of the most mortifying incidents of the war but that the international movement could yet reverse its failure by unifying in a great world campaign for an early and permanent peace.[59]

The fact that the words 'permanent peace ' were used indicates that, unlike Litvinov, the *Labour Leader* was contemplating peace following negotiation, not unilateral peace as Litvinov was advocating. However, the international socialist movement, if they had followed the *Labour Leader*'s advice, would have been setting themselves an almost impossible task.

---

[55] Sheinis, Zinovy: *Maxim Litvinov*, p.77
[56] Ibid. p.79
[57] Ibid. p.77
[58] *Labour Party Report*, 1916, p.31
[59] *Labour Leader,* 11 February 1915, p4

On 14 February 1915 the conference of the Socialist parties of the Entente countries met. Sheinis is right to claim that the Bolsheviks were not invited. Nevertheless, Litvinov not only attended the conference as an uninvited guest, but also spoke. The *Labour Leader* mentions that the largest section of the International within the four countries which was not represented at the conference was the Russian Social Democratic Party, the strongest of the Russian parties, because they were not invited. It does not seem they were not invited because they opposed the war, although the Independent Labour Party who also opposed the war was invited.

Litvinov in his speech stated:

> Your conference calls itself a conference of the Socialist parties of belligerent Allied Countries of Belgium, England, France and Russia. Permit me to direct your attention to the fact that the Social Democracy of Russia as an organisation represented by the Central Committee which is accredited to the International Socialist Bureau has received no invitation from you. Permit me now to say a few words about the goals of your conference, that is to say what the political conscious Social Democratic workers have been expecting of you.

This statement implies that Litvinov considered the Russian workers were more important than other workers. The International Socialist Bureau had previously resolved that all Socialist parties should not approve war credits, but when the vote was taken it had not considered the position if Belgium was attacked. Belgium could never be a threat to any major power. Litvinov was advocating that, after Belgium was attacked, France and Britain should have torn up the treaty protecting Belgium. Litvinov should have had the courage to say so, particularly as he, Litvinov, at the pinnacle of his power, emphasised the importance of abiding by international treaties.[60]

Litvinov continued:

> We think before entering into any discussion of the problems of restoring the International ties between Socialist workers our Socialist duty compels us to demand:

> Firstly, that Emile Vandervelde, Jules Guesde and Marcel Sembat should immediately leave the bourgeois Ministries of Belgium and France.

> Secondly, the Belgian and French Socialist parties should break up the so-called 'national bloc agreement' of pro-war socialist parties.

---

[60] Sheinis Zinov Maxim Litvinov p.81; As for respect for treaties see Ch 13 No 51

Thirdly, all Socialist parties should abandon their policies of ignoring the crimes of Russian Tsarism and renew their support for the struggle against Tsarism of the Russian workers, who do not shrink from any sacrifice whatsoever, in their fight against Tsarism.

Fourthly, in fulfilment of the decision of the Basle Congress, we are offering our hands to those Social-Democrats of Germany and Austria who replied to the declaration of war by preparing propaganda of revolutionary action. The voting of war credits must be absolutely condemned.

The Social Democrats of Germany and Austria

have committed a monstrous crime against socialism and the International by voting for war credits and in coming to a truce with the Junkers, the priests and the bourgeoisie, but the Belgian and French Socialists have behaved no better.

However, no doubt many socialists in Belgium and France would have been most indignant when Litvinov stated that the Belgian and French Socialists had done no better than the German and Austrian socialists because France and Belgium had been attacked.

Litvinov continued:

Under no circumstances must Socialists cease to be socialists and join the chorus of bourgeois chauvinists or forget the chorus of the workers and join the bourgeois governments. German and Austrian Socialists are committing a great crime against Socialism when, following the example of the bourgeoisie, hypocritically assert that the Hohenzollerns and Hapsburgs are waging a war of liberation from Tsarism. No less a crime is committed by those who are saying that Tsarism is becoming more democratic and who evade the fact that Tsarism is strangling and destroying unhappy Galicia exactly as the German Kaiser is strangling and destroying Belgium.

Yet Litvinov's inconsistency is shown because he advocated that it was more important to bring down the Tsar than to save Belgium. Litvinov criticised those

who are silent about the fact that Tsarism has thrown into prison the parliamentary representatives of the working class of Russia and only recently condemned several Moscow workers to six years' penal servitude merely for belonging to the Social Democratic Labour Party.

Finally, he pointed out:-

Tsarism has oppressed Finland worse than before, that workers' papers and workers' organisations in Russia have been closed down, and that the thousands of millions of roubles required to continue the war are being wrested by the Tsarist clique from the starving peasants and destitute workers.

The workers of Russia hold out a hand of comradeship to those socialists who are taking action like Karl Liebknecht, like the Socialists of Serbia, and Italy, like the British comrades of the Independent Labour Party, several members of the British Socialist Party and our arrested comrades from the Russian Social Democratic Party in opposing the war.

We call on you to follow the road to socialism. Down with the chauvinism that is betraying the socialist cause. Long live international socialism.[61]

Sheinis states that Litvinov was not allowed to finish. Although a contemporary newspaper refers to Litvinov not being allowed to finish, presumably some time limit was placed on speakers and he certainly had time to convey the Bolsheviks' message.[62]

However, it would appear that if the socialists had followed Litvinov's advice, Germany might well have triumphed, without there being any guarantee that the revolution Litvinov was still predicting would happen. Nevertheless, it was a partial triumph for Litvinov because the conference agreed with many of the ideas he was advancing.

The following resolution was adopted: firstly, it was resolved:

The conference could not ignore the profound general causes of the European conflict, itself, a monstrous product of the antagonisms which tear asunder capitalist society and of the policy of colonial dependencies and aggressive imperialism against which international socialism had never ceased to fight and in which every Government had its share of responsibility.

This was a significant acknowledgment for the Belgian and French members to make.

Secondly,
the invasion of Belgium and France by the German armies is rightly denounced as threatening the very existence of independent nationalities and striking a blow at faith in treaties. Under these circumstances a victory for German imperialism would be the defeat and destruction of democracy and liberty in Europe.

---

[61] Litvinov's speech, *Labour Leader,* 18 February 1915, p.4
[62] Sheinis, Zinovy: *Maxim Litvinov*, p.81

Thirdly, the Socialist parties of Great Britain, Belgium, France and Russia

> do not pursue the political and economic crushing of Germany. They are not at war with the peoples of Germany and Austria, but only with the Governments of those countries by which they are oppressed. They demand that Belgium shall be liberated and compensated.

Fourthly,

> they desire that the question of Poland should be settled in accordance with the wishes of the Polish people, either in the sense of autonomy in the midst of another state or that of complete independence.

Fifthly,

> they wish that throughout Europe from Alsace-Lorraine to the Balkans those populations that have been annexed by force should receive the right freely to dispose of themselves.

Finally,

> while inflexibly resolved to fight until victory is achieved, to accomplish this task of liberation, the socialists [of the Allied countries] are none the less resolved to resist any attempt to transform this defensive war into a war of conquest which would only prepare fresh conflicts, create new grievances and subject various peoples more than ever to the double plague of armaments and war.

The declaration also

> expresses the hope that the working classes of all the different countries will before long find themselves united again in their struggle against militarism and capitalist imperialism. The victory of the Allied Powers must be a victory for popular liberty, for unity, independence and autonomy of the nations in the peaceful Federation of the United States of Europe and the world.

The declaration also expressed the hope that:

On the conclusion of the war the working classes of all the industrial countries must unite in the International in order to suppress secret diplomacy and put an end to the interests of militarism and those of the armaments makers and establish some

some international authority to settle differences among nations by compulsory conciliation and arbitration and to compel all nations to maintain peace.

The conference protested against the arrest of deputies in the Duma, the suppression of Russian socialist newspapers and the condemnation of the editors, as well as the oppression of Finns, Jews, Russians and German Poles.[63]

Lenin was well pleased with Litvinov's efforts. Writing in the *Sotsial-Demokrat* after the conference, Lenin stated that Comrade Litvinov carried out his task in speaking specifically about the treachery of the German Socialists. 'Only one truthful word was heard at the London Conference. It was the voice of Litvinov.'[64]

It was shortly afterwards that Maxim met his future wife Ivy. How Maxim and Ivy met is not clear, because Ivy wrote some fictional accounts of their meeting. According to Ivy's article in the *Observer* in 1976, she was attracted to this portly figure whom she saw several times 'haunting the pavements of Hampstead High Street.' One day, when she was in the post office, she discovered he was Russian. A *Washington Post* article mentions that the friendship blossomed after they met one day outside the public library.

In Ivy's papers there are other versions of Maxim and Ivy's courtship. Both Sheinis and Pope state Maxim and Ivy met in a friend's house. Pope is more specific – he states it was Leeper. However, Lady Leeper denied this. Certainly, she first met Maxim when he came to their house as a possible Russian tutor for her husband, but Lady Leeper met Ivy much later. Maxim and Ivy married at Hampstead Town Hall on 22 February 1916.[65] Two children called Misha and Tanya were born while they were together in England.

Living in Hampstead under the tutelage of her husband, Ivy made a good effort to conquer the Russian language; but according to Ivy, conjugal lessons were hardly a success. Ivy was a good deal more successful as teacher rather than student. She imbued her Marxist husband with an appreciation of literature. Maxim discovered new pleasures in reading about Miss Austen's polite spinsters and Anthony Trollope's parsons.[66] Pope claims that Litvinov became a British subject. However, a search of the registration records indicate this was not so.[67]

---

[63] As to the conference resolution of the allied countries: *Labour Leader*, 18 February, 1915p.4; *Herald*, 20 February 1915 p11; *Daily Chronicle*, 15 February 1915, p.7

[64] Sheinis, Zinovy: *Maxim Litvinov*, p.83

[65] As to how Maxim and Ivy met, see *Observer*, 25 July 1976, p.17; Sheinis, Zinovy: *Maxim Litvinov*, p.86; Pope, Arthur: *Maxim Litvinov*, p.111; Carswell, John: *The Exile*, p.76; letter from Lady Leeper to *Times*, 5 May 1971, p.21; *Washington Post*, 30 January 1977 H1

[66] *Life*, 12 October 1942, p.117

[67] Pope, Arthur: *Maxim Litvinov*, p.96

Litvinov is often portrayed as a poor émigré, but he had moved up the social scale. He was teaching Russian to a young Foreign Office official at a time when the Foreign Office was considered the elite of British society, being almost exclusively drawn from the public schools and major universities. Litvinov was at ease in such company because, instead of working on Leeper's Russian, both men spent most of their time talking about Russian revolutionary politics and as a result Leeper became the Foreign Office expert on Bolshevism.[68]

Ivy Litvinov was recovering from the birth of their son Mikhail when she received a telephone call from her husband asking her if she had read the London *Times*. She replied that she had not read it. According to Ivy's article in *Life*, she asked to see the paper. The nurse had said there was nothing in it − just a Zeppelin raid, but nothing new from the Front. She had not noticed another page stating that a revolution in Russia had taken place. However, when Maxim telephoned, he was so excited with the news of the Revolution that he had got into the bath without turning on the taps, stepping solemnly out to dry his dry body after soaking in the cold air of a London bathroom.[69] Next day, the news reached London that Grand Duke Mikhail refused to assume the throne.[70]

Sheinis tells us Litvinov, upon hearing of the Revolution, went to the embassy to demand that the Tsar's portrait be taken down.[71]

The socialist émigrés in London organised the London Committee for the Repatriation of Émigrés. The chairman was Maisky. Chicherin, who was to become the Soviet Commissar for Foreign Affairs, was the secretary and Litvinov played a leading role in the Committee. The LCRE attempted to negotiate the speedy repatriation of émigrés. Virtually the only way to Russia was the North Sea route via Norway; therefore, émigrés from Europe were flocking to England demanding to be repatriated, together with those who had been residing in Britain. At first the British government was reluctant to assist, but eventually, with the help of the Russian Chargé d'Affaires, the British Government agreed to allot so many places on the government ship *Jupiter* that travelled fortnightly between Aberdeen and Bergen.[72] The Committee took advantage of this by selecting for travel those likely to support the Bolsheviks, but Litvinov was not among the passengers.

Although Litvinov had told his wife if the Revolution called him he must return to Russia, he did not so return, his wife having given birth to a son. Maxim quoted Deuteronomy 24:5, which states that when a man has taken a new wife he should not go to war, but

---

[68] Ullman, Richard: *Anglo-Soviet Relations*, vol.1, p.60
[69] *Life*, 12 October 1942, p.118; Phillips, Hugh: *Between the Revolution and the West*, p.18
[70] Hosking, Geoffrey: *Russia & Russian*, p.392
[71] Sheinis, Zinovy: *Maxim Litvinov*, p.89
[72] O'Connor, Timothy: *Diplomacy and Revolution*, p.43

should be free at home for a year.[73] Would his life have been different if he had returned? What were the chances of him being leader if he had returned to Russia after Lenin instead of Stalin?

On 22 August 1917, Chicherin was arrested because of his association with Germans and pro-Germans at the Communist Club. It was alleged that Chicherin was a danger to public safety and the defence of the realm. He remained in prison until after the November Revolution. Then Trotsky told the British that not even the Ambassador would be allowed to leave Russia until Chicherin was released. In view of this threat, the British Government decided to release Chicherin. After he was set free, the British ambassador in Russia and other British subjects who had not been allowed to leave were now able to do so.[74]

---

[73] Phillips, Hugh: *Between the Revolution and the West*, p.19
[74] O'Connor, Timothy: *Diplomacy and Revolution*, p.44

2: A BOLSHEVIK AMBASSADOR

It was from the newspapers that Litvinov heard of the October Revolution on 25 October 1917 – 9 November (British date).[1] On 3 January 1918, the *Times* carried an announcement that Litvinov had been made ambassador of the Russian Socialist Republic to Great Britain.[2]

Maisky claims that in January 1918 Litvinov had all his bags packed ready to return to Russia, when he heard from Lenin that he, Litvinov, had been appointed Russia's representative in Britain. Immediately after this event, Litvinov sent a note to Balfour, British Foreign Secretary, informing him of his appointment. Litvinov requested a meeting. This was the first Soviet note. Although Balfour declined such a meeting, because the Bolshevik Government was not recognised, a Foreign Office official, Sir Reginald Leeper, was instructed to keep in touch with Litvinov. Leeper already knew Litvinov, who had taught him Russian, as detailed in Chapter 1.[3]

Sheinis, as might be expected, credits Litvinov with his first diplomatic triumph in obtaining Chicherin's release. Sheinis agrees with Phillips that the Russian Revolutionary Government announced that no British subject, not even the ambassador, Sir George William Buchanan, would be allowed to leave Russia until Chicherin was released. On 14 December 1917, the British Government had to perform a U-turn and agree to release Chicherin. However, it was not until 3 January 1918 that Chicherin was allowed to leave prison, when he travelled to Aberdeen to make the voyage across the North Sea to Bergen, from where he travelled to Russia.[4]

As long as Russia was in the war, however unattractive Bolshevism appeared to the British Government, from their viewpoint the most important task was to prevent a Russian withdrawal from the war. Lloyd George saw this was vital. On 21 December 1917, Lockhart was summoned to 10 Downing Street. Lloyd George, after asking Lockhart about Lenin and Trotsky, stated it was folly for the Allies not to open negotiations with the Bolsheviks and asked Lockhart to go to St Petersburg for the purpose of establishing contact with the Bolshevik Government.[5] Leeper arranged a meeting with Rothstein

---

[1] *Times*, 9 November 1917, p.7

[2] *Times*, 3 January 1918, p.6; Ullman, Richard: *Anglo-Soviet Relations*, vol. 1, p.60

[3] Maisky, Ivan: *Journey Into the Past*, p.61; and see Ch.1, No.68

[4] O'Connor, Timothy: *Diplomacy and Revolution*, p.45; Sheinis, Zinovy: *Maxim Litvinov*, p.100; Pope, Arthur: *Maxim Litvinov*, p.130; Phillips, Hugh: *Between the Revolution and the West*, p.23

[5] Lockhart, Robert: *Memoirs of a British Agent*, p.199

(described by Lockhart as an armchair revolutionary), who had lived in England for many years, and Litvinov at a Lyons Corner House. They quickly came to an agreement that both Lockhart and Litvinov would enjoy diplomatic privileges, including the cipher and the diplomatic bag, although Litvinov had already been able to obtain facilities to cipher Moscow from one of the members of the former Tsarist Purchasing Commission.[6]

Nabokov, the Russian representative of the Provisional Government, protested against even qualified recognition being given to its competitor, but to no effect. A number of concessions were made to Litvinov, including the right to grant visas, especially to Lockhart, to enable him to travel to Russia to represent Britain's interests there.[7]

On 11 January 1918, Litvinov wrote a letter for Lockhart to give to Trotsky. This said:

> The bearer of the letter is going to Russia with an official mission the exact character of which I am not acquainted. I know him personally as a thoroughly honest man.

However Litvinov had only met Lockhart once a few days before. Lockhart left Britain on 18 January 1918. In a memorandum to the Foreign Office written shortly after Lockhart arrived, he advocated coming to a working arrangement with the Russians and abandonment of support for counter-revolutionary elements in Russia in return for the cessation of Bolshevik agitation in Britain.

One of the factors which persuaded Lockhart to be less hostile to the Bolsheviks was his belief that 'the Bolsheviks will not last for ever.' In making that remark, Lockhart no doubt contemplated the early demise of the Bolsheviks, not the period of seventy years which was the life term of the Communist state. However, after Lockhart was arrested, as is shown later, he was no friend of Lenin's Russia.[8]

In an interview with the *Daily Chronicle* and reprinted in *The New York Times*, Litvinov justified the Bolshevik Revolution because it took

> the reins away out of the trembling hands of Kerensky and his associates and handing them over to the Soviets in which all the Socialist parties were represented. The moderate parties, standing as they do for the lower middle class or petite bourgeoisie and well-to-do peasantry, chose to desert the Soviets and left the power in the hands of the only party that remained in the Soviets. The Bolsheviks grew

---

[6] Maisky, Ivan: *Journey Into the Past*, p.61
[7] Lockhart, Robert: *Memoirs of a British Agent*, p.202; Nabokov, C: *The Ordeal of a Diplomat*, pp.210 and 223
[8] Lockhart, Robert: *Memoirs of a British Agent*, p.203; compare FO 371/3299/25 and 26 with FO 371/3344 /174035

into the majority due to the incapacity and inefficiency of the Kerensky government in tackling the problems of the Revolution and principally bringing peace nearer.

However, after the Second Revolution the Bolsheviks were willing to share the responsibility for running the country with other Socialist parties. Although the plan was backed up by the powerful Union of Railway Workers and by various army organisations, the Bolsheviks' invitation was refused by these other parties, notably the Mensheviks and the Socialist Revolutionaries of the Right, who hoped at that time for the speedy defeat of the Bolsheviks with the aid of Korniloffe and Kaledine.[9]

Litvinov used the same argument in his pamphlet *Bolshevik Revolution: Its Rise and Meaning*. Litvinov stated: 'Not a single sentence of death had been passed and the number of people arrested compares favourably even with Kerensky's regime.' Litvinov alleged that, under the Kerensky regime, many people had been arrested and hundreds who refused to fight had been executed.[10] Another edition was published in 1919, including an article written by Ivy giving wholehearted support for the Bolshevik Revolution. Like many others, Ivy had then a utopian view of the Bolshevik Revolution. In dealing with the Red Terror, she stated: 'During the first six months of the Revolution nobody was executed'; although Ivy admits: 'Such shedding of blood that took place was either due to open street fighting with armed rebels or else the uncontrollable, unforeseen and spontaneous action of the crowd.'[11] However, this was not so. One source identified that 884 people were executed between December 1917 and July 1918, and even Lenin's cousin, Viktor Ardashev, unknown to Lenin, was executed by the Cheka. Lenin only discovered his cousin's execution when Lenin ordered an official to convey his greeting to his cousin and was told his cousin had been executed.[12]

Similarly, Chicherin did not see anything wrong with the Terror. In a speech on 12 September 1918, when neutral countries expressed deep indignation at the regime of terror established in Petrograd, Moscow and other cities, Chicherin said :

To our enemies merciless wars and we are convinced that the masses of all countries terrorised by little cliques of exploiters will understand in Russia violence is employed only for the sacred interests of liberation of the masses, but they will not only understand us but follow our example.[13]

---

[9] *Daily Chronicle*, 4 January 1918, p.1;*The New York Times*, 5 January 1918, p.2
[10] Litvinov, Maxim: *Bolshevik Revolution t: Its Rise and Meaning*, 1918, p.44; reprinted in edition with Ivy's postscript 1919, p.32
[11] Litvinov, Ivy : *Bolshevik Revolution: Its Rise and Meaning*, p.50
[12] Figes, Orlando: *People's Tragedy*, p.632
[13] Chamberlin, William: *Russian Revolution 1917-1921*, p.76

Chicherin must be criticised for not making it clear that, unless limits were placed on any arbitrary powers, it is more than likely that, as happened in Nazi Germany and Stalin's Russia, such arbitrary powers will deteriorate into mass oppression. Further, Chicherin was encouraging vigilantes acting outside the law.

Meanwhile, Litvinov initially told Maisky that he, Litvinov, had no instructions from Moscow, no money or experienced staff or training for diplomatic work. 'I simply had to start from scratch.'[14] The document written by Litvinov for Lockhart to present to Trotsky confirms what Litvinov stated to Maisky. Litvinov commented that he had only heard of his appointment from newspapers. 'I hope a courier is bringing me the necessary documents, without which the difficulties of my position are greatly increased.' Litvinov also pointed out that the Embassy and Consulate had not yet been surrendered.

The document added that Litvinov was pleased with the reception received from the press.

'Even the bourgeois press readily affords me its pages to explain our position.' Despite war-time conditions, Litvinov enjoyed freedom of expression far more than he ever received in his own country, either before or after the Revolution. Litvinov continued, 'I have issued an appeal to the English working men in all the Socialist newspapers.'[15]

Litvinov persuaded the *Labour Leader* to publish an article written by him headed 'A Message from Maxim Litvinov, Plenipotentiary for Great Britain, to the Workers of Great Britain. The fact it addressed the workers rather than the Government to which Litvinov had requested to be accredited was not helpful if Litvinov's goal was to become the new ambassador. Litvinov wrote:

> The Russian people and the peasant government have done me the honour of choosing me as its representative to this country and entrusted me in this critical moment of history with the desire and aspiration of the Russian revolutionary democracy and of keeping it informed of those of British democracy. To this end I consider it is my first duty to put before you the real truth of the Revolution, particularly in its bearing on the war. Millions of people have been calmly doomed to death, whole countries to devastation, a whole generation of workers all over the world to privation; and at least one may hope that the masses are going to profit by their bitter lessons. Bled to death, bereft of millions of its sons, brought to starvation and utter misery but enlightened by years of Socialist propaganda and inured to revolution by former struggles, the proletariat of Russia suddenly arose and with one stroke freed itself of its bonds and with the battle cries "peace, bread, land and liberty" overthrew its rulers and oppressors. For ten months the working men have been the guardians of the Revolution by the widespread network of the

---

[14] Maisky, Ivan: *Journey Into the Past*, p.61
[15] Lockhart, Robert: *Memoirs of a British Agent*, p.203-204

Soviets [Councils of workers and soldier delegates] holding real power in their hands perrmeating the Revolution with the social ideas of their class. Unfortunately, at first some of the leaders were so ill-advised to share the power with these middle-class politicians and did everything they could to arrest the further development of the Revolution, to prevent the masses from realising their political and social aims and to force them to remain still involved in the War.

Ostensibly standing for peace, these politicians actually thwarted the peace movement by proceeding with the arrangement of secret diplomacy. They appealed to the proletariat of the Central Powers, but the obvious duplicity of their policy weakened their appeal, which met with little response, while at home their irresolute and wavering handling of the land question and other problems of the Revolution caused dissatisfaction and disillusion among the masses and fed the counter-revolution and reaction.

Alive to the dangers of the prolongation of the war and of counter-revolution, the workers and soldiers of Petrograd, Moscow and other towns found themselves compelled finally to break with the middle class and to restore full power to the Soviets.

Litvinov's criticism of the middle class was somewhat hypocritical, because he had himself become very much middle class.

So the second revolution, the true proletarian revolution, was brought about and a mighty class war began in Russia which is now going on. The second outbreak showed the capitalists and their lower middle class helpers a vision of its far-reaching possibilities and now it is they who would move heaven and earth if they could crush the victorious Russian proletariat. No means are too low for them to employ. They shrink from nothing, not even complete disorganisation of the economic life of the country, not caring how much they add to the troubles already heaped on the people by four years of war.

In the teeth of the bitter struggle the working men of Russia are creating new forms of state organisation, carrying on social reconstruction on a tremendous and lofty scale, providing homes for the homeless, introducing the eight-hour working day, giving land to the peasants, taking control over industry, nationalising the banks and insurance companies, and rebuilding the social structure in every direction. To reveal to the world the imperialist nature of this war, the secret treaties have been published and the decisive step has been taken to bring about a general, just and democratic peace.

The Soviets are forcing foreign countries to state clearly their war aims, thus opening the way for peace negotiations. By giving complete freedom to all small nationalities of the Russian Empire, they prove their unselfishness and sincerity of their treatment of the national or no-annexation question.

The revolutionary propaganda among German soldiers at the Western Front and prisoners of war is undermining the strength of German autocracy and militarism more effectively than the military victories could and has already provoked a strong peace movement in Germany and Austria. But these endeavours met with opposition not only from capitalists in Russia but from capitalists the world over. The Russian Revolution with its dash and vigour has become the focus of the hatred of international capitalism and now the prolongation of the war, in addition to its former imperialist aims, has another aim – to crush the Soviets and the Revolution. So the Russian workers are not only fighting their battles, but your battles too, and they will succumb unless the workers in other countries come speedily to their help.

Realise this. The further prolongation of the War must lead to defeat of the Russian Revolution and to the triumph of militarism and reaction everywhere. An immediate, just and democratic peace on the principle of "No annexation, no indemnities" will spell the downfall of militarism in all countries. This peace can be achieved if only Labour will speak with one voice and act with all its might. The Russian workers appeal to you to join them in their efforts to turn the scale. Labour speaks.[16]

However, Litvinov was expressing a very utopian view.

During January 1918, Litvinov addressed the Labour Party Conference and described himself as:

A refugee who now stands before you in the unusual role of a representative of his Government. We have no longer to protest against the friendship of your Government with the Tsar.

Litvinov asked the gathering 'to disabuse itself of the notion that the Bolsheviks have usurped power. This is false. Were they merely adventurers, they would have been swept away long ago.' Litvinov briefly sketched the history of the Russian Revolution and the rise to power of the Bolsheviks, which he said was

an object lesson to weak-kneed moderate socialists.

---

[16] *Labour Leader*, 10 January 1918, p.5

How ridiculous it was to hear from the lips of responsible statesmen that the Russian people rose to carry on the war successfully. It was a first class lie. The Russian workers, peasants and soldiers revolted against the War.

This pronouncement was received with a hurricane of cheers.

They revolted against it by revolting against its authors and advocates. Brest-Litovsk is the remarkable experiment of the Russian people justifying itself. Greater and more dramatic history has been made in three weeks than in three-and-a-half years of war. Principles which mean the death of imperialism have been asserted in such a way as to shatter the efforts of the whole capitalist War. If negotiations do not end in peace, a revolution in Germany, and perhaps let me add somewhere else (will take place).

Litvinov stated the principles of internal government that were laid down by the Bolsheviks:

The land has been given to the peasants. The factories are under the supervision of their shop steward committees. Superfluous apartments of the rich have been made available to provide shelter for the homeless. The banks have been nationalised and in short a nationalisation policy has been carried out in all the services of the community. The Army has been democratised and self-determination has been guaranteed to all nationalities of Russia.

The *Labour leader* reported that Litvinov in his final appeal stated:

The Russian worker has been fighting an unequal battle against the imperialists of all the world for democratic principles honestly applied. They have begun the proceedings for a general peace, but it is obvious they cannot finish it alone. I would say to the representatives of British Labour 'Speed up your peace.'[17]

When the Bolsheviks seized power, as far as external relations were concerned, the most urgent question for the new government was whether to continue Russia's participation in the war or whether to seek peace with Germany. Of course, this was important for France, Britain, the United States and their allies because, if the Russians made a separate peace, the chances of a decisive victory over the Germans would be much more difficult. Litvinov's idea that the populations of these countries should persuade their governments to end a war that had been so costly in lives, by opening armistice talks, was hardly practical politics. If armistice talks had been initiated by the Allies, Germany and Austria might well have demanded terms which the Allies could not possibly have accepted and then Germany and Austria would have used the peace offer for propaganda – that those

---

[17] *Labour Leader*, 24 January 1918, p.5

fighting Germany were near to defeat – to bolster their own subjects' morale.

Meanwhile, Litvinov wrote to both the Labour Party leadership and the trade unions informing them of his appointment. Litvinov expressed his confidence that he would obtain the full support of the British proletariat. He then followed up the letter with personal letters to the Labour leaders. Most adopted a friendly attitude. Anderson was particularly friendly and supportive, although Bowerman, the leader of the print union, was hostile.[18]

In his interview with the *Daily Chronicle* and *The New York Times*, Litvinov stated:

> A separate peace would be looked upon by the Bolsheviks as a disaster and a collapse of all their efforts, but the present conditions of Russia aggravated by the Civil War may make it inevitable. It is up to the democracies of the Allied countries to see that this calamity does not happen.

Litvinov then advocated:

> The peoples in the anti-German coalition should compel their governments to smooth the path towards a democratic peace. This, if it is to be done, it must be done now. Otherwise it will be too late. Russia has spoken. It is up to the workers of the allied nations to speak.[19]

Lenin, as early as December 1917, had been endeavouring to sue for peace by sending a man across no man's land to the German trenches.[20] This initiative led to successful talks. An armistice was signed on 15 December 1917, although it could be terminated by seven days' notice after 21 days.

The Germans' reason for the armistice was to give the Bolsheviks time to endeavour to persuade Russia's former allies to join in the talks; however, as might have been expected, they would not agree to the Soviet request. Eventually, the Treaty of Brest-Litovsk was signed on 3 March 1918.[21]

Sir George Buchanan described Litvinov's speech at the Labour Party conference as:

> openly preaching revolution. To allow an unofficial diplomatic agent to carry on revolutionary propaganda in our midst seemed to me inadmissible; yet were we to

---

[18] Maisky, Ivan: *Journey Into the Past*, p.65
[19] *Daily Chronicle*, 4 January 1918, p.1
[20] Debo, Richard: *Revolution and Survival*, p.27
[21] Ibid. pp.32. & 155

take disciplinary action against Litvinov, Trotsky would retaliate with reprisals take members of our embassy. Therefore, we had to choose between coming to terms with the Bolsheviks on the basis of complete reciprocity in all things or to break with them and withdraw our embassy.[22]

Buchanan recommended the latter course, more especially 'as there seemed some prospect of the allies affording material assistance to the loyal elements in South Russia who had not yet submitted to the Bolsheviks or the Germans.'[23]

However, the MP Joseph King disagreed that the speech 'was in any sense an interference in internal politics. It was an appeal to the Socialists and Labour men of this country to act in sympathy with them. It was really a lecture upon the Russian Revolution and Bolshevik Policy.' Further Mr King appealed to the Foreign Office to be more sympathetic to the Russian Revolution.[24]

When some MPs queried whether Litvinov should be permitted to continue his propaganda work in Britain, the Home Office Minister Sir G Cave stated:

> Litvinov is not an ambassador. He is not the representative of any recognised government. He comes here with the avowed object of engaging in revolutionary propaganda in this country. He is not bound by the conditions which regulate the conduct of every ambassador and every minister of a foreign power. However, we are most anxious not to embarrass the Foreign Office, but there must be a limit. Neither Mr Litvinov nor members of his staff can be allowed to continue this course of conduct any longer.

Sir G Cave admitted: 'Unless the British Government had some kind of relationship with the Bolshevik Government, British citizens in Russia might be in serious peril.'[25]

The socialist parties of the Entente were not persuaded to alter course. When they met in conference in February 1918, Mr Vandervelde was using very different language to that of Litvinov. Vandervelde's views were more realistic when he said:

> While holding the olive branch in one hand, we have to hold the sword in the other. We have been forced to take up the sword as the only means of defence. We must not forget we are able to assemble here because the Royal Navy hold the high seas and millions of Allied troops hold the line. If Germany was to succeed, the

---

[22] Buchanan, George: *My Mission to Russia*, p.256; No:17 *ante*
[23] Buchanan, George: *My Mission to Russia*, p.256
[24] *Hansard*, vol.103, 27 February 1918, 1495
[25] Ibid. p.1624

resolutions we pass would be a mere scrap of paper and of no more value than the Russian bank notes of the Russian state bank.[26]

On the last day, Mr Vandervelde toasted the absent Russian proletariat 'who had rendered great service by freeing Russia from Tsarist oppression. They had created great hopes and terrible disappointment'; no doubt referring to the dictatorial way the Bolsheviks were ruling Russia,

The Bolsheviks harmed their standing with the Second International by refusing passports to Mensheviks who wanted to attend the conference. This action was condemned by the meeting.[27]

In February 1918, a mutiny took place on board a Russian ship in the Mersey when the crew were threatening to kill their officers. Nabokov's information was that the crew members had travelled from Liverpool to London to see Litvinov.[28]

A memorandum from the Foreign Office relates how the commanding officer of the mutinous ship stated that, after the sailors had seen Litvinov, their attitude changed,[29] implying that they had become more militant. Nabokov informed Lord Hardinge, a permanent civil servant, of what had happened. However, Lord Hardinge made it clear that Litvinov's relation with the British Government was the business of the British Government, not Nabokov's.[30]

In fact, a police report confirmed that what Nabokov stated was correct. It claimed that Litvinov had received the sailors very well.[31]

In spite of what Lord Hardinge said, it is presumed that he informed the British Navy, who were obviously monitoring the situation. When there was a mutiny on one of the ships, the officers were summoned on board and voices were crying out 'shoot the officers', so the British navy came on board to prevent bloodshed, followed by the police, who took the men into custody. Some of the arrested sailors incriminated Litvinov,[32] and if Litvinov disapproved of the mutiny one would have thought he would have wanted to have made a public statement to that effect.

Basil Thomson, the British police officer, also alleged that Litvinov was seeking interviews

---

[26] *Times*, 24 February 1918, p.8
[27] Ibid.
[28] Nabokov, C: *The Ordeal of a Diplomat*, p.221; Ullman, Richard: *Anglo-Soviet Relations*, vol.1, p.79
[29] FO 371/3299, p.52
[30] Nabokov, C: *The Ordeal of a Diplomat*, p.223
[31] FO 371/3299, p.52
[32] Ibid.

with British, American, Australian and Canadian soldiers and inculcating them with Bolshevik ideas, as well as inducing British and American soldiers of Jewish descent to carry on propaganda in their regiments.[33] There was an occasion when thirty Royal Engineers American and Canadian soldiers were received in Litvinov's office. It was assumed that similarly Litvinov was encouraging them to state their grievances. [34]

In March 1918, Litvinov had his first diplomatic bag, but he was to be disappointed. Instead of the instructions Litvinov was anticipating he would obtain from his government, all he received were some money and Moscow newspapers. Nevertheless, with that money Litvinov could establish the Bolsheviks' first embassy. Ivy Litvinov acted as secretary and Litvinov obtained the services of three or four Russian émigrés. On the door was a brass plate: 'Russian People's Embassy.' Litvinov gave himself the title of Russian People's Ambassador.[35]

Litvinov states that he wrote to Konstantin Nabokov demanding possession of the Russian embassy, but was told that his request would only be granted if the Bolshevik Government was recognised by HM Government. In fact, this recognition did not happen for a further six years. However, in his memoirs, Nabokov states that even if the Bolsheviks should be recognised by the British Government, Nabokov would not regard such recognition as binding on him. 'I would most certainly take every step in my power, in order to prevent the property of the Russian state from falling into the hands of traitors.'[36]

Russian émigrés had not been forced to fight in the British army, if the Russian ambassador granted them exemption. Of the 25,000 of military age, only 4,000 were fighting in the British army. At the time of the treaty of Brest-Litovsk between Germany and Russia, the British War Cabinet determined to toughen their attitude, partly because they believed Maxim Litvinov would exempt all the Russian Jews from military service and decreed that either these Russian Jews should join the army, be interned or return to Russia, which was impracticable because of limited shipping capacity to Russia.

This brought forward what was probably the first official Bolshevik protest when Litvinov stated that he had been inundated with complaints from Russian citizens of military age about what they regarded as a great injustice in the application of conscription to these émigrés whose country was no longer at war.[37]

Later, Litvinov had been banned fron Britain because he had been accused of carrying on

---

[33] Ibid.
[34] Ibid.
[35] Maisky, Ivan: *Journey Into the Past*, p.63
[36] Nabokov, C: *The Ordeal of a Diplomat*, p.210
[37] Englander, David: *A Documentary History of Jewish Immigration to Britain, 1840-1920*, p.334

revolutionary activity. The question is did Litvinov carry on any revolutionary activities in Britain? I have come to the conclusion that he did, provided that the information upon which I base my opinion is correct. First, Litvinov, while he was unofficial ambassador to Britain, made a visit to Ireland to demonstrate the solidarity of the Russian Government with Irish freedom.[38]

Brigadier-General Henry Page Croft drew attention in a question in the House of Commons to Litvinov's various aliases and asked if he was involved in the bank robbery at Tiflis, and whether he was not a dangerous character who should be sent back to Russia at the earliest opportunity.[39] The police confirmed the aliases. They said that Litvinov had registered as an alien under a false name (Finkelstein) and married under a false name (Harrison), both of which were, as an alien, criminal offences. There were regular prosecutions for these offences. If Litvinov had been an ordinary Russian, he would certainly have been prosecuted. However the Foreign Office instructions prevailed that on no account must Litvinov be arrested even if, as the police believed, he might attend an illegal meeting to prevent Russians in the East End from being conscripted into the British army by the creation of what was described as 'an armed guard of powerful men.' Therefore, if Litvinov attended the meeting, instructions were to be given to the police that he was not to be arrested. The Secretary of State for Foreign Affairs stated that if Litvinov was deported it would be impossible to keep our existing relationship in Petrograd.[40]

Litvinov did not, however, suffer in silence, and, believing attack was the best defence, lodged an official protest about the contents of Sir Page Croft's question. Litvinov stated: 'I cannot but arrive at the conclusion that the British Government is deliberately seeking to provoke a conflict with the Government of the Russian Republic.'[41]

Following the armistice which Lenin had negotiated, there was acrimonious debate between the Left revolutionaries who did not wish to make peace with Germany and those led by Lenin, who realised that, as the Russian army had disintegrated, there was no alternative but to accept any terms the Germans offered. In a rare display of democracy in the Soviet period, following defeat by Lenin, Trotsky agreed to support Lenin to enable peace negotiations to be initiated. Then, if the resolution was not passed, Lenin threatened to resign. Trotsky abstained because he realised a divided party was exactly what Germany desired. The Bolsheviks placed their hope in a German revolution led by the German proletariat, but, in the absence of a strong revolutionary movement in Central Europe, no progress was made. Lenin rightly realised that without an army capable of resisting the Germans there was no alternative but to sue for peace. When the treaty of Brest-Litovsk

---

[38] Gitlow, Benjamin: *The Whole of Their Lives*, p.43
[39] *Hansard*, vol.103, 25 February 1918, 1100
[40] FO 371/3299, p.72
[41] Ibid. p.68

was signed, the Germans extracted most harsh terms. Russia was stripped of more than a quarter of its arable land and 40,000,000 people.[42]

After the treaty of Brest-Litovsk was signed, there was a marked deterioration in the relations between the British and Russian Governments. The British Government first considered and then sent a force to actively intervene in the Russian Civil War on behalf of the Whites.[43] However, Litvinov, in the booklet mentioned above, did not criticise those Russians who negotiated and signed the treaty. On the contrary, Litvinov argued, the Bolshevik Government had no alternative to signing the Brest-Litovsk treaty. It seems in this matter he was right, as the Provisional Government's greatest failure was to pursue an unpopular war which Russia was losing.

Litvinov said:

> The Russian army had been melting ever since the last months of the Tsarist regime. It had been melting away through wholesale desertion, which in turn arose from disease caused by hunger, from lack of munitions and general equipment and from a complete lack of faith in the Russian and Allied war aims.[44]

> They [The Bolsheviks] went to Brest-Litovsk relying solely on the revolutionary succour of the working class of the other belligerent countries, above all Germany and Austria-Hungary. It was in order to provoke that succour, that is, to kindle the fire of revolution in Central Europe, that Trotsky, the head of the Russian peace delegation, tried to prolong the negotiations even after their hopelessness had become apparent.[45] [Trotsky] made those speeches that did more to set the German people in opposition to the bourgeois class and Junkers rulers than all the declarations of the Allied statesmen put together had done in the preceding three-and-a-half years of war.

> Trotsky was confronted with the dilemma of either capitulating to the Germans completely, or renewing the war. As he would not do the former and would not do the latter, he broke off negotiations and declared Russia was out of the war, but refused to sign the humiliating terms of peace.

Although Lenin was wrongly predicting a revolution in Central Europe, nevertheless Trotsky stated: ' He would sign the peace treaty if either the Germans presented Russia

---

[42] *The New York Times*, 3 September 1939, Section 4 p.8
[43] Maisky, Ivan: *Journey Into the Past*, p.64; Sheinis, Zinovy: *Maxim Litvinov*, p.106
[44] Litvinov, Maxim: *Bolshevik Revolution : Its Rise and Meaning*, p.50; reprinted as 10 p.38 in 1919 edition
[45] Ibid. p.50 reprinted as above, p.39

with an ultimatum or denounced the armistice by giving the agreed seven days' notice.'

The Germans, however, did neither and, with a perfidy not easily matched in military history, immediately broke off the armistice and marched against a defenceless and partly demobilised Russia. The Bolsheviks gave in and signed the aggravated German conditions of peace.[46] [Treaty of Brest-Litovsk]

Litvinov reports:

Lenin's argument in favour of Brest-Litovsk was that no effective resistance was possible until Russia had been reorganised. With the Germans in the Ukraine, any attempt at resistance would be still more hopeless and those who were prepared to wait until the rising of the working class in Germany and Austria had already been deceived in their expectation when they thought that Germany would not be prepared to march for fear of their own people. On the other hand, if only they [the Bolsheviks] could get a respite, the Russian Socialist Republic would be firmly established and would in due course, even without actually fighting, exercise such a potent influence over the people of other territories that German rule not only in countries forcibly separated from Russia but also in Germany and Austria themselves would be destroyed. This view carried the day.

Then for the first time Litvinov expressed his own opinion by stating: 'The future will show to what extent it was right.'[47] Litvinov clearly expressed doubts, unlike other Communist leaders, as to whether the predicted world-wide revolution would occur. The unsympathetic British Government policy concerning Brest-Litovsk did not go unchallenged. After consulting with Litvinov, Ramsay Macdonald made a strong attack on government policy, reiterating much of what Litvinov was saying:

Who can deny that after the Kerensky military failure, Russia was beaten? Lenin and Trotsky, at least let us be fair and honourable to them, were face to face with this terrible problem; the same problem had faced Kerensky and which has become still more impossible. They had to settle Russia internally, to feed Petrograd, to organise transport, and to meet all sorts of plots and schemes for their overthrow. That was their internal problem. The external problem was to face the Germans. They could only face the Germans in one of two ways. They had either to say straight away: "We are beaten. Do what you like", or manipulate diplomacy and appeal over the heads of the German governing class to the German democracy and try and separate the German democracy from the German governing class. There was a man, Trotsky, a representative of a beaten nation, no army behind him, no force at his command, meeting those liveried uniformed representatives of German

---

[46] *Bolshevik Revolution : Its Rise and Meaning,*1918, p.52; reprinted as p.40 in 1919 edition
[47] Ibid. p.53; reprinted as p.41

militarism and in the end striking more deeply in the heart of Germany than you have done with your armies in the last three years. We stood by supinely, and everybody who understands the situation had their hearts broken by the incompetence of our government to seize the magnificent opportunity which the Brest negotiations gave.[48]

Both Maisky and Sheinis state that Litvinov arrived one day and found the landlord had taken possession of the Embassy premises at 82 Victoria Street because Litvinov had used the premises for dangerous propaganda. Litvinov brought an action, but the judge found that the landlord was justified in repudiating the agreement because Litvinov was using the premises for dangerous propaganda.

A Foreign Office memorandum appears wrong when it stated that it was the landlord who brought the action. Oddly enough, an MP Noel Billings, alleged that Litvinov had physically threatened to defy the landlord and police and asked the Home Office Minister to intervene. The Minister stated that he had heard of Litvinov's threat to physically defy the landlord, but not to defy the police, and no doubt the landlord would avail himself of his legal remedies.[49] Accordingly, the embassy had to be transferred to Litvinov's own house at 11 Bigwood Avenue, Golders Green.[50]

In the summer of 1918, Kerensky arrived in London. On the Wednesday afternoon of the Labour Party Conference, a surprise was sprung when the Secretary at the Conference without warning announced: 'The person on the platform was Kerensky, who had been closely associated with their work in the last year.' Kerensky, speaking in Russian and attended by an interpreter, said:

> Comrades, I am very much impressed by the reception accorded by the Conference. I do not take it as an expression of sympathy towards myself. I do take it as an expression of sympathy towards Russian democracy, which is suffering but is going to fight for the ideals that are so dear to all of you. I do feel it is my duty as a statesman and a man and a politician to tell you, English people, and people of the whole world, that the Russian people and the Russian democracy are fighting against tyranny and they are going to fight to the end. One can break the Russian people, but you cannot subdue them.

Then, quite wrongly, Kerensky asserted: 'The Russian people will shortly join you in the great fight for the great cause for freedom.' Russia did not again enter the war on the side of the Allies. Arthur Henderson, the Chairman, then said that the Executive thought they

---

[48] *Hansard*, vol.103, 12 February 1918, 44
[49] *Hansard*, vol.103, 27 February 1918, 1399; Maisky, Ivan: *Journey Into the Past*, p.66; Sheinis, Zinovy: *Maxim Litvinov*, p.110; FO 371/3299, p.54
[50] Sheinis, Zinovy: *Maxim Litvinov*, p.110

could not allow the opportunity to go by and they therefore asked the Conference to authorise the executive to invite Kerensky to join the fraternal delegates the following day and then more fully to address the Conference. There were loud shouts of agreement.[51] Then, oddly enough in view of what transpired afterwards, the Conference is reported to have agreed unanimously to Kerensky addressing the Conference as a fraternal visitor. As Henderson's biographer states, Henderson said that if the Conference wanted a card vote they could have one as to whether they would hear Kerensky. Clearly, if there had been a substantial number opposed to Kerensky speaking, there would have been a card vote, but when the motion was put, every hand in the hall was raised in assent.[52]

The *Times*, but not the official report, recorded that one delegate moved that Litvinov should also be invited to address the Conference, but Henderson, the Chairman, would not accept the motion. Then the official report stated that a point of order was raised by several delegates as to what was the reason for Kerensky's visit and whom did Kerensky represent? However, both the *Manchester Guardian* and *The New York Times* reveal that there were other objections. One delegate referred to Kerensky as 'a government plant.' The Chairman indignantly replied that to say such a thing in the presence of Mr Kerensky 'was an outrage.' Evidence that the vast majority of the Conference delegates agreed with Henderson emerged when one delegate insisted on speaking after he had been ordered by the Chairman to sit down. The Chairman put it to the meeting that the delegate be ordered to withdraw from the Conference and the vote was almost unanimous.[53]

When the visiting delegates were introduced the next day, one delegate shouted: 'What are the credentials of Mr Kerensky?' Arthur Henderson reminded the delegates correctly that the Conference had agreed that Kerensky should address them. Litvinov was in the public gallery and one delegate said, 'Are we going to hear Litvinov?'

Henderson reminded the Conference:

> Although many delegates disagreed with Litvinov, he was permitted, in a spirit of toleration and fair play, to address the Nottingham conference. Is it too much that we would give Kerensky a similar hearing? By spoken word on the previous day the Chairman had understood the conference wished to hear Kerensky. If necessary, the question should be put again and even a card vote taken. This should be done rather than bringing Kerensky to the platform and subjecting him to insult and humiliation.

Further proof beyond doubt that the majority of the delegates wanted to hear Kerensky was shown when it was put to the vote as to whether the Conference wanted to hear Kerensky.

---

[51] Official Labour Party Report, 1918, p.35
[52] Hamilton Mary Agnes: *Arthur Henderson*, p.182
[53] *Times*, 27 June 1918, p.8 *The New York Times*, 27 June 1918, p.4; *Manchester Guardian* 27 June 1918, p.5

The *Times* then stated: 'The overwhelming majority decided that they wanted to hear Kerensky.' *The New York Times* was more specific and stated: ' Only four delegates voted against it.'[54] Sheinis's statement 'Kerensky was met with expressions of hostility while Litvinov was cheered though he was not allowed to speak' was highly misleading.[55] If Sheinis wanted to be fair, he should have recorded that only four delegates voted against hearing Kerensky. It would be very unusual for any person, whether or not he was a delegate, to reply to a distinguished speaker's address. On the contrary, the *Times* stated that when Kerensky appeared on the platform there was an extraordinary enthusiastic reception, the delegates and the public singing 'Jolly Good Fellow.'[56]

Kerensky then gave his address as a fraternal visitor and took the opportunity of making an attack on the Bolsheviks. Much of what he said was true. Kerensky remarked that he was astonished the Bolsheviks had

> dispersed the Constituent Assembly, abolished freedom of speech, has made human life the easy prey of every red guardsman, has destroyed the liberty of the elections, even in the Councils of the Workmen, that has made an end of all institutions of self-government that have been elected by universal suffrage. The Bolsheviks claim that the present state of Russia is a dictatorship of the proletariat, although the most ruthless repression is applied against the democratic and socialist parties. War has been organised against the helpless population and every Russian citizen who refuses to recognise this method of government as perfect is declared counter-revolutionary.[57]

History proved that Kerensky's criticism was justified. It would have been otherwise if the Bolsheviks had regarded dictatorship as a temporary expediency rather than a permanent feature of Bolshevik government and Lenin had determined not to be an absolute dictator but to rule with the consent of the people confirmed by universal suffrage. What Kerensky stated about enemies of the people transpired to be absolutely correct. People declared as enemies of the people in one generation and often executed were rehabilitated in a subsequent period of communism.

Litvinov and others in the Bolshevik hierarchy might have been wiser to have taken Kerensky's criticism seriously. Clearly, the reception given to Kerensky indicated that the vast majority of the British Labour movement believed that a safer route to improve the prosperity of the working class was through the parliamentary route rather than by revolution.

---

[54] *Times*, 28 June 1918, p.8; *The New York Times*, 28 June 1918, p.3
[55] Sheinis, Zinovy: *Maxim Litvinov*, p.110
[56] *Times* 28 June 1918 p.3
[57] Labour Conference Report, p.60

Certainly, the *Herald* was very supportive of Kerensky. M S Fairburn stated: 'Kerensky was completely justified in attributing the warm welcome extended to him by the conference to the sympathy of British Labour towards Russian democracy.' However, Fairburn was equally critical of the Allied Governments 'who let Russia fall to pieces, rather than accept the plain truth that Russia was on the verge of ruin. Kerensky failed because, under direct pressure from the Allies, last summer he undertook the criminal and disastrous Galician offensive with a broken army and in open opposition to the declared aspirations of the Russian people.' However, Fairburn was equally critical of Kerensky's appeal for foreign intervention, 'rather than in the past only asking for sympathy and asylum.'[58]

The *Observer* remarked:

> The large majority of the conference took the Chairman's view that Kerensky's service to democracy during the early days of the Revolution entitled him not only to a hearing but an enthusiastic reception.

It claimed:

> The minority occupied an amount of time at the conference out of all proportion to its numbers and was largely composed of people who also wished the withdrawal of the Labour members from the Government.

The attitude of the bulk of the delegates towards them was shown by the remark of Jack Jones: 'While they [the minority] claimed they were asking for freedom, what they were really out for was scalps.'

In similar vein, another delegate remarked:

> There were people in the conference who would oppose anything. The conference was pro-Kerensky without being anti-Bolshevik and it recorded a warm reception to Mr Kerensky, as the previous conference did at Nottingham for Mr Litvinov. Whatever the differences between them, both had worked for democracy. Both had suffered abuse and misrepresentation from the English daily press.[59]

The *Herald* published a statement from Litvinov, who accused the Chairman of the Conference, Arthur Henderson, 'of allowing Kerensky to make a calumnious attack on the Bolshevik Government without letting me reply to his charge.' Litvinov refuted Kerensky's assertion that 'the Bolshevik Government did not represent the bulk of the population.'

---

[58] Fairburn article, *Herald*, 6 July 1918, p.8
[59] *Observer*, 30 June 1918, p.9

Litvinov reminded Kerensky:

> The continuance of the government in time of Revolution for eight months without a standing army, except voluntary detachments, without police and press censorship and indeed with greater freedom of speech and the press than exists in any other country immediately disproves allegations to the contrary. Kerensky and his friends, having convinced themselves of the futility of any counter-revolutionary revolts in Russia, are now coming abroad to seek foreign military intervention for the overthrow of the Soviets under the pretext of fighting Germany. Further, if Kerensky is successful in overthrowing the Bolshevik regime, it will not be replaced by a socialist or even a democratic government but by the most brutal and barbaric military dictatorship resting on foreign bayonets, with the inevitable restoration of Tsarism. Is the British proletariat prepared to take upon itself the responsibility before history for crushing the great Russian proletarian Revolution?[60]

According to Sheinis, there was a meeting at Caxton Hall of various Left-wing persons who sympathised with Litvinov.[61] I have been unable to find any independent report of the meeting. On 30 June, trade union members assembled at Caxton Hall. Mr J H Williams said: 'There were people who were prepared to condone all the misdeeds of Germany and enter into peace negotiations.'

The meeting passed a resolution 'repudiating the right of the Labour Party to end the political truce without any mandate from the workers.' The meeting was highly critical of the Bolsheviks who, they complained, 'were trying to restrict shipbuilding and the supply of munitions.' Clearly, they were not impressed with Litvinov's desire for early peace negotiations, but preferred to put their faith in the British Government.[62]

Later, in the summer of 1918, Litvinov decided that the centre of the interventionist movement had moved to the USA and accordingly advised Lenin, who agreed with him that Litvinov could do more for the Soviet Government in the USA than in Britain. Accordingly, Litvinov applied for a visa to the USA, but was refused.[63]

On 30 August 1918, an attempt was made on Lenin's life and, on 1 September 1918, Bruce Lockhart, who was accused of being involved in the plot to kill Lenin, was arrested.[64] As a

---

[60] Litvinov's answer: *Herald*, 6 July 1918, p.4
[61] Sheinis, Zinovy: *Maxim Litvinov*, p.109
[62] *Times*,1 July 1918, p.5
[63] Maisky, Ivan: *Journey Into the Past*, p.67
[64] Sheinis, Zinovy: *Maxim Litvinov*, p.111; Pope, Arthur: *Maxim Litvinov*, p.138; Maisky, Ivan: *Journey Into the Past*, p.67

consequence, Litvinov, who was still in England, was arrested. While in Brixton gaol he was treated perfectly decently. The lower ranks of staff such as gaolers openly sympathised with him.[65]

However, the British Government had lost their one link with the Soviet Government which previously had been supplied by Litvinov. While in prison, the British Government sent Leeper to see Litvinov, whose attitude was firm. Either the Government regarded Litvinov as a representative of the Soviet Government, in which case he must be released, or they regarded him as being under arrest, in which case they had no business coming and asking him to send a message in cipher. Leeper left, for the moment, empty-handed.

Litvinov's firm hand paid dividends because shortly afterwards he was released. The other members of the embassy who had been imprisoned were likewise released.[66] Litvinov then agreed to send the message. Subsequently, it was arranged that Litvinov would be free to leave Britain if Lockhart was allowed to depart from Russia; but the question as to who would leave first made agreeing the terms more difficult.

A similar scenario was unfolding in Russia between Lockhart and the Soviet authorities. Karakan was instructed to talk to Lockhart while he was in prison. Lockhart's attitude was similar to that of Litvinov. Lockhart pointed out:

> How absurd it was for him to be talking to me [about foreign affairs] if they thought he was a murderer and assassin. Karachan laughed and talked about the necessity of propaganda.[67]

Eventually, Litvinov's proposal that he should go first to Norway but would not leave Norway until Lockhart left Russia was accepted by the Foreign Office. Litvinov duly kept his word that he would not leave Norway until Lockhart was released. When Litvinov arrived in Norway he went to see the Norwegian Foreign Minister, but was told that any such agreement did not concern them and Litvinov could do what he pleased.

Clearly, Litvinov could have left Norway, but instead called on the British Mission and told them that he would not leave until there was news that Lockhart had crossed the border. When it was confirmed that Lockhart had crossed the border, Litvinov left for Russia.[68]

A report in *Pravda* on 26 October 1918 states that the staff from Litvinov's embassy in Britain arrived back in Russia the day before. It announces and explains Litvinov's stay in

---

[65] Maisky, Ivan: *Journey Into the Past*, p.67
[66] Ibid. p.68
[67] FO 371/ 3344/186867, 18 October 1918
[68] Maisky, Ivan: *Journey Into the Past*, p.69

Norway, then goes on to report that he would arrive in the next few days.[69] Litvinov did so arrive in Russia.

While Litvinov was the Bolshevik representative in Britain, I have no doubt that he carried out his duties enthusiastically, doing his best to promulgate the Revolution in which he then unreservedly believed. For example, he wanted his military representative to visit interned Russians in the Tower of London and at Deepcut, Aldershot, because their complaints were being ignored.[70] I can find no mention of his request being granted. I am sure Litvinov appreciated the strength of his position. He knew he could overstep the mark as appropriate since the British Government could not afford to expel him. However, I believe that a profound change took place between the time that he was imprisoned in Brixton and the time he arrived in Russia, when he had lost his revolutionary zeal. The reason for this was that he expected that the defeat of Germany would lead to a communist revolution; but when it did not occur, Litvinov quickly realised that revolution was not going to spread through Europe and it was a question of communism in one country.

Upon his returning to Britain, Lockhart reported to the Foreign Office. He stated that, in his opinion, the Bolshevik regime was stronger than at any time during its brief history. It possessed one attribute necessary for any government – physical power to enforce its decrees. For this reason it was a mistake for the Allies to count on such anti-Bolshevik elements as existed to fight the regime. The peasants might welcome a deliverer, but they would not be induced again to undergo the horrors of war. One course would be to abandon intervention altogether, secure the free and unhindered exit of the Czech troops and come to some working arrangement with the Bolsheviks. The advocates of this policy pointed out that this would absolve the British Government of the charge of suppressing an anti-capitalist revolution. They argued that Bolshevism could not be killed by the bayonet but should be allowed to die a natural death. Further, by not sending troops to Russia to fight the Bolsheviks, the Government could help to avoid serious labour trouble at home. The Soviet Government, if freed from the constant fear of outside interference, could become more moderate because the Bolshevik leaders would not be able to use Allied intervention as an excuse for internal repression.

Nevertheless, this was not the policy Lockhart now advocated, but immediate intervention on a larger scale to supplement the Allied forces already in Siberia and North Russia, while at the same time taking advantage of the defeat of Turkey to send an expeditionary force through the Black Sea to join Denikin's force and march on Moscow. Lockhart criticised the half-hearted assistance given to those opposing Bolshevism.[71] However, such an army might have met the same fate as Napoleon's and Hitler's armies.

---

[69] Sheinis, Zinovy: *Maxim Litvinov* p.113
[70] FO 371/3299/54
[71] FO 371/3344/174035

3: THE OSTRACISED STATE

Back in Russia, Lenin received Litvinov. The date of the meeting was not disclosed. Lenin welcomed the opportunity to hear first-hand of conditions in Britain. He appointed Litvinov to the Foreign Collegiate.[1]

At this time Russia was enveloped in civil war. Sheinis is undoubtedly wrong to say that Litvinov returned to a country without gendarmes.[2] The Cheka police had replaced the Tsarist police, but had adopted many of the practices of the Tsarist police, such as provocateurs and methods of torture to extract confessions. After all, many of the Bolsheviks had been inmates in Tsarist prisons; but instead of repudiating such undesirable practices, the Bolsheviks decided to adopt them. Conditions in Cheka prisons were generally worse than in Tsarist jails. A Government inspection team in October 1918 found overcrowded cells, no water and inadequate rations and heating. Half of the 1,500 inmates were chronically sick, ten per cent with typhus, and corpses were even found in the cells.[3]

However, Sheinis was undoubtedly right when he said that there was much hunger in Moscow and Petrograd. Typhoid killed people by the thousands in October 1918, and there were 3,134 cases of cholera registered in one month. [4] However, some responsibility for this situation rested with the Allies, who had sent troops to support those who were trying, by force, to overthrow the Bolshevik Government. The consequences of such intervention were that, during 1918 and 1919, a civil war raged in Russia between the Red Army under the direction of the Bolsheviks and the White generals assisted for dubious reasons by the USA, Britain, France and Japan.

Towards the end of 1919, the question arose as to whether the Soviet Union should be admitted to the Peace Conference. Although Lloyd George took the sensible view that the affairs of 200 million people could not be settled without hearing them, he was overruled by Clemenceau, who had the support of two members of Lloyd George's own cabinet: Balfour and Curzon. For that reason, Russia was not invited.[5] Litvinov's efforts to seek a rapprochement with the USA were rebuffed.[6]

---

[1] Sheinis, Zinovy: *Maxim Litvinov*, p.116
[2] Ibid. p.113; compared with Figes see below
[3] Figes, Orlando: *A People's Tragedy*, p.645
[4] Sheinis, Zinovy: *Maxim Litvinov*, p.115
[5] Ullman, Richard: *Anglo-Soviet Relations*, vol.2, p.87
[6] Sheinis, Zinovy: *Maxim Litvinov*, p.118

France had tremendous foreign investment in Russia. Prior to the First World War, 32.6% of all investment in Russia was French; but France had no enthusiasm personally to intervene, but preferred allowing Poland and Czechoslovakia to do the job.[7] Perhaps the USA's intervention was most surprising because, as Fischer stated, President Wilson detested Bolshevism, but armed force never appealed to him as a means of suppressing Bolshevism.[8] An important aim of President Wilson was to prevent Japan's domination of Siberia,[9] but on the instructions of the British cabinet, a cable was sent to President Wilson urging him of the need for Japanese intervention. Clearly, any effective military action by the Allies without Japanese intervention would need an increased military force. However, orders were given by the Allies without the President's consent. Faced with such a *fait accompli*, Wilson immediately joined the expedition, but stated that military action was only justified to protect the Czech army.[10]

On 3 August 1918, President Wilson proposed to Japan that each country send a few thousand men to Vladivostok.[11] However, Japan, who wanted to gain a foothold in Siberia, decided to pour a great many soldiers into Siberia and North Manchuria. Japan resented the American presence.[12] Antagonism arose between Japan and the USA over the running of the Siberian railway, which the Provisional Government had asked the USA to run.[13]

The Allies tried to blockade Russia. By 1919 the blockade was complete. For a year Russia could not buy medicines to cope with typhus and other epidemics.[14]

However, the White generals had no political strategy to govern the territories they won. They were mostly occupying territory inhabited by non-Russians: the Ukraine, the Caucasus and the Baltic. Like Hitler a little more than twenty years later, the White generals failed to comprehend that a compromise with non-Russian national aspirations was essential if they were to build a broad area of support among non-Russian people. The non-Russian population favoured some autonomy at least.[15] Further, the White generals failed to gain the support of the peasants, who feared a White victory, because the peasants might be forced to hand back the land seized since the Revolution.[16]

As is well analysed by Figes, the help of the Western countries was spasmodic. With one hand they gave military help to the White generals and with the other tried to foster peace

---

[7] Fischer, Louis: *The Soviets in World Affairs*, pp.230 & 231
[8] Ibid. p 226
[9] Ibid. p.132
[10] Ibid. p.133
[11] Ibid. p. 133 -134
[12] Ibid. p. 227
[13] Ibid. pp.135 & 227
[14] Ibid. p. 248
[15] Figes, Orlando: *A People's Tragedy*, p.571
[16] Ibid. p.572

talks. It was a disastrous policy because it ingrained into the Russian leaders a deep suspicion that the Western countries were prepared to go to any lengths to topple the regime.[17] As Litvinov said, 'We must be left to work out among ourselves our social experiment.'[18] The intervention was quite unjustified by international law.

On the other hand, as early as November 1918, Karakhan told Lockhart that if intervention was abandoned, 'the Bolsheviks would have been prepared to come to terms with the Allies and make commercial concessions which would be most favourable for the Allies.'[19]

By October 1919, the war was going well for the Whites. Denikin captured Oriel. The crucial arsenal of Tulia, which was the gateway to Moscow, was within a hundred miles. The Reds were determined to go to any length to defend Tulia. Thousands of peasants and bourgeois citizens were conscripted into labour teams. They felled trees to fuel the factories and dug trenches around the city. Hundreds of bourgeoisie relatives were held as hostages to be shot if the work was not done properly. The Reds amassed 200,000 troops, together with a cavalry unit established by Budenny, a former NCO in the Tsarist army.[20] The counter-offensive was completely successful. After finally capturing a railway junction on 15 November 1919, the Whites were in full retreat and never again did they threaten to break through on the central sector.[21]

Meanwhile, fighting had been raging around Petrograd since the White army entered Russia and mounted a northern offensive. Finland had declared its independence in 1918, and established a useful army. If, as the Germans did in 1941, the White generals had endeavoured to enlist Finnish support by giving them an assurance that their independence would be preserved, the White generals might have captured Petrograd. On the contrary, the White generals were openly pursuing a policy of wishing to restore Greater Russia which, if successful, would have spelled the end of Finnish independence. A further problem for the Whites was that, as soon as the army entered Russia, many of their Russian conscripts deserted and the army met opposition from the local population.[22]

On 10 October 1919, the Whites decided to make a dash for Petrograd. The White generals thought they had a good opportunity with the Bolsheviks being heavily involved on the Southern Front. The Petrograd offensive partly succeeded because it caused, as no doubt it was intended to do, panic among Petrograd's population. Lenin wrongly wanted to abandon Petrograd because he thought it could not be successfully defended.[23]

---

[17] Ibid. p.574
[18] *The New York Times*, 24 March 1920, p.5
[19] PRO FO 371/3344, letter from Lockhart to Balfour, 7 November 1918
[20] Figes, Orlando: *A People's Tragedy*, p.667
[21] Ibid. p.670
[22] Ibid. p.670
[23] Ibid. p.673

It was fortunate for the Bolsheviks that Trotsky disagreed with Lenin. Trotsky believed that Petrograd could be defended and, having taken command of the army, proceeded successfully to implement his belief. Although Petrograd had been affected by strikes since the Revolution, hundreds of workers armed themselves with rifles and rallied to defend the city. By mid-November 1919, the White army, in full retreat, had left Russian soil. It was only allowed to enter Estonia on condition it was disarmed.[24] However, it was not until 1920 that the White general Wrangel was finally driven from the Crimea and control taken of Transcaucasia, Azerbaijan, Georgia and Armenia.[25]

The civil war was over. It had been won by overwhelming popular support. The communist regime now had a chance to build a new democratic system of government in which private capital would play no or little part. Would individual greed among the population frustrate such attempts? Unfortunately, this proved to be the case, although it would take over seventy years to end the regime that Lenin had established.

While Litvinov was in London, as ambassador, he did his best to persuade the most important of left-wing sympathisers that the Allies had no right to intervene in Russia. In Ramsay Macdonald, a Labour MP, Litvinov found a strong advocate.

In August 1918 the British troops were landing in Archangel. Macdonald wrote an article for *Socialist Review* attacking the British Government for acting as their great grandfathers had acted when the then British Government insisted on restoring the Bourbons to the throne of France. Macdonald praised Lenin for giving Russia a chance to settle down and for saving her from a reign of terror.[26] Litvinov had less luck with the Labour Party Executive, which had neither approved nor condemned the Allied intervention in Russia, but accepted it as an accomplished fact.[27]

The British Government's policy of intervention was criticised by Clynes, one of the most moderate Labour politicians, who wrote in the *Observer*:

> I doubt whether the Government appreciates the depth of feeling that exists in the minds of thousands of workers with regard to Russia. The art of concealment has bewildered workmen. It has created suspicion and aroused anger far more than any other policy since the General Election. No reassurance can be found by merely shouting "Bolshevik" and we still await a simple and convincing statement of our military purpose in Russia. If only a small part of what has come from persuasive sources is true about the Bolsheviks, there is a great cause for lamentation if not for military resistance, but why should we not get at the truth? If the Government has

---

24 Ibid. p.674
25 Pope, Arthur: *Maxim Litvinov*, p.167
[26] Marquand, David: *Macdonald*, p.226
[27] Labour Party Executive Minutes, 18 September 1918

the truth it should reveal it in more convincing form than has yet been attempted by its spokesmen.[28]

Indeed, rather than justify the intervention, in his Guildhall speech on 8 November 1918 Lloyd George, in effect, put an end to intervention. Lloyd George later constantly criticised Chamberlain for not being more enthusiastic about British-Soviet co-operation, but he had clearly shown his sympathies were with the anti-Bolshevik forces. In his speech at the Guildhall on 10 November 1919, Lloyd George stated that he 'did not like the outlook in Russia', which sentiments were likely to please his audience of bankers:

A few weeks ago there was a prospect of an early issue. It was distinctly promising. Today the indications point to a more prolonged and sanguinary struggle. The daring raid on Petrograd has not come off. For a moment General Denikin's brilliant march towards Moscow has been temporarily checked.

Lloyd George then said:

'We cannot afford to continue so costly an intervention in an interminable civil war.' However he did not question whether it was either wise or moral to have become involved in the Civil War in the first place, if the result of a White victory would have been to replace one dictatorship with another.[29] While the Civil War was waging, Litvinov was carrying on his diplomatic duties, mainly abroad. His first important task was to travel to Sweden at the end of November 1918 with instructions to try and reach an amicable agreement with the Allies. Sweden still enjoyed diplomatic relations with Soviet Russia.

Litvinov was sent as a commercial attaché, but was actually empowered to enter into political negotiations. On 23 December 1918, Litvinov approached the ambassadors of Britain, France, Italy and the USA with the Soviet Government's peace proposals. The British Chargé D'affaires, Clive, through an informant, was told that Litvinov hoped to secure the end of intervention and some form of recognition of the Soviet Union. In return, the decree whereby foreign debts were repudiated would be rescinded, British subjects would be released and compensation paid for the murder of Captain Cromie. Litvinov approached Clive, who refused to have any discourse with Litvinov on the grounds that the Swedish Government forbade the Soviet mission from taking part in political activities.[30] In spite of the fact that Clive refused to discuss the proposals of 23 December 1918, the Imperial War Cabinet decided that Litvinov's proposal should be examined. Churchill led the opposition to any accommodation with the Bolsheviks, but the Australian Labour Prime Minister, William M. Hughes, disagreed with Winston Churchill and advocated the

---

[28] *Observer*, 15 June1919, p.16; Ullman, Richard: *Anglo- Soviet Relations*, vol.2, p.361
[29] *Times*, 10 November 1919, p.9
[30] Ullman, Richard: *Anglo-Soviet Relations*, vol.2, p.88

not unreasonable policy that: 'The Allies should immediately withdraw from Russia and the Russians should be entitled to adopt whatever sort of government they wished.'[31]

Notwithstanding the decision of the Imperial War Cabinet, the Allies sabotaged Litvinov's efforts by persuading the Scandinavian countries to withdraw their missions in Russia and break off diplomatic relations. On 30 January 1919, Litvinov and Vorovsky were expelled and had to return to Russia across Finland in a sealed train.[32]

On 23 January 1919, while in Sweden, Litvinov made a press statement. He admitted that propaganda had been carried out in Germany but denied any Soviet activity in neutral or Entente countries:

> While I represented the Russian Government in Britain, neither I nor any of my staff was engaged in any illegal propaganda. The same applies to Bolshevik diplomats in Scandinavia. Now, when the Entente nations are waging war in Russia and in Russian territory, we feel justified in engaging in propaganda work among the Allied troops. Any government in our place would do the same. With the end of hostilities and the withdrawal of these troops, there will be neither opportunity nor desire on our part to make foreign troops or citizens the objects of our propaganda. In regard to Germany, we do not deny propaganda work, but prior to the Revolution, Germany, despite the formal peace, continued to be the greatest danger to the Russian Revolution and our propaganda was an act of self-defence. Even now the Allies are attempting to make Germany a jumping off ground to attacking Russia and are even using, for this purpose, German troops with the connivance of Scheidemann's government.
>
> With the ceasing of the Allied war against the Soviets and a resumption of diplomatic intercourse, German-Russia relations will be put on a more formal footing and then the German Government will have as little cause for complaint about propaganda as other Governments at peace with Russia. Of course we shall continue to express our views through our press and literature, but this will not take the form of a direct appeal to citizens of other countries, and will be conducted by political parties, not the Government.[33]

However, Litvinov was not correct. The incident that occurred nearest in time to prove that he was wrong was in 1920, when he was advocating giving money secretly to the *Herald*. Litvinov stated: 'In Russian questions the *Herald* acts as if it is our organ.'[34]

---

[31] Ibid. p.90
[32] Sheinis, Zinovy: *Maxim Litvinov*, p.121
[33] *The New York Times*, 23 January 1919, p.2
[34] See Ch.9, Nos.22-25

Litvinov assured the correspondent:

> The Bolshevik Government were great friends of the freedom of the Press and political liberty and that the present suppression of all opposition in Russia was due to the fact that the other parties in a treacherous way had invited foreign troops to invade Russia to fight the Bolsheviks.[35]

Whether Litvinov believed then that there would be freedom of the press is not known, but for the whole of the seventy years that the Communists ruled there was never freedom of the press until the arrival of Gorbachev, and one of the reasons for the 1968 Soviet invasion of Czechoslovakia was the fact that their leadership introduced freedom of the press. However, during Litvinov's USA ambassadorship, he became a convert to the notion of press freedom, a rarity among prominent Communists.[36]

In concluding, Litvinov said: 'He was sorry that Paris had been chosen for the Peace Conference as it was the least suitable place for the Soviet representative to go.' He remarked: 'It was not President Wilson's fault that the Russian Government, which has been in power for fifteen months, was not represented at the conference.'[37]

A young diplomat, Bullitt, was sent by President Wilson to Russia on a fact-finding mission. Following a long conversation with Lenin, Chicherin and Litvinov, Bullitt put forward these proposals on 12 March 1919:[38]

1. All *de facto* governments of the territories of the former Russian Empire and Finland would remain in full control of the territories they occupied at the moment of the Armistice, the revision of the frontiers to take place only by self determination of the inhabitants. Each government would agree not to use force against any of the others.
2. The blockade shall be raised and normal trade relations restored.
3. The Soviet Government shall have the right of unhindered rail transit to the sea and the use of all former Russian ports and Finnish ports necessary for trade.
4. Soviet citizens shall have free right of entry into Allied countries and countries set up on the former Russian territory provided they do not interfere in domestic politics, and Allied citizens would have the similar right to enter Russia.
5. All governments on the former Russian territory and the Allied Governments shall grant an amnesty to all political prisoners on both sides and all prisoners of war shall be released.

---

[35] *The New York Times*, 23 January 1919, p.2
[36] See Ch.17, No.80
[37] *The New York Times*, 23 January 1919, p.2
[38] FRUS Russia, p.77

6. All foreign troops would be withdrawn from Russia and foreign military assistance to anti-Soviet Governments on the territory of the Old Russian Empire shall cease.
7. All Governments set up on Russian territory will recognise their share in the responsibility for the debts of the former Russian Empire.[39]

It was indeed a generous offer giving up the whole of Siberia, the Urals, Caucasus, Murmansk, Finland, a portion of White Russia and most of the Ukraine; an offer that should have been accepted, as Bullitt recommended. Bullitt further said, 'No real peace can be established in Europe or the world until peace is made with the Revolution.'[40] However, these terms did not appeal to either the French Prime Minister Clemenceau or Lloyd George, who gave as a rather feeble reason the hostility of the press, including the *Times*.

The result of the visit was that Bullitt became sympathetic to the Soviet Union, which no doubt influenced Roosevelt (following recognition of Soviet Russia) in 1933 to appoint Bullitt as the first ambassador to the USSR.

The leader of the *Daily Mail* on 27 March 1919 stated:

> To dream of peace while this plague spot remains in Eastern Europe is absurd. There can be no peace until Bolshevism is overthrown. Instead of talking, the Paris conference should call in Marshal Foch and give him power to act.[41]

During the Allied intervention the peasants and significantly many of the Tsar's senior officers sided with the Bolsheviks. Napoleon and Hitler lost huge armies in the East and a large Allied army might well have suffered the same fate, particularly if the Allied Army had to fight through a Russian winter.

Another significant event, which occurred in 1919, was the founding of the Third Communist International, followed in September by the establishment of an affiliated American party. All the important Bolshevik leaders attended, including, of course, Lenin and Litvinov. Lenin's opening statement was laughable for its inaccuracies. Lenin stated:

> The Soviet system had triumphed not only in backward Russia but also in Germany, the most advanced of the capitalist countries, and in Britain, the oldest of the capitalist countries. The victory of the world communism Revolution is certain.

As Payne rightly said, Lenin must have known the victory was far from certain. Lenin's bombast was very different to Litvinov's equivocal language at this time. He was already acknowledging that 'communism was a system which might or might not fail', as stated in

---

[39] Ullmam, Richard: *Anglo-Soviet Relations*, vol.2, p.148
[40] Ibid. p.149
[41] *Daily Mail*, 27 March 1919, p.4

chapter 2, when discussing his response to the Brest-Litovsk treaty. When Lenin proposed the creation of the Third International, only the German socialist Eberlein was not overwhelmed by enthusiasm – he insisted that he must consult his party. At first Lenin agreed to Eberlein's request, but in the night Lenin changed his mind and insisted on a resolution being passed declaring this conference the first of the Third International, in spite of the fact that there were only thirty-five delegates. Lenin made the ridiculous remark:'The Soviets had conquered throughout the whole world.'[42] This indicates that Lenin never truly wanted an international conference, but only one dominated by Russia and him.

Litvinov, on 1 January 1920, made a patriotic speech declaring:

> We have triumphed over Yudenich, Denikin and Kolchak because they had the people against them. It is untrue the army is led by German staff officers. Many officers of the Old Russian army are fighting in our ranks from conviction. [Litvinov was correct, as many of the old generals in the Tsar's army were supporting the Communist government.] Both East and West have much else to think about than war with Russia. The world wants peace and peace is coming all the more quickly as the Red Army demonstrates the power of Russia.[43]

Litvinov achieved further success when he was instructed to proceed to Dorpat to negotiate peace terms with the Baltic States. Talks opened on 17 November 1919 and Russia confirmed that, although the Baltic States formed an integral part of the Tsarist Russian Empire, the Bolshevik government was prepared to recognise their sovereignty.[44]

Furthermore, Russia successfully threatened the rest of Europe that she would unilaterally break the blockade. On 16 January 1920, the Peace Conference lifted the blockade. On 7 July 1920, the US State Department decided to lift their blockade.[45] Once Europe had lifted the blockade, if the USA had not taken such action she would have lost potential markets.

Before the talks with Estonia were finalised, Litvinov was instructed to proceed to Copenhagen to negotiate an exchange of prisoners captured by both sides in the Civil War. Britain had agreed to send an MP, O'Grady, to negotiate. In Copenhagen, Litvinov was soon conducting parleys with a host of powers.[46] It was not long before he achieved further success when he agreed an exchange of prisoners with Russia which, besides Britain, included the Scandinavian countries, Austria, Hungary, Switzerland, Holland, Belgium and

---

[42] Payne, Robert: *Life and Death of Lenin*, p.510
[43] *The New York Times*, 1 January 1920, p.3, and 24 March 1920, p.5
[44] Debo, Richard: *Survival and Consolidation*, p.136
[45] Fischer, Louis: *The Soviets in World Affairs*, Europe: pp.248 & 313; & USA: p.313
[46] Debo, Richard: *Survival and Consolidation*, p.137

Italy, as well as France. The agreement was signed on 12 February 1920.[47] Although the official talks were limited to prisoner exchange, Louis Fischer gives credit to Litvinov for unofficial talks which played an important role as an icebreaker for the subsequent Anglo-Soviet trade talks, which were successfully concluded on 16 March 1921.[48]

Litvinov proved to be such a good negotiator that Gregory in the Foreign Office complained that Litvinov had taken unfair advantage of O'Grady.[49] Sir H Greenwood was able to report to the House of Commons on 24 February 1920 that an agreement had been concluded[50] and on 19 March 1920 that the Russians had expressed great satisfaction.[51]

Krassin and Joffe replaced Litvinov as the Bolshevik Government's negotiators. Estonia received no encouragement from its neighbours to come to an agreement with Russia. In particular, Poland wanted its allies to assist it as it prepared for a Russian invasion. The Bolshevik Government was so keen to effect an agreement with Estonia that Chicherin offered reparations for the damage caused by the Soviets when in possession of the Baltic States. Subsequently, Estonia was offered 15 million gold roubles.

In 1920, Estonia decided that she would resume negotiations with the Soviet Government without the participation of any of Estonia's neighbours. The negotiations were successfully concluded, restoring diplomatic relations with Estonia, and the treaty of peace was signed at Dorpat on 2 February 1920.[52]

While Maxim was in Copenhagen, Ivy joined him during the summer of 1920 (their third child was conceived at this time), but returned to England.[53] However, Ivy was appalled at how the communist delegation, of which her husband was part, lived in grand hotels, wore fur coats and smoked enormous cigars. She had never seen her husband so plutocratic.[54] Litvinov left Denmark on 3 September 1920 and travelled to Norway, but his trip met with no success as he failed to negotiate a trade treaty.[55]

Litvinov's success was resumed when on 20 April 1920 he signed a treaty with France by which France agreed not to intervene in the affairs of Russia and not to co-operate in any aggressive measures against the Soviet Union.[56]

---

[47] Fischer, Louis: *The Soviets in World Affairs*, p.250
[48] Ibid.   p.295
[49] Debo, Richard: *Survival and Consolidation*, p.158
[50] *Hansard* 24 February 1920, vol.125, 468
[51] *Hansard*,18 March   1920, vol.126, 2361
[52] Debo, Richard: *Survival and Consolidation*, pp.137-141
[53] Carswell, John: *The Exile*, p.98
[54] Ivy Litvinov's archives, Box 1
[55] Fischer, Louis: *The Soviets in World Affairs*, p.252
[56] Ibid.   p.251

On 26 April 1920, Poland invaded Ukraine without even a declaration of war on the pretext that they came to liberate the Ukraine from Soviet power.[57] The campaign proceeded so well that on 7 May the Polish army took Kiev.[58] A suggestion that Poland started the war as a preventative measure because they were about to be attacked seemed unlikely.[59]

The former British Prime Minister Asquith had no doubt, as he stated in a speech to the House of Commons:

> Poland started an aggressive adventure on her own. Poland was a party to the original Covenant of the League of Nations to which, by the way, she is now appealing. She did not apparently ever dream of invoking its sanction for the enterprise. What was her object? Her avowed object, as the conflict proceeded, was to get rid of this comparatively limited frontier, not an ungenerous frontier which had been accorded to her at the Peace Conference, and go beyond it to the ancient boundaries of the Poland of 1772. It was a purely aggressive adventure. She used the armaments with which she had been supplied or promised for the purpose of self-defence in order to prosecute an offensive campaign. It was a wanton enterprise which ought to have been formally repudiated by the united voice of Europe.[60]

No doubt Litvinov would have fully approved the contents of the speech and the failure of governments in Europe to condemn Poland's aggression increased the suspicion of the Soviet Government that Europe was again preparing to try and topple the Bolshevik regime by force. Most countries were either supportive of Poland or indifferent. George V's behaviour immediately after the invasion of Russia by Poland, namely sending a message of 'congratulations and sincere good wishes to Pilsudski on the occasion of Poland's national holiday', appears entirely inappropriate. [61]

Rather than weaken the Soviet regime, Europe's action strengthened it. Various Tsarist officers such as General Brusilov rallied to the Soviet Government's call to save Mother Russia and the Red Army successfully counter-attacked. Kiev was retaken on 13 June 1920. Minsk fell on 11 July 1920. Brest-Litovsk fell on 4 August.[62] The Polish army was driven out of Russia. After some debate among the relevant politicians as to whether to stop at the Polish border, those who favoured continuing won the day. Trotsky was the

---

[57] Debo, Richard: *Survival and Consolidation*, p.213
[58] Possony, Stefan: *Lenin the Compulsive Revolutionary*, p.335
[59] Walters, Francis Paul: *History of the League of Nations*, p.96 Possony Stefan: *Lenin the Compulsive Revolutionary* p335
[60] *Hansard* 10 August 1920, vol.133, 274
[61] Debo, Richard: *Survival and Consolidation*, p.215: GB Ch.9, No.19
[62] Fischer, Louis: *The Soviets in World Affairs*: Kiev, p.259; Minsk, p.260; Brest-Litovsk; *Times*, 4 August 1920, p.10

most prominent person who favoured both stopping at the Polish border and supporting open diplomacy which would enable the Polish people to see who was responsible for the outbreak of hostilities. This would not necessarily have altered the opinion of most Poles, including the working class, who were deeply hostile to Russia.

Trotsky thought a Russian invasion of Poland would only unite the Poles under Pilsudski, although this was a case where Litvinov wanted to act deviously.[63] However, when the Polish army was on the brink of disaster, the Soviet offensive halted just outside Warsaw. Notwithstanding the fact that Poland had provoked the war, with the Polish army in full retreat there was extreme gloom in London and Paris. The *Times* stated that in view of the Russian offensive, 'the outlook is ominous.' [64] Even the internationalist Robert Cecil was saying:

> We had got to the absurd and ironical position that our principal hope was based on the moderation of the Bolshevik Government. Could anything have been more absurd than that we should be placed in such a position?[65]

On 28 July Russia made a formal protest to France that they had broken the agreement of 20 April 1920 by giving military aid to Poland.[66]

However, in Europe working class people and the trade unions gave considerable help to Russia. In Britain, after it was thought that Lloyd George might be contemplating giving military help to Poland, British workers, not only refused to load cargoes bound for Poland, but British Labour established a Council of Action, to stenuously oppose any military `assistance being given to Poland. They wanted no war with Russia. [67] In Czechoslovakia, the railwaymen held up trains for Poland. In Danzig, German dockers refused to unload Allied munitions ships.[68]

Russia's hopes of a decisive victory were dashed. Defeated outside Warsaw, the Red army started to fall back. On 23 August, Russia admitted the Red Army had abandoned Brest-Litovsk.[69]

On 6 October 1920, a preliminary treaty was agreed, to be embodied in a formal document on 18 March 1921. In order to obtain a quick settlement, Russia had been generous. She

---

[63] Ullman, Richard: *Anglo-Soviet Relations*, vol.3, p.208; Deutscher, Isaac: *Prophet Armed 1891-1921*, p.459; as to Litvinov, see chapter 5, No.69

[64] *Times* 6 August 1920, p.11

[65] Ibid. p.12

[66] Fischer, Louis: *The Soviets in World Affairs*, p.25; see No 56 ante

[67] Ibid. p.265

[68] Machay, Robert: *Poland 1914 to 1931*, p.156; Carr, Edward: *Bolshevik Revolution*, vol.3, p.212

[69] *Times*, 24 August 1920, p.10

had agreed that 3,600,000 inhabitants would be incorporated into Poland, of whom no more than a million were Poles. However, the Polish invasion stirred Russia deeply. For the first time the Bolsheviks now called for national not civil war. They let loose patriotic instincts and chauvinistic emotions beyond their control. To the conservative elements, this was a war against a hereditary enemy with whom they could not reconcile themselves – a truly Russian war, although waged by Bolshevik activists.[70]

Privately, Lenin had to admit the Polish revolution, about which he had been optimistic, had failed. Lenin said:

> The peasants and workers stultified by the partisans of Pilsudski and Dashinsky defended their class enemies, permitted our brave Red Army to die of starvation and ambushed and killed them.[71]

In view of the anti-Russian feeling in Poland caused by the former disappearance of the Polish state, why should Lenin have thought otherwise? Possony stated:

> The Polish and German proletarians had not allied themselves with the Soviet proletariat, preferring national independence and democracy to Bolshevism. Politically this was an even greater blow than the military defeat.[72]

Possony was absolutely right. The Polish Socialist Party appealed to fellow socialists abroad, saying that they were mistaken if they thought that only the Polish bourgeoisie was defending Poland. 'The Polish proletariat is filling the ranks of the army. Peasants and workmen are hurrying to defend the Mother Country.'[73]

However successes for Soviet diplomacy in 1920 were the recognition of the Communist regime by Lithuania on 12 July, by Latvia on 11 August and Finland on 24 October. Accordingly, the new Soviet Government formally abandoned its claim to these territories of former greater Russia.[74] On the other hand, it was less successful in its devious attempt to help the *Daily Herald*.[75]

In January 1921, Litvinov became political and commercial envoy to Estonia, one of the few countries with which diplomatic relations had been established, and took up his appointment, his credentials being signed by Lenin.[76]

---

[70] Deutscher, Isaac: *Prophet Unarmed 1921-1929*, p.459
[71] Fischer, Louis: *The Soviets in World Affairs*, p.271
[72] Possony, Stefan: *Lenin the Compulsive Revolutionary*, p.338
[73] *Times*, 19 August 1920, p.9
[74] Pope, Arthur: *Maxim Litvinov*, p.164
[75] See Ch.9, Nos.23-25
[76] Sheinis, Zinovy: *Maxim Litvinov*, p.142

It was, of course, not only practicable but normal for a diplomat serving abroad to be accompanied by his wife, so Ivy set out in an advanced state of pregnancy to join Maxim. She went to Oslo, then called Christiana, where Maxim and Ivy's third child was born. The child was named Sigard, but it only lived for a few days. Nevertheless, Ivy continued with her two other children to join her husband in Estonia. When Ivy arrived in Estonia she was naturally still distressed because of the child's death, but Ivy describes how Maxim warmed her heart by asking eagerly what he had been like. Maxim said he had lost a part of himself; not like some of Ivy's friends, who showed their hatred of Bolshevism by writing to Ivy to say perhaps it was for the best.[77]

Notwithstanding being ambassador to Estonia, Litvinov was constantly required to return to Moscow. In May 1921, Lenin wanted Litvinov to supervise Russia's foreign currency.[78] This included the sale of Church property abroad. The Sovnarkom had appointed Trotsky head of a commission to confiscate moveable valuables from churches.[79] This property was to be used for famine relief. However, in spite of the Bolsheviks' anti-religious ideology, a conscious decision was taken not to destroy works of religious art, but generally over a period to close churches and transfer such works of religious art to museums in the hope they would be considered purely as secular objects.[80] Litvinov's attitude to religion, particularly Judaism (as he was a Jew), is discussed later.[81]

On 23 August 1921, Litvinov was back in Moscow in connection with the delivery of German and Swedish locomotives. In September 1921, with Lenin in the chair, Litvinov's advice was sought in connection with the granting of concessions.[82]

Between 1921 and 1923, Russia suffered a terrible famine. A non-Russian leading director of the Russian Red Cross, Dr Lodygensky, said:

> The crisis cannot be exaggerated and was far worse than the terrible famine of 1891. The 1921 famine covered a greater area, affected a larger number of illiterate people who failed to understand any element of their plight except hunger; they wandered around aimlessly in vast masses.

Dr Lodygensky confirmed reports that the areas most affected were the hitherto fertile regions of European Russia. Industries were closing down. The famine panic had brought river transport of wood and fuel materials to a standstill. The great mining regions, including Donetz, together with the oilfields of Baku and Grozny were slowly being

---

[77] Carswell, John: *The Exile*, p.98; Ivy's papers, Box 6
[78] Sheinis, Zinovy: *Maxim Litvinov*, p.149
[79] Brovkin, Vladimir: *Bolsheviks in Russian Society*, p.239
[80] Ibid. p.251
[81] Ch.19, Nos.27-31
[82] Sheinis, Zinovy: *Maxim Litvinov*, p.150

paralysed. [83] However, the Allies, by their intervention in Russia's civil war, which caused it to be prolonged, were partly responsible. A letter signed by the US President and British, French and Italian Prime Ministers offered material help to alleviate the famine, provided that all troop movements were suspended.[84] This was a condition to which a sovereign state would not be likely to agree and for that reason the offer of help was rejected.

However, no doubt the famine was one of the reasons for the communist U-turn – the New Economic Policy (NEP) was announced by Lenin at the 10th Congress to replace War Communism which, between 1917 and 1921, stemmed not from a structured plan but from the need to win a civil war and overcome by brutal means all those who opposed the regime. All businesses employing more than ten people had been nationalised. This included internal trade, so in agriculture the State became the sole producer and distributor.

It was the Government's duty to distribute the food among the urban population and administration was centralised. Such a poor job was done that about a third of the population in the cities migrated to the countryside either in search of food or to return to their villages if they had family or friends there. However, much black market trading took place, more in kind than in money. The Government printed money, so inflation reached such monstrous proportions that one rouble in 1913 was worth 2,400 roubles in 1920. Exchange and barter were therefore replacing money. Peasants, having no faith in the currency, grew less or hid their surplus as the state requisitioned such food.[85]

Lenin said, 'Only an agreement with the peasants can save the Socialist revolution in Russia until a revolution takes place in other countries.'[86] The purpose of the changed policy was to encourage the peasants to increase production, so the requisition of the peasants' surpluses was replaced by a tax. Tax rebates were given to peasants who increased the amount of land they cultivated. The peasant was free to determine how his land was to be cultivated and he was given security of tenure. However, it did not affect the previous policy of encouraging the amalgamation of the least profitable, most backward and smaller farms.[87]

When the NEP was introduced there were virtually no state credit institutions. During the period of War Communism industrial enterprises had received advances from the state budget. Now, as trade was to be restored, some credit institutions would be needed, so a state bank – Gosbank – was therefore formed for the purpose of assisting private enterprises.[88] However, Ivy Litvinov, in her unpublished memoirs, tells us that Maxim

---

[83] *The New York Herald Tribune*, 21 August 1921, p.7
[84] Fisher, Harold: *Famine in Soviet Russia*, p.16
[85] Grey, Ian: *Fifty Years in Soviet Russia*, p.146
[86] Carr, Edward: *Bolshevik Revolution*, vol.2, p.278
[87] Ibid. p.289
[88] Ibid. p.348; Gosbank is the State Bank

'was terribly depressed. He felt everything had been sold at the U-turn in policy, although he knew it had to be.'[89]

While the congress was proceeding, the Kronstadt mutiny took place, an indication of general discontent rather than, as Sheinis portrayed, sailors being influenced by counter-revolutionaries.[90] After carrying out the October Revolution, the working class had hoped to achieve its emancipation, but the result was an even greater enslavement of the human personality.

> The powers of the police passed into the hands of the communist usurpers who, instead of giving the people freedom, instilled in them the constant fear of falling into the torture chambers of the Cheka, which in their horrors far exceeded the gendarme administration of Tsarist Russia.[91]

Lenin's attitude towards the famine was curiously remote, cold and disinterested. He seemed to regard the famine as one more obstacle that had blocked his path since he became undisputed leader of Russia. Lenin personally made one appeal for help:

> The capitalists of all countries are taking revenge on the Soviet republic. They are making new plans for further excursions, interventions and counter-revolutionary conspiracies. We are convinced that the workers and small farmers from all over the world who live by their labour will come to our rescue with still greater energy and self-sacrifice.[92]

Lenin did not explain how the millions of tons of food needed to avert the famine were to be transported. Although the Patriarch, with Lenin's permission, appealed to Christians of the entire world to help the hungry women and children, the most effective appeal was Gorky's telegram to Herbert Hoover, the Chairman of the American Relief Association, appealing 'to all honest people' to help the Russians in their fight against starvation.[93] The USA alone probably had the resources and capability to mount a huge rescue operation.

When Litvinov told Lenin during the talks on the famine with the USA that the Americans had insisted upon the right to select the areas where the relief would be distributed, Lenin was at first extremely annoyed. He told Litvinov not to let the USA 'be insolent.'[94] Further evidence of Lenin's lack of concern for the famine was his effort to smash civil society that had begun to flourish in the final years of the Tsar's regime. Between July and August 1921

---

[89] Ivy's papers, Box 7
[90] Sheinis, Zinovy: *Maxim Litvinov*, p.143
[91] Avrich, Paul: *Kronstadt*, p.241
[92] Payne, Robert: *The Life and Death of Lenin*, p.539
[93] Phillips, Hugh: *Between the Revolution and the West*, p.48
[94] Ibid. p.48

Russian social activists and the church attempted to organise collections for the hungry. However, the Government first restricted and then prohibited their efforts. In August and September 1921, the Government-controlled newspapers made an appeal for people to give freely, but the public may well have been less enthusiastic to give to the Government than to funds outside the control of the bureaucracy.[95]

On 9 August 1921, Moscow announced that M Litvinov, representing the Central Executive Committee, arrived in Riga to carry on conversations with W F Brown, a representative of Mr Hoover. This eleventh-hour substitution of the first and foremost Bolshevik foreign plenipotentiary for non-political personages such as Gorky or Tchinchuk clearly indicates the Soviet intentions of trying to open negotiations with the USA.[96] On 11 August 1921, Litvinov stated:

> We would gladly accept all humanitarian aid that may be offered to us, but any attempt to take away any of the prerogatives of the Soviet Government or any of its powers we reply *non possumus*.[97]

On the following day, *The New York Times* stated that the famine

> may achieve the overthrow of the Bolshevik government because the masses belittle the government for the reason it has abandoned its first principle of communism.[98]

The tone of the article made it perfectly clear that the writer was not divorcing politics from humanitarian issues, and it can be assumed that the administration similarly had considered the political implications of the famine relief. No doubt the foreign papers were studied by the Foreign Commissariat, particularly one as famous as *The New York Times*.

Litvinov proceeded to Riga to carry out conversations with W F Brown, the representative of Mr Herbert Hoover – the new US Secretary of Commerce in the Harding cabinet. However, it was not easy to reach agreement. In order for the negotiations to succeed, it required someone as capable and flexible as Litvinov to negotiate for American help, rather than the authoritarian tone of Lenin's demands. However, even Litvinov seemed to lack the passion to obtain help that he showed in other political spheres which interested him. Payne states that Litvinov seemed to be more concerned with drawing up an elaborate protocol than in getting immediate help.[99] When the USA objected, both to the length and

[95] Brovkin, Vladimir: *Bolsheviks in Russian Society*, p.238
[96] *The New York Times*, 9 August 1921, p.3
[97] Pope, Arthur: *Maxim Litvinov*, p.173
[98] *The New York Times*, 11 August 1921, p.1
[99] Payne, Robert: *Life and Death of Lenin*, p.539

complexity of the document, saying, 'After all, Mr Litvinov ought to remember that what we want is to get help into Russia', Litvinov stated: 'Food is a weapon.' The reason why almost all foreign ministers or their officials insist on a complicated document is for fear that the other party may find a loophole. Accordingly, if the agreement did not produce the intended effect, the foreign minister will be blamed. Did Litvinov share Lenin's view that the sacrifice of millions of lives was a price worth paying to defend the revolution? If so, it was hypocritical, because there is plenty of evidence that the communist elite, including Litvinov, were not themselves making any sacrifices in their standard of living.[100] It could be argued that the difference in the standard of living had become wider between the communist elite and the poor than it was in 20th Century Tsarist Russia.

The USA were right to insist on the condition that they could control where the aid went, because the Bolsheviks misled the USA as to where the worst areas of famine occurred, wrongly stating that the areas of Kiev and other Ukrainian cities were not famine areas. Eventually, it was found that in some areas of famine in the Ukraine, rather than utilise the food available for distribution, it was actually being shipped to other famine areas.[101] Negotiations were difficult as the USA argued that there must be freedom of movement and also United States' nationals in Russia must be free to return to the USA. Litvinov was prepared to admit that 'there was too much suspicion on one side and lack of confidence on the other.'[102] However, Litvinov stood firm on the right to expel any American found guilty of engaging in political or commercial activity.[103] Eventually, having sought instructions from his superior, Hoover gave way.[104] This was a triumph for Litvinov. In the midst of the negotiations, Ivy said to Maxim, 'How sad it is that we have to appeal to the USA to help', and Maxim replied that 'You too feel for the honour of Russia.'[105] Ivy had not yet arrived in Russia and therefore was still believing it was the land of Utopia.

Thereafter, an agreement between the USA's representative Brown and Litvinov was concluded and signed on 20 August 1921. Litvinov did not allow a political opportunity to be lost. After stating that he was greatly pleased with the successful conclusion of the negotiations, he then made the political point that it was the first agreement between the people of the Soviet Union and the USA. After all, Mr Hoover represents the people of the USA as he is one of the foremost figures in American political life.[106] Next day, at the formal signing of the agreement, Litvinov paid warm tribute to Mr Brown, Herbert Hoover and the USA's relief programme. However, Brown was annoyed with Litvinov when in his speech after the signing ceremony Litvinov said:

---

[100] See No.54 *ante*

[101] Fisher, Harold: *Famine in Soviet Russia*, p.251

[102] Weissman, Benjamin: *Hoover & Famine Relief to Soviet Russia*, p.63

[103] Fisher, Harold: *Famine in Soviet Russia*, p.60

[104] Weissman, Benjamin: *Hoover & Famine Relief to Soviet Russia*, p.62

[105] Phillips, Hugh: *Between the Revolution and the West*, p.49

[106] *New York Herald Tribune*, 21 August 1921, p.1

I hope this first meeting between representatives of the Russians and USA will be followed by others which will bring the two peoples together and which will make them understand we have been kept apart by misunderstanding which otherwise would not exist. It is with this hope I leave the room.

Therefore, Brown in his speech in reply omitted reference to Litvinov's comments, but 'thanked Litvinov for his sincere co-operation in the negotiations' and expressed 'the hope that both parties would co-operate earnestly to the end so that the Russians might get the greatest possible benefit from the aid the USA was extending.' Brown expressed hope that 'the USA relief effort would save some lives.'

The Latvian Premier, Meyerowitz, who was hosting the conference, expressed gratification at the successful termination of the negotiations and gave a warm tribute to the work of the USA's Relief Agency; but Meyerowitz then trod on much more sensitive ground. He reiterated Litvinov's remarks that he 'was convinced that the common interests of both nations represented here will lead to other steps towards mutual understanding.'[107] On the other hand, Britain and France came in for criticism from the Soviets. *Pravda* ridiculed the efforts of the Entente to get down to business.[108] Lenin wrote to Molotov on 23 August 1921 voicing his fears that, in view of agreement with the USA, there was going to be an influx of US nationals:

> I propose the Politburo order that a commission be created to prepare to work out and operate intensive surveillance and information on the foreigners through the Cheka and other organs.[109]

Once the relief effort was put into place, even Lenin started to appreciate the philanthropic nature of the famine relief, as the ailing leader had shown a keen interest in the attitude of Herbert Hoover to the relief effort. However, in some Soviet quarters the relief work of the USA was an offence against the dignity of the Socialist state, but this was not Litvinov's view. He blamed the extreme communist wing for the growing hostility within the party towards the mission.[110]

Although initially funds were provided through the Red Cross, on 14 November 1921 a bill was introduced in Congress, and subsequently approved, requesting an appropriation of 20 million dollars towards famine relief. [111] Aid continued until 1923 when, as a result of a good harvest, it was no longer needed.

---

[107] *The New York Times*, 21 August 1921, p.1
[108] Entente, *New York Herald Tribune*, 19 August 1921, p.2
[109] Volkogonov, Dmitri: *Rise & Fall of the Soviet Empire*, p.64
[110] Weissman, Benjamin: *Hoover & Famine Relief to Soviet Russia*, p.165
[111] Browder, Robert Paul: *Origins of Soviet-American Diplomacy*, p.20

Russia acknowledged the success of the US mission. Pavlovich, a Bolshevik scholar high in party circles, wrote in 1922:

> The aid rendered to Russia by the United States was grandiose, even unprecedented. The Soviet Government and the worker-peasant masses shall never forget the great assistance which the Transatlantic Republic afforded to the Russian people.[112]

On 16 June 1923, the USA's representatives gave an informal dinner, which both Litvinov and his chief, Chicherin, attended. Chicherin made a formal speech in a most eloquent way, personally praising the head of the US mission, Col Haskell,

> who with such tact and consummate skill and with such energy and devotion, has carried out in Russia his responsible and arduous task and is leaving behind the kindest memories.

Rather than extol the virtues of communism, Chicherin described the world's premier capitalist country in glowing terms:

> Who but yesterday took possession of a gigantic virgin continent and turned it into a miracle of most perfect technique of production and culture can, better than anyone else, understand the similar aspirations and hopes of the Russian People who have from their bitter past inherited a great part of two continents which had remained in a primitive state as a result of a barbarous regime and oppression in the past.

One wonders why Chicherin was a communist; but then Chicherin made a political point.

> He hoped that the USA possessed of its incalculable technique and accumulated fruit of its gigantic production may enter into close economic co-operation with the peoples of Russia confronted with the task still more formidable.[113]

But the USA would for another ten years turn a blind eye to such a request.

In 1926, the Great Soviet Encyclopaedia stated that the American Relief Association (a philanthropic organisation set up by Hoover to feed the starving children of Europe)

> distributed almost two billion individual rations in a year and a half, provided drugs and other medical supplies to hospitals, sanitary facilities and improvement in the

---

[112] Browder, Robert Paul: *Origins of Soviet-American Diplomacy*, p.21
[113] Fisher, Harold: *Famine in Soviet Russia*, p.397

water supply. When its work was over, it left Russia. At the height of its activity, the ARA distributed supplemental food to approximately ten million people.[114]

As mentioned, motives of the USA might have been partly influenced by the hope of gaining political advantages, but there can be little doubt that, without American help, thousands if not millions might have died. It seems that the USA's help raised the profile of the USA with the Russian public as well as most of the communist elite. When the American note in 1929 concerning the Soviet-Chinese dispute was officially condemned, a peasant woman said,

> The Americans are good people. We would have died in Samara province in the hunger years and my son knows it. He is a commander in the Red army now and says he will never fight the people of the USA.[115]

Although Weissman gives the credit to Hoover, President Harding deserves much praise. It was he as President who gave authority and enthusiastic backing to the relief effort. The President expressed the hope that 'all those in the USA who were charitably inclined will give support either to the Relief Organisation or such organisation as may undertake to co-operate with that administration.' In due course, President Harding persuaded the Congress to provide the necessary funds.[116]

However, by 1928 the Communist leadership had decided to belittle the American efforts, complaining that the reason why help was given was to relieve a crisis in the USA arising out of the food prepared in huge amounts for an imperialist war.[117] This was not Litvinov's view, because later in the same year Litvinov displayed that exceptional courage that he exercised from time to time when addressing the Central Executive: 'We do not forget that during the difficult years of the famine the people of the USA gave us vital help.'[118]

At the beginning of the Cold War the Soviet historians distorted history. In a lecture in 1947, N Rubinshtein stated:

> The aim of this diplomacy of condensed milk was clear. The US Imperialists wanted to create relief committees made up of counter-revolutionaries and anti-Soviet agents so as to send to Soviet Russia a whole army of spies and undercover agents.[119]

---

[114] Weissman, Benjamin: *Hoover & Famine Relief to Soviet Russia*, p.184
[115] *The New York Times*, 5 December 1929, p.2
[116] *The New York Times*, 19 August 1921, p. 1; No. 111 ante
[117] Weissman, Benjamin: *Hoover & Famine Relief to Soviet Russia*, p.184
[118] Ibid.
[119] Browder Robert Paul *Origins of Soviet-Americn Diplomacy* p.21

In October 1921, Litvinov was recalled permanently to take up the post of Deputy Commissioner, and Alexander Stark became the new ambassador to Estonia.[120]

Ivy finally arrived in Moscow in autumn 1921 and lived in a portion of a grand old building directly across from the Kremlin that belonged to a wealthy sugar merchant before the Revolution and subsequently became the British Embassy.

When Alliluyeva committed suicide, Stalin gave Litvinov one of his personal dachas, a comfortable ride from their downtown quarters waited on by staff, all of whom were secret police agents. The children romped about in the spacious grounds that few Russians at that time ever saw. 'We were not supposed to do anything for ourselves', Madam Litvinov remembers. 'With great awe they say she actually goes to the shops. We were not meant to do that because we might have been poisoned.' In a period of shortages and even famine, security police were responsible for bringing the Litvinovs whatever they needed.[121]

When the sugar mansion was turned over to the British Embassy, the Litvinovs received a large apartment nearby. Before they moved in, Ivy was taken to see all sorts of furniture, mainly in teak, which had been seized after the Revolution: 'They gave me a list and the commander told me to put my tick against anything I wanted. That is how we furnished our home.'[122]

In that article Ivy does not convey her sense of disappointment. However, in her unpublished memoirs she states that she thought she was going to the land of Utopia.

> Because people had no hope of getting new ones, they kept things that would have been thrown away in normal times. I used to walk about in Moscow looking into the ground floor windows seeing(rooms) piled to the ceiling with things.[123]

Ivy tells us that initially she was terribly bored, but Maxim, as a loving husband, did his best to alleviate the situation, in spite of his arduous duties as Deputy Foreign Commissioner. He used to take Ivy to the theatre every night, normally to scc ballet. Although initially Ivy thought it was hideous, she came to love ballet.[124]

However, the capitalist powers were reluctantly having to accept that the Bolshevik regime was, at least in the short term, going to stay. Russia was invited to the next major conference at Genoa in 1922.

---

[120] Sheinis, Zinovy: *Maxim Litvinov*, p.151
[121] *Washington Post*, 30 January 1977, H1; *Observer*, 25 July 1976, p.17
[122] Ibid.
[123] Ivy's papers, Box 1
[124] Ibid.

The new Deputy Foreign Commissar could face the future with some confidence and deserved his promotion. The attempt of the Allies to undermine the new regime had miserably failed and had not only consolidated the regime but gave it a valid excuse for persistent abuse of the human rights of its citizens. Lenin obviously had confidence in Litvinov's ability as a diplomat. Litvinov can be credited with two outstanding achievements as a senior Russian diplomat. Firstly, there was the prisoner exchange scheme in 1920;[125] and secondly, the agreement in respect of famine relief in 1921.[126]

---

125 No. 47 ante
126 No. 96-111 ante

4: ACCEPTANCE OF BOLSHEVIK RUSSIA

The first major international event following Litvinov's appointment as Deputy Commissar was a conference – the Washington Conference – which took place between November 1921 and February 1922. The main participants were the USA, France, the British Empire, Japan and Italy. It had two main purposes, one of which was to discuss disarmament. It achieved limited success with regard to naval disarmament by fixing maxima in respect of total tonnage of battleships, cruisers and aircraft carriers, although inconsistently not in respect of submarines. Further, Britain, the USA and Japan agreed not to build any new fortifications or naval bases on the islands of the Pacific and to support one another if their rights were threatened by any other power. Secondly, the conference confirmed a mutual obligation to respect the independence of China and to maintain the principle of the open door, which meant equal opportunities for trade and investment.[1]

One would have thought that the other participants in the conference would wish the Soviet Union, as a Pacific power, to be similarly bound, but such was still the hostility of the capitalist powers to communism that Russia was not invited. Therefore, with considerable justification, Chicherin protested, expressing

> his Government's extreme astonishment at learning of the intention to convene a conference without its participation. Although the Russian Republic and the Far Eastern Democratic Republic rule over on the shores of the Pacific, the powers which took the decision of meeting in Washington did not consider it necessary to invite the Russian and Far Eastern Democratic Republic to this conference.

Chicherin confirmed the futility of calling the conference without the Soviet Union's participation as he made it clear: 'The Russian Government will not recognise any decision taken at the above-mentioned conference inasmuch as this gathering is being held without its participation', although he added that his government 'can only give a warm welcome to disarmament of any kind.'[2]

On 6 January 1922, in view of the high level of unemployment in Europe, a conference of a number of Allied powers took place at Cannes, at which it was resolved to call an international conference at Genoa, to include Germany and the Soviet Union. It was the first conference to which the Soviet Government was invited. In addition, the conference

---

[1] Walters, Francis: *History of The League of Nations*, p.163
[2] FRUS 1921, vol.1, p.41; Degras, Jane: *Soviet Documents on Foreign Policy*, vol.1, p.249

hoped to resolve two matters – Germany's reparations and Russia's repudiated debts.[3] On 17 January 1922, the Politburo determined that the invitation should be accepted and agreed the composition of the delegation.[4] The decision to hold the conference and invite Russia was widely welcomed in the Soviet press.[5] Originally, Lenin was to attend, but changed his mind because of his health.[6] However, the delegation had received detailed instructions from him which were approved by the Politburo on 8 February 1922.[7] In order to improve the image of the Communist regime, a new legal system had been introduced. Among measures introduced were the strengthening of the inviolability of the home, the privacy of the postal and telephone service, and the limiting of the power of arrest. Nevertheless, Hodgson, who admired Litvinov, and therefore whose opinion was more balanced than most diplomats, pointed out that 'arbitrary arrests and convictions continued to take place whatever the law might provide.'[8]

At the Eleventh Party Conference, Lenin was undoubtedly right in pointing out that the party had taken steps to select a delegation of the best Soviet diplomats in Chicherin and Litvinov. However, less accurate was his remark: 'The success of the delegation in achieving the Soviet Government's desired aims would depend in part on the skill with which the delegation conducted themselves at the conference.'[9] The best negotiators would have been unlikely to have made progress unless the Allies as well as Soviet Russia were prepared to make concessions. Lenin continued, 'Whatever its outcome, the development of economic relations between Soviet Russia and the outside world would undoubtedly continue as the interests of the capitalist states demanded it.'[10] Litvinov was no doubt content that the policy of co-existence was now welcomed by the Soviet State. However, *Izvestiya* acknowledged on 11 January 1922: 'The conference would not succeed if the Allies made demands on Russia that they had been unable to achieve by military means.'[11]

On the way to Genoa the Soviet delegation, including both Chicherin and Litvinov, had stopped over in Berlin and presented a draft treaty in roughly the same form as Rapallo a fortnight later. It seems that Chicherin was very much the architect of the treaty. 'The aristocratic diplomat aimed at splitting the capitalist West with a specific strategy competing with London and wooing Weimar Germany.'[12] However, the Germans, still hoping to reach a satisfactory arrangement with the West, refused to sign.

---

[3] *Survey* of *International Affairs* 1920-1923 p.20
[4] White, Stephen: *Origins of Détente*, p.105
[5] Ibid. p.109
[6] Ibid. pp.105 & 108
[7] Ibid. p.107
[8] Ibid. p 100
[9] Ibid. p 109
[10] Ibid. p.109
[11] Ibid. p.109
[12] Fink, Carole: *Genoa Conference*, p.129

On 10 April 1922, the Genoa conference opened. Lloyd George called it : 'The greatest gathering of European nations that had ever assembled on the Continent. We meet on equal terms.'[13] The Germans had been admitted as equals for the first time since their defeat in the First World War. Naturally, Russia's opening speech was delivered by Litvinov's boss Chicherin, who made it clear that Russia adhered to the policy of co-existence and advocated co-operation between states representing the two systems of property. He came not

> with the intention of making propaganda for their own theoretical opinions but in order to engage in business relations with the governments and with industrial and commercial circles of all countries on the basis of reciprocity, equality and full and unconditional recognition, ... to open up Russian frontiers deliberately and voluntarily for international transit, to grant for cultivation millions of acres of its most fertile land and to grant rich coal and mining concessions.

In a rare excursion into domestic policy, following recent measures taken by the Russian Government, Chicherin announced Russia's intention to meet the requirement of the Cannes resolution with regard to the legal guarantees necessary for economic collaboration between Russia and countries, based on private property.

Chicherin then stated:

> All efforts made to restore the world economy are in vain as long as the threat of new world wars hangs over Europe, wars perhaps more destructive and devastating than the war we have just lived through.

Chicherin then proposed a general limitation of armaments with absolute prohibition of its most barbaric forms of warfare such as poison gas and aerial bombardment. Further: 'Russia is equally prepared to limit its own armament on condition of full and unconditional reciprocity.'[14]

To support his communist credentials Chicherin then advocated the official participation of workers organisation. He proposed utopian ideas that he would not support any coercive measures but as with the Kellogg Pact it will be seen any pact without any such measures to deal with countries that break any pact, was likely to be ineffective.

As so often occurred, I am sure Litvinov agreed with Chicherin's action in endeavouring to bring disarmament to the top of the agenda. The conference now sprang to life. Barthou jumped to his feet and scolded Chicherin for exceeding the conference's agenda. Lloyd

---

[13] Ibid. p.152

[14] Degras Jane Soviet *Documents on Foreign Policy* vol 1 p. 298

George, acting as peacemaker, implored Chicherin not to overload the conference.[15]

Litvinov was not optimistic at the start of the Genoa Conference. His view was that France had decided to sabotage the conference whatever the cost. Litvinov believed that Lloyd George remained in power by favour of his Conservative colleagues in the Cabinet. This meant that in Russian matters Lloyd George still ran into serious difficulties from the Conservative members of his Cabinet and his friend Churchill.[16] This speech shows, as often happened, Litvinov correctly predicted what would happen. On 6 October 1922, the coalition government led by Lloyd George fell.[17]

On Saturday 15 April a meeting was arranged between the Allies and the Soviet Union. At that meeting the Allies, having formulated their financial claim against the Soviet Union, were shocked to hear of the Soviet Union's claim for 50 million roubles, representing the destruction of one third of Russia's pre-war wealth caused by the Wars of Intervention. With considerable justification, Litvinov stated that Russia had received no benefit from the long struggle, no colonies, no reparations, no Alsace-Lorraine, no Mesopotamia. Litvinov was quite firm. He would not acknowledge any war debts. Indeed, his instructions from Moscow would not have allowed him to do otherwise.

Why Litvinov rather than Chicherin was assigned this important task we do not know, but we do know that Lloyd George ridiculed the Soviet figures and the whole notion of presenting a bill in connection with Allied intervention. He reminded Litvinov: 'The Allies, who had gone to war over a Slavic quarrel, had paid dearly and received little.'[18] This was hardly correct, as it was the German invasion of neutral Belgium, as far as Britain was concerned, which made war inevitable.

Although Lloyd George was correct that Britain had gained little at great cost, France had wanted the war and Britain's support to regain Alsace-Lorraine, forcibly taken by Germany following France's defeat in the 1870 Franco-Prussian War. Lloyd George also claimed that Brest-Litovsk[19] had violated the 1914 agreement between Tsarist Russia and Britain concerning the prosecution of the war against Germany.[20]

In 1940 France broke a treaty with Britain when on the verge of defeat, but at the end of the conflict France was rewarded with a zone in occupied Germany and a permanent seat on the UN Security Council.[21]

---

[15] Fink, Carole: *Genoa Conference*, p.154
[16] Phillips, Hugh: *Between the Revolution and the West*, p.54
[17] Taylor, A P: *English History 1928-1945*, p.192
[18] Fink, Carole: *Genoa Conference*, p.169
[19] See Ch.2, No.21
[20] Fink, Carole: *Genoa Conference*, p. 169; White, Stephen: *Origins of Détente*, p.139
[21] See Ch.14, Nos.76-78

The meeting was adjourned and reassembled at 4.30pm, when Chicherin spoke. He endorsed what Litvinov had stated earlier in the day and challenged Lloyd George's view on the causes of World War I. This conflict, he stated,

> had originated in an Anglo-German quarrel, not a Slavic one. Brest-Litovsk came as a result of Russia's collapse, which to some extent was caused by Western shells that did not explode or were sent to Italy

not unlike Britain's fiasco at Gallipoli.

Chicherin then said he

> deemed the whole issue of war debt was one that solely concerned the Allies who had profited from the war. Russia had sustained 54% of the Entente losses, expended 20 billion gold roubles and, having been almost crushed by the Allied intervention, was now emerging from the Revolution and the defeat of the White armies and felt free of any burden to its former allies.[22]

However, the records indicate that it was Chicherin not Litvinov who was the most conciliatory. Chicherin pleaded for Lloyd George not to insist on restoring private ownership in the Bolshevik state.[23] Chicherin stated he would have to consult Moscow and Lloyd George agreed to a delay of three to four days.[24]

Further, the adjournment very much served Russia's interest as the Germans knew the meeting was taking place and were elated when they received a telephone call that the Russians were prepared to meet the Germans the next day.

On the next day, Easter Sunday 16 April, there were separate meetings between Rathenau and Chicherin and between Litvinov and the German representatives Maltzan and Gaus. Perhaps hearing of the meeting, and anticipating a possible Russo-German agreement, Lloyd George invited the German representatives Wirth and Rathenau to tea. Wirth was unavailable, so Rathenau declined Lloyd George's invitation and the final agreement which came to be known as the Rapallo Agreement was reached at 6.30pm on that day.[25]

Both countries agreed to forego all war indemnities (including the maintenance of war prisoners). Germany renounced all claims in consequence of nationalisation of private property, provided the Russian Government did not satisfy similar claims from other states.

---

[22] Fink, Carole: *Genoa Conference*, p.169
[23] Ibid. p.169
[24] Ibid. p.170
[25] Fink, Carole: *Genoa Conference*, p.173.

Diplomatic and consular relations were resumed. Both countries agreed to assist in the economic development of each other.[26]

Britain, France and the other Allies wrote a letter of protest to Germany. They said:

> By inviting Germany to Genoa, and by offering representation to her on equal terms, the inviting powers proved their readiness to waive memories of war and grant Germany the opportunity of honest co-operation with her former enemies in the European tasks of the conference. To that offer of goodwill and fellowship Germany has replied with an act that destroys the spirit of mutual confidence which is indispensable to international co-operation. In the circumstances we do not feel it fair or equitable that Germany, having effected her own arrangement with Russia, should enter into the discussion of the conditions of an arrangement between these countries and Russia and therefore assume the German delegation by their action renounced further participation in the discussions of an agreement between Russia and the various countries represented at the conference.[27]

Germany in reply justified its action because:

> Germany recognised the Russian Soviet Republic several years ago. Before normal diplomatic relations could be established, it was necessary for the two countries to conclude an agreement to liquidate the consequences of the war. The negotiations entered into by the two countries in this connection had already reached a sufficiently advanced stage to allow for the conclusion of an agreement.

> The agreement with Russia was especially important for Germany in that it placed her upon a peace footing without involving the prospect of indefinite indebtedness with one of the great nations which had taken part in the war and permitted the establishment of friendly relations unhampered by the burden of the past.

On the other hand, the Allies had

> initiated separate negotiations with Russia. Germany came to Genoa earnestly desiring to co-operate with all nations in the reconstruction of a suffering Europe and relying upon an international spirit of solidarity in matters of mutual concern.

> The proposals set forth in the London programme ignored German interests. Their acceptance would have led to oppressive demands for reparations from Russia.

---

[26] Rapallo Treaty, English translation in Cmd.1667, p.51; Ch.8, No.70
[27] DBFP, 1st series, vol.19, p.443, No.76

This matter was finally closed when Germany agreed she would not participate in those matters upon which she had come to an agreement with Russia.[28]

Lenin was so alarmed at developments that he obtained Politburo approval for a telegram to be sent to Chicherin insisting 'the refusal to restore private property must be maintained. Concessions should be made only on condition that a satisfactory loan was obtained and Chicherin was informed that if he deviated from his instructions he would be publicly disowned, and relieved of his responsibilities.'[29] At this time all the indications were that Chicherin and Litvinov were in accord. Both diplomats felt that Russia should refrain from using the conference for Communist propaganda because economic assistance from the West was essential for the reconstruction of Russia.[30]

In communications with Moscow, Chicherin indicated that the Allies would grant economic assistance only after the Soviet Government had agreed to compensate the former owners. Litvinov also argued in telegrams to Moscow, 'A Western loan was unlikely to be obtained unless there was some agreement to compensate the former owners, and the Allies would refuse even to discuss such an arrangement unless private claims had been recognised.' However, two junior members of the delegation went further. Krassin suggested: 'Pre-war debts should be recognised but without interest. Further compensation payments should be paid to former owners, the sum involved being covered by a loan which in return would be covered by the issue of foreign bonds to the former owner concerned.' Ioffe suggested: 'Financial compensation could be paid, without conceding the right to expropriate private property, by the issue of state bonds over a ten-year period.'[31]

Accordingly, by 19 May the Genoa Conference had collapsed. The countries that had gained most from the conference were Russia and Germany, not because of what had happened in the conference, but outside. The treaty of Rapallo had made both Germany and Russia instantly stronger. Because France and Britain were divided, both were considerably weaker – Lloyd George stated that he was in favour of recognising the Soviet Union. He considered it was essential that there should be a pact containing provisions not only that the Soviet Union would not attack Poland and Rumania, but also that Poland and Rumania should agree not to attack the Soviet Union; and it was not possible to achieve this without recognising Russia. 'You might as well ask Germany to sign a treaty without recognising the country that signed it.' Another reason Lloyd George gave was: 'He did not see how European trade could be revived without bringing the Soviet Union into the economic circle.' Then Lloyd George added, 'He was not prepared to recognise a communist Soviet Union if the Communists were gaining an upper hand.'[32] Surely this was

---

[28] Cmd, 1922, 1667, p.54
[29] White, Stephen: *Origins of Détente*, p.180
[30] Ibid. p.113
[31] Ibid. p.181
[32] Rowland, Peter: *Lloyd George*, p.569

an attempt to interfere with a state's internal affairs. The Soviet Union was constantly blamed for such interference.

Following Rapallo, Phillips states that Chicherin went to Germany to take a well-deserved rest.[33] However, Trotsky was annoyed with Chicherin's performance and sent him a stiff note, proposing that Radek should replace Chicherin as Foreign Commissar, since Trotsky claimed,

> Chicherin had not defended Soviet interests with sufficient determination at the Genoa Conference and Chicherin should have placed an ultimatum before the powers and having increased instead of having decreased the enemies of the Soviet Union. mentioning Sweden and her refusal to conclude a trade agreement which had taken Litvinov more than a year to conclude.

However no explanation was forthcoming as to why this was Chicherin's or Litvinov's fault. The letter ends by stating, 'The Red Army will now apparently have to correct the mistakes of Soviet diplomacy with its guns.'[34] I feel it is Trotsky's motives that were suspect – he wanted to promote his friends at the expense of Chicherin, a typical example of the infighting that the communists argued was characteristic of democracies and which did not take place in the worker state.

Chicherin had been responsible for Rapallo, and there is no evidence that a tougher stance would have brought more benefits. In spite of any disagreements with Chicherin during the conference, Lenin obviously had confidence in Chicherin, as he remained Foreign Minister, an appointment which until 1930 Stalin did nothing to alter when he assumed the reins of power. Phillips rightly describes the Rapallo treaty 'as the crowning glory of Chicherin's diplomatic career.'[35]

Between the Genoa and Hague conferences, Litvinov was busy. He achieved another success when on 5 June 1922 he laid the groundwork for Czechoslovakian friendship by negotiating a treaty whereby Czechoslovakia refused to recognise any other Russian government, recognised Russia's trade monopoly and both the Soviet Union and Czechoslovakia agreed not to carry out propaganda on each other's territory.[36] A friendship blossomed between the two countries which had disastrous consequences when, in 1948, following the Communist coup, Czechoslovakia virtually lost its freedom as an independent state.

---

[33] Phillips, Hugh: *Between the Revolution and the West*, p.54

[34] White, Stephen: *Origins of Détente*, p.200; *Times*, 22 June 1922, p.9

[35] Phillips, Hugh: *Between the Revolution and the West*, p 56

[36] Pope, Arthur: *Maxim Litvinov*, p.188

In view of Chicherin's ill health, Litvinov was appointed Chairman of the Russian delegation to the Hague Conference.[37] The conference started on 26 June 1922 and Litvinov held a press conference.

Litvinov informed the journalists that Lenin's health had broken down. A German doctor had travelled from Berlin to see Lenin and had advised him to take a long rest. He had resumed his official duties against the advice of his doctors, but his health had again broken down and he was now taking a prolonged rest. The question of putting somebody else in charge had never been raised, but Lenin's official work was temporarily being carried out by Rykov and Rustzar. There would be no change of internal or external policy.

In reply to a question put to Litvinov as to what goods or credits the Soviet Union required before it honoured its pre-revolutionary debts and whether it insisted on cash, Litvinov replied, 'We can do with some cash.' Litvinov made it perfectly clear that it did not matter whether the loan came from the government or private persons, as long as they received the loan.[38]

Litvinov laid before the conference a much wider list of concessions to foreign capitalists than had previously been proposed. Previously, such concessions had been limited to unused natural resources. Now they were available for the development of existing factories and installations.[39]

The format of the conference was that that there would be three non-Russian commissions consisting of all the 26 countries attending the conference, and one Russian commission. Initially, in order to explore ways of obtaining a settlement, three sub-commissions consisting of representatives from both Russia and the other countries met, but the commissions made virtually no progress.

Litvinov procured the one and only plenary session of the conference, which was held on 19 July 1922. In a desperate attempt not to let the conference end in total failure, Litvinov stated that he proposed to submit to Moscow a recommendation to acknowledge pre-war debts. He was prepared to admit the general principle of compensation for foreign property seized by the State without making it a precondition for credits, providing that the terms and conditions could be agreed between the Soviet Government and the foreign creditors within two years.[40] Litvinov, having received no instructions from Moscow since the previous week, made his latest offer on his own initiative. '[41]

---

[37] Phillips, Hugh: *Between the Revolution and the West*, p.56
[38] *Times*, 27 June 1922, p.7
[39] Carr, Edward: *Bolshevik Revolution*, vol.3, p.428
[40] Fink, Carole: *Genoa Conference*, p.298; Fischer, Louis: *The Soviets in World Affairs*, vol.1, p.362
[41] *The New York Times*, 20 July 1922, p.7; *Times*, 20 July 1922, p.10

Britain was in favour of continuing the conference. Their representative, Phillip Lloyd Greame, stated: 'He attached great importance to Litvinov's plan and felt it represented a new epoch in the negotiations.' Lloyd George had previously told the French:

> Every state has the compulsory right to acquire property whatever its nature on payment of just compensation. Whether the Russian Government makes restitution of private property or pays compensation is a matter solely for the Russian Government.[42]

However, France and Belgium wished to terminate the conference on the grounds that

> if the Soviet Union was sincere, they could have made the proposal long ago to recommend to Moscow recognition of Russia's pre-war debts and the principle of compensation for seized property of foreigners and they were merely trying to gain time and break the front of the powers.[43]

As the other members were not prepared to wait seven days, the conference dispersed on a note of complete rupture. *The New York Times* proudly proclaimed that the Allies had triumphed at the conference and the principle was laid down that there can be no accommodation with the way the present Communist government was run.

The Soviet Government, it claimed, appeared to think that their way would triumph and 'one by one other nations will be seeking terms. Other governments think the contrary. Time will tell.'[44]

On this occasion it was Litvinov and the Russians who would be right. Other governments did, one by one, including eventually the obstinate USA, recognise the Soviet Union without being repaid any of the pre-Communist debts owed to the governments and their nationals.

By failing to give any credits to Moscow, not a penny of pre-Bolshevik debts was ever satisfied. Even if initially modest credits had been given, until it was seen whether the Soviet Union would abide by its financial commitments, there was a good chance that the Soviet Union would have honoured its commitments.

Following Rapallo, there were no complaints by the German Government that the Soviet Union had not honoured its financial commitments. Indeed, in 1945 Western experts said that the Soviet Union's record in meeting obligations to suppliers was excellent.[45]

---

[42] Fischer, Louis: *The Soviets in World Affairs*, vol.1, p.360
[43] *The New York Times*, 20 July 1922, p.7
[44] Ibid.   22 July 1922, p.4
[45] Ibid.   3 June 1945, p.21

The other peculiar objection was that if the proposed Litvinov agreement had been accepted, negotiations would have taken place between the Russian government and individuals rather than between the Russians and other governments.

> It offered untold opportunity for dissemination of Bolshevik propaganda because it meant that every small bondholder in Europe would have a direct interest in the welfare of the Soviet Government and would be put into direct communication with it. Their hope of eventual payment would lie in the perpetuation of the Soviet regime. These people would be interested in having their governments help the Russian Government into permanent power.[46]

If that is what influenced the allies, it was a forlorn hope, as the Soviet Government held on to permanent power as firmly as any dictatorship. The Soviet regime survived for seventy years. As a result of the rejection of Litvinov's final offer, the Soviet Union's creditors received absolutely nothing. However, if the Soviet offer had been accepted, the creditors might have received some payment, if only to impress the governments of those creditors who were owed money by Russia.

Litvinov duly reported his rejected last offer to the Commissariat of Foreign Affairs and stated that in view of the immediate rejection of the offer there can be 'no doubt whatever as to who was responsible for the breakdown of the Hague Conference and for the failure to reach agreement between Russia and the other states of Europe.'[47]

It seems that Litvinov was right. He had been as conciliatory as any Soviet politician would be on Russia's pre-war debts and, instead of taking such an opportunity when the situation presented it, other countries' hatred of Communism prevented them from so doing, with the result that nothing was recovered.

Previously, Litvinov, who was to become the great champion of collective security, had informed a *New York Times* correspondent that 'collective bargaining had never appealed strongly to the Soviet Government and now the coast was clear for dealing with individual nations.'[48]

After the breakdown of the conference on 23 July 1922, Litvinov held a large press conference in Berlin on 25 July 1922, where he had travelled immediately after leaving The Hague. Litvinov spoke first in German, then in English, and answered questions in both languages. He observed:

---

[46] Ibid. 20 July 1922, pp. 1 & 7.
[47] Degras, Jane: *Soviet Documents on Foreign Policy*, vol.1, pp.322 to 327
[48] *The New York Times*, 20 July 1922, p.1

> The French press is shouting triumphantly about the result of the Hague Conference. I wonder why this jubilation is justified. What did France achieve by wrecking the Hague Conference in order to demonstrate the united front of the non-Russians. The failure of the Conference means that the Russian question cannot be settled in a joint conference. Europe would have to wait fifty years to make Russia accept the maximum demands of France and Belgium.[49]

Although the conditional offer made by Litvinov was repudiated by the Soviet Government,[50] it seems it was well pleased with the way Litvinov had conducted the Hague Conference, unlike the Genoa Conference. *Pravda* on 22 July wrote 'Litvinov's speech had unmasked the allies, who wanted to skin us alive.' Further, Litvinov's speech was praised by Lenin on 31 October 1922, who stressed that Soviet foreign policy had secured success in the face of governments of all countries.[51] Lenin was right. Within two years the Soviet Union had been recognised by the three remaining great powers of Europe. Germany had already recognised the Soviet Union by the treaty of Rapallo.

It seems that it was very much on Litvinov's initiative that the Soviet Government decided to call a disarmament conference of those states that bordered the Soviet Union, which met in December 1922. All accepted, except Rumania, and sent delegates. Rumania did not, because she would only participate in the conference if the Soviet Union recognised Bessarabia.[52] The conference opened on 5 December 1922. Litvinov was the chief Soviet representative, as Chicherin was absent at the Lausanne conference.

Litvinov took the initiative. He stated the Russian Government was unable to put forward proposals as to the limitation of naval armaments, alluding to the absence of an invitation to the Washington Naval Disarmament Conference, and then offered to reduce its army from 800,000 to 200,000 men, providing neighbouring countries did the same. Further, it was proposed that military budgets be limited; and finally Litvinov put forward a very sensible suggestion that there should be a neutral zone on each side of the frontier to prevent frontier incidents which threatened peace.

Poland, supported by the other non-Russian delegates, wanted a non-aggression pact and an arbitration clause in the case of any dispute. The Soviet Union, with justification, was chary of accepting provision for arbitration because it was the world's only non-capitalist state. However, Russia was breaking new ground when, for the only time, it indicated that it was prepared to accept any feasible scheme of arbitration, save that of the League of Nations, which Russia considered a more or less disguised organisation of war victors in order to perpetuate the oppressive peace treaties.

---

[49] *The New York Times*, 26 July 1922; Press conference, p.26
[50] Fink, Carole: *Genoa Conference*, p.300; Phillips, Hugh: *Between the Revolution and the West*, p.57
[51] Sheinis, Zinovy: *Maxim Litvinov*, pp.172 &175
[52] Carr, Edward: *Socialism in One Country*, p.440

Finland made the valid point that troop reduction might not be in the interest of the smaller states. It was easier to defend a small country with 200,000 men against an army of a million than an army of 20,000 against 100,000 adversaries. It does not appear that Litvinov had an answer to this concern of small states.

Prince Janusz Radziwill, the Polish delegate, first paid tribute to the Lithuanian delegate, which was gracious of him in view of the disputes over Memel and Vilnius,[53] and then expressed Poland's desire for peace in general and with Russia in particular. Litvinov then proposed a 25% reduction in military forces. Poland declared it would reduce her forces to 280,000. It was clear that, as the League of Nations report had stated, the Polish army strength was 295,734, and this represented only a 4% reduction. When the Polish delegate said that he would not discuss Poland's military budget, and made no further concessions, the conference was doomed to failure.[54]

Litvinov telegraphed Chicherin to report that he was prepared to agree a non-aggression pact with an arbitration clause. Litvinov then related the problems with the Polish figures and concluded this threatened the breakdown of the conference.[55]

Walters criticised Litvinov's proposals on the grounds that he wanted an immediate answer and if the proposals were made in good faith the Soviet Union would not have refused to establish expert committees.[56] However, expert committees at the League of Nations Disarmament Conference eventually achieved nothing.

The Russians hoped the proposals initiated by Litvinov would have a favourable effect on American public opinion. Indeed, one spokesman said the USA 'is the only power besides Russia genuinely willing and able by virtue of its strong position to advance the cause of world disarmament.' However, although the USA was prepared to promote disarmament, it was not prepared to allow verification, so any scheme would have been ineffective.[57]

As none of the other countries were prepared to accept the Soviet proposals, Litvinov wound up the conference. Nevertheless, it can be argued that the conference was a triumph for Litvinov because it was the first major win for Soviet Russia in European democracy 'by appealing to advanced bourgeois opinion in Western countries.' The unilateral declaration that the Red Army would be reduced by 200,000 men 'strongly appealed to widespread sentiments in favour of peace.'[58]

---

[53] *The New York Times*, 4 December 1922, p.3

[54] Pope, Arthur: *Maxim Litvinov*, p.195; Phillips, Hugh: *Between the Revolution and the West*, p.69; Fischer, Louis: *The Soviets in World Affairs*, p.380

[55] Phillips, Hugh: *Between the Revolution and the West*, p.69

[56] Walters, Francis: *History of the League of Nations*, p.228

[57] *The New York Times*, 4 December 1922, p.3; Ch.6, No.114

[58] Phillips, Hugh: *Between the Revolution and the West*, p.70

Commenting on the Disarmament Conference, Litvinov stressed to the US correspondent Duranty a theme which would be the cornerstone of Litvinov's policy. Soviet Russia needed for reconstruction the money now spent on the army. This, however, applied to her neighbours as well, so she had the right to expect the proposals for general disarmament would be welcomed. They were not and the conference failed. Litvinov stated:

> Poland and one or two other border states are virtual pawns in the hands of certain militarist powers opposed for their own reason to a real reduction of European armies, but the armament burden is so heavy nowadays on the European peoples that no government openly dares to admit its unwillingness to disarm or to decline an invitation to a disarmament conference. Accordingly, Russia's neighbours felt they must accept the invitation to Moscow.

Before the conference called by Litvinov met, Poland, Latvia, Estonia and Finland held a meeting at Revel to decide on a common form of action 'in order to kid the public', as Litvinov put it, 'of the respective countries into the belief they were really desirous to reduce their armies. These representatives put forward the same specious proposal of a pact of non-aggression as Senator De Jouvenal had advanced at the last congress of the League of Nations in reply to Lord Cecil's demand for a real reduction of forces.'[59]

In spite of the failure of the Moscow Disarmament Conference, it appears that the Soviet Government was not pessimistic. The Foreign Commissariat, reviewing 1922, commented that if 1921 had been the year of diplomatic recognition, 1922 had been the year of entry into the world arena. After Genoa, it added, no major international problem could be resolved without Soviet participation.[60]

One major socio-economic problem facing the Soviet Union was that the peasantry did not receive an adequate return for its produce.[61] Eventually, a committee was appointed to try and rectify what was termed the scissors crisis.[62] By the end of 1923 the gap between industrial and agricultural prices was closing, helped by the fact that for the second successive year the harvest in 1923 was excellent.[63]

In 1923 an anti-religious campaign had been moderated to conciliate the peasants and a large agricultural exhibition first mooted in 1921 was held.[64] There was a drive supported by Trotsky for greater efficiency in industry by cutting costs, including dismissing workers. Trotsky admitted that the necessity of dismissing workers was a 'hard, very hard

---

[59] *The New York Times*, 15 December 1922, p.14

[60] White, Stephen: *Origins of Détente*, p.200

[61] Carr, Edward: *Interregnum*, p.14

[62] Ibid. p.104

[63] Ibid. p.118

[64] Carr, Edward, *Interregnum*, p.86

nut', but thought it was a lesser evil than concealing unemployment caused by inefficient production.[65] The result was that unemployment rose from half a million in September 1922 to a million and a quarter in 1923.[66]

However, there were frequent strikes. Labour relations were damaged because wages were often in arrears. When in August 1923 there was a mass strike in the engineering works at Sormoa, the workers were told that workers had not been paid in the South for May or June 1923.[67] On 4 January 1924, it was announced that a special commission would be established to monitor and ensure the prompt payment of wages.[68]

At the 1924 party conference, held from 16 to 18 January 1924, an unsuccessful attempt was made to reverse the Politburo's policy of promoting the NEP, which was led by Pyatakov. He condemned the policy of giving encouragement to the commercial element of the NEP instead of seeking to strengthen the state economy and the co-operatives. Molotov supported the official line. Mikoyan stated that the programme of the opposition pointed the way back to war communism.[69]

In foreign affairs the first important event of 1923 was the action of France in invading the Rhineland because France was owed reparation payments by Germany. The Soviet Union supported Germany. Her condemnation of France's action could not have been stronger. A resolution of the Central Committee dated 13 January 1923 stated,

> The right of the German people to self-determination is trodden underfoot. Germany's disorganised economy had suffered a new and shattering blow. Cruel poverty and unprecedented oppression threatened the working people of Germany, while all Europe will witness an increase in economic dislocation. The world again is thrown into a state of pre-war feverishness. Sparks are flying in the powder cellar created by the Treaty of Versailles.

Britain did not support France either, so France's action assisted the Soviet Union because it caused a split in the alleged anti-Communist coalition.[70]

The League of Nations did not act after Poland seized the port of Memel in 1923. The Soviet Union sent a number of protests at the failure of the League, as Litvinov saw it, to protect small states. The failure to restrain Japan in 1931 has often been regarded as a turning point in the fortunes of the League, but as early as 1923 the League had failed to

---

[65] Carr Edward *Interregnum* p.22

[66] Ibid. p.47

[67] Ibid. p.93

[68] Ibid. p.124

[69] Ibid. p.128

[70] Carr, Edward: *Interregnum*, p.155; Degras, Jane: *Soviet Documents on Foreign Policy*, vol.1, p.368

restrain an aggressor although it would have been much easier to have done so than against Japan in 1931.[71]

Towards the end of 1923 the Soviet Union's desire for recognition, particularly among the major powers, received some response. On 30 November 1923 Mussolini declared that Italy agreed that full diplomatic relations with the Soviet Union should be restored.[72] Although this declaration caused confusion in the ranks of the Italian Communist Party, *Izvestiya* regarded it as the first breach in the united front against Soviet Russia, and the Soviet commentator, Shtein, commented that hitherto the Western countries had hoped to bargain political recognition for payment of private debts and restoration of private property. 'To Mussolini belongs the merit and honour of driving the final nail in the coffin of this hope.'[73] *De jure* recognition duly took place on 3 February 1924.[74]

As a result of a British General Election and the formation of a Labour Government, in January 1924 the Soviet Union received an even greater prize of recognition from Britain.[75] Later in the same year France recognised the Soviet Union, after a Socialist government under Herriot gained power.[76]

Litvinov was, no doubt, particularly pleased that Britain had recognised the Soviet Union, but there is nothing to indicate that Chicherin was not equally pleased. Litvinov showed his pleasure but also his toughness in an interview to *Pravda* explaining that Britain and Italy 'had at long last abandoned the illusion that recognition would only be to the advantage of the Soviet Republics', and for other countries recognition was now of 'incomparably greater importance than for the Soviet Union itself.' In the case of future proposals when countries desired to restore diplomatic relations with Russia, the answer would be 'no negotiations and no preliminary settlement of any question whatever; recognition must be unconditional and unrestricted.'[77]

The Soviet Union also achieved diplomatic recognition from Greece, Norway and Sweden.[78] However, the Soviet Union failed to achieve its remaining major objective in terms of recognition by other states. It would take another ten years before Litvinov achieved the biggest prize − recognition by the USA The Soviet Union's relations with USA were made more difficult by the re-election of the Republicans in the USA and the Conservatives in Britain. Notwithstanding such elections' Carr commented:

---

[71] See Ch.12 No2
[72] Carr, Edward: *Interregnum*, p.249
[73] Ibid. p.p.249-250
[74] Ibid.
[75] Ch.9, No.40
[76] See Ch.8, No.3
[77] Carr, Edward: *Interregnum*, p.251
[78] Ibid. p.251

When the Soviet Union seemed to have attained a new peak of political, economic and financial stability at home, it had also been readmitted to the circle of European powers as a full member.[79]

This was in spite of the fiasco of the Soviet leadership agreeing to support a *coup d'état* in Germany which miserably failed.[80] However, although this could have caused the end of German-Soviet rapprochement, it did not because Germany realised it needed the Soviet Union just as the Soviet Union realised it needed Germany.

Lenin died on 21 January 1924, but this made little difference because the Soviet state had functioned without the dictator since 1922 on account of his illness. Throughout this time the Soviet state had made considerable progress. Although supporters of Lenin would argue that this was to Lenin's credit because he had put into place a government that could function without him, it also begs the question as to whether a free communist society which Gorbachev attempted to create could not have been put into position at that time.

What was Lenin's opinion of Litvinov who was sent by Lenin at the height of the intervention to Stockholm at a very difficult time? Ehrenburg states that Lenin told Litvinov:

> It was essential to try and find reasonable men and to assess differences of opinion in the camp of the victors, the resentment of the defeated, the workers' movements, the appetite of potential concessionaires and the standing of scholars and writers.[81]

Why was Litvinov's boss Chicherin not sent? We can only presume that Lenin thought that Litvinov was the best person and Lenin must have had a very high opinion of Litvinov. Why was Litvinov not appointed Foreign Commissar rather than Chicherin? Litvinov had a loyal Bolshevik past, whereas Chicherin had been a Menshevik. However, Chicherin had been employed in the Tsar's foreign Commissariat, which tipped the scale in favour of Chicherin. It is to Lenin's credit that he wanted the best person for the job, so the fact that Chicherin had been a civil servant under the Tsar's regime and a Menshevik did not prevent him from being appointed to the top Foreign Office job. Further proof of the high regard that Lenin had for Litvinov was that, in spite of being ambassador to Estonia, Litvinov was constantly required to return to Moscow.[82]

In the post-Stalin period Lenin was revered and many felt how much better the fate of Russian communism and international communism would have been if a successor had

---

[79] Carr, Edward: *Interregnum*, p.253
[80] Ch.8 No 80
[81] Ehrenburg, Ilya: *Post-War Years*, p.277
[82] See Ch.3, No.78

been found who had a greater similarity to Lenin. This stifled discussion on his merits. However, Lenin was a dictator. As Debo stated, Lenin's two aims were 'to personally retain power and imbed for ever his principle of revolution.'[83]

Andrew Roberts, in an article in the *Daily Mail* on 21 August 2004, stated that Stalinism was simply the inevitable conclusion of Marxism and Leninism:

> Most of the crimes were planned by Lenin long before Stalin ever came to power. Murderous class hatred, rather than love of one's neighbours or betterment of the human race, let alone the perfection of society, already lay at the heart of Bolshevism and the massacres were already well under way when Lenin died in 1924.[84]

Lenin still retained his sense of humour. Chicherin's typist, instead of finishing a letter sent to Lenin with 'Communist greetings' as was customary, typed by mistake 'capitalist greetings.' When the mistake was discovered, Barmine unsuccessfully sent a Narkomindel employee to try to retrieve the letter before it reached Lenin, but was unsuccessful.

However, upon receiving the letter, Lenin roared with laughter.[85] I am by no means sure Barmine is correct when he states that nobody then would have dreamed of putting down such mistakes to sabotage or counter-revolution. The implication is that there was lack of of humour in Stalin's Russia among the elite but this is by no means certain.[86] On one occasion when Ernest Bevin, British Foreign Secretary, made an irreverent joke about Lenin to Molotov, Troyanovsky (Molotov's interpreter) was so shocked that he said, 'In the Soviet Union we do not joke about Lenin.' Nevertheless, it sent Molotov into gales of laughter.'[87]

Considering the changes involved in the transition from Leninism to Stalinism, Volkogonov rightly points out that many of Stalin's abuses, secret police, secrecy and privileges for the elite commenced in Lenin's time. Regarding terror, for example, Lenin, having established the Cheka Secret Police, approved the following statement:

> In the present situation the security at the rear by means of terror is an absolute necessity. ... It is essential to protect the Soviet State from class enemies by isolating them in concentration camps and that anybody involved in White Guard organisations, conspiracies and rebellions be shot.[88]

---

[83] Debo, Richard: *Survival and Consolidation*, p.135
[84] *Daily Mail*, 21 August 2004, p.28
[85] Barmine, Alexandre: *Memoirs of an Ambassador*, p.154; *One Who Survived*, p.117
[86] Ch.17, No.29
[87] Smith, Walter: *Moscow Mission 1946-1949*, p.62
[88] Volkogonov, Dimitri: *Lenin*, p.234

Similarly, Lenin took a harsh line in connection with the Church. In late 1918 at least ten church hierarchs as well as many clergy were executed.[89]

The communist elite, including Litvinov, had a very privileged lifestyle, even in a period of famine. The highest officials had the right to go on vacation and rest cures in foreign sanatoria, for which the party paid in gold roubles. In 1921 no fewer than six officials were receiving medical care in Germany at a time when the country was begging for help from the USA to avert famine. In 1922 the number of persons receiving special benefits exceeded 17,000. In September of that year it was raised to 60,000. As early as 1920 one, Adolph Ioffe, complained to Trotsky:

> From top to bottom and from bottom to top it is everywhere the same. On the lowest level it is a pair of shoes and a soldier's shirt, higher up an automobile, a railroad car, the Sovnarkom dining room, quarters in the Kremlin or the National Hotel and on the highest rung, where all is available, it is prestige, prominent status and fame.[90]

Whereas the secret police might have been necessary to protect the infant state, privileges for the few, particularly when they were clouded in secrecy, were the exact opposite to what Marx would have anticipated. When Lenin heard in May 1921 that 'there was another sanatorium to be established for Sovnarkom', he wrote to Molotov:

> I fear this may provoke reproach. I would ask that the Orgburo look at this question most carefully. It may be more rational just to name this home sanatorium no. 9.

As Volkogonov rightly states, 'Future Central Committee officials would learn how best to hide their sanatoria, hospitals, clinics, studios, restaurants and special shops from the public gaze.' [91]

The growth of a favoured bureaucracy was another feature of the state under Lenin. In one rural district in the Ukraine there were sixteen bureaucrats during the Tsar's reign. It now had 79. Whereas in 1913 there were 856,000 workers in Russian industry and 58,000 white-collar workers, in 1919 the number of workers employed in Russian industry had declined to 807,000 and the number of white-collar workers rose to 78,000. Further, even at the lowest level the communist civil servant had access to goods not available to the ordinary citizen, as well as opportunities to obtain bribes and tips.[92]

Ehrenburg confirms: 'Litvinov spoke of Lenin with veneration.'[93] Litvinov respected Lenin in a way he never respected Stalin. Tanya Litvinov maintains that her father thought

---

[89] Volkogonov, Dimitri: *Lenin*, p.234

[90] Pipes, Richard: *Russia Under the Bolshevik Regime*, p.442

[91] Volkogonov, Dmitri: *Rise & Fall of Russian Empire*, p.79

[92] Pipes, Richard: *Russia Under the Bolshevik Regime*, p.445

[93] Ehrenburg, Ilya: *Post-War Years*, p.277

one of Lenin's strength's was that he was prepared to acknowledge his mistakes – unlike Stalin.[94] With disaster in Russia in the early 20s, the population starving and towns half-deserted, Lenin shifted his policy away from War Communism towards the New Economic Policy, allowing small private businesses and the peasantry to flourish.

Ivy stated:

> I used to think Lenin was a sort of saint. I now think he was a wrong-headed saint, but still he was a man of integrity and culture; but what could one man do?

Implying that Lenin was head and shoulders above the others in the Politburo, including Trotsky, she indicated that, like her husband, she was not a Trotsky supporter. In her unpublished memoirs she stated: 'The dictatatorship of the proletariat was supposed to last a short time. They thought they'd ride the storm.'[95]

Carswell was right to state, confirmed by Litvinov's daughter Tanya, that Litvinov's disappointment in the Bolsheviks began even in the days of Lenin, when Litvinov considered the Revolution was taking the wrong direction.[96] One can assume that Litvinov was unhappy about some of the repressive measures initiated by Lenin, although it may be it had nothing to do with this because, from the draft of Ivy Litvinov's unpublished memoirs, 'Maxim was also unhappy about the U-turn away from communism towards the New Economic Policy.' Ivy says, 'He was terribly depressed.' Although Ivy states that Maxim felt it had to be, he felt everything had been sold.[97] This indicates that Litvinov's main concern was the deviation from communist principles rather than the harsh terror which Lenin had set in motion. Litvinov became highly critical of the Stalin regime, but Litvinov never appears to have realised that many of the abuses, lack of respect for human life, bureaucracy and secret privileges for the Communist elite were initiated by Lenin, only to be perfected by Stalin.

Although on the night of Lenin's death Litvinov was very upset, he was also apprehensive. He feared a bloodbath. However, he considered Trotsky would have been worse.[98]

---

[94] Tanya
[95] Archives, box 1
[96] Carswell, John: *The Exile*, p.200; Tanya
[97] Tanya
[98] Tanya

5: CHICHERIN AND TROTSKY

As far as the Soviet Union's foreign policy was concerned, when Stalin was taking over the reins of power, he had no desire to change his team. In the early days of Stalin's regime, Litvinov told his wife: 'The happiest time was when he was Deputy Commissar, as he loved work.' Sheinis agrees and described: 'The eight years from 1922 to 1930 as 'tranquil'compared to the preceding and subsequent troubled and trying times.'[1] This is rather strange in view of constant references by others to the antagonism between Chicherin and Litvinov, although such allegations appear exaggerated.[2] This alleged antagonism must have been personal, as Chicherin and Litvinov appeared mainly in agreement on foreign policy. We do not know whether Litvinov would have liked to have progressed to the ruling elite and was disappointed that he never became a member of the Politburo or until 1934 a member of the Central Committee. In spite of what Litvinov told his wife, Litvinov was ambitious to the extent that he wished to be in charge of his country's foreign policy. However, unlike Eden, who aspired to and obtained the top job, there is no evidence that, as far as we know, Litvinov ever aspired to the top job.

1925 was dominated by the Treaty of Locarno, which was a treaty of non-aggression between France and Germany, who accepted the loss of Alsace-Lorraine. Great Britain and Italy agreed that if either France or Germany committed aggression against the other, then Britain and Italy would come to the defence of the country attacked.[3]

The Soviet Union did not like the treaty. With considerable justification, they regarded the pact as an integral part of Britain's anti-Soviet activity. However, Britain was acting as she had done for centuries in seeking to maintain the balance of power in Europe. Clearly, as happened in 1939, a cosy relationship between Germany and the Soviet Union would upset that balance of power. The British motives for Locarno could not have been made clearer than a speech by the Under Secretary of State for the Colonies:

> The struggle at Locarno as I see it was this. Is Germany to regard her future to be bound up with the fate of the great Western powers or is she going to work with Russia for the destruction of world civilisation? The Foreign Commissar was brought from Moscow to try and prevent this. The significance of Locarno is

---

[1] Tanya's tape at Imperial War Museum; Sheinis, Zinovy: *Maxim Litvinov*, p.177
[2] Barmine, Alexandre: *One Who Survived*, p.119; *Memoirs of a Soviet Diplomat*, p.217; Bessedovsky, Grigory: *Revelations of a Soviet Diplomat*, p.95; Fischer, Louis: *Men and Politics*, p.125; Fischer, Louis: *Lenin*, p.274; O'Connor Timothy *Diplomacy and Revolution* p.58
[3] Cmd 1925 2525

tremendous. It means, as far as the present government of Germany is concerned, it is detached from Russia and is throwing in its lot with the Western powers.[4]

In view of this statement, it was not surprising that the Soviet Union was hostile to Locarno. Further, the Under Secretary of State was misleading his audience, because Germany had no intention of detaching herself from the Soviet Union, as is indicated by the commercial treaty with the Soviet Union which they continued to negotiate notwithstanding Locarno.

Chicherin said:

> There were innumerable proofs that the British Government was pursuing a policy of encirclement in regard to the USSR. The Conservative Government does not want the differences between Britain and the USSR to be smoothed out. British policy in regard to the pact of guarantee (Locarno Treaty)was an integral part of its basic anti-Soviet policy.

However, Chicherin then stated: 'British plans to separate Germany from the USSR ran contrary to the declared wishes of the German Government.'[5]

Unlike other important assignments which fell on the Narkomindel, such as the prisoner exchange and the famine relief,[6] Chicherin dominated the negotiations with France and Germany, although Litvinov twice visited Berlin in June and September to protest against Germany's intended move to the West, but without effect. However, Chicherin, playing on German suspicion of Poland, employed subtler methods. He visited Poland immediately before a visit to Berlin.

On 12 October 1925, just before the German Chancellor Stresemann left for Locarno, the Soviet-German Commercial Treaty was signed in Moscow by Litvinov and Brockdorff-Rantzau. Its significance was the declaration that the Rapallo Treaty would continue to be regarded as the foundation for regulating German-Soviet relations.[7] The close relationship between Germany and Russia continued, as both needed each other.

In a press statement made by Chicherin on 21 December 1925, he stated that the Locarno Treaty gives Britain

> the opportunity of exerting strong pressure on the German Government, as a result of which Germany might be compelled, even against its own wish, to change its

---

[4] Coates, W P S: *History of Anglo -Soviet Relations*, p.217; *Observer* 25 October 1925 p13
[5] Degras, Jane: *Soviet Documents on Foreign Policy*, vol.2, p.57
[6] See Ch.3 Prisoner Exchange, No.47; Famine, Nos.85-119
[7] Carr, Edward: *German-Soviet Relations*, p.85

attitude to the Soviet Government. We shall follow with friendly attention the policy which the German Government will pursue.[8]

Chicherin did not need to have any concerns about the continuation of the German-Soviet friendship because on 6 December 1926 Chicherin, in a press statement, was able to report: 'Since my visit to Berlin last year, relations between Germany and ourselves and our international position have established themselves more firmly, despite the efforts of the enemy camp', which was of course referring to Britain.[9]

However, the reason why the Locarno Treaty did not add to the pacification of Europe was that it gave Germany the impression that, although Britain was prepared to intervene in Western Europe, she gave notice that if Germany attacked in the East, Britain would give Germany a free hand. At the time of the treaty, Austen Chamberlain received much praise as the architect of Locarno, which was considered such a major contribution to peace that he received the Nobel Peace Prize. However, this was an occasion where the Nobel Committee for Peace was wrong and Stalin was right, because on 21 December 1925 Stalin said Locarno 'hides the seeds of a new world war.'[10] Austen Chamberlain formally disassociated Great Britain from France's Eastern alliances saying: 'For the Polish corridor no British Government ever will or can risk the bones of a British grenadier.'[11] Further, France was not prepared to treat Germany as an equal party and constantly frustrated Germany's attempts for equality in armaments.

Litvinov cleverly pointed out in his speech to the Central Executive Committee:

> If Locarno, as its authors try to convince us, is really aimed at the pacification of Europe, at a real improvement and consolidation of relations between European States, then its advocates would warmly welcome the treaty [the Soviet-German Commercial Treaty] as strengthening friendship between two nations. But if, as we always suspected, one of the aims of the Locarno Treaty is the formation of a united anti-Soviet front and the isolation of our Union, then we must admit that the treaty signed today does really contradict the spirit of Locarno and we can only rejoice that we have succeeded to some extent in depriving Locarno of its anti-Soviet sting.[12]

It is quite clear that Litvinov was right, as the British Government did not welcome Rapallo, as this made Germany and Russia stronger and increased their ability to withstand

---

[8] Degras, Jane: *Soviet Documents on Foreign Policy*, vol.2, p.78

[9] Ibid. p.144

[10] *The New York Times*, 21 December 1925, p.10; Grayson, Richard: *Austen Chamberlain and the Commitment to Europe: British Foreign Policy 1924-1929*, p.65

[11] Taylor, A J P: *English History 1914-1945*, p.222

[12] Degras, Jane: *Soviet Documents on Foreign Policy*, vol.2, p.108

pressure from Britain. Therefore, Britain's hope that the Locarno Treaty would cancel the benefits that the Rapallo Treaty gave to Russia and Germany did not succeed. However, subsequently in the 1930s Litvinov praised Locarno. In the debate on the League of Nations report in September 1935, Litvinov stated:

> Unfortunately, for reasons over which we have no control, we did not succeed in associating in this work of peace all the states belonging to the eastern part of Europe and we therefore could only conclude mutual pacts with France and Czechoslovakia, having the same aim as a regional pact. There can be no doubt that these pacts have fulfilled the strengthening of the feeling of security, thus performing in the East of Europe the same functions as does the Locarno Pact in Western Europe.[13]

Litvinov can be criticised for inconsistency.

The Soviet Union was criticised for supporting the General Strike in Britain, and thus interfering in British internal politics.[14] 1926 proved to be a year of tranquillity only interrupted by the British General Strike. 1927 was a torrid year for the Soviet Union. On 23 February 1927 Chamberlain warned the Soviet Government against defaming, attacking and offending the British Empire.[15] Three days later Litvinov replied, asserting the right of the Soviet Union to discuss international affairs.[16] On 6 April 1927, the Chinese police raided the Soviet Embassy in Peking and published documents alleging Soviet revolutionary activity in China. On 5 May 1927, Litvinov called the foreign press to the Narkomindel and denounced these papers as fraudulent and forgeries.[17]

On 12 May 1927, the building used by the Russian Co-operative Society (ARCOS) and Soviet Trade Delegation was searched, in breach of article 5 of the 1921 Trade Agreement, looking for a missing War Office document. On 17 May, Litvinov formally protested, condemning the raid as violation of the trade agreement; but rather than taking note of the protest, the British Government requested Parliament to approve the breaking off of diplomatic relations with the Soviet Union, which was approved by 357 to 111.[18] On 26 May 1927, Litvinov severely criticised Britain's decision to break off diplomatic relations in no uncertain terms.[19] In Britain the CID, contrary to the advice of the Foreign Office, thought that the Soviet Union was such a threat that plans for war had been drawn up.[20]

---

[13] Ibid. vol.3, p.145

[14] Ch.9, No.63

[15] Pope, Arthur: *Maxim Litvinov*, p.219

[16] Ibid. p.219

[17] See Ch.7, Nos.36 & 37; Pope, Arthur: *Maxim Litvinov*, p.219

[18] Ch.9. *Hansard*, vol.206, 26 May 1927, 2195-2326

[19] Ch.9, Nos.81 & 82

[20] Grayson, Richard: *Austen Chamberlain and the Commitment to Europe: British Foreign Policy 1924-1929*, p.266

Chicherin, who was in failing health, was absent from November 1926 until June 1927, so he could receive treatment in Germany and the French Riviera for diabetes and polyneuritis.[21] During this time Litvinov was in charge of the Narkomindel. O'Connor claims that Litvinov did not send regular reports to Chicherin.[22] Indeed, while in Germany, Chicherin, on 3 June 1927, criticised the way the leadership were allowing relations with Germany to deteriorate and stated he was going to return to the Soviet Union to submit his resignation. However, as Stalin indicated he would not accept Chicherin's resignation, he did not resign; but when he returned to the Soviet Union in June 1927 he was determined to repair the damage.[23]

The Soviet Union, together with other non-League members, the most important of which was the USA, were invited by the League to participate in the Preparatory Commission for the General Disarmament Conference. The Soviet Union was displeased that Geneva had been chosen as the meeting place because diplomatic relations with Switzerland had not been restored following their rupture after Vorovskii, a Soviet diplomat, had been murdered in Switzerland in 1923 and the suspected assassin acquitted. While Chicherin was away sick in 1927, Litvinov attempted to reach accommodation with the West. It was on Litvinov's initiative that an agreement had been reached with Switzerland which resulted in the Soviet Union's participation in the Preparatory Commission, although it was Chicherin who announced such participation.[24] O'Connor claims that Chicherin opposed such a conference.[25] However, I do not think O'Connor is necessarily correct. As Chicherin was continually interested in good relations with Germany, he would have welcomed the close collaboration between the German and Soviet representatives which occurred at the disarmament talks.

When Litvinov finally attended the Disarmament Conference, as Chairman of the Soviet delegation, with his very first speech he put forward the radical suggestion that all military forces, whether on land, in the sea or air, be dissolved, all weapons be destroyed and the scrapping of all military vessels and aeroplanes.[26] During the conference Austen Chamberlain met Litvinov at a time when there were no diplomatic relations, but, although courteous, Chamberlain raised the question of the close connection between the Communist International and the Soviet Government. Litvinov's reply was that the Soviet Government could not prevent the Comintern from expressing its views, and although the Conservative party in England might be responsible for the Conservative Government, the Conservative Government is not responsible for the activities of the Conservative party.[27]

---

[21] O'Connor, Timothy: *Diplomacy and Revolution*, p.153

[22] Ibid. p.154

[23] Ibid. p.158

[24] O'Connor, Timothy: *Diplomacy and Revolution*, p.158

[25] Ibid. p.159

[26] Disarmament, Ch.6, No.62

[27] Pope, Arthur: *Maxim Litvinov*, p. 239

There is no doubt that Litvinov endeavoured to enhance Moscow's prestige by Soviet participation in conferences, pacts and agreements, and there is much evidence to suggest that, in the public sphere, Litvinov was never happier than when attending such meetings, which is shown by his enthusiastic speeches at the League of Nations. Litvinov fought for the Soviet Union's adherence to the Kellogg Pact of 1928, by which states agreed to renounce war.[28]

Although it was alleged that Chicherin was suspicious of such international meetings and fought against them, Fischer correctly stated that Chicherin 'meticulously prepared for the Genoa Conference.'[29] In a letter to Fischer, Chicherin stated: 'I am and have always been an absolute, undiluted, unmixed, unwavering, unswerving enemy of our joining the League of Nations.' Barmine states, like Fischer, that Chicherin had no sympathy for the League of Nations, which he regarded as a thinly disguised coalition of the victors against the vanquished. Chicherin proposed to set up, under the protection of the Soviets, a League of Peoples to which the wronged, the oppressed and the exploited should be included on exactly the same footing as the dominant powers. In contrast to the League of Nations, this League of Peoples was to become a centre of international justice between peoples.[30] Undoubtedly, a just criticism of the League was its failure to include among its principles racial equality.[31]

However, Litvinov was a late convert to the League, and was equally scathing of the League in the 1920s.[32] Chicherin favoured, and it can be argued he initiated, what Litvinov would energetically pursue – the policy of non-aggression pacts with separate states rather than collective security through the League of Nations. In a press statement on 6 December 1926 Litvinov said:

> We are gradually realising our programme of direct negotiations with separate states in which we see the possibility of ensuring peace. In our opinion membership of the League of Nations does not increase our security but decreases it.[33]

In spite of Britain's hostility, in May 1927, the Soviet Union accepted an invitation to attend the World Economic Conference.[34] Unlike the World Economic Conference of 1933, Litvinov did not attend; but one of the delegation, Sokolnikov, when he addressed the conference, stressed:

---

[28] Ch.6, No.36

[29] Fischer, Louis: *Lenin*, p.570

[30] Fischer, Louis: *Men & Politics*, p.143; Barmine, Alexandre: *One Who Survived*, p.117; *Memoirs of a Soviet Diplomat*, p.153

[31] Ch.12, League of Nations, No.41, for criticism of League Covenant

[32] Ch.12, Litvinov criticism of League, No.7

[33] Degras, Jane: *Soviet Documents on Foreign Policy*, vol.2, p.146

[34] Fischer, Louis: *The Soviets in World Affairs*, p.727

If improvement of economic relations between the Soviet and capitalist countries resulted from the deliberations at Geneva, prosperity and the cause of world peace would be advanced and the conference justified.

He was speaking very much in Litvinov's language. This remark prompted the French socialist M Jouhaux to remark: 'Soviet Russia had abandoned her idea of a Communist world revolution.'

Mr Ossinski also of the Russian delegation proposed the following radical remedies:

'The annulment of all war debts', a step with which the USA (as main creditor would be very unlikely to agree), 'the increase in the wages of industrial workers, the re-establishment of the eight-hour day and also the establishment of complete real liberty for trade unions'; although trade unions in the Soviet Union certainly did not enjoy complete freedom. Mr Ossinski also stated that there should be 'introduction of real assistance for the unemployed', as well as 'increasing taxes on the rich.'[35] Mr Ossinski did not say why these measures would restore the world's economy.

Mr Ossinski then put forward further radical political proposals:

> The abolition of all barriers to the passage of surplus population from one state to another; the abolition of the system of protectorates and mandates; the withdrawal of all foreign troops from colonial territories; the cessation of all military intervention in China; the cessation of all forms of economic boycott against Soviet Russia.

Mr Osinski also advocated total disarmament. The workers and peasants were to control the liquidation of all equipment and installations; hardly the best people to assess whether disarmament has occurred.

The results of the conference were meagre. The conference adopted the reports of the three commissions which it had established (Agriculture, Commerce and Cartels, and Industrial Ententes). The report on cartels and industrial ententes was a very guarded document and obviously a compromise between a number of conflicting views. 'It does little more than sum up the advantages and disadvantages of this kind of organisation.' The conference considers: 'These agreements should not lead to a rise in prices, to the detriment of the consumer, and they should give due consideration to the interest of workers.' A number of delegates abstained, but the Soviet delegation was the only delegation to vote against the motion, saying: 'Capitalist combines exploited workers and consumers.'[36] Two days later,

---

[35] *The New York Times*, 8 May 1927, p.21
[36] *Times*, 21 May 1927, p.13

when the final report of the conference was adopted, which included the reports of the various commissions, the Soviet delegation abstained after an agreement that the report should contain a declaration welcoming their participation in the conference 'irrespective of any differences in their economic systems.' [37]

In an interview for *Izvestiya* on 2 June 1927, Ossinski rightly stated:

> The decisions of the conference were extremely abstract and unsubstantial, but by attending the conference the Soviet Union established contact with many bourgeois countries and made contact with representatives of many commercial and industrial circles of many bourgeois countries. In these meetings the Soviet delegation and the individual members vouchsafed exhaustive information on the situation in the USSR. This will undoubtedly bear fruit in the future of our trade missions abroad. Even if only for this purpose, I consider it is extremely important for the USSR to participate in future conferences of this nature.[38]

No doubt Litvinov would entirely agree with such sentiments.

Soviet agriculture following the famine of the early 20s recovered slowly until in 1926 grain output was 76.8 million tons. Thereafter, it again went into decline. However, these figures were not impressive compared with the 81.6 million tons in 1913, although the population had increased by 14,000,000 people.[39]

The Soviet Government committed the mistake of increasing prices for animal products but lowering grain prices in order to provide the cities with meat and dairy produce. From mid-1927, in the countryside as well as in Moscow and other big cities, a severe shortage of certain basic foods and essential goods was felt. By 1928 exports of grain had been virtually reduced to nil. A number of factories were threatened with closure, because grain exports paid for the imports the Soviet Union required for industrialisation, so imports were curtailed.[40] Chicherin in the previous year had supported Stalin in a proposed relaxation of the way foreign companies conducted business in the Soviet Union in order to stimulate the economy. Stalin said: 'We would not agree to the modification of our foreign trade monopoly if our trade was bright and rosy; but, as we all know, unfortunately it is not the case.'[41] Stalin was most complimentary about his Foreign Commissar, stating: 'When I suggested relaxing the foreign trade monopoly a year ago, only Comrade Chicherin was on my side, but all the other members of the Politburo and Central Committee thought the reconsideration was not timely or urgent.'

---

[37] Ibid. 24 May 1927, p.15
[38] Degras, Jane: *Soviet Documents on Foreign Policy*, vol.2, pp. 214-.216
[39] Hosking, Geoffrey: *History of the Soviet Union*, p.125
[40] Reiman, Michal: *Birth of Stalinism*, p.38
[41] Ibid. p.128

Then Stalin stated: 'It can hardly be doubted that Comrade Chicherin is better informed about the mood in foreign economic circles than any of us.'[42] This is hardly a remark Stalin would have made if in 1927 Stalin was antagonistic to Chicherin. It was against this background that Chicherin, with the support of Stalin, proposed, in the face of considerable opposition, 'the relaxation of the foreign trade monopoly measures.'[43]

Litvinov supported Chicherin. In a letter to ambassadors, Litvinov instructed the ambassadors to keep silent on the economic decline of the Soviet economy. He commented: 'I agree with Comrade Chicherin in being worried about the course of events.'[44]

1927 also saw the start of the Five Year Plan, as Stalin tried to rapidly industrialise the Soviet Union, terminating the New Economic Policy, about which Litvinov had been unenthusiastic and which attracted much criticism. By 1928 Stalin had also decided to blame the downturn in the economy on sabotage by both Soviet and foreign workers. On 5 March 1928 the Politburo decided to charge a number of Russian and German engineers. This was no doubt Stalin's decision.[45] Why Stalin decided to choose German workers with whom the Soviet Union enjoyed excellent relations rather than nationals of other countries hostile to the Soviet Union is a complete mystery and not a clever move?

In September 1928 Chicherin again departed for Germany for a long period of rest and medical treatment.[46] Litvinov was once more in charge. If Bessedovsky is correct, Chicherin wrote to Stalin in 1928, while Chicherin was abroad, demanding that Stalin choose between himself and Litvinov.[47] At this time it seems Chicherin was reluctant to return. The chief of the medical staff, Dr A Levin Karakhan, was dispatched in late November to investigate in order to prevent any scandal, as the Soviet leadership wanted Chicherin to return to the Soviet Union. However, Chicherin still displayed independence. He returned of his own free will on 6 January 1930. By 1929 Chicherin was the Foreign Commissar in name only. All power had passed to Litvinov, partly on account of Chicherin's long absence,[48] a situation that appeared to have had Stalin's blessing.

Almost immediately Litvinov achieved success when he negotiated the Litvinov protocol.[49] Further although diplomatic relations with Britain were restored, diplomatic relations between the Soviet Union and China remained severed.[50]

---

[42] Reiman, Michal: *Birth of Stalinism*, p.129
[43] Ibid. p.39
[44] Ibid. p.141
[45] O'Connor, Timothy: *Diplomacy and Revolution*, p.159-160 ; and see Ch.8, No.96
[46] Ibid. p.161
[47] Bessedovsky, Grigory *Revelations of a Soviet Diplomat*, p.95
[48] O'Connor , Timothy: *Diplomacy and Revolution*, p.162
[49] Ch.8, No.57
[50] GB Ch.9, No.103; China Ch. 7 No 40

In a letter to Molotov, Stalin criticised the tactics Litvinov employed as being too conciliatory and overlooking the revolutionary aspect.[51] In spite of these criticisms, Stalin's decision to promote Litvinov from Deputy Commissar to Commissar the following summer was not affected.

On 4 December 1929 Litvinov made a fine speech to the Central Committee which, in a letter to Molotov, Stalin described as 'pretty good.'[52] The speech mainly dealt with the problems of China and Great Britain, praising the Soviet Union's unchanging, steadfast and methodical foreign policy. On the other hand, Litvinov reported pessimistically about the Disarmament Conference and the rejection of the Soviet Union's plans for a rapid reduction in armaments. He also referred to the hostility which the capitalist countries always exhibited towards the Soviet Union and in fine rhetoric made a savage attack on the capitalist and social democratic press, which

> with unswerving energy for the past twelve years have continued to heap abuse on the Soviet Union and its representatives, to invent all kinds of incidents that never took place, to misrepresent the actual position of affairs in the Soviet Union, to exaggerate our difficulties which are inevitable in the gigantic task we have set ourselves, to belittle our successes and achievement, to attribute to us sins never committed, employing the sham revelation of faked witnesses, faked documents and other scurrilous methods. Not only the press, but even some of the governments are not above the flagrant use of the dregs of White Russian exiles for the forging of documents.[53]

Actually, much of what Litvinov said was true. Both the Zinoviev Letter (a supposed document from the Comintern which advocated the intensification of revolutionary propaganda in Britain, not least in the armed forces, which helped to bring down the first Labour government in 1924) and the War Office Document that led to the ARCOS raid were probably false.[54] However, what Litvinov did not then understand or want to understand was that this criticism of the press was not restricted to attacks on the Soviet Union, was not necessarily mendacious and is still relevant today. However, after Litvinov's ambassadorship in the United States he revised his opinion of the democratic Press. [55]

The mid and late 1920s were dominated by the rift between Trotsky and Stalin, resulting in Trotsky's downfall. Trotsky had much respect for Lenin. In Trotsky's farewell article

---

[51] Lih, Lars: *Stalin's Letters to Molotov*, p.174 No 44
[52] Lih, Lars: *Stalin's Letters to Molotov*, p.183 No.53
[53] Documents, 1929, p.191
[54] See Ch.9, No. 53 (Zinoviev letter), No.76 (Arcos raid)
55 *The New York Times* 3 January 1952 p.9; Ch 17 No.80

following Lenin's death, Trotsky stated, 'In each of us lives a small part of Lenin, which is the best part of all of us.'[56] Trotsky certainly did not praise Stalin.

In October 1926, after calling Stalin the 'grave digger of the Revolution', Trotsky was expelled from the Politburo. In October 1927 Trotsky, after publishing a letter criticising Stalin's version of the October Revolution and detailing Stalin's rift with Lenin, was expelled from the Central Committee. After Trotsky tried to mount a demonstration on 7 November 1927, the anniversary of the October Revolution, Trotsky was expelled from the Communist Party. On 17 January 1928 Trotsky, the hero of the October Revolution and the founder of the Red Army, was exiled to a remote city on the Chinese border. On 10 February 1929 he was deported to Turkey.[57]

Litvinov held the view that if Trotsky had assumed the leadership he, as a proponent of world revolution, would have been worse than Stalin.[58] Was Litvinov right? Litvinov appears to have supported Stalin against Trotsky, but Litvinov did not realise that the presence of Trotsky, who supplied credible opposition to Stalin, was the best guarantee against Stalin becoming a complete dictator.

It was Trotsky, not Stalin, as Reader Bullard, the Commercial Counsellor of the British Embassy, correctly stated, who built the Red Army.[59] It was Trotsky's brilliant leadership in 1919 when Petrograd was threatened that saved the city, a major factor in the Bolsheviks winning the Civil War.[60] If Trotsky had been leader in 1940 and 1941, it is difficult to see him ignoring the warning signs of the coming German invasion.

During the period of War Communism, Trotsky was initially an enthusiastic supporter, seeing it 'as a means and foremost as an instrument for the rapid socialisation of Russia.' Nevertheless, with the Soviet economy in crisis, Trotsky did not voice any objection when NEP.[61] was first debated and introduced. He himself had initially advocated the principle underlying it a year before it was introduced,[62] although he continued to be a leading proponent of comprehensive planning. He believed that, at least in the early stages of a planned economy, the state should be conciliatory towards the private sector and help to develop it. Planning should develop within a mixed economy until the socialist sector by its growing predominance, gradually absorbed, transformed or eliminated the private sector.[63]

---

[56] Tucker, Robert: *Stalin Revolutionary*, p.287
[57] Ward, Chris: *Stalin's Russia*, pp.15 & 16
[58] Tanya
[59] Bullard, Reader: *Camels Must Go*, p.162
[60] Civil war; see Ch.3, pp.15-25
[61] Ch.3, Nos.85-89
[62] Deutscher, Isaac: *Prophet Unarmed 1921-1929*, p.39
[63] Ibid. p.100

However, private enterprise has proved to be resilient and might well have continued to flourish unless closed down by decree. None of the Communist leaders were consistent. On some occasions they were guided by revolutionary zeal, on other occasions they were guided by pragmatism. Politicians of capitalist states are often similarly motivated. Nobody could be more inconsistent than Churchill on the question of appeasement, opposing it in respect of Nazi Germany, but supporting appeasement of Fascist Italy and Japan.

Litvinov told Fischer: 'The prospect of world revolution disappeared on 11 November 1918.'[64] and would be reprimanded by Stalin because the policies he was advocating were not sufficiently revolutionary. [65]

Trotsky was more reluctant than Stalin or Lenin to abandon the idea of imminent revolution, at least in Germany. Trotsky criticised the inept Soviet leadership shown in the 1923 German Communist uprising. Trotsky wrote an article in 1924 in which he stated: 'How was it possible to let slip an exceptional revolutionary situation of a universal historical character?'[66]

I think Trotsky was wrong. The Germans, who felt they were superior to the Russians, would not have wanted to side with the Russians against the German Government, any more than the Polish workers would support the Red Army when it invaded Poland, a concept that Lenin failed to comprehend.[67] Did Trotsky actually believe that if he had been in charge of the organisation of a revolution in Germany it would have been successful? As I have previously indicated, I believe even with the best organiser, such revolution would have failed. However, a sad factor was that Trotsky, Stalin or Lenin never thought there was anything morally wrong in breaking the spirit of the Rapallo agreement. I think it was fortunate for the Soviet Union that, on the assumption that Germany was aware of the Soviet Union's involvement, Germany did not herself repudiate Rapallo which would have left the Soviet Union entirely isolated in Europe.

Further, Trotsky appears inconsistent and two-faced. In a 1923 interview, Trotsky stated that the prospect of a general European communist uprising was receding. When the correspondent of the *Manchester Guardian*, Arthur Ransome, asked Litvinov to explain the contradiction between Soviet national government and the Communist International, Litvinov suggested that the best person to answer the question was Trotsky, because he was a member of the Communist International and a member of the Soviet Government. Trotsky's reply was far from revolutionary. Ransome asked Trotsky 'why he did not treat the French occupation of the Ruhr as a revolutionary stimulus', to which Trotsky replied:

---

[64] Fischer, Louis: *Men and Politics*, p.124
[65] Letter: Stalin to Molotov, No.44, p.174
[66] Carr, Edward: *Interregnum*, p.229
[67] See Ch.3, No. 71

Certainly we are interested in the victory of the working class, but it is not at all in our interest that the revolution should take place in a Europe exhausted and drained of blood, and the proletariat should receive from the hands of the bourgeoisie nothing but ruins, as we received them after Tsarism and the Russian bourgeoisie. If, however, the bourgeoisie should succeed in dragging Europe into yet another devastating war, this would first mean the bleeding and destruction of primarily those generations of working class who are the bearers of the future and secondly the economic beggary of Europe. The result might be the most severe lowering of European culture over a long period and accordingly not the approach but, on the contrary, rather the postponement of the revolutionary perspectives.

Then agreeing with Litvinov on the importance of peace, Trotsky said: 'That is why from a revolutionary point of view we are vitally interested in the preservation of peace.'[68] There are other instances where Litvinov and Trotsky were in agreement. An occasion when Litvinov agreed with Trotsky was in respect of the Soviet-Polish War in 1920. Whereas Chicherin made secret conciliatory proposals to Poland, even after the Polish offensive had begun, Litvinov opposed such secret proposals. Trotsky intervened and firmly sided with Litvinov and urged the Politburo to stop the overtures. Pilsudski saw in them signs of Soviet weakness and as they had been made secretly they failed to move Polish opinion towards peace. Trotsky demanded a return to open diplomacy. However, on this occasion it was Litvinov who was devious as he stated: 'Our mistake was that we artificially delayed negotiations instead of beginning them by putting forward Armistice negotiations that their fulfilment would require long enough to enable us to occupy Lemberg, Mlava and Warsaw.'[69]

However, unlike Litvinov, it appears Trotsky's offer to open up negotiations with the Poles was made in good faith, as Trotsky wanted to stop at the Curzon line.

Another occasion on which it appears that Litvinov and Trotsky held the same view was that the Soviet Union should recognise Rumania's right to Bessarabia, but they were successfully opposed by Chicherin.[70] As Trotsky was on the Left of the Bolshevik Party, one would have expected him to be one of the many who criticised the famine relief organised by the Americans in 1921. In fact, Trotsky praised the USA 'for unforgettable aid to the hungry masses of Russia.'[71]

The evidence is that Litvinov believed that following the 1918 armistice the chances of world communist revolution had ended. Did Chicherin share the same view? He probably

---

[68] Degras, Jane: *Soviet Documents on Foreign Policy*, vol.1, p.375
[69] Ullman, Richard: *Anglo-Soviet Relations*, vol.3, p.208
[70] Carr, Edward: *Bolshevik Revolution 1919-1923*, vol.3, p.346
[71] Fitzpatrick, Sheila: *Russia in the Era of NEP*, p.245

did not. In 1921 Chicherin asked O'Grady, a British Labour politician who had been sent by the Coalition Government to negotiate a prisoner exchange, whether revolution was imminent and appeared surprised when O'Grady made it clear that revolution in Britain was not imminent.[72]

Trotsky could be cruel, as he was when he suppressed the Kronstadt mutiny with great ferocity. [73] The comparison with the brutal suppression of the *Potemkin* mutiny in 1905[74] is obvious, giving ammunition to those who argue that the similarities between the Tsarist and Bolshevik regimes was far greater than their differences. However, we do know that Trotsky severely and in my opinion unfairly criticised both Chicherin and Litvinov – Chicherin for not being sufficiently robust at the Rapallo Conference; and Litvinov for taking a year to negotiate a treaty with Sweden.[75] As it was against Litvinov's nature to be dilatory, I can only assume there was a good reason for the delay.

Chicherin's ancestors were aristocratic and he had moved in high social circles, unlike Litvinov. Occasionally, Chicherin could not forget this fact. Once, when a comrade asked Chicherin whether he wanted red or white wine, Chicherin answered, 'Just as it properly should be – first the white, and then the red.'[76] Once, Chicherin telephoned Litvinov and when Ivy told him her husband was in the bath, Chicherin demanded to speak to Litvinov. Ivy refused to get him out of the bath. Chicherin said, 'I will have him arrested.'[77]

O'Connor assumes, without giving any authority, that Litvinov and Chicherin were often in disagreement, particularly concerning Germany; but at this time, when diplomatic relations with Great Britain were first difficult and then severed by Britain, I am quite certain that Litvinov also wished to have the best possible relations with Germany. I believe many commentators have exaggerated the differences between the policy that Chicherin and Litvinov tried to pursue and wrongly suggest that they were always at loggerheads. Although they came from different social backgrounds and were entirely different in character and working methods, people in such circumstances sometimes get on better than when both are similar. Certainly, there was rivalry between Chicherin and Litvinov, but the statement that whenever Chicherin said 'Yes', Litvinov said 'No', appears to have been exaggerated.[78]

On 17 January 1927 Litvinov stated that Chicherin was entirely right to apply all his strength to the renewal of normal relations between the USSR and Mexico.[79] Again, like

---

[72] *Times*, 13 December 1934, p.21

[73] Pipes, Richard: *Russia Under the Bolshevik Regime*, p.382

[74] Ch.1, No.21

[75] See Genoa Conference, 1922, Ch.4, No.4 to No 31; *Times*, 22 June 1922, p.9

[76] Hilger, Gustav: *Incompatible Allies*, p.110

[77] Tanya

[78] See no 2 ante

[79] Degras, Jane: *Documents on Soviet Foreign Policy*, vol.2, pp.152 & 153

Litvinov, Chicherin in 1921 urged recognition of the Soviet Union's foreign debts.[80] Scott's statement that Litvinov's language when accepting League membership was far removed from Chicherin's view of the League as a capitalist conspiracy is wrong. Litvinov used similar language to describe the League in the 1920s.[81]

Fischer agrees that both Litvinov and Chicherin thought that, following the rupture with Britain, the war scare orchestrated by Stalin was exaggerated.[82] Both were horrified at the arrest of five German engineers in connection with the Shakhty trial, although the German diplomat Hilger states they were only extremely worried.[83]

Unlike Chicherin, Litvinov enjoyed entertaining foreign guests and undertook this task with enthusiasm.[84] This greatly assisted his rise to prominence. He had plenty of opportunity to exhibit his talents before he became Chief Commissar in 1930. Chicherin preferred to work at night. O'Grady, the British Labour MP who had been sent to negotiate the prisoner exchange with Litvinov, recalled being summoned to see Chicherin at midnight.[85]

During the time Litvinov was first Deputy Commissar, and initially when he became Commissar, he allowed foreign correspondents to travel, except to forbidden areas, and to meet ordinary Russians. Also, Litvinov encouraged the ambassadors and diplomatic staff abroad to travel and receive hospitality from non-communists in the country in which they were serving, thereby being able to understand not only the politics and economics but also the purely human aspects.[86] It is probable that Litvinov placed more emphasis on individual freedom than Chicherin, with his background of being in the Tsarist diplomatic service. Litvinov's views on so-called Soviet Democracy are discussed in Chapter 16. [87]

Both Hilger and O'Grady state that Chicherin's desk was full of dusty old files. Litvinov received visitors behind an empty desk, which attested to his systematic methods. Litvinov would not bother to give his staff details. He did not waste any time and he was skilful in distributing the work among his staff.[88] However, in conjunction with Lenin, Chicherin knew how to use the services of his deputy Litvinov, who was sent to Sweden to negotiate prisoner exchange in 1920 and the famine relief in 1921. Both assignments were successful, so Hilger may well be guilty of not giving Chicherin the praise that he deserves.

---

[80] Fischer, Louis: *Lenin*, p.559
[81] Scott, William: *Alliance Against Hitler*, p.201; see League of Nations, Ch.12, No.7
[82] Fischer, Louis: *Russia's Road From Peace to War*, p.172
[83] Fischer, Louis: *Russia's Road From Peace to War*, p.184; Hilger, Gustav: *Incompatible Allies*, p.220
[84] O'Connor, Timothy: *Diplomacy and Revolution*, p.53
[85] *Times*, 13 December 1934, p 21
[86] Hindus, Maurice: *Crisis in the Kremlin*, p 51
[87] See Ch.16, Nos.34, 36 & 40; Ch 8 No 93
[88] Hilger, Gustav: *Incompatible Allies*, p.111; *Times*, 13 December 1934, p.21

Hilger was one to claim there were many conflicts between Litvinov and Chicherin. For Chicherin, Rapallo was the pillar of Soviet foreign policy. To Litvinov it was a political expedient just like any other measure, although he was not blind to the benefits of Rapallo. From the evidence I have studied, it appears that Litvinov was just as keen on the Soviet-German co-operation which resulted from the Treaty of Rapallo. He realised the benefits it had brought to the Soviet Union, if only, because of the continued hostility of Britain, there was no sensible alternative policy.[89]

Bessedovsky states that rivalry between Chicherin and Litvinov became acute in 1927, but this may be erroneous. Indeed, the Foreign Office defector Barmine stated that the Litvinov group fought bitterly against Chicherin for control of the Foreign Office and finally he stated, 'It was quite impossible for Chicherin to work with Litvinov.'[90]

When Litvinov replaced Chicherin, who retired in 1930, Litvinov wanted his own men in key positions in his commissariat, as did Molotov nine years later. However, unlike Molotov, Litvinov did not wish to liquidate those dismissed. Litvinov removed both Chicherin's deputies, Gregory Sokolnikov, who was sometimes summoned to the Politburo for meetings to give advice on financial matters, and Karakhan, who hobnobbed with Stalin, Mikoyan and Ordzhonikidze. This gave Karakhan the opportunity of going over Litvinov's head. Karakhan was made ambassador to Turkey, although we know Litvinov had a poor opinion of Karakhan.[91]

Litvinov should have acknowledged that Chicherin's achievement at Rapallo was 'gigantic', as did Chossudovsky in a *Times* article in 1972. [92] Litvinov's biographer, Phillips, acknowledged: 'Rapallo was the crowning glory of Chicherin's career.'[93] During the years following Rapallo, the Soviet Union obtained recognition from most countries, the most important being France and Britain, but until 1933 did not succeed with the USA.

Chossudovsky rightly states that Chicherin was a Germanophile. However, Chicherin's sole guiding star was that the foreign policy of his party and his government should achieve:

> The external consolidation of the first state of workers and peasants which he himself had helped so much to define. He fought with all means at his disposal against any sign of anti-Soviet machination and was prepared to play on the differences and contradictions between the powers to frustrate hostile designs.[94]

---

[89] Hilger, Gustav: *Incompatible Allies*, p.111
[90] Barmine, Alexandre: *One Who Survived*, p.119; *Memoirs of a Soviet Diplomat*, p.217; Bessedovsky, Grigory *Revelations of a Soviet Diplomat*, p.95
[91] Fischer, Louis: *Man and Politics*, p.126, No 110 post.
[92] *Times*, 24 November 1972, p.14
[93] Phillips, Hugh: *Between the Revolution and the West*, p.55
[94] *Times*, 24 November 1972, p.14

This was very similar to Litvinov's policy and to Britain's foreign policy in Europe over many centuries, when Britain aimed at maintaining the balance of power between European states, a fact which casts doubt on Pope's description of Litvinov as a new kind of diplomat.[95]

Various historians have stated that Chicherin was not interested in Europe, only Asia.[96] In common with Litvinov, Chicherin saw clearly the importance of good relations with other European continental powers. Chicherin went out of his way to improve relations with France at the time of Locarno.[97]

Chicherin was probably less interested in Britain and, if it was possible to have excluded Britain from Europe, he would have done so; but, as a realist, he did not pursue policies of which there was no chance of success − Yet in 1919, at the time of the Brest-Litovsk treaty, Chicherin told Lockhart, 'Negotiations were going badly and now was the great opportunity for Britain to make a friendly gesture towards Russia.'[98] Chicherin never visited Britain after his inglorious inprisoment in 1918.[99]

It is undoubtedly true that Chicherin continued to stress the importance of the Soviet Union's relationship with Germany. For example, in a letter to Rykov and Stalin dated 18 February 1927, Chicherin criticised Bukharin for his speeches that had a negative attitude to the relationship between the USSR and Germany. 'This was particularly dangerous because of the deterioration of the relationship between the USSR and Britain.' Chicherin said: 'At a time when the British are working against us, we must take care of our relationship with other states. We have to nurture such relationship.'[100]

On 11 March 1927 Chicherin warned against underestimating the hostile action of Britain and criticised those who thought that Britain would not sever relations with the USSR. 'I protest against naïve and harmful delusions. Moscow should not close its eyes to the British campaign against us as it continues and develops.'

Further Gromyko then correctly states: 'It is well known Chicherin was right.' Britain was shortly to sever diplomatic relations with the Soviet Union. Litvinov had dispatched a firm note to Britain in reply to its complaints on various matters, including assistance to workers during the General Strike in 1926. In view of Chicherin's attitude towards Britain, one would have supposed he would have agreed with Litvinov's tough line. On the

---

[95] Pope, Arthur: *Maxim Litvinov*, p.189

[96] This is not correct see ch.8

[97] Ch.8, No.10

[98] Fischer, Louis: *Lenin*, p.165

[99] Carr, Edward: *Foundations of a Planned Economy*, vol.3, p.32

[100] O'Connor, Timothy: *Diplomacy and Revolution*, p.154; *Izvestiya*, 5 December 1962, p.2

contrary, Chicherin dispatched a letter to Stalin and Rykov, Litvinov's superiors, warning them:

> The British Government was prepared to break off diplomatic relations with the Soviet Union and the Narkomindel should have responded to Britain in a conciliatory manner to mollify the moderate Conservatives in the Cabinet.[101]

Gromyko assumes, in his article of 1962, that this criticism was directed only against Stalin; but I think it was also directed against Litvinov, as he wrote the letter to which Chicherin objected.[102]

On 3 June 1927 Chicherin, while in a sanatorium in Germany, wrote about incidents that were detrimental to Soviet-German relations. Chicherin was exasperated 'by some comrades who can do no better than ruin all our work by attacking Germany, spoiling everything once and for all.'[103] When Voroshilov, at the May Day Parade in 1929, made a speech attacking the Weimar Republic, Chicherin dispatched a letter to the Politburo stating that the speech would do irreparable damage to German-Soviet relations.[104]

Although Litvinov is regarded as the one person in the Soviet hierarchy who would, within limits, speak his mind, credit for frankness belongs more to Chicherin, who was prepared to criticise Government foreign policy, which was of course Stalin's policy, where Chicherin thought it was appropriate.

Equally important was Chicherin's successful efforts to improve relations with Asian countries, mainly Turkey, Afghanistan, Iran and China.[105]

Fischer rightly states that Chicherin incorporated into Soviet diplomacy some of the traditional suspicion of the British Raj in Central Asia. No doubt Fischer was right when he said that Persia and Afghanistan were as important to Chicherin as they were to Lenin and to Stalin.[106]

It is alleged that Stalin disagreed with Litvinov over Afghanistan and that Stalin supported Chicherin. Litvinov's view was that it would not be wise for the Soviet Union to become involved in a dispute with Great Britain over Afghanistan.[107] However, Stalin supported Litvinov rather than Chicherin in respect of adherence to the Kellogg Pact.[108]While

---

[101] O'Connor, Timothy:*Diplomacy and Revolution*, p.154; *Izvestiya*, 5 December 1962, p.2

[102] O'Connor, Timothy: *Diplomacy and Revolution*, p.154; *Izvestiya*, 5 December 1962 and see No. 101 ante

[103] O'Connor, Timothy: *Diplomacy and Revolution*, p.158; *Izvestiya*, 5 December 1962

[104] O'Connor, Timothy: *Diplomacy and Revolution*, p.162

[105] *Times*, 24 November 1972, p.14

[106] Fischer, Louis: *Men and Politics*, p.125

[107] Ibid. p.129

[108] See Ch.6, No.38

Chicherin advocated that in China the Kremlin policy ought to be to further and deepen the revolution, Litvinov argued for caution and stated that the Soviet Government should play the Chinese trump card only for the purpose of putting pressure on Britain with the aim of reaching an agreement with her. Hilger was told that in a conference on this problem. Chicherin, with great agitation, accused Litvinov of wanting to sell China down the river. Litvinov replied with an obscene remark that 'it was better to sell China down the river than to miss the bus on concrete political opportunities.'[109]

An example of the difference between the concerns of Chicherin and Litvinov is an argument between them concerning Karakhan. Chicherin appeared to have had complete faith in Karakhan, while Litvinov had a poor opinion of him. Litvinov, in a letter to Kopp, the first Soviet chargé d'affaires in Japan, described Karakhan 'as a rogue and adventurer, a dull-witted journalist, a good-for-nothing diplomat.' As for Borodin, Litvinov called him 'a suspicious character.'

> Borodin is a crook who sprang from the depths of the Chicago Stock Exchange, where he is known as Gruzenberg. He has a code of his own, giving him direct access to the Comintern, which does not think it necessary to expose his intrigues, big or little.[110]

It has been assumed by many that Chicherin was dismissed for reasons other than ill health, namely that he had fallen out with Stalin; but this may not be so. All commentators appear to have overlooked the fact that in 1928 Chicherin stated that he wanted an improved relationship with the capitalist countries to encourage foreign investment. This policy had Stalin's enthusiastic support and was approved by the Politburo in late 1927 and early 1928. Stalin said: 'It can hardly be doubted that Comrade Chicherin is better informed about the mood in foreign investment circles than any of us.'[111] It was rare for Stalin to acknowledge that someone was more knowledgeable than himself. Incidentally, Chicherin also had Litvinov's full support. Therefore, as late as 1928, Stalin was very complimentary about Chicherin.

When Chicherin died, the official reason given for his dismissal was 'In 1928 the diabetes from which he was suffering started to interfere with his activities. Chicherin was released from his duties in 1930.' Ill health rather than disagreement with Stalin may have been the real reason for Chicherin's removal as Foreign Commissar.' *Izvestiya*, summarising Chicherin's character, described him:

> As highly educated, an exceptional diplomat and a sophisticated art lover. A continuing terminal illness burdened his last years, which forced him away from

---

[109] Hilger, Gustav: *Incompatible Allies*, p.112
[110] Dallin, David: *Rise of Russia in Asia*, pp. 240-241
[111] Reiman, Michal: *Birth of Stalinism*, pp.39-40

his circle of friends and active work and led to an early death bed.[112]

Chicherin's obituary in the *Observer* was generous to him.

> Chicherin was an aristocrat who renounced a fortune in order to spend it on the revolutionary movement. He carried this into his dress. He would wear the shabbiest of clothes, not because he could not afford better, but because he believed he was serving the movement.[113]

However, unless Germany was providing him with free medical care, he was not so frugal about expending the Soviet Union's precious foreign currency on his medical care in Germany.[114]

Obituaries in the British and foreign press, including the English-speaking *Moscow News*, were also favourable.[115]

A funeral service was held on 9 July 1936. At the service, according to Fischer, 'Krestinsky gave a halting tribute mixed with criticism.' If Krestinsky did make any critical remarks, *Izvestiya* certainly did not publish them. Neither can I find any reference to this in the foreign press, which *Izvestiya* confirms were present. If critical remarks were made, surely sooner or later they would have been published. *Izvestiya*, reporting the funeral, stated that Litvinov, among others, sent flowers, although there is no mention of Litvinov attending. Perhaps he was out of the country. Sorrowful friends and comrades of Chicherin came to pay their respects. All day officials of the Foreign Commissariat came to take their places by the coffin.[116] Finally, Krestinsky and Stomoniakov, both of whom would be killed in the purges, took their places.[117]

On 5 December 1962 former Foreign Minister Gromyko officially rehabilitated Chicherin in an article in *Izvestiya*. Gromyko acknowledged that, 'Stalin had distorted Chicherin's considerable contribution to Soviet history.'[118] However, Gromyko mentions no specific criticism of Chicherin by Stalin and it seems Gromyko is complaining about the failure of Soviet history to give Chicherin the importance and prominence he deserves. Surely Gromyko is right.

However, neither Chicherin nor Litvinov can escape some responsibility for the purges.

---

[112] *Izvestiya*, 8 July 1936, p.2
[113] *Observer*, 12 July 1936, p.10
[114] O'Connor Timothy ' *Diplomacy and Revolution*' p 153 and 161 No 46 ante and chapter 4 No 90
[115] *Moscow News* 15 July 1936; *Times* 8 July 1936 p. 16
[116] , *Izvestia*, 8 July 1936, p. 5 ; Fischer Louis *Men and Politics* p. 143
[117] See Ch.16, No.79 (Stomoniakov)
[118] *Izvestiya*, 15 December 1962, p.5

Chicherin endorsed the Red Terror in the early days of the revolution.[119] In speeches Litvinov, too, endorsed Stalin's terror against Trotsky in the 30s.[120]

Both Chicherin and Litvinov lied when they considered it was justified. Two German students entered the Soviet Union in 1924 with a view to travelling to the remotest part of the Soviet Union. They were arrested and Chicherin accused them of being hardened criminals without a shred of evidence, although the students were released shortly afterwards.[121]

Litvinov stated that the little republics surrounding Russia such as Armenia and Georgia (which had formerly been part of the Tsarist Russian Empire) would be given full freedom as to whether to join the Soviet Union, knowing this was a blatant lie. Russia would never have agreed to allow them their freedom. Litvinov could also be devious. [122]

Again, Litvinov lied when he said that the Comintern and the Soviet Government were separate entities and that the Comintern was not controlled by the Soviet Government.[123]

Persecution was particularly directed by Stalin against foreigners who had married Russians. When Arcadi Berdichevsky was arrested in 1937 for having been friendly or acquainted with a Trotskyist and received five years' imprisonment in an Arctic concentration camp, cards came regularly to his wife Freda until they suddenly stopped. Freda suspected that her husband had been killed but, when the British Ambassador, Chilston, took up the matter, Litvinov assured him that Arcadi was still alive, although he had already been executed.[124] However, British politicians and civil servants also lied when they thought that lying would bring sufficient benefit to justify the moral dilemma.[125]

---

[119] Chamberlin, William: *Russian Revolution 1917 to 1921*, p.78
[120] See Ch.16, No.77
[121] See Ch.8, No.93
[122] Ullman, Richard: *Anglo-Soviet Relations*, vol.3, p.208' ; Ch 3 No. 63
[123] See Comintern, Ch.9, GB, Nos.4 & 5
[124] Beckett, Francis: *Stalin's British Victims*, p.93
[125] Ch.17, No.65, Katyn

6: DISARMAMENT

Although the preparatory talks of the Disarmament Commission of the League of Nations had been established in 1925, the USSR did not attend the first three sessions because Switzerland refused to apologise for the killing of a Russian delegate, Vorovsky, while attending the second Lausanne Conference. He was murdered while dining in a Swiss hotel. The suspected assassin was acquitted.[1] Finally, in April 1927 the Swiss Government apologised, so Stalin and Chicherin decided that Litvinov should represent the Soviet Union at the Disarmament Commission. This decision was consistent with Chicherin's efforts to attract foreign capital, a policy which I am confident had Litvinov's support.[2]

On 30 November 1927, while attending the Disarmament Preparatory Commission, Litvinov stated to the Commission that his Government proposed the destruction of all weapons, warships and military aircraft. However, his proposals for immediate total disarmament were rejected. Then Litvinov suggested disarmament by gradual stages.

In a speech on 14 December 1927, Litvinov criticised the League of Nations' lack of progress in disarmament. He maintained that many countries, since the Great War, rather than decrease their armaments, had in fact increased them. Litvinov stated:

> In 1913, at the zenith of the pre-war militarism, the great powers had 5,759,000 men under arms. This included 1,129,000 soldiers belonging to the countries which were subsequently defeated (Germany, Austria-Hungary and Bulgaria). These countries now only have 198,000 men under arms or 931,000 fewer than before the War and, if we remember, instead of 1,350,000 men in the old Tsarist army, we have now only 562,000 men of the Soviet Union, then we see that the victorious and neutral countries, having crushed German imperialism, have been induced by pressure of fresh and constantly growing competition to increase their armies by 1,183,000 men.[3]

Eventually, Mr Paul-Boncour rose to criticise Litvinov's speech. He said:

> Mankind has for centuries perceived this simplicity and has desired to take such steps as they, the Soviet delegation, propose and the wars which have been repeated

---

[1] Phillips, Hugh: *Between the Revolution and the West*, p.89

[2] Reiman, Michal: *Birth of Stalinism*, p.38

[3] Preparatory Minutes, Series 5 Memorandum submitted to Disarmament Conference

and the after-effects which are still almost part of our flesh and bones have not been avoided.

They were working on the basis of article 8 of the Covenant; we have to settle what are the minimum requirements compatible with national security and international obligations necessary for the purpose of common action.

Even if I consider the other method is the better one, I think that when we have reached such a definite stage in our work we should be making the gravest of mistakes if we change our procedures now. We should, as an old proverb, which probably exists in many languages, puts it, be 'changing horses in crossing the stream.' Supposing you had total disarmament; if there was no international organisation taking charge of security, if you had no international force to ensure the maintenance of this security, if you had no international law such as we are endeavouring to lay down here, a powerful and populous nation would always have the power when it wished to do so on a small nation equally disarmed, less populous and less well equipped to resist an attack which might be made upon it.[4]

When reporting to the Central Committee, Litvinov was extremely scornful of Paul Boncour's argument. Boncour had claimed :

Fulfilment of our plans for total disarmament would deal a heavy blow to small nations, which should total disarmament take place, would find themselves in an unequal position in comparison with economically stronger states.

Litvinov argued:

Would small nations be less insecure after their powerful neighbours have disarmed than they are now when, in addition to economic, financial, territorial and other superiority possessed by the great powers, the latter also enjoy the immense advantage of greater armaments?[5]

It was agreed, with Litvinov's concurrence, that the Soviet proposals would be adjourned to the next session, so all the Commission achieved was to appoint a new committee on security; but one wonders why the Preparatory Commission had waited two years to appoint the committee rather than decide on it at the first session.

---

[4] Paul Boncour speech, Preparatory Minutes, Series 5, pp.13 & 14; *Times*, 1 December 1927, p.16
[5] Coates W.P. *Russia's Disarmament Proposals* p.30

On 14 December 1927 Litvinov reported to the Central Committee. The speech was highly critical and sarcastic. Litvinov said:

> The projected programme of the Preparatory Commission and its methods of work should fully insure an unlimited number of sessions and meetings for many years to come and the opponents of disarmament need have no fear of the outcome of the work of the League of Nations and its Preparatory Commission. But even this work of a snail's pace tempo of the Preparatory Commission is alarming to some. So, at the last session of the League of Nations, supplementary measures were taken, not only to prevent premature disarmament, but even the discussion of the problem of disarmament. For this purpose the so-called security committee was conceived and created. The new child of the League must occupy itself with considerations of the supplementary guarantees of security for members of the League; in other words, guarantees of the secure digestion of the fruits of conquest of the World War and the territorial plunders which were executed outside the Versailles, St Germain and other treaties.[6]

Litvinov stated the reason the capitalist countries were participating in this Preparatory Commission was 'because their Governments must take heed of public opinion which is demanding guarantees against future war, and demanding the lifting of the burden of militarism. Therefore, they could not state frankly they do not desire disarmament.'[7] However, Litvinov observed: 'The German delegate supported generally our efforts to hasten the work of the Preparatory Commission.'[8] Weizsacker tells us that from 1929 there was close collaboration between himself, Boris Stein. and Litvinov. Stein comments: 'They attacked the goings on at Geneva with biting logic.'[9]

Although Phillips, Litvinov's biographer, in an otherwise uncritical work, took issue with Litvinov using the Conference for propaganda, his performance cannot be compared unfavourably with other great powers who had not in the slightest way achieved anything constructive as far as disarmament was concerned. The Litvinov shock was exactly what the Conference required. He was entitled to state that the Soviet Union was prepared to totally disarm if other nations did likewise.

Litvinov is also criticised for ignoring French security arrangements. At that time France's armaments far exceeded those of any other European country. It could be argued that French fear was unfounded. Germany had a justifiable complaint that she had been denied the option of rearming on the understanding that other countries would reduce their level of armament so as to be roughly equal to Germany's.

---

[6] Coates, W P: *Russia's Disarmament Proposals* , p.27

[7] Ibid. p.30

[8] Ibid. p.32

[9] Weizsacker, Ernst: *Memoirs*, p.65

Phillips makes the valid point that Litvinov might have been more successful if he had initially proposed a more realistic programme of partial disarmament;[10] but, as France had no intention of agreeing to any substantial reduction of its forces, it would not have made the slightest difference to the outcome of the Soviet proposal.

Further, Britain's hostility to the communist Soviet Union was such that Britain would not have allowed the proposal from Soviet Russia to be the one that was finally approved. Nevertheless, Litvinov certainly enlivened the debate, if nothing else. The Disarmament Conference failed miserably to achieve anything significant before it became irrelevant.

The fifth session of the Preparatory Commission took place between 19 March 1928 and 24 March 1928. Litvinov repeated his call for general disarmament. He then stated that he had received addresses in favour of his proposals from trade unions and other bodies throughout the world, and complained that there had been 'no fewer than 14 different commissions and other League organs devoted over 120 sessions and 111 resolutions.' He hoped there would be no further multiplication of sub-committees. Litvinov stated that the Soviet Union was prepared to abolish its armed forces as soon as other states simultaneously took a similar view.

At this session Litvinov received support from Rouchdy Bey, the representative from Turkey, who was attending his first session of the Preparatory Disarmament Commission.[11] Rouchdy Bey hoped that Litvinov's proposals would be discussed by the Preparatory Commission and not referred to a sub-committee, as Litvinov later confirmed in his speech to the Central Executive Committee.[12]

The British representative, Lord Cushendun, led the attack against Litvinov's proposal, which on 23 March was rejected by the Preparatory Commission. Cushendun stated:

> The whole basis of the world policy of the Soviet Government as expressed by both their leading men and by Government owned newspapers has been to produce by some means or other armed insurrection We ought to be told whether the Soviet Government has now decided, in contrast with their recent policy, no longer to interfere in the affairs of other nations and to leave to all nations complete liberty to maintain and develop [their] own institutions in any way they like. Unless they are prepared to give us some such an assurance as that, we are faced with the unpleasant fact that they themselves and their policy will be, as they have been recently, the largest obstacle to the carrying out of any far-reaching proposals as they themselves have now put before us.[13]

---

[10] Phillips, Hugh: *Between the Revolution and the West*, p.88
[11] Preparatory Disarmament Minutes, Series 6, pp.239 & 240; *Times*, 20 March 1928, p.15
[12] Preparatory Disarmament Minutes, Series 6, p.243
[13] Ibid. Lord Cushendun speech, Series 6, p.245 @ 247

Litvinov then presented to the Commission detailed proposals for partial disarmament, but he damaged the Soviet Union's case with a gesture towards proletarian internationalism.

He proposed that the process should be supervised by an equal number of representatives from the legislative bodies and trade unions and other workers' organisations participating in the present convention.[14] The French delegation objected that the Soviet Union's proposal would result in the Preparatory Commission restarting its work;[15] a strange objection, because at that time the Commission had achieved nothing upon which all countries had been able to agree. However, the German delegate, Count Bernstorff, supported Litvinov's proposal. He remarked:

> He had been a member of the commission for two years and on no less than twenty occasions speakers have stated that our work was entirely useless because the Soviet Union was not represented, but now that the Soviet Union are to be with us for the first time and say they desire to discuss matters with us, the fact is to be taken as a pretext to do nothing.

The Germans then attacked not so much the Treaty of Versailles itself as the failure of the victorious powers to abide by it and start their own disarmament.[16]

Litvinov reported to the Central Committee on 21 April 1928 and showed how inconsistent the Disarmament Commission had been:

> The bourgeois press first of all started to express fear of the League disarmament energies being paralysed by the fact that outside the League there was a powerful state as the USSR with a large army and allegedly being unwilling to disarm. It was impossible to keep on repeating the assertions without making any attempt to invite the Soviet Union to take part in the disarmament work.[17]

Litvinov criticised the League 'for holding it in a country to which the League of Nations knew the Soviet Union was unable to send delegates' because of Vorovsky's assassination as previously mentioned. The Soviet Union at once accepted the invitation in principle and as soon as the external obstacles were removed (Switzerland apologised), 'did in fact send a delegate for active participation in the work of the commission.'

---

[14] Phillips, Hugh: *Between the Revolution and the West*, p.97; Preparatory Disarmament Minutes, Series 6, p.354

[15] Phillips, Hugh: *Between the Revolution and the West*, p.97; Preparatory Disarmament Minutes, Series 6, p.293

[16] Phillips, Hugh: *Between the Revolution and the West*, p.97; Preparatory Disarmament Minutes, Series 6, p.299

[17] Degras, Jane: *Soviet Documents on Foreign Policy*, vol.2, p.304

The Soviet Union's proposals, as Litvinov described them, 'for complete general disarmament' were rejected. Several speakers pointed out in tones of reproach :

> The Preparatory Commission had already worked out at their first three sessions, methods of solution for disarmament-[partial disarmament, of course]-had already drawn up draft measures, and that by our new draft convention we were setting all this work to naught and annulling all the labour already expended. [18]

However after three years it was difficult to see what had actually been achieved. Nevertheless, the Soviet Union's proposals for total disarmament were not rejected but adjourned to the next session.

One of the many arguments against general disarmament was:

> Article 8 obliges members of the League to disarm only to the degree required by their own security, while other articles envisage military sanctions against countries attacking any member of the League which sanctions require troops.

However, Litvinov said:

> It would be cheaper and more advantageous for Governments to change an article in the League Covenant than pay millions of pounds for maintenance of armies and navies.[19]

Litvinov put forward the interesting argument that, as the USA had proposed:

> The prohibition of war as an instrument of national policy, it might have been thought that the USA would have supported our policy for total disarmament because if we have no intention of making or threatening war, why spend millions of pounds of peoples' money on the maintenance of those armies and navies?[20]

Finally, Litvinov warned:

> So long as other Governments keep up such an irreconcilable position about disarmament, we shall not weaken the defensive power of our state, but will keep a careful watch on the movement of our innumerable enemies.

I believe Litvinov correctly described Soviet foreign policy when he said:

---

[18] Ibid. p.305
[19] Ibid. p.307
[20] Ibid. p.311

The primary aim of Soviet policy and Soviet diplomacy is to secure peaceful conditions for our internal creative work without infringing on the national interests of any other state. The Soviet Government will not allow itself to be deflected from the path of that peaceful policy of which its proposals to all nations for complete, immediate general disarmament is a striking manifestation.[21]

However, the proposals despised by most of the delegates won for Litvinov much favourable publicity in radical circles in the Western countries eager for disarmament and which were already impatient at the slow progress of the commission. The national joint Council of the Labour Party, the Parliamentary Labour Party and the Trades Union Congress passed a resolution expressing their sense of great importance of the proposals of general and simultaneous disarmament which was put forward by the USSR delegation at the Preparatory Disarmament Commission in Geneva on 30 November 1927.[22]

When Litvinov reported to the Central Committee on 10 December 1928, he produced figures showing that the Red Army had only 3.8 soldiers for each 100 inhabitants, whereas France had 9.2 soldiers, and France was spending £1.92 per inhabitant against the Soviet Union's £0.52 per inhabitant.

Further, France's military expenditure in 1913 was £70 million sterling, whereas in 1929 it was £78.5 million. However, in the period before the First World War there was much more need of military expenditure. Then France had to reckon with a German Army of 800,000, whereas in 1928 it was restricted to 100,000. However, the Soviet Union could rely on no outside support 'and along the entire length of our Western border are countries which are heavily armed and are continuing to arm and have every reason to believe they can count upon the help of the French army.'[23]

Litvinov also stated:

Whilst the imperialist countries decline to accept our proposals, they must pay certain tribute to the anti-war feelings among the working class and pacifism among the small bourgeoisie. They dwell on their love of peace unceasingly. The word peace is always on their lips and it is inconvenient politically to admit they do not wish to disarm. The only test of our sincerity would be the acceptance of our proposals and then if the public was actually convinced of our insincerity it would only be necessary to adopt these measures to bring about our exposure. [24]

---

[21] Ibid. p.313

[22] Carr, Edward: *The Russian Revolution from Lenin to Stalin*, p.174; Labour Party Conference Report, 1928, p.31

[23] Documents, 1928, p.178

[24] Ibid. p 176

The Kellogg Pact arose initially out of a statement by Briand proposing a pact between the USA and France, renouncing war and endeavouring to flatter the USA by saying:

> Ten years have gone by since the US nation, with its magnificent enthusiasm, associated itself with the Allied Nations for the defence of threatened liberties and in the course of those years the same spirit of justice and humanity has not ceased to inspire our two countries.[25]

Finally, Briand's statement included the observation:

> The renunciation of war as an instrument of national policy is a conception already familiar to the signatories of the covenants of the League of Nations and of the treaty of Locarno. Any engagement subscribed in the same spirit by the United States with another nation such as France would greatly contribute in the eyes of the world to broaden and strengthen the foundation upon which the international policy of peace is being raised.[26]

No doubt the French were hoping to encourage increased USA participation in world affairs, but their efforts proved useless. The USA did absolutely nothing when France was attacked and defeated by Germany in 1940.

Further, the Pact was little more than a hopeful aspiration, as there was no mechanism for enforcing breaches. France was no doubt wishing to steal a march on Britain in creating the special relationship with the USA, so loved by British Prime Ministers Churchill, Thatcher and Blair.

The idea of having some special treaty with France was criticised in a memorandum by the American chief of the Western European division, Marriner, who stated:

> The vague wording and lack of precision in the draft seemed also to give effect of a kind of perpetual alliance between the USA and France which would certainly serve to disturb the other great European powers, England, Germany and Italy. This would be particularly true as it would put the neutral position of the United States in any European War in which France might be engaged extremely difficult since she might deem it necessary to infringe upon our rights as a neutral under this guarantee of non-aggression,

 but that was actually exactly what France did desire.

The memorandum continued,

---

[25] FRUS, 1927, vol.2, p.611
[26] Ibid. p.612

Certainly a single treaty of this nature would raise the question of an alliance with a country outside the American hemisphere.[27]

Similarly, events were to prove that the value of the Pact as an instrument to assist peace turned out to be negligible because, as the *Times* leader stated on 3 March 1929,

> We would all like to abolish war by a general declaration, but we all know rebels, aggressors, traitors with bold, bad, revengeful tempers may burst out at any moment and cloud the bright prospects of a permanent peace. There must be sanctions and penalties somewhere.[28]

Kellogg, according to a *Times* editorial, did not claim: 'The treaties or arbitration, conciliation or even those renouncing war afford a certain guarantee against war, but he believes and rightly that the world is making great strides towards the pacific adjustment of international disputes.'[29]

Although it was agreed that the original signatories would be limited to the USA, Japan and the signatories of the Locarno agreement, which included Britain, her Dominions and India, there was provision that all countries would afterwards be invited to accede to it.[30] Britain was cautious and, much to the USA's annoyance, suggested preliminary meetings of jurists and Foreign Ministers, both of which proposals were rejected.[31]

Britain stated:

> There are certain areas in the world, the welfare and integrity of which constitute special and vital interest for our peace and safety. His Majesty's Government have been at pains to make it clear in the past that interference with these regions cannot be suffered. Their protection against attack is to the British Empire a measure of self-defence. It must be clearly understood that His Majesty's Government in Great Britain accept the new treaty upon the distinct understanding that it does not prejudice their freedom of action in this respect.[32]

Britain therefore was not prepared to sign the pact unconditionally, encouraging other countries to make similar reservations. Luckily, it was only France that did so, but their reservation was much more limited than Great Britain. It stated that she adhered to the Pact

---

[27] FRUS, 1927, vol.2, p.617
[28] *Times*, 3 March 1928, p.13
[29] Ibid.   17 March 1928, p.13
[30] FRUS, 1928, vol.1, p.32
[31] Ibid. p.47
[32] Ibid. p.68

'subject to the maintenance of existing treaties and freedom of action for all signatory powers against a power guilty of breaking the treaty.'[33]

Secretary of State Kellogg travelled to Europe to participate in the signing ceremony in Paris on 27 August 1928. The countries that had been selected as the original signatories also signed.[34] The negotiations which resulted in the creation of the Kellogg Pact and which took place between the fifth and sixth sessions of the Disarmament Conference would seem purely to have been for political advantage and diverted energies away from the Disarmament Conference, where the nations' efforts would have been better spent.

Although the Soviet Union was not invited to the preliminary discussions, Litvinov's handling of the Kellogg negotiations shows that he was prepared to appease where he considered it appropriate and the Soviet Union agreed to sign the Pact. Without any procedures or armaments to enforce the Pact, it was always purely a utopian ideal. However, Kellogg was extremely childish in refusing to have any contact with the Soviet Union, all communications having to be through France.

Chicherin opposed Soviet adherence, which was not unreasonable. As he stated, the Soviet Union could not sign unless she could determine the character of the document. In what was probably Chicherin's last act of significance as Foreign Commissar, on 4 August 1928 he gave a press conference. He continued his unbridled opposition to the Pact and its makers:

> Since last December the powers had been discussing a pact to outlaw war. Yet it has never occurred to them to ask for the Soviet Union's participation. Was it not therefore patent that the pact was an instrument for the isolation of the Soviet Union and the struggle against Bolshevism?[35]

I think Chicherin was wrong. I believe the main reason for Briand's initiating the Pact was to try and forge a special relationship with the USA, and Kellogg's motives were political − to show the American public and the world that the Republican administration was taking positive steps to prevent war.

Litvinov's recommendation was to adhere to the Pact. In his report to the Central Committee on 10 December 1928, Litvinov gave as the reason:' The states that signed the Kellogg Pact assumed a certain moral obligation to public opinion.' [36] It is not clear how

---

[33] FRUS, 1928, vol.1, p.86
[34] *Times*, 28 August 1928, p.13
[35] Fischer, Louis: *The Soviets in World Affairs*, p.778
[36] Documents 1928, p.175

far Litvinov was influenced by economic overtures from Germany or an opportunity to force Poland into a separate peace agreement with the Soviet Union. Even before the ratification by the Soviet Union, Poland first of all stated that she initially wished to discuss a treaty with the Baltic States.

Fischer believes the reason why Stalin decided to overrule Chicherin and support Litvinov was because Germany eagerly desired the Soviet Union to adhere to the Pact. Also, if the Soviet Union adhered to the Pact, it would help in improving relations with the USA. Accordingly, Chicherin's objections were overruled and the Sovnarkom accepted that at some time the Soviet Union would adhere to the Pact. I think, however, Fischer is correct to say that Stalin, as did Litvinov, favoured being on the world stage.

We have no evidence to assess whether, if Litvinov had not been involved in the negotiation, Chicherin would have been able to persuade Stalin not to adhere to the Pact. We just do not know. In *Road from Peace to War,* Fischer states that Bukharin, who was influential at this time, supported Chicherin;[37] but in his earlier work he states that Bukharin supported Litvinov. Pope agrees Bukharin supported Litvinov.[38]

When Litvinov summoned Herbette to receive the Soviet Union's adherence to the Pact on 29 August 1929, Litvinov told Herbette that the Soviet Union wished to make reservations. Herbette told him that no reservations could be made unless all parties accepted them. Litvinov then said that this meant that the Soviet Union might well make reservations, but Herbette insisted that he had no authority to transmit them. When Litvinov asked Herbette what would happen if his answer was therefore in the negative, Herbette said he would accept it. When Litvinov handed to Herbette Moscow's adherence to the Pact, it contained reservations.[39] The first was that Moscow refused to accept the British and French reservations.[40] Second, the Soviet Union declared that pacts outlawing war had no effect unless accompanied by disarmament.[41]

The Soviet Union was the first country to ratify the Kellogg pact on 9 February 1929.[42] Subsequently, the USA's Senate ratified the Pact by an almost unanimous vote of 85 to 1. [43] Notwithstanding his criticism of the Pact, Litvinov, however, made it the reason for a comprehensive agreement in Eastern Europe known as the Litvinov protocol.[44]

---

[37] Fischer, Louis: *Russia's Road from Peace to War*, p.186
[38] Pope, Arthur: *Maxim Litvinov*, p.241; but see Fischer, Louis: *The Soviets in World Affairs*, p.775
[39] Fischer, Louis: *The Soviets in World Affairs*, p.780
[40] See Nos 32 & 33 *ante*
[41] Fischer, Louis: *Russia's Road from Peace to War*, p.187
[42] Fischer, Louis: *The Soviets in World Affairs,* p.780
[43] Bailey, Thomas: *Diplomatic History of the American People*, p.650
[44] Budurowycz, Bohdan: *Polish- Soviet Relations*, p.29

On 15 April 1929 a further session of the Preparatory Commission took place. On 16 April 1929 Litvinov again quite rightly complained of the lack of urgency of the Preparatory Commission. He reminded the Commission:

> At the third session, completion of its first reading was postponed owing to the differences of opinion it aroused. At the fourth session it was found impossible to continue the work on account of persistence of these difficulties. At the fifth session the French delegate, supported by the delegate of Great Britain, stated that there was a chance of arriving at an agreement concerning these difficulties outside the sphere of the Commission, which decided once again to postpone work on the draft until the desirable negotiations had taken place. Over a year has elapsed since then, but the President had not been able to tell us anything at all about the present state of controversies evoked by this draft convention. So far as we are permitted to know, not only have these questions not been softened, but they have actually become still more acute and rendered more complicated by new questions. While France and Great Britain may have arrived through negotiation at a solution satisfactory to their respective interests, new differences have arisen to take the place of those settled, this time between the Anglo-French compromise and the point of view of the United States and Italy. As far as we can tell, negotiations for the settlement of these differences have not yet begun.

Litvinov was becoming the flag-bearer of people around the world who hoped and prayed the Commission would at least reach some kind of agreement. Continued postponements were the worst option.

Litvinov continued:

> We characterised the map drafted out by the Commission as a blind alley. Nothing happened between the fourth and fifth sessions to cause us to qualify our opinion. At the fifth session certain delegates thought they saw light and the Commission decided there was a way out of the blind alley. It is therefore permissible to ask whether it is worthwhile to persist in the same direction, to go on wasting more time in order to try and dig us out of the blind alley or whether it would not be more reasonable and economical to attempt a new path suggested by us which is at least free of the obstacles that have encumbered the work of the Commission for the past two years.

Litvinov finished his speech by stating:

> As for the Soviet delegation, it has already considered and still considers general and complete disarmament to be the most effective guarantee of peace in the present condition. The draft convention for such complete disarmament was,

however, rejected by the Preparatory Commission and the Soviet delegation can only advance it again at the Disarmament Conference if convened. At the same time the Soviet delegation advanced a proportionate progressive reduction of armaments which would immediately diminish the menace of war to a considerable extent and might become a stage for further disarmament. It is this draft convention that I recommend to the attention of the sixth session of the Preparatory Commission, supporting the proposal for it to be placed first on the agenda not merely for its rejection on formal grounds, out of fear for its novelty and devotion to the old paths, even when these are erroneous, but for the detailed study and consideration of its contents. I am profoundly convinced that nothing but an acceptance of such proposals can lead the Commission out of its difficulties, recompense it for the time and work spent in vain and bring about the recognition that the Preparatory Commission has at last readily taken up the question of disarmament.[45]

On 19 April 1929, although Lord Cushendun lacked the courage to say so, he was coming to agree with Litvinov that the Preparatory Commission was becoming a farce. Lord Cushendun stated: 'Unless a good deal was reached at the present session the Commission would make itself the laughing stock of the world.'

Lord Cushendun's criticisms were similar to the sentiments expressed by Litvinov but, rather than Lord Cushendun acknowledging he had similar views to Litvinov, he showed his anti-Soviet bias by saying, 'That no doubt would be gratifying to the Soviet delegation… and therefore I hope that we shall not give them that satisfaction.' It appears these remarks were neither justified nor clever. On the contrary, the evidence is that the Soviet Union wanted peace to enable the Five Year Plan then in progress not to be interrupted. Soon afterwards, in view of the 1929 financial crisis, any markets, even Soviet markets, would be welcome, as Hodgson had advised earlier when economies were healthier.[46]

Lord Cushendun's action seems to have been taken with the intention of trying to annoy the one Soviet politician who was most likely to pursue pro-British policies. Lord Cushendun also said, as Britain was not 'a major military power', he felt confident that 'Britain would be able to agree to any proposal which met general consent.' Lord Cushendun was able to show that Britain's 'military expenditure had been regularly reduced since 1919, while active service naval personnel had been reduced from nearly 150,000 in 1914 to under 100,000 in 1929.'[47]

This session of the Conference finally adjourned on 6 May 1929. Even after four years of talks, the *Times* leader of 7 May 1929 rightly stated:

---

[45] Preparatory Disarmament Minutes, Series 8, pp.12-15
[46] See Ch.9, No.70
[47] Preparatory Disarmament Minutes, Series 8, p.42; *Times*, 20 April 1929, p.11

It has not even been possible so far to limit the amount of war materials in stock or in reserves, nor yet to pass a resolution in favour of limiting military budgets. All that could be agreed upon was that publicity should be given to expenditure on materials of war for land armaments.

The *Times* rightly pointed out: 'This is not a great step forward.'[48]

However, the *Times* might have mentioned that if this tiny step forward had taken four years to achieve, most of the delegates would not have seen the Disarmament Conference brought to fruition in their lifetime. In fact, the *Times* leader agreed with Litvinov, in spite of the *Times* earlier disparaging remarks.

The final meeting of the Preparatory Commission took place in November and December 1930.

Litvinov spoke on 6 November 1930 and reminded the Commission of the various speeches delivered in recent League of Nations meetings, such as the statement of the Danish Foreign Minister that 'Europe seems more disturbed than at any time since 1924', and the comment of the Belgian Foreign Minister that 'at the present moment the atmosphere was charged with electricity and the rumours of war are growing like gas fumes.' As so often occurred, Litvinov correctly predicted the future. He said:

> Irresponsible, reckless, aggressive groups of parties were gaining influence in some states, while others were opposing attempts at disarmament. The War budgets of the five biggest countries increased by 27% during the time the Preparatory Commission had existed.

Litvinov ridiculed the French idea that arbitration and security must precede disarmament, arguing, as Britain, Germany and Italy had done on other occasions, that the situation now required disarmament more than ever as a prerequisite for security. Not only was this idea rejected, but this speech annoyed the Chairman, who instead of ordering the speech to be made orally in French, as the rules provided, ordered that a written copy of the speech would be provided later. Elements of the press objected, as most only knew French. [49]

One of the matters which was discussed at the session was naval armaments. Unlike air and land armaments, the major naval powers had reached an agreement to limit their navies in 1922 at the Washington Conference. Now the same powers were renegotiating the treaty, while the Preparatory Commission was sitting. It was quite prepared to leave naval disarmament to the major naval powers in the hope that they would reach agreement, which they substantially achieved at the London Conference in 1930 and it was agreed that

---

[48] *Times*, 7 May 1929, p.17

[49] Preparatory Disarmament Minutes , Series 10, p.18; *The New York Times*, 7 November,1930 pp.1 & 9

such agreement would be included in the draft convention for discussion at the Disarmament conference.

The Soviet Union was ignored as a naval power in respect of the London Conference, which appears ludicrous. The Soviet Union, as she was not a party, could have built her navy to any size she determined. Litvinov, at the November session, proposed further reductions, one of which was that capital ships were limited to 10,000 tons all of which were rejected. The question of the naval disarmament was only reached in the latter part of the Disarmament Conference on 2 May 1933. Again little progress was made as there were numerous amendments which were not determined but it was agreed it would be considered as a first reading of the chapter on Naval Armaments. Negotiations between Anthony Eden and the other delegates would continue and if, as seems likely, no agreement was reached the amendments would come up at second reading when the commission would be in a position to proceed to a vote.[50]

Count Bernstorff's criticism of the progress made by the Preparatory Commission was very similar to that made by Litvinov. Count Bernstorff stated,

> It may be that some delegates here are under the impression that my Government might be induced to accede to a convention which, instead of leading to genuine disarmament, would merely serve as a cloak for the actual state of the world's disarmament, or even worse would make it possible to increase these armaments. This, in my opinion, would be tantamount to renewing German signature to the disarmament clauses of the Treaty of Versailles.

This brought a strong rebuke from Lord Cecil, who said:

> It is to me quite astounding that anyone who has followed the proceedings of this Commission – any serious and responsible person, not carried away by passion and prejudice – should make such a statement as that. Let me remind the Commission very shortly what we have agreed to with regard to land armaments. We have agreed to the separate limitation of the total numbers. We have agreed to a separate limitation of officers, non-commissioned officers and professional soldiers of every army. We have therefore agreed inferentially and as a necessary consequence to limitation of those soldiers who are neither officers, non-commissioned officers nor professional soldiers in conscription countries. I do not see how a limitation of numbers could proceed farther than that. We have further agreed to a limitation by budgetary limitation of the total expenditure on armaments which included land

---

[50] Litvinov's proposals: Preparatory Disarmament Minutes, Series 6, pp.350 & 351;Series 10 p.167; Disarmament Conference p518 to 528; *Survey of International Relations* 1930, pp.110-112; Mahaney, Wilbur Lee: *The Soviet Union, the League of Nations and Disarmament*, p.94

armaments. It does seem to me that, in the face of these facts, which are incontrovertible, to say we have done nothing which can result in the limitation of land armaments is to make a statement absolutely devoid of foundation.[51]

Litvinov agreed with Count Bernstorff. Both the USA's delegate, Gibson, and the *Times* agreed with Count Bernstorff, not Lord Cecil.[52]

Count Bernstorff was surely right to propose a resolution to the effect that the Disarmament Conference be called not later than 5 November 1931. He said:

> If the Council decides to call a conference on 5 November 1931, we shall have ten months in which to prepare for the conference. If ten months are not enough, then ten years would not be enough either.[53]

Count Bernstorff was, no doubt, influenced by the growing power of the Nazi movement in Germany. Litvinov left before the end of the final session of the Preparatory Commission. In Berlin he correctly predicted the outcome of the Disarmament Conference. He stated:

> If the delegates to the World Disarmament Conference come with the same instructions which the delegates to the Preparatory Disarmament Commission brought along, there will be neither disarmament nor even the slightest reduction in armaments.

Then, in sarcastic mode, Litvinov observed:

> It would be better to leave the preparation for the forthcoming Conference to reliable clerks instead of consuming the time of representatives of thirty nations.[54]

Gibson, the USA's representative, had sounded an optimistic note at the beginning of the final session when he stated:

> For four years we have endeavoured to reach an agreement. There has been a long and direct conflict of opinion; views that have been maintained with vigour and yet our friendship with those with whom we have differed ... has grown as steadily and as surely as with those who have shared our views. I take this as a good omen for

---

[51] Preparatory Disarmament Minutes, Series 10, pp. 261-262
[52] *Times*, see No. 48 *ante*; Gibson: seeo. 56 *post*
[53] Preparatory Disarmament Minutes, Series 10 p.322; Mahaney, Wilbur Lee: *The Soviet Union, the League of Nations and Disarmament*, p.101
[54] *The New York Times*, 28 November 1930, p.12

the spirit in which all nations will enter the General Disarmament Conference and try to convert our text from a theory into reality.

His optimism would not be justified.

However, Gibson had anticipated and feared that 'a number of general statements would be made at the final session of the Preparatory Commission and there would be an excessive amount of congratulations' by the members,[55] although they had achieved little. Gibson privately admitted in a report in 1931:

> The Conference cannot be expected to achieve more than a minimum programme, as far as limitation of armaments is concerned, that there will be no reduction and that the most that can be hoped for is a stabilisation of existing armaments.[56]

So Litvinov was right.

Further, Gibson commented:

> In spite of this discouraging situation, it was realised that some effort must be made. Disarmament is one of the principal missions of the League of Nations and if, after twelve years of existence and the conclusion of the work of the Preparatory Commission, no effort is made to reach an agreement, the League will suffer a serious blow. Further, if the whole question were allowed to go by default, no matter what the practical difficulties existed, Germany would inevitably seize upon this for demanding revision of the disarmament provisions of the Versailles Treaty on the grounds that the other powers have no intention of carrying out a general measure of disarmament foreshadowed in the preamble of part 5 of the Treaty of Versailles.[57]

The USA's policy in any case was cautious. Although the US Government was in favour of governments giving the fullest possible information, not only on expenditure but also on numbers, weight and units of material, the US Government instructed its delegate that on no account was he to agree to any budgetary control. Further, the USA Government

> is therefore in favour of including a broad escape clause which will merely specify that the nation which believes its security threatened shall, after a public statement of the reasons for this belief, be freed from its obligations.[58]

---

[55] FRUS, 1930, vol.1, pp.200 & 201
[56] Ibid. 1931 vol.1, p. 472
[57] Ibid. p.473
[58] FRUS, 1930, vol.1, p.189

The Soviet Union objected to the escape clause on the grounds that it facilitated evasion by a state under the Convention. Surely the escape clause could and would have been abused and from our knowledge of Mussolini and Hitler it is clear that such fears were justified.

The draft convention having been agreed by the Preparatory Commission, it was for the Council of the League to agree when the Disarmament Conference should open. The date eventually chosen was 2 February 1932, which Litvinov finally attended rather than the Preparatory Commission. Then, ironically, just as the Conference was due to commence came the news that the Japanese had bombarded the Shanghai railway station. After a few hours' delay for delegates to consult their governments, the Disarmament Conference finally got under way.[59]

The chief historian of the League of Nations stated:

> Year by year the difficulties of agreement had grown, and never more swiftly than in the last year [prior to the Conference], during which the organs of the League had been condemned to almost total inaction with regard to disarmament. The plea that the great powers must be given more time to prepare the understandings necessary for success had again and again proved little more than pretence. Its utter falsity was demonstrated, when in the early weeks of the Conference, three of the powers concerned, France, United States and Italy, put forward fresh schemes of their own, reproducing, of course, the main propositions they had always maintained but with various new proposals and arguments on which the others had not been consulted. Thus the long and laborious preparatory work was almost as though it has never been. The draft convention drawn up by the Preparatory Commission was brushed aside, and the Conference had, as material for its discussions before it, a series of plans which the delegates now saw for the first time.[60]

When finally the Disarmament Conference started, in Litvinov's first speech to the Conference on 11 February 1932 he painted a pessimistic picture. Events proved he was right to assume this attitude. Litvinov stated:

> The general impoverishment resulting from the war has intensified the demand for outlawing war. These demands cannot be satisfied by the stabilisation or the insignificant reduction of armaments but by finding the means to abolish the institutions of war.

Litvinov further stated:

[59] Walters, Francis: *History of the League of Nations*, p.484
[60] Ibid. pp.500 & 501

In our day there are no continents which are isolated politically or economically. There are countries whose territory spreads into several continents. In Europe there are but few neighbouring countries which have no serious territorial disputes. There are now longer stretches of frontiers, the validity of which is more sharply disputed than before the outbreak of the last war. What guarantees have we that these disputes will not cause a general conflagration if but one of the European nations will be drawn into war?

Then, in an overt criticism of the Kellogg Pact, Litvinov asked

What can prevent this? International organisations and pacts? But we see that such organisations and pacts could neither prevent nor stop the hostilities in the Far East.

Then, in further criticism of American presidents, who harped on the force of public opinion, Litvinov stated:

Perhaps public opinion, but public opinion is even more impotent. Just what is public opinion? When and where can it be unified and serve a single aim? Public opinion which finds its expression in the press and in public organisations serves different interests, varied in different countries, and within these various countries the interests of individual capitalist groups, individual enterprises and even individual persons.

Nor can we see a guarantee against war in the reduction of armaments, especially if the reduction is not to be very substantial and is not carried out with a view of hindering war. The Soviet delegation believes that we must strive to make war impossible since it means suffering for the masses, both of the victorious and defeated countries, as was evidenced by the consequences of the last war.

With considerable skill, Litvinov then rightly drew attention to the weakness of any international army.

What guarantee have we that this international army will be made use of or used in time before the weaker participant is definitely crushed? Further, what guarantee is there that a decision will be arrived at as to who is the aggressor and that it will be applied to the real culprit?

It seemed clear to Asquith, and I agree, that Poland started the Russo-Polish war of 1920, but the eminent historian of the League of Nations, Walters, thinks: 'Poland were justified invaded Russia because Poland had beaten off an attempted Soviet offensive.'

It always seemed clear to Martin Gilbert (who is a historian of international renown) that the initiators of the Six Day Arab-Israeli war in 1967 were those Arab countries that interfered with Israel's rights to use international waters; but for over forty years many have tried to argue otherwise.[61]

However, Litvinov did not deal with the valid point made by Paul-Boncour that, even without armaments, small nations would be at the mercy of the larger nations whose industrial capacity would be greater. Soldiers, even when disbanded, would still be soldiers.

Although the Soviet Union desired general disarmament, Litvinov had no illusions about the fate reserved for such a proposal, but made it clear that he 'will discuss any proposal aimed at the reduction of armaments and the further such reduction goes, the more readily will the Soviet delegation take part in the work of the Conference.'

Litvinov further declared:

> The readiness of the Soviet Union to disarm to the same extent and at the same rate as will be agreed upon by other powers and first and foremost those actually at its borders may agree.

Litvinov also praised

> the successful accomplishment of the First Five Year Plan, of colossal achievement in every sphere of economic construction, It seems obvious to the Soviet Delegation that has been obvious from the beginning,-must by now be as clear as daylight to all and sundry- namely that the Soviet Union requires neither increase of territory, nor interference in the affairs of other nations to achieve its aim and could therefore do without army, navy, no military aviation and all other forms of armed forces.[62]

On 20 February 1932 Litvinov spoke at a luncheon organised in his honour by the US Committee at the Disarmament Conference, in spite of the fact the USA had not recognised the Soviet Union. The theme of his speech was that security was not a substitute for disarmament in securing peace:

> The [Preparatory] Commission has spent a great deal of time in discussing the question of security, but this has produced no results. Surely no one can object to security. Neither does the Soviet delegation; but we contend that under the social and economic conditions prevailing in most countries they will only be secure

---

[61] Gilbert, Martin: *Israel, a History*, p.368
[62] *Moscow News*, 17 February 1932, pp.1 & 3; Disarmament Minutes, Series A, p.81

when no one will be in a position to attack such countries and there will be no way of occupying foreign countries and subjugating other nations.

The exponents of the opposite conception interpret security only in the sense of equalising or more or less equalising the opportunity for winning the war by means of a redistribution of armaments or even the increase of armaments (the concept of the 'balance of power').

Security of this kind was known also in the pre-war period. In the final analysis what does this kind of security mean if not the old traditional principle of 'the balance of power', the guiding principle of pre-war diplomacy? Was it necessary to go through the horrors and privations of the World War to prepare for this Conference, in the course of thirteen years to draft and conclude all manner of pacts and international conventions, in order to return in the end to the old principle of international diplomacy, only somewhat modified and spiced with new slogans?

Litvinov was right to criticise the concept of the balance of power so beloved of Britain, because it did not prevent the First World War, although the 'balance of power' regained credibility by preventing the Cold War from leading to the Third World War. Litvinov continued, 'We have not yet reduced the existing military formations by a single unit.'[63] Subsequently, when the Soviet proposal for general total disarmament was put forward, only Turkey supported it.[64]

On 22 June 1932 President Hoover made a dramatic, comprehensive and meaningful proposal which advocated, among other matters, a plan to reduce land forces by one third, and to abolish battleships, submarines, heavy mobile artillery, bombing planes and bombardment from the air. Gibson referred to it as: 'Without doubt the biggest day we had at Geneva.'[65] These proposals were very similar to Litvinov's proposals which he had been advocating since 1928, and which were met with contempt.

Litvinov at the Conference supported President Hoover's proposals for reduction of armaments by one third of a country's existing strength. Litvinov said he

welcomed in the main the proposals that had been made by the USA's delegation, the more so because to some extent they proceeded along the same lines as the Soviet proposal which was not accepted. They included some of the most important principles which the Soviet delegation put forward in the Preparatory Commission and at the Conference, namely the objective method of proportional reduction relatively between nations being maintained, because any attempt to infringe that

---

63 *Moscow News*, 27 February 1932, p.2,

64 Ibid. 3 March 1932, p.1

65 Disarmament Minutes, Series B, p.121; Mahaney, Wilbur Lee: *The Soviet Union, the League of Nations and Disarmament*, p.136; FRUS, 1932, vol.1, p.215; *Moscow News* 26th June 1932 p.1

relativity might render the Conference's work completely useless. The United States' proposals were to some extent different from the Soviet proposals and would require consideration.

At least Litvinov tried to inject some urgency into the proceedings, saying:

> For his part he would propose that the discussion be not too long postponed so that the delegations may have an opportunity to, at least, express their attitude in principle towards the proposal of the President of the United States. In this way he hoped the work of the Conference would really begin.[66]

No doubt Litvinov was thinking ahead and support for the USA's proposals would assist him in his ambition to obtain diplomatic recognition for the Soviet Union from the USA. However, I think it would have been far more shrewd for Litvinov to have given, like Italy, unqualified approval to President Hoover's proposals, which would have been embarrassing to the French and British with their reservations and also to President Hoover in view of his hostility to the Soviet Union. Gibson reported to the President: 'Italy accepted the plan in its entirety and in its details, not only in principle but also in its application.'[67]

The President's proposals were not helpful to Germany. There would still not be equality of armaments. Nevertheless, the German representative praised the plan by approving

> the principle on which President Hoover's message was based, namely the magnitude of the defensive power of the nations, the need of strengthening it and hence for reducing their aggressive power.

As to the actual substance of the United States' proposals, the German representative considered at first sight they seemed very moderate. It was hoped that during the discussion the Conference would be able to agree on still more vigorous and decisive measures in the matter of reductions. He had a special reason for expressing that hope namely, the more substantial the reduction the easier it would be to solve the problem of legal equality, an equality that was based on the Covenant and the establishment of which was one of the essential conditions for the Conference's ultimate success.[68]

Britain had reservations about any further reduction of naval armaments which would vary the agreement reached at the London Conference.[69] France prevaricated when they should

---

[66] Disarmament Minutes, Series B, p.128

[67] FRUS, 1932, vol.1, p.216

[68] Disarmament Minutes, Series B, p.129

[69] FRUS, 1932, vol.1, p.194

have realised that, with Hitler's advent, time was no longer on their side. Paul Boncour told Gibson:

> It would be difficult if not impossible for France to go as far as the President's plan without further agreement for security in the form of a mutual assistance pact among European powers and, since it would take some time to reorganise the French military service in order to make the reduction provided for, we would not be willing to reach an early agreement to sign the treaty.[70]

However, in view of the growth of the extreme Right in Germany, France should, as Gibson, the US representative had realised, that time might be of the essence if any agreement was to be reached. On 25 June 1932 Gibson correctly predicted, 'If the Conference breaks up without any real achievement it will only be a matter of time before Germany denounces the military clauses of the Versailles treaty and in this she would have a good deal of sympathy from public opinion in the United States and Great Britain.'[71] France would never again have a chance of agreement on disarmament and within seven years was to be totally defeated.

Because of opposition from France, the Hoover plan was never put to the vote, but there was a vote on a compromise resolution prepared by Benes who, when putting the resolution to the vote, admitted its imperfections, and considered it should be only 'the first step towards the important solutions which the whole world is awaiting.'[72] However, the Hoover proposal had been so watered down that it did not contain the reduction of one third in land armaments, battleships and submarines.

Litvinov certainly did not welcome Benes's proposals, saying:

> If the resolution was apparently intended to represent the summary of all the achievements of the Conference during the six months of its existence and of the preparatory work which had preceded it, as well as maximum progress of work for the next stage, it must be generally recognised that the resolution would bring bitter disappointment to all those persons and organisations that had set all their hopes of peace on the Conference.

Litvinov continued:

> Although the resolution began with an assertion that the time had come when all nations must adopt substantial and comprehensive methods of disarmament in order

---

[70] FRUS, 1932, vol.1, p.227
[71] FRUS, 1932, vol.1, pp. 234 & 235
[72] Walters, Francis: *A History of the League of Nations*, p.511; Disarmament Minutes, Series B, p.161; *Moscow News,* 23 July 1932, p.1

to consolidate the peace of the world, all its subsequent content represented the utter negation of that assertion. On the contrary, they [the content] would seem to constitute a recognition of the fact that the States represented had not found the time ripe for the final adoption of a single decisive step towards disarmament.

Litvinov then embarked on a detailed criticism of the Benes plan. He criticised the fact that:

Nearly a month had gone by since the United States' proposals had been put forward. Had the General Commission come at once to grips with that proposal, serious results could have been achieved, again subject to conditions that the declarations and pledges contained in the proposals really corresponded to the intentions of the Governments represented.

Litvinov correctly stated:

The method of objective reduction recommended by the Soviet delegation in the Preparatory Commission and at the present Conference had not at first been supported in any quarter. That method was now contained in the United States proposals to which a number of other delegations had acceded. From numerous letters and resolutions of various national and international organisations, the Soviet delegation learned with satisfaction that its position was receiving wider and wider recognition.[73]

Litvinov therefore proposed an amendment to bring the proposals roughly in line with President Hoover's proposals by stating that a reduction of one third shall apply to all categories of armaments, but this reduction would not apply to countries with armies of less than 30,000 personnel or to countries subject to disarmament by virtue of other international agreements.[74] This was a constructive resolution. Germany would still be bound by the Versailles treaty, but the French army would be reduced by one third to bring it nearer the strength of the Germany army. The amendment was defeated by 30 votes to 5 with 16 abstentions.[75] However, Litvinov should be given credit that support for the Soviet Union's position was growing.

Benes' resolution was then passed without enthusiasm. 41 countries voted for it. Germany and the Soviet Union voted against it, with 8 abstentions.[76] Not only did Germany vote

---

[73] Litvinov's speech: Disarmament Minutes, Series B, p.164; *Moscow News*, 24 July 1932, pp.1 & 2; Mahaney, Wilbur Lee: *The Soviet Union, the League of Nations and Disarmament*, p.140

[74] Disarmament Minutes, Series B, p.166; Mahaney, Wilbur Lee: *The Soviet Union, the League of Nations and Disarmament*, p.141; *Moscow News,* 26 July 1932 p.1

[75] Mahaney, Wilbur Lee: *The Soviet Union, the League of Nations and Disarmament*, p.141

[76] Walters, Francis: *History of the League of Nations*, p.511; Mahaney, Wilbur Lee: *The Soviet Union, the League of Nations and Disarmament*, p.142

against it, but on 22 July 1932 the German delegation made it clear that she would be unable to accept the resolution and would not take part in the future labours of the Conference before the question of Germany's rights had been satisfactorily cleared up. A further serious blow was struck at the League when, on 14 September 1932, Germany gave notice of 'her intention to withdraw from the Disarmament Conference because her right to equality was not being recognised.' However, Von Neurath made it clear that if conditions changed he would return. He remarked:'The German Government is more than ever convinced that thorough-going general disarmament is urgently necessary for the purpose of ensuring peace' and then held out a life-line to the Conference by saying: 'It will follow the labours of the Conference with interest and will determine its further attitude by the course which they may take.'[77] When the Disarmament Conference reconvened on 21 September 1932, the German delegate was absent.[78]

On the British side, the youthful Eden had arrived at the Foreign Office. Unlike many Conservative politicians, Eden worked hard in persuading Germany to return to the conference table and an attempt was made to satisfy German demands by stating that the new convention would replace the German disarmament provisions in the Versailles treaty. The governments of the United Kingdom, France and Italy declared,

> One of the principles that should guide the Conference should be to grant to Germany and other Powers disarmed by treaty, of equality of rights in a system that would provide security for all nations.

Germany agreed to return to the conference table.[79]

A new British plan was lodged with the Bureau on 4 November 1932 and by the French on 17 November 1932. Then it was agreed that the Conference should adjourn to enable discussions to take place between the great powers.[80] Litvinov remarked caustically, 'If the General Commission should be adjourned until agreement had been reached by the great powers, the governments might be able to come to Geneva to sign a convention already drawn up.'[81] Here he was expressing the sentiments of small nations who were of the same opinion.

When the General Commission of the Disarmament Conference reconvened on 6 February 1933, it had before it the British and French plans.

---

[77] Disarmament Minutes of Bureau, Series C, of 14 September 1932, p.3; Mahaney, Wilbur Lee: *The Soviet Union, the League of Nations and Disarmament*, p.142
[78] Mahaney, Wilbur Lee: *The Soviet Union, the League of Nations and Disarmament*, p.143
[79] Disarmament Minutes, Series B, p.208; Eden, Anthony: *Memoirs, Facing the Dictators*, p.27
[80] Mahaney, Wilbur Lee: *The Soviet Union, the League of Nations and Disarmament*, p.143
[81] Mahaney, Wilbur Lee: *The Soviet Union, the League of Nations and Disarmament*, p.144; Disarmament Minutes, Series B, p.211

While the second session of the Disarmament Conference, which convened in January 1933, continued to discuss disarmament, momentous events of great significance had occurred in Germany with the election of Hitler as Chancellor, which would change the course of history. 'The Nazi leaders were openly inspiring the youth of the country with the desire for war, aggression, and revenge.'[82]

On 6 February 1933, in a speech to the League of Nations, Litvinov, although actually speaking on the debate on the French plan, made perhaps the most significant speech of his career arguing what is and what is not aggression in international affairs that the speech warrants a detailed analysis. Litvinov acknowledged that there was no escape from the problem of security because:

> It has been raised by so great a powerful state as France, whose representatives have declared, until it has been solved, they cannot undertake any obligation with regard to the reduction of armaments. Therefore, if we want to advance, and just not go round and round, we shall have to consider with all seriousness the French proposals, and make up our minds whether there is any possibility of reaching an international agreement based upon these and other proposals which may be made on security by other delegations, proceeding subsequently to questions of disarmament, or whether such an attitude will prove impossible, in which case we shall have to admit that owing to the attitude of some states the whole problem of disarmament and security is insoluble and that it is not through an international conference that humanity will rid itself of the heavy burden of armaments and the scourge of war. In either case, some clarity will have been shed on the fate of the Conference.

Unlike other delegates, Litvinov had shown remarkable realism.

Then Litvinov proceeded to state:

> The capitalist world as a whole had not finally reconciled itself to the existence of the land building up socialism and this irreconcilability breeds hostility to such a country. In such circumstances it is permissible to enquire whether the Soviet Union may expect a fair attitude towards it. A moment's thought will show why the Soviet Union, as long as the present attitude lasts, cannot agree to acknowledge as binding upon itself the decisions of such international organisations as the Assembly or Council of the League of Nations, existing international tribunals, or arbitration courts, although by no means rejecting on principle the idea of international co-operation or arbitration. It is natural enough in such cases we must

---

[82] Walters, Francis: *A History of the League of Nations*, p.549

demand a composition of these organs as would guarantee us the same measure of impartiality and fairness as is enjoyed by capitalist states.

This might have been difficult because no capitalist country was likely to agree that the Soviet Union would have majority voting rights and vice versa, and if voting rights were equal between Soviet Russia and the capitalist countries there might be deadlock.

Litvinov continued:

> Whatever is its composition, any international organ that had to determine which party was the aggressor would be confronted with extreme difficulties because there is no universally acknowledged definition of aggression, but in practice as well as in theory, multitudinous discordance prevails on this point. This is demonstrated among other things by the reservations made when signing the Briand-Kellogg Pact. What is the meaning of these reservations? Do they amount to an insistence of certain states on freedom of action, pact or no pact, in certain cases and in certain parts of the world? What these cases or localities are, is left to each state to decide. What it may be asked are those guarantees that circumstances that have hitherto been made a pretext for war will not be regarded in such cases?
>
> If we wish to see in action the Kellogg Pact together with the extension proposed by the French delegation and to secure the minimum of authority, impartiality and confidence in the international organ to be called into life by these extensions, we shall have to give it instructions for its guidance and that means first defining war and aggression and the distinction between aggression and defence and once and for all condemning those fallacious justifications for aggression with which the past has familiarised us. The Soviet delegation has attempted to embody the ideas in a draft declaration which it offers for your consideration.

Litvinov then submitted a document that defined aggression as:

a) Declaration of war against another state.
b) The invasion by its armed forces of the territory of another state without a declaration of war.
c) Bombarding the territory of another state by its land, naval or air forces or knowingly attacking the forces of another state.
d) The landing in or introduction within the frontiers of another state of naval, land and air forces without the permission of the government of such state or the infringements of the conditions of such permission, particularly as regards to duration, sojourn or extension of area.
e) The establishment of a naval blockade of the coast or port of another state.

The following acts cannot justify an attack:

a) The internal situation of a given state as for instance political, economic or cultural backwardness of a given country.
b) Alleged maladministration.
c) Possible danger to life or property of foreign residents.
d) A revolutionary or counter-revolutionary movement, civil war or disorders or strikes.
e) The establishment or maintenance in any state of any political, economic or social order.

However, the most significant aspect of the declaration was that no state should intervene in the affairs of another state on the grounds of human rights. The USA has constantly acted according to this principle, such as in Cuba and Chile, as well as USA and Britain in Iraq. Litvinov gave examples of cases where he regards war as unjustified where in the past they were justified, such as:

> The desire to exploit the natural wealth of some territory, infringement of some international agreement, measures taken by some states encroaching on the material interest of another state, defence of nationals who are voluntarily residing in a foreign country at their own risk.

This last point suggested that Stalin should have *carte blanche* to deal with Metro Vickers employees whose arrest was to take place a month after this speech.

Litvinov concluded by stating:

> I do not think there are any left to doubt the peaceful disposition of the country which I represent. It is true there are sceptics and cynics who seek to weaken the significance of this peace policy by the assertion that the Soviet state requires peace to carry out its socialist construction. We do not deny that, but do such people imply it is only the Soviet State which can build itself up and develop in peaceful conditions and other conditions, not peaceful, are required for the development of the capitalist states? We gave every State represented here the opportunity to display such disposition by accepting our proposals for a disarmament and non-aggression pact.[83]

The speech shows that Litvinov had abandoned the normal Communist rhetoric. He was no longer suggesting that capitalist countries needed wars – a mistaken concept as, of course, countries like Sweden have built and retained a successful economy without any such wars.

---

[83] *Moscow News*, 10 February 1933, pp.1 & 3; Disarmament Minutes, Series B, pp.234-239

Meanwhile, Litvinov's definition of aggression which had been referred to the Political Commission was initially favourably received and examined by them. Most of Litvinov's proposals were included in a report of the Political Commission which was presented to the General Commission on 24 May 1933.[84]

Eden led the attack on it, opposing any rigid definition of aggression, and, like his predecessor Austen Chamberlain, maintained:'Such a definition would be a trap for the innocent and protection for the guilty.' However, in 1946 the British Government supported Litvinov's definition of aggression by accusing the Soviet Union of not complying with Litvinov's definition of aggression, and Finland made similar criticisms against the Soviet Union in 1939.[85] The Chairman of the Commission, Nicholas Politis, supported Litvinov. He did not think that the element of rigidity to which Eden objected represented more than the usual differences between 'the Anglo-Saxon and the continental system of law.'[86] The matter was adjourned for the delegates to endeavour to formulate a compromise definition of aggression. However, although, in spite of the opposition of Germany, Hungary, Italy, Spain, Switzerland and Britain, the majority preferred Litvinov's definition of aggression [87] was a triumph for Litvinov. In a press statement, Litvinov said that, when he realised there was little chance of early acceptance, he initiated negotiations and completed a convention with the majority of Eastern European states by which his definition of aggression was accepted, although certain states 'found our proposed definition of aggression inconvenient and embarrassing.'[88] He was probably thinking of Germany and Britain, who both opposed his definition: Germany because of Hitler's designs, but also Britain, who wished for no limitation on the way it enforced law throughout its Empire because Britain desired to retain the right to bomb troublesome areas.

The French plan for a pact of mutual assistance between the nations of continental Europe was debated on 7 March 1933. On 9 March 1933 M. Massigli stated: 'As long as nobody knew in most cases whether a state would have to count solely on themselves', France would not be prepared to sacrifice a considerable part of their means of defence. The French plan proposed a reduction of land forces of the states of continental Europe to a uniform general type – that of national short service with limited weapons not adapted to launching a sudden offensive – and was very vague compared with the Hoover plan. More controversially, France wanted all European powers, including Britain (on the grounds that France was not satisfied with the British guarantee under the Locarno Treaty), to provide

---

[84] Mahaney, Wilbur Lee: *The Soviet Union, the League of Nations and Disarmament,* p.150

[85] Disarmament Minutes, Series B, p.512; Eden's support for Litvinov speech: *Times,* 28 January 1946, p.4; Finland: *The New York Times,* 12 December 1939, p.1

[86] Disarmament Minutes, Series B, p.515; Mahaney, Wilbur Lee: *The Soviet Union, the League of Nations and Disarmament,* p.150

[87] Disarmament Minutes, Series B, p.517; Mahaney, Wilbur Lee: *The Soviet Union, the League of Nations and Disarmament,* p.150

[88] Mahaney, Wilbur Lee: *The Soviet Union, the League of Nations and Disarmament,* p.152

specialised army units and air force units for the League of Nations.[89] Although Eden was much more sympathetic to the aspirations of the Disarmament Conference than all of his governmental colleagues, he was unimpressed with the French plan and stated that Britain refused to enter into any commitment in Europe. In any event, the French plan was useless as it met with opposition from both Italy and Germany. Baron Aloisi of Italy stated, 'I am bound to say I have not found in the plan a single specific datum to allow us to anticipate an immediate and effective reduction in armaments.' Nadolny for Germany stated, 'It contains no concrete proposals for bringing about a real and decisive disarmament in the qualitative sphere or for effectively limiting material.'[90]

Five countries voted against it, the most important of which was Germany, as well as Italy, Austria, Hungary and the Netherlands. The reason given for this was the fact that it did not include Britain, who only agreed to support the resolution if the words 'Continental Europe' were included.[91]

Unlike many older members of the Conservative party who were sceptical, Eden was still optimistic 'good might still come from the European discussions.' Cadogan wrote to Eden while he was away from London in Yorkshire and observed:

> This blessed Conference will fail unless it is taken properly in hand. We are the people who ought to do that. The French won't. If the Italians do, then the French won't follow. The Germans would wreck everything. The Americans talk big when there is nothing doing. We are the only persons who could make it a success. If the Conference is not driven along hard it will fail. The Conference cannot survive many more pauses or adjournments.[92]

The Cabinet endorsed a new British plan and Macdonald and Simon set off for Geneva. The fact that both the Prime Minister and Foreign Secretary travelled to Geneva shows the importance now given to League business. Ramsay Macdonald should be applauded for making a last-ditch effort to save the Conference by personally presenting the British plan on 16 March 1933.

Macdonald stated:

His delegation has felt perhaps an intervention at the moment would rather speed up the Conference's business and facilitate its completion and aimed at preventing an

---

[89] Massigli: Disarmament Minutes, Series B, pp.346 to 348
[90] Disarmament Minutes, Series B, Massigli's speech: pp.346 & 348; Aloisi's speech: p.217; Nadolny's speech: p.220
[91] *Survey of International Affairs, 1933,* p.245
[92] Eden, Anthony: *Memoirs, Facing the Dictators,* p.28

adjournment at this moment, which would be the most heart-breaking confession of failure in which the Conference could indulge.

For the first time Macdonald put on the agenda the question of actually completing the work of the Conference. He quoted from a person whom he described as a colleague in the promotion of peace, who stated:

> Either Germany is given justice and freedom, or the Disarmament Conference will risk destruction. The disarmed states want justice and freedom; the armed states must make their contribution to disarmament. The disarmed states must be prepared to make their contribution in helping to establish confidence, goodwill, security and mutual understanding.

He further described his speech as: 'not a shop window affair. It was not a message from Mars.' Macdonald 'wanted to warn the delegates the plan would satisfy no one.' How could it? He was too old to believe that whenever four or five were gathered together, to say nothing of sixty, to come to an agreement upon anything that afflicted them in common, 'the man amongst them who thought he was going to get everything that satisfied him' and, therefore was a 'good patriot or nationalist', was not – 'he was a very ordinary common fool.'

Macdonald presented what he intended to be a compromise plan. Under the plan, both France and Germany would be limited to 200,000 troops, but the smaller nations of Italy and Poland were surprisingly allowed the same number of troops. The limit on the size of guns was 105mm, although guns up to 155mm might be retained. All tanks were to be limited to 16 tons and there was a general prohibition against aerial bombing. Macdonald retained the exception, originally inserted by the 1924 Conservative Government, that it would not apply to aerial bombing for police purposes in outlying areas.[93]

In the absence of Litvinov, his deputy Stein argued against this in a sarcastic speech which might well have been drafted by Litvinov. Many delegates no doubt felt that Stein's indignation was fully justified:

> No instances were known of any Government having ordered its own population to be bombed from the air except where the population lived in outlying areas such as colonies. If the authors of the draft were firmly convinced that the outlying areas, probably because of the remoteness from the centre of administration, must receive, if he might so put it, the fruits of modern civilisation in the form of bombs dropped from the air, it would at all events be necessary and logical to say in advance in which region the population would enjoy the unhappy privilege. Nobody can deny that the Soviet Union would be entitled, if it so desired, to avail itself of this

---

[93] Macdonald's speech: Disarmament Minutes, Series B, p.352; Documents, 1933, p.144

exception and in relation to the centre of the Union any point in its immense territory might be regarded outlying. He need not say that nothing was further from the Soviet Union's thoughts than the idea of applying to the population of the Union a measure of the kind previously condemned by the Conference.

Further, Stein, with considerable justification, rejected the compromise suggested by Rumanian, Czechoslovak and Yugoslavian delegates that aerial bombing for police purposes should be prohibited in Europe but allowed elsewhere. 'He saw no reason why the population of the entire continental mass except the European part of it should have the unhappy privilege of being attacked from the air.'[94]

The *Times* leader praised the Macdonald plan, again criticising the Disarmament Conference, as Litvinov had often done, for its slow progress.

> Macdonald yesterday made a brave attempt at Geneva to stir the Disarmament Conference into a burst of decisive activity and at the same time gave direction and precision to its labours. It had lost its way. He has put the British plan on the path for a definite goal.[95]

However, within days Macdonald's speech was severely criticised by Winston Churchill, who said:

> In view of the tumultuous insurgency of ferocity and war spirit, the pitiless ill-treatment of minorities, the denial of the normal protection of society to a large number of individuals solely on the grounds of race that was occurring in Germany, he thought it was most unwise to advocate any action that would weaken France.[96]

The trouble was that Churchill was advocating the breaking of a term of the Versailles Treaty which provided that the victorious countries in the First World War would reduce their armies to the level of Germany. Britain and France's mistake was not treating earlier the Disarmament Conference with a greater sense of urgency so that an agreement was reached before Hitler came to power. Indeed, it would have removed from the German people a grievance which might have prevented Hitler from becoming popular in Germany.

Walters states that Hitler, if the press now under his control reflects his view, seemed not unfavourable to the British Plan.[97] If ever there was a case for diplomacy where it is better to accept proposals which were not ideal because the chance would not come again, this was the occasion. The Chairman of the Disarmament Commission and the British National

[94] Disarmaments Minutes, Series B, p.535
[95] *Times* leader, 17 March 1933, p.15
[96] Churchill's speech: *Hansard*, vol.276, 13 April 1933 2786 @ 2793
[97] Walters, Francis: *A History of the League of Nations*, p.544

Labour politician Henderson worked tirelessly to recommend acceptance of the plan, realising that its rejection would lead to unfettered German rearmament. The French, however, rather than accepting it, amended it to make it more favourable to themselves.

Nadolny's reaction to Macdonald's speech supports Walters's contention. Nadolny

> warmly congratulated Macdonald on his resolve to submit to the Conference a draft convention with a view of finishing its work. ... He noted with satisfaction that the draft convention submitted by Macdonald was to bring about a substantial measure of disarmament. He hoped it would be possible to obtain the general consent of the Conference for a convention based on that idea. He wished to make it clear that the aim which Germany had set before herself at the present Conference was to take her place at the side of the other states as an element of peace.

However, Nadolny ended on a more cautious note. He said that 'he would venture to reserve judgment until he had examined it [Macdonald's plan].'[98] Walters then shows inconsistency by stating, in spite of his previous remarks, that Nadolny, the head of the German delegation, 'showed himself to be stiff and uncompromising.' Nadolny's speech was in marked contrast to his speech about the French plan, which Nadolny had previously criticised on the grounds that it lacked substance, as previously stated. [99]

Litvinov's criticism of the Preparatory Commission and Disarmament Conference was fully justified. With events in Hitler's Nazi Germany unfolding, speed was of the essence, but discussion of the plan proceeded, in Litvinov's words, 'at a snail's pace'[100] until the Easter adjournment on 27 March 1933 and continued after 25 April 1933 upon the resumption of the Disarmament Conference.[101]

In order to bring fresh life to the Conference, the new President Roosevelt spoke on 16 May 1933. The President referred to the increase of armaments about which Litvinov had constantly complained, and then asked the Conference 'to take at once the first definite steps' to reduce the armaments 'as outlined in the Macdonald Plan and requested no nations shall increase its present armaments over and above the limitations of treaty obligations.' This was a direct appeal to Germany

Roosevelt asked all nations to confirm 'they would send no armed force of whatever nature across their frontiers' and concluded with these words: ' If any strong nation refuses to join with genuine security in these concerted efforts for political and economic peace, the

---

[98] Disarmament Minutes, Series B, p.358
[99] Walters, Francis: *A History of the League of Nations*, p.544; and see No. 90 *ante*
[100] See No.6 *ante*
[101] Mahaney, Wilbur Lee: *The Soviet Union, the League of Nations and Disarmament*, p.159

civilised world will know where the responsibility for failure lies.'[102] Eden, who was not an unqualified admirer of Macdonald, gave him the credit for persuading Roosevelt to make the speech.[103] However, moral responsibility as suggested by Roosevelt was unlikely to influence ambitious and troublesome dictators.

On 17 May 1933 Hitler addressed the Reichstag. He began his speech with an attack on the Treaty of Versailles and considered both political and economic aspects. He said:

> If the statesmen of Versailles wanted to bring lasting peace to Europe by means of the Treaty then, instead of falling victims of the dangerous and sterile conception of expiation, punishment and reparation, they should have recognised and followed the profound truth that the lack of necessities of life has always been and always will be a source of conflict between peoples. Instead of preaching the idea of extermination, they should have considered how far a reorganisation of international, political and economic relationships could best be undertaken so as to do justice so far as possible to the vital needs of every nation. It is not wise to deprive a people of the economic resources necessary for its existence without taking into account the fact that the population, dependent and relying on them, will still remain and will still have to be fed.

Hitler was actually right, and, after the Second World War, the USA, having destroyed Germany with her Allies, paid for Germany to be rebuilt by way of the Marshall Plan. Economically, Hitler said, 'The Treaty of Versailles is to blame for having inaugurated a period in which financial calculations appear to destroy economic reason.' Surprisingly, Hitler made the following thoroughly misleading statement: 'No fresh European war could improve the unsatisfactory conditions of the present day.' Then he stated:

> The boundless love and loyalty for our own national traditions make us understand the national rights of others and make us desire from the bottom of our hearts to live with them in peace and friendship.[104]

Hitler sent a telegram to the President of the Commission, the contents of which were by no means lacking justification. Hitler pointed out that recent events proved the Conference had no chance of achieving its purpose and (in the same terms as Litvinov) the heavily armed states had no intention of either disarming or fulfilling their pledge to satisfy Germany's claim for equality of rights. She forthwith withdrew both from the disarmament talks and the League of Nations.[105] Germany's decision to refuse to participate further in

---

[102] Roosevelt's speech, 1933 Document, p.194

[103] Eden, Anthony: *Memoirs, Facing the Dictators*, p.39

[104] Hitler's speech, Documents 1933, p.196

[105] Disarmament Minutes, p. 646; Walters, Francis: *A History of the League of Nations*, p.550; Eden, Anthony: *Memoirs, Facing the Dictators*, p.46; *Moscow News* 16 May 1933 p.1

the Conference for the reduction and limitation of armaments dealt a death blow to the Disarmament Conference.

On 29 May 1934 Henderson convened a general meeting which, although the words were never spoken, was considered to be the final meeting of the Disarmament Conference. Litvinov took the opportunity to make a major speech, but his thinking on rearmament had been somewhat transformed. Litvinov stated:

> The question is no longer one of disarmament itself since that is only a means to an end, but of guaranteeing peace and, since this is so, the question naturally arises cannot the Conference feel its way towards other guarantees of peace or at any rate might it not increase the security of at least those states, which cherishing no aggressive designs, are not interested in war and which in the event of war may become only the object of attack?

Litvinov thus rejected the communist theory that wars are a necessary ingredient of capitalist states and that the sole way of ending wars is total disarmament, a view which Litvinov cherished at the beginning of the Preparatory Commission of the Disarmament Conference.

However, Litvinov made it clear that there must be

> no question of military alliances or of division of states into mutually hostile camps or still less a policy of encirclement. Care must be taken not to create universal pacts which would exclude any state wishing to participate, thus countering the feeble German argument that they were being encircled.

What Hitler did not like was that these pacts made it more difficult for Germany to break out of its borders at the time of his choosing.

Litvinov then asked, 'Who can say whether the reinforcement of security and the effect it would have on aggressively inclined governments, will create conditions that would enable us to take up once more the problem of disarmament with a greater chance of success?' Litvinov realised that now, with Hitler re-arming, it was crazy to talk about disarmament, although many peace groups in the democracies were not prepared to accept that unpleasant fact.

Litvinov then made his main proposal that 'the Disarmament Conference be transformed into a permanent body concerned to preserve by every possible means the security of all nations and to safeguard universal peace.'

Litvinov continued:

Hitherto, peace conferences had normally been called upon the termination of wars and have, as their object, the division of spoils of war, the imposition on the vanquished of painful and degrading conditions, the redistribution of territory and the refashioning of states, thus hatching out the germs of future wars; but the conference which I have in mind should sit for the prevention of war and its terrible consequences. It should work out, extend, and perfect measures for the strengthening of security. It would give a timely response to impending dangers of war and to appeals for aid, to SOS calls from threatened states and it should afford timely aid [to such states] within its power, whether such be moral, economic, financial or otherwise.

Surely these tasks were intended for the League of Nations. Litvinov continued:

Today, when the peril of war stood before men's very eyes, it was feasible to consider a special body, with all its activity, concentrated upon one objective – the preventing or lessening of the danger of war.

Then Litvinov endeavoured to justify a new body separate from the League. His view was that the League of Nations was too strictly bound by its statutes, while he thought, 'The tribune of the conference might be more accessible, more free, more responsive to the needs of the moment' – this was perhaps wishful thinking. However, although the Soviet Union was not yet a member of the League of Nations, Litvinov, in view of his past criticism of the League, now made it clear that he no longer wanted to set up a body in opposition to the League: 'Let the Conference continue to be considered an organ of the League using the services of the League. Let it maintain its closest contact with the League.'[106]

The delegation of the USA issued a pessimistic press release which stated:

27 months ago and more have passed since we met, in the high hopes to frame a general disarmament convention; now we once meet again but with hopes dimmed. One great power has chosen to withdraw from the Conference (and) certain powers are not talking in terms of reduction of armaments but in terms of mere limitation and others of actual increase.[107]

On 5 October 1934 Bullitt, the US ambassador to the Soviet Union, conferred with Litvinov in Moscow. Litvinov said he thought that war was inevitable and all the Soviet Union could do was to strengthen the Red Army. He then said: 'I think we had better use the few millions we might pay you for debt settlement on guns and tanks.' Litvinov reiterated his plea for a permanent peace commission with a council consisting of the

---

[106] Disarmament Minutes, Series B, p.660
[107] FRUS, 1934, vol.1, p.79

present members and the USA. Litvinov said that the leading European powers desired US participation in the maintenance of a permanent peace commission in which they could participate without becoming a member of the League. Litvinov said his task would be tremendously lightened if he could know the USA would participate and asked Bullitt if he could obtain the US Government's views as soon as possible. Bullitt agreed to ask his government, but 'he would not be surprised if the answer was long in coming.' Bullitt reminded Litvinov that the question of adherence to the League was still a question of major political importance which aroused violent emotions in the USA and 'Litvinov's proposals would certainly be criticised in the USA as a method of entering the League by the back door.'[108]

In November 1934 Hugh Wilson, the new US delegate to the Disarmament Conference, met Litvinov at a dinner. Wilson told Litvinov: 'Although the USA was profoundly interested in the disarmament situation, they divided in their minds political problems, and especially European political problems in which they firmly refused to concern themselves.'[109] On 31 December 1934, when the US Government was asked about its attitude to a permanent Peace Commission, Cordell Hull replied: 'Political phrases of Litvinov's proposals would not permit the US Government to make any affirmative commitment.'[110] Unfortunately, Litvinov's efforts to obtain the USA's approval for further participation in Europe failed, as did Churchill's efforts. Litvinov saw clearly that US involvement in Europe was of prime importance in deterring Hitler. Had Litvinov succeeded, a world war might have been prevented. Litvinov's failure led to the involvement of both countries in a new world war.

As for control of armaments, Litvinov, when proposing total disarmament on 19 March 1928, initially stated that disarmament had to be enforced by on-site inspections, but it should be supervised by an equal number of representatives of legislative bodies and of trade unions and other workers' organisations.[111] As for partial disarmament, on 21 September 1932 Litvinov remarked: The need for supervision was unanimously admitted.' – he was absolutely wrong, as the USA would not agree to supervision. Litvinov continued, 'The Soviet delegation insisted that very rigorous supervision should be established. It asked that, contrary to the draft convention, the members of the Commission should not be chosen by governments but by legislative bodies, trade unions and peace groups.'[112] However, Litvinov now considered as premature any discussion on control of armaments until the degree of disarmament had been approved. Litvinov's alleged remark that to consider control in advance of determining disarmament was like 'a discussion on

---

[108] FRUS, 1934, vol.1, p.154
[109] Ibid. p.190
[110] Ibid. p.216
[111] Phillips, Hugh: *Between the Revolution and the West*, p.96
[112] Slusser, Robert Melville and Eudin, Zenia Joukoff: *Soviet Foreign Policy 1928-1934*, p.374

the frame of a picture before the picture was painted' did not appear in the speech.[113] It is difficult to imagine that Stalin would have agreed to independent verification of disarmament in the territory of the Soviet Union.

However, even if agreement had been reached on disarmament, it is likely the Disarmament Conference would still have been a failure because on 7 January 1933 the USA made it clear that 'any proposal for setting up any form of international supervision of privately owned factories would be certain to arouse strong opposition on the part of the American public and this would be clearly reflected in Congress.'[114]

Although complete disarmament, as initially proposed by Litvinov, was not practical, he achieved as much as any of the delegates by stressing that the purpose of the Conference was not stabilisation but a meaningful reduction in armaments. Eventually, but too late, this idea was reflected in the proposals of President Hoover in June 1932 and of Macdonald in March 1933. The other great powers would have done well to have accepted either plan. Litvinov strove to cajole the Disarmament Conference into making more rapid progress. He gained support among many ordinary citizens in various countries, among whom were many who had suffered the horrors of the previous war. These individuals actually prayed that there would be real disarmament. Litvinov also increased the prestige of the Soviet Union, particularly during the latter part of the Conference, because support for some of his ideas, particularly the notion of defining aggression, started to increase. The British delegates who took delight in criticising Litvinov achieved nothing constructive.

As far as delay was concerned, many delegates agreed with Litvinov but lacked the courage to say so. However, the only chance of success was if the capitalist countries had agreed measures of supervision among themselves and put such proposals to the Soviet Government or alternatively the capitalist countries could have accepted the Soviet proposals so there was an opportunity to put Stalin to the test.

---

[113] *Izvestii* 23 September 1932
[114] FRUS, 1933, vol.1, p.2

7: CHINA AND JAPAN

In Litvinov's speech following his appointment as Commissar on 25 July 1930, he stressed that foreign policy was determined by 'the worker and peasant masses which finds its expression in the decision of the Soviet Government.' [1] In fact, foreign policy was never, during the whole of the Communist period, determined other than by the supreme leader, who was subject in some cases to the influence of the communist elite.

There is evidence that, following the famine in 1921, the population in the countryside was more grateful to the USA than the Soviet Government.[2] We do know that, at the close of the Second World War, the USA was tremendously popular among the general Soviet population. The hostility of Soviet intellectuals in late 1945 might have also been reflected in the public at large when the USA opposed the Soviet Union taking over various Eastern European countries, but had done little to prevent Nazi Germany acting similarly.[3]

In democratic countries governments do not necessarily represent what the majority of the voters desire. At least, because there is a free press and uncensored public debate, it is easier to gauge what the public thinks than in authoritarian states.

A change of foreign minister in a democratic country is not likely to bring forth a major change of policy, which in the USA is determined by the President and in Britain by the Cabinet under the great influence of the Prime Minister. However, the change of foreign minister in a democratic country, as it did in the Soviet Union, often brings a change of style. Litvinov's style was entirely different from his predecessor, Chicherin, and would be entirely different from Molotov, Litvinov's successor, as Maisky stated.[4] Having lived in a democratic country,[5] Litvinov should rightly be criticised for making comments which he must have known were misleading to his own citizens.

In the nine years during which Litvinov was Commissar, he would have to deal with all the major powers of the world, during the turbulent 1930s, but it would be the Far East that would bring the first crisis of his time in charge of foreign policy. The crisis arose from an armed conflict between China and Japan.

---

[1] Degras, Jane: *Soviet Documents on Foreign Policy*, vol.2, pp. 449-451
[2] See Ch.3, No.115
[3] See Ch.18, No.2
[4] Maisky, Ivan: *Memoirs of a Soviet Ambassador*, p.211
[5] Litvinov's stay in England: see Chs.1 & 2

Since the Revolution, the Soviet Union had clashed with Japan and China over the Chinese railway. The USA also became involved. In 1896 China had agreed to allow Russia to construct a railway from Chita to Vladivostok on Chinese soil.[6] However, at the close of the Russo-Japanese war, Russia ceded to Japan the railway from Kwangchentze to Dairen, some 475 miles of track. South Manchuria was within the Japanese sphere of influence.[7] When Kerensky assumed power, following the 1917 February Revolution, the USA was asked to run the railway and appointed an American, John Stevens, as Chairman. When the Bolsheviks came to power, the Allies arrogantly considered themselves the heirs of the line and asked the USA to manage it. This action did not please Japan, who wanted to take the opportunity of Russia's internal turmoil to gain a foothold in Siberia.[8] After much friction caused by Japan and threats from the USA, an agreement was reached between Japan and the USA on 8 January 1919 which provided that John Stevens would remain Chairman of both the Chinese and Trans-Siberian railway, to the extent that it was not in Bolshevik hands. American troops would guard the eastern spur of the Trans-Siberian railway and Japanese troops the Chinese Eastern Railway.[9]

The Manchu dynasty, a monarchy which had ruled China since 1644, was toppled in 1911 and in theory a democratic Chinese state was established with a parliament.[10] The largest party in the new parliament was the Kuomintang, a nationalist movement formed in 1912. The leader of this movement was a non-Marxist nationalist leader, Sun Yat-sen. The Kuomintang was dedicated to the expulsion of the privileged foreigners from China, and the overthrow of all those Chinese authorities that permitted foreigners to have these privileges.[11] However, Yuan Shikai emerged as a dictator and dissolved parliament, but died in 1916.[12] China was in effect controlled by a number of warlords. There was still, in theory, a central government in Peking, but the only effective work it undertook was handling foreign relations with the foreign embassies situated in the capital.[13]

Both Inner and Outer Mongolia had been part of the Chinese Empire under the Manchus; but, with the fall of that dynasty, Outer Mongolia proclaimed its independence and accepted Tsarist Russian protection. Inner Mongolia remained part of China.[14] However, in the autumn of 1919, with Russia involved in civil war, China took its chance, invaded Mongolia and presented the Mongolian ruler with a petition. Bowing to *force majeure*, China signed an agreement to the effect that Mongolia would be reunified with China.[15]

---

[6] Fischer, Louis: *The Soviets in World Affairs*, vol.2, p.530
[7] Ibid. p.531
[8] Fischer, Louis: *The Soviets in World Affairs*, vol.2, p.531
[9] Ibid. p.531
[10] Moise, Edwin: *Modern China*, p.44: Manchus
[11] Carr, Edward: *Socialism in One Country*, vol.3, p.688
[12] Moise, Edwin: *Modern China*, p.46
[13] Ibid. p.46
[14] Ibid. p.5
[15] Dallin, David: *Rise of Russia in Asia*, p.187

The Russian Civil War then engulfed Mongolia. One of the White generals, Ungern Sternberg, wished to create a single dictatorship in Inner and Outer Mongolia. With political views similar to the Nazis, he hated democracy, political freedom, communists, socialists and Jews.[16]

In March 1921 the Mongolian Communist Party was formed at a town on the border between Russia and Mongolia. On 5 July the Red Army entered Mongolia in pursuit of Ungern Sternberg and, following the defeat of his army by the Red Army, Ungern Sternberg was captured and executed. The Mongolian Communist Party pretended it was a nationalist party, not a Communist party allied to Moscow, in order to increase its support among the local population.

On 5 November 1921 a treaty between Outer Mongolia and Russia was signed recognising the two governments, but not mentioning China, and in spite of the fact that the Bolsheviks despised secret treaties, it was not published.[17] When the Chinese heard of the treaty and asked for an explanation, Russia denied its existence. China was not convinced and accused Moscow of imperialism: 'Is it going the same way as the old Tsarist Government?' Moscow accused China of imperialism because it wanted to bring Outer Mongolia under Chinese rule. Dallin made the apt remark that for China to hold Outer Mongolia under Chinese rule 'was branded as imperialistic, while Russia's control was considered liberation.'[18]

The Chinese Communist party, founded in 1921, was only a group of intellectuals and so the Soviet Union forged an alliance with the nationalist movement, the Kuomintang. Communists were encouraged to join the Kuomintang as individual members.[19] On 6 October 1923 Stalin sent a Comintern agent, Borodin, to China in order to assist the Kuomintang in its revolutionary struggle and thereby increase the prestige of the Communist Party.[20] In 1922 Chicherin declared that China and the Soviet Union were natural allies.[21]

On 5 September 1924 the Soviet Central Committee of Trade Unions decided to form 'A Hands off China Society.' A meeting was organised at the Bolshoi Theatre which was addressed by Radek. Several foreign communists spoke and a circular letter was sent to communist parties in Europe and the USA appealing for support and urging them to create similar societies in their own countries.[22]

---

[16] Ibid. p.188
[17] Dallin, David: *Rise of Russia in Asia*, p.191
[18] Ibid. p.194
[19] Carr, Edward: *Socialism in One Country*, p.688
[20] Dallin, David: *Rise of Russia in Asia*, p.212
[21] Fischer, Louis: *The Soviets in World Affairs*, p.550
[22] Ibid. p.709

Between 1921 and 1924, because of China's firm stance on Outer Mongolia, an agreement between Russia and China could not initially be achieved. However, after long and tedious negotiations, the Soviet-Chinese Treaty of 1924 was concluded. The Soviet Union formally acknowledged Chinese sovereignty over Outer Mongolia without it affecting the *status quo*. Mongolia became a fully communist state and would remain so until the fall of the Soviet Union in 1990. The Soviet declarations of 25 July 1919 and 27 October 1920, whereby the Russian Bolshevik Government renounced all special privileges enjoyed by Tsarist Russia, were confirmed.

This treaty led to the restoration of diplomatic relations with the Chinese Government in Peking, still recognised by the Great Powers as the legitimate Chinese Government; although in the south an alliance had been concluded by Soviet Russia with the rising star – the Kuomintang. This shows that the Soviet Government was deciding questions of foreign policy pragmatically, instead of being guided by revolutionary hope, although Karakhan 'had turned the Soviet mission into the centre of nationalist and radical activity in Peking.'[23]

Sun Yat-sen died in Peking on 12 March 1925. Two documents were found. One exhorted the Kuomintang to carry on revolutionary work and called for the abolition of unfair treaties. The other note was a letter of farewell addressed to the Central Executive Committee of the Soviets in the USSR. It praised the Soviet Union's support for the Left and described the USSR, created 'by the immortal Lenin', as an 'inspiration to the oppressed peoples of the world.' The Chinese leader predicted that 'the Kuomintang would be bound up with you in the historic work of the final liberation of China and other exploited countries in the great struggle from the yoke of imperialism.' His note concluded by

> expressing the hope that the day would soon come when the Soviet Union will welcome a friend and ally in a mighty, free China, and that in the great struggle for the liberation of oppressed peoples both these allies will go forward to victory hand in hand.[24]

A wave of industrial unrest followed Sun Yat-sen's funeral. Since the large factories were almost all foreign owned, the strikes were regarded as anti-foreign as well as anti-capitalist. The situation deteriorated after the deaths of 12 demonstrators fired on by Shanghai police under the command of British officers. The strikes spread to Hong Kong.[25]

---

[23] Jacobs, Dan M: *Borodin*, p.166; Dallin, David: *Rise of Russia in Asia*, p.204
[24] Carr, Edward: *Socialism in One Country*, p.717
[25] Ibid. p.719

However, on 20 March 1926, Chiang Kai-shek started a campaign to humiliate the Soviet Union. The political commissars attached to the army, most of whom were Communists, were arrested and the Soviet military advisors were confined to their quarters.[26]

Litvinov, speaking before the Central Committee, openly sympathised with the Kuomintang movement on the basis of its programme – the revival of a free and fully democratic China. In a speech on 24 April 1926 Litvinov praised the policy of the Kuomintang Government in Canton because it pursued a policy which is of the 'greatest benefit to the broad masses of the population', and had been praised by the London *Times* stating: 'Canton is more nearly a Government than any Canton has had for some years.' Among the Government's achievements was stated to be

> the reunification of the province of Kwangtung and its determination to put down corruption which has been the bane of China. Canton is clean and more or less peaceful.[27]

Did Litvinov believe what he was saying or was this part included in his speech on the instructions of Stalin? We have no way of knowing, but by this time it seems that Litvinov probably predicted the policy of aligning with Chiang Kai-shek would end in failure. On balance, it seems that this part of the speech was on instructions from Stalin, as he had taken a special interest in China.[28] In spite of the Soviet Union being humiliated by Chiang Kai-shek, Stalin was prepared to turn the other cheek in the hope that the Communist alliance with the Kuomintang would continue.

On 1 July 1926 Chiang Kai-shek started his march northwards with the aim of overthrowing the Government in Peking established by the 1911 revolution. It was the biggest military operation between the wars.[29] Chiang Kai-shek's army pushed forward with little opposition. By August 1926 it had reached the Yangtze river, but thereafter met stiffer opposition as it moved towards Shanghai.

Having taken Nanking, Chiang Kai-shek continued his northern advance. By 18 March 1927 his army was within twenty miles of Shanghai. [30] 'However, he had no intention of sharing power with the communist-led radicals in Shanghai.'[31] In the city on 21 March 1927 the Communist trade unions had planned a co-ordinated attack – a military assault led by Chiang Kai-shek from outside and an armed uprising led by the Chinese Communist Party (CCP) from within. On that day at noon, 800,000 workers responded to a call for a

---

[26] Ibid. p.779

[27] Degras, Jane: *Soviet Documents on Foreign Policy*, vol.2, p.114; *Times*, 24 March 1926, p.17

[28] See 57 *post*

[29] Fenby, Jonathan: *Generalissimo Chiang Kai-shek*, p.114

[30] Moise, Edwin: *Modern China*, pp..61-63

[31] Jacobs, Dan M: *Borodin*, p.241

general strike. An hour later an armed uprising took place and within nineteen hours the last major points of resistance had been successfully taken. 'Shanghai, one of the great cities in the world with a population of 3,250,000, had fallen to Chinese workers led for the most part by the CCP and its sympathisers.'[32]

On 24 March 1927 Chiang Kai-shek's troops entered Shanghai, determined to crush all radical elements in the city. Chiang Kai-shek wished to receive all the credit for its capture and portrayed the army as being solely responsible for its fall.'[33] Chiang Kai-shek established his own government, which replaced the provisional government set up at the time of the workers' takeover. Martial law was imposed, and all meetings, strikes and demonstrations were banned. The radical trade unions were replaced by unions organised by Chiang Kai-shek. All over China trade union headquarters, usually the centre of resistance of the Left, were smashed and union officials were arrested and shot.

Whereas the Communist International described Chiang Kai-shek a traitor and an ally of imperialist bandits, Stalin was very reluctant to similarly condemn Chiang Kai-shek. [34]

In Peking, when it was realised that Chiang Kai-shek had decided to liquidate the Chinese Communists, on 6 April 1927 Chang Tso-lin (a dictator who ruled over Manchuria and parts of northern China, including Peking) decided to act. Chinese soldiers entered the Soviet Embassy compound. The Soviet employees and Chinese sympathisers in the embassy tried to burn their papers, but the police were able to extinguish the fire so that a huge assortment of papers could be removed for examination by the Chinese. Fifteen Russian and eighty Chinese employees were arrested. Fifteen of the Chinese employees were executed.[35] In protest, on 6 April 1927 the Soviet Union withdrew its chargé d'affaires, but permitted its consulates to function.[36]

On 6 May 1927 Litvinov declared:

> The only documents of which a photograph had been taken were forgeries, as it had been drafted with an old process not seen since the Revolution and is a clumsy forgery probably executed by a Russian White and is proof that general documents of a compromising character were not found. As no inventory was made in the presence of Soviet diplomats, Chang Tso-lin will doubtless be able to publish photographs of numerous documents definitely proving that the Soviet Government interfered in Chinese internal affairs, inspired anti-Soviet pogroms and other

---

[32] Ibid. p. 241
[33] Ibid. p. 243
[34] Dallin,,D: *Rise of Russia in Asia*, p.229
[35] Jacobs Dan M: *Borodin* p 244;
  Degras, Jane: *Soviet Documents on Foreign Policy*, vol.2, p.200
[36] Fischer, Louis: *The Soviets in World Affairs*, vol.2, p.737

nonsense that nobody believes. We are here facing a widespread plot to compromise the Soviet accredited representatives in China and to worsen the relations between the USSR and other countries, in particular Japan.[37]

However, when Litvinov challenged the authenticity of the documents in a speech during May 1927, he might well have concentrated on the fact that the raid was in flagrant breach of international law. Within a week Britain followed suit with the Arcos raid.[38] This shows the disdain with which the Soviet Union was treated in the pre-war period. Stalin's reasonable wish was to build up his country's industrial and military might so that in the post-war period no country would dare to treat the Soviet Union other than with proper respect.

After the Chinese attack on the embassy in Peking, Litvinov went to the Politburo and vehemently demanded that agents of the Comintern be excluded from the embassies. Certain members of the Politburo pointed out that the work of the Comintern agents was indispensable since the aim of all politics was world revolution. Litvinov replied: 'He was in charge of the Commissariat of Foreign Affairs, not world revolution, and he must protect the Commissariat's embassies abroad.' He added: 'If they transferred him to the Comintern he would watch the interests of world revolution, but while he remained at the Commissariat he was going to look after that and nothing else.' It is probable that, in spite of what Litvinov said publicly, he did not entirely agree with the actions of his own government; but it is not clear whether he disagreed entirely with Stalin's policy of interfering in internal Chinese affairs or was unhappy that the agents were in the embassy.

However, when various Soviet documents were released from the archives and published during the sixties and seventies, they were found to be identical to those published by the Chinese at the time, which seemed to indicate that what the Chinese stated was correct.[39]

Following an attempted Communist uprising at Canton on 11 December,1927 the Chinese Government severed diplomatic relations with the Soviet Union.[40]

In 1927 Borodin's American wife was arrested on a steamer on the Yangtze, accused of carrying propaganda leaflets. When Borodin's wife was freed, she and Borodin both left China for good, arriving in the Soviet Union on 6 October 1927, just after Moscow had ordered an end to the united front with the Kuomintang. Borodin's mission had been a complete failure. Borodin, in speaking to a Swedish official, said, 'I came to China to fight for an ideal, but China itself, with its age-old history, its countless millions, its great social

---

[37]*The New York Times*, 6 May 1927, p.3. What the *New York Times* states does not agree in a number of aspects with the statement as published by Jane Degras in *Soviet Documents on Foreign Policy*, vol.2, p.200.
[38] See Ch.9, No.76
[39] Bessedovsky, Grigory: *Revelations of a Soviet Diplomat*, p.97; Jacobs, Dan M: *Borodin*, p.244
[40] Fischer Louis:*The Soviets in World Affairs* .p737; FRUS, 1927, vol.2, p.38

problems and its infinite capacities, astounded and overwhelmed me.' With regard to the Kuomintang, which Stalin had sent Borodin to support, Borodin observed, 'The Kuomintang, like all bourgeoisie parties, was a toilet which, however often you flush it, still stinks.' This remark confirmed Litvinov's assessment. Stalin did not blame Borodin too much, as he survived the Great Purges of the 1930s, only to be arrested in 1949 because Stalin thought Borodin was too friendly with foreign Communists. He died in a Siberian prison camp in 1951.[41]

By June 1928 Chiang Kai-shek's troops finally reached Peking, then under the control of the dictator of Manchuria, Chang Tso-lin. He had pursued an anti-Soviet policy and was in control not only of Manchuria but also parts of northern China, including Peking, from where he ruled. When Chiang Kai-shek's army approached northern China in 1928, Japan warned both Chang Tso-lin and Chiang Kai-shek that, if civil war spread to Northern China, Japan might act. Further, Japan advised Chang Tso-lin to vacate all Chinese territory except Manchuria. Chang Tso-lin realised that without allies he could not oppose Chiang Kai-shek. Chang Tso-lin returned to Manchuria, where he was assassinated by Japanese officers in the hope that Chang Tso-lin's son, Chang Hsueh-liang, would be more susceptible to Japanese pressure. However, upon becoming dictator he allied himself to the Kuomintang Government and became a serious opponent of Japan.[42]

The Imperial City was taken by Kuomintang forces amid great rejoicing in Nanking, where Chiang Kai-shek was residing. In July 1928 Chiang Kai-shek visited Peking and was host at a dinner for the diplomatic corps, the international community having acknowledged Chiang Kai-shek's government as the true government of China.[43]

From 1927, in spite of Chiang Kai-shek's decimation of the Communist Party, there continued to be civil war with Chinese Communists under Mao, who operated independently of Moscow and sought a power-base not among the proletariat but among the peasants. In contrast to Soviet policy towards the richer peasants, the kulaks, in the USSR, Mao's principal strategy was to gain support among the richer peasants who were still able to retain some land. Unlike their Soviet counterparts, they did not face liquidation. Accordingly, Mao was able to win control of large areas of land, although from time to time these areas were attacked by Chiang Kai-shek's troops.[44] By 1931 some Communists who had fled China for Moscow clandestinely returned to China and proceeded to criticise Mao's wise tactics of avoiding a head-on clash with Chiang Kai-shek – overall, Mao was outnumbered by Chiang's troops. Instead, Mao waited patiently until he could attack isolated enemy units and capture their equipment.

---

[41] Fenby, Jonathan: *Generalissimo Chiang Kai-shek*, p.158
[42] Moise, Edwin: *Modern China*, p.83; McCormack, Gavan: *Chang Tso-lin in North East China, 1911-1928*, p.248
[43] Fenby, Jonathan: *Generalissimo Chiang Kai-shek*, p.181
[44] Moise, Edwin: *Modern China*, p.76

Even before the rise of Chiang Kai-shek, serious trouble occurred due to the action of Chang Tso-lin in interfering with the Chinese railway. On 20 September 1924 an amicable agreement was reached by the Soviet Union nominally with the Chinese Government concerning the Chinese Eastern Railway, but actually with the effective leader of North Manchuria, Chang Tso-lin. The agreement granted China further concessions, particularly their right to acquire the railway after sixty rather than eighty years.[45]

Litvinov, in his speech on 24 April 1926, complained that the Soviet Government 'would like to remain on friendly terms with Chang Tso-lin the ruler of Manchuria if he himself does not make this impossible by hostile attacks or a hostile policy.'[46]

After the Soviet Union resisted an attempt by Chang Tso-lin to transport his troops on the railway free of charge, the Chinese arrested Ivanov, the Russian Director of the Railway. It took an ultimatum from the Soviet Union to have Ivanov freed.[47]

Neither the Chinese nor Chang Tso-lin or his son Chang Hsueh-liang had justification for any complaint about the way the railway was run. Between 1924 and 1928 the number of passengers more than doubled and freight rose from 3,000,000 tons to 5,429,000 tons. Under the 1924 Treaty, the Soviet Union was required to increase the proportion of Chinese employed on the railway to 50% of the total workforce. In fact, the Soviet Union succeeded in increasing the Chinese employees to well above 50%, so by 1928 the railway employed 13,300 Russians as against 17,841 Chinese.[48]

In breach of every obligation of international law, Chang Hsueh-liang, like his father, seized the railway on 10 July 1929 without any warning or preliminary presentation of any claims. He acted in violation of existing agreements for the joint administration of the railway and justified his action on the grounds that Bolshevik propaganda was being conducted in Manchuria.

When the Soviet Union protested, China, on 17 July 1929, defended its action. Whereas her allegations that the Soviet Union had violated the agreement were groundless, more valid were China's claims that the Soviet Union was pursuing subversive propaganda on Chinese territory and that Chinese citizens were being arrested on Soviet territory. The Soviet Union suggested that China's action was inspired by foreign imperialists, but even somebody as sympathetic to Communist Russia as Fischer agrees there is no evidence that London or Washington were in any way implicated in this action.[49]

---

[45] Fischer, Louis: *The Soviets in World Affairs*, p.548
[46] Degras, Jane: *Soviet Documents on Foreign Policy*, vol.2, p.115
[47] Fischer, Louis: *The Soviets in World Affairs*, vol.2, p.795
[48] Ibid. p.798
[49] Ibid. p.796

Litvinov had deep sympathy for China because of the exploitation it suffered. So it must have been with some sadness that he made the following press statement on 6 September 1929:

> While maintaining the greatest firmness and calmness in the face of these new provocative anti-Soviet attacks, the Soviet Government will not allow itself to be misled by the diplomatic manoeuvres of the Nanking generals or by the falsely pacifistic declarations of their representatives in Geneva, but will, as before, take and strengthen all measures necessary to defend the interests of the workers' and peasants' state and restore its rights.[50]

In the Soviet Union there was a pleasing indication that the regime had not yet become a completely totalitarian dictatorship. Many in the Soviet Union argued that it was repugnant for a Communist country to fight a war against a weak nation for the privilege of operating the railway on another's territory; but this was not Stalin's opinion. He decided to pursue a strong policy. Litvinov had his doubts about becoming involved in internal Chinese politics, but he felt that China, having previously reached an agreement, should abide by that agreement, and that strong action should be taken to safeguard the Soviet employees.

Fighting broke out on the Chinese-Soviet border on 16 August 1929. In the absence of diplomatic relations between China and the Soviet Union, the German ambassador who looked after the Soviet Union's interests tried to assist in the resolution of the matter, but the attempt failed. The Soviet Union's position was conciliatory in the sense that she was prepared to replace the present administrator and assistant if the Chinese would be willing to appoint a new chief, but the Chinese rejected the Soviet offer.[51]

After China, allegedly with the help of White Russians, had made incursions into Soviet territory, Soviet troops entered Manchuria on 16 November 1929. With Chicherin away and Litvinov in charge of the Narkomindel, the threat presented by China indicated that the Soviet Union had decided to take a tougher line; but Soviet appeasement in the early 30s in the Far East suggests that the change of personnel did not suggest a change of policy.

On 18 November 1929 the Soviet Union decided with the help of their allies, the People's Republic of Outer Mongolia, to take the offensive and decisively defeated the Chinese army. The show of force caused Chang Hsueh-liang to cable Litvinov that he was prepared to negotiate, which offer Litvinov accepted. Negotiations commenced and on 22 December 1929 a new agreement was signed between the Soviet Union, China and Chang Hsueh-liang, returning the railway to mixed Chinese-Soviet management. This military operation was a considerable triumph for the Red Army. As *The New York Times* commented on 28

---

[50] Degras, Jane: *Soviet Documents on Foreign Policy*, vol.2, p.395
[51] Dallin, David: *Rise of China in Asia*, p.267

November, the Soviet military action 'assumes the aspect of another punitive act, but on a larger scale than hitherto.' Fischer commented: 'They had given the Chinese a severe slap, humiliated them by disarming 10,000 troops and scared Chang Hsueh-liang into a settlement by a relatively small operation which led to no entanglements.'[52]

On 3 December 1929 the USA delivered a note to the Soviet Union and China reminding them of their obligations under the Kellogg Pact to renounce war. Litvinov stated on 4 December 1929 that the note cannot be regarded other than putting totally 'unjustifiable pressure on the negotiations' between the governments of the Soviet Union and Manchuria and 'consequently cannot be considered a friendly act. In conclusion, the Soviet Union cannot but help expressing its astonishment that the United States, which by its own desire has no official relations with the Soviet Union, finds it possible to supply it with advice and directions.'[53] When Litvinov considered it appropriate he was not afraid of being firm, even with those countries with whom he was striving for better relations, particularly the USA.

The next day Litvinov, with much justification, criticised the Western powers for the way in which, while in theory they allowed China to keep its freedom, they exploited China for the Western powers' economic benefit. Litvinov said:

> It ill became foreigners who had oppressed China in the past, whose armed forces are still encamped on Chinese soil and whose gunboats were still anchored in Chinese ports to cast stones at the Soviet Union, who has abandoned its territorial rights and even now did not occupy an inch of Chinese territory, despite extreme provocation. Perhaps Mr Stimson (US Secretary of State) did not know, but unfortunately there was no Soviet envoy at Washington to inform him. Why judge on Nanking's version alone. Had Mr Stimson consulted Mukden before he sent his intervention note or did he obtain this information from J J Mantel, whose Soviet phobia was notorious?[54]

J J Mantel was an American railway manager who had been appointed during the troubled Civil War time to manage the Trans-Siberian Railway.[55]

In his 1929 speech to the Central Committee, Litvinov spoke of the Soviet Union's relationship with China in the following terms:

> It is because the history of the relations between the Chinese rulers and our Soviet

---

[52] *The New York Times*, 28 November 1929, p.2; Fischer, Louis: *The Soviets in World Affairs*, vol.2, p.801

[53] *The New York Times*, 4 December 1929, p.1; Degras, Jane: *Soviet Documents on Foreign Policy*, vol.2 p. 408

[54] *The New York Times*, 5 December 1929, p.2

[55] See no 9 ante

Union in recent years is a history of single handed on their part tearing up of voluntary concluded agreements, of raids and arbitrary expropriation and the brutal treatment of Soviet officials in China. There cannot be the least doubt that without the silent and active encouragement of the other powers in the early stages of the conflict and without being able to count on the all-pervading anti-Soviet hostility the Nanking Government would never have decided upon the provocative policy which led to the present situation.[56]

Litvinov spoke the truth, as none of the great powers showed any concern at the way the Soviet Union had been treated.

China was probably the greatest failure of Soviet foreign policy in the 1920s. The policy of interfering in China's affairs had brought little dividend. It appears it was Stalin personally who supported the alliance of Communists and the Kuomintang. Others, including Chicherin, had argued against it, so Stalin had ordered that Chinese affairs be transferred from Narkomindel to a special commission of the Politburo.[57]

A serious conflict had occurred between Chicherin, who supported Borodin, and Litvinov, who had a poor opinion of Borodin and thought that Japan would prove to be a more effective ally than China. Litvinov was in favour of coming to terms with Japan over spheres of influence. In 1925 Stalin rejected such a policy as being contrary to revolutionary Communism, although a safer policy would have been to establish spheres of influence.[58]

Whereas it could be argued that the British, by their raid on the Arcos trade mission, had infringed the Soviet Union's diplomatic immunity, Britain had not physically harmed any Soviet citizen, unlike China. Discussions between Stalin and Litvinov reveal that Litvinov wanted to avoid the Soviet Union being drawn into a dispute with the Chinese from which the Soviet Union might find it hard to escape. In conversation with Hilger, Litvinov asserted that too much attention was being paid to China for too little reward.[59]

Nevertheless, Stalin saw the possibilities of instigating revolutionary activity by taking a tough line. On 29 August 1929 Stalin wrote to Molotov, and expressed his view:

The point is really to use our tough position to unmask completely and to undermine the authority of Chiang Kai-shek's Government [which Stalin considered] was a government of lackeys of imperialism for attempting to become the model of national government for colonial and dependent countries. There can

---

[56] Documents, 1929, pp. 192 & 193
[57] Dallin, David: *Rise of Russia in Asia*, p.227
[58] Dallin, David: *Rise of Russia in Asia*, p.241
[59] Hilger, Gustav: *Incompatible Allies*, p.112

be no doubt that each clash between Chiang Kai-shek and the Soviet Government, just as each concession Chiang Kai-shek makes to us (and he is already starting to make concessions) is a blow against Chiang Kai-shek and exposes Chiang Kai-shek's Government as a government of lackeys of imperialism and makes it easier to carry out the revolutionary education of the workers in Colonial countries (and the Chinese workers above all). Litvinov and Karakhan (and they are not the only ones) don't see that. So much the worse for them.[60]

Stalin's comments did not mention it was he who had previously supported Chiang Kai-shek. However, on the evidence it appears that Litvinov might well have been right in reaching the conclusion (arrived at earlier by Borodin) that the Soviet Union was little able to influence Chinese events.

Japan, following two successful wars against China and Tsarist Russia in the late 19th and early 20th centuries, had already occupied Korea, giving her a common border with Manchuria, and had encroached on part of that region. She had occupied the tip of the Ladong Peninsula through which the Chinese Eastern Railway ran. Two former major ports, Dalian and Port Arthur, were also occupied by Japan.[61]

During the late 1920s, whereas Soviet relations with China had been turbulent, relations with Japan, since the final withdrawal of their intervention force from Siberia on 3 September 1922, had been remarkably tranquil. Two events outside the control of the Soviet Government discouraged Japan from having any major dispute with the Soviet Union. Japan was greatly weakened by a devastating earthquake in 1923 and a US anti-immigration bill, specifically aimed at the Japanese, passed by the US Congress in 1924. This encouraged Japan to recognise the Soviet Union in May 1925.[62] Japan was granted considerable concessions in Siberia. Japan moved closer to the Soviet Union in order not to be isolated.

It was Japan's policy to prevent the reunification of Manchuria with China, which might threaten Japan's position in South Manchuria. She therefore favoured the USSR's interest in North Manchuria, which it was hoped would help to exclude Chinese interest. Presumably, Japan regarded the Soviet Union as less of a threat in South Manchuria than China. The Soviet Union certainly wanted to exclude any of the other great powers who might be more sympathetic to any former supporters of the White cause.

In Litvinov's speech to the Central Executive Committee during December 1928, he was able to report:

---

[60] Stalin's letters to Molotov, edited by Lars T Lih, Olev V Naumov and Oleg V K Khlevniuk, letter 44, p.174

[61] Terms of peace in Jukes, Geoffrey: *Russo-Japanese War 1904-1905*, pp.86-87

[62] Fischer, Louis: *The Soviets in World Affairs*, p.555

The normal commercial and economic relations which had developed between the two countries are proof of the mutual advantage accruing. The conclusion of the fisheries agreement between the two countries created the necessary basis for exploitation of our rich supplies of fish in the Far East in conformity with our laws and interests.[63]

In 1929 Litvinov, while similarly reporting optimistically on Soviet-Japanese relations, gave an ominous and correct warning:

> There were certain groups who aim at impairing these relations. I express my belief that this group will be frustrated in the future, as they have been in the past, and my faith in the desire of the Japanese Government as well as the Japanese people to preserve and develop loyal and neighbourly relations.[64]

However, it was in this part of the world about which few people had and still have much knowledge that political events, following limited Japanese military action, resulted in the first open challenge by a major power to the authority of the League of Nations.

In September 1931 Japan invaded Manchuria. The news reached Geneva on 19 September 1931, when the League's Council was in session, so within a few hours of the news the Council was discussing the crisis.[65]

The Japanese representative was conciliatory: 'The military action was only a local incident that the Japanese Government intended to settle without delay by direct negotiations' with the Chinese Government. 'In any case, not having received full instructions, the Japanese representative stated that he must ask for a short adjournment', which the League Council reluctantly accepted.[66]

Three days later the Japanese delegate informed the Council: 'There had been no military occupation' and 'Japan intended to withdraw the military action when Japanese lives and property were no longer in danger, which it was hoped would be very soon.' His government was anxious to enter into direct negotiations with the Chinese and the best thing the Council could do would be to refrain from all intervention. Japan had been a loyal member of the League which could have been criticised if they had taken draconian action at that time. Accordingly, on 30 September 1931, the Council adopted a resolution, with the consent of both parties, 'repeating the reassuring messages that had been made' that Japan 'had no territorial designs in Manchuria and would continue to withdraw its

---

[63] Documents, 1928, p.187
[64] Ibid. 1929, p.213
[65] Walters, Francis Paul: *History of the League of Nations*, p.470
[66] Ibid. p.472

troops in proportion as safety was assured to Japanese nationals' ... and 'called upon both parties to prevent any extension of the conflict.' It further resolved 'to meet in a fortnight's time unless the situation was cleared up in the meantime.'[67] However, the first sign that Japan might not be honest over its intentions in Manchuria came when, not only did the Japanese air force bomb Chinchou, but warned the population to have nothing to do with Chang Hsueh-liang.[68]

On 5 October 1931 the League received a strongly-worded letter from USA's Secretary of State, Stimson, urging it to assert all its pressure and authority towards regulating its action in relation to Japan and informing the League that the USA, through its diplomatic representative, will endeavour to reinforce what the League does; but the fact that Stimson's statement was merely hot air is indicated by the course of events in 1937 when, upon a full-scale invasion of China by Japan, the USA did nothing. Briand, the acting Chairman of the League, took the initiative in persuading his colleagues to invite the USA to participate in discussions, because, if the Japanese action was found to be unjustified, it would be in breach of the Kellogg Pact as well as the League Covenants. In spite of Japan's objections, the USA was invited and did send the USA's Consul General in Geneva, Prentiss Gilbert, to take his seat at the League's Council table.[69] Afterwards, Gilbert, in the face of criticism in the American press from isolationists, was instructed not to attend any more Council meetings.[70]

The League acted with considerable determination on 24 October 1931 when it passed a resolution, which the Japanese representative refused to accept, calling on Japan to evacuate the territory she had seized within three weeks and, when the evacuation had been completed, 'Japan and China should enter into direct negotiations for the settlement of all questions at issue.'[71]

The USSR, who was not then a member of the League, did not in any way condemn Japanese action at this stage. Instead, in December 1931, Litvinov offered a non-aggression pact,[72] an act of appeasement greater than the universally condemned Munich agreement.

In the early 1930s there is every reason to believe that Stalin was as anxious as Litvinov to keep the Far Eastern front quiet to concentrate on Europe. Their concern over the Japanese threat was shown by the decision of the Politburo on 23 December 1931 to establish a commission to include Litvinov to develop measures to reduce the military threat from the

---

[67] Walters, Francis Paul: *History of the League of Nations*, p.473

[68] Ibid. p. 475

[69] Ibid. pp.475 & 476

[70] Ibid. p. 477

[71] Ibid. p. 480

[72] Browder, Robert Paul: *Origins of Soviet-American Diplomacy*, p.50

Far East. The commission decided and implemented a rapid rise in defence expenditure in the Far East.[73] However, both Stalin and Litvinov agreed that diplomacy was necessary to appease Japan and offered her a non-aggression pact which Japan rejected at the time of the Manchurian incident. Similarly, Stalin was enthusiastic to obtain the non-aggression pact with Japan in April 1941.[74]

At a time, when Litvinov had considerable influence on Soviet foreign policy, the Soviet Union's caution was guided by the belief that the Manchurian incident was the beginning of a widely supported anti-Soviet campaign. However, it seemed abundantly clear both at the time and subsequently that the Soviet Union's fears were unfounded. Did Litvinov really believe that the Manchurian Incident was part of an anti-Soviet campaign? I think not, as he had not believed that the Soviet Union was in peril of being attacked in 1928.[75]

John Simon became Britain's Foreign Secretary on 17 November 1931. He correctly appraised the situation when he wrote to Macdonald:

> Japan does not mean to withdraw her troops until she gets much more satisfaction than she is likely to obtain from China out of mere persuasion. On the other hand, the only thing the Council [of the League] can do is to avoid threatening sanctions and to give good advice and appeal to everybody to behave.[76]

The reason was that no confidence was felt in London regarding the likelihood of the USA taking active steps against Japan.

A J P Taylor confirms this:

> There was a legend that Stimson had proposed joint action but Simon had turned down the proposal. The legend was totally untrue and was made no truer by Stimson repeating it later. Stimson should have disclosed that President Hoover rebuked him for running the risk that USA might become involved in international affairs and warned him not to do it again.[77]

It should also not be overlooked that there was hardly any support for a policy that could lead to a conflict with Japan. A further consideration was that 'the conspiracy theory [put forward by the extreme advocates Lord Cecil and Philip Noel Baker] has had a long run, despite the fact that the historical evidence to support it is completely lacking.' Awareness

---

[73] Watson, Derek: *Molotov*, p.112
[74] See Ch.15, No.118
[75] See Ch.5, No.82
[76] Roskill, Stephen Wentworth: *Hankey, Man of Secrets*, p.27
[77] Taylor, A J P: *English History 1914-1945*, p.372

of lack of means was also present. It was realised how little we could do to deter Japan.[78] Thorne rightly compares British policy towards Japan in 1931 with the USA policy following the 1956 abortive Hungarian Revolution, in that no effective military measures could be taken as the possible price of endeavouring to compel the other party to back down could have resulted in a Third World War.[79]

If Britain was to use force it could not have been at a worse time. From an economic standpoint, military action would have been disastrous. Roskill, who has studied Hankey's papers, asked whether any government in peacetime had ever faced such intractable problems. Although compared with the 1980s unemployment at two to three million might not have appeared so acute, exports had fallen to little more than half their 1929 value. Despite the cuts which brought about the fall of the 1929/1931 Labour Government, a large government deficit was still in prospect.[80] Was it proper that the National Government, whose primary purpose was to restore the nation's finances, should be diverted from its course within a month of its being elected? If the Labour party had won the 1935 election, it would have been of no benefit to their agenda of social reform to have inherited a bankrupt economy.

In any case, Britain realised how militarily weak she was. On 28 February 1933 the Chief of Staff noted that the army thought that Hong Kong could only hold out against a Japanese attack for 21 days, while it would take 38 days for the main British fleet to reach Singapore, which was still not secure or defendable.[81]

As Japan did not comply with the League's resolution, on 10 December 1931 a report known as the 'Lytton Report' was commissioned by the League.[82]

The USA's Secretary of State informed China and Japan that the USA would refuse to recognise any situation between Japan and China brought about by force. Britain declined to follow Stimson's lead and delayed endorsing his position until Simon could carry the other members of the League with him, which he did in March 1932,[83] so non-recognition became a League principle.

Japan used the difference between the USA and Britain to its advantage. However, perhaps it would have been wiser for the USA to have endeavoured to agree a joint approach with Britain and surely the government of the USA had no right to anticipate that Britain would support USA policy without asking Britain?

---

[78] Roskill, Stephen: *Hankey, Man of Secrets*, p.27
[79] Thorne, Christopher: *The Limits of Foreign Policy: The West, the League and the Far Eastern Crisis, 1931-1933*, p.76
[80] Roskill, Stephen: *Hankey, Man of Secrets*, p.23
[81] Andrews, E M: *Writing on the Wall*, p.110
[82] Walters, Francis Paul: *History of the League of Nations*, p.480
[83] Ibid. p.487

The British note stated:

> His Majesty's Government stands by its open-door policy for international trade in Manchuria which was guaranteed by the Nine-Power Treaty signed in Washington during 1922. The Japanese representative at the Council of the League of Nations stated on 13 October 1931 that Japan was the champion in Manchuria of the principle of economic activities of all nations. Further, on 28 December 1931 the Japanese Government stated that Japan adhered to the open-door policy and would welcome participation and co-operation in any Manchurian enterprise. In view of these statements, his Majesty's Government have not considered it necessary to address any formal note to the Japanese Government on the lines of the USA Government's note, but the Japanese ambassador in London has been requested to obtain confirmation of these assurances from his government.[84]

Stimson, in his autobiography, stated the note

> was entirely silent as to the preservation of sovereignty, independence and integrity of China, the Kellogg-Briand Pact and the assertion of the principle of non-recognition of the fruits of unlawful aggression. It thus ignored entirely the question of world peace and China's integrity, which we deemed to be the most important features of the note.[85]

Alexander DeConde rightly states that: 'Hoover was opposed to any kind of sanctions, economic or military, insisting that they meant the penalties of wars except shooting. The only sanction he would support was public opinion.'[86] However, there is no evidence that world public opinion would in any way have influenced Japan. Hoover subsequently confirmed his opposition to sanctions in his memoirs, stating: 'On the question of sanctions' Hoover disagreed with his Secretary of State Stimson. 'Ever since Versailles I have held economic sanctions meant war when applied to a large nation.'[87]

Sumner Wells, the Under Secretary of State, said that the refusal of the British Government to concur with the action of the USA did much to create in the US hostility towards British policy and:

> To place the burden squarely on the British Government is not only unfair but unrealistic. The USA did not offer the slightest assurance to the British Government or to any other government of the League that the United States was

---

84 *Times*, 11 January 1932, p.13
[85] Stimson, Henry: *Far Eastern Crisis Recollections and Observations*, p.101
[86] DeConde, Alexander: *History of American Foreign Policy*, p.527
[87] Hoover, Herbert: *Memoirs*, p.366

prepared to take any action of a minatory character that would have the least effect.[88]

On 28 January 1932 the Japanese switched their attention to Central China when they seized Shanghai. Although President Hoover wanted to address a joint appeal to the Emperor of Japan, signed by both King George V and himself, the British Prime Minister Ramsay Macdonald refused.[89] Secretary of State Stimson visited Europe in May 1932 and there was agitation for economic sanctions by the Chinese and internationalists.

Hoover instructed his Secretary of State to include a statement that the President was opposed to economic sanctions.[90] If the USA had been prepared to use economic sanctions and if Britain had done the same it might have influenced Japan, but economic sanctions, without both USA and Britain applying them, and excluding oil, would surely have failed.

Those who emphasise the significance of Japanese aggression in Manchuria on the decline of the League are absolutely correct. However, as neither the USA nor Britain were prepared to even impose economic sanctions under any circumstances, it is quite wrong for either to blame the other for failure to stand up to Japan.

Alfred Zimmern admitted in 1935:

> None of the major powers was willing to take the lead in action against aggressors. None was even willing to promise publicly co-operation if and whenever the others took action.[91]

It is my view that the USA overestimated the effect of non-recognition, unless either or both USA and Britain threatened force and were prepared to use force if other methods failed. Even if Britain had supported the USA's note regarding non-recognition, it would not have been effective without a credible threat of force. The great powers, including the Soviet Union were unwilling

> to take any action and the impunity with which Japan was able to proceed upon her course and withdraw from the League were the direct causes for the decision reached two years later by the Italian Government to undertake the conquest of Abyssinia. It also contributed to the decision of Adolf Hitler when he came to power a year later to embark upon the creation by force and violence of his greater Germany.[92]

---

[88] Welles, Sumner: *Time for Decision*, p.216
[89] Hoover, Herbert: *Memoirs*, p.374
[90] Ibid. p.376
[91] Zimmern, Alfred: *The League of Nations and the Rule of Law*, p.418
[92] Welles, Sumner: *Time for Decision*, p.217

As the Soviet Government received no response from Japan concerning their offer of a non-aggression pact, they not unreasonably took a more belligerent attitude.

On 4 March 1932 *Izvestiya* published an article stating:

> Since September, the Soviet Government had done everything in its power to continue proper relations with Japan, despite the direct interest the Soviet Union must have in any activities in Manchuria. However, the Japanese Government had chosen to continue anti-Soviet acts and accusations to the point where the Soviet Union was forced to take cognizance of them and in return informed Tokyo that she was aware of the underlying plans of the Japanese for aggression against the Soviet Union.[93]

Finally, the Lytton Report was published in October 1932. Although it found many of Japan's complaints justified, it censored Japan for resorting to force before peaceful means had been exhausted. Drummond, the Secretary of the League, sent a copy of the Report to those non-members of the League who had signed the Kellogg Pact and invited those countries to co-operate with a Consultative Committee set up by the League. The Soviet Union was such a country.

It might have been expected that Litvinov and his government would have been pleased that the Lytton Report recognised the important interest which the Soviet Union had in the region, as owners of the Chinese Eastern Railway, and on account of the long border which it shared with Manchuria. It is clear that any solution of the problems in Manchuria which ignored the important interests of the USSR would risk a future breach of the peace and would not be permanent.[94]

Litvinov's response was hardly encouraging to those who wanted to take a firm line against aggression. Litvinov pointed out:

> Thirteen of the twenty-two nations involved in the Advisory Committee of the League did not maintain any relations with the Soviet Union, and it is permissible to doubt whether such states could really take into consideration the interests of the USSR. The USSR intended to follow a course of strict neutrality, although it would naturally look with favour on action to secure a just and speedy termination of the conflict.[95]

Again was this not appeasement ?

---

[93] Browder, Robert Paul: *Origins of Soviet-American Diplomacy*, p.51
[94] Lytton report, League Document 132, pp.vii, 12
[95] Moore, Harriet: *Soviet Far Eastern Policy 1931-1945*, p.23

Sheinis takes the traditional communist view criticising the softly-softly approach of the USA and Britain. He also espoused the view of communists and fellow travellers that virtually every act of foreign policy was motivated by hatred of the USSR. The argument was that, because Britain and the USA took no action, they hoped that Japan would be bogged down in a war against China and would then inevitably come to grips with the Soviet Union

There is no evidence that the motives of the USA and Britain, in not taking action, had any connection with the Soviet Union; but, as explained above, the reasons were largely economic. Both were in the grip of the worst economic depression that either country had experienced. Britain, as we have seen, knew she was in no position to defend her Far Eastern interest in any military confrontation with Japan. Sheinis alleged, peculiarly, that the motive of the Lytton Committee in travelling to the USA and Japan before going to China and Manchuria 'was to prompt Japan to mount fresh provocation against the Soviet Union.'[96] Again, there is not a shred of evidence to support this theory. Sheinis failed to mention that the Soviet Union's approach to the conflict was also weak.

The League was asking for the Soviet Union's help, although many of its members were still refusing to recognise the Bolshevik Government, and on this ground it could be argued that it was unreasonable to expect the Soviet Union to assist the League.

In his survey for 1932, Mr A J Toynbee sums up the policy of the Soviet Government towards the Japanese military adventure:

> It was one of invincible restraint and impenetrable reserve. So far as it concerned their rights and interests and assets on Manchurian soil, they steadfastly responded to Japanese encroachment by turning the other cheek and their settled policy was evidently one of a policy of peace, at any price, short of actual invasion of Soviet soil.[97]

Later, many who wished to attack the Chamberlain policy of appeasement criticised Simon's policy towards Japan, in order to belittle Chamberlain's policy at and after Munich. Whereas Liddell Hart was absolutely right to say that 'military action was difficult', he was wrong to say that 'economic or moral pressure', as he advocated, without the participation of the USA would have in any way deterred Japan. Liddell Hart criticised those who argued 'that no direct British interests were involved because Japan had attacked British interests in China.'[98] However, Britain without the USA's active participation would probably have lost any war against Japan.

---

[96] Sheinis, Zinovy: *Maxim Litvinov*, p.213
[97] *Survey of International Affairs,* 1932, p.533
98 *Headway*, October 1938, p.14

One of the problems of economic sanctions is what do you do if they fail? As in Iraq following the first Gulf War, more and more countries begin to defy them. Indeed, one of the problems of economic sanctions is: what do you do if they fail? Indeed, Litvinov was also guilty of hypocrisy and fuelled the mythical theory as to the efficacy of economic sanctions. In 1938 Litvinov stated: 'One threat of sanctions by the League of Nations or one conference between Britain, USA and the Soviet Union would have been enough for Japan to have retreated and dropped its prey.'[99] Litvinov very much underestimated Japanese determination once they had decided on an aggressive path and it would not have been an easy military and naval operation for the USA and/or Britain to defeat Japan. Hoover was told that a war between Japan and the USA would be won, but the victory would take six years to secure on its own and two years if Britain put their entire fleet under the joint command.[100]

When Japan commenced its invasion of Manchuria, there were no diplomatic relations between China and the Soviet Union. These had been severed in 1927. There is every reason to believe that, once Litvinov was in charge of the Foreign Commissariat, he strove to restore diplomatic relations with China, which he eventually achieved on 12 December 1932. It has sometimes been argued that Litvinov concentrated on European politics. However, he took the opportunity to emphasise:'The Soviet Union had freed China from unequal treaties, the extra-territoriality and other rights wrung by Tsarist imperialism and agreed to transform the railway concession into a commercial undertaking under the joint management of the USSR and China.'[101] Here, no doubt, he was speaking from the heart and with pride.

As the Japanese invasion of Manchuria interrupted the operation of the Chinese Eastern Railway, on 2 May 1933 the Soviet Union proposed to sell its interest in the railway to Japan for 160,000,000 yen. In a press statement, Litvinov justified the sale.[102] Was this not appeasement? The sale did not then proceed because, in Litvinov's words, the Japanese offered 'a paltry ridiculous sum of 130,000,000 yen.' Eventually, the Soviet Union accepted the Japanese offer of 140,000,000 yen. The agreement was completed on 12 March 1935.[103] However, the sale did not please China, who stated:

> While the Soviet Union might have deemed it fit to surrender her own interests in the Railway to a third person, be it real or fictitious, China can never recognise any party as a successor to any rights and interests in the railway. No railway can be

---

[99] Degras, Jane: *Soviet Documents on Foreign Policy*, vol.3, p.293

[100] Thorne, Christopher: *The Limits of Foreign Policy: The West, the League and the Far Eastern Crisis 1931-1933*, p.76

[101] Degras, Jane: *Documents on Soviet Foreign Policy*, vol.2, p.551

[102] Press statement of Litvinov, printed in Moore, Harriet: *Soviet Far Eastern Policy 1931-1945*, p.222

[103] Ibid. p.42

held by any person or organisation in the territory of China without her explicit consent. The Soviet Union's present action constitutes, without a shadow of doubt, a direct violation of China's contractual as well as sovereign rights. The painful fact that the Chinese people have been prevented by circumstances for which they were not responsible from exercising its rights in connection with the administration of the Chinese Eastern Railway does not in the least affect the validity of the provisions of the agreement of 1924 nor the status of the railway.[104]

The Soviet Union's reply was set out in *Izvestiya*:

> Every thinking Chinese patriot knows the USSR would have been deeply happy if it had been possible to turn over the Railway to the great Chinese people, friendship with whom is especially valued by the people of the USSR; but the Chinese people are not masters of the situation in Manchuria and they would gain nothing if the CER [Chinese Eastern Railway] became an object of war, which might destroy this Far Eastern Railroad.[105]

Was this, again, not appeasement, which Litvinov constantly condemned?

When Litvinov made his speech on 29 December 1933 he stated, in respect of Manchuria

> We were only trying to obtain from Japan one thing – the observance of our commercial interest in the Chinese Eastern Railway, because we have no other interests in Manchuria. In spite of all the solemn promises, the representatives of Japan in Manchuria soon began a direct attack on our interests, endeavouring to make quite impossible the management of the CER jointly with the Chinese or Manchurians as provided for in the agreement, disrupting the working on the line itself. … The whole world was surprised at our composure.

Litvinov correctly diagnosed Japan as: 'The darkest storm cloud on the international political horizon.' Although the Soviet Union subsequently joined the other major powers in condemning Japan's action over Manchuria, the Soviet Union, at least initially, was in no way prepared to take stern measures, as Litvinov later admitted in this speech. He gave two reasons for refusing to participate in the international actions at this time:

> The first reason was because USSR did not believe in the sincerity and consistency of the States taking part in this action, but chiefly (second reason) because we did not seek, as we do not now, an armed conflict with Japan.

Is this again not appeasement, which Litvinov would later consistently condemn?

---

[104] Press statement ,printed in Moore, Harriet: *Soviet Far Eastern Policy 1931-1945*, p.45
[105] Ibid.

Litvinov accused Japan of violent action against Soviet employees of the railway.

He further stated:

> The question of war against the Soviet Union for the seizure of the Maritime provinces and the entire Far Eastern region is being discussed by Japanese statesmen, including official representatives of the Japanese Government, as well as the press. The matter is not merely confined to conversations, but a considerable number of troops have been concentrated in Manchuria along our frontier, war material is being brought up and roads and railways built. The threat has occurred not only for the violent seizure of our line by Japan but a direct threat to our frontiers. With such a state of affairs there is nothing left for us to do except to enter upon strengthening our frontiers.

Litvinov did not make the normal accusation that the capitalist nations were encouraging Japan to attack the Soviet Union; but, on the contrary, he said that Japan's 'operation against China and her possible operation against us is condemned by the whole civilised world.' Litvinov criticised 'the provocative acts of the Japanese' and he warned that 'Japan is feverishly preparing for war, which can be no other than aggressive since no one is threatening the safety of Japan.' Litvinov also said, 'In our argument with Japan even the capitalist world admits the correctness of our stand and attributes aggressive measures exclusively to Japan.' Litvinov added, 'The capitalists do it, not out of love for us, but because if they approved of Japan's operation and political methods and thus strengthened her position, then tomorrow they may find the same methods directed against their own interests.'

In respect of China, Litvinov stated that 'normal diplomatic relations had been resumed', and it is interesting to note he used the words 'the great Chinese Republic.' He asserted: 'We have accepted the proposal of the Chinese Government for a non-aggression pact.' Then, referring to Japan, although not by name, Litvinov claimed that China was suffering from the invasion of a foreign enemy and deep internal discord. His next remark was ambiguous: 'While strictly adhering to the policy of non-intervention, we are watching its struggle for national unity with the greatest sympathy.'[106] Soviet policy was hardly honest. On the one hand the Soviet Union was supporting China against Japan and on the other allowing the Comintern to operate in China.

At the 17th Conference of the Soviet Communist Party in January 1934, Stalin stated:

> The relationship between the USSR and Japan is in need of serious improvement. Japan's refusal to sign a pact of non-aggression, which Japan needs no less than the Soviet Union, emphasises that all is not well in the domain of our relations. The

---

[106] Litvinov's speech, *Moscow News*, 6 January 1934, pp.4 & 14

same thing must be said of the interruption of negotiations on the Chinese Eastern Railway which took place through no fault of the USSR and also in regard to the fact that Japanese agents are committing intolerable, outrageous action on the CER, illegally arresting its Soviet employees and so on.

In addition:

> A section of the military in Japan is openly preaching in the press the necessity of a war with the USSR and the seizure of the maritime provinces with the open approval of another section of the military while the government of Japan pretends that this does not concern it, instead of calling the incendiarists of war to order. It is not difficult to understand that such circumstances cannot but create an atmosphere of unrest and uncertainty. Of course we will persistently continue our policy of peace in the future and will endeavour to secure an improvement in our relations with Japan since we desire an improvement of these relations, but here everything does not depend on us. We must at the same time adopt all measures to guard our country against surprises and be ready to defend against attack.[107]

In emphasising the need for defence and the wish to live in peace, the phraseology was remarkably similar to that of Litvinov.

During 1934 Chiang Kai-shek made a concerted and (in the short term) successful attempt to defeat the Communists in the South. As a result of these tactics and to avoid annihilation, Mao decided to break out and therefore started what became known as the Long March, which propelled the Communist army six thousand miles from the south to the north of China. It started with a force of 90,000 men, but as it had to encounter running battles on the way, at the end it was reduced to 20,000 men. The Long March has been compared to Hannibal's trek across the Alps and Napoleon's retreat from Moscow. It was longer than either and certainly more difficult. At the completion of the Long March the Communists were far from decimated, but operated in separate small units in the northern part of China, where their presence was only slightly less of a menace than it had been when previously concentrated in a single Communist area.[108]

By 1936 a remarkable U-turn had been effected because of the threat posed by Japan. Although the Sino-Japanese war did not break out for another year, in October 1936 the Chinese Red Army was ordered to cease taking the offensive against Chiang Kai-shek's forces. This change helped to stimulate dissatisfaction among Chiang Kai-shek's forces. Chiang Kai-shek was dramatically taken prisoner by one of the Chinese officers, General Chang. The part of the army that supported this rebellion complained that, instead of concentrating the Army's efforts on defeating the rising danger from Japan, they were

---

[107] Stalin's speech, *Moscow News*, 3 February 1934, p.4
[108] Karnow, Stanley: *Mao and China*, p.44

concentrating their efforts on fighting Chinese Communists. The rebels demanded that Chiang Kai-shek's forces stop harrying the Communists and respond to the demands for an internal truce and for co-operation with the Red forces against Japan. Eventually, after mediation (Chiang Kai-shek's wife was involved), Chiang was released unharmed and returned to Nanking. His release was made the occasion for widespread public rejoicing and demonstrations. The regional commanders in all parts of China, who had abstained from all overt attempts to exploit the crisis in their own interests, united in fervid expressions of congratulations to Chiang Kai-shek.[109] As in the case of the attempted *coup d'etat* against Gorbachev in 1991, the conspirators, when they realised that the Communist elite was not going to give them general support, surrendered rather than cause bloodshed. Lack of support from the military elite forced General Chang to surrender and face trial. Although at a court martial Chang was condemned to ten years' imprisonment, he was almost immediately released.[110]

In a major speech in December 1936, although criticising an agreement between Germany and Japan, Litvinov is silent on China, instead entirely directing his efforts to Europe with the crisis of the Rhineland.[111]

Now a much greater threat appeared for China – a possible invasion by Japan. As so often occurred, Litvinov correctly forecast the future, saying it might come at any moment. He was not so wrong. The major invasion of China by Japan would occur in the following year.[112]

---

[109] *Survey of International Affairs,* 1936, p.886
[110] Ibid.
[111] *Moscow News*, speech, 9 December 1936, p.5
[112] See Ch.15, No.83

8: LITVINOV'S SUCCESSES WITH FRANCE, POLAND AND GERMANY

During the 1920s the Soviet Union's relations with Germany had been satisfactory. This situation was only interrupted by two needless trials of German citizens, no doubt initiated by Stalin. Relations with Britain while there was a Conservative Government had been either poor or non-existent. Relations with France had for the most part been lukewarm, but relations with Poland, particularly after 1925, had improved. During the early 1930s Litvinov expended much effort in improving relations with both these countries with considerable success, but his efforts to improve relations with Britain were made more difficult by Stalin's action in making accusations of sabotage against employees of British companies, and arresting Soviet citizens employed by the British embassy.

FRANCE

Even before Litvinov was appointed Deputy Commissar, he seized the opportunity of trying to improve relations with France. An occasion presented itself when a representative of French commercial interests arrived in Copenhagen. Litvinov stated in the spring of 1920: 'Russia wished to pay its debts, but it cannot do so until the Civil War is over on the different fronts created against us by France.' Litvinov argued, 'It was to France's advantage to be on good terms with Russia.' Britain wanted to weaken Russia by supporting all the small states. British policy was aimed 'at reducing both Russia and France to slavery.'[1]

In June 1922, when the future leader of the Radical Party, Herriot, went to Moscow, the first attempt was made by a French politician to improve relations with the Soviet Union which had been frozen since the Bolshevik Revolution of 1917. Herriot on that visit pledged to recognise the Soviet Union, if his party was elected to office. In June 1924 when Herriot, as leader of a Left coalition, was appointed Prime Minister, it was anticipated that recognition by France of the Soviet Government would quickly follow. Herriot's main preoccupation in the summer of 1924 was relations with Germany, as well as paying a visit to Britain's new Prime Minister Macdonald. [2] It was not until September 1924 that Herriot appointed a commission to draft the terms of recognition, appointing De Monzie as its Chairman − one of those most enthusiastic for France to recognise the Soviet Union. After the final details were negotiated between the Soviet Ambassador to Britain,

---

[1] Debo, Keith: *Survival and Consolidation*, p.159
[2] Carr, Edward H: *Socialism in One Country*, p.38

Rakovsky, and De Monzie on 28 October 1924, Herriot announced *de jure* recognition of the Soviet Government and the readiness of France to exchange ambassadors.[3]

It was not made a condition of the restoration of diplomatic relations that the Soviet Government acknowledge the former Russian Government's outstanding loans to the French Government, but it was agreed that such debts might be acknowledged if a loan to the Soviet Government was made available and that these matters would be subject to later negotiations. However, subsequently the Soviet Union and France were unable to reach an agreement. As usual, the Soviet Union insisted that France must give the Soviet Union a long-term loan if the debts were to be acknowledged. The problem was that France's resources were such that she was less able to make such a loan than the British Government, even if the French Government had been willing.[4] Krassin arrived in early December 1924 to become the Soviet Union's first ambassador to France, and Herbette, the first ambassador to the Soviet Union, arrived in January 1925.[5]

Herriot's foreign policy had been marked from the beginning by a strong desire to keep in touch with Britain. Recognition of the Soviet Union by France was similar to the aims of Macdonald's Labour Government, but the situation was entirely changed by the election in Britain of the anti-Soviet Baldwin administration. Chamberlain, the new British Foreign Secretary, hastened to Paris to endeavour to discourage the French Premier from too close a Soviet-French collaboration.[6]

The fall of the Herriot government in April 1925[7] decreased the chance of an agreement with the Soviet Union. Painlevé, the new Prime Minister, was more hostile to the Soviet Union than Herriot. Briand, the Foreign Minister, was less interested.[8] By September 1925 further talks to settle the outstanding Russian debt in return for a loan reached deadlock.[9] Krassin returned to Moscow to be replaced by Rakovsky, with the intention of improving relations with France.

With the Locarno Treaty looming, and Germany moving in step with Great Britain, any deterioration in Franco-Soviet relations was most unwelcome in Moscow. Chicherin arrived in Paris on 30 November 1925 for the purpose of assisting in strengthening Franco-Soviet relations, only to find that his Foreign Office counterpart had left for London to sign the Locarno Treaty. Chicherin tactfully retired to the Riviera[10] until Briand came back to Paris, when Chicherin immediately returned and talks proceeded. Although nothing

---

[3] Carr Edward: *Socialism in One Country* p.40

[4] Ibid. p. 44

[5] Ibid. p. 42

[6] Ibid.

[7] Ibid. p. 44

[8] Ibid. p. 419

[9] Ibid. p. 420

[10] Ibid. p. 421

concrete was agreed during the talks, Chicherin gave a very optimistic interview, published in both *Izvestiya* and *Le Temps*, referring to 'the profound change in the state of mind and in public opinion in France with regards to my country.'

In a further press statement in Berlin, Chicherin stated, 'There are no serious difficulties', at the same time comparing it favourably with the consistently hostile attitude of the British Government.[11] Those who try to portray Chicherin as being primarily interested in Asia are surely wrong, as, particularly in 1925, Chicherin had devoted many months to the Soviet Union's relations with Germany and France.

The Soviet Union, still wanting to settle the debt problems with France, sent another delegation.[12] However, the negotiations again reached deadlock. The Soviet delegation hardened its attitude, firstly on account of France's action in recognising the Locarno Treaty in March, thus dashing any slender hopes that might have been entertained in Moscow of detaching France from her partners.[13]

The second factor was the fiasco of Germany's attempt to be admitted to the League of Nations, which encouraged Germany not to allow negotiations with the Soviet Union to deteriorate.[14] The formal talks between France and the Soviet Union dragged on until June, when they were adjourned.[15]

Meanwhile, in July 1926 Poincaré had reappeared as Prime Minster with a spectacular mandate to save the Franc.[16] Negotiations between the French and Soviet Governments on the Soviet debts and credits broke down. How far French foreign policy was influenced by the deteriorating relationship of the Soviet Union with Britain, that led to the ending of diplomatic relations, is uncertain, but relations between Britain and the Soviet Union steadily deteriorated, which eventually led to the breach of diplomatic relations.[17]

Relations between the Soviet Union and France were hindered when, on 10 June 1926, France signed a treaty with Rumania in which France agreed to assist in maintaining, even if necessary by war, the existing *status quo*. On 10 October 1926 the Soviet charge d'affaires protested, reiterating that the Soviet Union had never accepted that Bessarabia should be part of Rumania,[18] although on 6 December 1926 Chicherin reported an improvement in their relations with France.[19]

---

[11] Carr, Edward: *Socialism in One* Country p.421
[12] Ibid. p.423
[13] Ibid. p.424
[14] Walters   *The History of the League of Nations, p.*321
[15] Carr Edward: *Socialism in One Country,* p.425
[16] Ibid.
[17] Ch.9, No.77
[18] Degras, Jane: *Soviet Documents on Foreign Policy,* vol.2, p.137
[19] Ibid.   vol.2, p.146

In 1929 Litvinov describes the relationship with France as 'normal although strained', but commented that if 'the French bourgeois press, as a whole, reflects in the slightest degree the opinion of the French Government's attitude to us, then those relations must be regarded as very unsatisfactory.'[20]

On 26 June 1930 Stalin called France 'the most aggressive of nations.' A few months later, an outcry against Soviet dumping, chiefly of wheat, gave the French Government the opportunity to flaunt a similarly low opinion of Stalin's regime.[21]

However, just before Litvinov's formal appointment as Foreign Commissar in July 1930, he had already endeavoured to improve Franco-Soviet relations, with meetings on 26 February 1930 and on 10 March 1931. Litvinov stated: 'Although France had played a more active role in the foreign intervention after the Revolution, he nonetheless considered Britain the real culprit.'[22] Clearly, this shows the ruthless politician. Although Litvinov wanted to improve relations with Britain, he did not mind what he said about Britain to others if it helped Litvinov achieve his foreign office objectives. Molotov also gave strong support to improving relations with France; but, until the scare created in France by the proposed customs union between Germany and Austria on 21 March 1931, France gave no importance to improved relations with the Soviet Union.

It was Hitler's rise to power that caused French politicians to realise that the Soviet Union could be a useful ally. On 29 August 1932 Germany suggested that she and France should engage in confidential negotiations about the immediate application of equality of rights in armaments. France rejected Germany's overtures for bilateral talks.[23] Herriot told the British:'The solution could only be found in equality of status in eventual disarmament. There must be no rearmament by Germany.'[24] It was an idle threat because, even if France had the military means, she lacked the political will to prevent the rearmament of Germany.

By the end of September 1932 France was so concerned about German rearmament that she had discarded her passive attitude towards a rapprochement with the Soviet Union.[25] France's ally, Rumania, initially participated in talks with Litvinov, who quite clearly was working for a reconciliation with Rumania, although the Soviet Union would not abandon its claim to Bessarabia. The Rumanian ambassador to Britain, Titulescu, resigned so that he could speak openly with regard to the proposed Franco-Soviet Non-aggression Pact, which he regarded as a serious error. He argued it would weaken Rumania's occupation of Bessarabia, a curious argument as the proposed pact did not affect Bessarabia. He was then

---

[20] Documents, 1929, p.211

[21] Scott, William: *Alliance Against Hitler*, p.1

[22] Phillips, Hugh: *Between the Revolution and the West*, p.209, notes 6 and 7

[23] Scott, William: *Alliance Against Hitler*, p.60

[24] Ibid.   p.61

[25] Ibid.   p.64

appointed Foreign Minister.[26] Nevertheless, Herriot was not prepared to delay the finalisation of the proposed Franco-Soviet Pact and he gave notice of that fact at his party's conference, which met between 3 and 6 November 1932. Following negotiations, the Franco-Soviet Pact was signed on 29 November 1932.[27]

The most important provision in the Pact was that the two governments promised not to resort either to war or aggression against each other and, should either party be an object of aggression by one or more third parties, the other party agreed not to give aid or assistance to the aggressor during the period of the conflict.[28]

The Russians were well pleased that the negotiations for the treaty had been successful. *Izvestiya* stated:

> Just as the signing by Germany of a similar pact at Locarno did not remove those interests out of which was created the friendly attitude between the German people and the Soviet Union, similarly the policy of rapprochement between the Soviet Union and France should not injure these relations. Our relations with Germany have been and are still directed towards the mutual interests of both peoples.[29]

Poland was pleased with the Pact because it believed it complimented and reinforced their own.[30]

France claimed the Pact would end the liaison between the Reichswehr and the Red Army,[31] and would block Soviet support for Germany,[32] although in 1939 the Soviet Union failed to abide by the Pact. Coincidentally, Herriot was Prime Minister both when France recognised the Soviet Union in 1924 and when the Franco-Soviet Pact was signed in 1932. In 1924 he was influenced by a romantic comparison of the French and Russian Revolutions gained during his visit to Russia in 1922. However, by 1932 this view had no doubt changed.

Herriot had watched the unscrupulous battle waged by French Communists. Further, the Soviet Union had become far more of a totalitarian state under Stalin's leadership than when France recognised the Soviet Union in 1924. Nevertheless, in 1934 Herriot quite rightly stated: 'France was not strong enough to ignore the advantage of political co-operation with the Soviet Union.'[33]

---

[26] Scott William, *Alliance against Hitler,* p.68
[27] Ibid.   p.69
[28] Ibid.
[29] Ibid.   p.72
[30] Ibid.
[31] Ibid.   p.72
[32] Ibid.   p.69
[33] Ibid.   p.71

When addressing the Central Executive Committee on 29 December 1933, Litvinov spoke optimistically of the rapid significant improvement in relations with other countries: 'Our relations with France after the signing of the Non-aggression Pact have made rapid strides.'

Litvinov was most generous to France concerning her frequent change of governments when he said:

> We have the advantage of a stable government and a stable foreign policy, while in France the government is frequently changing, with possible alteration in political orientation. In so much as the French people sincerely desire peace, and it is just that desire which joins us to France, we need not fear particularly that a change of government will hinder the development of our close relations.

Litvinov then praised Herriot in glowing terms as 'one of the most prominent and brilliant representatives of the French people and one who reflects their peace-loving sentiments.'[34] Such language was in stark contrast to Litvinov's words about many of Britain's politicians.

1934 was, as far as the Soviet Union was concerned, a highly successful year in Franco-Soviet relations. France, after gaining the support of her allies, Britain and Poland, successfully campaigned for the Soviet Union to become a member of the League of Nations with a permanent seat on the Council.

POLAND

The Provisional Government under Kerensky had announced that it would assist in the forming of an independent Polish state composed of all territories where the Poles were in the majority.[35] The Poles were further encouraged when the new Bolshevik government published a decree annulling all treaties and agreements concluded between the government of the former Russian Empire with Germany and the Austro-Hungarian Empire concerning the partition of Poland.[36] All seemed (from the Polish viewpoint) to be going to plan, although the final boundary between Russia and Poland had not been finally settled before Poland, in my opinion without justification, invaded Russia in 1920. Following the Peace Treaty of Riga, territory was incorporated into Poland where only 30% of the population were Poles.[37] The reason the Bolsheviks agreed to lose so much of their territory might have been that the more non-Poles there were in that area, the greater the chance of a successful revolt by the ethnic Rumanian and Russian people.

---

[34] *Moscow News*, 6 January 1934, p.4
[35] Konovalov, Sergyei: *Russo-Polish Relations*, p.33
[36] Ibid.
[37] Ibid.   p.36; and Ch.3

No sooner had the Russo-Polish war finished than the Polish general Zeligowski, in October 1920, seized the Lithuanian town and district of Vilnius. The Soviet Government disapproved, even after the award of the district to Poland by the Conference of Ambassadors in 1923, the effect of which was to sanction use of force. It appeared an unfair decision in any event on its merits. In Vilnius town, Poles were outnumbered by Jews. Outside the town of Vilnius, Poles were numerically insignificant.[38] Of more international significance was the fact that the rule of the League of Nations had been flouted by force.[39]

Further relations between Poland and Lithuania continued to be hostile, but relations between Lithuania and the Soviet Union were better than with any of the Soviet Union's Western neighbours. However, this was purely a marriage of convenience. During the Second World War the majority of Lithuanians tended to side with the Germans. It is difficult to criticise Lithuania for doing so because, whereas the Germans occupied Lithuania for three years, the Soviet Union would occupy Lithuania for almost fifty years. Nevertheless, at the conclusion of the Second World War the Soviet Union returned Vilnius to Lithuania.[40] When, in 1991, Lithuania regained her independence, Poland had abandoned any claim to it.

Following the Russo-Polish war, Poland continued to be hostile to the Soviet Union. Postal and railway services between Poland and the Soviet Union were not restored until 1925.[41] Several conferences were organised between Poland, Finland, Estonia and Latvia for the purpose of agreeing action in their relationship with the Soviet Union, the last of which was on 16 January 1925. The Soviet Union objected, protesting that such agreement was tantamount to an alliance against Soviet Russia. Finland acceded to the objection and rejected such joint co-operation against the Soviet Union in the summer of 1923. By 1925 Latvia took a similar view to Finland, saying, 'We do not wish to become an enemy of one country by drawing closer to another.'[42]

The continued hostility between the Soviet Union and Poland appeared to have been the fault of Poland. However, in June 1925 a Polish trade delegation visited the Soviet Union and Chicherin stopped at Warsaw en route to Berlin on the eve of the Locarno agreement being signed.[43] Again, it seems that Chicherin was as keen as Litvinov to improve relations with Poland. Chicherin stressed: 'The conclusion of a lasting agreement between Poland and the USSR would have a profound influence upon the whole international complex of forces and relations.'[44]

---

[38] Ibid.. p.38
[39] See Ch.12, No.2
[40] Kiaupa, Zigmus: *History of Lithuania*, p.405
[41] Fischer, Louis: *The Soviets in World Affairs*, p.519
[42] Ibid. p.519
[43] Ibid. p.520
[44] Budurowycz, Bohdan: *Polish-Soviet Relations*, p.5

In his 1926 speech to the Central Committee of the Soviet Communist Party, Litvinov correctly stated, 'We attach great importance to a stable and lasting relationship with our nearest Western neighbours, in particular with Poland.' Litvinov reminded Poland: ' There are Polish people who cry out about the danger threatening Poland from the East', but that 'restoration and consolidation of Poland's independence would not have been possible without victory of the Revolution over Tsarism.' Litvinov also referred to the benefits of trade between Poland and the Soviet Union which 'could provide a big market for a considerable part of Polish industry now idle.'[45]

However, Litvinov stated, 'We do not and are not prepared to recognise Poland's protectorate, open or concealed', acting as 'manager of the external relations of all the Baltic states.' Litvinov lamented not only the failure of Estonia and Latvia to conclude non-aggression pacts, but 'also assaults on the Soviet Union's diplomatic couriers' in Latvia, the investigation of which was not being pursued with 'the energy and thoroughness which the Soviet Union had the right to count.'[46]

Moscow's concern that, following Pilsudski's coup on 1 May 1926, relations between the Soviet Union and Poland would deteriorate proved unfounded.[47] Louis Fischer's comment that 'overt hostility now replaced attempts at settlement' is incorrect, although Soviet proposals for a non-aggression pact and for disputes to be settled by a mixed conciliation court were met with a cool reception in Warsaw. While Pilsudski was quite prepared to eliminate trifling every-day friction and settle at least some of the outstanding differences, he did not believe in the possibility of a large-scale détente between Poland and the Soviet Union. Moreover, the conversations between the Soviet Union and Poland stalled when Voikov, the Russian diplomat, was assassinated in June 1927.[48]

The Soviet Union still feared an anti-Soviet alliance in which Poland would, as the Soviet Union's biggest neighbour, play a crucial part. Litvinov therefore realised it was in the Soviet Union's interest to deter Lithuania from coming to an agreement with Poland over Vilnius,[49] which, as described above, Poland had seized in 1923; another example of Litvinov as a ruthless politician beneath the veneer of a warm character. Pilsudski and Beck should be criticised for failing to distinguish between unimportant matters such as Vilnius and other factors that could affect the very existence of the Polish state. However, from 1927, although Chicherin was still nominally Foreign Commissar, Litvinov was more and more achieving the role of its head, and relations between the Soviet Union and Poland continued to improve, following the course initiated by Chicherin, notwithstanding the fact that Vilnius was still in Polish occupation.

---

[45] Degras, Jane: *Soviet Documents on Foreign Policy*, vol.2, p.111
[46] Ibid.   vol.2, pp.112-113
[47] Fischer, Louis: *The Soviets in World Affairs*, p.520
[48] Budurowycz, Bohdan: *Polish-Soviet Relations*, p.7
[49] Ibid.   p.6

Both Poland and the Soviet Union were signatories to the Kellogg Pact. Once Stalin had resolved to sign the Pact, Litvinov proceeded with considerable energy. On 29 December 1928 Litvinov proposed to Lithuania and Poland that they sign an additional protocol bringing into immediate effect the provisions of the Kellogg Pact. Poland replied in early January with a proposal that it should include Rumania. Poland had a military convention with Rumania because the Soviet Union claimed Bessarabia. This was the reason why diplomatic relations between the Soviet Union and Rumania had not been re-established since the Bolshevik Revolution. The acceptance by the Soviet Government of the Kellogg Pact indicated it had no immediate intention of using force to regain Bessarabia. The Pact, a triumph for the energy with which Litvinov pursued his foreign policy objectives when he had unambiguous instructions, was signed on 9 February 1929 by representatives of the USSR, Latvia, Poland, Estonia and Rumania. Lithuania, Persia, Danzig and Turkey adhered later.[50] It would keep the peace in Eastern Europe until Poland broke ranks in September 1938 by her aggressive policy towards Czechoslovakia. Perhaps this was why Litvinov had little sympathy for Poland in and after the Second World War.[51] The Soviet Union ratified the Pact on 13 February 1929. Latvia ratified it on 5 March, Estonia on 16 March and finally Poland and Rumania on 30 March 1929.[52]

In a triumphant speech, Litvinov stated when countries

> who have undertaken the obligation to renounce war under a General International Treaty solemnly declare and affirm through a new international act without waiting for these obligations to take effect between all the nations of the world, they have decided to carry out these obligations immediately with regard to a limited group of countries, they assume a double obligation of peaceful character with regard to those countries. Every one of the participants of the protocol undertake before the whole world the task of safeguarding peace within a defined geographical area in so far as it is in its power and the more apprehensions that sector caused formerly the more important is our action of today.[53]

Izvestiya similarly wrote a praiseworthy article reminding its readers that the USSR 'was the first to ratify the Kellogg Pact four days after signature.'[54]

In 1918 Rumania had annexed Bessarabia, former territory of the Russian empire, but as the Soviet Union had not accepted the annexation this caused much friction between the two countries. In 1931 Rumania had made it known that the Soviet Union had indicated it would not use force in line with its commitment under the Kellogg Pact. In a rare case of

---

[50] Fischer, Louis: *The Soviets in World Affairs*, pp.783 & 784

[51] See Ch.13, No.109

[52] Fischer, Louis: *The Soviets in World Affairs*, p.784

[53] Slusser, Robert M: *The Soviet Foreign Policy 1928-1934, Documents and Materials*, Doc.20, p.166

[54] Ibid. p.168, No.21

co-operation between the Soviet Union and Poland, both tried to obtain Rumania's co-operation and talks proceeded. However, when agreement was about to be reached, a new Rumanian Government was elected. Although Poland, like France, originally made the pact conditional on Rumanian participation and Rumania reaching with the Soviet Union a satisfactory arrangement over Bessarabia, eventually Poland, like France, agreed to sign a non-aggression pact with the Soviet Union which was ratified by the Polish President on 26 November 1932.[55] Next day, the Pact was also ratified by the Soviet Central Executive Committee. *Izvestiya* commented enthusiastically that relations had been repaired with 'the strongest state on the Soviet Union's Western frontiers.'[56]

Meanwhile, the Disarmament Conference was slowly proceeding without making much progress. In February 1933 Litvinov had put forward a definition of aggression, which had been well received but not agreed by the Disarmament Conference in the face of vigorous opposition from Britain. In June, while attending the World Economic Conference, Litvinov was active in persuading virtually all the countries in Eastern Europe, including Rumania, to sign a fresh convention containing Litvinov's definition of an aggressor as amended and agreed by the majority at the Disarmament Conference. The countries that were eventually included were the Soviet Union, Afghanistan, Estonia, Latvia, Persia, Poland, Rumania, Turkey, the Little Entente and Finland.[57]

In his address to the Soviet Central Executive Committee on 29 December 1933, Litvinov for once was optimistic about relations with Poland. He stated:

> He was particularly satisfied with the progress we have observed in the attitude of Polish public opinion towards our union. This progress indicates that wide circles of Polish public opinion are also coming to the conclusions which we arrived at a long time ago that between the Soviet Union and Poland the closest co-operation is both possible and necessary and there appears no objective reason to hinder its development.[58]

GERMANY

Soviet-German relations were much influenced by the Soviet hatred of the German Social Democrat Party. In 1914 the Social Democrats, in defiance of previous declarations, voted for war credits to enable the Germans to prosecute the war, which, until its final phase, the Social Democrats supported. 'For German workers and most of their leaders the Russians were still a backward and barbarous people without efficiency, without education and

---

[55] Budurowycz, Bohdan: *Polish-Soviet Relations*, p.23
[56] Scott, William: *Alliance Against Hitler*, p.68
[57] Mahaney, Wilbur Lee: *The Soviet Union, the League of Nations and Disarmament*, p.167
[58] *Moscow News*, 6 January 1934, p.4

without a serious workers' or trade union movement.'[59] However, by 1917 a significant minority of Social Democratic Party members who opposed the war formed a new party, the Independent Social Democratic Party.[60] This included a revolutionary cell called the Spartakusbund, who on 31 December 1918 formed the German Communist Party, which in its early years remained minute compared with the Social Democratic Party.[61]

In the middle of 1919, after spasmodic street fighting, one of Germany's most prominent Communist leaders, Rosa Luxemburg, was arrested and murdered by nationalist thugs while trying to escape.[62] On 13 March 1920 a general, Von Luttwiz, and civil servant, Kapp, organised what came to be known as the Kapp Putsch. No doubt the leaders of the Putsch hoped the army would support them, but the army, realising that their involvement would bring about civil war, remained passive. When a general strike was called, the Putsch collapsed. Initially, the strike was not supported by the German Communist leaders. However, the rank and file Communists were much more enthusiastic about the strike than their leaders, who were forced to change their attitude and gave half-hearted support for the strike. Roberts says: 'Its most sinister aspect had been unreliability of the army', who had told the government that 'the soldiers could not be expected to fire on their own comrades who took part in the Putsch and the participants were not punished.'[63]

On 24 March 1920 Litvinov declared:

> The Soviet Union will repulse any secret German advances seeking an alliance against the Entente. We do not wish to talk of other military combinations whatsoever. The only military danger that forces us to keep our army is Polish militarism, which Germany militarily is supporting. We are offering a loyal peace to Poland, but will not accept conditions which include in her frontiers Russian people on the grounds that they are being protected from Bolshevism.[64]

However, Litvinov was wrong that Germany would support the Polish war against Russia because, when Poland invaded Russia in April 1920, Germany did not at first assume any lively interest in the war; but when the Red Army struck back, German workers' sympathies for Russia increased, and Danzig dockers refused to handle munitions shipped to Poland through that port.[65] Membership of the meagre 50,000-strong German Communist Party rose to a respectable 350,000. The German Independent Social Democratic Party proved to be a major source of recruits.[66]

---

[59] Carr, Edward H: *German-Soviet Relations*, p.5
[60] Ibid.   p.6
[61] Ibid.   p.7
[62] Carr, Edward H: *German-Soviet Relations*, p.8
[63] Roberts, J M: *Europe 1880 to 1945*, p.464
[64] *The New York Times*, 24 March 1924, p.5
[65] Carr, Edward: *German-Soviet Relations*, p.35
[66] Ibid.   p.42

However, any optimism by the Bolsheviks in Moscow was soon dashed. On 16 March 1921, following disturbances in a mining area in central Germany, the Reichswehr moved in and suppressed the riot with considerable brutality, carrying out arrests and executions on a large scale.[67] On 17 March 1921 the German Communist Party thought their hour had come and staged an insurrection. Leaders of the German Communists became involved in fights, not only with the police but with the mass of ordinary workers who preferred to stay at their jobs. The Central Committee of the German Communist Party had been humiliated and on 31 March they called off the action without gaining any advantage.[68]

This radically affected the attitude of the Bolshevik Government in Moscow. When the 3rd Congress of the Comintern met in Moscow, the atmosphere was pessimistic on account of the failure of the Communist uprising in Germany. Both Lenin and Trotsky realised, as Litvinov had long suspected, that Europe was not yet ripe for revolution and that they had better concentrate on building socialism in one country. Lenin said:

> It is plain at a glance that after the conclusion of the peace, however bad that was, we did not succeed in provoking a revolution in the capitalist countries.

Trotsky's opinion was similar:

> We see and feel that we are not so immediately near the goal to the conquest of power to world revolution. In 1919 we said to ourselves it is a question of months. Now we say it is perhaps a question of years.[69]

In 1922 the Rapallo Treaty was signed between Germany and the Soviet Union. Both countries agreed to forego all war indemnities (including the maintenance of prisoners of war). Germany renounced all claims in consequence of the nationalisation of private property, provided the Soviet Government did not satisfy similar claims of other states. Diplomatic and consular relations were resumed. Further, both countries agreed to assist in the economic development of the other. Germany accordingly played a key role in enabling the Soviet Government to modernise its army and Germany was able to rebuild its army on Soviet soil and escape the restrictions of the Versailles Treaty.[70]

It is uncertain whether there was military collaboration between Germany and the Soviet Union in late 1921 prior to the signing of the Rapallo Treaty. The first attempt at collaboration, according to Hilger, was made by General Von Seeckt in April 1919. A Turk, Enver, a friend of German Commander-in-Chief Von Seeckt, was appointed to make contact with the Russians. He was captured by the British, but managed to escape. Hilger

---

[67] Ibid. p.45
[68] Ibid.
[69] Ibid. p.47
[70] Rapallo English translation, published in Cmd.1667, p.51; and see Ch.4, No.26

had no knowledge of Enver's reception in the Soviet Union, but Hilger did not take the view that these German feelers met with any success.

However, two years later the initiative came from the Russians. Hilger states that a Russian emissary was sent to Germany in autumn 1921 to sound out officials of the Foreign and War Ministries for aid in starting an aeroplane industry in the Soviet Union. In 1922 an agreement was reached whereby the Junkers factory was granted a concession to manufacture aeroplane motors in a plant at Fili, eight miles from Moscow. At the same time a German-Soviet joint stock company, Bersol, was established for the purpose of manufacturing poison gas.[71] However, there is a letter from Von Seeckt to Hasse of May 1922 (about a month after Rapallo) which indicates that no agreement on military action had been reached, although Von Seeckt ardently desired such an agreement and hoped: 'The enemy would believe it already existed.'[72]

Krestinsky became the first Soviet ambassador to Germany. Brockdorff-Rantzau was the first German ambassador to the Soviet Union, although on 14 February 1919 he had denounced the Russian Bolsheviks in the Weimar Parliament; and also, in a memorandum to the German President and Chancellor, he stated, 'The grave disadvantage of the Rapallo agreement lies in the military fears bound up in it. A German-Soviet Alliance would excite British suspicions and drive Britain into the hands of France.' Presumably, nothing in Moscow was known of Brockdorff-Rantzau's reservations on the merits of Rapallo.

Chicherin warmly welcomed the new German Ambassador to the Soviet Union when he arrived in Moscow to take up his diplomatic post, and a firm friendship sprang up between the two men.[73] In September 1922 Krassin, who was travelling through Smolensk, noted that the airdrome was full of German aviators.[74] Although Rathenau, who had negotiated the Rapallo agreement, was assassinated, this was the result of anti-Semitism rather than anti-Soviet feeling.[75] Increase in trade between Germany and Russia was promoted by Rapallo. In 1921, the year the Anglo-Soviet Trade Agreement was signed, Soviet Russia had taken 29% of her imports from Britain and 25% from Germany. In 1922, the year of Rapallo, 32.7% of the Soviet imports came from Germany and only 18.8% from Britain.[76]

On 11 January 1923 France occupied the Ruhr because of non-payment of reparations. This proved to be a good moment for the Soviet Union to show loyalty to its new ally. Both the All-Russian Union Central Executive Committee inside the Soviet Union and the Communists in Western Europe (at the 4th Congress of Comintern, held at the beginning

---

[71] Hilger, Gustav: *Incompatible Allies*, p.193
[72] Carr, Edward: *German-Soviet Relations*, p.60
[73] Carr, Edward: *Bolshevik Revolution*, vol.3, p.437
[74] Ibid.   p.436
[75] Ibid.   p 434; *Pope A. Maxim Litvinov* p.188
[76] Ibid.   p.434

of January 1923) denounced the Versailles Treaty and the imperialistic policies of the Western Powers towards Germany.[77] A further protest by Comintern was made on 27 August. This declared: 'The German proletariat to be in danger and invited workers of all countries to protest at the occupation of German territory.'[78]

However, the Soviet Union's support for Germany was deceitful, as at the same time a *coup d'etat* was being planned by the Comintern with the Russian Government's approval. Trotsky saw the French occupation of the Ruhr as a great opportunity for the German Communists to seize power. Carr states that Stalin was extremely cautious, but gives no authority for this assertion.[79] In spite of Stalin's alleged caution, the Politburo decided to fix the date of the German revolution as 7 November 1923. The proposed revolution was a complete fiasco. The only significant illegal challenge to authority occurred in Hamburg, where a few hundred Communists attacked and occupied several police stations, seizing their arms. They remained masters of the city for 48 hours. The Communist insurgents fought desperately with the police but, with the assistance of the army, the police had no difficulty in quelling the uprising.[80]

At the beginning of 1925 the Soviet Union's economic situation was changing for the better, but her efforts to improve relations with the major capitalist countries were becoming increasingly fruitless. Against this background, Moscow was more and more preoccupied with the need to woo Germany from an increasing Western orientation. Negotiations for a Soviet-German treaty opened in November 1924.[81] In December 1924 Chicherin, with the approval of the Politburo, submitted a neutrality pact to Germany by which the Soviet Union and Germany agreed: 'Not to enter into political or economic alliance or agreement with third parties directed against the other and to co-ordinate its action with that of the other in respect of joining or sending an observer to the League of Nations.' Chicherin, playing on chronic fears of a German approach to France, proposed that the Soviet Union would assume an obligation not to conclude an agreement with France against Germany, providing that Germany assumed a corresponding agreement in respect of Great Britain, *vis-à-vis* the Soviet Union.[82]

Stresemann, the German Foreign Minister, had determined that, while he wanted to keep in touch with the Soviet Union, Germany would not conclude any agreement with the Soviet Union until Germany had successfully completed negotiations with the West. However, once Stresemann had come to terms with the West, he could then reinsure himself by an agreement with the East.[83] Stresemann considered it was more in Germany's interest to pursue further rapprochement with France and Britain. He argued that, if the Soviet Union

---

[77] Carr, Edward H: *Interregnum*, p.155
[78] Ibid. p.203
[79] Ibid. p.205
[80] Ibid. p.222
[81] Carr, Edward: *Socialism in One Country*, p.253
[82] Ibid. p.257
[83] Ibid. p.262

was really interested in 'deepening German-Soviet negotiations', it must welcome a step that would strengthen Germany's position in European politics. He claimed that, under clauses 16 and 17 of the League covenant, Germany would be able to protect her neutrality by exercising her right of veto. Finally, Germany's membership of the League Council would enable her to counteract 'all anti-Soviet tendencies.'[84]

The German Ambassador to the Soviet Union, Brockdorff-Rantzau, was most unhappy with Stresemann's proposals and hastened to Berlin in order to argue with Stresemann that the Soviet proposals should be accepted because further delay in considering them would be regarded by the Soviets as an indirect rejection. Brockdorff-Rantzau was unable to persuade Stresemann to change his policy.[85] Brockdorff-Rantzau even suggested that if the Soviet Union was treated badly she might come to an agreement with Poland to guarantee Poland's Western border,[86] which, since the Treaty of Versailles, Germany had always disputed; but this did not affect Stresemann's decision.

Litvinov was now put in charge of the Commissariat as Chicherin was ill. Carr queries whether this was 'a diplomatic illness.'[87] Litvinov's attitude towards Locarno had been bitter but resigned. He observed: 'If Germany entered into the League, the Soviet Government would not declare war or break off diplomatic relations and would even remain ready as before to receive any concrete proposals of the German Government. However, he saw no possibility of reaching any positive result on important questions such as the ethnographical frontiers of Poland.'[88] Such comments showed Litvinov's pro-German orientation in the pre-Nazi period (which he shared with Chicherin) and also his anti-Polish sentiments, which he would continually harbour.[89] Litvinov further stated that he did not like the Soviet Union to be used in this way and told Stresemann, when Litvinov passed through Berlin on 13 June 1925, that he was 'very distressed by the state of German-Soviet relations.' He thought that the German attitude to the negotiations created a very 'odd impression.' Litvinov described British foreign policy as 'completely anti-Soviet and feared Germany would be drawn into the charmed circle of British policy.'[90]

However, there appears no discernible difference between the policy that Chicherin had previously pursued and that which Litvinov was now pursuing. Chicherin had said in his speech at the 3rd Union Congress of Soviets in May 1925 that British 'policy consists in officially denying any hostile intention towards us; yet in fact everywhere we turn we meet the opposition of British agents. Is the British Government getting ready to stramgle us us,

---

[84] Carr Edward *Socialism in One Country*, p. 260
[85] Ibid.   p.261
[86] Ibid.   p.267
[87] Ibid.   p.261
[88] Ibid.   p 261
[89] See Ch.17, No.64
[90] Carr, Edward: *Socialism in One Country*, p.266

or is it, on the contrary, trying to isolate us and so strengthen its position in relation to us or is it trying to create an atmosphere more favourable to itself for negotiations?' Chicherin further predicted that 'as soon as Germany sat down with her former enemies in Geneva, the other nations would be strong enough, in spite of the wishes of the German Government, to prevent it from continuing its existing friendly relations with the Soviet Union.'[91] It seemed that again both Litvinov and Chicherin were agreed that Britain was pursuing an anti-Soviet policy and were worried that Germany might be forced to pursue such a policy once the Locarno agreement was finalised.

Although the Soviet Union was disappointed when Germany signed the Locarno agreement, they took comfort in the continuation of the secret military alliance and the German desire to prevent an exclusively Western orientation. Accordingly, the relationship which Germany enjoyed with the Soviet Union was better than with any other country.[92]

Another difficulty for German-Soviet relations arose out of two trials in Germany. On 10 February 1924 several alleged Soviet agents in Germany were put on trial, including Skoblevsky, who had played a leading role in organising the abortive Communist uprising in October 1923. Among the accusations was a plan to assassinate Von Seeckt, head of the army, and Borsig and Stinnes, two German industrialists. Sentence of death was passed on Skoblevsky, as well as two Germans.

Stresemann refused Krestinsky's plea to intervene. Litvinov asked the German Foreign Minister to ensure that the Soviet Embassy was not mentioned; but, as the Weimer Republic was a democracy, a minister had no power to interfere with a judicial decision. There is no way we can know whether Litvinov understood democracy sufficiently to enable him to realise he was asking the impossible by requesting an executive in a democracy to interfere with a legal process. Meanwhile, in October 1924 two young German students, Wolscht and Kindermann, had entered Russia for the purpose of travelling to the remotest parts of the Soviet Union. En route to Moscow they had met an employee of the German Embassy in Moscow, Hilger, who had given the students a visiting card. The students were arrested and the visiting card given to them by Hilger was found. The two students remained in custody for some time to be used as hostages should any Soviet citizen face difficulties in Germany.

The German ambassador appealed to Chicherin, who alleged without a shred of evidence that Wolscht and Kindermann were 'hardened criminals.' After the verdict against Skoblevsky, Wolscht and Kindermann were put on trial and likewise sentenced to death. However, neither sentence was carried out and an exchange of the condemned took place in due course.[93]

---

[91] Ibid.   p.264
[92] Carr, Edward H: *Russian Revolution from Lenin to Stalin*, p.173
[93] Hilger, Gustav: *Incompatible Allies*, p.140

On 21 December 1925 Chicherin gave a press conference stating: 'Fears of Locarno do not in the least extend to the intentions of the German Government, whose goodwill was not in doubt.' However, what worried him was: 'The treaty gave the British Government the opportunity of exercising strong pressure on Germany, as a result of which Germany might be compelled, even against its own wish, to change its attitude to the Soviet Government.'[94]

In Litvinov's report to the Executive Committee on 26 April 1926 he reported with satisfaction that the Treaty of Berlin had been signed in which both countries 'will be guided by their recognition of general peace.' Germany was not prepared to state directly as a member of the League of Nations that she would not participate in any sanctions imposed by the League against the Soviet Government, but she did assure the Soviet Union by giving

> notice of its possible conduct should there arise in the League of Nations any aspiration not in accordance with the basic idea of peace and unilaterally directed against the USSR.

Further,

> The German Government declares the question whether the USSR is in armed conflict with a third power, the aggressor, can be decided by the League of Nations in a manner binding on Germany only with the consent of Germany.[95]

The tenor of Litvinov's speech indicated that he was satisfied with Germany's good faith, and desired, in spite of Locarno, to keep relations with Germany cordial.

Chicherin was distressed by the arrest of 3 German and 50 Soviet engineers: the Shakhty Case. They were accused of industrial sabotage and wrecking. According to Stalin, the bourgeoisie specialists, in co-operation with former owners of industrial enterprises, were subverting the Soviet Government's efforts to industrialise the country. On 7 September 1928 the Court gave its verdict. Eleven of the fifty Soviets were sentenced to death, two Germans were acquitted and a third was sentenced to one year's imprisonment. All were quickly released.[96]

The Disarmament Conference provided an opportunity for further collaboration between Litvinov and Weizsacker, the State Secretary of the German foreign office, and Boris Stein, a Soviet delegate to the Disarmament Conference. Litvinov definitely supported continued Russo-German friendship, even if Chicherin was more enthusiastic. At the time

---

[94] Degras, Jane: *Soviet Documents on Foreign Policy*, vol.2, p.78
[95] Ibid.   p.106
[96] O'Connor , Timothy (Chicherin): *Diplomacy and Revolution*, p.160

when the Soviet Union had decided to participate in the disarmament talks, further evidence that Litvinov wished German-Soviet friendship to continue and prosper was shown by his statement to Stresemann that Russo-German collaboration 'was the most significant result of the Soviet Union's first appearance at Geneva.'[97]

When Litvinov spoke of Germany in his speech to the Central Committee of the Soviet Communist Party on 10 December 1928, he praised Germany 'because she has established normal relations and at times even friendly relations towards us and she has availed herself of all the advantages which are at present offered by co-operation with a state of 140 million inhabitants.' At the same time he gave a warning when he referred to 'individual Government departments in Germany and by the public in Germany that sought to destroy these relations,' such as the action of a group of banks in joining the International Association for the Protection of Former Creditors of Russia.[98] However, a year later, again in a speech to the Central Committee, Litvinov expresses 'sympathy for Germany's efforts to free herself from the shackles riveted upon her by the Versailles Treaty' and refers to 'the fundamental objective conditions which produced in their time the Rapallo Treaty and our long-term friendship which continues generally to operate.' Litvinov's astuteness is shown when he refers to 'people, groups, organisations and even parties who have as their object a radical alteration of Germany's whole policy in favour of anti-Soviet machinations in exchange for illusory economic and political gains.' This represents an early reference to the possible danger of Nazism.[99]

In the summer of 1930 Litvinov told the German Foreign Minister, Curtius,

> his government wanted to plan its imports and exports more carefully so the earlier haphazard methods could be ended. It wanted to concentrate its trade more upon those countries with which the Soviet Union stood in friendly relations,

implying that Germany was one such country.[100]

Litvinov confirmed his desire for the best possible relationship between Germany and the Soviet Union by sending congratulations to the German Foreign Minister Julius Curtius, on an official Soviet announcement of congratulations on the final evacuation of the Rhineland by the Allies and the once possible theme of Germany's liberation from the fetters of Versailles.[101] On the German side, Neurath, who was shortly to be appointed his

---

[97] Dyck, Harvey Leonard: *Weimar Republic and Soviet Russia 1926-1933*, p.111; and see Weizsacker, Ernst von: *Memoirs*, p.65

[98] Documents, 1928, p.184

[99] Documents, 1929, p.210

[100] Dyck, Harvey L: *Weimar Germany and Soviet Russia 1926-1933*, p.221

[101] Carr, Edward H: *German-Soviet Relations*, p.102

Country's Foreign Minister, was campaigning actively for ratification of the extension of the Berlin Treaty, renewed on 24 June 1931.[102] In a conversation with Esmond Ovey, British ambassador to the Soviet Union, in July 1931 Litvinov had become pessimistic about Germany, rightly anticipating the emergence of a fascist government.[103]

Against a background of growing support for Hitler in Germany, Litvinov tried desperately to maintain German-Soviet friendship. 16 April 1932 was the tenth anniversary of Rapallo. Litvinov proposed that this should be marked by a Soviet-German lunch with appropriate speeches. Bruning accepted the lunch, but declined the speeches. Litvinov made a speech to the German Press.[104]

Subsequently, the Reichstag ratified the prolongation of the Rapallo Pact.

Moscow News commented:

> At the present time, ten years after the signing of Rapallo, at a time when the imperialists were preparing intervention against the USSR and on the basis of the world crisis, the imperialists are now attempting a new and political enslavement of Germany and it becomes important to assert the principle of Rapallo in the relations of the two peoples.[105]

The economic crisis was especially severe in Germany. A coalition government had been formed between the Centre Parties and the Social Democrats. When, in view of the financial crisis, the Centre parties wanted to cut social benefits, the Social Democrats decided to leave the coalition.[106] Bruning was installed as Chancellor, but had no Reichstag majority and ruled by decree. Although support for Hitler was growing, it was not enough to oust Hindenburg when Hitler stood against him in the election for the Presidency in March 1932.[107] Armed with this mandate, Hindenburg started freely to exercise emergency powers, as he wanted men in power who would work with the Nazis. Hindenburg erroneously thought the Nazi's could be tamed. In May 1932 Hindenburg brought pressure on Bruning to resign so Hindenburg could install Von Papen as Chancellor. Bruning's cabinet was divided as to whether to fight the President by defying him and appeal to Parliament. Bruning decided to resign.[108] Hindenburg now acted with greater audacity. In July 1932, by presidential decree, he dismissed the Social Democratic Government in Prussia, where they were still ruling, on the pretext of the failure of the Prussian police to act against the Communists. The Prussian police were under the control of the Social

---

[102] Heineman, John L: *Neurath, Hitler's First Foreign Minister*, p.99
[103] DBFP, 1st Series, vol.25, p.215, No.139
[104] Carr, Edward H: *German-Soviet Relations*, p.103
[105] *Moscow News*, 18 April 1932, p.2
[106] Roberts, J M: *Europe, 1880 to 1945*, p.468
[107] Ibid.
[108] Ibid.

Democrat Government, but the government chose not to resist the Presidential decree.[109] Even before Hitler had come to power, owing to the connivance of Hindenburg, democracy in Germany was in tatters.

At the Disarmament Conference Litvinov went out of his way to express his regret to his German colleagues that relations between the two delegations differed sharply from those established between Count Bernstorff and himself in the Preparatory Commission.[110]

Maisky states that Litvinov told him in 1932:

> The Weimar Republic was on its last legs. We cannot cherish any illusion in that respect. If not today, then tomorrow. Hitler will come to power and then the situation will change at once. Germany will be transformed from our friend to our enemy.[111]

Was Maisky being truthful? There is no corroboration. It is clear that Litvinov immediately appreciated the danger. He was fully aware of Hitler's plans for expansion eastwards as set out in *Mein Kampf.* Tanya states that they had a copy at home and as early as 1933 Litvinov had no illusions as to the danger faced by the Soviet Union if Hitler gained power.[112]

In the General Election of 31 July 1932, the Nazis more than doubled their vote to 13,765,781, and won 230 seats. The Communist vote was also rising, to the detriment of the Social Democrats, who now had only 133 seats against the Communists' 89 seats.[113] When fresh elections were called in November 1932 the Communists gained seats at the expense of the Social Democrats. The Communists then had 100 seats, compared to 121 won by the Social Democrats. The National Socialists had wanted the election so the electorate could endorse certain proposals of Hermann Goering concerning Reichstag procedure, but it had not brought the National Socialists any dividend, as their vote had declined from 37.4% to 33.1% and their seats had declined to 196.[114] Nevertheless, on 30 January 1933 Hitler was appointed as Chancellor by Hindenburg.[115] Thus, he had become Chancellor constitutionally.

One detrimental effect of Locarno had been to drive the German Social Democrat and Communist parties further apart and, not even when Hitler became a serious contender for the Chancellorship, could the rift be healed. It was entirely different in France and Britain,

---

[109] Ibid.   p.469
[110] Carr, Edward H: *Twilight of the Comintern*, p.54
[111] Maisky, Ivan: *Who Helped Hitler?*, p.16
[112] Tanya
[113] Clark, Robert T: *Fall of the German Republic: A Political Study*, p.381
[114] Ibid.   p.422
[115] Roberts, J M: *Europe, 1880-1945*, p.468

where Communists would often give covert support to non-Communist socialist parties at elections.[116] An alliance between the Social Democrats and the Communists might possibly have prevented Hitler gaining power, as the Social Democrat and Communist votes were roughly equal to the votes of the Right; but Stalin would not contemplate such a move. However, Carr is of the opinion that, even if the Communists and Social Democrats had combined, the Reichswehr would have used force rather than contemplate a joint Social Democrat-Communist Government.[117]

Hitler, having gained power constitutionally, then, through the Nazi party, proceeded to try and terrorise his opponents. The Communists were blamed for a mysterious fire in the Reichstag on 27 February.1933.[118] However, the Communist Party was the one party to which the fire was of no advantage. This was not true of the National Socialists, and they took full advantage of it. Overy is probably right that it was not the work of the Nazi Party.[119] Fresh elections were called; and, in spite of Nazi terror surrounding the election, the Nazis only polled 43.9%.

On 16 March the National Socialists proposed a decree giving absolute power to the government. Although the Centre Parties were coerced into supporting the decree, the Social Democrats bravely voted against. The voting was 441 in favour and 91 against the decree. Following the vote, the Chairman of the Reichstag declared that the Reichstag was dissolved until it pleased the government to again convene it. Hitler had established a dictatorship constitutionally, and had abolished the Republic by legal means.[120]

However, what is clear is that Litvinov desperately tried to remain friends with Hitler's Germany. He himself took the initiative by suggesting a joint guarantee of the Baltic States.[121]

Nadolny, the German ambassador to the Soviet Union, tried hard to obtain approval, but eventually informed Litvinov of Berlin's refusal to discuss the proposal. Litvinov published the rejection,[122] but this does not mean that he was anti-Germany and pro-France; only that, if relations between Germany and Russia deteriorated, Litvinov wished to make it clear that this was the fault of Germany.

Hilger, who was on the staff of the German embassy in Moscow, stated that the Soviet Union's attitude to the rise of National Socialism was ambivalent. There was, at first, actual welcome to Hitler's accession to power, because they believed it would not last very

---

[116] Carr, Edward: *Russian Revolution From Lenin to Stalin*, p.179
[117] Carr, Edward H: *German-Soviet Relations*, p.107
[118] Clark, Robert: *Fall of the German Republic: A Political Study*, p.482
[119] Overy, Richard: *The Dictators*, p.187
[120] Clark, Robert: *Fall of The German Republic: A Political Study*, p.486
[121] Scott, William: *Alliance Against Hitler*, p.158
[122] Ibid. p.159

long and his fall would speed the proletarian revolution in Germany.[123] It is quite clear that this optimism was not shared by Litvinov.

However, it appears that Litvinov's objection to Hitler was because of the danger of the Rapallo agreement ending. He realised correctly that the Soviet Union would be very much weakened internationally in such circumstances. The military threat to the Soviet Union would increase proportionately. Litvinov saw it as his duty to try and prevent the termination of the Rapallo accord, although National Socialism was repugnant to Litvinov, as was Stalin's so-called communism. The only difference was that whereas communism had the right principles, those of National Socialism were inherently evil.[124]

On the other hand, illogically, the belief in Moscow was that a National Socialist Government would understand it was in Germany's interest to continue the Rapallo agreement because, as Doletsky stated to Hilger, it was in their long-term interests.

Doletsky told Hilger in confidence that the Soviet press had been instructed to avoid all appearance of interfering in Germany's political crisis and even to refrain from criticism of German policy, although an extremely critical article on German foreign policy had been written in the English-speaking *Moscow News*. All they feared was that the accession of Hitler might be followed by a rather disturbing period of transition before normal relations could be achieved. The Soviet Communist Government was eager to establish contact with the National Socialists for the purpose of preventing any temporary difficulties.[125]

Scott claims that Krestinsky and Voroshilov tried to avoid action that would prevent a return to Rapallo and that Litvinov wanted to push rapprochement with France and enter the League. I believe Litvinov also wanted the Rapallo policy with Germany to continue.[126]

On 1 March 1933 Litvinov wrote to Neurath:

> We have no intention of altering our relationship with Germany, but we certainly cannot look kindly upon the prospect of an anti-Soviet bloc including Germany. Until now it appeared possible to forestall such a bloc by exerting pressure on Berlin, but if this turns out to be insufficient we will of course not hesitate to exert pressure in Paris.[127]

In the course of an interview, Litvinov reiterated to Neurath, 'the Soviet doctrine of non-

---

[123] Hilger, Gustav: *Incompatible Allies*, p.252
[124] Tanya
[125] Hilger, Gustav: *Incompatible Allies*, p.253
[126] Scott, William: *Alliance Against Hitler*, p.159
[127] Roberts, Geoffrey: *The Soviet Union and the Beginning of the Second World War*, p 10

interference in internal affairs of Germany, but made it clear that … this does not mean that Soviet Nationals could be ill-treated with impunity.'[128]

On 7 March 1933 Radek said: 'There was no victory [for the Nazis] since the Nazis had failed to crush the Communists.'It does seem that the Soviet leadership, except Litvinov, had not yet taken the Nazi threat sufficiently seriously. Radek continued:

> The Nazis were incapable of improving the economic situation. It will be rqually impossible to rule a great country against the wishes of the toiling masses. But there is not the slightest doubt, it will be equally impossible to rule the country without a programme and in addition to rule by adventurous methods.[129]

Moscow News commented:

> The National Socialists have come out with a broad statement of policy and this was done by Herr Hitler in a speech broadcast on 3 March 1933 on all German radio stations.

> [Hitler] found himself without any definite principles and not to one of the burning questions was he able to give an answer, nor does he know how to reply to them. His whole speech was received with the greatest amazement as an attack on the Soviet Union. Even the enemies of Germany failed to understand why the National Socialist leader took the opportunity of attacking the only state that does not entertain hostile feelings to Germany. It is highly embarrassing to reply, but what can one do? Herr Hitler started the discussion and he must not complain if we are obliged to reply. During the last year the best internationally known bourgeoisie economists have visited the Soviet Union and studied its economic development and written books about it in which they have tried to draw some lessons from the victorious proletariat which is embodying the dreams of the finest representatives of mankind. It is true we are not a sufficiently rich country, but we are rising, while in Germany only one third of the factories are operating and the toiling masses are plunged into monstrous destitution.[130]

However, Hitler made a conciliatory speech to the Reichstag on 23 March 1933:

> In regard to the Soviet Union, the Reich Government is determined to cultivate friendly relations which are productive for both parties. The Government of the National Revolution above all views itself capable of such a positive policy with regard to Soviet Russia. The fight, against communism in Germany, is our internal

---

[128] *The New York Times*, 3 March 1932, p.5
[129] Slusser, Robert M: *Soviet Foreign Policy 1928-1934, Documents and Materials*, p.360
[130] *Moscow News*, 10 March 1933, p.4

affair and we shall never tolerate interference from outside. The national political relations with other powers to which we are related by mutual interests will not be affected by this. Our relations with other countries will continue to warrant our most earnest attention in future, in particular our relationship to the major countries overseas with which Germany has long been allied with friendly ties and economic interests.[131]

On the same day Churchill in the House of Commons severely criticised Hitler's oppressive regime[132] and followed this up with a further speech on 13 April, particularly referring to persecution of Jews in Germany after three months of Nazi rule.

> You have the dictatorship. You have militarism and appeal to every kind of fighting spirit from the reintroduction of duelling in the colleges to the Minister of Education advising the plentiful use of the cane in the elementary schools. You have the martial and pugnacious manifestations and also ... the persecution of the Jews of which so many Honourable Members have spoken and which appeals to everyone who feels that men and women have a right to live in a world where they are born and have a right to pursue a livelihood which similarly has been guaranteed them under the public laws of the land of their birth.

In contrast, the Soviet leaders and Litvinov, which perhaps, as he was Jewish, was more surprising, took the traditional view of the British and US Governments that countries should not interfere in the internal affairs of another country, although I would have thought that the principle of communism was that all people are equal.

Wise advice was given to Moscow by Alexandrovsky, a political counsellor in the Soviet Embassy in Berlin, when he stated on 18 April 1933: 'Hitler cannot exist without a big foreign policy and this means extreme adventurism and ultimately war and intervention against the USSR.'[133]

Krestinsky certainly was extremely suspicious of Nazi Germany, although normally regarded as pro-German. Krestinsky wrote to Khinchuk that, even if Nazi Germany normalised its relations with the USSR:

> It would not signify a final reorientation of the Hitler Government. It would mean for us a definite breathing space which, the longer it is, the more favourable it will be to the international position of the USSR.[134]

---

[131] Domarus Max , *Hitler's Speeches and Declarations 1932-1945 p.271@ p. 283*
[132] *Hansard*, vol.276, 23 March 1933 538 and 13 April 1933, 2786
[133] Roberts, Geoffrey: *The Soviet Union and the Beginning of the Second World War*, p.11
[134] Ibid.

However, in early May 1933 an article more supportive of the new regime appeared in *Izvestiya*. It stated the Soviet people

> desired to live in peace with Germany in spite of their attitude towards Fascism. Public opinion has never harboured any plans against the integrity of German territory. It requires no change or revision in policy towards Germany.[135]

Litvinov protested to the German Ambassador, Dirksen, against the anti-Soviet remarks of Rosenberg, but he stressed: 'It could have friendly relations with National Socialist Germany as with Fascist Italy.'[136]

In June 1933 at the World Economic Conference, Hugenberg, the German Economics Minister, tried to submit a memorandum to the Conference in which Eastern Europe including the Ukraine was clearly marked as Germany's sphere of economic expansion. Although Hitler could just be advocating increased trade with the Soviet Union, Litvinov did not so regard it, but interpreted it as 'an open call to colonise Soviet territory.' It caused acute bitterness and worry in Moscow. As the Soviet Union interpreted it as a demand for living space in the Soviet Union, the German delegation refused to submit the memorandum, but Hugenberg distributed it among the delegates. Following the Soviet Union's protest, Hitler obviously did not at this stage wish to break with the Soviet Union. He disavowed his minister, sacked him from his cabinet and ordered his return to Germany.[137]

Krestinsky's alleged German orientation is shown to be false when in a letter to Khinchuk, the Soviet ambassador in Germany, Krestinsky accused the German Government of preparing

> to participate in a German coalition against us and is prepared to expand its military power to war with us and requires only two things, armaments freedom, and compensation at the expense of the USSR. We must of course remember that the friendly assurances of the German Government are not to be believed and that in the further estrangement are the political plans of Germany to enter into war with us and that the present position is only a temporary respite.[138]

Following the traditional principles of British foreign policy that states are not concerned with a foreign state's internal policy but only with its foreign policy, in September 1933

Litvinov stated:

---

[135] Slusser, Robert M: *Soviet Foreign Policy 1928-1934, Documents and Materials*, Doc.96, p.526 @ p528
[136] Ibid.　p361
[137] Hilger, Gustav: *Incompatible Allies*, p.257
[138] Roberts, Geoffrey: *The Soviet Union and the Beginning of the Second World War*, pp.12 & 13

> We of course sympathise with the suffering of our German comrades, but we are the last people who can be reproached for allowing our feelings to dictate our policy. The whole world knows that we can and do maintain good relations with capitalist states of any brand, including the fascists. We do not interfere in the internal affairs of Germany and we do not interfere in the affairs of other countries and our relations with her are conditioned not by her internal policy but by her external policy.[139]

When Krestinsky had the chance to meet Hitler on the way to a holiday, he did not avail himself of the opportunity, apparently thinking that no useful purpose would be served. Litvinov, in contrast, took the opportunity to see the Foreign Office when he passed through Berlin en route for Washington for the recognition talks, but his talks with the Foreign Ministry made no progress.[140] This, of course, further indicated that the assertion that Krestinsky was pro-German whereas Litvinov was anti-German is erroneous.

A stupid speech by Piatnitsky at the 13th Plenum of the ECCI shows how little the Soviet leadership except Litvinov appreciated the seriousness of the rise to power of Hitler.

Piatnitsky stated:

> In spite of the incredible terror, it is easier to work among the German proletariat now in the sense that social democratic workers and the non-party workers who followed social democrats and also the workers of the reformist unions are becoming disillusioned in significant numbers with the policy of social democracy. ... Because of the changed situation in Germany and the heroic work of the Communist Party, the Communists no longer encounter the resistance which the trade union bureaucrats and the Social Democratic Party were formerly able to offer.

Piatnitsky appeared pleased that the German Social Democrats had been annihilated, rather than being distressed that Hitler had gained power. However the person most at fault was Stalin who was not prepared to consider changing his attitude to the Social Democrat.

Also, Piatnitsky badly overestimated the ability of the Communists to offer any serious opposition to Hitler. He claimed: 'Even the German fascists are compelled to admit they have failed to smash and exterminate the Communist Party of Germany.'[141] If the Nazis never exterminated the Communist Party, they had certainly smashed it. Such significant opposition that arose in Germany during the Hitler era did not come from the Communists.

---

[139] Carr, Edward H: *German-Soviet Relations*, p.110
[140] Hilger, Gustav: *Incompatible Allies*, p.261
[141] Slusser, Robert M: *Soviet Foreign Policy 1928-1934, Documents and Materials*, Doc.106, p.556; *Izvestiya*, 7 March 1933

On 29 December 1933 Litvinov, in his key speech to the Central Committee of the Soviet Communist Party, first recited with approval 'the extremely valuable economic and political advantages gained by Germany and Russia' that the post-Rapallo policy reaped. However, without mentioning Hitler by name, Litvinov stated:

> A political leader found himself in office and later at a wheel of a ship of government who at the time of our best relations with Germany openly opposed these relations, preaching a rapprochement with the West for common offensive against the Soviet Union.

I believe that Litvinov was wrong in his assessment. I do not believe that Hitler ever believed that Britain and France would join with him in aggression against the Soviet Union. Nor would Hitler's Germany have welcomed such a policy, as they would then have owed France and Britain a debt. The possibility of a rapprochement between Germany and the Western powers is further undermined by the fact that Britain would probably have passively stood aside on a German invasion of the Soviet Union.

Litvinov went on to describe Hitler's views:

> The founder of this new policy explained in detail in a literary work his conception of the future policy of Germany. According to this conception, Germany was not only to conquer all the territory which had been taken from her under the Versailles Treaty, not only to conquer lands in which there were any German minorities, but by fire and sword to pave the way for expansion in the East without stopping at the borders of the Soviet Union and to enslave the people of this Union.

Litvinov proceeded to say:

> It sometimes happens that an opposition party coming to power strives to forget the slogan it has used against its political opponents. This was not the case in the present instance. We for one are unaware of a single responsible statement that would have erased the conception made by me. The literary work in which the conception is preached continues to circulate in Germany without any expurgations in new editions, including an edition in 1934 as the year of publication.

Litvinov, at the end of his speech, made it clear that he wished the best possible relations with Germany as with other states, no doubt thoughts with which both Stalin and Molotov agreed. Litvinov was right in saying the Soviet Union 'will benefit from such relations.' Litvinov, no doubt, stated with absolute conviction: 'We on our side are not striving for expansion in either East or West or in other directions. We feel no enmity to the German people.' How did his thoughts change when he saw the destruction of his country by the

German army between 1941 and 1945? He gave an assurance to Germany that he believed the Soviet Union would never encourage other states to make attempts at expansion. He then said that he hoped Germany would now 'contradict the statements she has made about Eastern expansion not only to the present but also to the time when she will have greater forces for realisation of those aggressive ideas which her present leaders have been preaching before their advent to power and which some of them are also preaching now.'[142]

Stalin similarly stressed a new German policy, although likewise not mentioning Hitler by name, which reminds 'one of the policy of the late Kaiser who occupied at one time the Ukraine and undertook a march against Leningrad, having turned the Baltic States into a jumping off place for such a march.'[143]

Now Litvinov tried without success to construct the Eastern Locarno, a regional defence pact between the Soviet Union's eastern neighbours. The main principle of this was that each nation would commit itself to aid each other in the event of an attack. Germany was not prepared to support the Eastern Locarno Pact. and instead wished to construct an anti-Soviet Pact.[144]

In May 1934 Germany ratified a protocol of 1931 extending the 1926 German-Soviet treaty, which indicates that Hitler wished to keep in touch with the Soviet Union so he could keep his options open.[145] An editorial in *Izvestiya* stated:

> If German policy actually aims at the establishment and consolidation of neighbourly relations with the USSR, we will only welcome it both in the interests of the two powers and also of the world in general. So far the Reich Chancellor's declaration did not make it clear what is meant by the important mutual interests of the new government or the policy of the new government towards the USSR. In view of the fact that the Government's plans are little known, a more concrete statement would have clarified the situation.[146]

However, following police raids on Soviet premises and molestation of Soviet citizens in Germany by the police on 3 April 1933, Litvinov again presented an official protest.[147]

In spite of his hostility to Nazi Germany, Litvinov made a final effort to appease Germany when he visited Berlin for the last time in June 1934. Litvinov proposed a non-aggression

---

[142] *Moscow News*, 6 January 1934, p.4

[143] Stalin's speech, *Moscow News*, 3 February 1934, p.3

[144] Budurowycz, Bohdan: *Polish- Soviet Relations*, p. 67

[145] Slusser, Robert M: *Soviet Foreign Policy 1928-1934, Documents and Materials*, p.361; Heineman, John *Neurath, Hitler's First Foreign Minister*, p.99

[146] Slusser, Robert M: *Soviet Foreign Policy 1928-1934, Documents and Materials*, p.360

[147] Ibid.

pact between Germany and the Soviet Union guaranteeing the independence of the Baltic States.[148]

This was probably the time when Litvinov assured Neurath that the Soviet Union considered it quite natural that Germany should treat Communists in the same way as enemies of the state were treated in the Soviet Union.[149] Did Litvinov say this to emphasise that Soviet policy at that time was not to interfere in the internal affairs of other states or was it a veiled criticism of Stalin's internal policy? If repression took place in the Soviet Union against opponents of the regime, then complaint could not be made if other countries adopted similar methods.

In 1934 Hitler was privately indicating that he did not wish to end the post-Rapallo relationship between Germany and Russia. Neurath noted with pleasure: 'The Chancellor is convinced about the importance of the Russian problems and about the necessity to maintain our political economic and political and military political lines.'

Neurath considered that Hitler would not allow any change to occur in German policy towards the Soviet Union.[150]

When the German Ambassador complained to Litvinov that the estrangement in Soviet-German relations was due to the Soviet Government's attitude to the Nationalist Socialist regime in Germany, Litvinov stated, 'Both Governments should maintain friendly contacts in order to secure agreement on all political and economic questions and welcomed the possibility of restoring relations of confidence.'[151]

However, Litvinov was not prepared to wait for Hitler's decision. Hitler's absent seat at the League of Nations had now been replaced by the Soviet Union. An alliance had now been created between France and the Soviet Union to oppose Hitler's expansion. If France had been prepared to supplement the Franco-Soviet agreement with a military pact and the French politicians had instructed its army to prepare for a major offensive against Germany if any of its allies were attacked, the Second World War might never have taken place. The failure of France to adopt either course finally led Stalin to the reasonable conclusion that there was a grave danger of the Soviet Union being involved single-handed in the fight with Germany while France sought the safety of the Maginot Line and Britain the Channel. Once the Soviet Union had come to terms with Germany, the Second World War was inevitable.

---

[148] Carr, Edward H: *German-Soviet Relations*, p.115
[149] Heineman: John L: *Neurath, Hitler's First Foreign Minister*, p.99
[150] Ibid.
[151] Librach, Jan: *Rise of the Soviet Empire*, p.67

9: LITVINOV, COMINTERN AND BRITAIN

Although in 1931 Litvinov had to turn his attention to Far Eastern affairs, most of his time and energy were spent on European questions concerning the Continent's major powers. Relations with democratic Germany and fascist Italy had, during the 20s, on the whole been tranquil. Relations with Poland and France had often been difficult, but Soviet relations with Britain had been worse.

When Litvinov was finally, officially in charge of foreign relations, he used his best endeavours and considerable energy to mend bridges. He achieved only limited success. In particular, the activities of the Comintern, founded in March 1919, would cause friction with Britain. The Comintern was described by the former chargé d'affaires, Hodgson, as:

> The organisation which the Party has fashioned for bringing about, through world revolution, the universal dictatorship of the proletariat. The Union of the Soviet Republics is the image in whose likeness the world is to be recreated.[1]

This suggests that the Comintern was never a truly international organisation. Lenin saw the Comintern as an organisation to promote Soviet interests. If, after the First World War, the Communists, as many feared, had gained control in Germany, they might have devised a different model; but this would have been unacceptable to Lenin.

The Comintern caused constant friction with Britain. On 1 June 1921, at a conference of the Comintern, all the speakers made it clear that their aim was the undermining of Britain's colonial Empire in the Far East. Dr Nuorteva, Director of Propaganda, after drawing attention to the gigantic task accomplished by the Eastern Secretariat during the past six months, said:

> The whole of our agency at the present moment is directed to elaborating a system for supplying the Eastern organisation with all they require. Up to the present time the work has been considerably interfered with by the alertness of the colonial administration, but in the near future, with the inevitable changes in the life of Persia, we shall have at our disposition in the immediate neighbourhood of India a base ample and sufficient for our task.[2]

Litvinov was given the duty of replying to these allegations. He denied that some of the

---

[1] Hodgson's description is at DBFP, 1st Series, vol.25, p.416, No.256
[2] Cmd Papers, 1927, 2895, enclosure No.2, p.6

alleged speeches had been made at the Comintern conference, but he did not deny the Nuorteva speech had been made. However, he stated:

> The Russian Government wishes to take this occasion to emphasise, as it had done many times before, that the mere fact that the Third International has, for obvious reasons, chosen Russia as the seat of their Executive Committee and some members of the Russian Government in their individual capacity belong to the Executive Committee, give no more justification for identifying the Third International with the Russian Government than the Second International having its seat in Brussels or counting among its members M. Vandervelde, a Belgian Minister, or Mr Henderson, a British Cabinet Minister, gave justification for rendering identical the Second International with the Belgian or British Governments. Moreover, the Executive Committee consists of thirty-one members, among whom are five Russian including three who do not belong to the Russian Government.[3]

It is clear that both Lenin and Stalin controlled the Third International, and certainly would never have approved of the Third International taking action not in accordance with their wishes. Further, Stalin took steps to liquidate any foreign member of the Comintern who disagreed with him and it was finally Stalin who determined to dissolve the Comintern in 1943. On the other hand, the Second International was never government-controlled, nor did any one country control it.

There can be no doubt Litvinov knew that what he was saying about the Comintern was untrue. For example, he sent letters of instructions to his ambassadors in 1928:

> It should be only by way of an exception that you answer the propaganda of ultra-lefts and bourgeoisie's anti-Bolshevik organisations in any official statements. The rest is not up to you; in general the struggle against ultra-left propaganda will be carried out through the joint efforts of the Central Committee and the Comintern.[4]

In private, far from disapproving of Comintern activities, Litvinov was stamping his approval on such activities and disproving the notion put forward by Stalin and other Communist leaders that the Comintern was separate from the Soviet Government, over which the Soviet Government had no control. US Communists thought that Litvinov had promised too much by agreeing 'not to permit the formation, on US territory, of any organisation or group which has, as its aim, a change in the political or social order of the whole or any part of the USA, its territories or possessions ' to which Litvinov responded:

---

[3] Cmd Papers, 1927, 2895, 29 September 1921, enclosure to No.3, pp.12 & 13
[4] Reiman, Michal: *Birth of Stalinism*, p.140

The agreement with the USA was between governments and not between the US Government and the Communist International. The Comintern is not restrained by the Soviet Government and is free to carry on any activity it deemed necessary. After all, Comrades, you should know by this time how to handle the fiction of the tie up between the Comintern and the Soviet Government. Don't worry about the letter. It is a scrap of paper which will soon be forgotten in the realities of Soviet-American relations.[5]

However, apparently, what Litvinov disapproved of was the Comintern using embassies for their activities. After the Chinese attack on the embassy in Peking, Litvinov went to the Politburo and vehemently demanded that agents of the Comintern be excluded from the embassies. Certain members of the Politburo pointed out that the work of the Comintern agents was indispensable since the aim of all politics was world revolution. Litvinov replied that he was in charge of the Commissariat of Foreign Affairs, not world revolution, and he must protect the Commissariat agencies established abroad. He added that if he was transferred to the Comintern he would watch the interests of world revolution, but while he remained at the Commissariat he was going to look after that and nothing else.[6] From this evidence it appears that Litvinov, in spite of any utterances to the contrary, did not disapprove of Comintern activity, providing it was kept separate from the work of the Foreign Commissariats so that it did not jeopardise the embassies' activities.

However, Litvinov rightly pointed out that Russian propaganda was not restricted to Communist Russia but applied equally to the Russian Government under the Tsars. In 1929 Lloyd George, in a debate in Parliament, referred to a previous speech where Joseph Chamberlain complained about the Tsar's Foreign Secretary's denial of carrying out propaganda against India. Joseph Chamberlain said, 'You cannot believe a word the Russian Foreign Secretary said, but nobody ever dreamt, least of all Joseph Chamberlain, of breaking off relations with Russia.'[7]

Russia still considered Britain the 'greatest capitalist power.'[8] This was not correct, as certainly by the 1920s, Britain had been replaced by the USA. However, democratic Britain was now far stronger than France or Germany, also both democracies. Tanya, Litvinov's daughter, confirms that, having lived here and married an English wife, her father found much to admire about Britain.[9]

The upper echelons of British society, including the Foreign Office, were unjustifiably antagonistic to Soviet Russia. They were worried that the Bolsheviks might succeed in bringing revolution to Britain. These fears proved to be entirely unfounded. In 1931, with

---

[5] Gitlow, Benjamin: *The Whole of Their Lives*, p. 265.
[6] Bessedovsky, Grigory : *Revelations of a Soviet Diplomat*, p.97
[7] Documents, p.208; *Hansard*, vol.231, 5 November 1929, 916
[8] See No. 48 post
[9] Tanya

the country in chaos, due to the 1929 financial crisis, the British electorate did not swing from the Labour Party to the Communists, but voted Conservative. Rather than perceiving Litvinov's position favourably on account of his moderation, in fact the Conservative Right hated him more than the conventional Communist politician. The Conservative MP, Henry Channon, described Litvinov as 'the dread intriguer.'[10] The reason why they feared Litvinov was because he took a more reasonable attitude over many matters compared with fellow Communists. Litvinov was therefore more likely to be able to influence anybody to the Centre or Left of centre of British political life. One would have thought that it was very much in Britain's interest to bolster Litvinov's position as Foreign Commissar, because his successor would be less likely to be so pro-British. Litvinov often became frustrated with British policy and the anti-Soviet element in British society, but he believed that, if there could be good relations with Britain, without too much loss of prestige, that should be the aim of Soviet foreign policy. On this point there was not any basic disagreement with Stalin, although Stalin's approach was purely pragmatic. He seemed to have had more respect for Germany and the USA.

The anti-Bolshevik section of British society included the Foreign Office. A memorandum of 25 October 1918 describes a new danger in Europe no less deadly than the Kaiser's Germany:

> The first duty of the League is to settle the Russian problem and declare war on the Bolsheviks. The longer Bolshevism is left the more dangerous it will be. If it is dealt with now, a comparative small army from the Urals might advance on Moscow and put it down by force; whereas, if decisive action is postponed, it may spread West and the task will be much more difficult and will require a larger army.'[11]

Chicherin has been portrayed as having little interest in Britain. The evidence does not support this. In 1918, at a time when negotiations with the Germans were going badly, Chicherin told Lockhart: 'Now was the great opportunity for Britain to make a friendly gesture towards Russia.'[12]

In 1920 Litvinov went to Copenhagen and successfully negotiated with O'Grady, a British Labour MP, a mutual exchange of Civil War prisoners. The reason why the negotiations did not take place in Britain was because Litvinov was refused entry. When questioned in the House of Commons, Bonar Law wrongly stated: 'Litvinov was refused entry because of his alleged previous activities.' This answer was highly misleading, because Litvinov left the country as part of the Anglo-Bolshevik agreement, under the terms of which British diplomats were allowed to leave Russia, and if it had not been for Litvinov's personal co-operation, the

---

[10] Channon, Henry: *Diaries*, p.164
[11] FO 371/3344, 174035
[12] Fischer, Louis: *Life of Lenin*, p.165

agreement might never have been effected.[13] What was surprising was that Bonar Law's incorrect answers were not challenged by any Labour MP who had far more sympathy for Soviet Russia.[14] Although it is my belief that Litvinov was engaging in some revolutionary activity while unofficial ambassador to Britain, that was not the reason for his expulsion.

However, the implementation of the prisoner agreement proved more difficult than had been anticipated. Shortly afterwards, 124 prisoners of war and 727 civilians arrived in Britain from Russia. All Russian prisoners, together with a good many more in Western Europe, were repatriated to Russia.[15] One of the problems was that there were various prisoners held in the Republic of Azerbaijan. Even if the Republic was not under the direct control of the Communist regime in Moscow, the latter had great influence. However, the Azerbaijan Government tried to make the exchange conditional on the exchange of some Kemalist Turks held in Malta.

Under pressure in Parliament, Lloyd George stated on 3 June 1920: 'An undertaking to release British prisoners is an indispensable principle to renewal of trading relations with Russia.'[16] In addition, Curzon, the British Foreign Secretary, gave an ultimatum: 'Unless, by 10 October 1920, we have definite evidence that the conditions laid down have been complied with, we shall take whatever action necessary to secure their release.' Chicherin and Litvinov were right to take Britain's threat seriously. A British warship detained a Finnish vessel and removed six Bolshevik detainees who had been allowed to sail from London on the assumption that the exchange would take place without delay. However, when Admiral Webb requested permission to bombard Odessa from land and in the air, permission was refused.[17]

Chicherin, in a letter to Krassin, said, 'It must be recognised that all elements hostile to Russia have become extraordinarily more insolent and full of hope.' Therefore, he said, 'The Soviet side should carefully appraise its statements and actions. There was no need to give those elements, which sought a rupture, a handle on which they could pull.' Chicherin also radioed to Litvinov that Curzon's note 'renders urgent the exchange of prisoners.'[18] In spite of the perception that Chicherin was only interested in Asia and Germany, this evidence clearly shows he was as enthusiastic as Litvinov about the importance of reasonable relations with Britain. Eventually, the Russian Government offered its good services to send a delegate to Azerbaijan if Britain would do likewise. After procrastination and delay on behalf of the Azerbaijan delegate, an agreement was finally signed on 1 November 1920 that the British prisoners at Baku should be freed.

---

[13] Ch.2, No.68
[14] *Hansard*, 1920, 10 May 1920, vol.129, 55
[15] Ullman, Richard: *Anglo-Soviet Relations 1917-1921*, vol.3, p.401
[16] *Hansard*, vol.129, 3 June 1920, 2032
[17] Ullman, Richard: *Anglo-Soviet Relations*, vol.3, p.409
[18] Ibid.

Meanwhile, relations between the Soviet Union and Britain were damaged by the action of King George V, who, immediately after the invasion of Russia by Poland, had sent Pilsudski a message of congratulations and 'sincere good wishes' on the occasion of Poland's national holiday.[19]

Moreover, Litvinov continued to be very suspicious of Lloyd George. After Krassin had written that peace with Great Britain was possible, Litvinov stated: 'Lloyd George's amiability was merely a façade, meant to confuse the Soviet Government and lead them to make needless concessions to Poland and Persia.'[20]

Although it was kept secret at the time, one visitor received by Litvinov in Copenhagen was Francis Meynell, a young director of the *Daily Herald*. He arrived in late July 1920 with a request for financial support for the *Herald*. This caused Litvinov to become embroiled in a controversy concerning that newspaper, as the money was apparently raised from the sale of jewellery smuggled into Britain. At that time any money transactions with Russia were forbidden. When a scandal erupted, Meynell resigned his directorship.[21]

However, perhaps unwisely, the Soviet Union decided to give financial support to the *Daily Herald*, which, although it was close to, was not controlled by the Labour Party and trade unions. The Labour leader, Lansbury, should be criticised for appealing to the Soviet Union for financial support in spite of the dire financial situation of the fledgling Communist state. A letter appeared in the *Times* which purported to be written by Litvinov to Chicherin on 11 July 1920. This letter stated:

> If we do not support the *Daily Herald*, which is now passing through a fresh crisis, the paper will have to turn to a Right trade union. On Russian questions it acts as if it is our organ. After Lansbury's journey to Moscow earlier in the year, the *Herald* has moved considerably to the Left and decidedly advocates direct action in support of the Soviet regime. It needed £50,000 in six months, after which once again it hoped to be on firm ground. I beg for an early and favourable answer because there is no hope of establishing a purely communist newspaper at this time.[22]

When Lansbury was asked to contradict the statement alleged to have been made by Litvinov on 11 July 1920, Lansbury stated, 'I have no knowledge Litvinov ever made that statement. Certainly we are not anybody's organ and never have been.' The *Herald* leader

---

[19] Debo, Richard: *Survival and Consolidation*, p.215

[20] Ibid. p.217

[21] Lansbury, George: *Miracle of Fleet Street*, p.150; Shepherd, John: *George Lansbury*, p.187

[22] *Times*, 19 August 1920, p.10; Shepherd, John: *Life of George Lansbury*, p.187; Lansbury *Miracle of Fleet Street* p.146

on the same day stated: 'We have received no Bolshevik gold, no Bolshevik paper, no Chinese bonds.'[23]

Thereafter the directors of the *Daily Herald* declared:

> We had no knowledge of any money offered to the *Daily Herald*, but now the matter has been brought to our attention we have decided not to accept the offer. We hold the strong belief that the British Labour movement and all loyal readers of the *Daily Herald* recognise the ever increasing value of the *Daily Herald* to the movement and will support the paper to the full extent of its financial requirements.[24]

Kamenev, the President of the Russian delegation to Britain, told certain British MPs 'In my capacity as its chairman, I have never given or offered any subsidy either to the *Daily Herald* or other newspaper whatever, or to any editor or proprietor of any newspaper.' However, the Lloyd George Government alleged that Mr Kamenev's statement was not true, because diamonds, having been brought over by the Russian delegation, were sold.

A sum of between £40,000 and £50,000 was raised for the benefit of the *Daily Herald*. It was claimed that the only reason why the *Daily Herald* would not accept Russian money was because it was no longer a secret. However, the *Daily Herald* stated sarcastically: 'Until we were appraised that the secret could no longer be kept, we did not know there was any secret to be kept.'[25]

As far as I am aware, neither Litvinov nor the Russian Government ever denied that Litvinov's statement was made and the evidence would seem to suggest that the gift was made and that it was Litvinov who proposed the gift should be made to the *Daily Herald*. It appears that Chicherin was not so keen because of the adverse effect on public opinion in Britain if it was discovered that the Russian Government was subsidising the *Daily Herald*.

Chicherin's desire to improve relations with Britain is further shown by a letter written in March 1920, which stated:

> Let Britain look on the trip of Krassin as a serious trip for the foundation of commercial relations and not a preliminary contact without final or precise decisions. It is especially important for us that we obtain concrete commercial results and not merely declarative statements. The very fact that the delegation is composed of such experts is a sign that concrete business decisions are expected.[26]

---

[23] *Daily Herald,* 20 August 1920, p.1;   Lansbury, George:*Miracle of Fleet Street,* p.146
[24] *Daily Herald,* 15 September 1920, p.1;   Lansbury, George *Miracle of Fleet Street,* p.147
[25] *Daily Herald,* 16 September 1920, p.1;   Lansbury, George *Miracle of Fleet Street,* p.149
[26] Debo, Richard: *Survival and Consolidation,* p.157

In March 1921 a trade agreement was negotiated. This contained the provision that gold sent as payment for merchandise would not be confiscated.[27]

However, immediately after the agreement was signed, the British Government and even more the British press began to complain about Communist propaganda. Finally, the British Foreign Secretary sent a note of protest to the Soviet Government, charging it with responsibility for intrigues against the British Government.

Litvinov replied:

> The British Foreign Office has been misled by a gang of professional forgers and swindlers, and had it known the dubious sources of its information, its note of 7 September would never have been produced.

Litvinov stated: The British Government's complaints of anti-British activities in India, Persia, Turkistan, Angora and Afghanistan

> to a certain extent are based on the above-mentioned fictitious reports and speeches, but the Russian Government wishes to state most emphatically that, after the conclusion of the Anglo-Russian agreement … it had given strict instructions to its representatives in the East to abstain from any anti-British propaganda.

At the same time Litvinov claimed :

> True to the principle of self-determination, the Soviet Government and its representatives exercise the greatest respect for the independence of the Eastern countries in giving up the privileges and concessions forcibly extorted from them by the Tsarist Government.

However, the Indian independence movement inspired by Gandhi was deep-rooted and Moscow was unlikely to have any more influence on it than it did in relation to the nationalist movement in China.

Litvinov continued:

> Still the Russian Government has done its utmost in honouring its undertakings and has endeavoured to obviate any cause of friction and misunderstanding.

Litvinov went on to say:

---

[27] Ullman, Richard: *Anglo-Soviet Relations*, vol.3, pp.397 -453

The Russian Government, on its part, feels compelled to place on record that the attitude of the British Government has lately been far from friendly towards Russia.

Litvinov also said:

The imprisonment by British authorities in Constantinople of a number of Russian trade agents and their expulsion without any charge having being preferred against them, the co-operation with the French Government in the so-called 'Russian question', the continued support given to French schemes tending to frustrate every effort on behalf of various countries and international bodies to bring some help to the famine-stricken population of Russia, and lastly the presentation of the British note itself of 7 September with its grave charges based merely on imaginary facts and unchecked loose information obtained from dubious sources at a time when France was inciting Poland and Rumania to make war on Russia, do not belong to the category of facts that would induce the Russian Government to believe that it is the sincere desire of the British Government to foster friendly relations between the governments and peoples of the two countries.[28]

This shows that, in spite of being pro-British, Litvinov was prepared to be tough with Britain if he thought the occasion demanded it.

In 1922 the coalition under Lloyd George fell, to be replaced by a Conservative administration. Lord Curzon, who was violently anti-Communist, became Foreign Minister.[29] On 23 March 1923 the British Chargé d'Affaires, Hodgson, handed a curt but polite note to the Narkomindel containing a plea that the death sentence on Butkevich, a Soviet citizen, should not be carried out.[30] On 4 April a reply was received from Weinstein on the letterhead of the Western Department of the Russian Government, stating that he was instructed by the People's Commissar of Foreign Affairs to point out :

Russia being an independent country and a sovereign state has the undeniable right of passing sentences in accordance with its own legislation on people breaking the law of the Country and that every attempt from outside to interfere with this right and to protect spies and traitors in Russia is an unfriendly act. It is necessary to mention that, simultaneously with your note, Chicherin received a telegram from the representative of the Irish Republic in France on the same subject in which the signatory, in asking for mercy on behalf of Cieplak, says: "He is doing so in spite of the hypocritical intervention of the British Government, which is responsible for assassination in cold blood of political prisoners in Ireland, where 14,000 men, women and young girls are treated in a barbarous and inhuman fashion in

---

[28] Cmd Papers, 1927, 2895, No.3, pp.12 @ 16, 29 September 1921
[29] Taylor, A J P: *English History 1914-1945*, p.193
[30] Cmd Papers, 1923, 1869, Letter No.1, p.3, 30 March 1923

conformity with the will of Great Britain, while British control over cables prevents the civilised world from learning of the horrible details of these atrocities." If similar facts, which have taken place under British rule in India and Egypt, are taken into consideration, it is hardly possible to regard an appeal in the name of humanity and sacredness of life from the British Government as very convincing.[31]

Hodgson stated that he could not accept the note in its present form.[32]

Weinstein stated:

> Taking into consideration that your note of 30 March cannot be qualified, otherwise as an entirely inadmissible attempt at interference in the internal affairs of the independent and sovereign RFSSR, the People's Commissariat for Foreign Affairs cannot acknowledge that the expressions employed in the answering note were inept or not suitable to the circumstances of the case. The People's Commissariat regrets that you find it not possible to transmit to your Government the note handed to you, but intended for it, and consequently it only remains to find other means for acquainting the British Government with its contents. In any case, in view of the publication both of your note and of the reply, the People's Commissariat for Foreign Affairs trusts that the contents of the latter are already known to the Government and that in the future it will refrain from attempts of any kind at interfering in the internal affairs of the Soviet Republics.[33]

I do not know why Weinstein rather than Litvinov or Chicherin replied. If a rash individual had responded to Hodgson's initial letter, one would have expected the second letter to have been written by either Litvinov or Chicherin. One cannot believe that Chicherin would have agreed to such a response in view of his rebuking Litvinov for writing un-diplomatic correspondence; or was Litvinov the author of the letter and, in view of the likely hostility to it, pretended it had been written by one of his staff ?

After a month of reflection, the Foreign Office dispatched a strong note through its Moscow Chargé d'Affaires known as 'the Curzon Ultimatum.' It complained about the anti-British activities of the Soviet representatives in Teheran and Kabul, as well as propaganda in India and the work of the Comintern generally, the abandonment of which it demanded immediately. Other complaints were about the death of a British agent and the imprisonment of another (their status was not contested, though the charges against one of them were described as false) as long ago as 1920. The final demand was for the withdrawal of Weinstein's two notes. If the demands in the Curzon ultimatum were not met within ten days, the 1921 Anglo-Russian trade agreement would be denounced, and

---

[31] Cmd 1869, 1923, No.2, p.3, 31 March 1923
[32] Ibid. No.3, p.4, 1 April 1923
[33] Ibid. No.4, p.4, 4 April 1923

Hodgson was instructed to leave Moscow. This was no idle threat, as if no reply was received or if Hodgson considered it unsatisfactory, he was instructed to leave Moscow without the necessity of taking further instructions.[34]

As far as the Soviet Union was concerned, the danger of Allied intervention in the Soviet Union had increased because at the same time the French general, Foch visited Poland, followed a week later by the British chief of the Imperial General Staff. The Russian Government gained the impression that the Polish army was being prepared for an attack on the Soviet Union.[35] The Soviet Union was so alarmed and frightened that they were prepared to concede almost all the demands of the Curzon note, even offering some compensation for the treatment of the two British agents.

Chicherin, rather than deal with the matter personally, chose Litvinov to sign a long note in reply which was conciliatory in tone, making it clear:

> In spite of reiterated misunderstandings, the Soviet Republic highly value their present relations with Great Britain and endeavour to preserve and develop them in the interests of general peaceful, economic restoration of ruined European peoples of the Soviet Union as of Britain, and are therefore ready for the most favourable and peaceful settlement of existing conflicts.[36]

Meanwhile, Chicherin spoke at a demonstration at the Bolshoi Theatre, stating: Lenin's death has filled the enemies of the Soviet Union 'with the naïve confidence that the Soviet power is deprived of its firmness and could be overthrown from pressure from without. We firmly await our enemy before the threshold, and we believe he will not have the courage to attack.'

Litvinov spoke on occasions just as harshly on British policy. On this occasion, although one might have thought that Trotsky, with his revolutionary zeal, would have welcomed with relish an out and out struggle with Britain, he made it clear he did not relish it, stating:

> In the present tense situation in Europe this would be a life and death struggle; It would be a struggle that would last for months, perhaps years, which would swallow up all the resources and forces of our country, which would interrupt our economic and cultural work for years. That is why we say: "May this cup pass from us."[37]

---

[34] Ibid. No.5, pp.5-13, 2 May 1923
[35] Carr, Edward: *Interregnum*, p.169, Foch
[36] Cmd 1874, 1923, pp.2-8, 13 May 1923; Degras, Jane: *Soviet Documents on Foreign Policy*, vol.1, p.384@ p.391
[37] Carr, Edward: *Interregnum*, p.171

Until the fall of the Conservative Government at the 1923 general election, Curzon was now in more conciliatory mode. Krassin was appointed to enter into negotiations and on 16 June 1923 a final note from Chicherin wound up the correspondence.[38]

The situation entirely changed when the Conservative Government was defeated in the 1923 British General Election. Both the Labour party, who formed a minority government, and the Liberal party, who gave Labour some support, favoured *de jure* recognition of the Soviet Government.[39]

Macdonald, the new Labour Prime Minister, took the initiative by sending a telegraphic message to Britain's Moscow representative, Hodgson, on 1 February 1924, informing him of HM Government's decision 'that the British Government was prepared to recognise the Union of Socialist Soviet Republics as the *de jure* rulers of those territories of the old Russian Empire that acknowledged their authority' and inviting the Soviet Union to send representatives to London to draw up a full treaty to settle all differences between the two countries. The matters named that needed to be discussed were: the validity of treaties completed before the Revolution, claims and propaganda. Rakovsky replied, expressing satisfaction with the British note and stating that he would travel to Britain as he had been appointed chargé d'affaires.[40] Litvinov showed he had yet to abandon the veneer of a revolutionary by stating: 'The British working class had always been the true ally of the working class of the Union of Soviet Socialist Republics', but then returned to more diplomatic language by holding out a hand of friendly fraternal greetings to the British people and empowered the Soviet Government to enter into negotiations. On 8 February Rakovsky, having arrived in London, had his first meeting with Macdonald.[41] Finally, on 14 April 1924 a formal conference opened to try to reach agreement on the various matters outstanding.[42]

However, the day the conference opened a number of leading bankers presented a memorandum, which they released to the press, demanding, among other matters, recognition of debts both public and private and restitution of private property to foreigners.[43] Two days later McNeill, a Conservative spokesman, wrote a letter to the *Times* stating that if Macdonald abandoned claims against the Soviet Government, a future Conservative British Government would not be bound by it.[44]

Meanwhile, on 8 February 1924 Hodgson travelled to the Soviet Union to take up his position as chargé d'affaires, immediately seeing Litvinov (Chicherin being temporarily absent), who 'expressed his profound satisfaction and that of his Government at the step

---

[38] Cmd 1890, 1923, No.4, pp.2-8, 13 June 1923; Carr, Edward: *Interregnum*, p.173
[39] Taylor, A J P: *English History 1914 -1945*, p.209
[40] DBFP,1st Series, vol.25, p.333, No.207
[41] Ibid. p.343, No.216
[42] Ibid. p 463, No.275
[43] Carr Edward, *Socialism in One Country*, p.23
[44] Ibid. p.23; *Times*, 16 April 1924, p.15

taken and his hope that it would result in a real and permanent improvement in the relations between the two countries.' Hodgson was invited to attend the Supreme Soviet, when Litvinov announced the British desire for the restoration of diplomatic relations with the Soviet Union, which was well received and approved unanimously. Shortly afterwards, Hodgson saw Chicherin, 'whose attitude throughout the meeting was marked by great cordiality.' Hodgson thought: 'He (Chicherin) was animated by a friendly disposition and will approach the pending negotiations in London in a conciliatory spirit.'Chicherin informed Hodgson of the proposal to appoint Rakovsky as the Charge d'Affaires.[45]

Whereas one would have thought the Soviet Government would have wanted to cultivate such an important ally as the British Labour Government, the Soviet Government immediately created difficulties by arresting any Russian who called at the legation to seek information, which brought forth a strong protest from the British Chargé d'Affaires, Hodgson.[46] Although Litvinov's advice was regularly sought on foreign policy over which he had some influence, unlike a British Foreign Secretary, Litvinov had no influence over security matters, which always had to take precedence, to the detriment of foreign policy objectives. After considerable deliberation and a sharp division of opinion in Cabinet, a strong group of Left-wing politicians – Morel, Lansbury, Purcell and Wallhead – intervened in an attempt to prevent the talks from breaking down. Accordingly, the Labour Cabinet decided to make an agreement possible by guaranteeing a loan available to the Soviet Union of £30,000,000. This was subject to satisfactory arrangements being reached with the bondholders and those former owners of property in the Soviet Union who were British and whose property had been nationalised. However, after informal and formal meetings, eventually, by 12 August, a formula had been found whereby the former owners' claims were not prejudiced. The commercial treaty was signed on 8 August 1924.[47]

Undoubtedly, the Soviet leadership was enthusiastic that the commercial treaty had finally been signed. A communiqué of the Narkomindel welcomed it as 'laying the foundation of new relations between the USSR and the greatest world capitalist power' and it appears reasonably clear that the policy of improved relations of the Soviet Union had both Chicherin's and Litvinov's enthusiastic support. Although they both wanted better relations with Germany, they did not want this at the expense of better relations with the United Kingdom. Kamenev described it as 'indubitably a turning point in the whole world situation of our union and as an international act in which the full equality of rights of our political and economic system with the system of the greatest political world power is guaranteed.'[48]

---

[45] DBFP, 1st Series, vol.25, p.344, No.217
[46] Ibid. pp. 382-383, Nos.238 & 239
[47] Carr, Edward: *Socialism in One Country*, vol.3, p.27
[48] Ibid.p.27

Chicherin was as pleased as anybody that Great Britain had at long last recognised the Soviet Government, saying:

> What does this treaty really include? First, that which has been unattainable, before settlement of the question of Imperial debts, has been made a component part of the question of our receiving a loan, and, moreover, in such a form in such a combination that we obtain from this transaction a tangible advantage. Moreover, the private recognition of old obligations in the actual text of the agreement signed by the British Government is regarded as an exception to our decrees regarding the cancellation of loans and the nationalisation of property. Consequently, the British Government has put its signature beneath a recognition of the fact that this partial concession is an exception from our decrees. This amounts to international recognition of these latter.[49]

Hodgson took up his appointment as chargé d'affaires and stayed at his appointment until the rupture in 1927. He liked and respected Litvinov and was confident that Litvinov worked wholeheartedly for good relations between Great Britain and the Soviet Union.[50]

However, the treaty needed the approval of Parliament. The Liberal party, upon whom the minority Labour Government needed its support, refused to support the Bill, but this was purely academic as on 8 October 1924 the Labour Government was defeated on a vote of censure condemning the withdrawal of a prosecution against John Ross Campbell, editor of the *Communist Weekly* for alleged incitement in the army. Constitutionally, the Labour Cabinet would appear to have acted correctly, as it was the Attorney General who eventually advised the withdrawal of the prosecution after being told that the editor responsible, who had an excellent war record, was only the acting editor. However, it can be assumed that the Attorney General was also told that if he persisted in the prosecution, 'bitter hostility would be incurred from the Left wing of the Labour Party.'[51] Parliament was dissolved and elections fixed for 29 October 1924.

During the election campaign, a letter was published, allegedly written by Zinoviev, the president of the Communist International, to the British Communist Party, with instructions to carry out all kinds of seditious activities. Many, including the eminent historian A J P Taylor, had their doubts and apparently George V had similar doubts as to whether the letter was genuine.[52] Zinoviev denied sending the letter, stating that he was in the Caucasus. Rakovsky delivered a direct message from Litvinov who demanded : 'An adequate apology and punishment of both private and official persons involved in the

---

[49] FO 371/10500, p.231

[50] *Times* (Hodgson), 11 November 1941, p.5

[51] Marquand, David: *Ramsay Macdonald*, p.365

[52] Taylor, A J P: *English History 1914-1945*, pp. 219-220;
  Carr, Edward: *Socialism in One Country*, p.29; Nicolson, Harold: *George V*, p.402

forgery' and proposed an impartial arbitration court for establishing whether the Zinoviev letter was a forgery. Macdonald might well have been wise to have agreed to an international arbitration court. It would probably have held that the letter was a forgery, which would have discredited those who were trying to sabotage improved relations with the Soviet Union. Instead, Macdonald acted timidly. The Foreign Office immediately assumed that the letter was genuine, saying: 'We have heard definitely on absolute authority that the Russian letter was discussed at a recent meeting of the Central Committee of the Communist party of Great Britain'; but it might well have been the alleged copy. The Zinoviev letter came to the attention of the Foreign Office on 10 October 1924, and the Foreign Office advice was not tendered to Macdonald until 15 October. In spite of the fact that a Cabinet Committee of the Labour Government on 31 October was 'unable to come to a positive conclusion as to whether the letter was genuine', Macdonald, on the advice of the Foreign Office, refused to accept the note.[53] Further evidence it was a forgery came to light in the 1970s as a result of research by the historian Michael Kettle, who believed that the signature on the letter was similar to that of Sydney Reilly, the Secret Service's master spy.[54]

The Conservatives easily won the 1924 General Election with 48.3% of the vote and 419 seats. *Izvestiya* described the vote as 'a deserved defeat for the Labour party.'[55] This was hardly an apt remark to describe Macdonald's continued fight not only to obtain recognition for the Soviet Union but also to obtain the loan for the Soviet Government thus risking the survival of the Labour Government. However, the result was not particularly bad for Labour who, although they lost thirty-eight seats, increased their vote by 1,000,000. This was disastrous for the Liberals, who had been unwise to bring down the Labour Government. The Liberal party, who did not have the funds to fight the election, fielded 100 fewer candidates than in 1922, losing one hundred and eighteen seats, including that of Asquith, and their seats declined to 40. It appears that those with Left-wing sympathies were little affected by the Zinoviev letter, but many Liberals voted Conservative to keep Labour from office.[56]

Austen Chamberlain, who was the new Conservative Foreign Minister, immediately adopted an anti-Soviet stance. He informed Rakovsky that he could not recommend the treaties of 1924 to Parliament, and secondly Chamberlain told a lie when he said: 'The information in the possession of HM Government leaves no doubt whatever in their mind of the authenticity of the letter.'[57] There is no evidence that the new Conservative Government ever submitted the Zinoviev letter for any sort of expert examination. If the

---

[53] DBFP, 1st Series, vol.25, Foreign Office Advice No.264, p.433; Labour Cabinet Conclusions, p.439, No.264; Rakovsky letter in Degras, Jane: *Soviet Documents on Foreign Policy*, vol.1, p.471
[54] O'Reilly, see *Sunday Times*, 15 February 1970, p.4; and Prem 13/3251
[55] *Izvestiya*, 31 October 1924
[56] Taylor, A J P: *English History 1914-1945*, p.220; Marquand, David: *Ramsay Macdonald*, p.387
[57] DBFP, 1st Series, vol.25, p.447, No.266

government had done so and the opinion had been that the letter was authentic, surely the Conservative Government would have been keen to publish their findings. It is difficult to see what this attitude achieved. It certainly did not strike a blow at the Bolshevik regime. It did make it easier for those in the Soviet Union who favoured an autocratic Communist regime, because they were able to portray the need for tough internal policies to protect them in a hostile world.

The Treaty of Locarno was the most significant political event of 1925. Its purpose was to bring Germany back into the community of nations. The Soviet Union believed the treaty was directed against them. This was not necessarily so, but it certainly was intended by Britain to lessen Germany's dependence on the Soviet Union.'[58]

However, Litvinov was entirely of the same opinion, describing 'British Foreign policy as completely anti-Russian.'[59] On 22 September 1925 *Pravda*, in a leading article, described British actions as: 'Nothing less than a systematic and prolonged preparation of war against the USSR.'[60] However, in April 1926 Litvinov struck a conciliatory note, making it clear that the Soviet Government, since the advent of the Conservative Government, had never refused to negotiate and detected a ray of hope when a handful of Conservative MPs voted against the Government's refusal to extend export credits to the Soviet Union.[61]

On the positive side of Anglo-Soviet relations, an extensive commercial agreement was signed by the British mining company Lena Goldfields, which had extensive mining interests in Russia before the Russian Revolution. Lena Goldfields, with the help of US private commercial money, invested a considerable amount of money to bring the mines back into production.[62]

Relations between the Soviet Union and Great Britain began to deteriorate following the attempt of the Soviet Union to give financial support to the British workers who participated in the 1926 British General Strike. On 8 May 1926 *Izvestiya* stated: 'The whole world's working class watches with the greatest delight the British working class's gigantic struggle' and were sharply critical of the fact that the TUC General Council subsequently called off the strike, describing it as a 'betrayal of the General Strike.' The Soviet Chargé d'Affaires defended the action on the grounds that the Soviet Government had never sent any money for the purpose of the strike, but wrongly stated that the Soviet Government does not interfere with the right of the trade unions to dispose of their funds as it wished.[63] It is quite certain that the Soviet Trade Unions would not have done anything

---

[58] Ch 5 No 4.
[59] Ibid. p.266
[60] Ibid. p.274
[61] Ibid. p.418
[62] Ibid. p.415
[63] Degras, Jane: *Soviet Documents on Foreign Policy*, vol.2, p.118

against the will of their leaders. However, the TUC refused to accept a gift of £25,000, although the Co-operative Society accepted a gift of £200,000.[64] Further, *Izvestiya* was a government newspaper. A further Narkomindel note on 27 June complained about a speech by Churchill, although 'it noted with satisfaction the British Foreign Secretary Austen Chamberlain's statement of the undesirability of the severance of diplomatic relations between the two countries.'[65] Litvinov, who realised the damage of the disclosure of the help offered to the strikers, set about trying to repair the damage. He wisely sought the help of Robert Boothby, an up and coming star in the Conservative party, to restate the Soviet Union's desire to reopen negotiations.[66] However, on 16 June 1926 Joynson Hicks led the attack in Cabinet, complaining that Chamberlain's policy on the Soviet Union had not been tough enough and pressing for a rupture. However, the Cabinet did not favour a rupture at this stage.[67]

The British Government was continually receiving resolutions from various trade associations such the Aberdeen National Association of Importers and Exporters and the Manchester Association of Importers and Exporters condemning the British Government for any action that might result in any improvement in relations with the Soviet Union.[68]

Litvinov, with the debt matter unresolved, as so often, took the initiative by suggesting to Hodgson, in August 1926, that Britain and the Soviet Government initiate conversations to settle outstanding difficulties. Hodgson complained about the Soviet Government's action in the British General Strike and also about allegations in the Soviet press that the British Government were carrying out a number of anti-Soviet steps, such as intriguing in the Baltic States or setting up a dictatorship in Poland.[69]

However, in a letter dated 26 October 1926, Hodgson in Moscow complained to the Foreign Secretary that great harm was being done to British interests by the anti-Communist rhetoric. Hodgson reminded his Foreign Secretary:

> In the first place we had signed a trade agreement as long ago as 1921 and in 1923 we went a step further by conferring on the Soviet Government *de jure* recognition.

He gave four reasons for criticising Britain's position.

> Possibly we did wrong on both occasions, but nothing shows, by going back now upon what we did then, we should improve matters. Second we have let

---

[64] Grayson, Richard S: *Austen Chamberlain and the Commitment to Europe,*
British Foreign Policy 1925-1929, p.261
[65] Degras, Jane: *Soviet Documents on Foreign Policy*, vol.2, p.121
[66] Gorodetsky, Gabriel: *Precarious Truth*, p.175
[67] Ibid.
[68] FO 371/10500, Aberdeen p.64 Manchester p.65
[69] FO 371/11787, p.38

it be known upon several occasions in the past six months that HM Government have every intention of maintaining its relationship with the Soviet Government unless the latter do something quite intolerably offensive. Third, the outbursts of enthusiasts carried away by their legitimate emotions are liable to prejudice our position in dealing with problems which, being in relation with the Soviet Government, we have to solve by discussion with that Government. Fourth, the Soviet Union whatever her political complexion, is a market and we badly need markets. The red bandit battle cry may conceivably serve a useful purpose in the political warfare at home. On this question I can offer no opinion. I can, however, lay it down as a proposition that in so far as our relations with Russia are concerned, the expressions of resentment which it epitomises are definitely detrimental to our essential interest. That we should be alarmed at the activity of Soviet agitators is an admission of weakness which is hailed with delight over here.

Yet the most pressing aspect is the commercial one and here the anti-red campaign does positive and immediate harm which it is impossible to calculate in pounds sterling. It creates a policy of insecurity which makes the Soviet Government hesitant about placing orders in Britain, causes British firms to fight shy of Russian orders and frightens British banks from financing them.[70]

Anti-Soviet behaviour in Britain was matched by Soviet press allegations, such as Britain was intriguing with the Baltic States and others in conspiracies detrimental to the Soviet Union, to which Litvinov replied on 26 August 1926: 'It was impossible for him of late to know all that the British Government was doing', but under pressure hinted that 'nothing had transpired of a nature to substantiate the accusations made in the Soviet press.'[71]

Somewhat delayed, on 23 February 1927 Chamberlain sent a note to the Soviet Union quoting what his political opponent Ramsay Macdonald had said on 24 October 1924:

No government will tolerate an arrangement with a foreign government by which the latter is in diplomatic relations of a correct kind with it, whilst at the same time a propagandist group organically connected with that foreign government encourages and even orders subjects of the former to plot and plan revolutions for its overthrow.

Chamberlain charged the Soviet Government with seditious activities in Britain during the 1926 General Strike, stating: 'We must be ready for anything and must continue to support the miner's strike with un-relaxed energy.' Further, Chamberlain complained about continuing to conduct a campaign against British interests in China. However, the British

---

[70] Ibid. p.81
[71] Ibid. pp. 39 to 41

Government had damaged its case because the Prime Minister had allowed Ministers to make remarks that encouraged disaffected Russians to rid themselves of the Soviet Government. Chamberlain ended his note by stating: 'His Majesty's Government is not concerned with the domestic affairs of the Soviet Union nor with its form of government', which was not correct in view of British Ministers' constant criticism of communism and the Soviet Government.

The British note continued:

> All we require is that the Soviet Government should refrain from interference with purely British concerns and abstain from hostile action or propaganda against British subjects. We consider it is necessary to warn the Union of Soviet Socialist Republics in the gravest terms that there are limits beyond which it is dangerous to drive public opinion in this country and that a continuance of such acts as have been complained of must sooner or later render inevitable the abrogation of the Trade Agreement, the stipulations of which had been so flagrantly violated, and even the severance of ordinary diplomatic relations.[72]

However this letter was sent almost twelve months after the General Strike and indicated that, even if further breaches occurred, it did not necessarily mean the severance of ordinary diplomatic relations, This supports the view that Chamberlain was not enthusiastic about sending the note, as he did not wish a rupture. Chamberlain, in his farewell interview with Rakovsky, rejected Chicherin's assertion that his (Chamberlain's) policy 'was directed to the isolation of the Soviet Union', but Chicherin's assertion was not unreasonable.[73]

Unlike the conciliatory reply to the Curzon note when Chicherin was in charge, Litvinov was determined to go on the attack in his reply. He referred to the fact that many of the difficulties of relations between Britain and the Soviet Union had arisen as a result of the forged 'Zinoviev letter' and that the Soviet Union 'had agreed, however, in view of the special political role the letter might play, to any expert examination of the letter, and agreed to recognise the decision of an arbiter'; a rare occasion when the Soviet Union consented to be bound by an arbitration. The British refusal to agree to arbitration 'could not be otherwise understood than as a withdrawal of the accusation.' Litvinov states that nobody can have any doubts, 'including circles in the Labour Party', that the letter was forged. Litvinov gave a reminder: 'There exists no agreement which limits freedom of speech and of the press within the confines of the two countries', but rightly referred to anti-Soviet remarks by members of the Conservative Government such as the Secretary of State for India, who described the Soviet Government, 'As a band of murderers and robbers'; and the Chancellor of the Exchequer, Winston Churchill, who had described the

---

[72] Cmd 2895, 1927, No.14, pp.45-63 @ p.49
[73] Carr, Edward: *Socialism in One Country*, p. 414

Soviet Government: 'As a band of international conspirators collected from the dregs of big towns of Britain and America which has despotically taken possession of all the enormous resources of what was once the famed mighty Russian Empire.'[74] Although Churchill rightly described the Communist regime as despotic, he failed to mention that the Russian Empire was similarly despotic.

The harsh nature of Litvinov's reply was criticised by Chicherin, who was in Germany and dispatched a note to Stalin and Rykov warning that the British Government was prepared to break off diplomatic relations with the Soviet Union and that the Narkomindel should have responded to the note in a conciliatory fashion in order to mollify the moderate Conservatives in the Cabinet. Further, Chicherin urged the Soviet leaders not to underestimate British intentions,[75] which is proof of Chicherin's deep interest in Europe, his understanding of the British political scene and the importance to the Soviet Union of maintaining relations with Britain.

On 12 May 1927 the building used by the Russian Co-operative Society and the Soviet Trade delegation was searched, in breach of article 5 of the 1921 Trade Agreement, for a missing War Office document.[76] On 17 May 1927 Litvinov formally protested, condemning the raid as violation of the trade agreement; but, rather than taking note of the protest, the Conservative Government requested Parliament to approve the breaking of diplomatic relations, which was approved by 346 to 98.[77] One person who did not believe that the raid was justified was Hodgson, the British chargé d'affaires, who described the raid as 'deplorable.'[78]

A *Manchester Guardian* article also stated:

> A first and hasty reading of Mr Baldwin's statement in the House of Commons might give the impression, which was doubtless the one intended, that the Russian trade delegation and its instrument, Arcos, had been engaged in a melodramatic conspiracy suddenly and unexpectedly exposed by the vigilance of the police. The more closely one examines the nature of the charges, the vaguer and less sensational are they seen to be. There is nothing to compare with the famous 'Zinoviev letter', which gave detailed instructions to the British communists on how to secure ratification of the Anglo-Russian treaty and went on to specify methods for the seduction of the army with a view to the complete success of an armed insurrection.

---

[74] Cmd 2895, 1927, No.15, pp.64-69

[75] O'Connor, Timothy: *Diplomacy and Revolution*, p.154

[76] Northledge and Wells: *Britain and Soviet Communism: The Impact of Revolution*, p.43; Litvinov criticism, Cmd 2895, 1927, No.17, pp.70 & 71

[77] *Hansard*, vol.206, 26 May 1927, 2195-2326

[78] *Times*, 11 November 1941, p.5 (Hodgson)

Will communist propaganda, in this country, be any less for the closure of the trade delegation and the departure of the Russian Chargé d'Affaires? unless we are to deport all communists, British as well as Russian, which is impossible. There is no reason why it should be. Will British trade benefit? Quite the contrary. Will Europe in general be more tranquil for the widening of the chasm? Quite the contrary. Less than a year ago, when Austen Chamberlain was invited to break with Russia and had as much ground for doing so as he does today, Austen Chamberlain said in the House of Commons that the breach would give us no weapon for fighting disorder or revolution in our own borders, would create divisions where we want to seek union, and would, in its echoes abroad, increase the uncertainty, increase the fears, increase the instability of European conditions, which it is and ought to be our chief object to remove. There are various possible explanations for the change of policy. It may be that the Government has once more basically surrendered to the continuing pressure of their own diehards. They may have found it difficult otherwise to put the raid in a favourable light. To have turned a blind eye to the document would have been to make the raid look ineffective and Sir William Joynson Hicks looked foolish. Moreover, awkward questions about diplomatic immunity would have been pressed. On the other hand, to publish the documents and do nothing might have been called feeble. The facts of the case strongly suggest that the Government has simply blundered into an action that they had not thought of taking when the raid was planned, and (of) which Sir Austen Chamberlain in his heart still disapproves.[79]

Northledge and Wells, in retrospect, many years later, criticised the break, stating that Britain was not much freer from industrial conflict after 1927 than it had been before.

If it was, it had nothing to do with Anglo-Soviet relations. British capitalism was no healthier. It might even be said that Britain's failure to build up trade with the Soviet Union in the years 1927 to 1929 when diplomatic relations were restored during which time the Soviet Union was undergoing intense industrialisation if anything aggravated the decline in trade which helped to produce mass unemployment in the 1930s.

The notion, as Northledge and Wells say further:

so dear to ministers who ordered the Arcos Raid that these nervous eminently respectable men of the Labour Party. were so debauched with Moscow gold as to act as firebrands for the Kremlin, while watching their union members play football with the Police, was too laughable to be taken seriously.[80]

---

[79] *Guardian*, 25 May 1927, p.10
[80] Northledge and Wells: *Britain and Soviet Communism: The Impact of Revolution*, p.45

In a public statement on 25 May 1927, Litvinov's criticism of the decision could not have been stronger:

> The British Government, whose programme is one of merciless struggle against its own workers and the enslavement of India, China and Egypt, could not admit the existence of the Soviet Union, which sympathises with the class struggle and of oppressed people, and the British Government only waited to attack the Soviet Union in the hope of finding allies. Having failed to do so, it had decided to attack the Soviet Union openly and independently, expecting to draw in other states later. As the missing document has not been found and as Premier Baldwin has been quite unable to justify the Scotland Yard scenario on police grounds, who can doubt that the rupture is not on account of the raid but the raid is the result of an intention to break relations.[81]

In Litvinov's reply to the formal British note severing diplomatic relations, on 28 May 1927, he was only slightly less critical of the British Government rejecting Britain's allegations that the Trade Mission had misbehaved, stating:

> The decision was no surprise to the Soviet Government. It had already for long been aware that a rupture of diplomatic relations with the Union of Soviet Socialist Republics was being prepared by the whole policy of the present British Conservative Government, which has declined all proposals of the Soviet Government for the settlement of mutual relations by means of negotiations. The lack of results of the search of the Trade Delegation premises, which was carried out with utmost thoroughness over several days, is the most convincing proof of the loyalty and correctitude of the official agents of the Union of Socialist Soviet Republics. The Soviet Government passes over with contempt the insinuations of a British Minister regarding espionage by the Trade Delegation and considers it beneath its dignity to reply to them. The Soviet Government places on record that the British Government had no legitimate ground for a police raid on the extra-territorial premises of the official Soviet agent.

It appears clear that Litvinov was right that there was no justification for the raid, which was also in breach of international law as well as a breach of diplomatic immunity.

Litvinov was not correct when he said, 'For the whole world it is quite clear that the basic cause of the rupture is the defeat of the policy of the Conservative Government in China', as it was the Soviet policy in China that had been defeated. Finally, Litvinov stated: 'The peoples of the Soviet Union cherish no enmity to the peoples of the British Empire and

---

[81] *The New York Times*, 26 May 1927, p.7

wish to maintain with them normal and friendly relations.'[82]

In spite of the fact that the General Council of the TUC had been accused by *Izvestiya* of betraying the 1926 General Strike, it now sprang to the defence of the Soviet Union.

In a letter to Baldwin dated 13 May 1927 it stated:

> The Trade Agreement of 1921 is regarded as a valuable means of regularising the commercial relations between the two countries. The General Council finds it difficult to believe that the representative of any other national state should be treated in this summary fashion, and I have to record the protest against a step that cannot fail to have an injurious influence on relations between Great Britain and Soviet Russia.[83]

We now know that the evidence that the Soviet Government had stolen the manual relied solely on evidence of a former dismissed employee of the Soviet Trade Mission. It was agreed that the name of the individual should be kept confidential. Although an officer of MI5 interviewed the dismissed employee, and was stated to be impressed with the truth of the statement, there is no other way of knowing whether the witness was genuine or that the dismissed employee was acting under a grudge.[84]

Pope alleged that, in June 1927, Chamberlain again tried to create a united front against the Soviet Union, calling a secret meeting of British, French, German, Belgian, Italian and Japanese representatives to discuss the Soviet problem. Chamberlain emphasised the danger of Bolshevik propaganda, not only in Britain but to all Europe and Asia. Briand disagreed, saying that the Bolsheviks had not proved disturbers of peace, but rather a barrier to chaos.[85]

The Foreign Office maintained that the Soviet Union was unlikely to attack British interests in Asia, although the CID took a different view. War plans had already been drawn up for a war against the Soviet Union. The war plans were actually approved in January 1928.[86]

There was widespread suspicion by the British hierarchy towards the Soviet Union, including the pro-British Litvinov. British foreign policy was aimed at preventing any close relationship between the Soviet Union and Germany. However, as Britain was

---

[82] Cmd 1927, 2895, No.17, pp.71-72
[83] National Archives, K3/15
[84] Ibid.
[85] Pope, Arthur: *Maxim Litvinov*, p.222
[86] Grayson, Richard: *Austen Chamberlain and Commitment to Europe. British Foreign Policy 1925-1929*, pp. 266 to 267

continually hostile to the Soviet Union, she should certainly not be blamed in seeking new allies, including Germany. Apparently, the enthusiastic League of Nations supporter Lord Cecil did not look favourably on the close relationship between Count Bernstorff and Litvinov at the Disarmament Conferences. Lord Cecil once said to Count Bernstorff: 'You call Litvinov by his Christian name'; to which Bernstorff said: 'No, his Jewish name.'[87]

In December 1927, at Litvinov's instigation, while Austen Chamberlain and Litvinov were both attending the Disarmament Conference, a meeting took place. Afterwards, an agreed press statement was released, 'acknowledging that Litvinov, having asked Sir Austen Chamberlain for an interview, a meeting had taken place which gave occasion for a frank exchange of views upon the relationship between the Soviet Government and the British Government. It was not, however, found possible to reach any basis of agreement within the course of the interview.'[88]

In a passionate speech to the Central Committee on 10 December 1928, Litvinov attacked Great Britain. He gave three reasons for Great Britain breaking off diplomatic relations:

> First, it was intended to place the Soviet Union in such a position where it would accept any new terms that were dictated to it. Second, it was intended to ruin the prestige of the Soviet Union in the Near East; and third, by setting an example to other states to bring about the complete isolation of the Soviet Union and to strike a crushing blow to us.

He said these three British aims all ended in failure. The Soviet Union had not

> availed itself of the trading facilities and credits amounting to £15 million provided by a powerful English financial group because we found better openings elsewhere. Our relations with countries in the Near East and Turkey have never been as satisfactory as at present and Britain's action in breaking off diplomatic relations has not been followed by any other country.[89]

The breaking of diplomatic relations had achieved nothing but had been detrimental to trade. The chief person to blame was Winston Churchill, who, as a senior member of the Cabinet, fuelled anti-Bolshevik feelings without the prospect of any material gain.

In the 1929 General Election, the Conservative party was defeated and the Labour party again became the largest political party and formed a minority government with Liberal support.[90] On 15 July 1929 the Labour Government notified the Soviet Union of its desire:

---

[87] Weizsacker, Ernst von: *Memoirs*, p.65
[88] Pope, Arthur: *Maxim Litvinov*, p.239; DBFP, Series 1A, vol.4, Nos.159-161
[89] Documents, 1928, p.181
[90] Taylor, A J P: *History of England 1914-1945*, p.270

To re-establish the machinery of the normal diplomatic relations with the Union of Soviet Socialist Republics. To this end, HM Government invite the USSR to send a responsible representative to London in order to discuss with the Foreign Secretary direct the most expeditious procedure for reaching as rapidly as possible a friendly and mutually satisfactory settlement of the outstanding questions between the two countries, including those relating to propaganda and debts.[91]

The new Labour Government had decided that, before diplomatic relations were restored, the approval of Parliament would be obtained, although in 1924 the first Labour Government had restored diplomatic relations without seeking Parliamentary approval.[92]

V S Dovgalevsky was sent by the Soviet Government to Britain, but only to discuss the procedure for resolving disputed matters, not on their substance. At the first meeting in London on 31 July 1929, Arthur Henderson the new Labour Party Foreign Secretary informed Dovgalevsky that the British Government could establish diplomatic relations only through Parliament, whose next session started on 29 October 1929.[93] In order not to lose the intervening three months, Arthur Henderson proposed that negotiations on disputed matters be commenced immediately. Moscow rejected this offer and on 1 August 1929 Dovgalevsky was instructed to return to Paris.[94]

However on 4 September 1929, Foreign Secretary Arthur Henderson decided to take the initiative because, when attending the 19th General Assembly of the League of Nations, he made the following statement:

The actual resumption of relations cannot take place until a report has been made to Parliament. In the meantime, there is plenty of work to be done and the interval between now and the opening of Parliament would usefully be occupied in arranging the procedure and programme for subsequent negotiations, which I hope will lead to the settlement of outstanding matters between the two countries. The desire of the British Government is to re-establish relations as soon as possible on a friendly and stable basis and the invitation to the Soviet Government to send a responsible representative to London in order to discuss the most expeditious procedure still stands.

Litvinov immediately responded: 'If the declaration of the British Foreign Secretary is to be understood in the sense he desires again to meet a representative of Soviet Government to discuss "only procedure" into which will naturally include the formation of the agenda

---

[91] DBFP, 2nd Series, vol.7, p.7, No.3

[92] See no.40 *ante*

[93] DBFP, 2nd Series, vol.7, p.14, No.10

[94] Ibid. p.15, No.11

of future negotiations, no objection will be made by the Soviet Government.'[95]

On 7 September Litvinov indicated in a press statement:

> No objection would be made on the part of the Soviet Government, which is ready to take corresponding steps as soon as the British Government states the time and place of negotiations on procedure.[96]

Further, the Labour Government determined that they were prepared to leave in abeyance the question of debts until after the resumption of diplomatic relations, but had decided to take a strong stand on the question of propaganda. In the 1924 treaty that led to the resumption of relations, both Britain and the Soviet Union had agreed:

> To restrain all persons and organisations under their direct or indirect control, including any organisation in receipt of any financial assistance from them, from any act overt or covert liable in any way whatever to endanger the tranquillity or prosperity of any part of the territory of the British Empire or the Union of Soviet Socialist Republics.

Unlike the situation in respect of debts, the Labour Government required an undertaking from the Soviet Union at the date of exchange of ambassadors. However, this was contrary to Foreign Office advice that had suggested:

> The only answer was to induce the Soviet Union to agree a formula whereby they solemnly undertook not to assist any organisation with funding and to take action against its responsible head on the territory of the Union if its agents in any part of the world were shown to have acted in contravention of this agreement.[97]

The delay did not please the Soviet Union. Molotov gave to the Moscow Communist Party conference the official Soviet version of their conversations with Britain for publication in the Soviet Union. Foreign Secretary Henderson is represented as trying to show 'he can obtain from the Soviet Union concessions that the Conservatives were quite unable to get as a prize for the renewal of relationship and as no imperialist state has so far obtained.' According to Molotov, Henderson:

> is acting as a representative of the entire imperialist world, but he is in fact only blowing soap bubbles of illusion and already British Government circles seem to begin to understand that such dreams are hopeless. The Soviet line remains fixed and no claims will be discussed until after full diplomatic relations have been

---

[95] DBFP 22nd Series vol p.17 no12
[96] Ibid.
[97] Ibid. p.12, No.9 and p.24, No.18

restored. The struggle over the conditions for the renewal of diplomatic relations helps the Soviets to expose the Labour party's real bourgeoise character, which is one of Russia's main international aims.[98]

Molotov's attack on the 1929 Labour Government was endorsed in Litvinov's speech to the Central Committee.[99]

However, we now know there was a divergence of opinion between Stalin and Litvinov. It appears the decision to reject Britain's offer of negotiation pending approval of Parliament was not what Litvinov recommended. Stalin wrote to Molotov on 29 August 1929, stating:

> The Politburo's decision on Litvinov's proposal was correct. The point is not only to achieve recognition without getting lost along the way. Our position, which is based on the exposure of the Labour Government, is an appeal to the best elements of the working class of the whole world. Our criticism unleashes the proletariat's revolutionary criticism of the Labour Government and helps the cause of the revolutionary education of workers of all nations (Britain above all). It helps the communists of the world educate the workers in the spirit of anti-reformism. It is a crime not to use a God-given occasion for this purpose. Litvinov does not see and is not interested in the revolutionary aspect of policy, but the Politburo should take all this into account.

Stalin, as did many of the Communist elite, had a hatred of moderate Labour parties, which apparently was not shared by Litvinov.

It is not at all clear what the differences were between Stalin and Litvinov. The only two matters of dispute between the Labour Government and Litvinov were whether Dovgalevsky should remain in Britain to negotiate during the Parliamentary recess or whether the Soviet Union should give any undertaking concerning the Third International. It rather looks as if Litvinov was in favour of making some concession to Britain, presumably fearing that the negotiations might break down; but Stalin opposed such concessions.[100]

Dovgalevsky returned to Britain and, after two meetings on 27 September and 1 October 1929, a protocol was agreed as to the questions to be decided when diplomatic relations were restored. Henderson, rather surprisingly, was prepared just to accept a repeat of the undertaking agreed in 1924, rather than trying to obtain a more stringent stipulation, as advised by the Foreign Office. Dovgalevsky readily agreed.[101]

---

[98] *The New York Times*, 21 September 1929, p.7
[99] See No.105 *post*
[100] Lih, Lars T: *Stalin's Letters to Molotov*, p.174, No.44
[101] DBFP, 2nd Series, vol.7, pp.34 & 35, No.22; and see No.97 *ante*.

Although Dovgalevsky agreed to that wording, when Henderson indicated he 'regarded the undertaking under the 1924 Treaty and the above undertaking covered propaganda by the Third International', Dovgalevsky stated that he had no authority to discuss questions of interpretation. Leventall is therefore correct that Henderson, instead of trying to continue to come to an agreement about propaganda, 'papered over' the differences,[102] so an early agreement could be reached. Parliamentary approval was obtained by 324 votes to 199.[103]

In a speech to the Central Committee on 4 December 1929, Litvinov stated:

> We easily weathered the rupture which the Conservatives believed we would regard as nothing short of a catastrophe. We did not crave pardon. We did not walk in sackcloth and ashes and we made no proposal to the Conservative Government.

However, this was not quite correct, as Litvinov had tried to improve relations by meeting Austen Chamberlain. but these talks although courteous had failed to make any progresss whatsoever.[104]

Litvinov continued his speech by saying:

> In industrial circles, there were serious doubts as to the wisdom of such tactics employed by their government which not only failed to speed up a settlement of the questions in which they were interested and brought them no advantage, but even caused economic loss to Britain. The dispatch this year to Moscow of a trade delegation was an expression of this doubt, as was a search instituted by the City of London itself for fresh channels through which a settlement on questions vital to Great Britain might be reached. It had become increasingly obvious that the card of breaking off diplomatic relations played by the Conservative Government in their anti-Soviet game has been trumped.

Litvinov then said:

> In view of the promises made by the British Labour Party in the 1929 election campaign, we were not a little astonished when the new British Government, instead of a simple intimation of their readiness to re-establish normal diplomatic relations invited us to send a plentipotentiary to London for negotiation. It is true that these negotiations, according to the text of the formal invitation, were to be confined to the procedure for the examination of the substance of disputed questions which must take place after the restoration of normal relations. It seemed to us that even the procedure could have been examined with advantage when

---

[102] Leventhal, F M: *Arthur Henderson*, p.157
[103] *Hansard*, vol.231, 5 November 1929, 895-1010
[104] See No.88 *ante*

negotiations of the substance of the claims were instituted. Our policy consists, while firmly maintaining our fundamental position and our essential rights, in not quarrelling over trifles and especially over merely technical points. We therefore dispatched to London Comrade Dovgalevsky, previously informing the British Government that the conversations could only touch upon procedure for the negotiations and not the nature of disputed points.

However, when Dovgalevsky arrived in London, he was told by the British Foreign Secretary:

> As the first session of the new Parliament was over, and the new session would not open for three months, and without Parliament the new government does not renew relations, would it not be a good thing to utilise this spare time by actually examining and settling the actual disputed questions?

Litvinov took a firm stand and recalled Dovgalevsky.

Litvinov successfully achieved what he desired. Henderson, requested that if Litvinov ordered the plenipotentiary to return, it would be on the understanding 'to keep the conversations exclusively to the question of procedure.'

The second meeting between Comrade Dovgalevsky and Arthur Henderson actually concluded with the signing of a protocol which contained an undertaking for the immediate restoration of diplomatic relations and Henderson promised to submit this protocol to Parliament for ratification, which protocol provided for future negotiations on outstanding matters.

Litvinov recorded with pleasure

> the restoration of normal relations with Great Britain which, we have no doubt, fully accords with the interests of the British people also. All sincere lovers of peace cannot fail to welcome the cessation of hostilities between the two such powerful states as ourselves and Great Britain.[105]

It appears from the available evidence that Stalin was right and Litvinov was wrong, because, although Litvinov was more prepared than Stalin to be conciliatory, there was no need for the Soviet Union to make any concession. By standing firm, Stalin was still able to achieve diplomatic recognition, without conceding anything on the question of whether propaganda by the Third International was in breach of the Soviet Union's undertaking concerning propaganda. Therefore, when Stalin wrote that Rykov, Litvinov and Bukharin were shown up, Stalin was right in the sense they had been proved to be wrong. However,

---

[105] Documents, 1929, pp.200-202

although Stalin states that Henderson was also shown up, I do not think this was so. Stalin prides himself that the reason Henderson yielded was because 'of the power and the might of the USSR'.[106] However was not likely to be the reason. Henderson yielded because presumably he thought that was the right course. Having campaigned in the 1929 General Election to resume diplomatic relations with the Soviet Union, the Labour Government would have suffered loss of prestige if the negotiations with the Soviet Union had failed. The Labour Government had been just as keen to recognise the Soviet Union in 1924, when no doubt the Soviet Union was weaker.[107]

However, while Litvinov was only Deputy Foreign Commissar, his efforts to improve relations with Britain were frustrated by two actions no doubt orchestrated by Stalin. The first problem was the action of arresting the former Russian employees of the British Legation.[108] Second was the action in arresting and bringing before the criminal court Russian employees of the British company Lena Goldfields. When the company was accused of wasteful and dishonest conduct, it withdrew its employees, claimed compensation under the terms of the concession and was awarded £12,965,000 as compensation. However, eventually, by negotiation the Soviet Union agreed to pay £3 million compensation over twenty years and £1,067,500 was eventually recovered.[109]

Henderson, in a statement to Parliament, admitted

> in breach of the agreement by which diplomatic relations were restored, there was propaganda [not, as a Government report stated, representations were made five times to the Soviet ambassador about Soviet propaganda], but that if diplomatic relations were again severed there is no guarantee it would alter the position [of propaganda] in the slightest degree, although it might stop the flow of orders which have begun to come in and are likely to come in within the next few months. It might stop them to the detriment of this country and the punishment of our people who are suffering from unemployment.[110]

As far as trade was concerned, the progress since the restoration of diplomatic relations had been disappointing. In 1930 the Soviet Government sold for cash £25 million of their exports to the United Kingdom, while exports to the Soviet Union from the United Kingdom amounted to less than £7 million.[111] In view of the 1929 financial crisis, Britain now desperately needed export markets.

---

[106] Lih, Lars T: *Stalin's Letters to Molotov*, p.182 No 51
[107] See No.40 *ante*
[108] DBFP, 2nd Series, vol.7, p.54, No.42
[109] DBFP, 2nd Series, vol.7, p.58, No.45
[110] Ibid. p.748, Appendix to Anglo-Soviet Relations 1929-1931; and *Hansard*, 6 June 1930, vol.239, 2625 @ 2630
[111] DBFP, 2nd Series, vol.7, p.753, Appendix to Anglo-Soviet Relations 1929-1931

Therefore, Soviet foreign policy was aimed at attacking the British Labour Party, who in the 1920s had constantly showed sympathy and friendship to Soviet Russia. The real problem with the cardinal feature of the so-called communist system as devised by Lenin was dominance by the Soviet leader, until such policy was rejected by Gorbachev. Stalin, as with the other Soviet leaders, only wanted friends who believed that every action, such as the Nazi-Soviet Pact, must be in the long-term interests of the proletariat; but Stalin preferred to be without foreign friends rather than have friends like the British Labour Party, who would consider and debate every directive from Moscow. However, there is every reason to believe that this was not Litvinov's view, and he stated in 1932: 'We have had and still have good relations with Labour.'[112]

Sokolnikov was appointed the new Soviet ambassador to Britain. Unlike the situation in 1924, much to King George V's annoyance, it was agreed to exchange ambassadors rather than chargé d'affaires in both capitals. As the Bolsheviks had murdered the King's cousin, the King tried to avoid contact with diplomats from the Soviet Union. Protocol required the sovereign to receive, shake hands with and entertain fully fledged ambassadors. However, when the new ambassador, Mr Sokolnikov, presented his credentials, the King pleaded illness and the new ambassador was received by the Prince of Wales; but in 1930 the King was finally forced to shake hands with Sokolnikov at a levee and the Queen received the Ambassador and his wife at Buckingham Palace. In 1933 the King was not pleased when, at a garden party, he had to shake hands with Litvinov.[113]

Esmond Ovey, who was appointed ambassador following the resumption of diplomatic relations, took up his position in December 1929. In Ovey's first dispatch on 13 December 1929, he described Litvinov 'as being more innately fanatical' than Ovey 'had anticipated.'[114] In Ovey's second dispatch of 15 December 1929, he stated that both from his conversation with Litvinov and official utterances, Ovey 'is not very hopeful, nor I fear is there much hope that were he to adopt a more reasonable attitude he would have any power to affect the group which not only governs the country but remains, as far as can be ascertained, in almost monk-like seclusion in order to avoid any contamination with the western ideas of the heads of the foreign missions.'[115] Certainly, the memorandum indicates that Ovey was pessimistic about improving Soviet-British relations, although it does appear that, as Ovey's and Litvinov's personalities clashed, they failed to enjoy the cordial relationship that normally existed between Ovey's predecessor Hodgson and Litvinov and two of Ovey's successors, Seeds and Clark-Kerr.

In 1932 Sokolnikov was replaced as ambassador to Britain by Maisky, who was the ideal person, being an enthusiastic Litvinov supporter. Both Litvinov and Maisky had lived in

---

[112] Maisky, Ivan: *Who Helped Hitler?*, p.17
[113] Rose, Kenneth: *George V*, p.369
[114] DBFP, vol.7, p.51, No.40
[115] Ibid. p.53, No.41

London in the pre-revolutionary era and they became life-long friends. It appears reasonable to infer it was Litvinov's influence that gained Maisky the position. He became an outstanding ambassador, making many friends and, although the majority were to the Left of Centre, some were Conservatives, the most important of whom being Winston Churchill.

Before Maisky arrived to take up his appointment, Litvinov had instructed Maisky that relations with the Labour and Liberal parties were good, and although all positive steps should be taken to improve relations with Labour, what was important was to improve relations with the Conservatives, who were the real bosses in Britain. This indicates clearly that in spite of the hostility of the Conservative party and Government to the Soviet Union, Litvinov wished to have good relations with a British Conservative Government.

It was the Conservative party's foolishness in not responding to Litvinov's overtures which achieved absolutely nothing. Maisky prepared a press statement for Litvinov's approval. Maisky made it clear that the Soviet Union wished 'to live in peace and good understanding with Great Britain, as well as with all parts of the British Empire', indicating that they accepted Britain's colonial policy, which as communists one would have thought they might want to oppose. 'The USSR's policy is a policy of peace.' Maisky quoted, as evidence of the latter assertion, the list of non-aggression treaties concluded, and also the position of the Soviet delegation at the Disarmament Conference, which opened in February 1932:

> With all the greatest readiness does the USSR strive to develop friendly relations with Great Britain with which it has such a variety of contacts in the economic sphere. The successful fulfilment of the First Five Year plan which has led to a growth in the productive force of the USSR and the forthcoming Second Five Year Plan, the result of which will be a substantial rise in the prosperity of the working class in our country, represents a good foundation for development and the strengthening of Soviet-British economic and consequently political relations.

Maisky was then to pay compliments to Britain:

> I hope the common sense so characteristic of the British people and their unsurpassed ability to reckon with facts (and the fifteen years' existence and development of the USSR are an undisputable fact and which cannot be avoided) will greatly facilitate the fulfilment of this task being of the greatest benefit to the two countries and at the same time represent an exceptionally powerful international peace which would be particularly important in our disturbing and difficult times.

This indicates that, although Hitler was not yet in power, like Litvinov, Maisky was disturbed at the political outlook, particularly in Germany.

Maisky continued:

> Personally, I received my appointment as ambassador of the USSR in Great Britain with great satisfaction. During the past twenty years I have had more than once to live and work in your country and have become better acquainted with the British people and British culture. I also had a feeling of gratitude to Britain, which in the years before the Revolution granted me the right of asylum as a political exile. I should therefore feel particularly happy in promoting a cause of a rapprochement between the USSR and Great Britain.[116]

Within days of arriving, Maisky was faced with one of the many crises in British-Soviet relations between the wars when, on 17 October, Sir John Simon, the British Foreign Secretary, gave six months' notice to terminate the temporary trade agreement. Therefore, this speech of welcome, which Maisky had prepared, was cancelled on Litvinov's orders.[117]

Another crisis occurred in Anglo-Soviet relations when, on 12 March 1933, four employees of Metro-Vickers were arrested and were subsequently charged with numerous offences, including military and economic espionage, collecting much secret information of military and state importance, damaging equipment at the Baku power station, causing breakdown and also alleging bribery. Two Russian women secretaries and two Russian chauffeurs were also charged.

On 29 March 1933 a Tass communiqué was published in *Pravda* that Ovey visited Litvinov and stated, 'He had come to acquaint him of the measures the British Government would take if the trial which had been announced was not liquidated.'[118] However, Litvinov informed Ovey 'A definite decision had been taken to bring up the case for hearing in the immediate future, that the decision could not be changed, and if the ambassador in his statement regarding the measures of the British Government had the object of affecting the decision, then he might be assured that nothing would come of it.'

To this Litvinov added 'Such method of diplomacy, i.e. external pressure, might be sometimes successful in Mexico, but in the USSR they were doomed to failure in advance.'[119] Ovey had previously served in Mexico. However, when journalists asked Ovey to comment he refused, stating: 'His Majesty's Government will doubtless know

---

[116] Maisky, Ivan: *Who Helped Hitler?,* pp.17-20
[117] Ibid. p. 20; Ch. 10 No 43
[118] DBFP, 2nd Series, vol.7, p.380, No.306
[119] DBFP, 2nd Series, vol.7, p.380, No.306

how to deal with this incident.[120] The British Foreign Minister, Arthur Henderson, was so annoyed about the way that his ambassador had been treated, the Foreign Secretary recalled Ovey.

Bullard, a diplomat in the embassy, agreed that Litvinov was taking a very arrogant stand with the ambassador, and said Litvinov, on 9 April 1933: 'began by being very rude to the ambassador and insisted he could do just as he pleased with British subjects.'[121]

On 5 April 1933 a Bill was presented to Parliament to enable the government to ban Soviet goods. It was read a second time on the same day and the remaining stages in the Commons were passed the next day. The same month the Bill passed the Lords and received the Royal Assent. At once, 80% of Russian goods were banned.[122]

On 18 April 1933 two of the British engineers were found guilty and immediately deported. Two were sentenced to two and three years' imprisonment, respectively. Litvinov retaliated by stating that the plea for mercy could not come before the Supreme Soviet until November and the embargo prevented him from considering it sooner.[123]

In retrospect, Maisky blamed the ambassador Ovey, but he should not have been surprised that there was scepticism in Britain whether the charges were correct in view of the unsatisfactory state of the Soviet Union's legal system under which, in 1953, Maisky was arrested on the most dubious charges, after giving outstanding service to his country.[124] His idol, Litvinov, did not believe in the engineers' guilt. Ivy attended the trial of the British engineers and stated that Maxim had said that nothing would convince him that the engineers would deliberately destroy their own machinery.[125] Was Maisky, an intelligent man, so steeped in Communist ideology not to realise the imperfections of the Soviet legal system?

While the advent of Hitler had only a moderate influence on the British Right in their view on Anglo-Soviet relations, it had a significant effect on the Soviet establishment. An early indication was that *Izvestiya*, on 30 March 1933, wrote sympathetically about a speech by Winston Churchill made on 23 March 1933 opposing revision of the Treaty of Versailles.[126]

In Litvinov's speech to the Central Executive Committee on 29 December 1933, he referred to the practical common sense of the British. There is every reason to believe that,

---

[120] Ibid. p.380, No. .307
[121] Bullard, Reader: *Inside Stalin's Russia*, p.168; DBFP, 2nd Series, p.383, No.310
[122] *Hansard*, House of Commons vol.276, 6 April 1933, 1767-2034; and House of Lords vol.87, 11 April 1933, 506-539
[123] DBFP, 2nd Series, vol.7, p.483, No.418
[124] Kostyrchenko, Gennadii: *Out of the Red Shadows*, pp.203 & 300
[125] Ivy Litvinov's archives, Box 1
[126] Carr, Edward: *Soviet-German Relations*, p.114; *Hansard*, vol.276, 23 March 1933, 538

in view of his low opinion of France, he was desirous of maintaining the same good relationship he was building up with other countries. Litvinov admitted:

> The Soviet Union's efforts to improve relations with another great power, Britain, had not been realised or fully realised. Our relations with that country cannot boast of stability or permanency. I am certain that the British people as a whole are anxious to live in perfect peace and friendship with us.

Litvinov rightly refers with justification to those anti-Communist elements in Britain, comparing her unfavourably with many other countries. He said:

> There were certain elements that still cherish the fond dream of that general capitalist fight against the country of socialism that had been abandoned by the USA. However, since they can neither destroy nor upset this country of socialism, it is rather astonishing that, notwithstanding the renowned common sense of the British, there should still remain among them such quixotic snipers and partisans. As far as we are concerned, we are ready and desirous of maintaining the same good relations as with other countries.

Litvinov continued: 'Sincere and good relations between the big powers were not only an essential condition to, but a guarantee of, universal peace.'

Litvinov ended on a more optimistic note, 'hoping that a temporary trade agreement which is expected to be concluded shortly, by eliminating certain misunderstanding, will, we trust, make better relations between Great Britain and ourselves.'[127]

At the same conference, Stalin similarly criticised Britain: He recalled

> the pressure brought to bear on us by Britain, the embargo on our exports, the attempt to interfere in our internal affairs and put out feelers and hereby test our power of resistance. It is true nothing came of this attempt and subsequently the embargo was lifted; but the unpleasant taste it left behind is still felt in everything affecting Britain and the USSR, including negotiations for a commercial treaty, and these sallies must not be regarded an accident.

Stalin was right. He continued:

> It is notorious that one section of the British Conservatives cannot live without such sallies and precisely because they are not accidental we must reckon with the USSR also being attacked in the future, also menacing situations of every sort being created and the USSR being harmed.

---

[127] *Moscow News*, 6 January 1934, p.4

Privately, Stalin may not have been as concerned about the anti-Soviet section of the Conservative party as he stated he was, because he gave a warning that, because of the anti-Soviet section of the Conservative party, 'we must reckon with the USSR being attacked in the near future' thus justifying the need for terror.[128]

Eden, who had been appointed Lord Privy Seal to serve under the Foreign Secretary, Simon[129], was asked in 1934 by the French Foreign Secretary, Barthou, to support the Soviet Union's entry into the League of Nations. Eden persuaded his government to support this policy, although he admits it was not popular with some of his colleagues, particularly the older ones. Eden rightly was convinced that the League must gain from wider membership. whatever Britain's views on Soviet policy.[130] Surely he was right.

---

[128] Ibid. 3 February 1934, p.4
[129] Thorpe D *Eden the Life and Times of Anthony Eden* p 117
[130] Eden, Anthony: *Memoirs, Facing the Dictators*, p.98

Litvinov on Lenin's right in Red Square, Moscow May 1ˢᵗ 1919

Red Square, Moscow on the 2ⁿᵈ anniversary celebrations of the
'Great October Socialist Revolution.' Lenin (centre) Litvinov (right)

Lenin and Stalin, Gorky 1922

Chicherin and Litvinov

Statue of Lenin, Statue Park, Budapest

The Soviet delegation in Geneva with Anatoly Lunacharsky
and Maxim Litvinov (centre, sitting)

Litvinov addressing the League of Nations, Geneva, early 1930's

Maxim Litvinov and his wife Ivy

Signing of the 'Nazi – Soviet Pact,' August 1939
L to R – Ribbentrop, Gaus, Stalin and Molotov

Tania with the author (above) and author's wife (below)

10: THE DEPRESSION AND LITVINOV THE ECONOMIST

In October 1929 the dramatic decline in the US Stock Market caused a world depression. International trade declined. Unemployment rose alarmingly. The Soviet Government wrongly thought that the crash showed the inherent weakness of capitalism, but time proved it was wrong. After 1990 communism in the Soviet Union would be replaced by the capitalist system, which Litvinov derided. Much criticism has been levelled against capitalist governments during the depression era who did not pursue the policy advocated by Oswald Mosley, then a Labour Cabinet Minister. This consisted of 'planned foreign trade, public direction of industry and a systematic use of credit to promote expansion, instead of trying to produce balanced budgets.'[1]

However, statistics do not prove Mosley right. For example, in 1938 unemployment in Britain at 10.5% was lower than in Sweden at 10.9%, which endeavoured to pursue the policy called for by Oswald Mosley. When Roosevelt was elected in 1933, unemployment was almost 20%, and even with Roosevelt's New Deal it did not prevent a further recession, with unemployment back at 20%.[2] Where criticism can be made concerns the fact that more international co-operation could have lessened the impact of the economic crisis. Unfortunately, countries lowered export prices in order to sell surplus goods.

It was in the middle of this world crisis that Litvinov became Foreign Commissar in July 1930 and his speech on his appointment included a survey of economic affairs. He made it clear:

> In expanding its [the Soviet] economy we would like to be able to count on the further expansion of our economic intercourse with other states. The more our economy expands, the greater the field for the application of foreign techniques, foreign labour, the products of foreign industry and even of certain raw materials. Even here we are encountering inimical tendencies towards certain hostile capitalist groups who are conducting a campaign for severance economic relations with our Union. Their efforts appear to be directed against our exports

---

[1] Taylor, A J P: *English History 1914-1945*, p.285

[2] Unemployment in Britain and Sweden: Galenson, Walter and Zellner, Arnold: 'International Comparison in respect of the USA', in Kennedy, David M (ed): *A New Economic View of American History, Freedom from Fear: The American People in Depression and War, 1929-1945*, pp.86 & 142

3 Degras, Jane: *Soviet Documents on Foreign Policy*, vol.2, p.449

but in fact they are against our entire trade, for a reduction in our exports would necessarily mean a reduction in our imports. The foreign exchange connection between our exports and imports is so obvious that it is unnecessary to dwell upon it. At the present time, when the economic crisis is spreading so deep and wide, affecting almost all European and non-European countries, the exclusion from world trade of a country as vast as our union, which is growing stronger economically and which alone is free from depression, will scarcely be regarded as an appropriate measure in keeping with a realistic policy.[3]

However, in his 1933 speech Litvinov admitted that the Depression did have some effect on the economic life of the Soviet Union.[4]

The Soviet Union brought upon itself a major crisis by the imposition of collectivisation. It is not known when Stalin decided to viciously pursue such a policy against the kulaks (the richer peasants). As late as 27 June 1929 a decree on agriculture assumed the predominance of the private sector for an indefinite period.[5] Nove speculates that one of the factors which led to the U-turn was the desire of Stalin 'to eliminate the private peasant which produces capitalists from our midst.'[6] Such a policy was popular with many urban party members.[7] (While many Communists might criticise the kulaks, in fact their economic status was very modest by the standards of farmers in the countries of Western Europe.)[8]

In December 1929 Stalin announced the liquidation of the kulaks as a class.[9] They were not allowed to enter the collectives. By 1 July 1930 about 320,000 kulak households had suffered exile and the confiscation of their property. The poor peasants would take part in this free-for-all and would seize their neighbours' goods in the name of the party struggle.[10]

Serge describes the terrible features of collectivisation: 'Rather than hand over their livestock' (to the state), 'the peasants slaughter the beasts, sell the meat and make boots out of the leather.' Because of 'the destruction of its livestock, the country passes from poverty to famine, the result of which was bread cards in the cities, black market, a slump in the rouble and in real wages.'

---

[4] *Moscow News*, 6 January 1934, pp. 4 & 14; Nos 49 & 50 post
[5] Nove, Alec: *An Economic History of the USSR*, p.156
[6] Ibid. p.158
[7] Ibid.
[8] Ibid. p.159
[9] Ibid. p.166
[10] Ibid. p.167

In a Kuban market town whose entire population was deported, the women undressed in their houses thinking that no one would dare to make them go out naked. They were driven out (as they were) to the cattle trucks, beaten with rifle-butts. Train loads of deported peasants left for the icy north, from the forests, the steppes, and deserts. These were whole populations denuded of everything. The old folk starved to death in mid-journey, new-born babies were buried on the banks of the roadside.[11]

At the 15th Party Conference, Molotov stated:

> The progress of the private economy along the socialist path is a slow process and a long process. It will take quite a few years to move from the individual to a social [collective] economy. Whoever now tells you that we can apply a policy of total extraction of two to four million tons of grain, even if we only take it from the 10% of the peasants (that is not only from the kulaks but some of the middle peasants), then that person is an enemy of the workers and peasants.

At this Stalin shouted out 'Correct!'[12]

Indeed when Chuev asked Molotov what Lenin privately thought of NEP he said:

> NEP embraces both positive and negative. The dictatorship of the prioleteriat ruled but the bourgeoisie still remained.[13]

In Molotov's later life he expressed no regrets at the large loss of life. When asked by Chuev whether there would have been the same loss of life under Lenin in carrying out the collectivisation, Molotov's reply was:

> They say that Lenin would have accomplished collectivisation with fewer victims, but how could it be done in any other way? I renounce none of it. We carried out collectivisation relentlessly. Our measures were absolutely correct.[14]

This was rather different to the attitude of Stalin, who at least stated that the policy had been terrible, but in his opinion necessary, when Churchill courageously asked him whether the stresses of the war were as bad as the collective farm policy. Churchill stated that he 'thought you would have found it bad because you were not dealing with [a small number] of aristocrats but with millions of small men.' 'Ten million', Stalin said, holding

---

[11] Serge, Victor: *Memoirs of a Revolutionary*, p.247

[12] Medvedev, Roy: *Let History Judge*, p.78; Volkogonov, Dmitri: *Stalin*, p.163

[13] Cheuv, *Felix: Molotov remembers p.145*

[14] Ibid. p.146

up his hands. 'It was fearful'; but Stalin justified it on the grounds that the peasants would not mechanise and it was the only way to prevent famine.[15]

What was Litvinov's view on collectivisation? Some evidence suggests that, unlike his rival Molotov, Litvinov did not like it. In condemning Trotsky, Litvinov stated, 'Collectivisation was Trotsky's idea and terror his habitual language.'[16] However, in his speech of 24 May 1931, Litvinov came near to giving his stamp of approval when he spoke at the European Commission Conference:

> The fact that the Five Year Plan is being completed ahead of schedule and collectivisation of agriculture is rapidly taking place does not and will not lead to a reduction in the foreign trade of the USSR.[17]

It was in the political climate caused by the Depression that on 5 September 1929 Briand launched before the League of Nations Assembly a plan for a closer European union. He said, 'Among peoples constituting geographical groups there should be some sort of federal bond.' Following discussions with representatives of other States a memorandum, 'Sur L'Organisation d'un Régime d'Union Fédérale Européenne', was circulated to various European powers. This memorandum asked for comments and the replies, as one would expect, were varied.[18]

Although most favoured the idea provided it did not impinge on sovereignty, Britain echoed British Conservative opposition to the European Union many years later. While supporting co-operation in 'economic relations', Britain stated: 'The establishment of new and independent international institutions [was] neither necessary nor desirable.' The Netherlands correctly affirmed, 'If there was to be an effective international organisation, it was impossible to establish economic or moral union without limiting sovereignty.'[19]

Litvinov, when the Soviet Union joined the Commission for European unity never discussed sovereignty, but mainly saw the organisation as a useful forum to defend the Soviet Union's foreign and economic policy; but if Litvinov had been successful in obtaining agreement to his economic non-aggression pact, that would have limited the Soviet Union's sovereignty as well as that of all other participants.

Stalin, in his speech to the Communist Party of the Soviet Union, made it clear that he regarded the French initiative as 'the most striking representation of the bourgeoisie

---

[15] Churchill, Winston: *Second World War*, vol.4, 'Hinge of Fate', p.447

[16] Tanya

[17] *Moscow News*, 24 May 1931, pp.1 & 6

[18] *Survey of International Affairs, 1930* p.130; Beloff, Maxim: *The Foreign Policy of Soviet Russia*, p.42 Documents, 1930, pp.122 and 123

[19] Documents, 1930, pp.75-81

movement towards the intervention against the Soviet Union' and described 'France of today' as 'Fatherland of pan-Europe, the cradle of the Kellogg Pact, the most aggressive and militaristic country among all aggressive and militarist countries of the world. '[20]

On 7 October 1930 *Izvestiya*, in a highly critical article, spoke of the idea of European Union as an enterprise of Briand and the plan ran 'a gamut of contradictions' with which the League of Nations 'was absolutely unable to cope.'[21]

However, at the second session of the Committee for the Study of European Union on 16 January 1931, Germany and Italy urged the inclusion of the Soviet Union in the organisation, against the opposition of France and the rather lukewarm support of Great Britain,[22] although a Labour Government was then in power. Eventually, it was decided to invite the Soviet Union. It would have been ludicrous not to have done so given that the Soviet Union was a major European Power. The invitation was accepted with some misgivings. Litvinov stated:

> It must be evident to all concerned that without generally ensuring universal peace, and more particularly European peace, by eliminating the causes that threaten to disturb it, there can be no hope of the efforts to establish European solidarity in the economic or any other sphere achieving any degree of success. The bourgeois economists themselves acknowledge the indissoluble connection between political unrest which at present exists and which is growing more profound throughout the world with the constant increase in armaments which in some countries represent as much as 40% and 50% of the national budget.

Although Litvinov stated he was unclear exactly what would be discussed and with whom, the Soviet Government agreed to participate, realising it could not hope to have light thrown on these questions outside the meetings.

Finally, Litvinov stated, 'The Soviet Government has been guided by its desire to contribute [to the Committee] which with its help may be directed towards universal peace and particularly European peace.'[23] It is my opinion that Litvinov honestly believed he should use his best endeavours to preserve peace with the aim of enabling the Soviet Union to consolidate particularly its economic progress. He also considered that, if Stalin believed the Soviet Union was not under threat, he would construct a more liberal regime.[24]

Pravda summed up the position:

---

[20] Beloff, Max: *The Foreign Policy of Soviet Russia*, p.43
[21] Slusser & Eugin: *Soviet Foreign Policy 1928-1934*, p.55
[22] Beloff, Max: *The Foreign Policy of Soviet Russia*, p.43; *Survey of International Affairs,* 1930, p.141
[23] Degras, Jane: *Documents on Soviet Foreign Policy*, vol. 2, p.470
[24] See Ch.16, No.40

> The Genevan Pan-European conference will have to reveal to the great masses of the people with what methods and by what means, at what price and at whose expense they propose to restore the health of capitalism, which is suffering from the result of the world crisis. The Soviet Union does not fear such a discussion and will not flinch from it. It has in any event plenty of things to discuss with the Genevan doctors. By taking part in the work of the European Commission, the Soviet Union will wreck the plans of the leaders of the Commission for the secret elaboration of anti-Soviet projects. Let the game be played with the cards on the table.[25]

The commission had six meetings between 16 May 1931 and October 1932. On 18 May Litvinov addressed the conference. He started by telling the Chairman that by inviting the Soviet Union 'the Chairman had delighted geographers that Russia was all part of Europe' which *The New York Times* described as 'the only flippant remark.'[26] He then went on to claim that the present economic crisis was due to the very nature of the capitalist system.

Litvinov asserted that the economic crisis

> had its roots in the general situation rising [arising] out of the World War and post-war politics, including increased tax burdens, continued militarism and incessant growth of armaments. The cutting up of Europe into small parcels, the multiplying of frontiers and, in some countries, the form of reparations all increased suspicion and confusion, which were augmented by the disproportionate distribution of gold and unprecedented unemployment.

Whereas Litvinov is normally regarded as an advocate of collective security, this speech illustrates Litvinov the economist, and much of what he said was true, although it is much easier to state the causes of the unprecedented economic crisis than determine the correct remedies. He then said: 'In the final analysis, the world markets were regulated by the law of supply and demand. Raising artificial tariff barriers, the creation of industrial cartels to maintain high prices and the constitution of preferential systems on behalf of affiliated nations were political rather than economic expedients and could only add to the difficulties of Europe.' This was hardly a statement one would expect of a Communist.

Then Litvinov correctly suggested that Soviet exports 'did mitigate rather than intensify the world crisis.' The Soviet Union received from the USA 53.5% of her total tractor exports, the Soviet Union received from Britain about 12% of her textile machinery exports and from Germany about 25% of her total export of agricultural machinery, 21%

---

[25] Beloff, Max: *Foreign Policy of Soviet Russia*, p.43
[26] *The New York Times*, 19 May 1931, p.1

of the export of lathes and 11% of total export of other machinery. Soviet exports were in the majority of cases far less than under the Tsars.

Then Litvinov turned to allegations that the Soviet Union

> had a diabolical plan of trying to throw the capitalist commerce into confusion by flooding the world markets with cheap goods. Nothing could be sillier than this charge because such a plan would do no good and would result only in reducing the return the Soviet Union would get from her exports, a return which is vital to her Five Year Plan and industrialisation. It would not decide the fate of capitalism but would nevertheless pin down export receipts and consequently reduce imports to the Soviet Union, thus delaying the Socialist reconstruction.[27]

Litvinov continued:

> We do not deny that special conditions of agriculture in foreign trade in the Soviet Union allowed agricultural products to be sold at lower prices than can be offered in other countries. Those special conditions are the absence, thanks to the nationalisation of land, in the heavy calls of rent, lease and mortgage which are such a drain on agriculture in other lands, absorbing sometimes 70% of the cost of production and the elimination of private profits, exchange, speculation and middlemen.

Litvinov gave figures to show:

> Czechoslovakia, Poland, and Germany last year sold sugar abroad at prices considerably less those on the home market. He then cited examples of high wheat prices in Paris, Berlin and London to show what protectionist tariffs and dumping by monopolistic organisations were doing to impede commerce.

Litvinov then proceeded to specify the remedies. First, the situation required 'the abstention from war as a means for the settling of international conflicts.' Also necessary was 'the cessation of economic aggression, both avowed or concealed by countries or groups of countries against other countries or groups of countries.' Further, 'countries should solemnly endorse the principle proclaimed at the Economic Conference in 1927 of the peaceful co-existence of countries irrespective of their social, political and economic systems.'

'As a final and concrete demonstration' of what he called the Soviet Union's 'good faith in the matter of dumping', Litvinov made the following sensible suggestion:

---

[27] See Nos.37 & 45 *post*

Nations in the Commission should sign an agreement for the compulsory sale on the home market at prices not higher than those demanded on the foreign markets. This would have a beneficial effect on the mass of the population by increasing their purchasing power and helping to absorb over-production.[28]

The *Manchester Guardian* stated those who insisted on the invitation to Soviet Russia to attend the Comission of Enquiry into European Union were justified this afternoon when the Commission listened to a remarkable speech from Maxim Litvinov who praised the speech as being 'solid in substance, moderate in tone and extremely clever. It was the most practical contribution for discussion on the European crisis that we have yet heard.' The Manchester Guardian's reporter was right to add: 'This is the general opinion this evening except among those who are under the influence of undying prejudice.'[29] *The New York Times* stated, 'It was astonishing to see Litvinov as the apostle of peace and friendly competition in their [the Soviet] struggle for supremacy.'[30]

At the next meeting in September 1931, a report of the Sub-Commission on the Disposal of Grain was discussed. Francois-Poncet, the French representative, stated:

The June session foresaw the possibility of introducing a preferential regime governing grain crops in the countries of South-Eastern Europe. In this connection an agreement had already been reached between various countries. All these treaties will shortly be submitted to the League of Nations.

In discussions that followed, Litvinov declared that the Soviet Union had made its position clear in respect of preferential regimes at the last meeting of the European Commission. He would

therefore limit himself to discussing the features deemed objectionable by the Soviet Union. The judgements expressed and the report of the sub-commission revealed dangerous tendencies. Preferentialism means the bestowing of privileges on one group of exporting countries at the expense of another. It is nothing but legitimatised discrimination.

To Litvinov's enquiry as to whether the USSR was included in the preferential countries of Eastern Europe, the answer was in the negative. Litvinov then said:

Evidently, the sub-committee wishes to change the map of Europe and divorce the USSR from the rest of Eastern Europe. In view of the narrow stand taken by the

---

[28] Litvinov 's speech, May 1931: *Manchester Guardian*, 19 May 1931, p.6 ; *Moscow News*, 24 May 1931, p.1.
[29] *Manchester Guardian*, 19 May 1931, p.6
[30] *The New York Times*, 19 May 1931, p.1

Commission, the Soviet delegate is compelled to reject the proposals. It is needless to add that the decision of the sub-commission cannot interfere with the trade agreements of the USSR with other countries. Is this not proof that the only European state against which preferential treatment is directed is the Soviet Union? Either the dog is not muzzled or muzzled and all it can still bite the Soviet Union and is much inclined to do so.

François-Poncet in reply asserted:

There was no discrimination against the Soviet Union. Only the South Eastern European countries applied for help. The crisis does not affect the Soviet Union. There is nothing to fear in preferentialism. It is only a barking dog well muzzled.

The second matter that was discussed was Litvinov's proposal submitted in May for an economic non-aggression pact. Curtius on behalf of Germany, proposed a commission to study these proposals. *The New York Times* described it as: 'Litvinov's first important victory here.'

Litvinov opened the discussion with this claim:

The pact for economic non-aggression is founded on the principle of non-discrimination and will forbid a country to establish worse commercial relations with any one country than those existing with the rest of the world.

Litvinov urged that economic non-aggression was in the interest of all countries involved, regardless of their system of foreign trade. In conclusion, Litvinov stated that the project for non-aggression was presented by him as far back as May. At that session representatives of various countries asserted they could not act upon the proposal prior to learning the attitude of their various governments.

Litvinov continued by pointing out that in the last four months the representatives of the European countries have had ample time to acquaint themselves with their government's stand on this proposal. He therefore hoped it would be possible for this session to come to a definite decision on the essence of the project. Litvinov wanted a commission to be established without delay on the grounds that this had been done with the Cereal Committee. This was laying down very preferential tariffs which the Soviet Union considered as economic aggression against it.

François-Poncet said:

He did not find so much objection to the substance of the pact as to the procedure for its adoption. The idea of non-discrimination on the surface appears to be very just and arouses considerable interest, yet it is subtle and may raise many difficulties. In some instances discrimination is justified, as in the case of safeguarding against dumping. He suggested the question be carefully studied.

As to Litvinov's charge that nothing had been done for four months, François-Poncet claimed, 'The French Government had been too occupied with other matters' a poor argument. The French delegation proposed, 'The same be referred to the Economic Committee of the League of Nations.' Grandi, the Italian representative, rose to state that his government was ready to accept the idea formulated in Litvinov's proposals. Curtius, of the German delegation, too 'had expressed its sympathy with the Soviet project; and Litvinov was justified in demanding the matter be settled at this session.' Kollin, representing Holland, a country with which the Soviet Union had no diplomatic relations, suggested: 'The Soviet proposals be referred to a special committee of experts.' He pronounced, 'It is more important than the Kellogg Pact.' In company with the French delegation, the Swiss Chairman of the Committee, Motta, supported by Viscount Cecil, the British delegate, favoured referring the proposal for a non-aggression pact to the Economic Committee of the League. Litvinov wanted the pact adopted immediately, but accepted the German representative's (Curtius) proposal to establish a special committee to consider Litvinov's non-aggression pact proposals. This was supported by Italy, Lithuania, Poland and Ireland.

Litvinov argued in his rejoinder to François-Poncet and Madarjar, the Spanish representative, that their speeches contained contradictions:

> At the last session no objection was raised to the Soviet proposals and no Committee was appointed to study it. Now, as an afterthought, it is suggested it be referred to the League of Nations. The work of the League proceeds very slowly, while the crisis which is not depended sic (dependant) on the actions of committees, develops at a much faster tempo.

It was determined to submit Litvinov's proposals to an editing committee in order that the matter be referred to the next plenum of the European Commission. This was a modest victory for Litvinov,[31] who entertained to lunch those delegates whose countries had diplomatic relations with Soviet Russia. Litvinov was 'entering Geneva Society.'[32]

The Special Committee appointed at the September session of the Commission of Enquiry

---

[31] *Moscow News*, 7 September 1931, pp.1 & 3; *The New York Times*, 4 September 1931, p.10; and 6 September 1931, p.7

[32] *The New York Times*, 6 September 1931, p.7

for European Union held its first meeting between 2 and 5 November 1931. The Soviet representative was not Litvinov, but Sokolnikov, who stated:

> Soviet economic policy has never been directed towards sharpening the world economic crisis, but on the contrary has taken great pains to protect the rapid growing Soviet economy from the harmful influence that is gripping capitalist economy.

The Committee endorsed 'the general idea underlying the proposal for a pact of non-aggression' and recommended that, 'the economic relations should be guided solely by the necessities of economic life and not by any consideration explicitly derived from differences in their political and social systems.' Then the Committee adjourned its proceedings, having decided to meet again prior to the next meeting of the Commission in January 1932. As that meeting was also postponed, it was a good excuse to also adjourn the Committee, rather than attempt to resolve the differences in the Committee.[33]

The major problem Litvinov had to face in 1931 was complaints against the Soviet Union for dumping wheat. However, the fall in wheat prices was unconnected with any actions of Soviet Russia, because, as Christopher Addison, then British Minister of Agriculture, said, 'The world surplus was 233,000,000 cwt [hundredweight], but the Soviet Union was only responsible for 30,000,000 cwt.' Although in certain weeks there has been excessive supplies of Russian wheat and that has unduly depressed the market, at the same time the overwhelming reason for the present slump in trade prices is the enormous surplus in the world's stocks. [34]

At the time of the allegations against the Soviet Union that they were dumping goods in foreign markets at less than the market price, some elements were sympathetic towards the Soviet Union. Dirksen, a German diplomat who became Germany's last ambassador to Britain before the Second World War, complained that the Soviet Union's imports from the United States, with whom the Soviet Union had no relations, exceeded that of Germany, with whom of course the Soviet Union still had good relations. However, it seems that Litvinov agreed with Germany's complaint, because Litvinov told Curtius: 'The Soviet Government wanted to plan its imports and exports more closely with those countries [with whom] it stood in friendly relations.'[35] Dirksen nevertheless reported to the Foreign Ministry that the Soviet Union's eagerness to increase exports was a means to earn foreign currency and nothing else.

---

[33] Coates, W P: *A History of Anglo-Soviet Relations*, p.393, and Sokolnikov's speech in support, quoted in Slusser & Eugin: *Soviet Foreign Policy 1932-1934*, p.341; Document 66
[34] *Hansard*, vol.244, 30 October 1930, 266
[35] Dyck, Harvey: *Weimar Germany and Soviet Russia*, p.221; see Ch.8, No.100; Browder, Robert: *The Origins of Soviet-American Diplomacy*, p.34

It was questionable whether the Soviet Union was guilty of dumping. The meaning of the term is where countries sell surplus goods abroad below the price than they could be sold for on the home market. On the basis of that definition the charge was not justified, for there were no surplus goods in the Soviet Union. The purpose was to sell the goods abroad in order to pay for imports.[36] Stalin, in an interview with a Tokyo newspaper, offered this explanation:

> We can afford to sell wheat at lower prices than rival countries because we do away with all speculators and brokers. It is ridiculous to accuse us of dumping, since we do not sell our wheat any lower than production cost.[37]

However, another complaint, which was more justified, was that the Soviet Union was able to sell goods cheaply because, as was stated in a 1931 Foreign Office memorandum, some of the goods were produced by convict labour.[38]

What was absolutely clear was that the financial crisis had not been caused by any action of the Soviet Union. Hilger stated, 'The foreign trade monopoly enabled the Soviet Union to let political considerations determine its export policy, the placing of orders and the fixing of a price.' Hilger also alleges that they were so acting and reducing the price as an element of surprise.[39] However, 'the volume of exports was never large enough to affect market conditions by whatever practice was adopted.' Nor did the foreign trade monopoly enable the Soviet Union to sell goods cheaply, because they needed the hard currency to buy imported goods, particularly those which would facilitate the Five Year Plan.

If the Soviet Union was dumping goods, other countries were doing the same. For example, in Australia, under the Patterson Scheme, butter was sold in the home market at exorbitant prices while surpluses were dumped abroad.[40]

In 1914 Russia exported to Britain 51% of its total timber exports; but, because of the Civil War in 1918 and 1920, exports in those years were only 4%. Gradually during the 1920s, Soviet exports to Britain recovered. In 1927 it was only 16%, in 1928 it was 22% and in 1929 27%. Although following the financial crisis there was an accelerated increase in 1930 to 36%, rising to 40% in 1931, exports still had not recovered to the pre-1914 level and the increase was as much to do with the need of Soviet Russia to earn a greater amount of hard currency than with dumping.[41]

---

[36] Browder, Robert: *The Origins of Soviet-American Diplomacy*, p.34
[37] The *New York Times*, 26 November 1930, p.14
[38] DBFP, 2nd Series, vol.7, p.754
[39] Hilger, Gustav: *Incompatible Allies*, p.237
[40] Coates, W P: *A History of Anglo-Soviet Relations*, p.433
[41] *Financial News* supplement, 6 June 1932, p.24

Before what proved to be the final session of the Enquiry of the Committee for the Study of European Union, an Imperial Conference had been called which sat between 21 July and 20 August 1932. The Conference agreed to limited customs preferences between Britain and her dominions. Britain was persuaded to give six months' notice, which she was entitled to do, to terminate the Anglo-Russian Trade Agreement. However, the Foreign Secretary, Sir John Simon, made it clear that he remained anxious to promote trade between Britain and the Soviet Union. There was considerable criticism from those who would normally be expected to support Conservative policies;[42] hardly the right way to promote trade with the Soviet Union.The *Financial News* believed the reason for the termination of the Anglo-Russian agreement at this time was because Britain had agreed with Canada to do so. An oblique reference to an agreement between Canada and Britain to denounce the Anglo-Russian trade agreement was referred to in an article of the agreement with Canada which stated:

> If either government is satisfied that any of the preferences are likely to be frustrated by reason of the creation or maintenance directly or indirectly of prices of a class of commodities through state action on behalf of any foreign country, action will be taken to prohibit the entry of such foreign imports.[43]

The *Spectator* described the denunciation of the Russian Trade Agreement, which was part of a bargain exacted by Canada at the Ottawa Conference, 'as profoundly unfortunate. '[44] Concerning the suggestion that the Soviet Union was dumping timber, Mr Bamberger, a timber expert, stated:

> Russian and Siberian softwood are fine. The forests are old and the texture of the wood is mild and admittedly much of the timber is of exceptional quality. There has been no dumping of Russian wood.[45]

At a conference which was convened in Warsaw between certain agrarian countries of Eastern Europe (Bulgaria, Estonia, Hungary, Latvia, Lithuania, and Poland) and the more industrialised countries Rumania and Yugoslavia, customs preference was agreed between the eight states, but the industrialised countries Czechoslovakia, Austria and the Soviet Union were excluded.[46]

Other European countries were invited to participate in a conference at Stresa between 5 and 20 September 1932, but again the Soviet Union was not invited; so why these other

---

[42] Taylor, A J P: *English History 1914-1945*, p.333
[43] *Financial News*, 22 August 1932, p.1
[44] *Spectator*, 22 October 1932, p.522
[45] Coates, W P: *History of Anglo-Soviet Relations*, p.419
46 *Survey of International Affairs,* 1932, p.24

countries expected Soviet co-operation is a complete mystery. A fund was established to which all countries attending the conference would contribute, calculated on the volume of their foreign trade, from which compensation to wheat-exporting countries would be paid when a drop in the price of cereals occurred. The decision of the conference was not unanimous. Britain refused to participate in the agreement. It was intended that the proposals made by the conference would come before what transpired to be the final session of the Enquiry into European Union.[47] Litvinov was highly critical and said sarcastically:

> The Soviet Union had not been represented at the conference. The Stresa countries were supposed to consist of delegates from exporting and importing countries, especially from the east and centre of Europe. …

The conference

> assumed that the Soviet Union had neither imports nor exports. Soon the organisers of the conference may discover that the world did not contain all the countries marked on the map.

I believe it was a valid criticism by Litvinov, sarcastically spoken. The Soviet Union was only reluctantly invited to join the Study on European Union due to pressure from Germany and Italy. He was making the point that an invitation should have been initially made Further, the Soviet Union was also unjustly excluded from the Stresa Conference.

A meeting, which was in fact the final meeting of the Enquiry into European Union, took place in October 1932. The main business was how to bolster the price of cereals.

Litvinov made another fine speech. Dealing first with the purpose for which the conference had been called, Litvinov referred to a measure agreed at the Stresa conference to bolster the price of cereals which had established a fund from grain-exporting countries. If the price of wheat obtained on the international market was less than an agreed amount a payment from the fund would be made

According to Litvinov, the above measure

> was obviously prompted by the consideration that, owing to the drop in prices of cereals, exporting countries were having difficulties in covering the payments abroad for their own imports, past and present. Hence, a diminution in imports reacted on the industrial countries and created a factor in the general economic crises. The drop in the price of cereals impoverished the agricultural population and lowered its purchasing capacity, thus leading to the same results − that is to

---

[47] Ibid. p.23

say, for a restriction of industrial production and all its consequences. There could be no doubt that the agricultural countries would profit by such a scheme and from this point of view there would be no objection to it − unless it was from the contributors to such a fund; but in connexion with the question as to whether it would lead to the recovery of industry and alleviation of the crisis, many doubts were bound to arise.

Litvinov then made a valid critique of the scheme:

> What guarantees were there that the grain-exporting countries in their competition with each other and with extra-European markets in their fight for markets would not further lower prices counting upon the premiums?

He made the valid point that if this scheme resulted in a drop of Soviet exports there would be a reduction in Soviet imports.

> European trade might suffer as a whole more than it would gain by the total increase in the purchasing power of some countries by 75 million francs, which after all was coming out of 'their own pocket.'

Litvinov stated: 'He sincerely believed that the present crisis could not be cured or alleviated by any measures amounting to discrimination.' Then Litvinov used his sarcastic wit by reminding the Commission:

> Nearly a year had elapsed since he had submitted a proposal for the conclusion of an economic pact of non-aggression. After passing through a series of committees, that proposal had found lasting peace in one of them.[48]

The idea of some kind of European Union was then indefinitely postponed, only to be revived after the Second World War when Europe lay in ruins. Then the notion would be pursued with more vision, determination and success.

However, a much more grandiose scheme to try to eliminate the world depression was the holding of the World Economic Conference in London, which Litvinov attended. This occasion presented Litvinov with an opportunity to make another major speech. He started his speech with the words:

> Thanks to the specific nature of the economic system in my country, the world crisis has been unable to affect the steady development of its economic life. Such symptoms as over-production, the accumulation of stocks of goods for which no

---

[48] Degras, Jane: *Foreign Policy of Soviet Russia*, vol.2, pp. 541-543

market can be found, unemployment, wage cuts, increase in foreign indebtedness and bankruptcy are conspicuous by their absence. Yet the crisis is not without its unfavourable effect on our foreign trade.

It will hardly be an exaggeration to say that at least 60,000,000 are eking out a semi-starved existence in countries embraced by the crisis. At the same time there has been a catastrophic drop in the earnings of those still in employment and a corresponding drop in purchasing power and consumption, leading in its turn to accumulation of stocks in spite of a decline in production and an unprecedented shrinkage in foreign trade returns.

Later in the speech, Litvinov gave an example:

It was only the measures adopted by various countries undergoing the crisis causing reduction in the Soviet exports, that in 1932 forced the Soviet Union to revise its import plans. Even so, there was only a 20.2% reduction as compared with 1929, while the corresponding reduction in world trade amounted to 58.5%. The Soviet Union, while having no part in the creation of the conditions bringing about the world crisis, has itself been to some extent affected by the crisis in respect of its foreign trade. Although perfectly able, thanks to the success of the first Five Year Plan, to develop its own economic life independently of imports and foreign markets, my country has no desire to shut itself off from the rest of the world by economic barriers or to withdraw into its own economic shell and in spite of the ever-increasing productivity of its own industries it is not addicted to autarchy and has no objection to advantageous imports of foreign goods.

While in the rest of the world industrial production in 1932 fell by 33% compared with 1928, the Soviet Union's production rose by 219% during the same period. While in most countries the number of persons employed had gone down catastrophically, in the USSR the number of employed people went up during the previous four years from 11,600,000 to 22,800,000.[49]

However, it appears that the effect on the Soviet Union of the financial crisis was greater than Litvinov stated. As prices fell and competition to sell goods intensified, the value of Soviet exports but not the volume fell by just under 40% between 1929 and 1932, compared with a reduction of 70% in the USA, a 64% reduction in Great Britain and 58% in Germany.[50]

Litvinov went on to make this offer to the capitalist countries:

---

[49] *The New York Times*, 15 June 1933, p.7; *Times*, 15 June 1933, p.9
[50] Beloff, Max: *The Foreign Policy of Soviet Russia*, p.32

The Soviet Union, as a rule, draws its import quotas in accordance with plans in strict accordance with its export possibilities and credit facilities, but the Soviet Union could conceive of conditions such as lengthened credits, normal conditions for Soviet exports and other favourable factors which might induce it to revise its plans to a degree which would have no small influence in the alleviation of the crisis. ... According to our calculations, the Soviet Government, given such conditions, might agree to place orders abroad in the sum of $1,000,000,000.

Then Litvinov elaborated:

In the near future the Soviet Union could absorb $200,000,000 of ferrous metals; $100,000,000 worth of materials for the textile, leather and rubber industries; $400,000,000 worth of machinery, including railway equipment, to the value of $100,000,000; $35,000,000 of agricultural goods, including breed-stock; $50,000,000 worth of consumer goods such as tea, cocoa, coffee and herrings; and $50,000,000 worth of new ships, chiefly for industrial purposes such as fishing, seal-hunting and dredging and so on.

The significance of these figure will be more evident if it is realised that this amounts to 25% to 66% of the existing world stocks in respect of such metals as aluminium, nickel, copper and lead and 100% in respect of some of the consumer goods I have mentioned to a third of the annual world export of machinery and 100 per cent in respect of last year's ship-building output. The vast majority of countries represented here might be supposed to be interested in the export of the commodities I have enumerated. Such figures would be in excess of any plan already drawn up by the Soviet Government and do not apply to goods urgently required by it and to be ordered under present conditions.

By making such a suggestion, we are far from inviting the conference to lose sight of other aspects of the situation such as artificial obstacles and barriers in the way of economic relations. We should be the last to deny that the operation by States of methods of economic warfare in their economic relations is making worse an economic situation which is bad enough as it is. Herein must be included all forms of discrimination, tariff wars, covert or overt, currency wars, the discriminatory prohibition of imports and exports, and all forms of economic boycott.

I have already had occasion to recommend economic non-aggression and to propose the conclusion of a pact of non-aggression. Unfortunately, the proposal was itself the victim of aggression, taken prisoner and thrown into a dungeon, by one of the League of Nations' commissions.[51]

Experts were of the opinion that if the Soviet Union was granted long-term credits, she could absorb most of the surplus of goods which are at present unsaleable, and the Soviet Union had not failed to make a single payment in recent years. Germany, however, had to make advance payments to the Soviet Union so that payments could be maintained.[52]

Litvinov's speech gained the approval of *The New York Times*: 'What really thrilled the Conference was the speech by Max Litvinov, because it mentioned real money and envisaged for the delegates the prospect of getting some.'[53]

The Conference for which there were high hopes ended in failure. The main purpose of the Conference, which was to endeavour to stabilise international currencies, was doomed once President Roosevelt decided not to participate in any agreement to stabilise the dollar.[54] The *Times* summed up the Conference: 'Neither Macdonald nor any of the other speakers attempted to cloak the failure of the Conference to achieve any definite, practical results.'[55]

However, the Conference's chief benefactor was Litvinov, for reasons other than those for which the Conference was called. Following a meeting with Sir John Simon, it was announced, presumably as part of a secret deal, that the embargo on Soviet purchases would be lifted. The employees of Metro Vickers, imprisoned in the Soviet Union, were released the next day.[56]

The Conference gave Litvinov the opportunity to make contact with a considerable number of the delegates from Eastern European countries, who all accepted Litvinov's definition of aggression. They all participated in a formal treaty to that effect shortly after the Conference ended in July 1933.[57]

Further, Litvinov made contact with two important US statesmen, Secretary of State Hull and President Roosevelt's advisor Raymond Morley, and this was a contributing factor in the US's recognition of the Soviet Union four months later.[58]

As far as the Soviet Union was concerned, the question of payment of her debts, the issue which had caused such a fuss in the past, began to become insignificant. President Hoover

---

[51] *The New York Times*, 15 June 1933, pp.1 & 7; *Times*, 15 June 1933 , p.9

[52] Ibid. p.7

[53] Ibid. p.1

[54] Taylor, A J P: *English History 1914-1945*, p.335; Pope, Arthur: *Maxim Litvinov*, p.284

[55] *Times*, 28 July 1933, p.15

[56] Pope, Arthur: *Maxim Litvinov*, p.283

[57] Ibid. p.284; see Ch.6, No.88

[58] Pope, Arthur: *Maxim Litvinov*, p.284

had proposed on 20 June 1931, in view of the world financial crisis, to postpone repayment of the loans countries had received from the USA to fight the First World War provided the countries having the benefit of the moratorium similarly granted like postponement of their intergovernmental loans owing. A number of countries, including Britain, enthusiastically agreed. France did so only reluctantly.[59] In December 1932 France, Estonia, Hungary, Poland and Yugoslavia defaulted on their debts to the USA. Britain paid her instalment to the USA in full, but wanted to resist having to pay if nobody was paying the debts due to her.[60] In June 1933 Britain offered a token payment. Roosevelt gave an assurance that he did not consider Britain being in default.[61] A similar situation occurred in December 1933.[62]

In his interview with Duranty, Stalin very much supported his Foreign Commissar:

> What Litvinov said in London still holds good. We are the greatest demand market and are ready to order and pay for large quantities of goods, but we require satisfactory conditions of credit and what is more we must have the assurance we can pay. It is impossible for us to import unless we can export because we will not place orders unless we can pay for them when the time comes. Everyone has been surprised that we are paying, that we do pay and can pay. I know it is not customary to pay debts now, but we do. Other nations renig (renege) on their debts, but the Union of Socialist Republics does not renig (renege).[63]

Stalin was referring to the failure of most countries to repay their debts to the United States and the failure of countries owing money to Britain to repay them. The United States Congress took the initiative by passing the Johnson Act on 13 April 1934 prohibiting financial transactions with any foreign government in default.[64]

Roosevelt, however, wished to avoid humiliating Britain and stated that if Britain paid the current instalment, and not the arrears, she would not be considered to be in default. Britain replied, 'It was impossible to contemplate a situation in which they were called upon to honour their war obligations to others while continuing to suspend all payments of war obligations due to them.'[65] Ironically, Western democracies were now in a position similar to the Soviet Union in not honouring their international debts. The Communist Government punctiliously paid the debts they had incurred, and so on 3 June 1945 *The New York Times* described the Soviet Union as a good credit risk.[66]

---

[59] Documents, 1931, pp.114-118; Walters, Francis: *A History of the League of Nations*, p.458

[60] *Survey of International Affairs*, 1932, p.128; *The New York Times*, 15 June 1933, p.1

[61] Documents, 1933, p.124

[62] Ibid. p.130

[63] *The New York Times*, 28 December 1933, p.1

[64] Documents, 1934, p.194

[65] Documents, 1934, p.198

[66] *The New York Times*, 3 June 1945, p.31

The era of Litvinov the economist was over, as no more similar international conferences on economic issues took place and the premier concern became how to deter aggression by Germany, Japan and Italy. Stalin was well pleased with the performance of his Foreign Commissar in London. Pope tells us, presumably from his conversations with Litvinov, that 'his long fight for recognition [of the Soviet Union by the USA] was thus crowned by the important event now impending.'[67]

---

[67] Pope, Arthur: *Maxim Litvinov*, p.287

11: THE USA

.

Initially, President Wilson showed warmth towards the Bolshevik regime by stating that, despite its inability to render direct aid, the United States 'would avail itself of every opportunity to secure once more for Russia complete sovereignty and independence in their own affairs.' In reply, the Bolshevik Government expressed

> the gratitude of the Congress to the labouring and exploited classes for their message sent by President Wilson and voiced the hope that the happy time is not too distant when the toiling masses of all bourgeoisie countries will throw off the yoke of capitalism and establish a socialistic order of society.[1]

It was an unwise move, and contrary to later Soviet policy of trying to split the capitalist powers and persuade the USA to grant recognition to the Soviet Union.

There is every reason to believe it was on Litvinov's initiative that he particularly endeavoured to negotiate a rapport with the USA, whose growing importance and strength he recognised. Litvinov sent a personal letter to President Wilson dated 24 December 1918, quoted in Sheinis, which stated:

> The dictatorship of the working people and producers is not an aim in itself, but a means for building a new social system under which all citizens, irrespective of the class to which they previously belonged, will be given equal rights and the opportunity to work usefully.

With considerable justification, Litvinov said:

> One may believe or disbelieve in this ideal, but this does not justify the dispatch of foreign troops to fight against it or for arming and support of classes who seek to restore the old system of exploitation of one man by another.[2]

Further, Trotsky enquired through the Red Cross mission what aid Moscow might expect from the USA should the Soviets reject the treaty of Brest-Litovsk. Washington's response referred to the President's message indicating the inability of the USA to render direct aid, so the Soviet Congress voted to accept the treaty of Brest-Litovsk.[3]

---

[1] Browder, Robert Paul: *Origins of Soviet-American Diplomacy,* p.6
[2] Sheinis, Zinovy: *Maxim Litvinov*, p.119
[3] Browder, Robert Paul: *Origins of Soviet-American Diplomacy*, p.7

Although the USA intervention in the Civil War did nothing to improve the relationship with the Bolshevik regime, the latter believed that the United States had entered the campaign with reluctance, and had attempted to maintain a neutral position *vis-à-vis* Russia's internal strife. The Bolsheviks also recognised that the USA's intervention had helped to restrain Japan.[4] Therefore, it was always treated with less hostility than the intervention of Japan and the European powers. Karakhan, in conversation with Lockhart, stated:

> The USA had only intervened to protect the Czechs. He admitted that, in attacking the Czechs, Trotsky had made a political mistake, although he was fully justified by the bad faith of the French.[5]

President Wilson sent a young diplomat called Bullitt to the Soviet Union in the Spring of 1919 on a fact-finding mission. Bullitt saw Lenin, Chicherin and Litvinov. His report stated :

> He found Lenin, Chicherin and Litvinov full of the sense of Russia's need for peace and therefore disposed to be most conciliatory.

Bullitt finished his report by stating:

> Having seen the three leaders, there is no doubt whatever of a desire of the Soviet Government for a just and reasonable peace and the sincerity of their proposal and I will pray you will consider it with the deepest seriousness.

However, Bullitt was optimistic because:

> Lenin, Chicherin and others expressed in the most straight, unequivocal way the determination of the Soviet Government to pay its foreign debts and I am convinced there is no dispute on this point.[6]

In the course of discussions, Litvinov made, with Lenin's approval, the most unusual oral suggestion to Bullitt that the USA take over all Allied claims against Russia and cancel a corresponding amount of Allied debts to Washington. Litvinov thought it would be to the advantage of the Soviet Government to have only one creditor, as it was hopeful that the USA would offer better terms. Bullitt returned to see President Wilson, but the offer failed to interest the President. This caused Bullitt to resign from the American Peace Delegation. However, one advantage of the offer was that Bullitt became a Russian sympathiser, and on that account was appointed first US ambassador to the Soviet Union in 1933. One of the

---

[4] Browder, Robert Paul: *Origins of Soviet-American Diplomacy*, p.19
[5] PRO 3344/186867, 7 November 1918, p.289
[6] FRUS, 1919, Russia, pp.77 & 80

reasons why, no doubt, the USA rejected the offer was because Britain and France were regarded as better credit risks. This assessment did not anticipate that, following the Depression, both Britain and France, as well as all other European countries in debt to the USA except Finland, would default.[7]

This did not impress the President, who became extremely hostile to the Bolshevik Government. In a nationwide tour in support of the Versailles Treaty and League of Nations, Wilson referred to the Bolshevik government as 'the intolerable tyranny of their government, [which] cut off every way possible in which we might aid them.' [8]

On 3 December 1919 the USA's Secretary of State, Lansing, was extremely critical of Lenin's regime, saying: 'They have dragged Russia into a state of misery, of hideous brutality and of despair.'[9]

However, the USA showed sympathy for Kerensky's Russian Revolution. Lansing reported:

> The USA had obtained from Admiral Kolchak and his associates an assurance that they would direct their efforts, if they succeeded in driving the Bolsheviks from Moscow and Petrograd, to the democratic rehabilitation of the Russian state. They expressly repudiated all attempts to revive the former land system or to impose again on the Russian people the regime of caste and privilege which the Revolution destroyed.[10]

This was in direct contrast to Litvinov's allegations, but it was Litvinov who was probably correct. I believe it is doubtful whether the White Generals, if they had been successful in the Civil War, would have restored democracy and risked the Bolsheviks winning a democratic election.

Chicherin, as well as Litvinov, realised the importance of US recognition. President Wilson's refusal to recognise the Soviet Union was not in accordance with traditional US foreign policy which, like Britain, recognised any government, whatever its character, so long as it exercised control over the area of the state.

However, preliminary steps had been taken by the US administration to reduce their hostility to the Soviet Union. On 7 July 1920 a formal embargo on trade with the Soviet Union imposed since the Revolution was withdrawn, but at the same time US diplomats and consular officials were instructed to take no action which 'officially or unofficially,

---

[7] Browder, Robert Paul: *Origins of Soviet-American Diplomacy*, pp.11 and 12
[8] Dulles, Foster Rhea: *Road to Teheran*, p.156
[9] FRUS, 1920, vol.3, p.444
[10] Ibid. p.437; No 2

directly or indirectly assists or facilitates commercial or other dealings' between US citizens and Russia.[11]

On 10 August 1920 Secretary of State Colby wrote: 'It was not possible to recognise the present Russian Government as one in which relations common to friendly governments can be maintained.'[12] Colby confirmed the friendship of the people of the USA for the people of Russia and the desire to see Russia's territorial integrity maintained,[13] so that in 1920 it was refusing to recognise the independence of the Baltic states without the consent of Russia.

Nevertheless, the Administration completely opposed recognition. Colby said:

> The present rulers of Russia do not rule by the will or the consent of a considerable proportion of the Russian people.

> The Bolsheviks, although in number an inconsiderable minority of the people, through force and cunning, seized the powers and machinery of government and continued to use them with savage oppression to maintain themselves in power.[14]

> Further, they intended to use every means including diplomatic agencies to promote such revolutionary movements in other countries.[15]

Chicherin thought it was appropriate to make a tough reply. Whereas Chicherin could have pointed out the suppression of all opposition in Russia by the Tsar, he stated: 'Only in Russia were people free from exploitation by the privileged minority.'

Although there was much truth in this, the privileged minority had been replaced by another clique which came to stifle debate and suppress those who did not agree with it. Further, in 1920, this clique presided over a country with high unemployment and widespread hunger. Consequently, the so-called workers were far worse off.

With regard to propaganda, Chicherin stated: 'The Communist regime cannot be forced upon other people and the struggle must be carried on by the toiling masses themselves in their own country.' Chicherin then ended on a conciliatory note. In spite of the attitude of the US Government, the Soviet Government felt sure that 'friendly relations could be established and that far-sighted business leaders would see the advantage of commercial and diplomatic relations with Russia.'

---

[11] Ibid. pp.717-719; Carr, Edward: *Bolshevik Revolution*, vol.3, p.279
[12] FRUS, 1920, vol.3, p.466; Browder, Robert Paul: *Origins of Soviet-American Diplomacy*, p.16
[13] Browder, Robert Paul: *Origins of Soviet-American Diplomacy*, p.16
[14] FRUS, 1920, vol.3, p.466
[15] FRUS, 1920, vol.3, p.467

As the Bolshevik regime hoped that a Republican victory would lead to a resumption of relations, they took the opportunity, soon after President Harding took office, to send him a message. Litvinov, then ambassador to Estonia, sent a note dated 21 March 1921 and signed by the President of the All Russian Executive Committee which stated: 'From the first day of her existence Soviet Russia had nourished the hope of a speedy establishment of friendly relations with the great North American Republic.' Litvinov then made an attack on President Harding's predecessor, President Wilson, a Democrat. Litvinov pointed out:

> Even when US troops together with others participated in an attack upon Soviet Russia, the Russian Republic still expressed the hope of a speedy change of policy towards her and demonstrated this by its particularly considerate treatment of Americans in Russia; but President Wilson, who without cause and without any declaration of war had attacked the Russian Republic, showed during the whole of his administration a growing hostility towards the Russian Republic. The Soviet Republic absorbed in the work of internal reconstruction and building up its economic life has no intention of intervening in the internal affairs of the USA and the All Russian Central Executive Committee herewith makes a categorical declaration to that effect.[16]

The tenor of such a note was in sharp contrast to that of the 1918 note.[17]

However, President Harding left it to his Secretary of State Hughes to reply. He stated:

> If fundamental changes are contemplated involving due regard for the protection of persons and property and the establishment of conditions essential for the maintenance of commerce, the Government will be glad to have convincing evidence of the consummation of such changes and until this evidence is supplied this Government is unable to perceive that there is any basis for considering trade relations.[18]

However, although the USA was permitted to take such action against the Soviet regime as is permitted by international law, the USA had no right to tell an entirely independent country how to manage its economy, and in any case Hughes would be proved wrong. In fact, during the Great Depression, USA exports to the Soviet Union were most welcome.

Until 1922 the Provisional Government was still represented in Washington, but finally, on 5 June 1922, the ambassador, Bakmeteff, offered his resignation to Secretary of State Hughes and departed from Washington with full diplomatic recognition. It was alleged that

---

[16] FRUS, 1921, vol.2, p.763
[17] See No.1 *ante*
[18] Browder, Robert Paul: *Origins of Soviet-American Diplomacy*, p18; FRUS, 1921, vol.2, p.768

he (Bakmeteff) had bought real estate with Russian state resources in the United States, but he denied this.[19]

Some US industrialists did not share the reluctance of its Government to associate itself with the Soviet Union. The Soviets granted a concession to American groups in the spring of 1922 to mine coal in the Kuznetsk basin.[20]

US workers appeared not to have had the same sympathy for the Soviet regime as did their British counterparts. As Gompers, the Secretary of the American Federation of Labour, wrote to the Secretary of State in 1923:

> To the wage earners of the USA, the present tyranny in Russia is a thing despicable and intolerable in practice and any thought that the United States might under any circumstances extend official recognition, even in a modified form, to such villainous despotism is repugnant.

This brought forth the following reply:

> The seizure of control by a minority in Russia came as a grievous disappointment to US democratic thought which had enthusiastically acclaimed the end of despotism of the Tsars and the entrance of free Russia into the family of democratic nations. Subsequent events were even more disturbing. The right of free speech and other civil liberties were denied. Even the advocacy of these rights was declared to be counter-revolutionary and punishable by death.[21]

The allegations were undoubtedly true, but they were also true of the regime of the Tsars and no difficulty was encountered in continuing to recognise that regime, and for that reason it was understandable that the Soviet leaders were bitter.

Following the Revolution, Lenin, Trotsky, Chicherin and Litvinov realised that the USA was the principal source of capital and the Soviet regime needed this capital to develop its resources, much of which had fallen into decay following the upheavals caused by the Revolution and the civil wars. In 1919 Lenin said: 'He was in favour of economic relations with all countries, but particularly the USA.' In February 1920, Lenin stated: 'The USA is strong. Everybody is now in its debt. Everybody depends on it. Everybody hates the USA more and more.' Lenin then said, 'To attract the Americans we must pay them. They are business people. What shall we pay with? We shall answer this question with the help of concessions.'[22]

---

[19] *The New York Times*, 5 May 1922, p.1, 13 June, p.2, 20 June, p.6; FRUS, 1922, vol.2, pp.876 and 877

[20] Carr, Edward: *Socialism in One Country*, vol.3, p.481

[21] FRUS, 1923, vol.2, p.760

[22] Gaddis, John Lewis: *Russia, the Soviet Union and the United States*, p.91

Lenin, in 1918, dreamed of the Soviet Union's national resources being exploited with the help of USA capital. In 1921 a manganese concession was agreed. In 1923 a Soviet cotton trust successfully agreed to purchase cotton from one of the USA's largest cotton exporters, finance being provided by Chase National Bank. In the year 1923-1924, US exports to the Soviet Union rose to 223 million roubles, as compared with Soviet imports from the USA of 346 million roubles in 1913.

During the following year Soviet imports from the USA dramatically increased to 883 million roubles.[23] However, Soviet exports to the USA were far less than the imports, although in 1913 imports from the USA had only been slightly higher than Russia's exports to that country.[24]

In 1926 Trotsky stated:

> The Soviet Union needs US capital to increase its rate of development. For good capital and good technique, the Soviet Union is ready to pay good dividends. This is not absolute harmony, but in our imperfect world one should not reject even relative harmony.[25]

Similarly, in 1925 Chicherin was saying:

> The USA is virtually overflowing with free capital that seeks investment, while the USSR presents a magnificent picture of national resources waiting to be brought to fruition by capital. Great prospects, not only for the well-being of our two countries but for the future of the world economy, are linked with the future penetration of US capital into our country in fruitful work.[26]

Chicherin has often been portrayed as pro-German. However, his business sense was such that, when a concession was granted to a USA firm for restoring the mine at Chiaturi, Chicherin said: 'The Soviet Government preferred the Deutsche Bank, to Harriman [of the US State Department], but the latter (Harriman) had made such favourable proposals the Soviet Government could not refuse his offer.'[27]

However, if the Soviet Government wanted improved relations with the USA they certainly did not go about it in the right way. Trotsky remarked to the Communist Youth in Moscow: 'Revolution is coming in Europe as well as in the USA, systematically, step by step, stubbornly and with gnashing of teeth in both camps. It will be long, protracted, cruel

---

[23] Carr, Edward: *Socialism in One Country*, vol.3, p.480
[24] Ibid. p.480
[25] Ibid. p.488
[26] Ibid. p.483
[27] Ibid. p.484

and sanguinary.' Rather than repudiate such statements, Lenin in fact endorsed them. Lenin stated before the last congress of the Third International:

> Revolutionists of all countries must learn the organisation, the planning, the method and substance of revolutionary work. Then I am convinced that the outlook of world revolution will not be good but excellent.[28]

Trotsky and Lenin failed to understand that what they stated for internal consumption would be monitored by diplomats and the capitalist press. Such statements would influence the capitalist politicians even if the Soviet politicians tried to explain that their statements were only for internal consumption.

As Lenin, Trotsky and Chicherin rightly appreciated, there was a need for co-operation with US capitalism in order to build the Soviet economy, and it would be expected that Litvinov would be fully in agreement. In 1919 Litvinov had already told a USA representative, Buckler, whom Litvinov met in Copenhagen, that there was a possibility of the Soviet regime recognising the foreign debt of the previous Russian governments, but that his government would want foreign machinery and manufactured goods as a *quid pro quo*. Chicherin gave an undertaking that propaganda against foreign governments would cease when peace was made. He added that revolutionary propaganda was a means of retaliation and that, in certain Western countries, conditions were not favourable for a 1917-type revolution.[29] However, Chicherin should be criticised for speaking on matters over which he had no control. He had no power over the Comintern as he had no control over internal repression and, in such cases, foreign policy had to be subordinated to other factors.

Further, showing a somewhat hypocritical but pragmatic approach, Litvinov said:

> We generally object to trade with countries who have no relations with us, such as for example Switzerland and Belgium, making however an exception for understandable reasons for such a powerful country as the USA.[30]

The USA continued to grant visas to Soviet nationals, even if associated with the Soviet regime, provided the bona fide purpose of the visit was solely for trade or commerce between the United States and the Soviet Union.[31] Nevertheless, the USA could be accused of being petty when, following Alexandra Kollontai's appointment as ambassador to Mexico, she just wished to cross the USA to take up her appointment and accordingly needed to obtain a visa. However, she was refused on the grounds that being one of the

---

[28] FRUS, 1923, vol.2, p.763
[29] Browder, Robert Paul: *Origins of Soviet-American Diplomacy*, p.17
[30] Carr, Edward: *Foundations of a Planned Economy*, p.90
[31] FRUS, 1925, vol.2, p.703

outstanding members of the Communist party, present at the Third Congress of the Communist International and a member of the Soviet Diplomatic Service, she had been actively associated with the 'international communist subversive movement.'[32]

In 1926 Litvinov told the Central Committee that, if negotiations were opened with the USA, there was every reason to believe that the USSR could obtain agreement:

> We can only wait for a sign of equal readiness on the part of the USA Government. I am quite convinced that the course of events will automatically lead both sides to agreement and in future to very close economic collaboration. [33]

However, the USA was alarmed at the attempt of the Communist International to pursue revolutionary aims in South America. A US Communist stated at the sixth session of the Enlarged Executive Committee of the Communist International on 24 February 1926: 'The last and most important task of our party is the fight against imperialism. The time is not long distant when Latin America will become the China of the Far East, and Mexico the Canton of Latin America.'

The conference issued a statement that Latin America

> can and must become the basis of support of the liberation movement against imperialism. In the present state of things the nations living in Latin America are oppressed nations which will sooner or later be drawn into the struggle against the imperialism of the United States.[34]

Nothing that Stalin could have done, even under the cloak of the Third International, could have made recognition of the Soviet Union by the United States more unlikely. On the contrary, Litvinov, in his speech to the Central Executive Committee on 8 December 1928, spoke optimistically of

> the rapidity at which our relations were improving. Exports from the USA to the Soviet Union are increasing. Our industries are making increasing demands upon the technical strength of the USA, but that economic co-operation is unfavourably influenced by the lack of official recognition.

He proceeded to give a further indication of the Soviet Union's desire to have diplomatic relation established with the USA. He also stated that the USA 'was a country with which we have no quarrel or are likely to have in the future.'[35]

---

[32] FRUS, 1926, vol.2, p.911
[33] Degras, Jane: *Soviet Documents on Foreign Policy*, vol.2, p.111
[34] FRUS, 1927, vol.1, p.357
[35] Documents 1928 p. 185

At this time the Soviet leaders were debating whether to adhere to the Kellogg-Briand Pact, as fully discussed in Chapter 6. The Soviet Union's early signing of the Kellogg-Briand Treaty, according to Carr, created a favourable impression on the public of the USA and on the Secretary of State. This development raised Moscow's hope of a rapprochement. Fischer states that Chicherin, Litvinov and other Soviet statesmen no longer believed in the imminence of recognition, but had an intuitive feeling that sooner or later friendly relations would be discovered with the USA. Fischer also claims that Litvinov contributed much towards finally overcoming the opposition of Chicherin and other Soviet leaders, whose attitude towards the Kellogg Pact was either indifferent or hostile.[36]

Although there is no doubt that Litvinov was ambitious to obtain recognition by the USA, the evidence supports the view that Fischer was wrong. Given the opportunity, in the 20's both Stalin and Chicherin would not have hesitated to have gone to considerable efforts to gain recognition by the USA as they had done with France in 1924, in spite of considerable anti-Soviet activity in France, and also in the same year with Great Britain. In 1929, it is my belief, although Chicherin no longer had the reins of power, he would not have opposed the resumption of diplomatic relations with the USA. He had been as enthusiastic as Litvinov to obtain diplomatic relations particulalry from the major powers. No country which want recognition by the Soviet Union was ever refused.

The unwise decision of the British Government to sever diplomatic relations with the USSR gave an impetus to Soviet-US trade. Mikoyan told Fischer,

> After the break with Britain, contacts with the USA became much broader. USA's purchases of oil equipment, coal cutting and mining machinery, electrical appliances, automobiles, tractors, and agriculture machines should increase year by year. He favoured direct dealings with American firms in preference to trade through third nations.

A favourable impression of the Soviet regime in the minds of the public of the USA was further assisted by the dramatic rescue of an Italian polar expedition by Soviet aviators which was heavily reported in the US press without a single critical comment. The US Chamber of Commerce hastened to invite the heroic aviators to visit the USA which. invitation was accepted.[37]

Imports from USA to the Soviet Union for the year 1927/1928 were 50% higher than they had been for the years 1925/1926. In fact, 20% of the Soviet Union's total imports now

---

[36] Fischer, Louis: *The Soviets in World Affairs*, p.761; Carr, Edward: *Foundations of a Planned Economy*, p.92
[37] Carr, Edward: *Foundations of a Planned Economy*, p.91

came from the USA. However, the Soviet Union total exports to the USA were approximately 90% less than its imports, representing only approximately 3% of the Soviet Union's total exports. This shows how unbalanced was the trade between the two countries. [38] This illustrated how absurd was the Republican Party's refusal to have diplomatic relations with the USSR.

Meanwhile, as Stalin embarked upon rapid industrialisation directed by the state and was winding up the NEP, many of the concessions granted to US firms were no longer consonant with the growing power of Soviet industrial expansion. Many were wound up by mutual consent. Instead, the Soviet Union wanted to purchase equipment for the new factories and sought the employment of US engineers and technicians. US-Soviet trade was given an impetus by an exhibition held by the Soviet Society for Cultural Relations in the USA featuring Soviet products,[39] notwithstanding the fact that there were still no diplomatic relations between the two countries.

Following the Great Depression, the increase of exports from the USA to the Soviet Union was especially welcome in the USA. In 1930 and 1931 the Soviet Union was the largest purchaser of American agricultural and industrial equipment.

The increase of trade caused by the Soviet demand for technical aid in various fields of industry and agriculture caused some members of the Congress, such as Senator Wheeler of Montana, to warn the administration that, unless the USA revised its attitude, Germany and Great Britain would procure the greatest part of the Soviet trade.

Similarly, Senator Cutting called for a new approach to Moscow, minimising the danger of communism, and noting the Russian debt to the United States was too small to warrant it standing in the way of reconciliation.[40] In November 1930 Stalin sensibly asked Walter Durranty how the USA could withhold formal recognition and simultaneously continue to supply machinery and goods to be used in the economic expansion of the Communist regime. There was much truth in Stalin's view 'rather than trying to undermine the US system, Stalin could be accused of supporting capitalism by giving it markets during the Depression.'[41]

There is every reason to believe that Litvinov regarded achieving recognition by the USA of the Soviet Union as one, if not the most important aim, of his administration. Such views were entirely in accord with views expressed at various times by Lenin, Trotsky and

[38] Fischer, Louis: *The Soviets in World Affairs*, p.765
[39] Carr, Edward: *Foundations of a Planned Economy*, p.91
[40] Browder, Robert Paul: *Origins of Soviet-American Diplomacy*, p.31
[41] *The New York Times*, 1 December 1930, pp.1 & 7

Chicherin. If Litvinov could personally achieve recognition of the Soviet Union by the USA, it would be both a personal triumph for him and greatly increase his prestige among the Soviet hierarchy. Surely Litvinov was the person most likely to obtain that goal with his confidence, audacity and knowledge of the capitalist world.

The situation was dramatically changed by the defeat of the Republican President Hoover by Roosevelt in the 1932 presidential elections. Roosevelt in his election campaign had made it clear he favoured recognition of the Soviet Union.

Prior to the negotiations for recognition, Secretary of State Hull advised Roosevelt that, before Litvinov was invited to the United States, there should be negotiations on three points: non-interference in US affairs, freedom of religion for US citizens in the Soviet Union and debt settlement; but Roosevelt overruled Hull and invited Litvinov to come to the USA without any prior conditions.[42] Other countries had given unconditional recognition to the USSR and the question was whether the industrial might of the USA was such that concessions could be extracted. Certainly, in a memorandum of the State Department, detailed consideration was given to the conditions that should be imposed on the USSR as the price of recognition. En route to Washington, while in Berlin, Litvinov's remark that, as far as the Soviet delegation was concerned, he could reach agreement 'in half an hour, perhaps less', created an unfavourable impression.[43]

Max Litvinov arrived on 7 November 1933, the sixteenth anniversary of the Russian Revolution, in buoyant mood. A formal reception had been arranged by the President for the same day, shortly after his arrival.[44] On 8 and 9 November negotiations started, but no progress was made on the major issues, namely propaganda and debts. No minutes were kept, apparently, because of the completely unsatisfactory progress.[45]

However, in view of the Soviet rejection of any conditions whatsoever, the State Department had to report to the President that stalemate had been reached. Roosevelt intervened and it was arranged that, on 10 November, Litvinov would meet the President together with his Secretary and Under Secretaries of State, Hull and Phillips. The meeting lasted one hour, during which the President introduced some humour into the discussion by suggesting that they meet in the evening alone in private so they could, if need be, insult each other with impunity. They were closeted for three hours the same day. There was a further meeting of two hours on 12 November.[46] No negotiations took place on the next two days, presumably because Litvinov was awaiting instructions from Stalin.[47]

---

[42] Hull, Cordell: *Memoirs*, p.297
[43] Browder, Robert Paul: *Origins of Soviet-American Diplomacy*, p.127
[44] Ibid. p.129
[45] Ibid. p.133
[46] Browder, Robert Paul: *Origins of Soviet-American Diplomacy*, pp.133-135
[47] Ibid. p.134

A further meeting took place with the President on the morning of 15 November and a final meeting took place on 16 November, when the gentlemen's agreement was signed. If an agreement had not been reached, Browder stated that both the President and Litvinov would have suffered immeasurable loss of prestige both at home and abroad. However, I think the loss to the President would have been greater because his Republican critics, who were mostly opposed to recognition, would have boasted they were right all the time. Browder stated that, if Litvinov had been given the alternative of signing an agreement or relinquishing the prospect of US recognition, he would probably have complied with any US ultimatum. However, Browder may be wrong. In 1929, when it looked as if Britain was insisting on conditional approval, the Soviet Union was prepared to allow the negotiations to fail and used the failure for propaganda.[48] The Soviet Union was now in a stronger position because of her reconciliation with France and, to a certain extent Britain. Even if recognition by the USA had been refused, the Soviet Union's application to join the League of Nations would probably have still been successful.

Further, if a comprehensive agreement had been signed, the Soviet Union would almost certainly have not complied with the agreement. The President then would have been faced with the difficult decision of whether to break off diplomatic relations. However, Litvinov should be given due credit for charming the President sufficiently to gain what in effect was unconditional approval.

The major issue would be whether the USA could persuade the Soviet Union to acknowledge any and if so how much of the pre-war debt without the USA agreeing, as a condition of such acknowledgment, a loan. At the meeting of 15 November, attended by, Bullitt, the Acting Secretary of the Treasury, the President and Litvinov, a memorandum was agreed. Roosevelt told Litvinov the smallest sum Congress would accept would be $150 million, but Litvinov entered into a gentlemen's agreement that, over and above all Soviet claims against the United States arising out of the War of Intervention, a payment of $75 million dollars would be paid, although it seems unlikely Litvinov had authority to agree such a figure. Litvinov, no doubt to flatter the President, stated he had

> entire confidence in the fair-mindedness of the President and felt sure that when the President had looked at the facts about the loan to Kerensky, the President would not consider a sum greater than $75 million dollars was justified.

Litvinov had maintained that it would be found that the greater part was spent by Bakmeteff, the Kerensky Government's Ambassador to the USA, buying supplies for the Kolchak army, an anti-Bolshevik army.[49]

Litvinov told Roosevelt:

---

[48] See Ch.9, Nos.91-97
[49] FRUS, 1933, vol.2, p.804

As far as Litvinov, personally, was concerned and without making any commitment, he would be inclined to advise the Soviet Government to accept $100 million, if the President would consider that sum fair.[50]

As part of the negotiations, Litvinov entered into a gentleman's agreement covering a number various matters:

1. To respect scrupulously the right of the USA to order its own life within its jurisdiction in its own way and to refrain and restrain all persons in government service and all organisations of the government or under its direct or indirect control, including organisations in receipt of any financial assistance from it, from any act covert or overt [this surely must include the Comintern] to injure the tranquillity, prosperity, order or security of the whole or any part of the United States.[51]

2. With reference to freedom of religion, Roosevelt reminded Litvinov that the Government of the United States since the foundation of the Republic has always striven to protect its nationals both home and abroad in the free exercise of liberty of conscience and religious worship and from all disabilities or persecution on account of their religious faith and worship.

Litvinov quoted a Bolshevik decree of 23 January 1918 that every person 'may profess any religion or none.' Further, 'There was a right to conduct without annoyance or molestation of any kind, religious services and rites of a ceremonial nature.'[52] Litvinov must of course have realised that there was constant harassment of those professing to be Christians and, as Ivy and he were Jewish, also those who wished to practise that religion.

Litvinov also gave an assurance that:

Nationals of the USA will not be granted less favourable treatment than the nationals of the nations most favoured in this respect,

and provision for the nearest diplomatic or consular official to be immediately notified of any arrest of a US citizen. Further, requests for visits to a USA citizen by consular representatives shall be granted without delay, although the right for the Consular official to see the prisoner in private was not conceded.[53]

As for economic espionage was concerned, Litvinov gave an assurance: ' There was no

---

[50] Ibid.
[51] Ibid.p.805-806
[52] Ibid. p.807
[53] Ibid. pp.810 and 811

right under Soviet law to obtain economic information in respect of business and production secrets.'[54]

Senator Borah had campaigned for a long time for his country to grant recognition to the Soviet Union. When he heard of Roosevelt's plans, he wired the President: 'It would be in accord with the President's initiative and courage more than once disclosed in great emergencies.' Later, on 11 November, Litvinov acknowledged Senator Borah's help:

> You, I believe, were the first American in a high position to realise the full implications of amicable relations between your country and mine. The present occasion is in large measure the result of your vision and your persistent efforts.

When recognition was granted, Borah wired the President: 'Congratulations. It was a fine big, courageous thing to do.' Before Litvinov left the USA, Borah was going to deliver the address at a dinner in honour of Litvinov, but he could not attend on the grounds of illness. However, Borah's wire was the chief event in the evening.

> Profound gratification. Estrangement is at an end. Friendship, trade and commerce are to terminate sixteen wasted years. These two great peoples are entitled to live in friendship.[55]

At the end of his visit, Litvinov wrote a very appreciative letter to President Roosevelt:

> On leaving the USA I feel it is a great pleasure respectfully to convey to you my feelings for the high esteem as well as gratitude for the many tokens of attention and friendship you have been good enough to show me during my stay in Washington.

Although some of Roosevelt's aides had not been as enthusiastic as the President, Litvinov nevertheless 'thanked the whole executive and its various organs for their courtesies and care.' Litvinov then confirmed his optimism for the future by stating:

> My firm conviction that the official linking of the two countries by the exchange of notes between the President and myself will be of great benefit to our two countries and will also be conducive to the strengthening and preservation of peace between nations towards which our countries are sincerely striving. I believe that their joint efforts will add a creative factor which will be benefical to mankind.[56]

---

[54] FRUS, 1933, vol.2, p.812
[55] Johnson, Claudius: *Borah of Idaho*, p.366
[56] FRUS, 1933, vol.2, p.819

Roosevelt returned the compliment, describing it as 'a great personal pleasure to be able to meet you', and agreeing with Litvinov that 'co-operation of our two governments in the great work of preserving peace will be the cornerstone of an enduring friendship.'[57]

Roosevelt lost no time in appointing Bullitt as first ambassador to the USSR and two days later consented to Alexander Troyanovsky being the Soviet ambassador in Washington.[58]

Bullitt received a most enthusiastic welcome in Moscow when he arrived on 11 December 1933. He was met at the railway station by Troyanovsky and taken to the Hotel National, where the American flag was suspended over the entrance. On 12 December 1933 Bullitt lunched with Litvinov and his family, and on 13 December Bullitt presented his credentials to President Kalinin, who assured Bullitt that the Ambassador could travel to every part of the Union of Soviet Socialist Republics. Bullitt pointed out:

> It was like a continent rather than a country and in order to see much of it he would like to have a plane and if he [Kalinin] would permit me to use it without restriction.

Kalinin assured Bullitt there would be no objection.

The highlight was a dinner given on 21 December by Voroshilov at his Kremlin apartment. Stalin, Litvinov and Molotov were all present. Stalin, who had never previously seen an ambassador, proposed the first toast to President Roosevelt. Bullitt had a private conversation with Stalin, who stated that President Roosevelt, 'in spite of being the leader of a capitalist nation, is one of the most popular men in the USSR.' Stalin also stated, 'If you want anything day or night, you only have to let me know and I will see you at once.'[59]

Stalin was well pleased with the achievements of his Foreign Commissioner. At the 17th Party Conference, Stalin stated:

> The recognition of the USSR by the USA is of the most serious significance in the entire system of international relations. The question is that it raises the chance of peace, improves the relations between the two countries, strengthens the commercial ties between them and creates a basis for mutual collaboration. The point is that it will create a landmark between the old, when the USA was considered in various countries as a bulwark for all anti-Soviet tendencies, and the new, when this bulwark has been voluntarily removed to the mutual advantage of

---

[57] Ibid. p. 820
[58] Browder, Robert Paul: *Origins of Soviet-American Diplomacy*, p.151
[59] FRUS *The Soviet Union 1933-1938* p.55

both countries.[60]

The Soviet press joined in the enthusiasm which resulted from the US recognition of the Soviet Union. *Pravda*, on 19 November 1933, stated:

> The menace to peace of certain imperialist powers and the ominous portents in East and West gave the resumption of Soviet-US relations a special significance. 16 November will become an important date in the international relations of our epoch. The very fact that the present administration has renounced the traditional policy of non-recognition is in itself the most significant evidence of the strength and importance of the Soviet Union.[61]

However, Roosevelt's fault was that he was too inclined to take a more optimistic view than the facts justified. Roosevelt's confidence in the growing relationship between the Soviet Union and the United States would have been shattered if he had heard of a conversation that Litvinov had with the leaders of the US Communist Party. Litvinov stated: The letters that he had written were only scraps of paper soon to be forgotten in the realities of Soviet-US relations. However, Browder doubts the authenticity of what Gitlow states on the grounds that Litvinov would hardly have had the time to attend this meeting, although Hoover in his memoirs appears not to doubt the truth of Litvinov's supposed comment.[62]

According to Dubrowsky, the former director of the Soviet Red Cross in the USA, there is further evidence of Litvinov's bad faith. Litvinov stated, 'They wanted us to recognise the debts due to the USA'; and he was reported as saying 'I promised to negotiate. They don't know we are going to negotiate until Doomsday.' Litvinov said: 'The Americans wanted freedom of religion in the USSR. I gave that to them. I was tempted to offer to collect all the Bibles in the USSR and ship them to the USA.'[63]

In 1935 Bullitt complained that the presence of US citizens at the Third International was in breach of the undertaking that Litvinov gave when he assured the President that the Soviet Union would restrain any organisation in the USA in receipt of financial assistance from the Soviet Union from 'any act covert or overt [this surely must include the Comintern] to injure the tranquillity, prosperity, order or security of the whole or any part of the United States.' Litvinov's defence was that the President told Litvinov: 'He would hold him to strict accountability with regard to the Third International.' Litvinov's response was: 'He could not be responsible the Third International.' The President replied:

---

[60] *Moscow News*, Stalin's speech, 3 February 1934, p.4

[61] *Pravda*, 19 November 1933; Browder Robert Paul: *Origins of Soviet-American Diplomacy*, p.155

[62] Gitlow, Benjamin: *The Whole of Their Lives*, p.265; Browder, Robert Paul: *Origins of Soviet-American Diplomacy*, p.150; Hoover, Herbert: *Memoirs*, p.363

[63] *The New York Times*, 24 September 1939, p.22

'He would hold the Soviet Union responsable only in case of important injury to the interests of the United States.'

Bullitt stated that his memory was entirely different. He said:

> I recalled that Litvinov said he could make no promises about the Third International, but the President had told Litvinov that the President would hold Litvinov to strict accountability with regard to the Third International and he had subsequently signed the pledge.

Litvinov's explanation was that he had made that statement after signing the pledge. When Bullitt suggested: 'A discussion of our present relations might be more valuable than further remarks about the past,' Litvinov made it clear:'The Soviet Government would in no way restrain activities of the Communist International in the United States, or the Soviet Union or of US citizens who were Communists connected with the Communist International in the Soviet Union.' Litvinov then expressed, with his 'customary cynicism', the view: 'There was no such thing as friendship or real friendly relations between nations.'[64]

It is quite clear that Roosevelt made the mistake of accepting what he was told by Litvinov in good faith. Roosevelt made a similar mistake at Teheran that Stalin's offer for Roosevelt to stay in the Soviet embassy because it was more secure was genuine and not made for the purpose of spying on the President.[65]

Soviet policy towards the USA was inconsistent. The visit of two US warships to Vladivostok on 2 July 1937 was given wide publicity in *Izvestiya* and *Pravda*. During the previous three years, no article on the USA which was friendly in tone had been published in the Soviet press. Three reasons were advanced for the change of policy. First, there was a growing feeling that the formulators of foreign policy had underestimated the potential importance for the Soviet Union of friendship with the USA and overestimated the Soviet Union's ability to build dependable alliances in Europe. Second, there was the belief that the USA was planning to take a more active interest in world affairs, particularly in the Far East. Third, there existed a desire to strengthen Soviet prestige which had sharply declined of late by making it appear to the world that there was a rapprochement between the USA and the Soviet Union.[66]

At the same time, internally, the Soviet Union was waging an anti-foreigner campaign. US citizens were no exception. Even Louis Fischer, a Soviet sympathiser, stated that many of his Soviet acquaintances made it plain that they desired to have no dealings with foreigners

---

[64] Bullitt, William C: *For The President*, p.141
[65] Beria, Sergo: *Beria My Father*, p.93
[66] FRUS, *Soviet Union 1933-1939*, p.389

whatsoever. During July and August 1937 more than fifty US citizens who came to Leningrad on cruise ships for the purpose of spending several days in the Soviet Union were refused entry, notwithstanding the fact that their visas were in order.[67]

However, I am confident that Litvinov disapproved of Stalin's policy and would have wanted to deepen friendship with the USA, even showing deference to them by asking the US diplomat Marriner whether they would have any concern if the Soviet Union joined the League of Nations.[68]

Ultimately, the recognition of the Soviet Union by the USA considerably benefited the USA; as, of course, if the Soviet Union and USA had not enjoyed diplomatic relations in 1941, the speedy granting of lend-lease following Germany's attack on the USSR would have been more difficult. Further, the USA then had the opportunity of embarrassing the Soviet Union by insisting on recognition and the payment of the pre-1917 debts, even if payment was to be postponed. Hull, however, rejected this course of action on the grounds that it was not in the national interest.

---

[67] Ibid.
[68] Ibid. p.53

12: THE LEAGUE OF NATIONS

Although the Soviet Union had attended the Genoa and Hague conferences, these conferences were independent of the League of Nations. However, in March 1923 Chicherin recited the reasons for the undiminished hostility of the Soviet Union to the so-called League, which he described as 'this pseudo-international organisation.'[1]

There was already evidence that the League of Nations was ineffective. In the very first session, while the League was trying to resolve a dispute between Poland and Lithuania concerning Vilnius a Polish army crossed its border with Lithuania and captured Vilnius.

The League should have taken the most drastic action, such as suspending Poland from the League until the Polish army retreated behind its own frontiers; but the Polish army remained until 1939.[2] At least one of the reasons why no more drastic action was taken was because France would never have agreed, as Poland was France's ally in Eastern Europe; so Chicherin's criticism was justified.

Rakovsky, at the opening of Anglo-Soviet discussions at the London Conference on the question of peace and disarmament, went on to explain that a League of Nations would be acceptable to the Soviet Union only if it excluded 'coercion and measures of reprisals which can merely result in the selfish interests of certain states.'[3] However, in view of the hostile attitude of the Right in both Britain and France, such a stance was not unreasonable.

Chicherin declined to participate in a conference on the traffic in narcotics on the grounds that, under cover of instituting control of traffic in narcotics, 'the various governments are endeavouring to gratify their own commercial interest and obtain business advantage for themselves.'[4] It appears that Chicherin had no evidence that this was so.

In April 1925 the decision was taken not to attend a League of Nations conference on international traffic in arms, both because 'it was a fresh device to strengthen the rule of the imperialist powers over the weaker nations' and because the draft convention involved an attempt 'to interfere in the internal affairs of the Union of Socialist Republics.'[5]

---

[1] Carr, Edward: *Socialism in One Country*, p.451
[2] Walters, Francis: *History of the League of Nations*, p.107
[3] Carr, Edward: *Socialism in One Country*, p.452
[4] Ibid. p.453
[5] Ibid.

However, Chicherin made it clear when speaking to The third Union Congress of Soviets that the Soviet Union 'did not absolutely boycott the League' and rightly pointed out that the Soviet Union had already co-operated with the League on technical and health issues, as it was participating in the League's Public Health Committee.[6]

On 24 November 1925 Litvinov stated his government

> continued to see the League, not as a friendly union of nations working together for the common weal, but a combination of the so-called great powers for the purpose of usurping the right to dispose of the fate of weaker nations. The fact that Germany has been conquered and a militarily weak nation enters the League does not alter its nature. It is perfectly evident that certain nations intend to turn to their own profit, German participation, for execution of their plans generally and are hostile in their designs against the Soviet Union in particular? The Soviet Union more than anybody else is particularly interested in strengthening on a peace basis the independence and self-determination of all nations. From this viewpoint it would welcome the creation of international relations through which each nation would maintain their sovereign rights and all nations settle their respective misunderstandings in a friendly and peaceful way.

This was a utopian view.

The Soviet Union

> considers the existing League of Nations the least of all in approaching such organisation. The League has not fulfilled in the slightest way the hopes of its adherents. Not only has it failed to protect the rights and safety of small nations against military outrage by stronger powers, but on the main question, in which the whole of humanity is interested and which particularly interests the Soviet Union, namely disarmament, it has taken no steps whatsoever. The League is a mere screen for the further oppression of small and weak nations. It is chiefly a diplomatic stock exchange whereby by the stronger nations arrange their affairs behind the backs and at the expense of smaller and weaker nations. The Soviet Union, like the United States of America, intends as before to stand aloof from similar organisations.[7]

The attitude of the USA and the Soviet Union (before 1934) was very similar. Each became slowly more and more involved in co-operation with the various conferences and agencies of the League, although each remained aloof from its main purpose and refused to share its responsibilities. 'Let others bind themselves if they wish. We remain free.' These

---

[6] Ibid. p.454
[7] *The New York Times*, 24 November 1925, p.9; Pope, Arthur: *Maxim Litvinov*, p.334

were the words of Chicherin. They might equally have been the words of Hughes or Kellogg.

Each indeed, in pursuit of its national greatness and security, deliberately obstructed the growth of the League in its own part of the world. The United States prevented the full participation of the Western Hemisphere in the working of the covenant. The Soviet Union played a like role in relation both to the Asiatic people and to the small nations on its European frontiers.[8]

Litvinov persuaded Stalin to change the Soviet Union's attitude to the League from negative to positive, but there was no Litvinov in the United States. The USA continued on its feeble path until the demise of the League.

The Soviet Union had agreed to participate in the Preparatory Commission of the Disarmament Conference, but did not attend any meetings until November 1927 due to the assassination in 1923 of a Soviet diplomat in Switzerland, the acquittal of the suspected assassin and the failure of the Swiss Government to apologise until 1927. The apology enabled the Soviet Union to attend the 1927 World Economic Conference in Geneva. Litvinov was not among the delegates. Ossinski led the Soviet delegation.[9]

The radical change of attitude to the League of Nations was a direct result of the establishment of the Nazi regime in Germany. The Soviet Union's motives were clear because, as Walters correctly stated:

> Rosenberg was openly teaching that Germany's future lay in the acquisition and conquest of Ukraine and the Caucasus. The Soviet Union took the threat seriously. She had few friends and no allies. She had built up a network of treaties of non-aggression with all her neighbours from the Caspian to the Gulf of Finland, but they contained no obligation on either side to help resist aggression by others. By joining the League, she would be able to call on all its members for support if attacked by Germany. Membership of the League would also, she believed, reinforce her security in another way. Between her and Germany there lay a number of weak states. None of them could do much to hold up a German advance, but all were members of the League of Nations, and Germany could not violate the frontier of any one of them without laying herself open to the sanctions of the [League] Covenant. If the Soviet Union was also a member, the chances that her fellow members would in such a case carry out their obligations were much enhanced, with either economic or military sanctions.[10]

---

[8] Walters, Francis: *History of the League of Nations*, p.359
[9] See Ch.5, World Economic Conference, Nos.35-37; Budurowycz, Bohdan: *Polish-Soviet Relations 1932-1939*, p.7
[10] Walters, Francis: *A History of the League of Nations*, p.579

From speeches that Molotov made, it appeared he was of the same accord.

The attitude of Stalin changed under the influence of Litvinov and during autumn 1933 the Politburo approved the country's entry into the League of Nations. Stalin confirmed the change of Soviet attitude in an interview with *The New York Times*:

> Despite Germany's and Japan's exit from the League of Nations, or perhaps just because of it, the League may become a brake to hamper or retard military action. I would say, if the historical events were such that the League became a brake upon or an obstacle to war, it is not excluded we would support the League, despite its colossal deficiencies.[11]

On 26 January 1934 Poland signed a non-aggression pact with Germany. Litvinov should not have been concerned in view of his enthusiasm for entering into such non-aggression pacts, but he did worry because it could have been a cloak for possible joint action by Poland and Germany against the Soviet Union. Beck boasted to Litvinov that Germany now understood that Poland 'was not a weak young state.' Litvinov's perception was again right:

> [Litvinov] derided the idea that the Nazis had changed their ultimate goals since coming to power. ... We judge the aspirations of the Nazis, on the basis of their past publications, not on some political speeches that Hitler was now making, and in which he had switched over to some pacifistic phraseology.

Although Litvinov encouraged other countries of Europe to enter into non-aggression pacts with their neighbours, he made an exception in the case of Hitler because of his aims, which Litvinov already regarded as aggressive. Beck objected that Germany presented no immediate threat and if he was able to make Poland secure for the present that was sufficient, and he scolded Litvinov for looking too far into the future. Although Beck had thought that he had achieved some sort of security he was sadly misguided.[12]

On 12 February 1934 Beck paid an official visit to Moscow. Litvinov, in spite of his distrust of Poland's orientatation to Hitler, took the opportunity to improve Soviet-Polish relations, of which he spoke optimistically, stating:

> With profound satisfaction the changes that had taken place between the Soviet Union and Poland and the further successful development of this relationship have been expressed in instruments that have the most weighty significance not only for relations between the two countries but also for the cause of peace in general.

---

[11] *The New York Times*, 28 December 1933, pp.1 and 8
[12] Phillips, Hugh: *Between the Revolution and the West*, p.141

The cordial reception given to our airmen during their stay in Poland and the visit of the Polish Air Force squadron led by General Rayski to the USSR had led to the happiest of memories.

Then Litvinov personally praised Beck:

I should add all the facts I have enumerated demonstrating the profound process of rapprochement between the two countries coincides to a large extent with the period during which you, Mr Minister, were in charge of Polish foreign policy and therefore should be regarded as part of your personal endeavours.[13]

Although Budurowycz states that Beck's speech was more restrained and indicated he did not wish to extend political collaboration with the Soviet Union, in his book *Final Report*, Beck stated: The Non-aggression Pact was extended and the status of legations extended to embassies.'[14]

The final communiqué stated:

The conversations between M Litvinov and M Beck revealed a community of views in regard to many of the problems, as well as the firm determination of the two governments to continue their endeavours for a further improvement in mutual relations between Poland and the USSR, as also an all-round rapprochement between the peoples of both States. The foundation of such rapprochement is the pact of non-aggression and the definition of aggression and the convention for aggression concluded between the two countries. It was thought desirable to give these as permanent a character as possible.[15]

I think the statement in the communiqué stressed by Budurowycz that 'the future understanding between the two countries must be founded on existing agreements' is misleading. On the contrary, both countries pledged themselves to co-operate with each other in the spirit of these documents, with the purpose of preserving general peace. In order to take full advantage of 'the increasing possibilities of such co-operation', the Polish legation in Moscow and the Soviet diplomatic mission in Warsaw were raised to embassies. The communiqué did not stress that future understanding must be founded on existing agreements. Although the two countries did not enter into any new agreements, they both anticipated continued improvement in their relationship with each other.[16] There is every reason to believe that Litvinov wanted Soviet-Polish collaboration extended in

---

[13] Litvinov's speech, in Degras, Jane: *Soviet Documents on Foreign Policy*, vol.3, p.74
[14] Beck, Josef: *Final Report*, p.53
[15] Degras, Jane: *Soviet Documents on Foreign Policy*, vol.3, p.75
[16] Budurowycz, Bohdan: *Polish-Soviet Relations 1932-1939*, p.46

view of the German threat, while Poland did not want to take any action which Germany might see as directed against her.

When Litvinov was in Geneva in May 1934, following discussions between himself and the French Foreign Minister Barthou, a new pact for all the countries of Eastern Europe was mooted which included a non-aggression pact, but also provided for consultation between the participants and mutual assistance in case of unprovoked aggression by one of the signatories against another. France initially wanted the pact restricted to the Soviet Union, Germany, Poland and Czechoslovakia, but accepted Litvinov's request that the pact should include the Baltic States, as the Soviet Union feared that the Baltic States were particularly vulnerable to German attack.[17] Litvinov was enthusiastic to implement what came to be known as the Eastern Locarno, as was Barthou. However without the guarantee of Italy and Britain, an Eastern Locarno was not likely to be as effective as the Locarno Treaty.' Sir John Simon, the British Foreign Secretary made it clear Britain would not take on any new commitments in Eastern Europe. [18]

Britain, who was trying to persuade Germany to enter into a convention limiting armaments, was unenthusiastic about the whole concept of an Eastern Locarno. However, Barthou managed to persuade Britain to accept the concept, providing Germany was made a party to any agreement between the Soviet Union and France. Therefore, if Germany was attacked by the Soviet Union, France would be bound to come to Germany's assistance, and if France attacked Germany, the Soviet Union would similarly be bound to come to Germany's assistance.[19] Eventually, Estonia, Latvia, and Lithuania also agreed to participate in the pact. Litvinov frustrated Poland's efforts to persuade Estonia and Latvia to co-ordinate their efforts with Poland, which shows the progress Litvinov had made in being regarded by at least some of the Soviet Union's neighbours as a man who could be trusted.[20] Poland stated that she would only participate in the pact if Germany did likewise,[21] but Hitler was uninterested. He stated:

> The German Government cannot consider it a practical reality that she one day should be defended in her own territory by Soviet troops attacking the West or by French troops against an attack from the East.[22]

However, during the negotiations between France and the Soviet Union, prior to the Franco-Soviet pact being agreed and signed, France argued that she would be in considerable difficulty if the Soviet Union was not a member of the League. The essence

---

[17] Degras, Jane: *Soviet Documents on Foreign Policy*, vol.3 p.74; Scott William:E. *Alliance against Hitler* p.159

[18] *Survey of International Relations*, 1935, vol.1, p.66; *Hansard*,13 July 1934, vol.292, 694

[19] Scott, William E: *Alliance Against Hitler*, p.179

[20] Scott, William E: *Alliance Against Hitler*, p.186

[21] Ibid. p.187

[22] Ibid. p.186

of the French argument was that the pact could then be classed as a regional pact and would not infringe the Locarno agreement.[23]

Eden had been appointed Lord Privy Seal to serve under the Foreign Secretary, Simon. In 1934 the French Foreign Secretary, Barthou, asked Eden to support the Soviet Union's entry into the League of Nations.[24] Eden persuaded his government to support this policy. Eden was rightly convinced: 'The League must gain from wider membership, whatever our views upon Soviet policy.'[25] Surely he was right? Barthou also obtained the support of Italy.[26]

There was a minority who stubbornly opposed the Soviet Union's entry. Yet it was remarkable that, even those who intended to oppose the USSR's entry into the League, were prepared to accept that, if the Soviet Union was admitted, it would be proper for her to have a permanent seat on the Council. However, before any country could become a member of the League, an application had to be made, which was then scrutinised.

In 1931 it was determined that Mexico, who wanted to become a member, would receive an invitation, in which case it was unanimously decided that those states who issued the invitation must have been satisfied that the proposed new member was fit to join the League and no further scrutiny was required. However, as a small number of states wished to oppose and did oppose the Soviet Union's membership, France, Britain and Italy wished to ensure that there was no danger of the Soviet Union's application being refused. The League's lawyers therefore determined that, provided two-thirds of the members of the League issued the invitation, there would be no need for any scrutiny. None of the three who opposed the Soviet Union's entry decided to challenge the situation on procedural grounds.[27] On 15 September 1934 thirty nations, including Poland, cabled an invitation to the Soviet Union to join the League.[28] Another four indicated that they would support the Soviet Union's entry into the League.[29]

After some wavering, Poland was one of those countries who officially invited the Soviet Union to become a member of the League of Nations. Phillips is wrong to say:'The Poles were a leading force opposing Soviet entry into the League of Nations.'[30] However, Beck illogically expressed concern that once the Soviet Union was a member of the League she would disregard bilateral treaties. Although the Kremlin was quite ready to give a suitable

---

[23] Eden, Anthony: *Memoirs, Facing the Dictators*, p.97; FRUS, Soviet Union, 1933, p.53

[24] Eden, Anthony: *Memoirs, Facing the Dictators*, p.98

[25] Ibid.

[26] Walters, Francis Paul: *History of the League of Nations*, p.580

[27] *Survey of International Affairs*,1934, p.395; Walters, Francis: *History of the League of Nations*, p.581

[28] Budurowycz, Bohdan: *Polish-Soviet Relations 1932-1939*, p.62; *Times*, 16 September 1934, p.1
The New York Times, 16 Sepember p 1.

[29] *Survey of International Affairs*, 1934, p.400

[30] Phillips, Hugh: *Between the Revolution and the West*, p.141

assurance, Poland suggested that the obligations to which Poland and the Soviet Union had agreed should be extended to all members of the League. What worried Poland was that the Soviet Union might use the forum of the League of Nations to attack the treatment of Ukrainians and Byelorussians in Poland, as she had done previously and rightly so. Poland had, under the Treaty of Riga, guaranteed the rights of the Ukrainians and Byelorussians living in Poland, and the Soviet Union did likewise with Poles living in the Soviet Union. The great powers indignantly rejected these proposals, so Poland denounced the treaty containing guarantees to minority populations in Poland.[31]

Much to Barthou's annoyance, De Valera, the League's Chairman, stated that, in accordance with what had previously happened to proposals for new members, the Soviet Union's application should be referred to the Sixth Committee, one of whose duties was to consider new applications for membership of the League.

De Valera was prepared to support the Soviet Union's entry and he appreciated 'the need that her dignity would not be wounded', but he took the view that 'decisions of the League should be taken following debate, rather than settled beforehand in hotel rooms or by collecting signatures of delegates.'[32]

Motta, the Swiss representative, led the opposition to the Soviet Union's entry. Motta denounced Communism, the danger of world revolution, Soviet atheism and the persecution of religion. He did not believe that such a state would ever evolve towards democracy and tolerance. Was it wise to present the USSR with the added prestige of League membership?[33] However, Italy had remained a member in spite of the authoritarian nature of its regime.

Barthou led those who were in favour of the Soviet Union's membership. He said:

> France had suffered more financial loss from their Russian investments than any other country. No one could be more hostile to religious intolerance than he, but was it not, by association with others, that the Soviet Union was likely to become more tolerant?

Then Barthou mentioned the advantages of the Soviet Union's membership. 'The primary concern of the League was not internal doctrine but international action. The League's Assembly was there to promote and organise peace.'[34] Eden, in supporting Barthou, stated that: 'Britain's foreign policy had been based on the League ever since it was created and

---

[31] Budurowycz, Bohdan: *Soviet-Polish Relations 1932-1939*, p.63; Scott, William Evans: *Alliance Against Hitler*, p.199

[32] Walters, Francis Paul: *History of the League of Nations*, p.582

[33] Ibid. p.583

[34] Walters, Francis: *History of the League of Nations*, p.583

he welcomed the Soviet Union's contribution to the League's power and resources.'[35] Before De Valera took the vote, he appealed to the Soviet Union on behalf of not only 300 million Catholics but also other Christians. He suggested if this was not done, Christians would lose faith in the League.[36] When Hitler committed suicide, De Valera called on the German Ambassador in Ireland to express his regret.[37] If Litvinov was aware of this fact, he must have thought that De Valera had a peculiar sense of religious belief, as he appeared so concerned about the persecution of Christians in the Soviet Union but unconcerned about the slaughter of millions of Jews in the Holocaust.

The Sixth Committee recommended that the Soviet Union should be invited to join by 38 votes to three. The Soviet Union replied in terms that could be treated as a demand for admission. The next day the assembly proper, after a short debate, similarly voted to admit the Soviet Union, by 39 votes to 3 with seven abstentions. The three countries to vote against were Switzerland, Holland and Portugal. However, the vote to grant the Soviet Union a permanent seat on the Council was agreed by 40 votes to 0. Ten countries abstained.[38] After the vote Litvinov, as the head of the Soviet delegation, was expected to enter the conference hall, but had been allowed unwittingly to enter the hall before the vote.[39]

Litvinov, in his first speech to the League as a member, began by praising

> the initiative of the French Government, actively supported by the Governments of Great Britain and Italy and the sincere efforts made towards realising the initiative of the French delegation. I wish to thank personally that esteemed Minister of Foreign Affairs of the French Republic, M Barthou, and the Chairman of the League Council, Dr. Benes.

Litvinov rightly recalled:

> At the time when the League was formed to proclaim the organisation of peace, the people of our Union were not yet permitted to enjoy the fruits of peace. They were forced for a long time to defend with rifles in their hands their right to self-determination, their internal tranquillity, and their foreign independence. It is perfectly clear that the relations between the Soviet Government and the League of Nations could not differ from those between the USSR and the countries belonging to the League. Moreover, the people of the Soviet Union were apprehensive that

---

[35] Walters, Francis: *History of the League of Nations*, p,584; Eden, Anthony: *Memoirs, Facing the Dictator*, p.98

[36] Walters, Francis: *History of the League of Nations*, p.584

[37] Coogan, Tim Pat: *De Valera: Long Fellow, Long Shadow*, p.610

[38] Walters, Francis: *History of the League of Nations*, p.584

[39] *Times*, 19 September 1934, p.10; Sheinis, Zinovy: *Maxim Litvinov*, pp.262-263

These countries who had joined in the League would give expression to their collective hostility to the Soviet Union by co-ordinating their anti-Soviet activities.

Litvinov stated: 'If the Soviet Union had participated in drawing up the Covenant she would have objected to some of its points' and also to the fact that 'race equality was not included' in the articles establishing the League. However, these points were not of such vital importance as to prevent the Soviet Union from joining the League, the more so since new members entering an organisation can be 'morally responsible only for those decisions which have been adopted with its participation and consent.'

Litvinov did not say that the Soviet Union could not accept all the resolutions of the League, as stated by Sheinis.[40]

Litvinov then recalled that the Soviet Union had collaborated with other countries within the framework of the League in economic and political matters.

Litvinov acknowledged thirty delegates

> comprising the majority of League members representing all the larger and in any way important states in their message to the Soviet Government that the mission of the League is to organise peace and that the success of this mission demanded the collaboration of the Soviet Union. They knew that the State they were addressing, throughout the seventeen years of its existence, had not spared any efforts for the establishment of the best of neighbourly relations with all its own neighbours on the most stable foundations in effecting rapprochement with all countries which so desired.

There can be no doubt that it was the external threat from Germany and Japan which caused the Soviet Union to become a supporter rather than a critic of the League. Litvinov explained in his speech the new Soviet enthusiasm for the League by complimenting instead of criticising the League 'because of its intensified activity in preserving peace. Further aggressive elements are finding the framework of the League too irksome and are seeking to free themselves from it.'[41]

Litvinov received many messages of support from luminaries such as Bernard Shaw, Albert Einstein and Edward Herriot, the French statesman.[42]

Molotov, in a speech on 10 January 1936, stated:

---

[40] Sheinis, Zinovy: *Maxim Litvinov*, p.262
[41] Text of speech in *Moscow News*, 27 September 1934, p.3
[42] Sheinis, Zinovy: *Maxim Litvinov*, p.263

The first year of membership had fully borne out the correctness of the decision to join the League. Despite all its shortcomings inherent in the League of Nations as a capitalist state, the League has to a certain extent been a restraining influence on warmongers and aggressors.[43]

It was in an unusual area that Litvinov now made a favourable impact on an interest group in the Western World. Four days after the Soviet Union's admission, the International Committee of Women told Litvinov that they were striving to place women's equality on the agenda of the League of Nations. Litvinov was the first to sign the petition; but once he had signed it, Czechoslovakia, Turkey, Mexico, Chile, China, Panama, Siam, Haiti, The Dominican Republic, Argentina, New Zealand, Latvia and Yugoslavia also signed. The great powers were conspicuously absent. Although Litvinov stated that there was complete equality for women in the Soviet Union, this was never so. Throughout the seventy years of communism there never was equality for women in the Soviet Union. Women were appointed to far fewer top jobs, particularly during the stagnation period under Brezhnev. While Litvinov was leader of the Foreign Commissariat, he made no appointment of women as ambassadors, although Kollontai had, during the 1920s, become the world's first woman ambassador. One has the feeling that it was, surprisingly like the Holocaust, a subject to which he gave little attention, but it was valuable for increasing Litvinov's profile in the United States because, at a women's conference in 1934, he was praised for placing equality of rights on the agenda of the League of Nations.[44]

Carr rightly states that between the time when Russia entered the League until Litvinov's removal in May 1939, he became one of the League's most active supporters, loudly condemning aggression on all occasions in the most vigorous way.[45] In Sumner Welles' opinion, 'as long as Litvinov represented the USSR in the League, he strove with great ability to make the League work.'[46] Walters summed up the position:

> No future historian will lightly disagree with views expressed by Litvinov on international questions. Whatever may be thought of the policy and purpose of his Government, the long series of statements, the speeches in the Assembly and the Council, the Conferences, and the Committees of which he was a member between 1927 and 1939 [although Litvinov did not attend the League of Nations after 1938] can hardly be read without an astonished admiration. Nothing in the annals of the League can compare with them in frankness, in debating power, in the acute diagnosis of each situation. No contemporary statesman can point to such a record of criticism justified, and prophecies fulfilled.[47]

---

[43] Molotov report to the Government, 10 January 1936, p.47
[44] *The New York Times*, 23 September 1934, p.12, and 18 November 1934, part 2 p.3
[45] Carr, Edward H: *German-Russian Relations*, p.115
[46] Sumner Welles, Benjamin: *Time for Decision*, p.29
[47] Walters, Francis Paul: *History of the League of Nations*, p.712

As Poland would not agree to join the Eastern Locarno if Germany did not participate, by the end of September 1934, the Eastern Locarno was dead. Eden commented:

> It can be argued that no decision taken by Poland in 1935 would have prevented Hitler and Ribbentrop from doing a deal four years later with the Soviet leaders to destroy Poland and the Baltic States. I am not so sure. The Polish leaders would have been wiser to throw in their lot whole-heartedly with the Western powers at a price that would have included the acceptance of an Eastern Locarno on the terms Litvinov offered. Such a policy could have had a number of consequences. The policy which Litvinov upheld of collective security and joint resistance to the German demands would have been strengthened. Had the Eastern Pact come into being, it would also have influenced German policy towards Czechoslovakia: not in its intention, but in its execution. It might even have averted Munich and the surrender to German demands there.[48]

In view of Beck's disparaging remarks, one wonders whether part of his apathy towards Hitler's Germany stemmed from a lack of concern for the fate of the huge Jewish population in Poland.

On 9 October 1934 Barthou was assassinated, which was a blow to the concept of the Eastern Locarno, as he had been a keen supporter.[49] The new Foreign Minister Laval was by instinct much more sympathetic to Germany. However, on 5 December Litvinov and Laval concluded an agreement to continue to pursue the concept of an Eastern Locarno.[50] Shortly afterwards the Eastern Locarno agreement was signed between the Soviet Union and France. A commercial treaty was also signed, resulting in a rapid increase in exports from France to the Soviet Union from 44 million francs in 1933 to 176 million francs in 1935.[51]

At the end of February 1935, before the next crisis arose, it had been decided that Eden and Simon would visit Berlin, but Simon wanted Eden to go to Moscow. On a rare occasion when Baldwin had sympathy for the Soviet Union, he expressed his view that it was wrong for two ministers to go to Berlin and only one to Moscow. However as Maisky, the Soviet Ambassador to Britain, had shown such a desire for the visit, and no objection was raisedy the Soviet Union, both Simon and Eden visited Hitler, but only Eden went to Moscow.[52]

The British Government produced a White Paper and announced modest re-armament.

---

[48] Eden, Anthony: *Memoirs, Facing the Dictators*, p.171
[49] Scott, William: *Alliance Against Hitler*, p.203
[50] Ibid. p.211
[51] Ibid. p.213
[52] Eden, Anthony: *Memoirs, Facing the Dictators*, p.125

Although Baldwin would forever be condemned for his failure to rearm sufficiently, the Labour Party opposed the White Paper. Attlee said:

> We believe in a League system in which the whole world would be ranged against an aggressor. If it is shown that someone is proposing to break the peace, let us bring the whole world opinion against her.[53]

Litvinov had already warned of the danger of believing that public opinion could stop aggression.[54] Afterwards, Austen Chamberlain, the former British Foreign Secretary, severely criticised Attlee's speech with the words:

> If war breaks out, and we become involved in a struggle and if the Honourable Member for Limehouse [Clement Attlee] is sitting on the government benches while London is being bombed, do you think he will hold the language he held today? If he does he will be one of the first victims of the war, for he will be strung up by an angry and justifiably angry populace to the nearest lamp post.[55]

On 15 March 1935, perhaps unwisely, France announced an increase in the period of conscription, just the pretext Hitler needed for denouncing those provisions of the Versailles Treaty limiting the size of the German army. On 16 March Hitler called in the British, French, Italian and Polish ambassadors and informed them that, contrary to the Versailles Treaty, conscription was being introduced and the size of the German army, on a peace footing, was to be increased to twelve corps and thirty-six divisions, thus increasing the army to about 600,000 men as against the limit imposed by the Versailles Treaty of 100,000. Hitler blamed the increase on the failure of the Disarmament Conference and recent rearmament measures in other states.[56]

In spite of Germany having broken the Versailles Treaty, Poland, in the absence of German participation, still refused to sign the Eastern Locarno Pact.[57] This amounted to a defeat for Litvinov, who had successfully negotiated the Litvinov protocol in 1929,[58] the Non-Aggression Pact in 1932,[59] and had obtained the acceptance by his neighbours of his definition of aggression in 1933.[60]

In March 1935 Eden and Simon travelled to Berlin, which gave Hitler the opportunity to boast that the Luftwaffe had already reached parity with Great Britain. The British

---

[53] *Hansard*, vol.299, 11 March 1935, 40
[54] See Ch.6, No.62
[55] *Hansard*, vol.299, 11 March 1935, 77
[56] Scott, William: *Alliance Against Hitler*, p.228
[57] Ibid. p.238
[58] Budurowycz, Bohdan: *Polish-Soviet Relations 1932-1939*, p.7; ch 6 No 44
[59] Ibid. p.23; Ch 8 No 50
[60] Ibid. p.29; Ch 6 No 88

Government hoped that either Hitler could be persuaded to return to the League of Nations, other than on terms that would be onerous to other members, or some arms limitation agreement could be agreed. The fact the visit was a failure is indicated by Eden's pessimistic report of the visit:

> There may be the only course of action open to us to join with those powers who are members of the League in affirming our faith in that institution and to uphold the principles of the Covenant. It may be the spectacle of the great powers of the League reaffirming their intentions to collaborate more closely than ever is not only the sole means of bringing home to Germany that the inevitable effect of persisting in her present policy will be to consolidate against her all those nations which believe in collective security, but will also tend to give confidence to those less powerful nations which through fear of Germany's growing strength might well otherwise be drawn into her orbit.[61]

Eden's thinking was far nearer to Litvinov's views than either Chamberlain, who thought he, not the League, would more likely be able to prevent the Second World War, or Churchill, who, although he believed he was a supporter of the League, was not prepared to support the League's robust condemnation of Italy for unprovoked aggression.

Eden arrived in the Soviet Union at a time of strain caused by the murder of Kirov. Surprisingly, in 1962 Eden stated that Kirov had been shot by the husband of a woman whom Kirov had loved, but there had apparently been a deeper political motive.[62] However, even at that time love appeared to have been the least likely motive for Kirov's murder.

Eden's meetings with Litvinov, Stalin and Molotov on 28 and 29 March 1935 reveal much of Litvinov's thinking on foreign affairs. Eden first described his meeting with Hitler:

> In producing a map, Hitler had repeated the encirclement argument showing the divisions of Hitler's neighbours. France had thirty-four divisions, Czechoslovakia seventeen divisions and the Soviet Union one hundred and one divisions.

Eden pointed out that the Soviet Government 'had plenty to do at home and plenty of territory to administer.' Hitler took a completely different view and regarded the Soviet Union as 'a serious menace from the point of world revolution and military aggression.' Litvinov asked whether Hitler mentioned German expansion in the East. Eden pointed out to the Chancellor that Herr Rosenberg's plan to expand in the East 'was a cause of apprehension and asked why Hitler allowed these plans.' At this remark both Hitler and Neurath merely laughed. Litvinov asked for Eden's conclusions from the conversation.

---

[61] Eden, Anthony: *Memoirs, Facing the Dictators*, p.142
[62] Eden, Anthony: *Memoirs, Facing the Dictators*, p.150 and ch 16

Eden said: 'The Governments who believe in the collective system shall have to hold to it even more strongly than before.' Then Litvinov asked what were the grounds for the Chancellor's fear of the Soviet Union? Eden replied that apparently 'Hitler fears both the military strength of the Soviet Union and the Soviet intention to promote world revolution.'

Hitler thought that Germany was a barrier to these threats.

Litvinov then told Eden

> After the Treaty of Rapallo, for many years relations were excellent. Rapallo contained no secret clauses.
>
> These relations continued until just before Hitler came to power, when Von Papen proposed to the French Government a secret agreement aimed at the Soviet Union. This was followed by the Hugenberg Memorandum at the London Economic Conference and the programme of aggression in *Mein Kampf.* The original plan was to attack France and then to attack in the East. Since then the plans have changed. The plan now is to leave France alone but attack in the East. Von Neurath has assured the Soviet Government that nothing has changed in the attitude of the German Government towards the Soviet Union and that what Hitler and Rosenberg are saying is purely of historical interest. The Soviet Government is not satisfied with this explanation. If Hitler's and Rosenberg's books continue to be the basis of education in Germany, then that can only mean that Germany takes these plans seriously. Words are not enough. The Soviet Union wants deeds.
>
> To test the German expressions of goodwill I proposed to Germany the conclusion of the Baltic pact that would include a reciprocal guarantee by Germany and the Soviet Union of the integrity of the Baltic States. The pact was to be open to access of other powers. Although the German ambassador of the day, Nadolny, was in favour of this pact, the German Government rejected any endeavours to negotiate a pact without giving any substantial reason.[63] I made a somewhat similar proposal to Poland, namely a joint declaration of common interest in the independence of the Baltic States. Beck initially accepted a joint declaration of common interest in the maintenance of the independence of the Baltic States, but, immediately after the conclusion of the German Polish agreement, the Polish ambassador informed me that his Government could not enter into such a declaration. German's refusal of the Baltic Pact has increased apprehension in the Soviet Union and also in France. Hitler, however, is not the only man in Germany, the Reichswehr being much less

---

[63] Eden Anthony *Memoirs*, Facing the Dictators p.147

hostile to any eastern pact and is always ready to make a bargain with the Soviet Union. The Soviet Government is concerned not only for its own frontier but for the peace of Europe.

This was very much Litvinov's own philosophy. He continued:

> The Soviet Union has enough work at home to keep it busy for half a century and it will take them decades to catch up with the rest of the world in technical development and the standard of life. We do not want to be disturbed and we believe that a war in Europe, even if we are not directly involved, will eventually drag us in. For this reason we strongly support the idea of collective security and approval of a central European pact as well as an Eastern pact.[64]

Litvinov was absolutely right when he said, 'Germany was trying to separate the other powers one from another.' Litvinov then said:

> There is some chance of persuading Poland to join the pact. That is where British policy might play a big part, because Poland now attaches great importance to what is said in London, particularly since Poland has quarrelled with France.

Litvinov believed:

> It might be possible to detach Poland from her present line, and draw her towards the Eastern pact. The alternative is a pact without Germany and Poland, but this would lose 50% of its value.[65]

Then Litvinov asked: 'Whether Eden considered the integrity of the Baltic States a British interest?' Eden replied: 'It would be extremely short-sighted of anyone to think that it is better to have war in the East to avoid a war in the West.'

Therefore Eden firmly rejected Neville Henderson's argument that as Hitler was determined to Eastern Europe we should in effect give him a free hand. [66]

Eden continued:

> The interest of His Majesty's Government in the Baltic States is not like the interest in Belgium and the Low Countries, although Britain is of course interested from the point of view of general security of Europe.[67]

---

[64] Ibid. p.148
[65] Ibid.
[66] Eden, Anthony: *Memoirs, Facing the Dictators*, p.148; and Ch.13, No.132
[67] Eden, Anthony: *Memoirs, Facing the Dictators*, p.149

Chilston wondered whether any Polish attack on the Soviet Union was credible. Litvinov thought Poland might attempt it if she had a promise of assistance from Germany. Eden 'could not conceive that Poland would attack the Soviet Union', although Litvinov was right to be concerned, as Poland had attacked Russia in 1920. Eden then told Litvinov that, in 1934, he thought there was a general basis for settlement with Germany. Eden considered that the French were unwise not to accept the offer. 'Now I find it very difficult to see what basis there is. Apart from Germany's attitude towards the League of Nations, I cannot see there is any prospect for an arms and security agreement.'[68]

In the evening Maxim and Ivy Litvinov gave a dinner in Eden's honour. Apart from Stalin, nearly[69] every commissar was there. Litvinov, in a short speech, referred to the fact, which subsequently proved correct, that 'never since the World War had there been such misgivings about the fate of peace as now.' Litvinov proposed the toast to the health of His Majesty the King, the first of such toasts in the Soviet Union since the Revolution.[70] However, the next day the toasts were omitted, although the text of the speeches was published. This indicated the devious way the Stalin Government often acted.

Also the following morning the talks continued and Litvinov rightly stated: 'His Majesty's Government did not believe in the aggressiveness of Germany.' Eden's reply was that: 'His Majesty's Government was not so convinced as the Soviet Government',[71] indicating that, in spite of Eden's later anti-appeasement stance, at this stage he was in favour of dialogue rather than confrontation with Hitler.[72]

The highlight of the visit was a meeting with Stalin, the first occasion on which he had received a political representative from the West. Eden was impressed by Stalin from the first, and when Eden wrote his memoirs in the 1960s his opinion had not subsequently altered.:

> (Stalin's) personality made itself felt without exaggeration. He had natural good manners, perhaps a Georgian inheritance. Though I knew the man was without mercy, I respected the quality of his mind and even felt a sympathy I have never been able to analyse. Perhaps it was because of the pragmatic approach. I cannot believe he had any affinity to Marx. Certainly no one could have been less doctrinaire.[73]

---

[68] Eden Anthony: *Facing the Dictators* p.149
[69] Ibid.
[70] Ibid. p.150
[71] Ibid. p.150
[72] Ibid. p.151
[73] Ibid. p.153

This was an indication, why, on the question of policy, Litvinov often related well to Stalin.[74] Eden telegraphed to the Government in Britain that Stalin 'was a man of strong oriental traits of character with unshakeable assurance and control whose courtesy in no way hid from us an implacable ruthlessness.'[75]

That evening Eden was invited to the Opera House to see the production of *Swan Lake*, where the old Imperial box was reserved for the honoured guests. The building astonished Eden with its old fashioned décor. As Madame Kollontai, the wise Ambassador to Sweden, remarked, 'We are a very conservative people.'[76] The British national anthem was played, followed by the Internationale. It was the first time the British National Anthem had been played since the Revolution. However, this did not please George V who, although he understood the value of contact with the Soviet Union as a deterrent to war, had most affectionate recollections of his cousin the Tsar. It did not seem to him good that the anthem should be played with the Internationale. Eden was suitably acknowledged by the audience with clapping both before the official announcement when Litvinov arrived in the box and when Eden's presence was officially announced to the audience.[77]

Early in Eden's visit, he handed to Litvinov a communiqué which seemed to please him. Towards the end of the visit Litvinov requested a number of amendments to a text to which Eden alleges Litvinov had previously agreed. Eden was told they had been requested by Stalin himself. Litvinov requested Eden to urge the signature of an Eastern Pact. It would have been most unwise for Eden to sign such a statement without Cabinet approval and naturally he declined. The final communiqué which showed the success of the visit stated:

> It was emphasised in the conversations by Stalin, Molotov and Litvinov that the, organisation of security in Eastern Europe and the proposed pact of mutual assistance do not aim at the isolation and encirclement of any state, but the creation of equal security for all participant .and that the participation in the pact of Germany and Poland would therefore be welcomed as affording the best solution of the problem. The representatives of the two Governments were happy to note that as a result of a full and frank exchange of views there is at present no conflict of interest between the two Governments on any of the major issues of international policy and this fact provides a firm foundation between them in the cause of peace.[78]

But for illness, Eden would have participated in a conference between Italy, France as well as Britain concerning German breaches of the Versailles Treaty, Germany having re-armed

---

[74] Ch.19, No.69
[75] Eden, Anthony: *Memoirs, Facing the Dictators*, p.157
[76] Ibid.
[77] Ibid.
[78] Ibid. p.160

in breach of the provisions of that treaty. Italy and Britain were guarantors of the Locarno Treaty entered into between France and Germany. When Laval called a meeting of the League of Nations Council, Mussolini suggested a prior meeting between the signatories of the Locarno Treaty other than Germany. The Soviet Union, not being a signatory of the treaty, was not represented. The decision of the meeting at Stresa accorded with France's wishes, because it decided:

> The three powers would oppose by all practical means any repudiation of treaties that may endanger the peace of Europe, and will act in close and cordial collaboration for this purpose.[79]

Immediately thereafter, an emergency meeting of the Council of the League was called to endorse the decision reached at Stresa. During the debate Litvinov quite rightly criticised the fact that the motion was restricted to treaty violations in Europe and this might be taken to mean that treaty violation outside Europe might go unpunished. In view of Mussolini's plans to invade Abyssinia, he might have taken the resolution to mean that he had a free hand in Africa. However, the French, who did not want anything to jeopardise the passing of the resolution, ended up empty-handed. Germany took no notice of the League's resolution and Italy not only invaded Abyssinia, but joined Hitler's camp.

Litvinov was remarkably conciliatory at the League Council meeting. The Council was invited to declare, and by thirteen votes to none, with Denmark abstaining, passed a resolution condemning Germany because

> Germany had failed in the obligations which lie upon all members of the international community to respect the undertakings they have contracted and admits no unilateral repudiation of international obligations.

> The British, French and Italian Governments are invited to continue the negotiations so initiated and in particular to promote the conclusion within the framework of the League of Nations (a plan) for a general settlement to be freely negotiated for the organisation of security in Europe and for a general limitation of armaments in a system of equality of rights, while ensuring the active co-operation of Germany in the League of Nations.

Litvinov reminded the League that the Soviet Union had not signed the treaty which Germany had broken and indeed disapproved of it; but, showing his anti-Nazi sentiment, Litvinov stated that the Soviet Union would support it, as he wished to emphasise that the Nazi programme was a programme of revenge and conquest that could only be countered by the creation of a strong international order. However, when Litvinov showed signs of rejecting the resolution unless the limitation to European affairs was removed, he accepted

---

[79] Stresa, *Survey of International Affairs,* 1935, vol.1, p.160

a sharp retort from Simon, Laval and Aloisa and withdrew his opposition.[80] There is no reason to believe that Stalin did not approve of this conciliatory approach, although my opinion is that it would have been better if Litvinov had stood his ground.

Britain was worried that, if Germany attacked the Soviet Union and France attacked Germany, Britain, pursuant to the Locarno Treaty, would be bound to go to war effectively in support of the Soviet Union, even though it was the policy of the British Government to avoid any military commitment in Eastern Europe. Eventually, Britain changed its mind in 1939 with its commitment to Poland and went to war. The trouble was that by the time Britain became involved in the fighting, Germany and the Soviet Union were allies. If, in 1935, Britain had come to a similar agreement with the Soviet Union, like the Franco-Soviet Pact, so that if either country was attacked by Germany, the one not attacked would go to the defence of the country attacked, Britain might have entered the war as an ally of the Soviet Union. However, eventually, much to Litvinov's delight, in May 1935 Britain stated: 'There was nothing in the Franco-Soviet treaty which either conflicted with the Locarno Treaty or modified its operation in any way.'

In spite of much hostility from the British Conservative politicians, Litvinov realised that Britain was a vital player in Europe. He said:

> At last we got it. The obligation undertaken by France to come to the support of the Soviet Union has been without binding authority until the declaration of Sir John Simon, which made French support of the Soviet Union in case of attack by Germany absolutely certain.[81]

Surely Litvinov was being over-optimistic. If the Soviet Union had been attacked by Germany, surely France would have sought safety in the Maginot Line, just as it did when Poland was attacked by Germany in 1939.

Finally, on 2 May 1935 France and the Soviet Union concluded the Franco-Soviet Pact, which provided:

> In the event of France or the Soviet Union in circumstances specified in article 15(7) being the object, in spite of the peaceful intentions of both countries, of an unprovoked attack on behalf of a European state, the USSR and reciprocally, France shall give each other aid and assistance.

Article 15(7) provided that, if the League Council failed to reach a unanimous decision, the members of the League reserved unto themselves the right to take action as they deemed necessary. The Soviet Union, no doubt advised by Litvinov, demanded how long France

---

[80] *Survey of International Affairs*, 1935, vol.1, p.164
[81] Scott, William: *Alliance Against Hitler*, p.250

and the Soviet Union would have to wait for a decision, but eventually Litvinov accepted that in practice it was to be left to France to decide for herself what was required of the League Council by way of speed,[82] again showing Litvinov's conciliatory approach.

In October 1935, after months of threats, Mussolini invaded Abyssinia. On 10 October, by fifty votes to one, the League appointed a Committee to initiate and supervise sanctions.[83] Even the German Government imposed restrictions on many materials.[84] However, the country that was initially guilty of appeasement was France, not Britain. Eden's policy of persuading France to impose effective sanctions on Abyssinia was thwarted by the French attitude. Laval, the French Prime Minister, told Eden: 'France was not prepared to do anything that would impair the existing harmony between Italy and France.' Eden rightly commented that he 'did not see how Laval proposed to tolerate the invasion of Abyssinia with France's obligations under the Covenant upon which his country's foreign policy rested.'[85] France continued to be reluctant to support sanctions in the face of threats by Mussolini that sanctions meant war. The sanctions were moderately successful in that Italy's exports were reduced by 50% and her imports by 40% between March 1935 and March 1936,[86] but it did not stop the war. It was this factor that inspired Hoare to secretly negotiate with France and Abyssinia the notorious Hoare-Laval pact by which the greater part of Abyssinia would be retained by Italy, but the King would retain a small area with a corridor to the sea. Litvinov was theoretically right to criticise any such compromise when he stated:

> This violates the Covenant of the League which guarantees each member's inviolability and the integrity of their territory in the name of which the League has both intervened in the conflict and begun to apply sanctions. The League cannot approve such a proposal.[87]

Eden regarded the suggested imposition of oil sanctions as 'timid and uncertain.'[88] Sir Samuel Hoare, the Foreign Secretary, realised that, if sanctions were to be successful, it was necessary to impose oil sanctions, but as France would not agree, it was better for Abyssinia, at least to retain some territory, than be totally defeated. This was not the view of the British public and the Conservative Government was prepared to sacrifice Hoare, who resigned. However, Hoare, in spite of subsequently being condemned as an appeaser, actually supported oil sanctions. He told the British ambassador in Washington that he was fearful that a delay in imposing sanctions would distress US public opinion.[89]

---

[82] Ibid. text pp.246 & 247; French text in Appendix 2
[83] Walters, Francis: *History of the League of Nations*, p.656
[84] Eden, Anthony: *Memoirs, Facing the Dictators*, p.292
[85] Eden, Anthony: *Memoirs, Facing the Dictators*, p.237
[86] Phillips, Hugh: *Between the Revolution and the West*, p.156
[87] Ibid. p.157
[88] Eden, Anthony: *Memoirs, Facing the Dictators*, p.293
[89] Ibid. p.294

However, there was much merit in Hoare's argument that the Hoare-Laval plan was the only practical way of saving any of Abyssinia, because if governments were not prepared to go to war, they had to negotiate. Hoare states in his autobiography: 'As far as I could judge, there was not a single government in the League who was prepared to go to war, least of all the French.'[90] However, what we do not know is whether Litvinov would have supported military action if other measures failed; but surely one cannot blame him if he was not asked.

Turning to the USA, at no time did Roosevelt indicate that, if the League imposed sanctions, he would endeavour to persuade Congress to impose quickly the necessary restrictions. The action the USA took was feeble. All that occurred was, as Cordell Hull stated:

> There had been an increase in the exports to Italy that could be used for war purposes and this class of trade is directly contrary to the policy of this government as it is contrary to the general spirit of the Neutrality Act.

The refusal of Congress to give Roosevelt the power to prohibit the export of commodities prevented him from giving any support to the League's sanction policy.[91] Italy did not have the military might of Germany, and if Germany only wanted to give limited assistance to Spain, why should it have wanted to save Italy in a war with Britain and France? However, Britain's fear was that she would be responsible for the brunt of the fighting. The service chiefs estimated it would take six to nine months to defeat Italy for the estimated loss of four capital ships, which was not an acceptable figure when our commitments were taken into account.[92] Further, it was vital that docking facilities in French ports were available because of the serious danger of air attacks.[93] However, Britain could have taken the lead and informed the other members that it would lead the operation, if and only if, other members gave adequate support in men and equipment.

Unlike France and the USA, the Soviet Union acted positively, for which we have Litvinov to thank. In a memorable speech in September 1935 Litvinov correctly stated:

> The Soviet Union had maintained invariably friendly relations over ten years with Italy and the invasion of Abyssinia does not directly affect the interest of our country. ... However, nothing in the Covenant of the League entitles us to discriminate between members of the League as to their internal regime, the colour of their skin, their racial distinction or the stage of their civilisation, nor to deprive them of their privileges by virtue of the membership of the League, and in the first

---

[90] Hoare, Samuel: *Nine Troubled Years*, p.191
[91] Eden, Anthony: *Memoirs, Facing the Dictators*, p.292
[92] Middlemas, Robert and Barnes, Anthony: *Baldwin*, p.876
[93] Ibid. p.858

place of their inalienable right to integrity and independence. In my mind the League should stand firm on the principle that there can be no justification for military operations except in self-defence.[94]

Litvinov's support for the League against Abyssinia was indeed praiseworthy because of the excellent relationship which the Soviet Union enjoyed with Italy, as he indicated when he addressed the Central Executive Committee on 29 December 1933.[95] Further, Litvinov told Eden on 22 January 1936 that the Soviet Union would participate in oil sanctions if other countries were involved.[96]

Surely no act did more to encourage Hitler to march into the Rhineland than the failure of France and England to take effective measures against Italy? The Conservative Right felt it was far more important to appease Italy for fear of driving her into an alliance with Germany than care about the fate of Abyssinia.

Churchill was an appeaser. He advised the Ministers 'not to try and take a leading part or put themselves forward too prominently', a rather cowardly approach, even if Churchill justified that decision because of Britain's lack of armaments.[97] Amery supported the Hoare-Laval pact, which was condemned by many. Amery noted in his diary that Sam Hoare

> opened with a clear, well-marshalled and most impressive statement of the reasons which made it dangerous to go on with oil sanctions when no other power had taken a single measure of military precaution and war was clearly threatened by Italy.[98]

Nevertheless, did Amery consider that militarily Italy was likely to be as efficient as Germany, if one compares her campaign in Abyssinia with the brilliant German campaigns in Poland and France? Amery had the support of Pownall, who said:

> Is it worth a European War with all its losses in life and money, with all the risks of it spreading into a general confrontation: just to stop a colonial war?[99]

In retrospect, Litvinov considers it was a great mistake not to have imposed effective sanctions,[100] so that the League could impose its will. He told Eden: 'Germany must be made to understand that a close understanding exists among the peaceful nations. [Those

[94] Degras, Jane: *Documents on Soviet Foreign Policy*, vol.3, p.139
[95] *Moscow News*, 6 January 1934, p.2
[96] Phillips, Hugh: *Between the Revolution and the West*, p.157
[97] Churchill, Winston: *Second World War*, vol.1, 'Gathering Storm', p.132
[98] Amery, Leopold: *Empire at Bay*, p.404
[99] Pownall, Sir Henry: *Diaries*, p.89
[100] Tanya

nations] must be strong. Germany only understands force.'[101] Litvinov is in good company. Unlike Churchill, Iain Macleod stated in his biography of Chamberlain:

> Historically, the Abyssinian crisis has been presented as a side show compared with the main drama of the German advance to world conquest. In fact, it was the turning point of the thirties. Hitler was not slow to act upon this evidence.[102]

On 7 March 1936 German troops marched into the Rhineland.[103]

I am sure both Litvinov and Macleod were right. If a firm hand had been taken, Mussolini would have had to yield and if not would have lost a war. However, we do not know, in the event of Britain becoming involved in a war with Italy, whether the Soviet Union would have given any assistance; nor do we know the extent to which France would have participated. However, Litvinov was at the zenith of his influence and there is no reason to think that the Soviet Government would not have co-operated militarily; but still there is the question of whether such help would have been effective. As we have seen, Germany had adopted a cautious attitude in the Italy-Abyssinian war and I believe this was caused by Hitler's fear that if Britain and France had declared war on Italy in 1935, she would have lost, and Germany did not wish to become involved in such a war if she was to be on the losing side.

Litvinov had worked hard to prevent the deterioration in relations with Germany which had threatened to occur during the early days of the Nazi regime and had tried to obtain Hitler's participation in an Eastern European security pact. Having failed to obtain Hitler's co-operation, Litvinov then worked speedily for an alliance with the European democratic states to rebuff German aggression. However, when Italy threatened Abyssinia, Litvinov had taken the strategic decision that the Soviet Union should be seen to stand shoulder to shoulder with the democracies trying to restrain Italy from conquering Abyssinia, a policy for which he succeeded in obtaining the Politburo's approval.

It was in this light that Kandelaki commenced his mission. His formal instructions were to explore the possibility of an improved relationship between the Soviet Union and Germany. I believe historians have been obsessed with the notion that Litvinov opposed such negotiations and wished to discredit Kandelaki. Such conclusions were wrong. Kandelaki had been posted to Berlin as a trade representative. According to Gnedin, Litvinov's press secretary, Kandelaki gave his colleagues the impression that he had confidential instructions from Stalin personally to go beyond economic subjects and he was actively attempting, irrespective of Litvinov and his co-workers, to 'build bridges between the Soviet and Hitler Governments.' However, no valid evidence has been

---

[101] Phillips, Hugh: *Between the Revolution and the West*, p.157
[102] Macleod, Iain: *Neville Chamberlain*, p.189
[103] See Ch.13 No 1

produced that Litvinov was opposed to such tactics. After all, Britain was doing the same; for example, Halifax visited Germany in 1937, to which Eden was generally opposed.[104]

At a meeting with Kandelaki, Schacht enquired what help was needed. Kandelaki stammered out 'an Eastern Pact', an ideal very near to Litvinov's heart, so it might well be that, rather than acting independently of Litvinov, he concurred with what Kandelaki was doing. Schacht, however, repeated that, as it was a political matter, Kandelaki must approach the Foreign Minister through the Soviet ambassador. Kandelaki finally stated that he would inform the Foreign Minister of the conversation.[105]

Another meeting took place on 30 October 1935 between Kandelaki and Schacht to discuss the implementation of the 1935 credit agreement, but Kandelaki left for Moscow that day.[106]

Following anti-Nazi remarks at the Congress of the Communist International in Moscow in July 1935, Soviet-German relations deteriorated, although immediately after signing the mutual assistance pact with France on 2 May 1935, the Soviet Union once more took the initiative and asked the Germans to agree on a non-aggression and consultation pact.[107]

Hilger tells us that Kandelaki's overtures about improving Soviet-German relations were reported to Neurath, who informed Hitler. He rejected the idea that an improvement in relations was possible at the present time.[108]

Ambassador Suritz returned to Moscow on 28 November 1935, but was most pessimistic about future Soviet-German relations. He reported:

> I met a great number of Nazis, including Goebbels and Rosenberg. I have also planned a number of receptions of my own to which I invited among others Schacht and also Verner Von Blomberg Minister of Defence.
>
> All my contacts with the Germans only strengthened my earlier conviction that the course against us on which Hitler had embarked will remain unchanged and we cannot expect serious alteration in the immediate future. For example, I am told that Hitler had three obsessions: hostility to the Soviet Union towards communism), the Jewish question and Anschluss. Hostility towards the USSR flows not only from his ideological attitude towards communism, but also forms the basis of his

---

[104] Eden, Anthony: *Memoirs, Facing the Dictators*, p.512: Halifax visit.
[105] Roberts, Geoffrey: *The Soviet Union and the Beginning of the Second World War*, pp.27 to28; Roberts, Geoffrey: 'Russo-German Relations 1933-1941', in *International History Review*, August 1994, p.473
[106] Roberts, Geoffrey: *The Soviet Union and the Beginning of the Second World War*, p.29
[107] Ibid. p 20
[108] Hilger, Gustav: *Incompatible Allies*, p.270

tactical line in foreign policy.[109]

Further, Gnedin, another official of the Foreign Commissariat, told an officer of the Nazi party that he had been sent to Berlin with a view to improving relations.[110] However, there is no reason to doubt that these contacts were not approved by Litvinov.

On 3 December 1935 Litvinov sent a pessimistic report from Suritz on Soviet-German relations to Stalin, accompanied by Litvinov's written opinion advising that economic relations should continue because 'a break in economic relations could lead to a break in diplomatic relations', which Litvinov clearly did not want.

However, Litvinov rightly stated:

> I would consider erroneous the gearing to Germany of all or most of our foreign orders in the coming years. This would be mistaken because we are rendering important support to German Fascism now experiencing the greatest difficulties in the economic sphere and also because we would, without any political benefit in the coming years, weaken economic interest in the USSR more advantageous to our country. The Hitler anti-Soviet campaign is not slackening but is taking on Homeric dimensions.

Roberts states that Litvinov then proceeded to criticise Kandelaki. However, it appears that Litvinov was only critical of Schacht because he said:

> Initially, I regarded with some scepticism the Tass report from Geneva of Schacht's report about the intention of Germany to divide Poland and the Soviet Ukraine. I instructed Comrades Potemkin and Rozenberg to check the report. The result of the investigation leaves no doubt about the reality of the said statement by Schacht. Thus, Schacht, to whom not very long ago Kandelaki offered our support, is supporting Hitler's aggressive strivings in the East.

Those who argue that these exchanges gave birth to the Nazi-Soviet pact are entirely mistaken, as there was no suggestion that there was any thought of a pact. The sole aim was the Soviet Union's desire for the preservation of peace and there is no reason to doubt that these contacts were not approved by Litvinov.

---

[109] Roberts, Geoffrey: 'Russo-German Relations 1933-1941', in *International Historical Review*, August 1994, p.475; Roberts, Geoffrey: *The Soviet Union and the Beginning of the Second World War*, pp.29 and 30
[110] Roberts, Geoffrey: 'Russo-German Relations', in *International History Review*, August 1994, p.478; Roberts, Geoffrey: *The Soviet Union and the Beginning of the Second World War*, p.34

However the next day 4 December 1936 Litvinov replied to Suritz stating he supported the Ambassadors stand. Litvinov said: He was against the Soviet Union takimg the bulk of imports from Germany to the detriment of other countries. 'There is no point of strengthening present-day Germany too much.' Litvinov rightly stated, 'It is enough to maintain economic relations with Germany only at a necessary level to avoid a complete split between the two countries.'[111] Litvinov also stated: 'As far as he knew, this was the view of the Government', which indicates a certain indecision on the part of the Politburo.[112]

I think Suritz was right when he assured Fritz von Twardowski on 10 December that the idea that Litvinov was opposed to better Soviet-German relations was entirely untrue.[113] After all, the more contact the Soviet Union made with the German Government, the more likely Litvinov was to determine how serious and imminent was the German threat. There were influential people who favoured giving Germany a free hand against the Soviet Union.[114]

Litvinov, even after Churchill became Prime Minister, feared the day when he might see the British and German fleets sailing together to attack St Petersburg.[115] Again, Suritz reported in writing to Litvinov on 13 December 1935 that 'the Nazi's anti-Soviet policy was being criticised not only from the Reichswehr, Schacht and from the Foreign Ministry, but also from sections of the Nazi party itself.'[116] However, Litvinov had previously criticised Schacht for offering his support in improving Soviet-German relations when he was in fact supporting Hitler's drive to the East.[117]

In 1936, following rumours of a German-Russian rapprochement, the advice was taken of the British Ambassador to the Soviet Union, who reported that he had no doubt the Soviet Union would not find it impossible:

> If other considerations favoured a rapprochement, the Soviet Government undoubtedly could, if they wished, dis-continue their anti-German propaganda and grasp the Nazi hand without experiencing any real uncomfortable reactions at home. Nothing worthy to be called public opinion has existed in this country for a long time.[118]

---

[111] Roberts, Geoffrey: *The Soviet Union and the Beginning of the Second World War*, p.33; Roberts, Geoffrey: 'Russo-German Relations, 1933-1941', in *International Historical Review*, August 1994, p.476
[112] Roberts, Geoffrey: *The Soviet Union and the Beginning of the Second World War*, p.33
[113] *International History Review*, August 1994, p.478
[114] Ch 13 No 132.
[115] Cadogan, Alexander: *Diaries*, p.389
[116] Roberts, Geoffrey: *The Soviet Union and the Beginning of the Second World War*, pp.34 and 35
[117] See No.111 *ante*
[118] FO 371/ 20347, pp.52-54

However, contrary to Litvinov's advice, Stalin had decided to accept the German offer of extended credit. Presumably, Stalin's main reason was that he felt such an agreement in the short term would assist the Five Year Plan. Kandelaki returned to Berlin in mid-December 1935. However, the negotiations nearly floundered because of German demands for the existing debts to be paid in hard currency or gold and Soviet complaints about restrictions on the type of exports, so that military equipment was not allowed to be exported to the USSR.[119] The fact that apparently the Soviet Union stood firm because of the refusal of Germany to export military equipment shows that Litvinov's counsel was still significant.

Nevertheless, the Soviet Union had been cautious in limiting their criticism of the German Hitlerite regime, but this would all change when, following the occupation of the Rhineland by the Reichswehr, the Politburo, presumably on Litvinov's advice, emphatically opposed the seizure.

The death of George V gave Litvinov an opportunity to visit London for the funeral, accompanied by his wife Ivy and General Tukhachevskii, who saw military and air establishments and visited some armaments factories which were supplying arms to the Soviet Union, and they stayed a fortnight.[120] This indicated the improving relations between Britain and the Soviet Union. Further, as often happens, leaders used the opportunity of a funeral for diplomatic activity. As *The New York Times* described it: 'Litvinov probably did not come all the way for the satisfaction of walking behind the Royal Coffin. Undoubtedly, Litvinov would like to persuade Downing Street to let bygones be bygones.'[121] Following the funeral, it was reported that nobody had been more pleased with the reception he had received than Litvinov.

The State dinner given by Edward VIII was confined to royalty because it was felt that members of the Royal family should not associate closely with the representative of the state who had slain the Tsar and his family. Litvinov was received after the dinner. Next day, 29 January, the King saw separately various foreign statesmen, including Litvinov, who stayed for about half an hour.[122] It is not correct that George V and Queen Mary had entirely stayed aloof from such encounters with Litvinov,[123] who lunched with Eden at the Foreign Office. The other guests were Alfred Duff Cooper and his wife. Afterwards, Litvinov was received by Baldwin at 10 Downing Street.[124] The allegation in *The New York Times* that Maxim Litvinov had damaged his reputation by repeating to all and sundry his version of what he and King Edward discussed was not substantiated by any British

---

[119] Roberts, Geoffrey: *The Soviet Union and the Beginning of the Second World War*, pp.35 and 36

[120] Bilainkin, George: *Maisky, Ten Years an Ambassador*, p.148

[121] *The New York Times*, 27 January 1936, p.9

[122] *Times*, 30 January 1936, p.14

[123] See Ch.9, No.113, regarding George V's efforts to avoid meeting the Soviet Ambassador

[124] Coates, W P and Z: *A History of Anglo-Soviet Relations*, p.549

newspaper or other evidence. According to *The New York Times*, the King asked why it was necessary to have a revolution in Russia? Litvinov tried to explain. The King then asked, 'Why did the Tsar have to be killed?' Again, Litvinov tried to explain. Litvinov then said: 'The King was just a mediocre young Englishman who reads no more than one newspaper a day.' Naturally, there was indignation at Litvinov's bad manners, for it almost sacred rule of British public life that nobody ever repeats what the Monarch has said in private conversation.[125]

While relations with Britain were improving, the low point of Soviet-German relations had been reached, with two speeches by Hitler in March 1936 containing declarations of cold war against Bolshevism.[126]

---

[125] *The New York Times*, 3 February 1936, p.1
[126] Hitler's speech, Domarus; Max: Hitler's *speeches and proclamations 1932-1945* , p.767

13: LITVINOV'S EFFORTS TO AVOID A SECOND WORLD WAR

Although the Treaty of Versailles had prohibited Germany from remilitarising the Rhineland, on 7 March 1936, Hitler announced to the Reichstag that German troops 'are at present reoccupying future garrisons of peace' in the Rhineland, and while he spoke German troops streamed across the boundary and entered all the main German towns in the demilitarised zone. Hitler's justification for this action was that the Franco-Soviet agreement:

> was directed against Germany and Locarno had lost its inherent meaning and ceased to exist. France had acted as if neither the Covenant of the League of Nations or Locarno were in effect.

Hitler stated: 'After three years I believe that today the struggle for German equality of rights shall be deemed concluded.' In respect of the Soviet Union, Hitler stated, 'I rejected and continue to reject co-operation with Bolshevism which lays claim to world rulership.'[1] while at this very time negotiations were proceeding between the Soviet Union and Germany.[2]

Although the Franco-Soviet Pact had been ratified by the National Assembly, it had not been ratified by the French Senate. Litvinov took the opportunity to press for its final ratification, instructing his ambassador in Paris to tell Flandin, the French Prime Minister, 'He can count on my full support at Geneva, but our public opinion is still agitated by what has happened to the Pact.' Litvinov's pressure was sufficient. At long last the Pact was ratified by the Senate by an overwhelming vote of 231 to 52.[3]

A meeting of the Council of the League of Nations was called and Litvinov attended. On 16 March 1936 *The New York Times* reported:

> Litvinov, the Soviet Foreign Minister, showed greater determination than any of his Council colleagues in opposing Germany's reoccupation of the Rhineland. Litvinov eloquently rejected the German Government's accusation of Germany being encircled.[4]

---

[1] Domarus, Max: *Hitler's Speeches and Proclamations 1932-1945*, p.767
[2] See Ch.12, No.119
[3] Haslam, Jonathan: *The Soviet Union and the Struggle for Collective Security*, p.98
[4] *The New York Times*, 16 March 1936, p.11; Degras, Jane: *Soviet Documents on Foreign Policy*, vol.3, pp.173 and 175

Condemning German action, Litvinov stated:

> If there is one state in the world which is threatened by no external danger it is Germany. I know of not a single country which makes any territorial claim on Germany and know of no literature preaching an attack on Germany. Attacks on a state do not and cannot take place without preliminary preparations, without the preliminary presentation of territorial claims and to train up people in the spirit of making them good. No such preparations are going on in a single country.

Litvinov then claimed Germany's real motive, as Hitler had specified in *Mein Kampf,* was to prevent any other power in Europe being in a position to challenge Germany's position as militarily the dominant power in Europe:

> If there was such a danger of a rival to Germany, *Mein Kampf* preached you must not only think it is your right but your duty to prevent such a state coming into existence by all possible means, including force of arms, and if such a state has come into being, it must once again be shattered.

Then Litvinov added:

> There are people who really see a particular expression of Germany's love of peace in the offer to France and Belgium of a treaty for twenty-five years to be guaranteed by Britain and Italy.

Although Litvinov had previously been one of Locarno's sternest critics, he was now a keen supporter of Locarno without expressing any reason for his change of attitude. Litvinov affirmed:

> People forget the Locarno treaty, which Germany has torn up, represented just such a non-aggression pact with the same guarantees and its validity was not for twenty-five years but for an indefinite period. The other difference was that the Locarno treaty included supplementary guarantees for France and Belgium in the shape of a demilitarised zone in the Rhineland. Thus, Hitler's new proposals amount to this. While depriving France and Belgium of certain guarantees which were provided by the Locarno treaty he [Hitler] wants to retain for Germany all the benefits of the treaty in its totality.[5]

---

5. *The New York Times*, 18 March 1936, p.15; Degras Jane; *Soviet Documents on Foreign Policy vol 3* pp.173 and 175

Litvinov's promotion of tough action against Germany in response to the remilitarisation of the Rhineland won him an unlikely audience. Litvinov, who was once hated by all good Conservatives in Britain as a dangerous agitator, visited the House of Commons and addressed a group of Conservative members on the European situation. Although the meeting was private, those who attended indicated that Litvinov took the opportunity to make a slashing denunciation of Nazi Germany along the lines of his speech to the Council of the League of Nations earlier in the week.[6]

Litvinov's views were very much supported by Churchill. However, it is by no means certain that, as Churchill claimed: 'If the French army had mobilised, Hitler would have withdrawn.'[7] It had always seemed the likely outcome of any war would have been that the German troops west of the Rhine would either have withdrawn or been overwhelmed; but, as in 1944/1945, it would have been difficult for the French army to have successfully crossed the Rhine, and it would not have been 'the simple police operation' that Churchill claimed it would have been. However, this option was purely academic as the French Cabinet was itself undecided on the right course of action. Only four Cabinet members were in favour of military action. Although it had been clear since Hitler came to power that German reoccupation of the Rhineland was only a matter of time, the French had prepared no military plans for such an eventuality.[8] Without a robust request from France for Britain to fulfil her Locarno commitment and enforce the Treaty by military action, there was no chance of such help from Britain. In any case, British military action would have had virtually no public support. British public opinion was summed up in the famous words of Eden's taxi driver: 'I suppose Jerry can do what he likes in his own back garden.'[9]

Litvinov continued to be disillusioned about the failure of the League to take action. In a telegram to the Foreign Office in London, Litvinov stated:

> He did not see what use there was coming to Geneva. Nothing ever seemed to result from his speeches. After each failure the League said it would make efforts to strengthen against the next trial, but nothing was done. We just waited for the next aggression. As to securing universal membership, he was convinced we went about it the wrong way. If those within the League bound themselves closely together and showed themselves determined, then in due course they would get universal membership. Germany could not remain outside the League, a really effective organisation which comprised the rest of Europe. We were always making concessions and we got nothing in return.[10]

---

[6] *The New York Times*, 20 March 1936, p.13
[7] Churchill, Winston: *The Second World War*, vol.1, 'Gathering Storm', p.152
[8] Eden, Anthony: *Memoirs, Facing the Dictators*, p.353
[9] Ibid. p.346
[10] FO 954, pp.24 and 261

Turkey took the opportunity, by peaceful means, to try to obtain a variation of the Lausanne Treaty of 1923, by which Turkey agreed not to fortify the Dardanelles. Instead of following the option of unilateral action favoured by Germany and Italy, Turkey decided to go down the legal route and wrote to the signatories of the Lausanne Treaty. Ataturk stated: 'The situation in Europe is highly appropriate for a variation of the treaty to give back to Turkey some of the sovereignty it had surrendered.' As a result of a conference in which the Soviet Union took part, it was proposed that Turkey regain its right to fortify the Straits area and introduce troops. Turkey was given the job of enforcing the convention giving unlimited right for commercial shipping. Litvinov agreed to submit the proposals to his government and a slightly modified version was agreed.[11]

Such an agreement, which enabled Turkey to have a stranglehold on Soviet military activity in the Black Sea, was to the detriment of the Soviet Union. *Pravda* complained, in its edition of 2 July 1936, that the agreement did not take into account Soviet interests. This reaction left Ataturk unmoved. Writing under the name of Yunus Nadi, Ataturk said: 'Friends should realise that Turkey would insist on measures to safeguard the country's full security.'[12] Nevertheless, the fact that the Soviet Union agreed to the revision shows the co-operative nature of the Soviet Union's foreign policy at that time.

In spite of the suspension of economic talks caused by German military action in reoccupying the Rhineland, an economic agreement with Germany was signed on 29 April 1936, but only to deal with the existing credit of 200 million marks. Haslam is probably correct that this was caused by the failure of Britain and France to take stronger measures against Germany following her Rhineland action.[13] Clearly, while the Germans might desire to be portrayed as the saviour of the world against Communism, German leaders appeared unanimous that they required trade with Russia for economic reasons.

The suspension of the trade talks was not what Germany desired and they were anxious to restart them. On 29 April 1936 Bessonov reported from Berlin that Schacht had asked Kandelaki when discussion about big credits might start again. The April credit agreement had provided the basis for a big growth in Soviet-German trade. Schacht wanted to exclude politics, which he said got in the way of business.[14] On the other hand, at a luncheon given by Kandelaki on 4 May 1936, the Soviet delegation of Kandelaki, Gnedin and Bessonov expressed their desire to discuss the unsatisfactory political situation between the two countries and gave their personal opinion that, despite increasing scepticism in Moscow, the Soviet Government still saw the possibility of achieving a political détente.[15]

---

[11] Terms of Lausanne Treaty Mango A *Atarturk* pp.387 & 388 revised version p.504
[12] Ibid. p.617
[13] Haslam, Jonathan: *The Soviet Union and the Struggle for Collective Security*, p.103
[14] Roberts, Geoffrey: *The Soviet Union and the Origins of the Second World War*, p.40
[15] Ibid.

In early May 1936 Herbert L Goering, an official at the economic ministry, who a month earlier had been appointed head of a new Raw Materials and Foreign Exchange Office, arranged for his cousin, Hermann Goering, to see Kandelaki. According to the German reports, when Goering saw Kandelaki on 13 May 1936, Goering told the Russian delegation he was pleased that a new credit agreement had been signed, which would be 'a pacemaker for further political understanding.'[16] Hermann told the Russians, 'If ever they felt they were making no headway, they should apply to him direct. He was prepared at all times to assist by word and deed.'[17] What Goering did not tell the Soviet delegation was that, having discussed the importance of developing German-Soviet business with German industrialists, they had decided to discuss the matter with the Fuhrer, whose attitude was not very sympathetic.[18]

However, on 22 May 1936 Suritz came to bid farewell to Neurath before going on leave to Carlsberg. Suritz expressed satisfaction over economic relations and asked whether any change in political relations might be expected. Neurath said he did not see any pre-conditions at present, but hoped that political relations would again proceed satisfactorily.[19]

There was a further initiative on the part of the Soviets, rather than the Germans. A German Foreign Ministry official, Hencke, reported in a memorandum of 3 July 1936 that Soviet Embassy counsellor Bessonov raised the question of a non-aggression pact and Henke spoke of three possibilities. Firstly, Germany might feel there is no need of one in the absence of a common border. Secondly, Germany might reject the pact because of existing treaties with France and Czechoslovakia. Thirdly, Germany might be prepared to supplement the 1936 Berlin Treaty with a non-aggression clause. Hencke stated that non-aggression pacts were indeed applicable to neighbouring states only, but Germany had no desire to attack the Soviet Union.[20] This has the mark of Litvinov stamped on it, who was keen on such pacts. It has been suggested from time to time by historians, such as Haslam, that the negotiations by Kandelaki had either been conducted secretly without the knowledge of Litvinov or without his approval. I believe the evidence does not support this interpretation. Stalin had shown his confidence in his Foreign Commissar because Litvinov was on the reviewing platform at the 1936 anniversary celebrations of the Russian Revolution with Stalin, who bestowed on him the Order of Lenin.[21] As late as April 1939 Litvinov was the architect of the proposals for the joint British, French and Soviet pact.[22]

---

[16] Ibid.
[17] Tucker, Robert: *Stalin in Power*, p.409
[18] Ibid. p.410
[19] Ibid.
[20] Ibid.
[21] Ch.16, p.31
[22] See No. 158 *post*

Litvinov was prepared to take a tough line with Germany and on 19 August 1936 wrote to Suritz: 'In the event of a positive reply to Soviet demands for the import of German military equipment, it would be possible to raise again the question of a new credit agreement.'[23] However, this action does not indicate that Litvinov was an unwilling participant in these negotiations. On the contrary, this letter indicates his view that no agreement should be reached unless the Soviet Union obtained the military hardware she desired. Litvinov wanted to test whether Germany was acting in good faith. If Germany did not want to export military hardware to the Soviet Union, it could be because Germany feared that the Soviet Union at a future date might attack Germany, A more possible reason in view of *Mein Kampf,* was if Germany wanted to attack the Soviet Union, Germany did not want the equipment used against them in such an attack. Unlike the situation in December 1935, the Soviet Union was now not so enthusiastic about the loan. They had difficulty in using up the existing loan and the Popular Front victories in France and Spain made an agreement between the Soviet Union and Germany less vital.

On 11 September 1936 Suritz telegraphed to Moscow asking whether a note of protest should be lodged in relation to the occupation of the Rhineland. Krestinsky's instructions on 19 September 1936 indicated that there should be no note of protest, although Suritz should show his displeasure with Germany at meetings.[24] Sensibly, the reason for the failure to make a formal protest was that the Soviet Union was not in a position to take any punitive action if Germany ignored her protest. Germany, also, was trying to isolate the Soviet Union by appealing to anti-communist sympathies in Western Europe. Therefore, to ignore such remarks was not what Hitler wanted.

On 13 September 1936, at the Nuremberg Party Conference, Hitler launched a major anti-Soviet campaign, suggesting by implication his intention to try and conquer Soviet territory. He stated: 'If the Urals, with their incalculable wealth of raw materials, the rich forests of Siberia and the unending cornfields of the Ukraine lay in Germany under National Socialist leadership, the country would swim in plenty.' One day later, Hitler stated:

> We must regard Bolshevism abroad as our enemy. We shall fight it as a world power if it tries to transfer its Spanish methods to Germany. It is not the intention of Bolshevism to free the nations of what is sick in them, but exterminate all that is healthy.[25]

Four days later, Voroshilov answered by declaring:

---

[23] Roberts Geoffrey *The Soviet Union and the origins of the Second World War* p.41
[24] Ibid p.42
[25] Documents p.295

I can assure you that the Soviet Ukraine will remain an impregnable outpost of the Great Socialist fatherland. The Soviet Union, particularly the Soviet Ukraine, has many enemies. Our enemies are miscalculating. The country solid, mighty, 170,000,000 strong is advancing in all directions in Socialist reconstruction and is able to rebuff any enemy.[26]

In October 1936 Goering left strict instructions, in spite of Germany's urgent need for Soviet raw materials, that all business with Soviets had to be non-political.[27] Haslam claims that the Soviet Union, acutely aware of Germany's economic difficulties, sanctioned further soundings by Kandelaki and his deputy Friedrikson, probably against Litvinov's advice. However, Haslam gives no evidence for that statement and Litvinov may well have approved these soundings by Kandelaki. As an experienced diplomat, he would have wanted to know as much as possible about the German leader's intentions.

On 14 December 1936 Goering and Suritz met. Goering reiterated what Schacht stated about his country's commitment to the further development of Soviet-German economic relations and said that a normalisation of political relations was also desirable. However, what happened in the political sphere depended in the first instance on what happened in the economic sphere. [28] Goering's answer was probably not honest. Germany needed the Soviet Union's exports in its planned domination of continental Europe and the Soviet Union had to be appeased sufficiently to obtain such exports.

If Stalin was hoping for better relations with Germany in 1937, his behaviour was certainly inconsistent. In early January,1937 a book called *Collapse of German Occupation in the Ukraine* was published, based on original German documents alleged to have been given to the USSR by mutinous German soldiers at the close of the First World War. This book stressed the cruelty of the German conquerors and quoted an order by the Chief of the German division: 'For every German or Polish soldier killed or wounded, the first ten Russian soldiers or inhabitants met shall be promptly shot.'[29]

Towards the end of December 1936, Kandelaki asked to see Schacht, who told Kandelaki that the only way in which trade between the Soviet Union and Germany would develop would be if the Soviet Government made a clear political gesture and 'the best thing would be for them to state, through their ambassadors, that they would refrain from communist agitation outside the Soviet Union.' According to Schacht, Kandelaki indicated that he sympathised with the views expressed by Schacht.[30]

---

[26] Documents , 1936, p.296

[27] Haslam, Jonathan: *The Soviet Union and the Struggle for Collective Security*, p.127

[28] Roberts, Geoffrey: *The Soviet Union and the Origins of the Second World War*, p.43

[29] *Moscow News*, 6 January 1937, p.4

[30] Roberts, Geoffrey: *The Soviet Union and the Origins of the Second World War*, p.43

On 8 January 1937 a report was drawn up by Litvinov for the Politburo. This body was no doubt seeking Litvinov's views and the report showed his deep involvement in negotiations with Germany.

> The Soviet Government has not only never shunned political negotiations with the German Government. At one time it even made a definite political proposal which was the non-aggression pact. The Soviet Government, by no means, considers its policy must be directed against the interests of the German people. It has therefore no objection to now entertaining negotiations with the German Government in the interests of improving general relations and peace in general. The Soviet Government does not refuse to negotiate through official diplomatic representatives. It agrees also to respect confidentiality and not to make publicly known our recent conversations or future talks, if the German Government insists on this.

Apparently, the reply proposed by Litvinov was approved by the Politburo and the talks between Kandelaki and the German Government were to continue; the only proviso was that, 'in view of Kandelaki's lack of political experience', he should not be solely in charge of the negotiation. If Stalin had charged Kandelaki to come to a secret deal with Germany, he would have wanted the negotiations to be solely with Kandelaki.

On 29 January 1937 Kandelaki returned to Germany with a verbal proposal from Stalin and Molotov to open up direct negotiations. Schacht said the request would be passed to the German Foreign Ministry and again commented that communist agitation would have to be dampened down.[31]

On 4 February 1937 Litvinov reported to Stalin that the Germans had requested further conversations between Neurath and Suritz. Litvinov suggested that he should arrange a dinner to which Neurath, Suritz and Kandelaki would be invited. There was a difference of opinion between the Russians, who wanted to keep the talks confidential, and the Germans, who opposed secrecy. Litvinov argued, although not necessarily correctly, that the reason for Schacht's aversion to secrecy was that Hitler wanted a loan from England and France. I cannot understand why Roberts thinks that what Litvinov said was intended 'to put the boot into Kandelaki.' Litvinov's advice was that the Soviet Union should do nothing until it heard from the Germans. All that was required was that Suritz, the Soviet ambassador in Berlin, should be empowered to authorise negotiations, the only proviso being that before negotiations commenced, France and Czechoslovakia should be informed. The Politburo had decided not to make any proposals themselves, but that Kandelaki and Suritz should receive any new German proposals. Stalin and Molotov approved Litvinov's advice,

---

[31] Conquest, Robert: *The Great Terror*, p.197; Haslam, Jonathan: *The Soviet Union and the Struggle for Collective Security*, p.127

indicating that he was still at the centre of the negotiations. This proves that Haslam is incorrect when he claimed, 'Kandelaki's soundings were the symptoms of Litvinov's waning influence.'[32]

In February 1937 Neurath discussed the whole matter with Hitler, who rejected the idea of political conversations.[33] On 21 March Schacht told Suritz that he saw no prospect of any change in German-Soviet relations.[34] Kandelaki returned to Moscow, only to face imprisonment or death, and Friedrikson suffered a similar fate.[35] The traditional view is that no further political negotiations between the Soviet Union and Germany would take place until after the Anschluss and Munich. However, economically it was business as usual. In 1937 it was mutually agreed that Soviet bills which fell due that year would be paid for, by delivery of goods, before maturity.[36]

Hochman has unearthed an interesting episode concerning the appointment of Yurenev as Soviet ambassador to Germany which challenges the traditional view on German-Soviet relations during this period. In spite of Hitler's anti-Soviet rhetoric, he gave a cordial reception to Yurenev, who was invited to present his credentials, not as normal for ambassadors, in the Reich Chancellery, but at Hitler's private apartment. Haslam argues that the reason why the new ambassador was received at Hitler's private residence was because, if the new ambassador had been received at the usual location in Berlin, protocol demanded a military parade.[37] However, in a rare streak of humanity, when Yurenev was summoned back to Moscow in December 1937 and shot, Hitler was so angry that firstly he told Schulenburg to inform Moscow that it was no good the Soviet Union sending a new ambassador to Berlin as it would by no means be easy to obtain Hitler's agreement. Secondly, Schulenburg was instructed to take leave of absence from Moscow for two months.[38] This episode indicates that at this stage Stalin had subordinated foreign policy concerns to the Great Purges. The new ambassador, Merekalov, was not appointed until June 1938.[39] Hitler, realising he might need Soviet imports temporarily, did not entirely shut the door to the Soviet Union.

How did the Great Purges affect Litvinov and what was the main thrust of his policy at this time? His main concern must have been, apart from his own survival, that many of his staff were imprisoned or executed. However, as Stalin was giving priority to the Great Purges, in a way Litvinov's authority in the day-to-day running of the Commissariat was probably

---

[32] Roberts, Geoffrey: *The Soviet Union and the Origins of the Second World War*, p.45; Haslam, Jonathan: *The Soviet Union and the Struggle for Collective Security*, p.128; Ch 19 No 87

[33] Roberts, Geoffrey: *The Soviet Union and the Origins of the Second World War*, p.46

[34] Ibid.

[35] Ibid.   although Robert Conquest is not so sure, in *The Great Terror*, p.216

[36] Hochman, Jiri: *The Soviet Union and the Failure of Collective Security*, p.120

[37] Haslam, Jonathan: *The Soviet Union and the Struggle for Collective Security* p.145

[38] Hochman, Jiri: *The Soviet Union and the Failure of Collective Security*, p.121

[39] *Times*, 28 June 1938, p.13

increased. It seems that at this stage Litvinov was as concerned as Stalin that options relating to Germany should remain open. In an interview with a *Le Temps* journalist, Litvinov stated:

> It is you, the French, who are interested in the preservation of the territorial clauses in Versailles. However, we have won nothing in Versailles. Therefore we have nothing to give. We [the USSR] will not be harmed by territorial revision. That is why we can disinterest ourselves. It [the eventual rapprochement with Germany] will not be a question of signing new treaties. Things can go otherwise.[40]

Does not this show, firstly, Litvinov's disappointment that, after his robust defence of Locarno following Germany's re-militarisation of the Rhineland, France had shown weakness? Secondly, it points to the fact that Litvinov had not shut the door to improved relations even with Nazi Germany, if he thought it was in the Soviet Union's interest. Although I may be wrong, I feel that this is what Litvinov believed and not what he thought Stalin wanted him to say.

However, Litvinov's policy of collective security would now receive a setback when, although the Czechs and the Russians were in favour of staff talks, the French held back. A French Foreign Office official stated that Germany continued to hate the Franco-Soviet Pact because they considered it was a real obstacle to German expansionist designs.

> I think the fundamental reason why they hate it so much and why it is valuable for the French is because it is an outward and visible sign to the whole world that the Soviet Government is on the side of the territorial *status quo* in Europe. I expect you have received the letter of 8 March and the importance of the Franco-Soviet Pact in preventing the Soviet Union from falling into the arms of Germany. As we have frequently reported from this Embassy, this is a question that is constantly in the minds of French politicians and journalists, irrespective of party, and it is for this reason that the newspapers of the Right refrain from more criticism of French policy towards the Soviet Union, which they dislike on other grounds.

This indicates the French view of the Pact as a talisman rather than a serious commitment which needed underwriting by military discussions.

It was stated that France was concerned, for which she had every justification, that Britain had in the past dismissed too lightly the possibility, however remote, of a change in Russian policy and the danger which it would entail for France and Britain.

---

[40] Hochman, Jiri: *The Soviet Union and the Failure of Collective Security*, p.121

Neville Chamberlain was entirely wrong. His assessment was shared by the French. Blum read the reports sent to him from the French ambassador in Moscow, who took the view there was no immediate likelihood of a change of attitude of the Soviet Union towards the Franco-Soviet Pact or of a closer relationship between Russia and Germany.[41]

On 15 April 1937 Litvinov returned to Moscow to approve the appointment of Potemkin as First Deputy Commissar.[42] I do not agree with Watson that Litvinov's authority was weakened by the fact that Potemkin took over the Western section of the Foreign Commissariat as Litvinov dominated the Foreign Commissariat, as he did the League of Nations. It was clearly Litvinov who was in charge and made the opening speech at the Brussels Conference on the Far East.[43] It was Litvinov who met De La Warr, the British Lord Privy Seal, in the critical days before Munich[44] and, according to Soviet documents, Maisky was clearly receiving direct instructions from Litvinov in 1938 and until Litvinov's dismissal in 1939.[45]

It is constantly being said, including by Watson, that Potemkin was a Molotov man; but Watson gives no evidence to support that contention and I cannot find any evidence of any antagonism between Litvinov and Potemkin. On the contrary, if Sheinis is correct, when Litvinov visited Potemkin in Paris, the two men seemed quite close to each other.[46]

Indeed, when Potemkin was appointed Deputy Foreign Commissar he is alleged to have told Willi Munzenberg he was 'leaving for Moscow with a heavy heart. Litvinov's retirement appeared certain and his departure from office would mean the end of a policy [in which] they both believed.'[47]

Potemkin was a cultured man, whom I think Litvinov would have respected. Potemkin spoke seven languages and before he entered the Foreign Commissariat was a Professor of History.[48]

Nevertheless, relations with Britain continued to improve. Edward VIII abdicated uncrowned in December 1936 and Litvinov was a guest at the Coronation of George VI in May 1937. Repeating the precedent established by the Foreign Office at the Coronation in 1911, four places away from the Queen, in the place formerly occupied by a member of the

---

[41] FO 21094, N216 229, 254,257
[42] Watson, Derek: 'The Politburo and Foreign Policy in the 30s', in *The Nature of Stalin's Dictatorship*, p.152
[43] See Ch.15, No.99
[44] See No.80 *post*
[45] *Soviet Peace Efforts* No 158. p. 260, 11 April 1939
[46] Sheinis, Zinovy: *Maxim Litvinov*, p.285
[47] Haslam, Jonathan: *The Soviet Union and the Struggle for Collective Security 1933-1939*, p.132
[48] *The New York Times*, 1 March 1940, p.4

Imperial House of Russia, sat Maxim Litvinov. Afterwards, a Russian battleship attended the King's review of his fleet at Spithead.[49]

The sanctions that the League imposed on Italy, which had previously been imposed in July 1936, because of Italy's invasion of Abyssinia, proved to be ineffective. Italy completed its conquest of Abyssinia. Therefore reform was discussed by the League, but after a debate no reform was in fact implemented. Litvinov reminded his audience that this debate had been brought about by the Italian-Abyssinian dispute. Litvinov, no doubt with sadness, stated:

> The League had failed to procure for one of its members the territorial integrity provided for by clause 10 of the Covenant and today is only able to express to that member its platonic sympathy. We must analyse it and draw from it all the lessons requisite to prevent similar action in the future.

He then complained of

> the striving to confine the action taken to the barest minimum. Even economic sanctions were limited in their scope and their function and, even in this limited scope, sanctions were not applied by all members of the League.

Whereas some countries, including Britain, wanted a voluntary system of sanctions, Litvinov had no doubt that economic sanctions must remain obligatory for all members of the League:

> It is only when sanctions are obligatory, will be removed the apprehension and mistrust that exists if in certain cases certain states, which have no direct interest in the conflict, undergo considerable sacrifice [whereas] in another case other disaffected states will act with less idealism. What is necessary is confidence that in all cases of aggression, independent of the degree of interest in a particular case, sanctions will be applied by all and this can only be obtained when sanctions are obligatory. It may be possible to conceive in individual cases – very rare it is true – when aggression may be stopped by economic sanctions alone, but I recognise that in a majority of cases economic sanctions must march parallel with military action. In an ideal League of Nations, military sanctions as well as economic sanctions ought to be binding on all.[50]

Litvinov had spoken in such passionate terms that the conclusion must be that he believed in what he was saying. Although clearly he could not have so acted without Stalin's agreement, it seems most probable that it was Litvinov who persuaded Stalin that full

---

[49] Coates, W P: *A History of Anglo-Soviet Relations*, p.574
[50] Speech, 1 July 1936; Degras, Jane: *Soviet Documents on Foreign Policy*, vol.3, pp.194 and 196-198

support for the Covenant of the League was the right course. Unlike Eden, Chamberlain's inclination was for personal and direct negotiations rather than invoking the League.

At the League of Nations in September 1936, Litvinov made another eloquent speech in which he stated he was convinced

> the aggregate power of all peace-loving states, both in the economic and in the military sense, their total resources in manpower and in the war industries surpasses the strength of any possible combination of countries which the aggressor might rally around him. I would object most strongly if, in the name of universality, the League was to set about to eliminate from the Covenant all that makes it a weapon of peace and a threat to the aggressor. I should object vigorously to anything that makes the League safe for aggressors. We must of course admit that a state which openly exalts the power of the sword against international obligations for which it does not conceal its contempt, a power which cynically calls on other states to adopt the same contemptuous attitude to their signatures at the foot of treaties with the object of finally destroying international confidence, cannot feel comfortable in a League of Nations which proclaims one of its principal aims to be the maintenance of justice and the scrupulous respect for all treaty obligations in the dealings of organised people with one another.[51]

Notwithstanding the Soviet Union's interests were not directly involved in the Italian-Abyssinian dispute or in the reoccupation of the Rhineland, Litvinov's country had given full vocal support to the defence of the *status quo* and sanctions imposed by the League, although in the 20s he had been one of the League's severest critics. I do not criticise Litvinov for changing his mind, but are we not entitled to know why? As the Soviet Union was not asked for military support, it seems to me a poor criticism that such support would have been ineffective.

Litvinov, in a speech to the League Assembly in September 1938, spoke in his most sarcastic mode:

> The aggressor states have grown immensely during the last three years. There exists an opinion that when some states announce a foreign policy based on aggression, on the violation of other people's frontiers, on the violent annexation of other people's possessions, on the enslavement of other nations, on domination over entire continents, the League of Nations not only has the right but the duty of declaring loudly and clearly that it has been set up to preserve universal peace, that it will not permit the realisation of such a programme and it will fight the programme by every means at its disposal.

---

[51] Speech, 28 September 1936; Degras, Jane: *Soviet Documents on Foreign Policy*, vol.3, pp.208 and 209

Naturally, at the least attempt to carry out aggression in practice there should be brought into play the appropriate measures and, according to the capacity of each member of the League, the collective action provided by article 16 of the Covenant.

There is, however, another conception, which recommends, as the height of human wisdom under cover of imaginary pacifism, that the aggressor be treated with consideration and his vanity be not wounded. It recommends that conversations and negotiations be carried out with him, for he be assured that no collective action will be taken against him and no groups or blocs be formed against him, even though he himself enters into aggressive blocs with other aggressors. Hitherto, the aggressor reckoned with the possible reaction of the League of Nations and showed a certain hesitation in preparing his aggression, carrying it out gradually and in proportion to his growing certainty that there would be no reaction at all. But now we are asked to reassure him beforehand that he need fear nothing from the hands of the League and henceforth the League will not apply to him either military or even economic or financial sanctions. At the very worst he is threatened with moral condemnation and that, in all probabilities, clothed in appropriate courteous diplomatic forms.[52]

How right was Litvinov.

However, the Soviet Union's insistence on the imposition by the League of compulsory sanctions was damaged in September 1938. Britain proposed that the sanctions covenant would no longer be compulsory. This proposal always seemed to me incredibly stupid, unless Britain wanted to sabotage the League rather than uphold it. A more sensible proposal of Britain was that when the Council was contemplating action to safeguard peace, the vote of the party or parties directly interested was not to be taken into account. As Poland and Hungary voted against, it was quickly defeated, but the Soviet Union inconsistently abstained.[53] However, as Litvinov had always previously maintained that sanctions, once imposed, must be compulsory, I cannot understand why he did not vote for the proposal, which would have facilitated League action against aggression.

Upon the Anschluss taking place, Litvinov rightly reported to the Central Committee: 'The annexation of Austria is the greatest event since the World War and is fraught with the greatest danger, not least for our Union.'[54]

Much sympathy in the Soviet Union was generated for Austria following the Anschluss. Tanya mentions meeting an Austrian refugee in the Soviet Union shortly afterwards and

---

[52] Speech, 21 September 1938; Degras, Jane: *Soviet Documents on Foreign Policy*, vol 3 pp.299 @ 301
[53] Walters, Francis: *A History of the League of Nations*, p.781
[54] Bullock, Alan: *Hitler and Stalin*, p.629

feeling embarrassed that nothing had been done.[55] However, looking at the newsreels it appears many Austrians welcomed the German Army. The newsreels show thousands of cheering supporters. I believe that if Hitler had held a free election, the Anschluss supporters would have been in the majority. It is possible that both Hitler and Stalin could have won fair elections, but dictators rarely agree to free elections in case they miscalculate public opinion.

Churchill condemned the Anschluss when he spoke in the House of Commons, but he quite rightly never suggested using force against Germany to oblige her to quit Austria, because it was not practicable unless one was to start a full war against Germany. In any event, Austria made no request for assistance. Churchill fully realised: 'Mastery of Vienna gave to Germany the military and economic control of the whole of the communications of South Eastern Europe by road, river and rail.' Although clearly Austria could not be saved, the long border between Czechoslovakia and German-controlled Austria meant Czechoslovakia was defenceless. Churchill advocated collective security with the words: 'What is ridiculous about collective security? The only thing that is ridiculous about it is we have not got it.'[56]

Churchill, no doubt, agreed with Litvinov, who had acted positively by suggesting a conference to consider the new situation. Joseph Davies, the US ambassador in Moscow wrote to the Secretary of State stating that Litvinov had told him during the course of a conversation: 'The European situation was extremely dangerous.'[57] Litvinov claimed that the disappearance of the Austrian state was not noticed by the League of Nations. France did not respond.

Britain's position was that a conference 'was inappropriate as it would divide Europe into two camps and would be branding Germany as an aggressor', which she clearly was. Bullock is right that the Western powers' response 'shows how far they still were from seeing the problem as clearly as Stalin (no doubt under the influence of Litvinov) did.' [58]

Following the Anschluss, Fischer, in an off-the-record talk with Litvinov, asked whether Litvinov was pleased at the firm stand taken by Britain and France. Litvinov said 'Yes', but indicated he mistrusted France and Britain, or rather the governments then in power. He said, 'Hitler is not through yet. The British and French want an agreement with Germany.'[59] He told Cripps that the men he most mistrusted were Chamberlain, Simon and Laval.[60]

---

[55] Tanya

[56] *Hansard*, 14 March 1938, vol.333, 95 to 99

[57] FRUS 1938 vol 1 p.445

[58] Bullock, Alan: *Hitler and Stalin*, p.630

[59] Fischer, Louis: *Men and Politics*, p.469

[60] Estorick, Eric: *Stafford Cripps*, p.280

In common with many politicians and members of the public, Tanya tells us her father regarded Czechoslovakia as one of the most democratic countries in Europe and personally felt there was a duty to defend it. He was sad at the loss of the Sudetenland, as he believed that this would result in the complete loss of Czechoslovakia. However, in fact Czechoslovakia was not the perfect democratic state it was held to be. As the eminent historian Toynbee stated at the time:

> It was an imperfect democracy even for the Slovaks while he [the historian Arnold Toynbee] was convinced for the Germans, Magyars and Poles, who account between them for more than one quarter of the whole population, the present regime in Czechoslovakia is not essentially different from the regimes in the surrounding countries.[61]

In his public statements at the time of Munich, Litvinov ignored the question of discrimination. He was in good company. Churchill did the same. It was left to Eden in the Munich debate in the House of Commons to acknowledge that there had been 'discrimination, even severe discrimination' against the Sudeten Germans, although he in fact abstained when in September 1938 the House of Commons debated the Munich agreement.[62]

The defenders of the Munich settlement argued that the state which had been established in 1919 was not a viable state. Like most of the new states established following the First World War, the creators of Czechoslovakia strove for the largest area possible, regardless of the wishes of minorities. In fact, the defenders of Munich were proved right by events much later in the century because Czechoslovakia no longer exists. When the State became a democracy, upon the fall of the Iron Curtain, Slovakia quickly decided to go its separate way.

The problem of the German minority had previously been solved in 1945 by expelling them as a race, a step which in 1919 would have been considered so barbarous that no self-respecting state would have contemplated it. Eleanor Rathbone, an independent British MP and a moderate feminist, was one of the few Britons who were prepared to criticise the expulsion of 2,500,000 people of German origin from Czechoslovakia during the winter months of 1946 because it might create large-scale starvation. This was in a speech to the House of Commons on 15 October 1945. Although it was not mentioned, some of these Germans had been anti-Nazi. Later, Eleanor Rathbone achieved limited success, because the Minister agreed not to deport pregnant women or young children during the winter months.[63]

---

[61] *Economist*, 24 July 1937, p.183

[62] *Hansard*, HC vol.339, 3 October 1938, 80

[63] A sympathetic view for those expelled; see *Hansard*, vol. 417, 26 October 1945, 766

There can be no doubt that Sheinis is correct when he states that Litvinov sought to avert an invasion of Czechoslovakia. Sheinis presumably quotes from Schulenburg's notes of a meeting with Litvinov on 22 August 1938, incorrectly stated by Sheinis to be 26 August 1938. Litvinov could not have been more supportive of Britain and France. Litvinov told Schulenburg that if Czechoslovakia was attacked, 'it was certain that France would attack Germany and Great Britain would be at France's side.' Litvinov was indeed blunt with Schulenburg. Litvinov told Schulenburg:

> In no circumstances would Czechoslovakia attack Germany. Even the wildest Czech hothead did not want war or to attack Germany. She was not so concerned about the Sudeten Germans. She (Germany) aimed at the annihilation of Czechoslovakia as a whole. She wanted to conquer the country. Naturally, Germany preferred to achieve her end by peaceful means. War was always a risk.

Litvinov rightly understood Germany's motives. Schulenburg criticised Litvinov for not telling Schulenburg 'what would be the form of possible Soviet help to Czechoslovakia', but Litvinov would have been crazy to disclose to a potential enemy the Soviet Union's military tactics.

Sheinis said that Litvinov told Schulenburg: 'The people of Czechoslovakia will fight for their independence as one man. We too will live up to our commitments to Czechoslovakia.' Nowhere does this appear in Schulenburg's text. It is uncertain what Sheinis hoped to achieve by misquoting the text. Litvinov told Schulenburg:

> If, however, it came to war, Germany would clearly be an unprovoked aggressor. It was certain that France would mobilise and Britain would follow France's lead. The British Government would no longer retreat, even if Chamberlain wanted to do so. The Soviet Union had promised Czechoslovakia her support. She would keep her word and do her best.[64]

However, what Litvinov did not disclose was that, under the Soviet Union's treaty with Czechoslovakia, the Soviet Union was only bound to fight if France did. It was perfectly reasonable for Litvinov to have previously negotiated this condition because there were many on the Right in Europe who would have been delighted to have embroiled the Soviet Union, fighting alone, in a war with Germany in order to weaken both the USSR and Germany. However, it was Czechoslovakia that insisted upon the above condition because Czechoslovakia did not want to be drawn into a war on the Soviet Union's side unless France was also participating.

On 16 September 1938 Fischer asked Litvinov (Fischer, as always, was obsessed with Spain) what Litvinov hoped would transpire in Spain if a European war broke out.

---

[64] *Documents on German Foreign Policy*, Series D, vol.2, p.629; Sheinis Zinovy *Maxim Litvinov* p. 290

Litvinov said he hoped France would send troops to Spain and Britain would do likewise (although I personally would have thought that the troops would be better employed elsewhere), but ended his conversation with Fischer as follows: 'There will be no war. Britain and France have sold out Czechoslovakia.'[65] These comments are consistent with what Andrew Rothstein recollected when he saw Litvinov on 1 September, and asked him what he thought would happen to Czechoslovakia. Litvinov said, 'Britain would sell the Czechs down the river.' [66]

Although it appears that Litvinov was uncertain whether France and Britain would resist Germany, he clearly did his best to deter Germany from attacking Czechoslovakia, for which Litvinov should be praised. If Litvinov had been instructed by Stalin to try and embroil France, Britain and Germany in a war so that the Soviet Union could sit on the sidelines and reap the benefit, I do not think Litvinov would have been so enthusiastic about deterring Germany.

In September 1938 Litvinov spoke to Jean Payart, the French chargé d'affaires. Litvinov pointed out that, under the existing treaty, France was obliged to aid Czechoslovakia in the event of a German attack, and he suggested that military experts of the three countries should gather and discuss military aid in order 'to defend Czechoslovakia in common; there must be preliminary discussion of how to do it.' He added: 'We are ready for it, but France turned the suggestion down.'[67] Chamberlain showed no enthusiasm for such a conference.

However, I believe that, had such a conference taken place, the Soviet Union would not have wanted to participate in defending Czechoslovakia. It would have become clear that France had no intention of mounting an offensive against Germany but would, as happened when Poland was invaded, have stayed behind the safety of the Maginot Line. Neither did Czechoslovakia show any enthusiasm for Soviet assistance if France was not prepared to fight. Eubank, in *Summit Conferences*, correctly stated that the critics of Munich assumed the Soviet Union would have been prepared to enforce the Versailles Treaty while French troops sat secure and safe within the Maginot Line. Eubank also stated that France had the means to attack Germany, but she had prepared no plans to do so.[68] However, France's best chance of victory was to attack Germany while the German army was occupied in an attack on Czechoslovakia.

Britain had no plans to attack Germany in 1938 because it had neither the army to give material help nor the air force, unlike in 1939. When senior British Cabinet ministers asked the French how they were going to prevent the Czechs being overrun, Daladier, the French

---

[65] Fischer, Louis: *Men and Politics*, p.529
[66] Sheinis Zinovy *Maxim Litvinov* p. 290
[67] Ibid.
[68] Eubank, Keith: *Summit Conferences 1919 to 1960*, p.48

Prime Minister, evaded the question, but instead asked of his British friends three questions: 'Would the British accept Hitler's plans? If not, would they bring pressure on the Czech Government to concede [against their wishes] or should France do nothing?' However, the questions were futile if there was no plan to save Czechoslovakia, in spite of the criticisms of Churchill, Attlee and Litvinov.

When Gamelin had a meeting with the British Minister of Co-ordination of Defence, Inskip, all Gamelin said was that he thought the Czechs could: 'hold out only for weeks, but not for months. He expected no effective help would come from the Soviet Union because of Polish and Rumanian opposition to the transit of Soviet troops.'[69] As Gamelin failed to reveal any plans for the French Army to save Czechoslovakia by attacking Germany, it was reasonable for the British Cabinet to assume there were no plans.

I cannot see that Litvinov would have been prepared to have recommended to Stalin that the Soviet Union participate in the defence of Czechoslovakia in these circumstances. Further, the Soviet Union had no common frontier with Czechoslovakia, so it needed to cross either Poland or Rumania and consent for this from the relevant countries was unlikely to be forthcoming.

The anti-Chamberlain lobby has always stated that, if Britain and France had fought Germany in 1938, the German generals would have been willing to oppose Hitler. As Eubank states: 'Their past record does not make them worthy of trust.'[70]

On 16 September 1938 Litvinov confirmed to Fischer that Poland would in no way give permission for Soviet troops to cross their territory and Litvinov estimated it would take the Soviets a month to force their way through Poland.[71] Poland had its own agenda. She was waiting for the opportunity to seize Teschen, which was a part of Czechoslovakia and had in its population many Poles.

Concerning Rumania, Fischer stated that on 11 September 1938 Litvinov met, among others, the Rumanian Foreign Minister, Nicolae Petrescu-Comnen, and the French Foreign Minister, Bonnet, at Geneva. Fischer claims that on that day the Rumanian Foreign Minister gave transit rights for Soviet troops and weapons. However, Bonnet did not disclose this at a Cabinet meeting the next day. Then later Fischer contradicts himself by stating: 'The Rumanians, not so hostile to the Czechs, would probably let us (Soviet troops) pass.' Would the Soviet troops which had to be transported by train through the Carpathian Mountains (as Churchill suggested) have arrived in time to be effective?[72] Even

---

[69] Eubank, Keith: *Munich*, p.172
[70] Eubank, Keith: *Summit Conferences 1919 to 1960*, p.48
[71] Fischer, Louis: *Men and Politics*, p.529
[72] Churchill, Winston: *The Second World War*, vol.1, '*Gathering Storm*', p.239

if Rumania had consented, Litvinov admitted: 'The railroads were poor and Soviet heavy tanks would have difficulty on poor bridges and highways.'[73]

Churchill also dwells on a pessimistic report of the German Army mentioning among other matters the deficiency of the German defences on the German-French frontier.[74] However, as France had no plans to invade Germany, this was irrelevant. As with Poland in 1939, Czechoslovakia would have been conquered by German troops.

Litvinov stated that help could come from the air, but doubt is cast on this assertion by the situation during the Winter War, when Finland was able to contain the Russian air force. At the beginning of the Winter War, the Red Air Force had 900 aircraft on the frontier, opposed by less than 100 Finnish aircraft; yet the Red Air Force lost at least 700 planes compared with Finnish losses of between 60 and 70.[75] In 1938 the Luftwaffe was vastly superior to the Soviet air force and, as the Finnish air force was able to inflict heavy losses on the Soviet air force, the Luftwaffe might have quickly annihilated any Soviet air force sent to Czechoslovakia.

In 1948 the USA Government permitted the publication of the communications before and during the period of the Nazi-Soviet Pact. In retaliation, the Soviet Government published documents showing the willingness of the British and French Governments to appease Germany before the Second World War. I refer to them as 'Soviet documents.' Unless I indicate otherwise, I believe they are genuine and this description applies to most of them. The 'Soviet documents' claim that Stalin told Gottwald, 'The USSR would render military assistance to Czechoslovakia, even without French participation, if Czechoslovakia defended herself and required assistance.'[76] However, I believe that statement is untrue. It is contrary to what Litvinov said at the time and it would have been most unwise for the Soviet Union to allow itself to be embroiled in a war with Nazi Germany in which France and Britain were not involved.

Many references have been made to the fact that the boundary between the area where the Sudeten Germans were living and Germany was the best fortified in Europe. This was totally irrelevant, as, with Austria in German hands, Czechoslovakia could be attacked from the rear. If Czechoslovakia had fought, it might have assisted Britain, France and the Soviet Union, but it would not have benefited Czechoslovakia. There were various predictions of how long it would take the German army to defeat the Czechs, but none of the predictions contemplated that the Czech army would ultimately have been successful. Masaryk predicted two months, Churchill three months and, according to Beria's son, his

---

[73] Fischer, Louis: *Man and Politics*, p.529
[74] Ibid. p.282
[75] *Fischer Louis Men and Politics*, p.529; Boyd, Alexander: *The Soviet Air Force Since 1918*, p.90
[76] Maisky, Ivan: *Who Helped Hitler?*, p.79; Gromyko, Andrei: *Soviet Peace Efforts on the Eve of World War 2*, p.577

father predicted at least six months.[77] Six months of modern warfare in a small country like Czechoslovakia would have left her devastated.

Before Chamberlain left for Munich he received the following report. At the Expansion Progress meeting on 27 September 1938, the Air Member for Supply and Organisation said:

> We have in the past few years been building an air force that is nothing but a façade. We had nothing in the way of reserves or organisation behind the front lines with which to maintain it.[78]

Was not Chamberlain right not to go to war in 1938 in view of that report.

Churchill agrees that Britain had five squadrons of Hurricanes and there was no reserve of parts for older aircraft since they were shortly to be replaced. Between 1939 and 1940 the British air force increased by 80%, whereas the German air force increased only by 20%.

Churchill rightly states that in 1938, as Germany had not occupied the Low Countries, there was no possibility of a decisive Battle of Britain. However, Churchill further admits that in 1938 London was defenceless against German air attack, but assumes that Londoners should have been prepared to suffer such bombing for the sake of Czechoslovakia. It is questionable whether the majority of Londoners would have agreed with Churchill.[79]

On 23 September 1938 De La Warr, the British Lord Privy Seal, and Maisky met Litvinov, and, according to Maisky, Litvinov reiterated that, if Britain wanted to participate in the conflict, a conference should be convened to work out a common plan. De La Warr suggested London, to which Litvinov consented. De La Warr expressed satisfaction with the proposals for the conference and said he must report back to London and talk about other details when a reply was received from London. Litvinov heard no more because of the Munich agreement.[80]

The Soviet Union made the first gesture towards the defence of Czechoslovakia by sending a number of bombers to Czechoslovakia over Rumanian territory, thereby infringing both Rumanian and Polish airspace.[81]

---

[77] Amery, Leopold: *Empire at Bay*, 24 September 1938 p.514 ; Churchill, Winston: *The Second World War*, vol.1, '*Gathering Storm*', p.246; Beria, Sergo: *My Father*, p.49

[78] Paper in archives of RAF Museum Hendon: 'Expansion of Royal Air Force', p.74

[79] Churchill, Winston: *The Second World War, vol.1, 'Gathering Storm'*, p.265

[80] Letter to the *Times*, 8 June 1971, p. 13

[81] Budurowycz, Bohdan: *Polish-Soviet Relations*, p.116

Beck, the Polish Foreign Minister, stated that the Soviet Union:

> during the critical days of September 1938, made, at our frontier in the Minsk Litovsk area, a somewhat theatrical military demonstration. Units of two army corps were moved from their garrison with a great number of motorised and armoured units marching in the direction of our frontier. I would not call it a serious demonstration, as it was known that no real mobilisation had been carried out, and in order to bring the cadres of the frontier Army corps up to establishment, the Soviet Government had to bring up 150 officers and non-commissioned ranks from other garrisons.[82]

Incidentally, Beck does not mention that neither France nor Britain had made a more serious attempt to mobilise and place their fighting services on a war basis.

In September 1938 Litvinov went to the League of Nations Assembly for the last time. He said:

> We abstained from all advice to the Czechoslovakian Government considering [it is] quite inadmissible that it should be asked to make concessions to the Germans to the detriment of its interests as a state. [The Soviet Government intends] to fulfil its obligations under the Pact and together with France to afford assistance to Czechoslovakia by the ways open to us. Our war department is ready to participate immediately in a conference with the French and Czechoslovak war departments in order to discuss the measures appropriate to the moment.[83]

Litvinov could not have made the Soviet position clearer, but the one person to whom this was not sweet music was Chamberlain. If the Red Army could prove to be an effective fighting unit, and in 1938, in spite of the purges, they defeated the Japanese army in the Far East, Chamberlain's belief that the Soviet Union could never make a reliable ally would be in tatters.

However, Sheinis makes the claim that Britain and France, 'blinded by their hatred of the Soviet Union, had betrayed the cause of peace in Europe.'[84] Sheinis did not mention that the British Government faced a number of problems if Britain had gone to war in 1938 over Czechoslovakia, particularly military weakness.

In 1970 Lord Butler's (RAB Butler) autobiography, *The Art of the Possible*, contains the assertion that 'the Soviet Union did not mean business. Litvinov had been deliberately

---

[82] Beck, Josef: *Final Report*, p.168
[83] Litvinov speech, 21 September 1938; Degras, Jane: *Soviet Documents on Foreign Policy*, pp.299 to 303
[84] Sheinis, Zinovy: *Maxim Litvinov*, p.290

evasive and vague', except when he said: 'If France acted, the Soviet Union would act too.'[85]

Lord Butler then quotes Wheeler-Bennett's argument that Munich was inevitable, giving as only one reason: 'The uncertainty whether the Soviet Union would fight.' I believe Lord Butler distorted what Wheeler-Bennett said because he states that the fundamental weakness of those opposed to Britain accepting the terms of the Munich agreement was because:

> No member of the House was sufficiently certain of himself to stand up in his place, with one exception, Duff Cooper, to say that the terms of the Munich agreement should be rejected at the price of war because no member of the House was sufficiently assured that the people of Great Britain would have endorsed such a rejection.[86]

However, from what Maisky states, and this is supported by other evidence, it was Britain not the Soviet Union which was devious, because Litvinov could not have made it clearer that the Soviet Union was prepared to fight. In this situation the most sensible course would have been to find out what help the Soviet Union could give. [87] Lord Butler's above comment was highly misleading, as he himself then refers to another reason for not opposing Hitler in 1938 – Britain's weakness in the air due to modernisation. 'Britain had only one fighter squadron with Spitfires and five in the process of being equipped with Hurricanes.'[88]

It was hardly surprising that Maisky was indignant, and on 8 June 1971 he wrote to the *Times* claiming:

1. Thirty [Soviet Union] infantry divisions had been deployed to areas adjoining the Soviet border. The same had been done in respect of cavalry divisions.
2. Units have correspondingly been plenished with reserves.
3. As regards our technical troops, air and armour units, they were in full readiness.[89]

On 11 October 1938 Lord Winterton made a public speech in which he explained: 'The concessions by the British and French to Hitler were inevitable because of the military weakness of the Soviet Union and its inability and therefore unwillingness to fulfil its

---

[85] Butler, R A B: *Art of the Possible*, p.70
[86] Wheeler-Bennett, John: *Munich, Prologue to Tragedy*, p184
[87] See Ch.19, No.55
[88] See nos, 78 and 79 ante
[89] Letter to the *Times*, 8 June 1971, p.13

obligations under the pact of mutual assistance with France concerning the defence of Czechoslovakia.'[90] It is difficult to think of another case where a Minister of the British Crown has deliberately told such a blatant lie concerning foreign affairs. Britain was also weak and it is unjust to complain about the Soviet Union when she had offered help and Britain had not been prepared to ascertain the nature of the help offered and whether or not it would have been effective.

Walters rightly states: The Soviet delegation stood out as champions of the victims of German, Italian and Japanese violence and as a protagonist of that considerable minority of League Members who demanded the maintenance of the covenant.[91]

Molotov, although he lacked Litvinov's eloquence and passion, supported the policy of his enemy Litvinov. Molotov blamed France 'because it denounced its treaty with Czechoslovakia and also France, Britain, Germany and Italy for getting together to defeat little Czechoslovakia.' He referred to German imperialism and stated: 'This does not mean the small and large robbers are satisfied. On the contrary, it only makes their appetites larger.'

However, in just over a year Molotov would be praising Germany. Molotov then, in very much the manner of Litvinov, argued that the Munich agreement was against Britain's and France's interests. Molotov asks: 'Have Britain and France gained greater respect for their rights in the eyes of German and Italian fascism? Rather the contrary; their international authority has been considerably shaken.'[92] Churchill would have approved of such language. The small robbers were Poland and Hungary, who had taken advantage of the situation to seize Czechoslovakian territory.

Maisky had every right to be indignant that, as the Soviet ambassador, he was virtually ignored during the Munich crisis, which must have been humiliating for Litvinov in Moscow. This showed to Stalin, in spite of Litvinov's efforts, that he was not accepted by France and Britain as in any way equal.[93] Chamberlain thought he was clever in excluding the Soviet Union from meaningful dialogue during the Munich conference, but the exact opposite was the true position.

Nothing would have frightened Germany more than being faced with an alliance involving the Soviet Union, Britain and France. In fact, the Munich conference benefited the Soviet Union. Upon the failure of the Munich agreement it was a propaganda victory for the Soviet Union because, as she had been ignored, she was not responsible for the consequences.

---

[90] Maisky, Ivan: *Who Helped Hitler?* p.88
[91] Walters, Francis: *History of the League of Nations*, p.783
[92] Molotov speech, in Degras, Jane: *Soviet Documents on Foreign Policy*, vol.3, pp.308 @ 310
[93] Ibid. p.307

The Soviet Union's admirers did not want to know about the cruelty practiced by Stalin. In the first post war election 38% supported the Communist Party the highest in Western Europe. [94] If Stalin's main aim, as Marx had envisaged, was to spread the dictatorship of the proletariat throughout Europe rather than promote Soviet interests, the jovial and engaging Litvinov, rather than the dour Molotov, would have been Communism's best ambassador. Of course, the Soviet Union's prestige was subsequently severely damaged when the Soviet Union signed the Nazi-Soviet Pact. It is therefore a mystery why the Czech people seemed to put more trust in Stalin than Britain or France.

However, not all of the Left were blameless. The British Labour Party was inept in pretending they were supported by Churchill in placing all the blame on Chamberlain while ignoring Churchill's other criticism of the failure of the Chamberlain Government to adequately re-arm.[95] Churchill said:

> The plea so often advanced that this was because they [the Labour Party] did not like the foreign policy, was feeble, for no foreign policy can have validity if there is no adequate force behind it.

Most Czechs should be grateful to the appeasers, whom they had despised so much. If war had broken out in 1938, Czechoslovakia would have borne the brunt of the conflict. Poland fought and lost six million people, 20% of its population, although this figure was so high because of the large Jewish population, which was liquidated. Only 100,000 Czechs died. Kennan, who was then in the US Embassy in Prague and became the American ambassador to the Soviet Union, stated:

> The benefit of the Munich agreement was that it has preserved for the exacting task of the future a magnificent younger generation disciplined, industrious and physically fit that would have undoubtedly been sacrificed if the solution had been the romantic one of hopeless resistance rather than the humiliating but the true heroic one of realism.[96]

Further, the Czechs would not practise what they preached. Having criticised appeasement so vigorously, Benes and Masaryk capitulated to Stalin in 1948 in the same way that they complained Chamberlain had capitulated to Hitler at Munich. Benes said to the Russians:

> The only salvation lies in a close alliance with your country. The Czechs may have different political opinions, but on one point we can be sure. The Soviet Union not only liberate us from the Germans. It will also allow us to live without constant

---

[94] Mamatey Victor: *History of the Czechoslovak Republic.* p. 404
[95] Churchill, Winston: *The Second World War*, vol.1, 'Gathering Storm', p.294
[96] Kennan, George: *Memoirs*, p.95

fear of the future. [97]

Finland was wiser, by keeping their distance from any major power, so after the Second World War, they kept their freedom whereas the exact opposite happened to Czechoslovakia.

When Czechoslovakia wanted only to consider applying for, but not accepting, Marshall Aid, the Czech leaders were summoned to Moscow to see Stalin and were told that unless they ceased participation in the Marshall Aid talks they were no friends of Moscow. Instead of telling Stalin that they were a sovereign state which was not going to be bullied, unlike Tito, they meekly complied.[98] Benes completely misunderstood the nature of Stalin's Soviet Union, the result being Czechoslovakia lost its independence for forty years.

When Britain and France declared war on Germany on 3 September 1939,

> it first awakened hopes among the Czech people for an early end of their subjugation. These hopes were dampened by the unexpected defeat of the Polish army. On the other hand, Czechs showed some satisfaction for Poland's collapse and the suffering of the Polish people.

This was because of the Polish decision to take advantage at Munich to the detriment of Czechoslovakia. This seemed to 'justify the Czech attitude of non-resistance by which freedom might have been lost but the country was left undamaged.'[99]

The essence of the Munich agreement was that the land in which the Sudeten Germans mainly lived should be transferred to Germany upon Britain, France, Germany and Italy giving a guarantee to safeguard the independence of the remaining territory of Czechoslovakia.[100]

On 4 October 1938, in the House of Commons, Inskip, Minister for Co-ordination of Defence, was asked, rightly, 'Whether the guarantee was to be joint and several?' He failed to answer the question and oddly was not pressed to do so by Mander, the Liberal MP who asked the question, or by any other MP. However Inskip did say that until the guarantee was drawn up it was not in force, but then gave the misleading answer that the Government felt 'a moral obligation to take steps to ensure the integrity of Czechoslovakia should be preserved.' [101]

---

[97] Ehrenburg Ilya *War Years* p.130
[98] BBC programme, 'Cold War', 1998
[99] Mamatey, Victor: *History of the Czechoslovak Republic,* p.306; and 97 *ante*
[100] Munich Agreement *Documents,* 1938, pp.214 and 289-290
[101] *Hansard* HC vol 339 4 October 1938 303

In the House of Lords, Lord Snell, the Labour peer, asked a number of questions of the Earl of Plymouth in the absence of Lord Halifax, the Secretary of State for Foreign Affairs. Lord Snell first asked: 'Whether the new frontiers may now be considered as finally fixed?' The reply was 'The frontiers between Czechoslovakia and Poland had now been definitely fixed.' However, the frontiers of Czechoslovakia with Germany and Hungary, 'though generally settled, [were] not finally fixed.'

> Since the new frontiers of Czechoslovakia are not yet been definitely fixed, the undertaking of Germany and Italy to guarantee Czechoslovakia has not taken effect; nor has there been any exchanges of views between the two governments as to the manner in which the guarantee would be combined and as to the conditions in which they shall operate.

However, the fact that two and a half months had passed since the Munich debate and the British Government had done nothing about the guarantee is evidence that the statement that a meaningful guarantee would be given was not made in good faith.

When the Earl of Plymouth was asked: 'When the guarantee by this Country of the new frontier will come into operation', the answer was: 'Many questions remain to be settled regarding the system of guarantees to be set up in favour of Czechoslovakia', although the Munich agreement had been sold to the British public clearly on the basis that the frontiers would be guaranteed by Britain, France, Germany and Italy. The Earl of Plymouth was asked: 'Whether the guarantee would be joint or several or joint and several', but he evaded answering the question, like Inskip in the Commons. Again, the Earl of Plymouth was not pressed to answer the question properly.

The final question with regard to Munich was: 'Whether the Governments of Her Majesty's Dominions beyond the seas' had been consulted. The Earl of Plymouth stated that, immediately after the Anglo-French proposal, the Dominions had been informed 'of the proposed participation of HM Government in an international guarantee of the new boundaries of the Czechoslovak State against unprovoked aggression', implying there would be an international guarantee by the British Government.[102]

One of the main defences of the Munich agreement was that, although Sudetenland had been surrendered to Germany, the British and French guarantee increased Czech security for the remainder of its territory. However, Britain was insisting on a guarantee jointly with Germany and Italy. If the guarantee was not operative, unless all the participants to the Munich agreement agreed, the Government was guilty of gravely misleading Czechoslovakia and the British public, because the guarantee clearly lacked substance. Harvey's diary discloses that the French wanted to give it 'at once and make it

---

[102] *Hansard*, HL vol.111, 17 November 1938, 119

individual',[103] but the British Government overruled the French Government, who did not press the point. Maisky was absolutely right when, on 25 November 1938, he stated:

> Despite the Munich agreement, Britain and France have in the last two months taken no step whatever in resolving the fate of Czechoslovakia. Germany and Italy have been given complete freedom of action in determining the boundaries of Czechoslovakia. … Official circles made no mention of Britain and France guaranteeing Czechoslovakia's boundaries. It is my impression that Chamberlain is laying the groundwork for a refusal to fulfil his obligation and is merely seeking a suitable form in which to do so.[104]

However, it is surprising that the only other Soviet leader to criticise Britain and France for failure to give the guarantee was Molotov. He commented that 'a division of Czechoslovak territory was made recently in Vienna without Britain and France.'[105]

In its leader on 3 January 1952, reflecting on the death of Litvinov, the *Times* rightly pointed out that it was Munich which was the dividing line. For some years 'instructions from the Politburo' and Litvinov's 'beliefs' ran together, but, after being sidelined at Munich, Soviet foreign policy prioritised its own security over the prevention of war. Soviet policy was

> to uphold the Litvinov foreign policy in keeping in touch with France and Britain, while at the same time dropping hints that the Soviet Union would consider an agreement with Hitler. … Even so, Stalin's mind was by no means made up. Stalin only reached a decision when war was clearly imminent and when the Western powers could not agree to give the Soviet Union the bases and right of passage in Eastern European countries which she demanded as the condition of an alliance.[106]

Bearing in mind Stalin's ruthless leadership, the British Cabinet, by not showing more enthusiasm for Litvinov's policies and failing to liaise with him at the time of Munich, helped to bring about the downfall of Litvinov. This may not have been apparent to them. It was unwise of them to undermine the person who was their best hope in the Soviet leadership. Litvinov had lived in England, his wife was English, and he was the most pro-Western Foreign Minister that the Soviet Union was likely to produce.

One person who was not concerned with the sidelining of Litvinov at Munich and the consequent threat to Litvinov's position, if not his life, was Chamberlain. *The New York Times* aptly stated, following Munich:

---

[103] Harvey, Oliver: *Diplomatic Diaries*, p.224

[104] Soviet Documents, 29, p.90, 25 November 1938

[105] Speech, 6 November 1938, in Degras, Jane: *Soviet Documents on Foreign Policy*, vol . 3 pp.308 and 310

[106] *Times*, 3 January 1952, p.5

> Litvinov is the father of the Russian-Czech alliance and her [the Soviet] entry into the League of Nations whereby he hoped to connect with Britain. On the face of things, the September events dealt him a severe blow. Not only is his position imperilled, but he risks the purge. Litvinov can now point out in Paris that if he returns to Moscow empty-handed, Britain and France risk losing their best friend in Moscow and the other school, which prefers an understanding with Germany, may now get control, denounce the Russian-French alliance and make a deal with Berlin. Litvinov may ask for how long Hitler may consult Mr Chamberlain once Germany has not only obtained Mittel-Europe and can draw on the Soviet Union's great resources?[107]

On 16 October 1938 Litvinov, to show his annoyance at what he saw as the capitulation of the Allies, stated, 'Henceforth the USSR only has to watch, from the shelter of its own frontiers, the establishment of German hegemony over central and south-eastern Europe.' He then went on to say that he had made the following remark to Lord Halifax:

> Once Germany's hegemony is solidly established in Europe and France neutralised, Germany will be able to attack either Great Britain or the USSR. She will choose Britain because it would offer a much greater advantage with the opportunity of substituting the German Empire for the British Empire and to succeed in this undertaking he will prefer to reach an understanding between USSR and Germany.

Litvinov said the same to Cripps.[108]

Britain and the Soviet Union shared common ground in their opposition to the fact that Poland had taken short-term advantage of the Munich crisis and seized Teschen. They took the same line once the *fait accompli* had been established, and Teschen had been incorporated into Poland. Not long after the handover, Litvinov was eager to forgive Poland for its wicked behaviour, one of Litvinov's worst actions in such a distinguished career. Potemkin arranged a meeting between Litvinov and the Polish ambassador to the Soviet Union, Grzybowski. On 26 November a joint communiqué was released simultaneously in both capitals. It stated: 'Relations between Poland and the Soviet Union would continue to be based on the existing agreements and that the two governments were also favourably disposed to the extension of the commercial intercourse between the two countries.' It also agreed: 'To settle some current and long outstanding difficulties between the two countries.'[109] Thus, Litvinov had performed a complete U-turn by first condemning and then accepting the annexation of Teschen by Poland. Czechoslovakia must have felt sorrow at the desertion of her ally, the Soviet Union.

---

[107] *The New York Times*, 2 October 1938, p.32
[108] Craig, Gordon: *Diplomats 1919-1939*, p.363; Estorick, Eric: *Stafford Cripps*, p.281.
[109] Budurowycz, Bohdan: *Polish-Soviet Relations,* p.130

Peculiarly, what Hilger describes as 'an oral understanding' was made in October 1938, that both the German and Soviet press and radio should henceforth restrain themselves and cease attacking each other. Schulenburg, the German ambassador to the Soviet Union, was the prime mover, and when the proposal was mentioned to Litvinov, it appeared to fall on fertile ground. There is no indication that Litvinov did not support it and Stalin gave his approval. Hilger believes his readiness to agree was the direct result of the Munich agreement.[110] Perhaps Litvinov intended it to be a warning to Britain and France that they should not take co-operation from the Soviet Union for granted.

Walters stated:

> After Munich and after the passive acceptance of defeat that characterised that assembly [of the League of Nations], the Soviet Government concluded it was useless to look to Geneva any longer. No spectacular change took place at first. Soviet experts found themselves unable to attend the meetings of the League committee to which they belonged. If a Soviet committee member died or resigned, it was indicated that Moscow did not desire the vacancy should be filled for the time being.

Litvinov did not attend the Council meeting in January 1939.[111] There is every indication that Litvinov and Stalin were still not far apart in their thinking. The common ground would appear to be that both men were agreed on the necessity of keeping in touch with Germany, however difficult or frustrating this was, because of the danger of Britain and Germany coming to some understanding, such as at Munich. The greatest danger to the Soviet Union lay in the possibility of an agreement between Germany and Britain, so that Germany would be free to attack the Soviet Union. In spite of all the rhetoric from Soviet sources, I believe the Left wing in Britain was strong enough to prevent any actual British encouragement of a German war against the USSR, or any assistance to Germany should such a war break out.

On 5 January 1939 the former German ambassador in Moscow, Rudolf Nadolny, and the Commercial Counsellor approached Merekalov, Russian ambassador in Berlin, and asked if negotiations with Germany for a 200 million mark credit agreement, suspended in March 1938, could be resumed. Merekalov returned to Moscow for instructions. On 8 January Mikoyan, the Soviet Commissioner for External Trade, replied that the Soviet Government was prepared to renew credit negotiations based on conditions proposed by Germany. Mikoyan suggested negotiations take place in Moscow. On 6 January Merekalov accordingly conveyed to Wiehl, the director of the Economics Section of the German Foreign Ministry, the instructions that Merekalov had received from Moscow. Wiehl was pleased with the news and said he would take further instructions from his superiors. On 17

---

[110] Hilger, Gustav: *Incompatible Allies*, p.289
[111] Walters, Francis: *History of the League of Nations*, p.783

January 1939 Merekalov returned to see Wiehl and Schnurre, when it was announced that Schnurre would go to Moscow at the end of January 1939.[112]

As was normal, Hitler received the diplomatic corps in January 1939 and observers noted he chatted with Merekalov longer than with any other diplomat. Merekalov reported back that Hitler greeted him and asked about living in Berlin, his family and his recent trip to Moscow. The German leader wished him success. Other government ministers and officials limited themselves to polite conversation.[113]

As Chamberlain saw no reason to form any alliance with the Soviet Union, he could not contemplate that Hitler might form an alliance with the Soviet Union. His erroneous assessment was that such talk was propaganda created either by his political opponents or by the Soviet Union. On 9 January 1939 Chamberlain wrote to his sister, informing her: 'He refused to abandon his policy of appeasement with Germany and adopt Winston's policy of a grand coalition against Germany.'[114]

However, in a speech at Llandudno, Lloyd George criticised Chamberlain:

> The Soviet Union was never approached. Surely this is not because of any aversion to authoritarian states. The Prime Minister has been cringing and crawling before dictators for months. The supreme diplomatic imbecility of snubbing the Soviet Union ought to be repaired without loss of time.[115]

Lloyd George might have been encouraged to use the words 'without loss of time' by the warm greetings Hitler bestowed on the Soviet ambassador.[116]

On 11 January 1939 Litvinov wrote to his ambassador:

> The fact that France and England would like to prod Germany to take action in the East is well known and is understandable. It is also true that they would like to direct Germany exclusively against us so that Poland would not be affected. Bonnet would like to isolate us from Poland.[117]

The friendly reception given by Hitler to Merekalov was probably the reason for the report in the *Sunday Pictorial* on 23 January 1939:

---

[112] Carley, Michael: *1939*, p.90

[113] Carley, Michael *1939*, p.89; Schuman, Frederick: *Night Over Europe*, p.278

[114] Taylor, A J P (editor): *Lloyd George, 12 Essays*, p.338

[115] Taylor, A J P (editor): *Lloyd George, 12 Essays*, p.337

[116] See No. 113 *ante*

[117] *Soviet Peace Efforts*, No.54, p.124, 11 January 1939

While the world awaits Hitler's most spectacular move, the Nazi leader, with his eyes on complete European domination, is planning in secret an alliance with the Soviet Union, Britain's ally in the last war. The plan is fast taking shape. This week Soviet and Nazi representatives will meet in a Scandinavian capital, probably in Stockholm. A definite approach was made to the Soviet Union by Hitler last week, after a reception in Berlin for foreign diplomats. The Fuhrer summoned the Soviet ambassador and had a forty minute talk with him. Hitler asked the minister to convey a personal message to Stalin, expressing a desire for negotiations between Berlin and Moscow. Nothing was disclosed in Berlin or Moscow, but two days later it was announced that Litvinov, the Soviet foreign minister, would not be able to attend the League of Nations meeting at Geneva as his presence in Moscow was indispensable. Significantly since then, attacks on Soviet Russia in the Nazi press have disappeared. Britain, France and the USA have come in for a heavy share of vituperation, but not a word is said against Stalin or Soviet policy. Hitler's decision to approach the Soviet Union was taken immediately after the Munich agreement. The Fuhrer knew that Stalin was bitterly disappointed with the attempted co-operation with Western democracies during the Czechoslovakian crisis. Herr Von Rosenberg, Hitler's advisor on Soviet affairs, reported to his leader that Stalin was faced with a choice of two policies. The first choice was to withdraw from European politics and seek closer co-operation with the USA. The second course was to forget ideological differences and try and come to terms with Germany and Italy. Secret agents informed the Nazi leader that many Soviet politicians favoured Soviet-US friendship. Hitler chose again his favourite weapon – the weapon that he had successfully wielded in the past – intimidation. The Ukrainian problem with heavy implications for Soviet Russia was pushed to the foreground. For weeks everybody believed that Hitler was planning an anti-Soviet campaign. Then, on 12 January, the Soviet Minister in Berlin was informed that Germany had no intention of invading the Ukraine. The secret negotiations in Scandinavia will be of a preliminary character. If negotiations proceed smoothly, Hitler will make a friendly gesture towards the Soviet Union in his speech before the Reichstag on 30 January.[118]

On 28 January 1939 the *News Chronicle* published an article by one of their correspondents, Bartlett, on the danger of German-Soviet rapprochement. This stated correctly:

The refusal to treat Russia as a potential friend of great military importance has had a bad effect on Moscow and looked back to 1922, when the failure to treat Russia on the basis of equality led to Rapallo. Especially, there is the belief in the City that

---

[118] *Sunday Pictorial*, 23 January 1939, p.1

if Germany indulges in the adventures they will take place in the East of Europe. This is highly improbable because Germany's only hope in the case of war would be a quick and sudden victory and no amount of wishful thinking can lead one to believe a lightning victory could be obtained over such a large and amorphous country as the Soviet Union.[119]

As Maisky knew Bartlett, the *News Chronicle* journalist who wrote the article, this could have been inspired by Maisky, who may have been acting on the instructions of Litvinov – to warn the British and French of the danger of a German-Russian rapprochement. This article may have been the reason why the Schnurre trip to Moscow was unexpectedly cancelled.[120]

Nevertheless, Chamberlain continued to consider that such action was a manoeuvre by those who opposed his policy of appeasement. Certainly, Cadogan took the warnings more seriously. He stated on 1 February: 'It seems to me that we must watch very carefully the development of any tendency towards a rapprochement between Germany and the Soviets.'[121]

On 19 February 1939 Litvinov wrote to Maisky in response to his assertion that opposition to appeasement was growing. Litvinov wrote that 'Britain and France had decided to avoid war in the coming years at all costs and I would say at any price'; but then admitted he might be wrong, by stating: 'I am making no claim that my diagnosis is absolutely correct. Any surprises are possible.'[122] From time to time, unlike most Soviet Communists, Litvinov was prepared to admit he could be wrong. Even Chamberlain was having a slight doubt about whether the policy of excluding the Soviet Union was sensible, because Britain suggested a visit to the Soviet Union by Hudson, a Trade Minister, in March 1939.

Therefore, in accordance with his instructions, on 19 February 1939 Seeds informed Litvinov: 'The British Government had decided to send Hudson, the Parliamentary Secretary to the Board of Trade to Moscow not for negotiations, but the establishment of contact with leading figures and discussion of possibilities for trade.' Litvinov was not filled with enthusiasm and informed Seeds: 'I could see no change in the line that had taken the form at Munich.' He cited the example of Spain:

> We only saw France and Britain, being unwilling and considering it unnecessary to put up any resistance to the demands of the aggressors who were endeavouring to justify or blur those demands.

---

[119] *News Chronicle*, 28 January 1939, p.1
[120] Carley, Michael: *1939*, p.90, Schnurre trip
[121] Dilks, David: *The Diaries of Alexander Cadogan*, p.146
[122] *Soviet Peace Efforts*, No.82, p.159, 19 February 1939

Seeds defended his government against Litvinov's criticism with the claim: 'He was convinced, however, that Britain was talking a completely different tone and was fully determined to defend her positions.'

Litvinov replied: 'He was happy to hear of the new mood among the ruling circles in Britain and would be even happier to see it in action.'[123] Once again, in Chamberlain's letters to his sister Hilda, he seems to have had more confidence in Hitler than in Stalin.[124]

Litvinov thought the visit of Hudson had no serious purpose. He stated:

> We do not know whether Hudson is planning to raise some political issue apart from a general discussion on the situation. I cannot even imagine what proposal Hudson can put to us in this field. Seeds has hinted that Hudson has some very serious proposals, but surely it must be in the field of economic relations. They may propose not only measures to increase trade but also credit and financial measures involving the settlement of old claims. It is possible that these claims are being dragged out of the archives in order to render impossible the advance of any agreement and to shift on us a responsibility that will be understood by the City. Therefore, while treating the English gestures with a certain amount of scepticism and mistrust, I consider them to be far from useless, particularly in view of the aggravation of our relations with Japan.[125]

Litvinov must be given credit for the fact he was one of the few Communist politicians to admit he might be wrong.[126]

Although Litvinov has normally been portrayed as pro-British, he nevertheless continued to be suspicious of British policy and, when he heard Hess had come to Britain in 1941, he thought that Britain had done a deal with Germany, so he was relieved by Churchill's speech.[127]

At about this time there was a dinner party attended by Maisky, Robert Boothby, Richard Law, Vernon Bartlett and J B Priestley. Maisky stated that the Soviet Union was 'obviously much wounded by Munich and Great Britain could expect no advances from her side, but an approach from London might be reciprocated.'[128] There is every reason to believe that both Litvinov and Maisky were doing what they could to encourage Britain to

---

[123] *Soviet Peace Efforts*, No.83, p.161,19 February 1939
[124] See No.148 *post*
[125] *Soviet Peace Efforts*, No.93, p.180, 4 March 1939
[126] See Ch.19 No. 47
[127] See Ch.17, No.7
[128] Taylor, A J P (editor): *Lloyd George, 12 Essays*, p.336; Aster S: *Making of the Second World War* p.156

make meaningful overtures to the Soviet Union to improve relations. At about the same time Maisky warned a Parliamentary Committee; 'There might be a change of policy.'[129] Nobody can argue that Litvinov and Maisky did not warn Britain of the possibility of a Nazi-Soviet Pact.

Eventually, Halifax became uneasy about Chamberlain's policy of trying to exclude the Soviet Union from participation in decision making. At a meeting of the Foreign Affairs Committee of the Conservative Party, he correctly described:

> Soviet Russia is something between that of the unconquerable steamroller and looking on her as entirely useless militarily. We cannot ignore a country with a population of 180,000,000 people.[130]

On 1 March Chamberlain made a dramatic appearance at the Soviet Embassy reception although Litvinov was not impressed. Maisky thought Chamberlain's action 'was motivated by the desire to placate the opposition.' On the other hand Litvinov was even more cynical:

> It is not excluded that even Chamberlain was having doubts as to whether there is a fear that the insatiability of the aggressor will force Britain and France to take up arms, and in anticipation of that eventuality, it would not be amiss to extend a feeler towards the USSR.[131]

Future events proved that Litvinov was right when he said, 'They were only dealing with a gesture and tactical manoeuvres, not with any genuine desire on Chamberlain's part to co-operate with us.' However, Litvinov thought that a Chamberlain Government would still be of some use to the Soviet Union.

Litvinov's fears of Britain passively standing aside, while the Soviet Union was attacked, were confirmed by a telegram from Henderson:

> Lebensraum for Germany can only be found in expansion eastwards and expansion eastwards makes a clash between Germany and the Soviet Union some day highly probable. With a benevolent Britain on her flank, Germany can envisage such an eventuality with comparative equanimity, but she lives in dread of the reverse and a war on two fronts, which was equally Bismarck's nightmare. The best approach to good relations with Germany is therefore along the lines of the avoidance of constant and vexatious utterances in matters of which British

---

[129] Ibid. p 338; Aster S: *Making of the Second World War* p.156
[130] Taylor, A J P (editor): *Lloyd George, 12 Essays*, p.338; Aster, Sidney: *The Making of the Second World War* p.156
[131] Carley, Michael: *1939*, p.95

interests are not directly involved and neutrality in the event of Germany being involved in the East.[132]

The views of Henderson, shared by many others, help to explain Stalin's March 1939 speech. Although often portrayed as pro-German, it certainly was not that, as he starts by condemning the aggressor states:

> In 1935 Italy attacked and seized Abyssinia. In the summer of 1936 Germany and Italy organised military intervention in Spain … Having seized Manchuria, Japan in 1937 invaded north and central China, occupied Peking, Tienstein and Shanghai and began to oust her foreign competitors from the occupied zone. At the beginning of 1938 Germany seized Austria and in the autumn of 1938 the Sudeten region of Czechoslovakia. At the end of 1938 Japan seized Canton and at the beginning of 1939 the island of Hainan.

> The war which has stolen so imperceptibly upon the nations has drawn over 500 million people into its orbit and has extended its sphere of action over a vast territory stretching from Tienstein, Shanghai and Canton through Abyssinia to Gibraltar.

By including Gibraltar, Stalin – like Litvinov and Attlee – was wrong, and Eden was right. The person who would prevent Germany obtaining Gibraltar would be Franco.

> The world war is being waged by the aggressor states who in every way infringe upon the interests of the non-aggressor states, primarily England and the USA, while the latter draw back and retreat, making concession after concession to the aggressors.

Litvinov had constantly criticised the action, or rather the inaction, of the non-aggressor states. Then, publicly approving Litvinov's policy, Stalin stated: 'The chief reason is that the majority of non-aggressive countries, particularly Britain and France, have rejected the policy of collective security.'

Stalin ended his speech by stating that the Soviet Union wishes to 'strengthen the international bonds with the working people of all countries who are interested in peace and friendship.' However, in his speech he constantly refers to Germany, together with Italy and Japan, as aggressor nations, which description would hardly place them in the club of those nations wanting peace. Therefore, the speech presumably indicated that he was not interested in improving relations with such countries. We know now that either Stalin changed his mind or that statement was not truthful. Further, his policy is 'the strengthening of business relations with all countries', presumably even such countries like

---

[132] Henderson, DBFP, 3rd Series, vol.4, 9 March 1939, p.210 No.195

Germany, who were aggressors. However, the speech does contain what most commentators consider was a hint to Germany in the following quotation: The Soviet Union's policy was 'to be cautious and not allow our country to be drawn into conflicts by warmongers who are accustomed to have others pull the chestnuts out of the fire';[133] the one sentence in the speech that is always remembered.

On 15 March 1939 German troops marched into Czechoslovakia. Channon wrote: 'What a day of shattered hopes.'[134] Litvinov sent the strongest possible note to the German ambassador, which stated:

> The Soviet Union knows of no state constitution that empowers its Head of State to abolish its independence without the consent of the people. It is difficult to believe that any people would voluntarily consent to the cancellation of its independence and its incorporation in another state, especially a people who has fought for its independence for centuries and has enjoyed an independent existence already for twenty years.[135]

However, as Litvinov regarded Czechoslovakia as one of the truest democracies,[136] he felt strongly that everything possible must be done to save Czechoslovakia. He must have obtained Stalin's approval before making such a condemnation.

Litvinov followed this note with the sensible suggestion that a conference be called between Britain, France, Poland, Rumania and the USSR.[137] However this found no favour with the Chamberlain Government.

When Chamberlain made a statement in the Commons, it has been maintained that he did not condemn Germany. This is not correct, because he stated quite clearly that he considered:

> Hitler had broken the Munich agreement which provided for fixation of the future frontiers of Czechoslovakia and laid down the limits of German occupation, which the German Government accepted. They have now, without any communication with the other signatories to the Munich agreement, sent their troops beyond the frontier there laid down. Even though it is now claimed that this has occurred with the acquiescence of the Czech Government, I cannot regard the method by which the changes have been brought about as being in accordance with the spirit of the Munich agreement.

---

[133] Stalin's speech, in Degras, Jane: *Soviet Documents on Foreign Policy*, vol.3, p.315
[134] Carley, Michael: *1939*, p.99
[135] *Soviet Peace Efforts*, .No.106 p.200,18 March 1939
[136] See No. 61 *ante*
[137] Bullock, Alan: *Hitler and Stalin*, p. 670

This scenario was exactly that of which Litvinov had warned Chamberlain about after Munich. However, the words in Chamberlain's speech which came in for criticism were:

> The aim of the government is now as always to promote peace. Though we may suffer checks and disappointments from time to time, the object we have in mind is of too great a significance to the happiness of mankind for us lightly to give it up or set it on one side.

However, Chamberlain should now have realised that such words must have been sweet music to Hitler, and confirmed Stalin's deepest suspicions. Loyal Conservative MPs, the press and the public were much more outraged by German action than Chamberlain. Within two days Chamberlain, addressing a Conservative meeting in Birmingham, took a stronger line. He said:

> We are told that the seizure of territory has been necessitated by disturbances in Czechoslovakia. If there were disorders, were they not fermented from without? Is this the last attack upon a small state or is it to be followed by another? Is this not a step in the direction of an attempt to dominate the world by force?[138]

However, Litvinov's proposal of a joint conference found no favour with Britain, who wanted the Soviet Union to participate in a joint declaration, as follows:

> It was agreed that Britain, France, the Soviet Union and Poland hereby declare that, in as much as peace and security are a matter of common concern and since European peace and security may be affected by any which constitutes a threat to the political independence of any European State, our respective governments hereby undertake immediately to consult together as to what steps should be taken to offer joint resistance to any such action.[139]

It was not unreasonable for Litvinov to be annoyed that Britain had rejected for the third time his suggestion for a conference, and no doubt was even more annoyed when, little more than a week later, Britain had given a guarantee to Poland without consulting the Soviet Union. Oliver Harvey, a Foreign Office diplomat, stated this in his diaries:'If we want to keep the Poles in, we cannot have the Russians in too, and the Poles are better military material immediately than the Soviet Union, in spite of their numbers and arsenals.'[140]

While the British response was lukewarm, Litvinov's strong stand found favour in USA.

---

[138] *Hansard*, 15 March 1939, vol.345, 431; Read, Anthony and Fisher, Alan: *Deadly Embrace*, p.62
[139] *Soviet Peace Efforts*, No.121, p.217; 21 March 1939
[140] Harvey, Oliver: *Diplomatic Diaries*, p.272

The Soviet chargee reported a tremendous growth in the prestige of the USA and interest in us. [141]

Hudson, the British Trade Minister, as planned, arrived in Moscow on 23 March. However, the purpose of the visit was contradictory. Whereas the official purpose of the visit was to bring the Soviet Union and Britain closer together, Chamberlain's letters to his sister made it clear that Chamberlain desired such collaboration only as a last resort. Litvinov saw clearly:

> Chamberlain's policy ... was to feel out the Soviet Government on its willingness to collaborate and conclude a possible military alliance. Of course, this does not mean that Britain is now striving for such an agreement. Britain only wants to have in hand all the elements necessary to make a decision in the future under appropriate circumstances.

A communiqué was issued at the end of the meetings which stated that discussions on the international situation had taken place. Cadogan thought the remark relating to the 'international situation' was undesirable and instructed Seeds to have it deleted, but his instructions came too late. Tass had already published it.[142]

It appears that, in spite of Hitler's outrageous conduct in invading Czechoslovakia, Cadogan wanted to appease Hitler and was frightened he might annoy Hitler. Britain's behaviour only increased Stalin's suspicion.

On 31 March 1939 Poland begged for and received Britain's assistance when threatened by Hitler. In Parliament Chamberlain stated that if Poland's independence was threatened and 'if the Polish Government considered it vital to resist the threat with their national forces', the British Government 'would feel it was bound at once to give them all their support.'[143] On the same day Maisky had been asked by Halifax whether Chamberlain could state that this declaration had the approval of the Soviet Government, but Maisky reasonably said that he could not answer in the affirmative without consulting Moscow.[144]

After the Polish declaration, Chamberlain had an exchange of views with Lloyd George. The latter asked about the Soviet Union. Chamberlain explained that, in view of the decision taken by Poland and Rumania, the participation of the USSR in defensive action was a difficult issue, but that according to his information neither the German General Staff nor Hitler would ever risk a war on two fronts. When Lloyd George asked about the

---

[141] *Soviet Peace Efforts*, No.119, p.214, 21 March 1939
[142] Hudson visit, in Carley, Michael: *1939*, p.109
[143] *Hansard*, vol.345, 31 March 1939, 2415
[144] Maisky, Ivan: *Who Helped Hitler?*, p.107

Second Front , Chamberlain referred to Poland. Lloyd George burst into laughter and said, rightly:

> Poland had no air force to speak of, an inadequate mechanised army … and that Poland was weak internally, economically and politically. Without active help from the USSR, no Eastern front was possible.

Lloyd George further stated:

> Without a definite agreement with the USSR, I consider your statement of today an irresponsible gamble of chance that can end up very badly.[145]

Beck paid a visit to Britain at the beginning of April 1939. He was pleased that Halifax and Chamberlain, unlike the French, 'had a marked distrust for the Soviets', and observed that 'we saw two imperialisms, the old Tsarist one and that of Communism.' At least Beck assured his hosts that Poland would not attempt to impede any efforts at an understanding between France and Britain on the one side and the Soviets on the other side, but warned his allies that no agreement signed by Britain and France without Poland's participation could create any new obligations for Poland. Beck also made the unrealistic request that 'Poland be given transit rights for war equipment from the Allied countries over the Soviet Union and have supplies of raw materials and Soviet goods which they would require for conduct of the war', without giving the Soviet Union any reciprocal rights. Beck also made clear his opposition to the French belief in the 'Soviet conception as the key for creating the European balance of power', vainly trying to convince himself that Poland, not the Soviet Union, would be of superior use in creating a second front.[146] It was Litvinov who again got it right with the statement: 'To hold back and stop aggression without us is impossible', and then said, 'Later is the Anglo-French appeal for help, the higher the price will be.'[147] Without a second front supported by the Soviet Union, France would be unlikely to be able to survive a German onslaught.

Ridiculously, Chamberlain was still convinced that the saviour was Poland, not the Soviet Union. Shortly thereafter, he wrote to his sister:

> I must agree with Beck, for I regard the Soviet Union as a very unreliable friend with very little capacity for active assistance, but with an enormous irritative power on others. Unhappily, we have to strive against the almost hysterical passion of the opposition, egged on by Lloyd George, who have a pathetic belief that Russia is the key to our salvation.[148]

---

[145] Lloyd George visit, in Carley, Michael: *1939*, p.114
[146] Beck, Josef: *Final Report*, p.177
[147] Carley, Michael: *1939*, p.118
[148] Ibid. p.126

However, events proved it was Chamberlain who was wrong and the others who were right, and the Soviet Union's help would be essential if Hitler was to be defeated. Once France was conquered, an invasion of Europe by Britain and the USA would have been virtually impossible without an Eastern front. In 1944, even with an Eastern front, conquering Normandy was no easy matter. If Rommel had unrestricted command so that the use of the Panzers in the battle had not been delayed, the invasion might not have succeeded.

It is surprising that, although Chamberlain constantly criticised the Soviet Union to his sister, he made no similar criticisms of Hitler, who had double-crossed Chamberlain. Channon, the Conservative MP, expressed similar sentiments. He described Maisky, who was trying to promote better understanding between the Soviet Union and Britain, as: 'The ambassador of torture, murder and every crime in the calendar.'[149] Of course, this comment was also applicable to Hitler's Germany, but there was no similar criticism.

On 7 April, the day that Italy occupied Albania, Ribbentrop told his Eastern European expert, Kleist, to start improving relations with Soviet diplomats. Kleist wisely arranged to have tea with Counsellor Astakhov, who was a career diplomat at the Soviet Embassy in Berlin and apparently one of Stalin's men. Astakhov stated: 'How absurd it was for Germany and the Soviets to fight each other over "ideological subtleties" instead of making a grand policy side by side as they had done so often in history.'

Astakhov stated: 'Stalin and Hitler were men who created that reality and did not let themselves be dominated by it.' It is extremely unlikely that, unless Astakhov had Stalin's confidence, he would have spoken in this way. However, following the meeting, Ribbentrop must have had second thoughts, because he told Kleist to have no further contact with Astakhov: 'I do not think the Fuhrer would wish that conversation to be continued.'[150] This seemed surprising, as it was during April 1939 that Hitler told Weizsacker that he was contemplating a reconciliation with the Soviet Union.[151]

Litvinov and Potemkin called in the Polish ambassador, Grzybowski. Potemkin stressed that, if Poland was attacked by Germany, it would need support from other great powers if it wished to protect its independence. When the Ambassador mentioned Poland's policy of neutrality, Litvinov retorted that he had not noticed it in the Munich crisis. The Ambassador stated that Poland would turn to the Soviet Union when necessary. Litvinov warned the Ambassador to take care not to do it too late. This was sound advice. On 11 April Hitler approved new war plans, Operation White, for the isolation of Poland and the destruction of its armed forces, if Poland failed to make the concessions Germany would

---

[149] Carley, Michael: *1939*, p.125
[150] Kleist, Peter: *European Tragedy*, p.16
[151] Weizsacker, Ernst: *Memories*, p.186

demand.[152] The concession required would, no doubt, be the return of Danzig to the Reich. As Beck was not prepared to make any concessions over Danzig, Poland would need all the help it could muster.

Litvinov now instructed Maisky to probe Halifax tactfully on the possible anti-Soviet character contained in Britain's projected pledges of aid to Rumania and Poland and that it would not be acceptable for Britain to associate itself with the Polish-Rumanian Treaty of 1921 whereby both countries offered military assistance if either was attacked by the Soviet Union. Thus, Rumania gained Poland's pledge to defend Bessarabia, if the Soviet Union, who claimed it, attacked.[153]

Litvinov also instructed Maisky to tell Halifax that the Soviet Union was entitled to expect that the treaty should make it clear that any aid to Poland was exclusively to protect her against German aggression, although the Soviet Union had no intention of attacking Poland.[154]

We do not know, as there is no indication, whether the purpose of this stipulation was whether one day the Soviet Union envisaged she might want to attack Poland. On the other hand was it not sensible to indicate that it was not purely against German aggression? This would counter the German criticism that Britain with other countries were attempting to encircle Germany.

Two events now show that Stalin was still supporting Litvinov's policy. Halifax advised Maisky at a meeting on 11 April that the British Government was contemplating further guarantees to Greece and Rumania. Halifax told Maisky that the British Government was moving towards a firm position against Nazi aggression. Maisky's reply obviously indicated that he was not convinced. He said: 'It was necessary not only to catch the aggressor but to anticipate their actions and thwart them.' Maisky also stated 'The only way to check aggression and guarantee peace was through a broad multilateral undertaking, rather than through bilateral or trilateral agreements.'[155] Halifax was disappointed he had not received a more enthusiastic response from Maisky, but the stance of the latter was hardly surprising after Chamberlain's conduct both over Munich and over the Polish guarantee.

Oddly, Litvinov was also critical that Maisky had not shown more enthusiasm about Halifax's overtures and, after having received Stalin's approval, sent a telegram to Maisky reprimanding him for being critical of Britain's preference for bilateral or trilateral treaties. Apparently, Litvinov believed that Maisky had been influenced by 'articles from our press

---

[152] Carley, Michael: *1939*, p.119
[153] *Soviet Peace Efforts*, No.158, p.260, 11 April 1939
[154] Ibid.
[155] Carley Michael: *1939* p.124

that may permit to itself greater liberties than an official representative.' On the other hand, Litvinov instructed Maisky to tell Halifax:

> The Soviet Government was not indifferent to the fate of Rumania and it would like to know how Britain contemplated help by itself and others for Rumania. We are ready to take part in such assistance.[156]

Resis is quite right to assume that Stalin considered Britain's unilateral guarantees to Poland, Romania and Greece enhanced – gratis – Soviet security; although Medlicott believes the British guarantee to Poland given on 31 March 1939 was not taken very seriously in Moscow. The Soviet Union realised that Britain and France had committed themselves irrevocably to defend the frontiers of Eastern Europe without securing explicit promises from other powers. 'The wily politicians of the Kremlin, not unreasonably, no doubt proceeded with thoroughly good consciences to take full advantage of the situation.'[157] Chamberlain had unintentionally strengthened the Soviet Union's position in the forthcoming negotiations with the Allies, although it had weakened the Soviet Union's position with regard to Poland.

On 15 April 1939 Litvinov sent a comprehensive proposal to Stalin for a tripartite agreement with Britain and France.[158] On 16 April Litvinov saw Stalin to discuss his draft. The Soviet leader approved it. Two matters appear clear. First, it was because of Litvinov's initiative that the tripartite pact proposals were submitted to Stalin. The Soviet records indicate that Litvinov submitted detailed arguments in favour of the proposed pact, which Stalin accepted. Litvinov stated that they ought not to wait for the other side to propose the very thing that the Soviets wanted. Litvinov summarised his proposals, which were for mutual assistance in case of aggression against the Soviet Union, Britain or France and support for all States bordering the Soviet Union, including Finland and the Baltic States. It also provided for rapid agreement on the form that such assistance would take. Further, there would be an agreement not to conclude a separate peace. As late as 16 April it appears that Stalin still had faith in his Foreign Commissar and had no immediate plans to remove him. Nor had any concrete proposals been initiated for a Nazi-Soviet Pact by either the Soviet Union or Germany. Litvinov said: 'We can expect urgent and complex negotiations with the French and especially the British. We need to monitor public opinion and try to influence it.'[159]

Now that the new proposals had the support of Stalin, Litvinov appeared to have been so enthusiastic that he summoned Seeds while he was enjoying a play at the theatre with his

---

[156] See DBFP, 3rd Series, vol.5, No. p.209 Carley Michael *1939* p 125
[157] Resis, Albert: 'Fall of Litvinov', *Europe Asia Studies*, No.52n, p.43; Medlicott, William: *Foreign Policy Since Versailles,* p.266
[158] *Soviet Peace Efforts*, No.171, p.273, 17 April 1939
[159] Carley, Michael: *1939*, p.128

wife. Litvinov was surprised that Seeds appeared annoyed at having his evening entertainment unnecessarily interrupted, and wished to return to his wife, who was still at the theatre.[160] Presumably Litvinov could have had the proposals conveyed to the Embassy with a request for Seeds to visit Litvinov urgently in the morning.

In spite of the warning by Lloyd George, Chamberlain, instead of requesting a report from his service chiefs as to the strength of the Polish army, requested reports from the service chiefs as to the strength of the Soviet army. Chamberlain was no doubt pleased with the critical remarks made about the strength of the Red army and overlooked the most important point, which was that the report stated that the greatest danger was a rapprochement between Germany and the Soviet Union. Macdonald was the only member of the Foreign Affairs Committee to have studied the report in detail. He referred to that part of the report which stated:

> If the Soviet Union was neutral or siding with Germany, Anglo-Franco economic warfare would be gravely embarrassed.[161]

Litvinov constantly gave warnings to Britain of the posibility that Stalin might come to terms with Germany.

Chamberlain made the fatal mistake of believing that the Soviet Government would agree to play a subordinate role controlled by Britain, which would determine when and how the Soviet Government would intervene to protect its own interests.[162] Litvinov would not have allowed his country to play a subordinate role any more than Stalin or Molotov would have done.

It appears purely incidental that the day after Litvinov saw Stalin about the proposed tripartite agreement on 17 April, the Soviet Ambassador saw the German State Secretary to press for the fulfilment by Skoda of a contract for the supply of armaments to the Soviet Union. This contract had been negotiated before the German invasion of Czechoslovakia. Litvinov himself had instructed his ambassador to see the German State Secretary. Litvinov did not instruct his ambassador to raise any political issues. A report in the captured Nazi documents indicates that Merekalov complained about anti-Soviet reports in the German press. If Merekalov did raise other political issues, he was not acting in accordance with Litvinov's instructions. Merekalov was either acting on his own initiative, or was acting on somebody else's instructions. However, if Merekalov had raised the question to impress those in Moscow, he would surely have included it in his report.[163] I

---

[160] *Soviet Peace Efforts*, No.170, p.272, 17 April 1939

[161] Aster, Sidney: *The Making of the Second World War*, p.165

[162] Carley, Michael: *1939*, p.115

[163] *Historical Journal*, October 1992, 35.4, pp.921-926; Sontag, Raymond and Beddie, James: *Nazi-Soviet Relations 1939-1941*, p.1

think Louis Fischer's statement about the initial negotiations which finally resulted in the Nazi-Soviet Pact is misleading. Fischer stated: It was important that negotiations with Germany, which were about to begin, remained secret.[164]

If Stalin wanted an agreement with the West, he would have negotiated openly with Hitler. Serious negotiations with Hitler did not start until three months after Litvinov's dismissal. The documents which were found in the German Foreign Office archives and published in 1945 certainly do not contain proof that Stalin never intended to come to an arrangement with the West.

We learn from the newly opened Soviet archives that even in July 1939 there were no pending political negotiations. Astakhov wrote to Molotov: 'I have no doubt that if we wanted to we could involve the Germans in far-reaching negotiations.' Molotov was still guarded, and maintained as late as 4 August 1939: ' Soviet policy was to continue with an exchange of views in general terms, but that more concrete discussions depend on the outcome of trade credit talks.'[165] It was at this time that the British and French military delegation was awaited. However, if Litvinov was deeply suspicious of Chamberlain coming to an arrangement with Hitler, it was natural for Molotov and Stalin to be equally suspicious. This was not unreasonable, as the British ambassador in Berlin was in favour of giving Hitler virtually a free hand in Central and Eastern Europe and in the light of this situation it was sensible for the Soviet Union to put out feelers to Germany.

When Roosevelt asked Hitler to confirm he would not attack various states, wisely he included the Soviet Union among those states because he realised that an attack on the Soviet Union would not be the solution to the problem of Hitler, but might start a war, the outcome of which it was impossible to predict.[166] If Chamberlain had made a similar declaration in respect of the Soviet Union, that would have given Litvinov confidence that Britain would not come to any arrangement with Hitler; but Chamberlain was not prepared to do that.

I imagine, in view of his poor opinion of Chamberlain, Litvinov was not surprised that Russia's proposal for an alliance would not be welcome, but he may have been taken aback by the attitude of the Foreign Office. Cadogan, in his diary, described Litvinov's proposals as 'mischievous.'[167] A Foreign Office report to the Foreign Affairs Cabinet Committee ttermed them 'inconvenient.'[168] There is a strong case for arguing that if Litvinov's proposals had been quickly and favourably considered, the Second World War might not

---

[164] Fischer Louis: *Life and death of Stalin,* p.162
[165] Roberts, Geoffrey: 'The Soviet Decision for a Pact with Nazi Germany', *Soviet Studies,* 1992, vol.44, No.1, pp.66 and 67
[166] Roosevelt speech, in *Documents,* 1939, p.204
[167] Cadogan, Alexander: *Diaries 1938-1945,* p.175
[168] CAB 27, 624, 309

have taken place. Churchill, on 7 June 1939, stated he 'much preferred the Russian proposals. They are simple. They are logical and conform to the main groupings of common interest.' Churchill further stated that the Soviet claim that the Baltic States should be included in the triple guarantee was well founded.[169] Three years later, Britain agreed a similar pact of assistance with the Soviet Union. In the meantime, its major ally France had been defeated, many of Britain's cities and towns devastated by German bombing and Britain's financial reserves decimated by the cost of the war. Litvinov's proposals were also conveyed to the French Ambassador.

As soon as the proposals reached the French Government, Bonnet's first reaction was entirely different from that of the British Government and Foreign Office. Bonnet saw the Soviet Ambassador, Suritz, who cabled that 'the first impression of the French is very favourable.'[170] However, Britain successfully persuaded the French Government to take no action until a common policy had been formulated. Although there were talks between the French and the British Governments, they both failed either to accept or reject the proposals until after Litvinov's dismissal on 4 May.[171]

Maxim and Ivy decided to adopt a girl. If Ivy found official parties boring the girl did not, and to the scandal of many, she started to make appearances at official functions.[172]

Litvinov's efforts to prevent the Second World War failed; but that was due to inaction by Chamberlain and Halifax, not Litvinov. He clearly saw that the only way to stop Hitler was for an effective alliance between Britain, France and the Soviet Union, and Litvinov persuaded Stalin that was the correct course. If Chamberlain had quickly accepted the offer of an alliance I do not believe Litvinov would have been dismissed. By pursuing the wrong policy, Chamberlain, the man of peace, made war certain.

---

[169] *Herald Tribune*, 7 June 1939, p.7
[170] Carley, Michael: *1939*, pp.129 and 130
[171] Litvinov's fall: see next chapter
[172] Carswell John *The Exile* p.139

14: THE FALL

Before Litvinov was dismissed, Sheinis claims that ambassadors, 'were sending their reports over his head direct to Molotov',[1] although I have found no evidence of this. On the contrary, there is evidence that Litvinov appears to have been giving Maisky direct instructions. Watson states that diplomats reported direct to Molotov and articles on foreign policy from members of the Commissariat, including Potemkin, appeared in the press without Litvinov's knowledge; but Watson gives no examples in support of such contention.[2] Sheinis's reference to Kandelaki is strange, because his negotiations with the Germans finished in 1937, since when he had taken no further part in diplomacy. It is my belief that Kandelaki's negotiations were undertaken with Litvinov's full knowledge.[3]

I have no doubt that Litvinov was distressed by the useless purge whereby hundreds of thousands of people were being shot, including many of his own ambassadors and diplomatic staff.[4] Prior to her father's dismissal, Litvinov's daughter Tanya tells us that her father was feeling very unhappy. He felt that something was happening behind his back and wondered whether Stalin could be negotiating with the Germans. Litvinov wrote a letter to Stalin: 'I cannot work any longer at the Foreign Commissariat.' Litvinov asked to be relieved of his post and to be given another. He took a long time to make up his mind. This is corroborated by Sheinis, who states that Litvinov thought, 'Things were happening behind his back.' As Litvinov felt he could no longer change anything, he sat down and wrote his resignation letter. 'Did this mean he should resign?' or 'would it not be cowardly to abandon his post at this troubled time?' He pondered and pondered before putting his resignation letter in his safe. Although Sheinis does not clarify this, presumably the only purpose of putting it in the office safe was in the expectation that his safe would be searched and Stalin would become acquainted with the contents of the letter.[5] Both the German and Russian archives indicate that in fact Litvinov was wrong and that there were at this time no pending negotiations with Germany.

Tanya never asked her father any questions about the political situation, except once. She said: 'I know war is inevitable, but could you not postpone it for fifteen years?' Her father said: 'You want your generation to be out of it', and Tanya admits that was probably what

---

[1] Sheinis, Zinovy: *Maxim Litvinov*, p.293
[2] Watson, Derek: *Molotov*, p.153
[3] As to Kandelaki, see Chs.12 and 13
[4] See Ch.16.
[5] Sheinis, Zinovy: *Maxim Litvinov*, p.293; Tanya

she did want. Her father then said that the world was hypnotised by war, but he did not think war was inevitable.[6] On this point he agreed with Chamberlain.

As far as Germany was concerned, the next event of real significance was Hitler's comprehensive speech on 29 April viciously attacking Roosevelt and the USA for interfering in Europe's affairs. In a two-hour speech, Hitler did not direct one word of criticism or abuse against the Soviet Union.[7] How did Stalin react to this cue suggesting better relations with the Soviet Union? Was not Stalin exasperated by Britain's failure to respond to what Stalin, with justification, considered were the reasonable proposals of his Foreign Commissar? Stalin may well have thought that Litvinov had not been tough enough with Britain and Molotov would be less tolerant.

On 19 April 1939 a meeting in Stalin's office took place. Present were Litvinov, Molotov Voroshilov, Mikoyan and Kaganovich. Boris Shtein, who had been in Helsinki to negotiate Finnish territory for Soviet bases, joined the meeting for the last 20 minutes, and, in addition, Beria also attended for the last forty minutes.

A further meeting on 21 April was attended by Maisky and Merekalov. Stalin asked Merekalov, 'Will Hitler start a war against us?' Merekalov, as far as he could remember, replied that Hitler would invade Poland in the autumn of 1939 and would endeavour to neutralise the Soviet Union while they dealt with France and would then attack the Soviet Union, which was a remarkably accurate forecast. No discussion took place and Stalin told Merekalov that he was free to leave.[8]

Apparently, a significant incident before Litvinov's dismissal was Maisky's stop in Finland when he was returning from London to Moscow, which has been disclosed by Sheinis. According to Sheinis, both Litvinov and Maisky had been requested to return temporarily to Moscow on 27 April. Clearly, Maisky could not have seen Stalin on 27 April, as stated by Sheinis. In fact, Maisky left Moscow for London on 25 April, as confirmed by the *Times*, and arrived in Stockholm on the same day. On 26 April he flew to Paris and arrived in London on 28 April. All these dates are confirmed by contemporary reports in the *Times*.[9] Sheinis reports that Maisky returned to Moscow via Helsinki and made a courtesy call on the Foreign Minister, Erkko, who had been ambassador in Moscow from 1929 to 1932. Erkko asked Maisky for his opinion on the European situation. Maisky gave a vague reply, which was reported in the press. Something that occurred gave offence to Stalin.[10]

---

[6] Tanya

[7] Hitler's speech, Documents, p.214

[8] Resis, Albert: 'Fall of Litvinov', *Europe Asia Studies*, vol.52, N01c2000, p..48

[9] *Times*, 25 April 1939, p.14; 27 April 1939, p.15; 29 April 1939, p.14; Bilainkin, George: *10 Years an Ambassador*, p.245; Maisky, Ivan: *Who Helped Hitler?*, p.119

[10] Sheinis, Zinovy: *Maxim Litvinov*, p.294

The gist of the conversation with the Finnish press, at the airport, where Maisky had arrived from London, as reported in the Helsinki *Sanomat*, was as follows: 'Do you have a prepared plan or agreement to take to Moscow?' asked a journalist. Maisky said: 'No, I have nothing in my pockets.' He even looked inside his breast pocket and showed he was returning to his homeland empty-handed. Maisky was then asked: 'How long are you staying in Moscow?' His reply was:

> Probably not for long, but no decision has been made on the length of my stay. It depends on the circumstances. At least long enough to talk to my Government and to report on the recent negotiations and express the views of members of the British Government on the current situation.

When he was shown a newspaper report regarding Soviet foreign policy, Maisky commented that he had not seen the news article before. When asked to comment on the issues contained in that newspaper article, the Minister answered again, with a grin, 'I don't know. I cannot say.'[11]

It appears that this report, and in particular the reference to the article concerning foreign policy, which was beyond the control of Maisky, offended Stalin. Certainly, a rational politician would not take offence; but Stalin was not rational and his staff learned to take this into account as when Molotov deliberately wrongly pronounced Narkomzyem instead of Narkomzem. [12]

Sheinis states there was a meeting between Stalin, Litvinov, Maisky and Molotov after Maisky's arrival in Moscow following his Finnish visit. Stalin complained to Litvinov: 'What right has Maisky to speak to Erkko?' Litvinov said: 'It was an ordinary conversation between two diplomats. Maisky could not avoid it.' Although Stalin had looked outwardly calm, puffing on his pipe, he was annoyed with Litvinov. It may be that Stalin was annoyed with Litvinov because he, Litvinov, had advised Stalin that the Soviet Union should make proposals to Britain and France for an alliance which had not been accepted and therefore the Soviet Union's prestige had been damaged. However, Molotov was described as: 'Being simply vicious, attacking Litvinov and accusing him of everything under the sun.'[13] It seems probable that Molotov was jubilant. He realised that he had finally managed to persuade Stalin to dispose of Molotov's rival, Litvinov.

It is a pity that Maisky apparently informed Sheinis of this affair but Maisky did not mention it in either of the two editions in his original autobiography in Russian, or in the English translation, although the English version is not an exact translation. Maisky made several changes for the benefit of his English readers. He took the opportunity to attack

---

[11] *Helsinki Sanomat*, 20 April 1939, p.3
[12] Tucker, Robert: *Stalin in Power*, p.586; Ch.19, No.108
[13] Sheinis, Zinovy: *Maxim Litvinov*, p.294

British and French policy and politicians.[14] Various historians have accepted what Sheinis said as true, but I am not so sure.[15] Resis mentions the meeting without comment.[16] He did not realise that Maisky could not have had the meeting in Moscow on 27 April, because Maisky was not in Moscow on that day, being on his way back to Britain. Resis is correct that Maisky arrived in London on 28 April but I believe he did not realise that Maisky left Russia on 25 April as he travelled by Stockholm and Paris. Resis having researched all the material about the meetings on 19 and 21 April found no mention of Stalin's complaint about Maisky's Finnish visit. This casts further doubt on the truth of what Sheinis reported of Maisky's description of what occurred. I believe the alleged meeting to which subsequent mention is made, where Litvinov remained seated while all the audience stood up and cheered at the time of the Nazi-Soviet Pact, is false.[17]

Further, Tanya had not heard of the alleged attack by Molotov at the April 1939 meeting or on the August 1939 occasion. If Sheinis recorded the wrong date, it is possible that this incident could have caused Litvinov's removal, although I feel it is unlikely. However, there is every reason to believe that Molotov would have done nothing to discourage Litvinov's removal. There must be some doubt whether the above meeting took place at all and significantly more so because there is no record of any meeting of a person employed in the Finnish Foreign Ministry with Maisky in their archives.[18]

At the May Day parade, Litvinov was on the reviewing platform next to Stalin. However, there was a difference because, whenever Litvinov caught Stalin's eye, as the massive parade passed, Stalin looked the other way. Actually, the fact that a person as ruthless as Stalin felt embarrassed showed the respect Stalin had for Litvinov. As Maxim and Ivy made their way home, Maxim told Ivy he 'had a bad feeling.' Ivy said: 'I have heard rumours from the wives.' Maxim's reply was: 'They are changing their policy', to which Ivy responded with the words: 'Damn that fool Chamberlain.'[19]

Litvinov's pending dismissal should not have been a surprise to him, as on 2 May an investigating panel of Molotov, Beria, recently appointed People's Commissioner for Internal Affairs, Malenkov, then secretary of the Central Committee, and Vladimir Dekanozov, Deputy People's Commissioner for Foreign Affairs and soon to be ambassador to Germany, assembled at the NKID building to interrogate one by one the high-ranking members of the foreign service. Litvinov was present, sitting quietly and

---

[14] Maisky, Ivan: *Who Helped Hitler?*

[15] See Watson, Derek: 'The Politburo and Foreign Policy in the 1930s', in *The Nature of Stalin's Dictatorship,* p.156

[16] See Resis, Albert: 'Fall of Litvinov' *Europe Asia Studies*, vol.52, N01c2000, p.48. Note 75

[17] Sheinis, Zinovy: *Maxim Litvinov*, p.298; No. 86 post

[18] Tanya, and letter from Finnish Foreign Ministry

[19] Read and Fischer: *Deadly Embrace*, p.74

dejected at the end of the table as the panel probed for evidence of a criminal conspiracy. The group interrogated Gnedin, who felt the inquisitors were searching for information which would compromise Litvinov.[20]

On both 2 and 3 May being the date of Litvinov's dismissal, he had received the British ambassador. There was another fruitless meeting with Sir William Seeds. On the same day, Litvinov sent a memorandum to Stalin: 'The English are not in a hurry to reply to us.'[21] Stalin's main concern appears to have been not about any adverse publicity in the West but that Soviet diplomats loyal to Litvinov might desert. On 3 May Stalin was said by Louis Fischer to have communicated with the head of all foreign embassies and legations, informing them of Litvinov's dismissal, which he attributed not to Litvinov's ill health, but to his refusal to work harmoniously with Molotov.[22] Now we have the text of these letters.

> In view of the serious conflict that has arisen between the Chairman of the Commissars Cde [Comrade] Molotov and the People's Commissars of Foreign Affairs, Cde Litvinov has requested to be released from his duties of Commissar of Foreign Affairs. The Central Committee has acceded to Comrade Litvinov's request. Cde Molotov has been appointed as People's Commissar of Foreign Affairs to serve concurrently as Chairman of the People's Commissars.[23]

Therefore, what Louis Fischer discovered was correct. Stalin acknowledged 'not that Litvinov had done anything disloyal to the Soviet State or been a Trotskyist', but had failed to work harmoniously with his superior Molotov.

Litvinov held a relationship with Stalin which no other Soviet politician enjoyed, even surviving after his interview with Hottelet was bugged.[24] Otherwise, he would never have survived. I have suggested various explanations, such as Stalin liked Litvinov for his wit; trusted that, as he was a loner, he would neither be invited nor agree to participate in any plot against Stalin; the incident at 1906 London Conference; Litvinov's respect for his knowledge of the Western World and Stalin had a foreign affairs expert if he wanted to liquidate Molotov.

In July 1939 Molotov criticised the way Litvinov ran the Foreign Commissariat by stating:

> Comrade Litvinov failed to ensure the pursuance of the party line of the CPSU Central Committee in the People's Commissariat. It is wrong to say that … [Litvinov] was non-Bolshevik. … But, as regards the choice and training of the

---

[20] Miner Steven in Craig: *Diplomats 1939-1979*, p.68
[21] Vaksberg, Arkady: *Stalin Against Jews*, p.88
[22] Fischer, Louis: *Life and Death of Stalin*, p.161
[23] Resis, Albert: 'Fall of Litvinov', *Europe Asia Studies*, vol.52, No.1, 2000, p.34
[24] See ch 1 No 41; Ch.18, No.16; ch.19, No. 68

personnel, the Commissariat was not quite Bolshevik because Comrade Litvinov was clinging on to a number of people alien and hostile to the party and to the Soviet state and displayed a non-party attitude to the new people who had come to serve at the Commissariat.[25]

A prearranged meeting with Stalin was held on the afternoon of 3 May. The detailed report is contained in Louis Fischer's *Life and Death of Stalin*. Molotov began the conversation. The Soviet Government intended to improve its relations with Hitler and if possible sign a pact with Nazi Germany. As a Jew and an avowed opponent of such a policy, Litvinov stood in the way. He was angry. He asserted that an alliance between Moscow and Hitler would spell disaster and sketched the possibilities. Litvinov argued and banged on the table. Stalin finally sucked his pipe and said, 'Enough.' Then, thrusting a paper in Litvinov's direction, Stalin said, 'Sign.' It was Litvinov's letter of resignation, which he signed. Louis Fischer claims his source is a conversation Litvinov had with two Americans.[26] I believe that one of the Americans was Maurice Hindus, a journalist, as his account is identical to what he has told. I believe that Hindus' source was Litvinov himself, as Hindus states: 'Now Litvinov is dead and cannot suffer punishment for frank talk with foreign journalists.'[27]

Fischer's statement that the meeting was perfectly amicable must be regarded as inaccurate. Stalin told Litvinov he was being replaced by Molotov, who was also at the meeting. Molotov apparently agreed that they were not blaming Litvinov personally, but felt it was time for a change.[28] However, Tanya Litvinov is of the opinion that Molotov said to her father, 'You take us for fools.'[29] If the meeting was amicable, then why would Molotov have needed to make this remark? Read and Fisher, apparently relying on what Litvinov recorded in his diary, quote Litvinov as saying: 'It is all over. I have been caught like a man stealing.' The same words were quoted by Bromage.[30] This fact increases the chance this is what Litvinov actually said.

Tanya Litvinov recalls her father telling her that he had a meeting with Stalin on the afternoon of 3 May. Presumably, from his demeanour, Tanya felt her father was concerned. Tanya similarly was so uneasy that she continually rang home, but could not obtain an answer. When she arrived home, in the meantime, her father had returned and gone to bed. In the morning Maxim and Ivy's adopted daughter told Tanya, 'Father has been demoted.' I went into my father's bedroom. I felt terribly sympathetic. Maxim said, 'Tanya, there is a new page in your life.' I thought, why does he talk about my life? It is

[25] Resis, Albert: 'Fall of Litvinov', *Europe Asia Studies*, vol.52, No.1, 2000, p.35
[26] Fischer, Louis: *Life and Death of Stalin*, p.62
[27] Hindus, Maurice: *Crisis in the Kremlin*, p.55
[28] Read & Fisher: *Deadly Embrace*, p.74
[29] Tanya
30 Bromage, Bernard: *Molotov*, p.186; and see No. 28 *ante*

his life.' I said: 'We ought to call mother.' Tanya called her mother, who said she 'has to wait for exams and how is Papa?' [31] Tanya on the telephone told her mother: 'We ought to be together.' It appears Ivy had already heard the news at her institute.and Tanya confirms that her mother immediately returned to Moscow. If Ivy had any hesitation as to whether she should return to Moscow, Tanya was positive that they should all be together. [32]

Previously Ivy had been confronted by a colleague who said 'You know Molotov? He will make a splendid Foreign Secretary.' A copy of *Pravda* was placed in Ivy's hands, and her attention drawn to a small paragraph announcing that Molotov, 'while retaining his position as Chairman of the Council of Commissioners, had assumed control of the Narkomindel.' [33]

There can be no doubt that Pope, Litvinov's first biographer, is wrong when he states Litvinov's departure as Foreign Affairs Commissioner was perfectly friendly, and claims Litvinov recommended his friend Molotov as his successor. Pope's view is that both Litvinov and Molotov realised that collective security as envisaged by Litvinov had broken down, and it was in the Soviet Union's interest to consider a rapprochement with Germany. Litvinov was unsuitable for the post of Foreign Minister both because he was Jewish and also on account of his anti-Nazi stance.

Surprisingly, there is support for the Pope version from Gedye's account in *The New York Times*. He states that in December 1938 Litvinov did offer his resignation to Stalin and asserted that as France and Britain 'were determined to head off Hitler eastwards … France and Britain should be recognised as the Soviet Union's most dangerous enemies.' Gedye claims that Litvinov favoured an approach to Hitler. However, in view of what Tanya said, Gedye's version of events must be considered unreliable.[34]

Pope told Roberts, when he wrote an article on Litvinov for *The Diplomats*, that Pope's account of his resignation had been confirmed by Litvinov himself, which indicates that Litvinov gave Pope false information.[35] If Pope, as a Communist sympathiser, did not want to disclose that the Communist party was not united, why did he need to perpetuate the false information after Litvinov's death by writing a letter to *The New York Times*?[36]

Much of Sheinis's account of what occurred on 4 May 1939 must similarly be discounted. Sheinis states that on that morning, the Foreign Commissariat building was surrounded by

---

[31] Tanya
[32] Ibid.
[33] Carswell, John: *The Exile*, p.145;Tanya
[34] *The New York Times*, 12 September 1940, p.10; Pope, Arthur: *Maxim Litvinov*, p.441
[35] Roberts, Henry, in Craig, Gordon: *The Diplomats*, p.374
[36] *The New York Times*,, 6 January 1952 Part 4 , p.8, letter from Pope

troops of the Commissariat for Internal Affairs. Molotov, Malenkov and Beria arrived at dawn and informed Litvinov that he was dismissed from the post of People's Commissar of Foreign Affairs. At 10am Litvinov went to his summer house. A platoon of soldiers was already there. As Litvinov's private telephone had been disconnected, he used the city telephone to get in touch with Beria. Around noon, Molotov and Beria returned to the Foreign Commissariat. Beria summoned Dekanozov, a Foreign Commissariat employee who was eventually promoted to Soviet Ambassador to Germany, where he served until the German invasion of the Soviet Union in 1941. Foreign Commissariat employees were not allowed to enter the building. They were kept in the lobby. Then they were summoned by Molotov, who told them that he was now People's Commissar for Foreign Affairs. Molotov also said that he would restore order with regard to personnel, a reference to the more relaxed attitude of Litvinov towards the diplomats under his control and the wider discretion allowed them.[37]

This is completely different from what Tanya Litvinov says occurred, an account which is supported by Read and Fisher and Louis Fischer. This version of events claims that Litvinov was informed of his dismissal in Stalin's office on 3 May.[38] Following Litvinov's dismissal, his office would, of course, be searched and, being a shy man, he was embarrassed that a half-bar of chocolate would be found.[39]

Molotov asked Litvinov to give him a list of people who Litvinov thought were the most knowledgeable. Although dispirited, Litvinov thought that, as Molotov was working for the same cause, he would give the names of those people whom he thought were the best people – and all disappeared within a week. Tanya has since met some of the dismissed employees. None bore a grudge. They all respected Litvinov's integrity. Tanya comments: 'In many ways my father was naive. He spent too much time in the West. He could have been a Western statesman.'[40] Carswell states that, after the guard around Litvinov's home had been increased, Maxim rang Beria on the direct telephone to the Kremlin to complain. Beria said to Maxim: 'You do not know your worth'; and thereafter Beria arranged for the line to be disconnected.[41] Tanya is the source.[42] Sheinis's version that Litvinov used the public telephone sheds doubt on other aspects of Sheinis's account.[43]

Although most statesmen in Europe, except those from Germany, Japan and Italy, were sad at Litvinov's departure, Beck was pleased. He previously referred to Litvinov as 'our notorious enemy.' One of the reasons for Beck's stance might well have been anti-Semitic

[37] Sheinis, Zinovy: *Maxim Litvinov*, p.295
[38] Tanya; Read & Fisher: *Deadly Embrace*, p.74
[39] Tanya
[40] Ibid.
[41] Carswell, John: *The Exile*, p.145
[42] Tanya
[43] Sheinis, Zinovy: *Maxim Litvinov*, p.295

because, referring to Litvinov, he stated: 'One could expect that the specific physiological anti-Polish complex of that man, a Litwak, a Russian Jew by origin, disappeared with his departure.' Beck was pleased with the appointment of Molotov, who 'immediately took the initiative to liquidate some trifling pending matters in dispute and in a short time we arrived at the conclusion of a very profitable commercial treaty.'[44]

This attitude shows that Beck was not fit to hold high government office. The dismissal of Litvinov paved the way for the Nazi-Soviet Pact, which destroyed the Polish state and the war that followed was responsible for the deaths of 20% of the Polish population. Many of the victims were Jews. Of course, it is possible Beck welcomed the German presence to solve the Jewish question in Poland by means of an attempt to liquidate all Polish Jews.

Hitler took Litvinov's removal much more seriously than Chamberlain. As the German Ambassador to the Soviet Union, Schulenburg was in Iran to represent Germany at the Crown Prince's wedding. Hilger, the First Secretary, was summoned to see Hitler, who asked two questions. The first was why Stalin might have dismissed Litvinov? Hilger said:

> According to my firm belief he (Stalin) had done so because Litvinov had pressed for an understanding with France and Britain while Stalin thought the Western powers were aiming to have the Soviet Union pull "the chestnuts out of the fire" in the event of war.

However, my belief is the real reason was the lukewarm response from London to Litvinov's offer of an alliance, and therefore I feel that Hilger may have been wrong. The second question Hitler asked Hilger was : 'Did I believe that Stalin might, under certain circumstances, be ready for an understanding with Germany?' Hilger mentioned the speech by Stalin of 10 March 1939, in which he stated: 'There was no visible ground for a conflict between the Soviet Union and Germany.' Hilger was surprised that, in spite of a detailed report of the speech made by the German Embassy in Moscow, neither Hitler nor Ribbentrop remembered Stalin's speech.[45]

When Litvinov resigned in 1939 only Communist sympathisers such as Bilaikan and Coates believed what the Moscow papers said; namely that he had resigned on the grounds of ill health.[46] Browder, the US Communist leader, was asked by undergraduates: 'Why Litvinov had been disposed of.' Browder gave the official version that when Litvinov resigned, 'it was for ill health.' Roars of laughter met this remark. Browder retorted: 'If you doubt his health was bad, let me ask you this. If for several years you had been had

---

[44] Beck, Josef: *Final Report*, p.190

[45] Hilger, Gustav: *Incompatible Allies*, p.296

[46] Bilainkin, George: *Maisky, 10 Years an Ambassador*, p.249; Coates, William Peyton: *Anglo-Soviet Relations*, p.609

been negotiating with Neville Chamberlain, wouldn't you be sick too?'[47] The only thing of which we can now be certain is that Litvinov was dismissed and did not resign.

In 1948 the Soviet Government published its explanation of the Nazi-Soviet Pact negotiations in *Falsification of History* in reply to the US Government's publication of the captured documents from the German archives concerning the negotiations between Germany and Soviet Russia. The Soviet Government admitted that the reason for Litvinov's replacement was not his supposed ill health, but because 'it was necessary to have in such a responsible post as People's Commissar for Foreign Affairs a political leader of greater experience and greater popularity in the country than Litvinov.' However with twenty years' experience in the service of the Foreign Commissariat and knowledge of a number of foreign languages, he was probably the world's most experienced foreign minister. On the other hand Molotov, besides being able to speak some German, had nowhere near Litvinov's foreign language skills and had no first-hand knowledge of foreign countries. *Falsification* further alleges that Great Britain and France, backed by the USA, were abetting the aggressors by spurring them on to start a war against the USSR.[48] Although many on the Right in Britain would not have shed any tears if Germany had attacked the Soviet Union, the USA was in fact not colluding with Britain and France. Britain and France were criticised by prominent people such as Joseph Davies in the USA for not being tough enough with Germany. However, there was something insincere about the USA's position because, in spite of her rhetoric, she was not prepared to give Britain or France any help other than economic.

The available evidence is that Stalin took the decision to dismiss Litvinov suddenly. Having approved Litvinov's initiative in making the comprehensive proposals on 18 April,[49] it appears illogical that Stalin, shortly thereafter, dismissed him; and it is my view that Stalin's decision was influenced by Hitler's speech on 28 April 1939 which, like his speech on 30 January 1939, 'did not make the customary attacks on the Soviet Union.' Even a devoted admirer of Chamberlain wrote that in 1939 it was widely noted that Hitler, in his Reichstag speech of 30 January 1939 and his reply to President Roosevelt on 28 April, deliberately refrained from his customary attacks on Stalin.[50] Further, Stalin was frustrated by the delay of Britain in replying to the Soviet proposals. I believe Litvinov's dismissal was a surprise to Germany. The German chargé d'affaires, Tippelskirch, reported on 4 May 1939 that Litvinov 'appeared on the tribune next to Stalin and there was no recent evidence of the instability of his position. Yesterday his name appeared on the platform as one of the honoured guests at the May Day parade. His dismissal appears to have been as a result of some unexpected decision by Stalin;'[51] which may indicate that

---

[47]*The New York Times*, 29 November 1939, p.14
[48] *The New York Times*, 10 February 1948, p.13; *Moscow News*, 11 February 1948, p.2
[49] See Ch.13, No.159
[50] Walker-Smith, Derek: *Chamberlain, Man of Peace*, p.393
[51] Vaksberg, Arkady : *Stalin Against Jews*, p.88

Stalin did not decide to dismiss Litvinov until after the May Day parade. Stalin might have taken the decision to dismiss Litvinov reluctantly.

I do not believe that, when Litvinov requested Stalin's approval for the proposal of an alliance with Britain and France, this was to distract attention from any forthcoming negotiations with Nazi Germany. Clearly, there was complete agreement between Stalin and Litvinov that the Soviet Union was interested only in an effective alliance where Britain and France would come to the defence of the Soviet Union if she was attacked, and presumably would also come to the defence of Poland. The Soviets did not have in mind an agreement which Britain and France would not effectively honour and that was what occurred when Poland was attacked in September 1939.

If Britain and France had accepted the 18 April offer of mutual assistance before 3 May and agreed to start military conversations at once, I believe Litvinov would not, at least at that stage, have been dismissed. Stalin would then have had to make the choice as to whether to proceed enthusiastically with the negotiations with Britain and France or to endeavour to come to an agreement with Hitler. However, in May 1939 there was no guarantee that Stalin would be successful in reaching an accommodation with Hitler. Stalin was a cautious politician and realised that if he made a serious mistake it might lead to his removal. Therefore, I feel, on balance, he would have decided to conclude a certain alliance with Britain and France rather than wait for the possibility of an alliance with Nazi Germany. Chamberlain should forever be criticised for indecisiveness in April 1939 rather than at Munich.

The *Times*, commenting on Litvinov's dismissal, correctly predicted 'the possibility of a bargain between the Soviet Union and Germany at the immediate expense of Poland and in the end at the cost of the Western Powers.' However, it suggested 'a more likely explanation was that Stalin, impatient at the delay in conclusion of an agreement between Britain, France and Russia, had chosen this drastic method of attempting to speed things up.'[52] These thoughts were echoed by Harvey, who stated: 'Does it mean the Soviet Union will turn from the West towards isolation and won't she inevitably wobble into Germany's hands?'[53] It was a pity that nobody in the British diplomatic corps was able to enjoy the close relationship that Litvinov enjoyed with Norman Davis who was head of the USA's delegation to the Brussels conference. In 1937 Litvinov said:

> He was in a difficult situation. If the powers did not intend to treat the Soviet Union on the basis of complete equality and put her on essential committees, they should never have invited her [to work with the Western powers]. The Soviet Union, once she had espoused the idea of working with the Western powers, had done so wholeheartedly, but had taken some terrible beatings in consequence. He had been

[52] *Times*, 5 May 1939, p.14
[53] Harvey, Oliver: *Diplomatic Diaries*, p.287

in two minds whether to accept the invitation to come to Brussels and it would be exceedingly difficult for him to return with completely empty hands. While he was given a pretty free hand in formulating Russian foreign policy, he must personally take the rap for any failures.[54]

Joseph Davies, in a memorandum analysing the reason for Litvinov's dismissal, stated:

> Stalin had no confidence in either France or Great Britain and feared that the Soviet Union might be involved in a European war and be left holding the bag. The Soviet Government is definitely devoted to peace, both because of economic and ideological reasons. The Soviet Government is intolerant and disgusted with the method of appeasement previously employed and that the aggressors will only understand positive and bold military alliances that are concrete in character and that these only can preserve peace.[55]

It is a pity that Davies had not persuaded Roosevelt and the US Congress to take stronger action against Nazi Germany. Davies continued with his report:

> [As] Litvinov in the past two years had been unsuccessful in persuading the Western Powers to this view, a new Foreign Minister is required who will project a hard realistic front in these negotiations, which will either secure adequate practical resistance to the aggressors or retirement of the Soviet Union into itself.

However, surely Davies should, in addition, have criticised the USA, which had also practised appeasement?

On 4 May 1939 the British Ambassador, Seeds, sent a telegram to London telling them of Litvinov's retirement which was a complete surprise, as Seeds had seen Litvinov in the morning. Litvinov told Seeds he could not see him in the afternoon. No doubt the reason was the prearranged interview with Stalin. Litvinov had given no inkling of his retirement.[56]

On the same day Seeds again reported to London. He was uncertain as to whether Litvinov's dismissal signified a change of policy to isolation.[57] However, a memorandum of 5 May 1939 from Phipps, British Ambassador to France, confirmed: 'Maisky in London, Suritz in Paris and Molotov have all given assurances that Mr Litvinov's resignation implies no change of policy, but none of them have explained what it does imply, of which I have no concrete evidence.' This memorandum further stated: ' It was

---

[54] Moffat, Jay: *Moffat Papers*, p.174
[55] Davies, Joseph E: *Mission to Moscow*, 4th impression 1943, pp.283 and 284
[56] Telegram referred to in Seeds's letter of 12 May; FO 371/ 23685, p.54
[57] FO 371/ 23685, p.16

unlikely to be a personal matter, despite rumours of intrigues against his chief by Potemkin, and there was Litvinov's difficult position created for him by distrust of his English wife.'[58] Further, Potemkin, on his journey to South-East Europe, assured his hosts that Litvinov's departure did not amount to any change of policy.[59]

On 8 May 1939, Seeds, had his first meeting with Molotov, and we know what transpired from Seeds's report to the Foreign Secretary on 9 May. After Molotov had assured Seeds that the Soviet Union's proposals made by Litvinov on 18 April still held good, Seeds justified the decision of his government in not agreeing to Litvinov's proposals on the grounds that it would take too long to complete the negotiations.[60] This was not a valid reason. The British Government acted with remarkable speed to make the declaration concerning Poland in March 1939 and to conclude the Anglo-Soviet Pact in 1942. Molotov also questioned Seeds thoroughly on Britain's claim that the Polish Government regarded any close co-operation militarily with the Soviet Union as provocation. Molotov took up the question and rightly argued that military conversations should start at once. Seeds made it clear that Molotov persisted in his questioning of the attitude of HM Government to military conversations.[61] Molotov had obviously done his homework, because Sir John Simon had confirmed in the House of Commons on 13 April that military conversations might start at once.[62]

On 12 May 1939 Seeds wrote a longer letter with his observations. One was that, as Fischer believed, Litvinov's dismissal was 'an abandonment of the policy of collective security in favour of isolation.' Seeds, however, was inclined not to adopt that explanation too readily. Seeds's view was that Stalin's action did not amount to a retreat from the Litvinov proposals of 18 April and that the Soviet Union is preparing to come to terms with the Axis powers.' Seeds did not endorse the anti-Soviet view that Litvinov had made the proposals 'in a form which it is difficult of acceptance by Her Majesty's Government and the French Government', and therefore had not made them in good faith.[63]

I believe Seeds is right in stating that Stalin hoped, by dismissing Litvinov, that the French and British Governments would be induced to accept the Soviet proposals for fear of a new and unwelcome orientation of Soviet policy. However this eventually was what happened following the failure of the British, French and Soviet military conversations, which resulted in the Nazi-Soviet Pact. Seeds was confident: 'The delay in replying to the Soviet proposals of 18 April1939 was undoubtedly unwelcome to the Soviet Government.'

---

[58] Ibid. p.22
[59] Gafencu, Grigore: *Last Days of Europe*, p.147
[60] FO 371/23066, p.91
[61] Ibid. p.93
[62] *Hansard*, vol.346, 13 April 1939, 138
[63] FO 371/23685, p.54

The second alternative, according to Seeds, is that 'Litvinov had given offence to Stalin by his too energetic advocacy of a certain policy or by a failure to anticipate certain developments: that an intrigue may have developed against him.' It is curious that Seeds linked the two above factors. If Litvinov had given offence to Stalin and he had so determined, no doubt Litvinov would have been dismissed. It would not require intrigue from others, which I would have thought was the least likely explanation. If Litvinov had given offence to Stalin, there might have been other evidence, of which there is none.

The third alternative was that, when the international situation 'can justifiably be said to expose the Soviet to greater danger than it has been for years past, Stalin desires to bring the conduct of foreign affairs more closely under the control of the Kremlin', as he did in May 1941 by replacing Molotov as premier with himself.[64] There is much merit in what Seeds stated that Stalin has decided to take the negotiations into his own hands.

Is Schuman correct that the British Government shared some responsibility for what happened?[65] Chamberlain saw no reason to strengthen Litvinov's hand by negotiating with more enthusiasm. The Foreign Office had confirmed this view in May 1939. However, should not the British Cabinet have given more attention to trying to strengthen Litvinov's position, given his pro-British orientation? *The New York Times* had considered this as early as 2 October 1938. [66] William Seeds was one UK diplomat who was distressed at Litvinov's departure. He regarded it as a retrograde step. Britain might well have prevented it, as Seeds wanted the Foreign Office to be more accommodating to Litvinov.

Seeds wrote to Sir Lancelot Oliphant saying: 'He was sad at Litvinov's disappearance. Talks with him were always stimulating. We had got to understand each other very well.'[67] The British Cabinet, before Litvinov's dismissal, must or should have foreseen that if they continued to deal with Litvinov in the way they were doing and failed to obtain for Litvinov any achievements, he would be replaced by a more pro-German Foreign Commissar. Collier of the Northern Department correctly pointed out: 'A trend towards isolation by Russia is now probable and this must in practice work in favour of Germany, because Poland can no longer be certain of receiving vital Soviet supplies in time of war. We have a chance of avoiding it by being more forthcoming on the vital question of reciprocal guarantees against aggression.'[68]

Sheinis states that Stalin wanted to destroy Litvinov, but is this so? Astakhov, the Soviet

---

[64] FO 371/ 23685, p.56; Roberts, Geoffrey: *The Soviet Union and the Origins of the Second World War*, p.72

[65] Schuman, Frederick: *Night Over Europe*, p.233

[66] *The New York Times*, 2 October 1938, p.32; No. 68 post

[67] FO 371/23066, p.246

[68] FO 371/23685, p.14-15

Chargé d'affaires in Berlin, had told Coulondre that 'for six months Litvinov's fall had been foreseeable as Stalin, while esteeming him [Litvinov], did not like him.' However this is not Miner's view and what is more important is not Litvinov's daughter, Tanya's opinion. [69]

.

Carswell may again be right by saying:

> At least a year before Maxim's [Litvinov's] dismissal and probably longer, the major decisions of foreign policy had been deliberately held in the balance at a level inaccessible to Litvinov by Stalin. To Stalin it would appear that if Maxim's policy of a combination to contain Hitler succeeded all well and good, and if it did not, its effect would be to drive "the bandits" to seek an agreement with Moscow.[70]

There appears no truth in a proposition argued by G. Roberts that the reason for Litvinov's dismissal was that he was against the proposed alliance with the British and the French, and Molotov was more in favour of it. Roberts chose not to see Litvinov's daughter before writing the article.[71] Tanya recalls that, before her father's dismissal, he was very unhappy with the thought that secret negotiations with Germany might be taking place without his knowledge.

However, the only certain fact was that Litvinov's departure was a matter of great significance. Unlike Hitler, Chamberlain and, to a lesser extent Halifax, influenced by their blind hatred of Bolshevism, distorted facts to feed their own ideological interpretation. On 5 May 1939, Halifax, in reporting to the Foreign Affairs Committee, justified the decision to reject Litvinov's offer on 18 April of an alliance (if Germany committed aggression with no-separate-peace agreement) on the grounds

> it would have little additional security. It would arouse the suspicion of our friends and aggravate the hostility of our enemies. [72]

Britain's friends were France who capitulated to the German onslaught but failed to abide by 'the no peace agreement', Poland whose army was defeated in three weeks and Rumania which in due course allied herself to Germany.

Molotov effected the alliance with Britain which Litvinov had tried to formulate and which Halifax and Chamberlain had spurned at a time when German bombers could, at will, bomb Britain and attack its shipping. The entire western coastline of Europe from the

---

[69] Roberts Henry in Craig's *Diplomats 1919-1939* p.375
[70] Carswell, John: *The Exile* p.146
[71] Roberts, Geoffrey: 'The Fall of Litvinov': A revisionist view , in *Journal of Contemporary History*, 1992, p.639
[72] CAB 27 624 p.311

Pyrenees to the north of Norway was in German hands. Chamberlain and Halifax completely misunderstood the fact that the most dangerous scenario would be any co-operation between Germany and the Soviet Union. Efforts to form a political and military alliance with Soviet Russia might have failed, 'but we have no right to assume that would have been the position.'[73] All the evidence indicates that Litvinov always considered the Soviet Union's interests were paramount. For this reason, if Litvinov had continued to be Foreign Minister after May 1939, he might have recommended a rapprochement with Germany; but there is every reason to believe that the foreign policy, as long as Litvinov was Foreign Minister, would be no less moral than that pursued by the wartime governments of Britain, France and the USA.

If Britain and France were to win any war with Germany, unless the USA participated, a watertight agreement with the Soviet Union in 1939 was in fact essential. If no such agreement with the Soviet Union was possible, at least a watertight agreement with Poland might have deterred Germany. The British Government believed the vague declaration given to Poland was sufficient and only entered into an agreement with Poland following the Nazi-Soviet Pact, over four months later, and only days before the invasion of Poland. The relationship between Poland and France was similarly farcical. On 19 May France entered into a military commitment. In the event of an attack on Poland, France would use the bulk of her forces to attack Germany; but the military convention was made conditional on a political agreement which was never signed, so the military convention was not binding. No doubt what was happening was being studied by German diplomats, who were able to report correctly to their superiors with considerable optimism that, if Poland was attacked, Britain and France would not give effective help.[74]

Just before the evacuation at Dunkirk in 1940, Gort was given orders that the safety of the British Expeditionary Force was to be his predominant consideration and therefore by implication he was to evacuate it if necessary, irrespective of the effect on Britain's allies' campaign. However, Eden had to remind Churchill that the Belgian King had not been told of the evacuation. As Belgium was Britain's ally and as Britain was fighting on Belgian territory, the King of Belgium and his Government had a right to know immediately.[75]

Eden was understandably nervous that the news would crack Belgian's resolve, already weakened by defeat. It was hardly surprising that, against the advice of his Ministers, The King, upon hearing the news, ordered the Belgian armed forces to surrender the following day.

---

[73] Mosely, Phillip: *A Foreign Affairs Reader 1922-1962*, p.208

[74] Prazmowska, Anita: *Eastern Europe and the Origins of the Second World War*, pp.153 and 156; Chamberlain's Guarantee to Poland, *Hansard*, vol.345, 31 March 1939 , 2415; Anglo-Polish communiqué dated 1939, in *Documents, Second World War*, p.129; Anglo-Polish Mutual Assistance Pact, in *Documents, Second World War*, p.469 .

[75] Eden, Anthony: *Memoirs, The Reckoning*, p.111

Before France's defeat in 1940 she constantly pleaded with Britain to send more aircraft, without considering whether this would leave Britain defenceless. Further, France broke the agreement with Britain at the beginning of the war whereby it had been agreed that neither Britain nor France would make a separate peace.[76] Britain was prepared to release France from the agreement, providing the French fleet sailed forthwith to British harbours or to a neutral country, so it was out of reach of the Germans, pending negotiations. Notwithstanding the agreement between Britain and France and in complete disregard of her obligations to Britain, France allowed her fleet to fall into Germany's hands.[77] Further, Paul Reynaud agreed with Britain that if peace was made with Germany, German airmen who were prisoners of war would be sent to Britain. Again, the Pétain Government did not honour this pledge and the German airmen, many of whom had been shot down by the RAF, were returned to Germany.[78]

With Molotov as Foreign Commissar, the USSR eventually proved a much better ally than France. Having held the German armies at Moscow, Leningrad and Stalingrad – the latter at crippling cost to Nazi Germany, who lost one sixth of their entire equipment – the Soviet Union then smashed the German Army at Kursk, making possible the invasion of Western Europe by the Allied forces.

At the time of the German offensive in December 1944, known as the Battle of the Bulge, Churchill appealed to Stalin to start an offensive on the Eastern Front. Stalin replied:

> It is most important to take advantage of our superiority. What we need for the purpose is clear flying weather and an absence of low mists that hinder aimed artillery fire. We are mounting an offensive, but at the moment the weather is unfavourable. Still, in view of our Allies' position on the Western front, GHQ of the Supreme Command has decided to complete the preparation at a rapid rate and to commence large-scale operations against the Germans along the whole central front not later than the second week of January.

Churchill replied, thanking Stalin 'for the thrilling news.'[79]

Chamberlain had taken a huge gamble in hoping Germany and Russia would exhaust themselves if they fought against each other. A Soviet victory would have been far less dangerous for Britain than a German victory, which would have made Germany all-powerful and a direct threat to Britain. In 1970 the US President Nixon was much wiser.

The possibility of a war between Communist China and the Soviet Union might seem an

---

[76] Reynaud, Paul: *In the Thick of the Fight*, pp.343 and 559
[77] Ibid. p.537
[78] Ibid. p.497
[79] Churchill, Winston: *The Second World War*, vol. 6, 'Triumph and Tragedy', p.244

attractive proposition to the naive. However, Nixon realised that such an eventuality would, in Kissinger's words, 'upset the global equilibrium.' Nixon took the most daring step of his presidency and told the Soviet Union that the USA would not stand idle if the Soviet Union attacked China. Nixon's experts warned him that such a step might jeopardise Soviet-American relations. The exact opposite happened, as, prior to the Kissinger visit to China, Moscow had been stalling on negotiations for a year. Then, within a month of Kissinger's China visit, the Kremlin invited Nixon to Moscow.[80]

Molotov is often portrayed as pro-German, but this is exaggerated. There was nothing pro-German about his remarks in 1936:

> In this book [*Mein Kampf*], Herr Hitler speaks explicitly of the necessity of adopting a policy of territorial conquest and makes no bones about declaring when we speak of new lands in Europe we can only think in the first instance of Russia and her border States.

He commented:

> German Fascism, having openly turned the country which has fallen into their hands into a military camp, which, owing to their position in the very centre of Europe, constitutes a menace not only to the Soviet Union. All this constitutes a growing menace to the peace of Europe and not of Europe alone.[81]

Molotov's speech of May 1939 was on similar lines:

> Meanwhile, the aggressor countries continue to adhere to their policies. Germany has snatched Memel. As you know, Italy is not far behind. Italy put an end to the independent state of Albania.

> After this there is nothing surprising in the head of the German state tearing up two important treaties, the Anglo-German Naval Agreement and the Polish-German Non-Aggression Pact. At the time they were concluded, great international importance was attached to the treaties, but Germany simply walks out of the treaties without regard to formalities. This was Germany's answer to the proposal permeated with the spirit of peace made by President Roosevelt.[82]

This speech could have well been made by Litvinov, particularly those generous remarks

---

[80] Kissinger, Henry: *Diplomacy*, pp.723 and 731

[81] Complete copy of speech, 1936, in Working Class Movement Library, Manchester; Degras, Jane: *Soviet Documents on Foreign Policy*, vol. 3, pp.153 and 154

[82] Molotov's speech, in Degras, Jane: *Soviet Documents on Foreign Policy*, vol.3, p.332

about President Roosevelt.

Then, in view of that rhetoric, why did Stalin and Molotov conclude the Nazi-Soviet Pact? I think the biggest fear was that, if the Soviet Union did not come to terms with Germany, Britain might have done so. Would Litvinov have agreed to a similar pact if he had still been Foreign Commissar?

Louis Fischer argued that 'Litvinov never by hint or word approved of Stalin's pact with Hitler.' All Ivy Litvinov stated was that 'the Nazi-Soviet Pact had not inspired her husband with much confidence.'[83] Nevertheless this does not prove that Litvinov would have rejected any overtures made by Germany, only that he would not have been surprised if Germany had broken any agreement and would have ensured that his country would have been as prepared as possible if Germany decided to invade the Soviet Union.

It has been maintained that negotiations between Germany and the Soviet Union commenced on 17 April 1939, the date of the first meeting between Weizsacker and Merekalov; but the evidence indicates otherwise. Even as late as 31 July 1939 it appears clear that there were no serious negotiations pending. So, if Britain and France had shown more enthusiasm, there is a good chance that a pact could have been concluded.

Astakhov, in his report to Potemkin, the Deputy Foreign Commissar, stated: 'I have no doubt, if we wanted to, we could involve Germany in far-reaching negotiations.' It is clear that Astakhov was not even encouraged to enter into negotiations, let alone come to an agreement.[84]

Another reason why Litvinov might not have concluded a pact with Germany, if he had desired such an alliance, is that Hitler showed considerable caution and nervousness in his decision to try and come to an arrangement with the Soviet Union.

As late as 2 August 1939 Hitler asked Neurath, former Foreign Minister and career diplomat at the time of the Weimar Republic, whether the German people would accept such an ideological shift from anti-communism to signing a pact with the Soviet Union. Neurath assured Hitler he 'could do what he liked with the party.'[85] Similarly, it seemed that the Russians were extremely suspicious of any German overtures.

Sheinis makes the claim that Litvinov attended a ballet performance of *Swan Lake* in honour of Ribbentrop's visit on 23 August 1939. The orchestra played the national anthem of Germany and the Internationale. Everybody stood. Neither Litvinov nor his wife rose.

---

[83] Archives Box 7 ; Roberts Henry *Diplomats* p.366; Fischer Louis *Great Challenge* p.46
[84] See Ch.13, No.165
[85] Heineman, John: *Hitler's First Foreign Minister* (Neurath), p.200

Then Nina Mirnaya, the wife of the dismissed Soviet diplomat Semyon Mirnaya, came up to Litvinov and said 'Hello.' Litvinov remarked. 'You are a very brave woman.'[86] Tanya Litvinov had never heard of the incident [87] and if anybody else witnessed it they have remained silent. Another reason to doubt the authenticity of the story is that, when Ribbentrop came to negotiate the Nazi-Soviet Pact on 23 August, Ribbentrop did not go to the ballet because there was not time. Ribbentrop did go to the ballet on the second occasion he visited Moscow on 28 September 1939 and gloated with his Soviet hosts over the conquest of Poland. Sheinis is also wrong in stating that this was Litvinov's first appearance in public since his resignation. He had been seen on a number of occasions.

Nevertheless, I believe that Litvinov, if he had been Foreign Commissar, would have approved the Pact. Sheinis states that, when foreign correspondents first asked Litvinov about the Pact, Litvinov evaded the question, but then decided to speak: 'I think this calls for a closer look, because among other things enemies of the Soviet Union ascribe to me what I never said.' He told foreign journalists: The imperialists in these two countries

> had done everything they could to goad Hitler's Germany against the Soviet Union by secret deals and provocative moves. In the circumstances the Soviet Union could either accept German proposals for a non-aggression treaty and thus secure a period of peace in which to redouble preparations to repulse the aggressor; or turn down Germany's proposals and let the warmongers in the Western camp push the Soviet Union into an armed conflict with Germany in unfavourable circumstances and in a setting of complete isolation. In this situation the Soviet Government was compelled to make the difficult choice and conclude a non-aggression treaty with Germany. I, too, would probably have concluded a pact with Germany although a bit differently.

Sheinis' contention is supported by what Litvinov is reported to have told Ehrenburg, 'The pact was absolutely necessary.'[88]

Where Litvinov differed from Stalin and Molotov is that Litvinov foresaw the danger of France being overwhelmed, an eventuality which Stalin and Molotov did not take seriously. Fischer stated:

> A wiser Kremlin would have kept out of the war and out of Finland in 1939, but fought when France was menaced. Roosevelt realised in 1940 that the USA's interests dictated maximum aid to Britain. Stalin should have realised that Soviet interests dictated aid for France.[89]

---

[86] Sheinis, Zinovy: *Maxim Litvinov*, p.298
[87] Tanya
[88] Ehrenburg, Ilya: *Post-War Years*, p.305; Sheinis, Zinovy: *Maxim Litvinov*, p.305
[89] Fisher Louis: *Geat Challenge* p.31

This danger was one reason why Litvinov, unlike Stalin, always foresaw the Nazi-Soviet Pact as a less favourable option than a satisfactory pact between Britain, France and the Soviet Union. When the Soviet Union was in dire danger from Hitler, Litvinov told Cripps he was 'relieved that things had turned out as they had.' [90] That indicates that Litvinov regarded a pact with France and Britain as the preferred option. It has been argued that Stalin and Molotov would have preferred a pact with Germany, provided Germany had abided by the pact and not attacked the USSR. Stalin was never at ease with the Anglo-American Alliance.[91] Stalin feared any increased fraternisation between Soviet and British and US citizens. However, was not Stalin right about the fact that, unless France attacked Germany when Germany attacked Poland, an alliance between France and the Soviet Union was not in the interests of the Soviet Union?

Volkogonov, a Russian critical of the Communist regime, was one of many to justify the Non-Aggression Pact. He said:

> Looking back, the Non-Aggression Pact appears extremely tarnished and morally an alliance with the Western democracies would have been immeasurably preferable. However, neither Britain nor France was ready for such an alliance. From the point of view of state interest, the Soviet Union had no other acceptable choice. A refusal to take such a step would hardly have stopped Germany. The Wehrmacht and the nation were tuned to such a degree of readiness that the invasion of Poland was a foregone conclusion.

Volkogonov then states that rejection of the Pact could have led to the formation of an anti-Soviet alliance and have threatened the very existence of the Soviet state. Volkogonov then refers to the secret talks involving British individuals with influence in Germany, but does not mention the fact that the British Government was not itself party to the talks.[92] How far they were in fact authorised by the British Government is unclear. However, the important fact is that there is little doubt that Britain would have demanded far harsher terms from Germany than did the Soviet Union, and for this reason I do not believe that the negotiations ever progressed beyond the preliminary stage. What was more surprising and open to criticism is the pact of friendship signed on Ribbentrop's second visit to Moscow on 28 September, which Volkogonov fails to mention in his biography of Stalin, However Volkogonov did criticise the Pact in *Pravda*, according to Nove, and what he says carries considerable force. While there may have been some justification for the Non-Aggression Pact signed the previous month, this declaration of ideological solidarity was unnecessary and confusing. 'Friendship with fascism – it is hard to explain such a sliding of Stalin and

---

[90] Estorick, Eric: *Stafford Cripps*, p.280
[91] Tolstoy, Nikolai: *Secret War*, p.275
[92] Volkogonov, Dmitri: *Stalin*, p.356; Gromyko, Andrei: *Soviet Peace Efforts Before World War 2*, p.450; Aster, Sidney: *The Making of World War II*, p.246

Molotov into a *de facto* denial of all their previous anti-fascist ideological declarations.'[93] Litvinov was right to describe Molotov as a fool. For example there is Molotov's bizarre action in congratulating Germany on the entry of her troops into Warsaw. [94] It must be assumed that Litvinov, even if he had approved of the need for the Nazi-Soviet Pact, would never have approved of the pact of friendship. This is only supposition, because he does not appear ever to have expressed an opinion on this Pact.

It is presumed that, if Litvinov had been in charge of the negotiations with Britain and France, he would have suspected, as Stalin and Molotov did, that Britain was not carrying out the negotiations in good faith. The Foreign Office confirmed to the US chargé d'affaires on 8 August 1939 that 'the military mission, which had now left for Moscow, had been told to make every effort to prolong discussions until 1 October 1939.'[95] Halifax disclosed to the Foreign Affairs Committee on 10 July 1939: 'Although the French were in favour of the military conversations commencing, the French Government thought that the military conversations would be spun out over a long time and as long as they were taking place we should be preventing Soviet Russia from entering the German camp.' Lord Halifax also misunderstood Hitler. On 19 July, just over a month before the signing of the Nazi-Soviet Pact, Halifax said: 'Hitler had a very low opinion of the Soviet Union, and our action [in aligning with the USSR] would confirm to him the idea that we were a weak and feeble folk.' [96] On the contrary what made Hitler worried was the thought of a joint pact between France, Britain and the Soviet Union.

I believe that the greatest argument against the military conversations was that if there were joint military discussions and the military commission disclosed information to Stalin, the latter might well pass on valuable information to Hitler for other benefits. Derek Smith was one of the few who perceived this difficulty. Although he does not believe that any such information was in fact divulged to Germany, Chamberlain and the Government ignored that difficulty and, as we have seen, thought of every other reason for non-collaboration with the Soviet Union. [97]

Stalin did not put the twenty-one months' grace won by the Nazi-Soviet Pact to good use. Ehrenburg states: 'He heard this both from military men and diplomats.'[98]

Following Litvinov's dismissal, contemporary and subsequent commentators speculated that Litvinov was in disgrace. This was not so. Litvinov continued to attend official functions and carry out his duties as a member of the Supreme Soviet and Central

---

[93] Nove, Alec: *Glasnost in Action*, p.47
[94] Bethell Nicholas *The War that Hitler Won* , p.114
[95] FRUS, 1939, vol.1, p.294
[96] 27 CAB 625 p.295
[97] Smith, Derek: *Chamberlain, Man of Peace*, p.394
[98] Ehrenburg, Ilya: *Post-War Years*, p.305; see Erickson, John: *Road to Stalingrad*, p.61

Committee.[99] Barmine tells us that during this period Litvinov sometimes appeared on the official tribune for special occasions.[100] Similarly, Cassidy saw Ivy and Maxim at the Bolshoi from time to time. In contrast to his appearance at the meeting with Beaverbrook in 1941, Litvinov was apparently, 'well-dressed, his clothes well-pressed and his flabby face well-shaven.'[101] There is every reason to believe that the one person who was disappointed that Litvinov was not in disgrace was Molotov. What is unknown is whether Molotov did anything to actively encourage Stalin to disgrace Litvinov, or whether Molotov kept his dislike for Litvinov to himself.

Although *The New York Times* in May 1939 stated that Litvinov shared a box with his former deputy, Potemkin, Tanya Litvinov feels that this observation does not tell the whole truth. It is true that Potemkin and her father were present in the government box, but Potemkin's wife turned around and wanted to ignore Ivy, perhaps for fear that Litvinov might be purged and therefore her liberty might be jeopardised. Ivy sarcastically said 'Oh, I had not noticed you.'[102]

Litvinov also attended the Supreme Soviet when the budget was presented. He was wearing a black suit and sat in the front row, chatting with Potemkin. Litvinov attended a number of sittings of the Supreme Soviet, most notably on the occasion of Molotov's statement on foreign policy, where he sat in the fifth row. However, there was no praise or recognition of Litvinov's work after he had held the position of Foreign Minister for nine years. Seeds thought his services might have merited some recognition.[103]

However, when Litvinov applied for a passport to go to Vichy two months later to take the waters, it was refused, presumably on the grounds that he might never come back.[104] In fact, Litvinov was only to leave the Soviet Union once after he attended the League of Nations meeting in September 1938 and that was to take up his appointment as ambassador to the USA in December 1941.

A report in *The New York Times* in July 1939 stated that, when Litvinov attended a meeting of the Supreme Soviet, he was directed to a place where there was an empty seat on either side. The reporter observed that no one spoke to him or appeared to recognise him. However, this is the only official meeting at which it is alleged that Litvinov was shunned and therefore it seems the reporter drew the wrong conclusion.[105]

Litvinov was present during the speech that Molotov delivered to the Supreme Soviet in

---

[99] Schuman, Frederick: *Night Over Europe*, p.233
[100] Barmine, Alexandre: *The One Who Survived*, p.121
[101] Cassidy, Henry: *Moscow Dateline*, p.65; Ch.17, Nos.18.20,23
[102] *The New York Times*, 19 May 1939, p.8; Tanya
[103] *The New York Times*, 1 June 1939, p.13; FO 371/23685, p.72
[104] Murray, Nora: *I Spied for Stalin*, p.125
[105] *The New York Times*, 27 July 1939, p.18

support of the Nazi-Soviet Pact. The British Embassy reported that, although Stalin was also present (he remained silent throughout the sitting), he did not seem fully at ease. However, Molotov enjoyed making his speech.[106]

On 31 October 1939 *The New York Times* reported an extraordinary session of the Soviet Parliament of Western Ukraine. Litvinov was among the deputies present, and he spoke to spectators and journalists.[107]

The British Embassy records confirmed that Litvinov was present in a conspicuous place at the 1939 anniversary of the Revolution by Lenin's tomb. He was standing on the outskirts of a group that included Stalin, Molotov, Kaganovich, Mikoyan, Andreev, Beria and Dimitrov. Litvinov was in full view of the diplomatic stand of foreign journalists, some of whom had no hesitation in exchanging salutations with Litvinov. *The New York Times* disclosed that about thirty members of the German Trade delegation, the German Military Attaché and members of a Finnish delegation watched the parade. The emergence of Litvinov wearing his usual flat cap was apparently a source of interest to the German delegation near the tomb. [108]As this was Litvinov's first public appearance for several months in such select company as Stalin's entourage, it may be supposed that Stalin may well have been finding some use for his talents and extensive knowledge of capitalist countries and their governments. There was continued media speculation outside the Soviet Union that Litvinov was leading the Foreign Information Service of the Russian Communist Party.[109]

The New York Times stated subsequently that Litvinov had been dismissed from the Foreign Information Service for sympathy with the Western powers, but this would appear to be without foundation. Records released since indicate that the speculation about the Litvinovs was erroneous, and Litvinov was never in charge of the Foreign Information Service; but according to Tanya her father did write some articles for academic magazines.[110]

The New York Times reported that Litvinov attended the 1940 celebration of the anniversary of the Bolshevik Revolution in civilian dress. Timoshenko gave the prominent person's address and stated:

> Stalin's policy of peace among the nations and ensuring the security of the Fatherland has resulted in new and remarkable victories of the peoples of this

---

[106] FO 371/23685, p.96

[107] *The New York Times*, 1 November 1939, p.9

[108] *The New York Times*, 8 November 1939, p10; FO 371/ 23685, p.183

[109] *The New York Times*, 15 November 1939, p.8; Tanya

[110] *The New York Times*, 22 January 1940, p.4

Country. The Soviet Union does not take part in the war. The Soviet Union has ensured the peaceful labour of the people of this country.[111]

Twelve months later, with German troops outside Moscow, Stalin's policy did not seem so wise to neutral observers.

Ivy describes this period of her life and relates how the family spent their time with their daughter-in-law in their Dacha seventeen miles from Moscow, although when the schools were open the whole family migrated to the family apartment in Moscow. Nevertheless, they still spent long weekends in the country. Two years passed while the family played bridge, read music, and went on long walks in the countryside with the two dogs Silky and Me-Too, together with an assortment of young dogs and pups, some of them the offspring of carefully picked sires and others the fruit of the illicit union of Silky and Me-Too. Ivy had two pupils for her English classes : Svetlana, the 13-year-old daughter of the gardener, and Ivy's 63-year-old husband. There was certainly rivalry between them, although both did very well.[112] Litvinov wrote to Stalin asking for a job. Not Stalin, but Zhdanov summoned him and offered him the position of Minister of Culture, which Litvinov refused on the grounds that it was not his field. Further, Litvinov stated that one cannot decree culture. As Tanya Litvinov was an artist, she described this as one of her proudest moments.This was surely a veiled criticism as to how the Soviet State tried to decree what works an artist should produce, the most high profile artist was the composer Shostakovich. Ehrenburg recollects the incident. There is some controversy as to when this incident took place. Whereas Sheinis states it occurred in 1940, Tanya believes it happened immediately after Barbarossa. Ehrenburg confirms that Litvinov wrote to Stalin, but says the incident took place in 1947 after Litvinov's retirement.[113]

On 21 February 1941 Litvinov was dismissed from the Central Committee of the Communist Party on the pretext of his inability to discharge his obligations as a member of the Committee.[114] According to Pope, this step was taken because Stalin wanted to give no offence to the Germans.[115] However, Maisky was elevated to alternative membership of the Central Committee, even though he was partly Jewish. Sheinis supposedly has given a fuller version of the event. Litvinov is alleged to have said:

My more than 40 years in the Party obliges me to say what I think of what has happened. I do not understand why I am being dealt with in such a peremptory style.

---

[111] Ibid. 8 November 1940, p.6
[112] *Life*, 12 October 1942, p.124
[113] Sheinis, Zinovy: *Maxim Litvinov*, p.298; Ehrenburg, Ilya: *Post-War Years*, p.279; Tanya
[114] *Times*, 22 February 1941, p.4; Pope, Arthur: *Maxim Litvinov*, p.460
[115] Pope, Arthur: *Maxim Litvinov*, p.460

Litvinov went on to say: 'It was necessary and possible to delay if not totally avoid war' and set out his views on what the Soviet Union should do *vis-à-vis* Britain and France. He said that 'Germany intended to attack the Soviet Union. Of this I am deeply convinced.' Then he said: 'There were hardly any Bolsheviks left on the Central Committee and quite a number of Mensheviks, one of them being Andrei Vyshinsky.'

While he was speaking, Molotov heckled.[116] No doubt Molotov was an unhappy man, as his wife had been simultaneously dismissed from the Central Committee.[117] Stalin rejected everything that Litvinov had said. When Stalin had stopped speaking, Litvinov faced him and asked: 'Does that mean you consider me an enemy of the people?' Stalin took his pipe, turned his head around and answered: 'We do not consider you an enemy of the people, but an honest revolutionary.'[118]

As far I am aware, Ehrenburg was the first person to publicly reveal what was stated at the meeting, but it is only the last sentence of what Litvinov is reputed to have said that is corroborated by Ehrenburg, and indeed Tanya has only heard what Ehrenburg stated. In her *Observer* article likewise Ivy Litvinov confirms only what Eherenburg states and not what Sheinis reports. Tanya thinks it is extremely unlikely that her father would have accused Vyshinsky of being a Menshevik. After all, Litvinov owed his survival to the fact that he did not become involved with any of the factions that surrounded Stalin. Further, in view of what Ivy said about her husband's surprise at Barbarossa, it is even less likely that Sheinis reported the speech accurately.[119]

I have been unable to verify whether Pope is correct about when Stalin reviewed the May Day parade in May 1941, Litvinov was present. I can find no mention of this in either the US or British press. Surely they would have commented if this had been so?[120]

Litvinov's inactivity did not last long. It would be all change with Barbarossa in just four months time.

---

[116] Ehrenburg, Ilya: *Post-War Years*, p.278; Sheinis, Zinovy: *Maxim Litvinov*, p.298 *Observer* 25 July 1976 p.17

[117] Kostyrchenko, Gennadii: *Out of the Red Shadows*, p.120

[118] Sheinis Zinovy: Maxim Litvinov p.298

[119] Tanya, Archives Box 7 ; Ch17 No.3

[120] Pope, Arthur: *Maxim Litvinov* p.460

15: SOVIET ALLIES, SPAIN AND CHINA

Litvinov's sympathies, as with millions of others on the Left, were with the Republicans. Like many others, both in Western Europe and in the Soviet Union, Tanya dreamed of fighting for the Republicans in Spain. This they considered to be the noblest of causes.[1] Indeed, a young poet described it as 'a struggle between the forces of good in the world and the forces of evil.'[2]

Those who considered Franco to be a fascist dictator on the model of Mussolini and Hitler were proved wrong. As Roberts stated:

> Franco did not take his debt to Hitler and Mussolini very seriously. Franco certainly did not intend to subordinate Spanish national interest to ideological fraternity. As in Portugal, the regime is best understood, not in terms of fascism with its disturbed middle class of Germany and Italy, but in terms of traditional authoritarianism, Both were backward countries superficially constitutionalised in the nineteenth century and, in both, conservatism was based on the enduring local forces of church, army and landholders.[3]

Litvinov wholeheartedly agreed with Attlee and Gunther that it was in the interests of Britain as well as the Soviet Union to ensure that Franco was defeated. Attlee could not have been more mistaken when, in a speech to the House of Commons on 31 January 1939, he said: 'I cannot understand the delusion that if Franco wins with Italian and German aid, he will immediately become independent. I think it is a ridiculous proposition.'[4] Even more surprising was Gunther's remark in *Roosevelt in Retrospect* that Spain was 'going down the drain and … [was] the worst failure in the whole record of Roosevelt's foreign policy.'[5]

It was Anthony Eden who correctly appraised the situation when, during a speech at Liverpool on 12 April 1937, he stated:

> Whatever the final outcome of the strife … the Spanish people will continue to display that proud independence, that arrogant individualism which is a characteristic of the race. There are twenty-four million reasons why Spain will

---

[1] Tanya
[2] Symons, Julian: *The Thirties*, p.118
[3] Roberts, John Morris: *A General History of Europe 1880-1945*, p.449
[4] Attlee, in *Hansard*, vol.343, 31 January 1939, 72
[5] Gunther, John: *Roosevelt in Retrospect*, p.326

never for long be dominated by the forces or controlled by the advice of any foreign power.[6]

Eden criticised Dalton for saying that Franco must not be allowed to win, to which Eden replied: 'If that is your view you have to take certain action to ensure a certain result and the only action that would be effective is actual intervention on our part.' If Britain had intervened in this sideshow, she would have consumed weaponry and troops that would have been desperately needed in 1940 and might have resulted in Britain's defeat in that year. Privately, Dalton agreed with Eden, as Dalton in his memoirs stated:

> I was far from enthusiastic for the slogan "arms for Spain" if this meant, as some of my friends eagerly did, that we were to supply arms which otherwise we should keep for ourselves, for I was much more conscious than most of my friends of the terrible insufficiency of British armaments against the German danger.[7]

In spite of the rhetoric of the anti-Franco camp that Eden privately was in favour of intervention, and that Chamberlain prevented it, I believe this is incorrect. Eden himself, on his own initiative, obtained Cabinet authority to appoint an agent to liaise with Franco and his supporters as early as March 1937, although the man chosen, Sir Robert Hodgson, did not take up his position until November 1937. The reason for this policy was to prevent German and Italian domination of a Franco Government and to maintain good relations with a victorious Franco regime. Hodgson's official task was limited initially to commercial issues.[8]

At the commencement of the Civil War, Chilston, the British ambassador to the Soviet Union, reported that the Soviet Union took no notice of the outbreak of the Civil War. However, on 3 August 1936, indignant popular meetings took place all over the Soviet Union. There appears no reason for the dramatic change. Half a million pounds was raised by workers all over the Soviet Union.[9] Tom Jones stated that Eden's instructions from Baldwin were that on no account should Britain fight with the Russians.[10] France suggested to Eden that a Non-Intervention Committee should be established. An invitation was sent out to Italy, Germany, the Soviet Union and Portugal, but Eden took the initiative and on 19 August 1936 it was announced that Britain had unilaterally decided to impose an arms embargo on both sides in the Spanish Civil War, without waiting for the other countries.[11] Both Germany, on 17 August, and Italy, with reservations on 21 August, also

---

[6] Speech of Anthony Eden on 12 April 1937, *Foreign Affairs*, p.192

[7] *Hansard*, 1 November 1937, vol.328, 592; Dalton, Hugh: *Fateful Years*, p.97

[8] Buchanan, Tom: *Britain and the Spanish Civil War*, p 59

[9] Eden, Anthony: *Memoirs, Facing the Dictators*, p.402; Jones,

[10] Buchanan, Tom: *Britain and the Spanish Civil War*, p.48; Jones Tom *Diary with Letters* p.231

[11] Eden, Anthony: *Facing the Dictators*, p.403

agreed.[12] The Soviet Commissioner for Trade issued an order prohibiting the export of war materials to Spain which was dated 28 August 1936.[13]

On 9 September a Non-Intervention Committee of all the major powers had its first meeting. The major players − France, the Soviet Union, Germany and Italy − chose to send their ambassadors. Britain provided the Chairman, William S. Morrison, a Government minister.[14]

An important element of the situation was that, if France and Britain had intervened, they could not be certain of victory. The Soviet Union's intervention could have similarly been hampered by supply difficulties in view of the distance of the Soviet Union from Spain and the quality of their weaponry might have made the Soviet Union's participation less effective than those opposed to non-intervention might have hoped. The reason that Litvinov gave for supporting non-intervention was his fear that the war could lead to an international conflict. The Soviet Union stated: 'She supported the non-intervention policy', in spite of the fact that she considered the principle of neutrality inapplicable to a war pursued by rebels against the lawful government, and on the contrary to be a breach of international law; on which point the Soviets were in agreement with the Spanish Minister for Foreign Affairs.

> The Soviet Government understands this unjust decision was imposed by those other countries which, considering themselves to be champions of order, have established a new principle fraught with incalculable consequences according to which it is permitted openly to assist rebels against their legitimate government.

However, privately Litvinov told Eden that the reason for his support was because he believed

> it would be rigorously enforced; but unfortunately, as a result of breaches of the agreement by some powers [Germany and mainly Italy], it had favoured the rebels.[15]

When the French first raised the question of non-intervention, Litvinov was on holiday, but when he returned he appeared to have been successful in supporting a policy of prohibiting the export of war materials to Spain. There appeared to have been differences of opinion between Litvinov and the doves on the one hand and the hawks on the other, but in such

---

[12] Haslam, Jonathan: '*The Soviet Union and the Struggle for Collective Security in Europe 1933 to 1939*', p.113

[13] Ibid. p.114

[14] Eden, Anthony: *Memoirs, Facing the Dictators*, p.407

[15] Degras, Jane: *Soviet Documents on Foreign Policy*, vol.3, p.210, speech on 28 September 1936; FO 954 24

situations it would be more unusual if there was not a range of opinions. If the Soviet Union had not agreed to non-intervention she would have been isolated, and if she had then not given effective help she would have been accused of letting down her ally. Further any failings would advertise the Soviet Union's military weakness. Surprisingly, this difference of opinion was revealed by *Izvestiya*, which stated: 'Had a Leftist uprising taken place against a Fascist dictatorship, those now clamouring for neutrality would be taking a very different view.'[16]

It is uncertain whether, if Litvinov had been able to determine the Soviet Union's policy, he would have preferred a policy of intervention; but his support for the non-intervention was because initially he thought it would be effective. According to a conversation with a British diplomat, Litvinov told him: 'The policy, if it had been rigidly enforced, would have been the proper one, but unfortunately as a result of breaches by some powers it had resulted in favouring the rebels.' He was critical of Britain and France's policy of not enforcing non-intervention. However, Litvinov was a realist who appreciated that effective active intervention by the USSR without the support of Britain and France was not likely to be successful and it was of benefit to his country to keep in the good graces of the Western democracies. Also, Litvinov gave priority to collective action to curb Hitler's ambitions. At this time the Soviet Union was independently pursuing another secret policy. Litvinov never gave any inkling to what extent he realised Stalin's fluctuating policy was being pursued independently of the non-intervention policy, but surely he must have realised what was happening? [17]

However, at a meeting of the Non-Intervention Committee on 9 October 1936, allegations were being made of breaches by Germany, Italy and Portugal. Eden saw Blum, who immediately told Eden they must do all in their power to make the policy effective. Notwithstanding these events, the French Prime Minister continued to consider that non-intervention was the correct policy. If it had not been for non-intervention, the Spanish Government would have suffered more than the rebels, because the German and Italian dictatorships could supply arms more readily to the insurgents than the democracies were able to do.[18] In any event, the British and French Governments were woefully short at that time of armaments.

Kennan alleges that, once Stalin had decided to assist the Spanish Republicans, the operation was put in place with remarkable speed and energy. The first load of arms, and tanks arrived as early as 26 September and was secretly unloaded at night. Advisers accompanied the armaments. Soviet officers were in effective charge of military operations on the Madrid Front. Kennan believes that this operation was originally conducted in good

---

[16] Haslam, Jonathan: *Soviet Policy in Europe 1933-1939*, p.114
[17] Traina, Richard Paul: *American Diplomacy and the Spanish Civil War*, p.38; FO 954 24, p.244 and see No. No.35 post.
[18] Eden, Anthony: *Memoirs, Facing the Dictators*, p.409

faith with no other purpose than saving the Republic. No effort was made to encourage the Spanish Communist Party to seize power.[19] It was claimed that the Soviet Union only sent military assistance to Spain when it was realised that Germany and Italy were not abiding by the Non-Intervention Agreement to which they had agreed. The Politburo, according to Krivitsky, took the decision to provide military aid to Spain as early as 31 August 1936.[20] If that is so, the Soviet Union never acted in good faith and the order prohibiting arms was merely a smokescreen.

On 23 October 1936 Maisky, no doubt on instructions from Litvinov, complained:

> The proceedings of the Committee have convinced the Soviet Government that at present there is no guarantee against further supplies to the rebel generals of war materials. In these circumstances, the Soviet Government is of the opinion that, until such guarantees are created, and an effective control over the strict fulfilment of the obligations regarding non-intervention established, those governments who consider supplying the legitimate Spanish Government as conforming to international law, international order and international justice are morally entitled not to consider themselves more bound by the agreement than those governments who supply the rebels in contravention of the agreement.[21]

On 26 November 1936, in a passionate speech to the 8th Extraordinary Session of the Supreme Soviet, Litvinov described Franco's policy as: 'An attempt to force upon the Spanish people a fascist system with the aid of bayonet, hand grenade and bomb.'

On 27 November 1936 Spain's Republican Government, protested at the League of Nations against Italian and German intervention in the Spanish Civil War. At the extraordinary session of the League Council on 12 December 1936, the League Council expressed the opinion:

> The good understanding between nations upon which peace depends ought to be maintained, irrespective of the internal regime of states and affirmed the duty of every state to respect the territorial integrity and political independence of other states.

The resolution also took note of :

> New attempts which had been made by the Non-Intervention Committee to make

---

[19] Kennan, George F: *Russia and the West under Lenin and Stalin*, p.309; Haslam, Jonathan: *The Soviet Union and the Struggle for Collective Security in Europe 1933-1939* p.118
[20] Thomas, Hugh: *The Spanish Civil War*, p.441; Krivitsky, Walter: *I Was Stalin's Agent*, p.98
[21] Coates, W P & Z: *A History of Anglo-Soviet Relations*, p.561

its action more effective, in particular by instituting measures of supervision and recommended members of the League who were also on the London Committee to spare no pains to render the non-intervention undertakings as stringent as possible.[22]

However, the Council rather cowardly refused to condemn Germany and Italy for intervening, although the Soviet Union had also intervened. Litvinov was probably annoyed at the decision of Spain to involve the League Council without the Soviet Union being consulted, as he did not attend.[23] Until 1939 Litvinov was very punctilious in his attendance at League meetings.

One of the features of the Soviet involvement in Spain was that, Soviet policy at that time advocated co-operation between communist parties and democratic Left-wing parties. Therefore the Soviet Union advocated loyal co-operation between middle-class liberals and the working class in Spain. The Communists had 'made themselves champions of the small bourgeoisie' against the collectivisation proposed 'by Anarchist and Left Socialists.' If Stalin had advocated such cooperation with the Social Democrats in the Weimar Republic, Hitler might have been kept from power.

However, there was great bitterness between the German Social Democrats and the Soviet Union. The arguments whether the decision not to advocate the same co-operation in the Weimar Republic that occurred in Spain was due to such bitterness that overrode a pragmatic approach or was a result of a serious error by Stalin, who did not believe either in the Hitler menace or that the Hitler regime would last, are finely poised. We do know that Litvinov opposed Stalin's policy of non-co-operation between the German Social Democrats and the Communists.[24]

In December 1936 the Soviet press called for the elimination of the heretical Marxist party of Catalonia (POUM) because that party had criticised, among other matters, the Zinoviev trial. The Spanish Prime Minister, Caballero, was told that Stalin was personally interested in its liquidation. It appears the Prime Minister disregarded Stalin's threat and took no action. On 15 May 1937 the Communist party managed to infiltrate the Barcelona police and seized the telephone exchange from the anarcho-syndicalist CNT unions, who had controlled it since the beginning of the war. Instead of fighting the Nationalists, the Communists and allied Republicans fought against the POUM and other Left-wing organisations. The Communists won this conflict after four days of fighting, the chief beneficiary being Franco. On 15 May 1937 the Communists in the Government demanded, no doubt on Stalin's orders, the suppression of the POUM.

---

[22] *Survey of International Affairs*, 1937, vol 1 p.266
[23] Carr, Edward: *Socialism in One Country*, p.28; Thomas, Hugh: *The Spanish Civil War*, p.571
[24] See Ch.19, No.152; Jackson, Gabriel: *The Spanish Republic and the Civil War*, p.361

The Prime Minister, Largo Caballero, refused to accede to Stalin's request, and the Communist ministers in the Spanish Government resigned.[25] Rather than cause further disunity, Caballero resigned, to be replaced by Stalin's choice, Negrin, a moderate Socialist. However, Negrin displayed 'that proud independence, that arrogant individualism which is a characteristic of the race', as portrayed by Eden,[26] and certainly was not prepared to be dictated to by Stalin. Although Stalin wished the Communist and Socialist parties to merge, Negrin said that such action was inappropriate for a democratic state.[27]

On Christmas Eve 1936 the British ambassadors in Berlin, Rome, Moscow and Lisbon were instructed to propose to the governments of the countries in which they were serving that measures be taken to stop volunteers from going to fight in Spain. On 10 January 1937 Eden took steps to prevent Britons from joining the fight in Spain.[28] Portugal quickly stated that they were willing to prevent the enlistment of volunteers or their transit through Portuguese territory if the other countries would do the same.[29] By the end of January 1937, Germany and Italy likewise stated that they would stop volunteers if other countries did the same.[30] The navies of Great Britain, France, Italy and Germany would function to supervise shipping and prevent volunteers travelling to Spain.

In the meantime, although Italy was contravening the Non-Intervention Agreement, Italy and Britain entered into an agreement on 2 January 1937 which stated that Britain and Italy, who are:

> animated by the desire to contribute increasingly in the interests of the general peace and security to the betterment of relations between them and between all the Mediterranean powers and resolved to respect the rights and interests of those powers, disclaim any desire, to modify, or as far as they are concerned, to see modified the *status quo* as regards national sovereignty of territories in the Mediterranean area.[31]

Sensibly, Eden had reservations about appeasing Mussolini:

> No amount of promises or understandings or renewed profession of friendship or even humble crawling on our part will affect Mussolini's course. On the other hand, a little plain speaking may. We must be on our guard against increasing the dictator's prestige by our own excessive submissiveness.

[25] Conquest, Robert: *The Great Terror*, p.410
[26] See No. 6 *ante*
[27] Jackson, Gabriel: *The Spanish Republic and the Civil War1931-1939*, p.402
[28] Eden, Anthony: *Memoirs, Facing the Dictators*, p.436
[29] Ibid.
[30] Ibid. p.438
[31] DBFP, 2nd Series, vol.17, p.754, No.530

However, Eden had to yield to the opinion of most members of the government as well as the Chief of Staff that Britain had to remove Italy from the list of countries with whom Britain might have to reckon.[32] These elements did not face up to the unpleasant fact that, however much Mussolini was appeased, there was no guarantee he would not join the Hitler camp.

The gentleman's agreement was a farce because Italy, by invading Abyssinia, had, instead of contributing to peace, brought Europe to the brink of war, and by helping Franco had not only broken an agreement but was assisting in changing the national sovereignty of Spain. This course of events was bound to increase Soviet suspicion, which should have been obvious to both Eden and the Foreign Office. Rather than being neutral, it implied that Britain was quite happy for Italy to assist Franco, and really desired a Franco victory, but was cowardly and would not say so.

However, by February 1937 the Soviet Union's military help started to taper off, to be replaced by limited economic aid. Kennan suggests that Stalin's action was influenced by the resistance of his colleagues to the arrest of Bukharin and the continuation of the purges, but there is no evidence for this view.[33] A more likely motive was Stalin's instinct for self-preservation, because the Spanish Civil War had aroused a spirit of heroism in support of freedom more in line with Trotskyism and such ideas might be exported to the Soviet Union. Further proof of this is what Modin stated that Stalin decided to attack the extreme Left, particularly Trotskyites and militants of the POUM before liquidating Franco,[34] but Stalin would leave it too late. Those who had served in Spain were tainted in Stalin's view and were singled out for harshness in the purges and were virtually all eliminated.

The defector Orlov, who worked for the NVKD in Spain, confirms that he was told by a General, whom Orlov did not want to name, that when the General returned to Moscow to seek further instructions, he was told that the Politburo had adopted a new line towards Spain. Until then, the policy of the Politburo was to assist Republican Spain by supplying armaments, Soviet pilots and tanks in order to bring about a speedy victory over Franco; but now the Politburo had revised its strategy. Stalin had come to the conclusion that 'it would be more advantageous to the Soviet Union if neither of the warring camps gained preponderant strength, and if the war in Spain dragged on as long as possible and thus tied up Hitler for a long time.' The Soviet General who informed Orlov of this was shocked by the Machiavellian calculation of the Politburo which, in its desire to obtain time, wanted the Spanish people to bleed as long as possible.[35] However, Litvinov's reported conversation with his wife indicates that, although he shared Orlov's distress at the continued agony of the Spanish people, he was prepared to accept that Stalin might have

---

[32] Eden, Anthony: *Memoirs, Facing the Dictators*, p.426
[33] Kennan, George: *Russia and the West Under Lenin and Stalin*, p.310
[34] Modin, Yiuri: *My Five Cambridge Friends*, p.56
[35] Orlov, Aleksandr: *Secret History of Stalin's Crimes*, 1953 edition, p.238, 1954 edition p. 244

been unable to give effective help, rather than attributing any failings to wilfulness on Stalin's part.[36] Kennan was right when he states that eventually Stalin's attitude to the Spanish Civil War was similar to Germany's, which was to give sufficient help to prolong the conflict in order to tie down its adversaries as long as possible.[37] We do not know whether Litvinov was aware of Stalin's tactics, but I think probably not, because of Litvinov's conversation with his wife, as related by Tanya.

Nevertheless, the Soviet Union had another problem in assisting Republican Spain, as they needed to use French ports. Often ships laden with Russian munitions stood in French ports waiting for authority.[38]

It appears that Republican Spain was tricked into releasing to the Soviet Union a vast quantity of gold and numerous rare and antique coins, which have never been accounted for by the Soviet Union.[39]

Attacks on shipping by submarines increased alarmingly during the summer of 1936. On 10 August a British tanker, *British Corporal*, was attacked off the Spanish coast,[40] and two vessels of the Spanish Government were torpedoed as far away as the Turkish coast.[41]

The idea of a conference to discuss the deteriorating situation was originally suggested by the French Foreign Minister Delbos and, after considerable discussion, it was agreed to invite all the Mediterranean powers as well as Germany.[42] Neither Germany nor Italy attended. Eden and Delbos agreed that the aim of the conference should be to organise naval patrols in the Mediterranean, so that unlawful attacks on shipping could be dealt with promptly.[43] Eden wanted to invite Italy but exclude the Black Sea powers. However surely France was right to insist upon the Soviet Union being invited?[44] Presumably, given the Soviet Union's spies in London, this fact was known to Litvinov before he argued his case before the Politburo. Litvinov gave the following four reasons for supporting the Soviet Union's attendance at the Conference :

1. The conference was conducted without the participation of Germany and Italy, which had attempted to get us the (USSR) excluded.
2. Britain and France rival Italian domination in the Mediterranean.
3. Recognition of our interests (USSR) in the Mediterranean.

---

[36] Tanya
[37] Kennan, George: *Russia and the West Under Lenin and Stalin*, p.311
[38] Fischer, Louis: *Men and Politics*, p.470
[39] Spanish gold, in Krivitsky, Walter: *I Was Stalin's Agent*, pp.99 and 131
[40] Eden, Anthony: *Memoirs, Facing the Dictators*, p.457
[41] Ibid. p.458
[42] Ibid. p.459
[43] Ibid. p.465
[44] Haslam, Jonathan: *Soviet Policy in Europe 1933-1939*, p.146

4   (There would be) a certain mitigation of the danger from submarines.[45]

The conference was held at Nyon, fifteen miles from Geneva, where the League of Nations was in session. Nyon was chosen rather than Geneva so that Germany and Italy would not have been deterred. However, Litvinov praised Britain and France for calling the Nyon conference. He described the calling of this conference

> as timely and appropriate. Consistent in its defence of the idea of collective security, the Soviet Union could not fail to respond to the call for the collective organisation of security for peaceful navigation on such an important waterway as the Mediterranean.

However, Litvinov regretted the absence of Spain from the conference. Referring to the loss of two Soviet ships, he gave a warning that the Soviet Union would have to take its own measures. It could not remain inactive in the hope that its interests might be defended by other states or an international organisation. Litvinov, commenting on Italy's absence, stated publicly:

> Only those states can refuse to take part in the conference, while having a merchant fleet and using the Mediterranean, think themselves guaranteed against piracy either because they are organising it as an instrument of their national policy themselves or because of their extreme intimacy with the pirates.[46]

Italy, after boycotting the conference, joined in the patrols in November 1937. Litvinov rightly stated: 'In accusing Italy of infringing the freedom of the seas, we cannot at the same time entrust her with the defence of freedom.'[47]

The conference encountered some difficulty when Britain and France suggested they would patrol the western Mediterranean while Russia and Turkey would patrol the Aegean in the north, and Yugoslavia and Greece in the south. Eden realised that the Eastern Mediterranean countries, including Turkey, with whom the Soviet Union enjoyed excellent relations, were most unwilling to have any involvement on the part of the Soviet Union. At first Litvinov objected to the exclusion of the Soviet Union, and by the end of the first day Eden was prepared for failure. However, Litvinov the next day agreed to a plan under which Britain and France would patrol the whole Mediterranean. Eden considered that Litvinov, realising how unpopular the Soviet Union was among the small states, was wise

---

[45] Ibid. p.148

[46] Degras, Jane: *Soviet Documents on Foreign Policy*, vol.3, p.252, speech opening session of Nyon Conference, 10 September 1937

[47] Buchanan, Tom: *Britain and the Spanish Civil War*, p.59; Haslam, Jonathan: *Soviet Policy in Europe 1933-1939*, p. 148

enough not to want to give publicity to that condition of affairs.[48] We do not know how far Litvinov acted on his own initiative, and how far he was acting on instructions from Stalin. However, the most likely reason for Litvinov's change of heart was that, if the conference had not been successful, the chief beneficiaries would be Germany and Italy.

Further matters that presumably influenced both Litvinov and the Politburo were the outbreak of the Sino-Japanese war in July 1937 and the Soviet Union's commitment to supply arms to China. The USSR was further influenced because they had suffered heavy losses. Between October 1936 and July 1936, 96 Soviet merchant ships were captured and three were sunk.[49]

Litvinov made a further speech on 14 September 1937:

> Thanking Britain and France for their considerate attitude to the wishes and proposals advanced by the Soviet delegation during the course of the conference, and welcomed the kind consent of Britain and France to take over the protection of the entire Mediterranean.

It is a pity that Sheinis gives no authority when he records a supposed comment from Litvinov that other delegates

> tried to prevail on me not to speak. The motive was to get on with the business and begin patrolling the Mediterranean. I said I welcomed strong action but, if the patrolling started half an hour late, no one would lose. Since we were not consulted before the conference convened, I said we could not sit idly by without stating our government's attitude.[50]

If that was what Litvinov said, Sheinis fails to explain why the public statements made by Litvinov were in a much more conciliatory tone.

The conference at the time was considered a triumph for Eden because it curtailed Italy's submarine attacks. However, as Britain had cracked Italy's codes, Eden was presumably aware that Mussolini had already suspended submarine attacks on 4 September 1937,[51] although the threat of the conference might have encouraged Mussolini to make the decision to suspend these attacks. Apart from an isolated attack on the British vessel *Endymion* in the spring of 1938, submarine attacks ceased.[52] Finally, the patrols were

---

[48] Eden, Anthony: *Memoirs, Facing the Dictators*, p.467
[49] Haslam, Jonathan: *Soviet Policy in Europe 1933-1939*, p.146
[50] Degras, Jane: *Soviet Documents on Foreign Policy*, vol. 3, p.254, speech on signing Nyon Agreement; Sheinis, Zinovy: *Maxim Litvinov*, p.281
[51] Buchanan, Tom: *Britain and the Spanish Civil War*, p.59
[52] Ibid. p.60

suspended in August 1938.[53] However, Eden's triumph was dampened because the Nationalists and their Italian allies then turned to aerial attacks on shipping to achieve their objects.[54]

The Spanish Government was disgruntled that the agreement did not protect her ships and made an urgent appeal to the League. The Spanish premier Negrin asked the League:

1. That the aggression of Germany and Italy be recognised as such.
2. In consequence of this recognition the League examine as soon as possible the means by which such aggression can be brought to an end.
3. That full rights once more be given to enable the Spanish Government to acquire all the war material the Spanish Government considers necessary.
4. That non-Spanish combatants be withdrawn from Spanish territory.
5. That measures to be adopted for security in the Mediterranean be extended to Spain and that Spain be granted her legitimate share in them.

Litvinov had stayed away from the December 1936 meeting of the League which dealt with a previous similar request from the Spanish Government; but now, unlike the other great Powers, he wholeheartedly supported the Spanish initiative.[55] Litvinov's change of heart was no doubt brought about by both the failure of the Non-Intervention Committee and also Litvinov's difficulty in justifying to his superiors his previous conciliatory stance, which had achieved little.

In a League debate on 21 September 1937, most of the delegates appeared reluctant to criticise Germany and Italy. Only Mexico's representative and Litvinov defended the Spanish Government. Litvinov said:

> Spain continues for the second year in succession to be subjected to organised foreign armies and its magnificent capital of Madrid and other cities daily undergo the most violent bombardment, which takes toll of tens of thousands of lives and vast material and cultural riches.[56]

When there arose the question of what resolution should be passed, Litvinov initially insisted upon Negrin's five points being incorporated, but Litvinov's tough stand was undermined when Britain and France persuaded Negrin not to name Germany and Italy as aggressors, although it was known at the time those countries were undoubtedly aggressors and nothing that history has unearthed since has altered the situation. A resolution was passed:

---

[53] Ibid.
[54] Ibid.
[55] *Survey of International Affairs*, 1937, vol 2 p.355
[56] Degras, Jane: *Soviet Documents on Foreign Policy*, vol.3, p.256

> Not merely has the London Non-Intervention Committee failed, despite the efforts of the great majority of its members, to which the Assembly expressed its appreciation, to secure the withdrawal of non-Spanish combatants taking part in the struggle in Spain, but it must today be recognised that there are veritable foreign army corps on Spanish soil which represents foreign intervention in Spanish affairs.

The resolution expressed the hope that 'diplomatic action recently initiated by certain powers [would] be successful in securing the immediate and complete withdrawal of non-Spanish combatants taking part in the struggle in Spain'; and, having appealed to Governments 'to undertake a new and earnest effort in this direction', it then finished with a warning to Germany and Italy: 'If such a result cannot be obtained in the near future, the members of the League who are parties to the Non-Intervention Agreement will consider ending the policy of non- intervention.'[57] 32 countries voted in favour, including Britain, France and the Soviet Union, but Portugal and Albania voted against it, so technically the resolution was defeated, as it required unanimity.[58]

However, far more than in the case of Abyssinia and Munich, the policy in Spain was considered sufficiently important that, on major matters, it was Stalin who determined the policy. There is a difference as, unlike the other crises of Abyssinia and Munich, Red army troops were committed. If the USSR had been called upon to intervene in Abyssinia and at Munich, Litvinov's authority would have been considerably restricted. Stalin's policy in the Spanish Civil War fluctuated. First, he gave help to the Spanish Republicans. The evidence appears to prove that when Stalin initially stated that the Soviet Union would abide by non-intervention; this was a smokescreen to hide intervention. However, there is abundant evidence that the policy of effective intervention which saved Madrid was replaced in December 1936 by a policy of endeavouring to liquidate in Spain those Left-wing movements that did not please Stalin. Finally, Stalin's motives became similar to Hitler, which was to allow the Civil War to continue in the hope that those Countries who Stalin then perceived as hostile to the Soviet Union would be weakened by their continuous involvement. Eleanor Rathbone, the moderate feminist and independent MP, who was normally so level-headed, was completely wrong. She observed:

> I am no admirer of any dictatorship, certainly not that of Stalin, but it is only fair to recognise in the sordid history of the Non-Intervention Agreement the one bright spot was the part played by the USSR. With far less to lose than ourselves and

---

[57] *Survey of International Affairs*, 1937, vol. 2, p.360
[58] *Survey of International Affairs,* 1937 vol. 2, p.362; Walters, Francis Paul: *History of the League of Nations*, p.728

France, by the triumph of fascism in Spain, that Government at least allowed themselves to be neither intimidated nor bluffed.[59]

Stalin's actions were certainly not influenced by the welfare of the Spanish people. I am sure Litvinov had the welfare of the Spanish people at heart, which was indicated by his speech[60] and by what Tanya Litvinov stated about her father's attitude towards Stalin's involvement in Spain.

Throughout the war there was constant argument whether a state of belligerency should be declared, but it was never declared. Until such time as a state of belligerency is declared, a rebel government is treated as an insurgency. Insurgents are entitled to the benefit of the humanitarian rules of war, providing the insurgency is for political reasons. If the insurgency is not for political reasons, the rebels are not insurgents but regarded as pirates. Neutral governments are free to help the parent state and refuse aid to the rebels. What has been criticised, particularly by Paul Preston, is that the Non-Intervention Agreement took away the right of the parent state to obtain the arms to which they were entitled by international law. There has been an argument that belligerency should have been declared if the rebels were occupying a substantial portion of the parent state, as Franco achieved in 1936. Belligerents are entitled to equal treatment from neutrals, to attack their opponents' territory and ships and to impose a blockade to prevent their opponents trading.[61] However, Maisky for the Soviet Union initially opposed the granting of belligerent rights to Franco. The Soviet Union rightly suspected that Germany and Italy, in spite of what they may have stated, had no intention of removing their forces. Therefore, Britain, France and the Soviet Union refused to grant belligerent rights to Franco's forces until the majority of combatants had left Spain and new reinforcements did not arrive. This was never achieved.

I have found one clue which points to a conflict between Stalin and Litvinov, although there is no guarantee it is correct. *The New York Times* stated that there was a conflict between Litvinov, who advocated the correct policy was to try and come to an agreement with Britain and France, and Stalin, who wanted to adopt a sterner line, in the hope people would believe he was supporting the Republican cause; but as we now know, he really wanted the Spanish Civil war to continue. *The New York Times* further indicated that Maisky, by pleading for greater latitude in trying to reach a compromise, was supporting Litvinov. Eventually, Maisky, however, agreed to the resolution, which rather indicates it was Litvinov who succeeded in persuading Stalin to adopt a more flexible stance.[62] However, as Britain's resolution was vague, Maisky nevertheless made it clear that the interpretation of the words 'substantial withdrawal' meant substantial.

---

[59] Rathbone Eleanor : *Can War be averted* p.65; No 35 ante
[60] No. 56 ante
[61] Belligerent rights defined in *Encyclopaedia Americana*, 1977, vol.3, p.515
[62] *The New York Times*, 29 October 1937, p.4

In February 1938 Italy suddenly became more co-operative. She wanted Britain's support in asking the League of Nations to recognise Italy's conquest of Abyssinia.[63] When the Council of the League discussed Abyssinia in May 1938, Emperor Haile Selassie made a spirited speech of condemnation against countries who wanted to recognise Italy's right to Abyssinia.[64] The only Council members who supported the Emperor were the Soviet Union, China and New Zealand.[65] This prevented the passing of any resolution, although Britain and France nevertheless proceeded to recognise Italy's conquest of Abyssinia.[66] No wonder Litvinov was suspicious of Britain and France, and Stalin even more so. If they could do such a U-turn with Mussolini, might they not do a similar deal with the much greater menace of Adolf Hitler?

The first meeting of the Non-Intervention Committee in 1938 took place on 5 July, when 27 nations reaffirmed their acceptance of the plan for the departure of volunteers. However, this proposal still needed the support of each side in the Spanish Civil War. The Republicans accepted, but Franco only gave conditional approval. He stated that he would only agree to withdraw 10,000 men, which was a ridiculous offer, as 17,000 volunteers had arrived in the last month from Italy. Further, Franco wanted to make the withdrawal of the 10,000 volunteers conditional on the granting of belligerent rights. The Soviet press was wholly critical.[67] Franco was never granted belligerent rights, but all the powers except the Soviet Union now suggested that Francis Hemming, the secretary of the Non-Intervention Committee, should go to Spain to try and reach agreement.[68]

However, the whole situation changed when Negrin announced at the League his intention to unilaterally cause to be withdrawn all non-Spanish combatants in the belief that there might be restored to it the right for the Republicans to purchase arms. In fact, this action caused Franco some embarrassment, because if he won the Civil War it would be said he only achieved it with foreign help.[69]

Litvinov's final involvement of any significance in the Spanish Civil War was his address to the Political Committee of the League while the deliberations at Munich were proceeding. Spain made the modest request that a League Commission be appointed to guarantee to the world that its voluntary withdrawal of non-Spanish foreign volunteers was being loyally executed. Surprisingly, some European countries, because of their fear of Germany and Italy, who were having increasing influence on what these countries said and did, were reluctant to support such moves. Instead, the Spanish request was referred to the

---

[63] Walters, Francis: *History of the League of Nations*, p.773

[64] Ibid. 773; *Survey of International Affairs*, 1938, vol. 1, p.151

[65] Walters, Francis: *History of the League of Nations*, p.773

[66] Ibid.

[67] *Survey of International Affairs*, 1938, Vol.1 p. 326 , 5 July Non-Intervention meeting

[68] Ibid. p 338

[69] *Survey of International Affairs*, 1938, Vol 1. p 330

Council, the result of which was to postpone any meaningful resolution. Litvinov, referring by implication to those countries who had opposed the Spanish request, stated:

> It cannot even bring down upon us the wrath of the present dictators of Europe, before whom some members of the League have now become accustomed to tremble. The Spanish people too are fighting for the right of self-determination, for its right to set up the internal regime it pleases, and to dispose of its natural resources and foreign trade.

Litvinov reminded the Committee firstly of Mussolini's reiterated statement: 'He will not tolerate the establishment in Spain of an internal regime that does not answer his own ideology and political interests' and, secondly, Chancellor Hitler's statement:'He seeks such a commercial policy in Spain as would answer his economic interest.' Litvinov contrasted

> the volunteers on the Government side who often went against the wishes of their Government and those on the other side whose Governments openly admit their part in sending combatants.

By granting the Spanish Government's request, Litvinov concluded:'The League could help in cleansing the international atmosphere to some extent from its accumulation of hypocrisy and lies.' When it was suggested that, if the League sent a commission, it should not preclude the Non-Intervention Committee from sending a commission, Litvinov pointed out that 'the Non -Intervention Committee's graveyard was more crowded than the League's.'[70] Although Negrin's request was opposed by Poland and Portugal, they could not prevent Spain's request being remitted to the Council, who agreed to send a commission of 15 from ten countries. Three months later, the Commission reported back to the Council not, as incorrectly stated by Walters, that the Negrin Government had faithfully fulfilled the withdrawal of the foreign volunteers, but that, of the 12,673 non-Spanish nationals serving with the Republican forces, 4,640 had left Spain. Although the Council approved the report, some countries did so reluctantly, not wanting to incur Mussolini's wrath, showing how correct Litvinov's September League speech had been.[71]

The withdrawal in early October of 10,000 Italian volunteers was a sufficient gesture for Chamberlain to bring into force the Anglo-Italian agreement.[72] However, because of French opposition, Franco was still not given belligerent rights, so the Soviet Union had achieved their object in preventing General Franco receiving belligerent rights. This did not matter as, with the fall of Barcelona in February 1939, Franco had won the Civil War.

---

[70] *The New York Times*, 30 September 1938, pp.1 and 10

[71] *Survey of International Affairs,* 1938 vol. 1 p.334; Walters, Francis: *History of the League of Nations*, p.790; and No.70 *ante*

[72] *Survey of International Affairs*, 1938, vol. 1, p.333

In March, 1939, for the sound reason that now that, as the Civil War was over, the Non-Intervention Committee had nothing to do, the Soviet Union withdrew. Similarly, the Germans and Italians refused to make any further payments. The only meeting of the Non-Intervention Committee to take place after July 1938 was on 20 April 1939, when it dissolved itself,[73] marking the demise of an inglorious organisation.

No doubt Litvinov passionately believed what he stated in that speech, his last to the League. His entire sympathy was for the Republicans in Spain and he was disappointed that Franco was not deposed when the Second World War was won by the Soviet Union and its Allies. In conversation with Fischer in 1938, Litvinov spoke sourly of the failure of Britain and France to support the Republican Government in Spain. 'Always defeats, always retreat.' However, privately, Tanya tells us that Litvinov was also equally unhappy with the way Stalin gave promises to the Spanish Republican Government he could not keep, thus prolonging Spain's agony.[74]

Neither did the end of the Spanish Civil War necessarily please Hitler, whose aim was the active intervention of the Soviet Government as well as Italy, Britain, and France. Hitler told his Generals on 5 November 1937: 'A 100 per cent victory for Franco was not desirable either.'[75] I can find no indication as to whether Litvinov was aware of German motives, but I suspect, in view of Litvinov's hatred for Franco, he allowed his normally sound judgment to desert him. What is surprising is that many historians since, such as Paul Preston in his mammoth biography of Franco, failed to consider this factor.

An early indication that Franco was going to keep his distance from Germany soon proved true. A rumoured state visit by Franco to Germany did not take place and a further rumour of a visit by Goering to Spain, after he had enjoyed a cruise in the Western Mediterranean, again did not take place. Instead, Goering had to return to Berlin.[76]

If Franco was to enter the war as Hitler's ally, he wanted colonial territory at the expense of France; but Hitler was pursuing a policy of friendship with Vichy France. When Hitler met Franco on 23 October 1940, Hitler completely failed to persuade Franco to enter the war. Franco wanted all of France's North Africa Empire.

Although Hitler wanted Gibraltar attacked with German specialists, Franco made it clear that, if Gibraltar was attacked, it would be with Spanish troops alone, again indicating how right Eden was when he said: 'Spain would never for long be dominated by a foreign power.'[77]

---

[73] Ibid. p.341

[74] Tanya

[75] German documents, p.37, 4th Series, vol.1, Document 19

[76] *Survey of International Affairs*, 1939 (On the Eve of War), vol 1 p.358

[77] See No. 6 *ante;* Preston Paul: *Franco* pp.394-400; Kershaw Ian: *Hitler,* p.329-330

In view of the unsatisfactory result of the meeting between Franco and Hitler, on 10 February 1941, at a meeting between Mussolini and Franco, a further attempt was made to persuade Franco to be more co-operative to the Axis powers. Mussolini asked Franco: 'Would Spain enter the war if given sufficient supplies and binding promises about his colonial ambitions?' Franco replied: 'Spain's un-preparedness and famine conditions would mean several months before she could join in the war', but emphasise:

> Spanish entry into the war depended on Germany more than Spain herself. The sooner Germany sends help, the sooner Spain will make her contribution to the Fascist world cause.[78]

No doubt Franco realised it was in the interests of Spain not to be on the losing side, and unlike Mussolini, correctly and in time predicted the outcome of the war. Preston states:

> For all his [Franco's] sympathies with the Third Reich, Franco was trying to take advantage of Axis difficulties exactly as he was exaggerating German threats to squeeze benefits from the Allies. The extent to which Franco was now coming into his own, ready to pit his native cunning against both Axis and Allies, was soon made clear. [79]

Franco was putting his country first. Although Franco made a pro-German speech expressing confidence in Germany winning the war and his contempt for 'plutocratic democracies', if he had been confident that Germany would win the war would he not have entered the war on Germany's side? Was not Franco's brother right that this speech might have been for internal consumption only?[80]

As so many of the British population were hostile to Franco, Britain could hardly expect any sympathy from Franco. I also think that Shirer was right, following Britain's success in the Battle of Britain, when he stated, 'The crafty Spaniard was not impressed by the Fuhrer's boast that Britain already is decisively beaten',[81] as Franco only wanted to join Germany and Italy if they were to be victorious.

Litvinov was disappointed that Franco was not deposed after the Second World War. In the Snow interview in the autumn of 1944, Litvinov said: 'Who would put Franco out? The Spanish people are powerless. The French won't move a finger. Do you see any sign of the British and French being dissatisfied?' However, Litvinov was pursuing an ideological agenda, not practical politics. He gave no indication in what way Franco was to be deposed. Clearly, Litvinov had no sympathy for Franco.

---

[78] Preston, Paul: *Franco*, p.422
[79] Ibid.   p.480
[80] Ibid.   p.442
[81] Shirer, William: *The Rise and Fall of the Third Reich*, p.814

His views were entirely different from Dalton, a pre-war Labour Shadow Opposition Minister who specialised in foreign affairs. He stated that before the Second World War he believed,

> as Germany and Italy were potential enemies of Britain and Franco was their ally, it was in Britain's interest that Franco should not win the Spanish Civil War. It was on this proposition rather than any extravagant eulogy of the Spanish Government that I based most of my public references to this most tragic struggle.

Yet Dalton admitted he was wrong in his assessment of British interests stating:

> When the Germans overran France in 1940 and reached the Pyrenees, Franco was neutral, and with remarkable skill maintained his neutrality until the end of the war. Hitler respected this and never forced his way through Spain to attack Gibraltar or crossed the Straits into Morocco.

Dalton further stated: 'Hitler would not have respected the neutrality of a Spanish Republican Government. If Franco had lost the Civil War, Hitler would have occupied Spain.'[82]

In 1937 the Sino-Japanese war opened, and, at its commencement, Japan achieved spectacular success. Shanghai was taken by the Japanese in November 1937 and Chiang Kai-shek's capital, Nanking, fell to the Japanese in December 1937. Hankow had become the Nationalist capital following the fall of Nanking, but itself was taken by the Japanese.

However, the fall of Hankow and the forced move of the Chinese capital to Chungking behind the Yangtze gorge in October 1938 did not lead to the triumph Japan had expected. Military stalemate followed, during which Japan unsuccessfully tried to capture the Changsha gateway to south China and wrestled with guerrillas who operated behind the lines in north China.[83]

Meanwhile, another major difficulty was that, as the Japanese army moved westwards in order to try and defeat Chiang Kai-shek, the Communists moved into areas vacated by the Japanese army, so by 1940 the Chinese Communist Party had control of an area in which about one hundred million people were living. Part of the Japanese army which otherwise could have been used to defeat Chiang Kai-shek's army had to fall back to deal with the Communist menace. Although the Japanese army was able to reduce the areas held by the Communists, they failed to annihilate them, so part of the Japanese army had to constantly

---

[82] Snow, Edgar: *Journey to the Beginning*, p 313; Dalton, Hugh: *Fateful Years*, p.97
[83] Moseley, George: *China: Empire to People's Republic*, p.80

continue operations against the Communists.[84] The Soviet Government, to show their support for China, offered a non-aggression pact.[85]

Long after Litvinov had ceased to have any influence on Soviet affairs at the end of the Second World War, Stalin initially followed a pragmatic and cautious policy towards China. Stalin encouraged the Communists and Nationalists to reconcile their differences,[86] underestimating the Communists' ability to win any war. Stalin was apprehensive lest a conflagration would lead to American intervention, although it is clear that Stalin had misjudged the position. Mao's China, unlike most of the Soviet Union's allies, would certainly not agree to play the junior partner for long and finally, by coming to an agreement with the USA, checkmated the Soviet Union,[87] as foreseen by Maisky.[88] Ironically, perhaps after all, a China ruled by Chiang Kai-shek would have been better for Soviet Russia.

Cordell Hull boasted that the USA had taken various steps to settle the dispute with China by direct appeals to Japan and China to stop the fighting. However, it was obvious that Japan was the aggressor. Cordell Hull stated it was quite clear to him: 'Germany, Italy and Japan had pushed rearmament so far that it was intended for offence, not defence.[89] He was in favour of 'parallel concurrent action rather than joint action' with the League.[90] However, as will be shown, the USA was not in favour of any meaningful action.

By 1937 it was obvious that Japan had embarked on an expedition of conquest in China, which, apart from any other considerations, was in breach of the 1922 Nine Power Treaty, to which the USA, Britain and Japan were parties. This treaty pledged respect for China's independence.

China appealed to the League after her approach to the signatories of the Nine Power Treaty had been ignored. The League referred the appeal to its Far Eastern Committee, which had been set up during the Manchurian crisis and on which the USA had been represented. However, Roosevelt should be criticised because he exercised extreme caution by instructing his minister in Berne to attend the meetings but to say or do nothing. The Far Eastern Committee, at least, condemned the Japanese bombardment, quite rightly rejecting Japan's contention of self-defence, and held Japan had violated the Kellogg Pact and Nine Power Treaty. China now urged that members of the League should do nothing to help the aggressor, but even this modest demand only found favour with the Soviet Union and New Zealand. Eventually, under pressure from New Zealand, Britain agreed to support a

---

[84] Moise, Edwin: *Modern China*, p.89
[85] Beloff, Max: *The Foreign Policy of Soviet Russia*, p.181
[86] Karnow, Stanley: *Mao and China*, p.52
[87] See Ch.14, No.80
[88] Ch.17, No.144
[89] Hull, Cordell: *Memoirs*, p.547
[90] Ibid. p.539

motion: 'Not to hinder China's resistance and that members should consider what help they could give.'[91] However, in spite of that resolution, the USA continued to be Japan's chief purveyor of oil, scrap metal and other materials for the war effort, as well as supplying similar goods to China to enable her to fight the war. The chief beneficiary of the war was therefore the USA, and if ever there was a case that supports the theory that the capitalist countries need wars, this was it.

The other odd matter was that, in spite of a full-scale war being fought, neither Japan nor China had declared war because, if they did so, the USA's neutrality law would have applied, so China or Japan could not have imported war materials from the USA and all other goods could only be supplied after full payment was made, and not in US ships. Japan had both the ships and the finance to comply with the neutrality legislation. China had neither.[92] However, Roosevelt lacked the courage to tell the people of the USA that the situation was a farce. Clearly, either he should have asked Congress to amend the neutrality legislation so that it only applied to Europe, or else he should have applied the Act, as it was not intended that parties could circumnavigate the Act by not declaring war. In 1939 the Neutrality Act applied to Britain and France until Lend Lease to Britain was implemented because they had declared war on Germany for an unprovoked attack on Poland. Roosevelt had repeatedly urged Britain and France to take a stand against Germany. The Soviets, including Litvinov, must have wondered why Britain always showed respect for the USA while being so hostile to the Soviet Union.

Now the countries in the ambit of the Nine Power Treaty which had previously ignored China's request for a meeting, agreed, at the request of the League of Nations, to convene a meeting. This has come to be called 'The Brussels Conference.'

In advance of the conference, Eden sent a memorandum stating that the conference could take three courses. The first possibility was to defer any action. The second course was to express moral condemnation, but he did not think this would have any effect. Therefore, the only other alternative was to actively help China by the imposition of sanctions. Eden quite rightly warned that there was a danger that Japan would make war against one or more countries imposing sanctions and therefore it would have to be a condition of any agreement that any other nations participating in the agreement would have to come to the help of any country which had imposed sanctions and was then attacked by Japan.[93] However, the USA intimated that consideration of sanctions did not arise, as the purpose of the conference was to resolve the conflict by agreement.[94] The US Government was not even prepared to declare that the USA would not recognise any alteration in the *status quo* of China or declare her unwillingness to lend money to Japan for the development of any

---

[91] Walters, Francis: *History of the League of Nations*, p.734
[92] Ibid.
[93] Hull, Cordell: *Memoirs*, p.550
[94] Ibid.   p.551

conquest by her.[95] Why Roosevelt felt that such a conflict could be settled by an agreement is a complete mystery.? If ever there was a case of appeasement, this was it.

Chamberlain had indicated to Eden that on no account would he agree to sanctions.[96] Davis, the US representative, suggested that an agreement might be reached on the basis of refusing credits and non-recognition of Japanese conquests. Eden apparently received authority to agree with Davis' proposal, but when Davis asked for authority from the US Government, he was told he had gone too far and that the President had not wished to use any word that might indicate that hostile action was a possibility.[97]

Germany politely refused to attend on the grounds that it was not a contracting party to the Nine Powers Treaty. Its motive no doubt was not to offend Japan.[98] Japan did not attend, accusing the Chinese Government of provocation and stating that it was endeavouring by every means to ensure respect for the rights and interests of foreign powers. It maintained it attached the highest importance to establishing lasting peace in the Far East, while in fact it was doing everything possible to ensure the Far East would not be peaceful.

When Litvinov addressed the conference, he stated:

> The Soviet Government has more than once had to make its position clear both on the general question of combating aggression as an international phenomenon and on the subject of particular cases when that aggression becomes active. All these statements were undoubtedly inspired by the Soviet Union's devotion to the cause of peace. With very few exceptions, governments of all other states are undoubtedly inspired by the same idea.

This view was very different to the traditional Marxist theory that wars are an essential ingredient of the capitalist system. Then Litvinov acknowledged, 'Divergences among them [different states] begin only when the question arises of going on from the general idea to the most effective method of maintaining peace or restoring it when it has been broken.' Litvinov made clear his support for the idea of the conference. 'In some cases the very fact of summoning a conference for joint discussions represents a definite action with a certain moral value.' Litvinov then paid a compliment to Belgium, 'expressing his gratitude to the Belgian Government for their efforts in organising the conference, as well as the cordiality with which they have received the delegations.' It seemed to me that, firstly, the conference failed to address the issue that this was not border skirmishes but was a full-scale invasion of China by Japan in which the great cities of China were being attacked and occupied. Secondly, the fact that all those powers were not prepared to stop

---

[95] DBFP, 2nd Series, vol.21, p.520, No.381
[96] Eden, Anthony: *Memoirs, Facing the Dictators*, p.539
[97] Ibid.
[98] Moffat, Jay: *Moffat Papers*, p.159

with a show of force the occupation of China by the Japanese encouraged Japan to continue with its adventure. As Litvinov put it: 'When it is a question of an aggressive attack by one state against another state and if that attack', as with Japan's attack on China,

> has been in some measure successful, there is nothing easier than for an international organisation to say to the aggressor take your plunder, take what you have seized by force and peace be with you, and to say to the victim of the aggressor, love your aggressor, resist not evil, which was now happening in the case of the Brussels Conference.

Litvinov continued:

> It does not represent a victory for the peace or the victory of peace-loving countries. That kind of response can only invoke new kinds of aggression. Yet the unity of all peace-loving countries is particularly necessary at the moment when aggressive countries are more and more uniting and consolidating their forces, thereby creating a menace to an ever-increasing number of states.

Whereas Litvinov strongly condemned the Disarmament Conferences, he decided to please the other delegates by stating:

> I am certain that the new conference will pursue the aim of not only restoring peace in the Far East, but of establishing a just peace, a peace which will not untie but on the contrary will bind the hands of the aggressors also for the future and in other parts of the world.[99]

However, it is doubtful whether he believed in the success of the conference.

Litvinov was not pleased when the conference wanted to appoint Italy, rather than the Soviet Union, to a committee. Litvinov quite rightly told Eden: 'The Soviet Union had far greater interests in the Far East than Italy.' Litvinov paid tribute to the courage of the Chinese, who were resisting 'with truly wonderful courage. China was receiving certain supplies from the Soviet Union, but these must of necessity be small due to the difficulty of transport.'[100] Britain did not want the Soviet Union on the committee, as it wrongly alleged the USSR had made trouble on whatever committee it sat – a most unfair comment, as the Soviet Union had co-operated in the League of Nations and Non-Intervention Committee.[101] Litvinov had lunch with Davis, the USA's representative, on 8 November 1937. Litvinov told Davis:'If the powers did not intend to treat the Soviet Union

---

[99] Eden, Anthony: *Memoirs, Facing the Dictators*, p.535; Degras, Jane: *Soviet Documents on Foreign Policy*, vol.3, p.262
[100] DBFP, 2nd Series, 21, p.456, No.343
[101] Moffat, Jay: *Moffat Papers*, p.171

on the basis of complete equality, and put her on essential committees, they should never have invited her.'

Litvinov told Davis: 'He was in two minds whether to attend', indicating that the decision whether he was to attend was his, so he still had considerable power. He said 'The Soviet Union, once she had espoused the policy of working with the Western powers, had done so wholeheartedly and had taken some terrible beatings as a consequence.' Litvinov took his deputy with him (not, as Davis stated, a high-ranking Russian), so Davis thought that Litvinov's power was on the decline. When Chicherin attended the Genoa conference, Litvinov accompanied him as his deputy.[102]

Whereas Cordell Hull agreed that Litvinov advocated a strong policy towards Japan, Roosevelt stated: 'If we were to avoid any ultimate serious clash with Japan, some practical means would have to be found to check Japan's career of conquest and to make effective the collective will of the countries believing in peaceful settlements.' Roosevelt stressed: 'The importance of mobilising moral force in all peace-loving nations.'[103] However, Roosevelt had no justification for taking such an optimistic opinion when the League, the Soviet Union and the USA had made it clear that they were not prepared to consider force in 1933, even when all other efforts, such as the US note in 1931 and the endorsement of the Lytton committee, had miserably failed.

The powers, including the USA, Britain, France and the Soviet Union, came to a rare unanimous decision:

> The conference strongly reaffirms the principle of the Nine Power Treaty as being among the basic principles which are essential to world peace and orderly progressive development of national and international life.[104]

China was most disappointed by the US action. Chiang Kai-shek quite rightly complained that the USA had bitterly criticised Britain for failing to support the USA over non-recognition in 1931, and now Britain was right to criticise the USA for not co-operating with her. Unjustly, Hull stated:

> A large body of public opinion argued that as USA's interest in the Far East was far smaller than Britain's and that Britain, being unable to protect her own interests, was trying to manoeuvre us in pulling her chestnuts out of the fire.[105]

Then why was the USA so worried about Japan in 1931 rather than she being prepared to

---

[102] Moffat, Jay: *Moffat Papers*, p.174; ch 4 No. 13-31
[103] Hull, Cordell: *Memoirs*, p.552
[104] Ibid. p.555
[105] Ibid. p.553

follow Britain's lead in not making any demands that could not be supported by force?

Sheinis criticised the Western powers because they did 'nothing to curb the aggressors in Asia.'[106] However, the Soviet Union in 1933 had done little to deter Japan's incursions into Manchuria. Sheinis somewhat cancelled out the argument by saying: 'The reason why Litvinov was more prepared to appease Japan rather than Germany was because he considered, quite rightly, that Nazi Germany was a greater threat than Japan.' Litvinov's and Eden's aims were identical. Both wisely realised that neither was strong enough to militarily assist China without the USA's participation and both were anxious for US co-operation. Indeed, Eden, in his report to George VI, stated:

> The main object of Your Majesty's delegation has been to ensure the closest co-operation with the USA. Even though such co-operation may not emerge in definite joint action in the present crisis, the future of world peace depends to so great an extent on Anglo-American co-operation that Mr Eden feels that no effort should be spared to consolidate it.[107]

What was the point of relying on US support if Roosevelt was intending to do nothing?

However, the fact is that the conference achieved nothing and co-operation is easy if one achieves nothing. Events in 1941 and 1942 proved that the policy of doing nothing was not wise. Roosevelt accepted the view of public opinion in the USA in 1937 that, as Japan was not a direct threat to the USA, on no account must any action be taken that would risk war with Japan. At Pearl Harbour, US public opinion was proved to have been wrong. Unlike the USA, Britain and the Soviet Union both took considerable risks in assisting China.

In 1938 Japan started to try and seize part of the Soviet Union's territory in Eastern Siberia. Zhdanov stated that the Commissar of Foreign Affairs should be more resolute with regard to 'one sortie after another on the part of provocative acts of agents of Japan and of the so-called Manchukuo taking place on our Eastern Borders.'[108]

This is a most unfair criticism because it appears that the only way to block Japanese aggression was by force, and clearly it was a matter for the Red Army acting under the direction of the Politburo whose duty was to direct when and on what conditions the Red Army should intervene. Although Carr drew attention to the fact that, from time to time, Soviet foreign policy was criticised for not being firm enough to strengthen the Foreign Commissar's position, certainly on this occasion, Litvinov and others understood it to be a genuine criticism.[109]

---

[106] Sheinis, Zinovy: *Maxim Litvinov*, p.282
[107] Eden, Anthony: *Memoirs, Facing the Dictators*, p.540
[108] *Moscow News*, 26 January 1938, pp.8 and 9
[109] Carr, Edward: *Socialism in One Country*, vol.2, p.233

On 31 July 1938 Japan launched an assault against the Soviet Union in Siberia. The Red Army, involved in the first war since the 1929 conflict in Manchuria, fought vigorously. Not resting on its laurels, as military deficiencies were discovered, a conference was called on 31 August with Stalin present. The British army Lieutenant-Colonel, John Brown, stated: 'There can be no doubt that the Soviet troops gave a very indifferent display'except for artillery.[110] This is an example of British anti-Soviet bias rather than a considered military criticism. The Red Army achieved their objective by halting a Japanese invasion more successfully than Britain and the USA did in 1941 and 1942. In 1939, upon learning that Japan intended to mount a general offensive, Zhukov attacked four days before the intended attack. During the fighting that lasted until a ceasefire was agreed on 16 September 1939, 18,500 Japanese were killed against 9,824 Red Army soldiers.[111] The result of the Red Army's victory was significant because Japan realised that the Russians would fight vigorously if Siberia was invaded. Accordingly, the Japanese realised that they would be likely to achieve easier success in the South by seizing British, American, French and Dutch possessions. Chamberlain should have taken notice that the Red Army was not as weak as he thought and hoped it was. If it was likely to be an effective fighting force, it was essential that an alliance with the USSR be formed without delay to make certain that it was fighting on the side of the Allies.

At least, as long as Litvinov was in office, the Soviet Union refused to be intimidated into not assisting China. The Soviet Union sent supplies by the Sinkiang route. When Japan protested, Litvinov robustly answered:

> The sale of arms including air planes to China is entirely in accordance with international law … just as, incidentally, arms are provided to Japan by many countries.

Previously, China was helped in the war against Japan by German advisers; but in order to show solidarity with Japan, these advisers were withdrawn in May and June 1938. Russian volunteers served with the Chinese as pilots, technical advisors and economic advisors, although they were not of the same calibre as the German advisers.

Soviet economic aid for China, although given little publicity, continued to grow. Beloff was one of the few to give this aspect of Soviet policy prominence. Chinese sources indicate that credits of £50,000,000 were granted to China in October 1938 and February 1939 in connection with the exchange of machinery and munitions for tea and other raw materials. According to Chinese sources, no political conditions were attached to these credits.[112] After the departure of Litvinov from office, a trade treaty between the Soviet

---

[110] Haslam, Jonathan: *The Soviet Union and the Threat from the East*, pp.118 and 119
[111] Ibid. p.132
[112] Beloff, Max: *The Foreign Policy of Soviet Russia*, p.185.

Union and China was signed in Moscow on 16 June 1939. This extended most favoured nation status to both sides. This was followed by a further credit of $150,000,000 in August 1939.[113]

Britain continued to supply arms to China until, in the face of threats from Japan, the Churchill Government agreed to close the Burma Road, the one route through which supplies could be brought to the beleaguered Chinese army.[114] Although Britain's action was due to its dire position in the European war, Churchill criticised 'appeasement from weakness.'[115] However, three months later, when Britain saw that the USA was adopting a much firmer policy towards Japan, because the USA indicated that she would oppose the taking over by Japan of the colonies of France, Britain and Holland, Britain decided to reopen the Burma Road, in spite of Japanese threats.[116]

On 6 January 1941 the Lend Lease Bill was submitted to Congress and enacted into law on 11 March 1941. This enabled China to receive supplies without paying for them and China received a limited amount of supplies by the Burma Road. This was eventually closed in 1942 when, following Pearl Harbour, Burma, as well as many other countries of South-East Asia, was conquered by the Japanese army and thereafter supplies could only be sent to China by the dangerous route of flying them over the Himalayas.[117]

There was a bombshell on 13 April 1941 when a neutrality pact between Japan and the USSR was signed. Japan and the Soviet Union pledged themselves to neutrality in the event of military action by any other power or powers against either signatory. The benefit for the Soviet Union was that, if Japan abided by the Pact and Germany invaded the Soviet Union, she would be spared a fight on two fronts. The Neutrality Pact did benefit China because, firstly, the Pact did not prejudice aid to China. Secondly, if the Soviet Union was attacked by both Germany and Japan, aid to China was likely to cease. Perhaps the greatest benefit to China was that the Pact undermined the tripartite pact by demonstrating Japan's unreliability as an ally.[118]

Molotov had given an assurance to the Chinese ambassador that nothing would be altered with regard to Soviet relations with China.[119] British, American and Soviet aid continued. Haslam states that the level of Soviet aid was well above American aid. Chiang Kai-shek told the USA that, up to 16 April 1941, the Soviet Union was continuing to supply aid and he did not expect that aid to stop.[120] Prior to the Soviet involvement in the European War,

[113] Ibid.
[114] Furuya, Keiji: *Chiang Kai-shek: His Life and Times*, p.646
[115] *Hansard*, vol.482, 14 December 1950, 1367 ; Churchill's complete speeches, vol.8, 8143
[116] Furuya, Keiji: *Chiang Kai-shek: His Life and Times*, p.653
[117] Moise, Edwin: *Modern China*, p.95
[118] Furuya, Keiji: *Chiang Kai-shek: His Life and Times*, p.684
[119] Beloff, Max: *The Foreign Policy of Soviet Russia*, p.376
[120] Haslam, Jonathan: *The Soviet Union and the Threat from the East*, p.156

the material supplied to China exceeded that of the USA.[121] This showed the success of this operation during the time when Litvinov was Foreign Minister.

Following the German invasion of the Soviet Union in June 1941, the Soviet Union needed all its resources to defend its country, so it was hardly surprising that in October 1941 it was stated that the Soviet Union was no longer able to continue the supplies.[122] Nevertheless, as late as 1942 the Chinese Minister of Economic Affairs was able to report a continuous flow of materials, carts and trucks from the railway head at Alma Ata towards Chungking. [123]

In contrast to Spain in the late thirties and early forties, the Soviet behaviour towards China appears to have been entirely honourable. The aid was unconditional.

---

[121] Ibid.
[122] Moore, Harriet: *Soviet Far Eastern Policy 1931-1945*, p.130
[123] Ibid.

16: INTERNAL POLICY

How far Stalin was involved in the murder of Kirov is still not clear. Stalin's daughter, a stern critic of her father's behaviour, wrote in *Twenty Letters to a Friend* that she did not believe he arranged it. However, in another passage of the same book and in another of her books, *Only One Year*, she implies the contrary.[1] According to Mikoyan's son, his father felt Stalin was in some way involved in the murder.[2] Khrushchev, in his Secret Speech, did not directly accuse Stalin of Kirov's murder, but claimed only: 'The circumstances surrounding Kirov's murder hide many things which are inexplicable and mysterious and demand a more careful examination.' Many years later Khrushchev asserted that the murder was arranged by Stalin.[3] Orlov has no doubt that the assassination was planned by Stalin.[4] Robert Conquest, an expert on the Purges, is also satisfied that Stalin took the most extraordinary decision of his career when he decided: 'The best way of ensuring his political supremacy and dealing with his old comrade Kirov was murder.'[5] Neither Overy nor Montefiore, however, believe Stalin organised the murder, but do not say why they reject Orlov's testimony or why they believe Conquest, an expert on the Purges, got it wrong. However, unlike Overy, Montefiore says: A 'whiff of complicity still hangs in the air.'[6]

Kirov, who was secretary of the Central and Leningrad Committees of the Communist Party, returned from a plenary session on 29 November 1934 to the Smolny Palace, from where not only Leningrad but the whole of the north-west of the USSR was controlled.[7]

At the 17th Congress the delegates were given ballot papers on which there was a list of names. The delegates crossed out the names they opposed, and voted for the names left unmarked. When the votes had been counted, there was a shock. Kirov received one or two negatives, the lowest number. Kaganovich and Molotov received 100 negatives each and Stalin received, according to Mikoyan's son, 292 negatives. When Kaganovich, managing the Congress, received the vote he ran to Stalin, who certainly ordered all but three of the negatives to be destroyed. When the vote was announced, Stalin was in the lead with 1056 votes and Kirov second with 1055 votes. Mikoyan's son later heard this from Napoleon

---

[1] Alliluyeva, Svetlana: *Twenty Letters to a Friend* (Penguin Books edition), 1968, p.124; but see her remarks at p.57 and in *Only One Year* p.143, where she seems to have different views
[2] Mikoyan, Stepan: *Autobiography*, p.193
[3] Khrushchev, Nikita: *Glasnost Tapes*, p.24; 'Anatomy of Terror' Secret Speech, p.33
[4] Orlov, Aleksandr: *History of Stalin's Crimes*, 1953 p.14, 1954 p.27
[5] Conquest, Robert: *The Great Terror*, 1990, p.36
[6] Overy, Richard: *The Dictators* p.51; Montefiore, Simon: *Stalin, The Court of the Red Tsar*, p.134
[7] Conquest, Robert: *Stalin and the Kirov Murder*, p.26

Andreasian.[8] 63 members of the counting commission were subsequently arrested. 60 were shot and three miraculously survived.[9] Stalin never again put himself up for election as General Secretary.[10] No doubt, Stalin became worried that Kirov was more popular than himself. The ovation Kirov received was as great as for Stalin at the 17th Conference.[11] Molotov regarded Kirov as a poor organiser but a good orator. Further, Kirov did not want to replace Stalin.[12] Knight suggests that whereas Kirov 'might have toed the line as others did', on the other hand he might have acted as a rallying point for those 'who wanted to oppose his [Stalin's] dictatorship.' Further, Knight suggests that Kirov 'would not have been a willing accomplice when the full force of Stalin's terror was unleashed in Leningrad.'[13] Knight's contention is supported by the fact that whereas most of the elite, including to a certain extent Litvinov, tried to anticipate what Stalin desired and acted accordingly, Kirov did not always do what Stalin wanted. In 1934, Stalin wanted Kirov to come to Moscow permanently. Whereas all the other members of the Politburo would have complied, Stalin accepted that, as Kirov had no desire to leave Leningrad, he would not come to Moscow until 1938. Again, when Stalin wanted Medved moved from the Leningrad NKVD to Minsk, Kirov refused to agree and, rarely for Stalin, he had to accept defeat.[14]

According to Orlov, Yagoda, the NKVD chief, acting on Stalin's orders, was to find a suitable person to go to Leningrad to procure the murder of Kirov. The man chosen was Zaporozhets, who had been imposed on the Leningrad NKVD by Moscow. However, Medved remained the chief. Then, Orlov states Zaporozhets procured a gun for Nikolayev in order that the assassination might be accomplished.[15]

Kirov was shot on 2 December 1934 and Nikolayev was arrested for the murder. Stalin immediately set out for Leningrad, accompanied by Molotov and other prominent persons among the leadership. They arrived in Leningrad 16 hours after the assassination.[16] Stalin and Molotov conducted the interrogation. Stalin remained in Leningrad for two days and put Yezhov in charge. When Stalin asked Nikolayev, from whom he received the pistol with which he had shot Kirov, Nikolayev said Stalin should 'ask' the deputy NKVD chief

---

[8] Mikoyan, Stepan: *Autobiography*, p.194

[9] Ibid.

[10] Overy, Richard: *The Dictators* p.52

[11] Ibid. ; Knight, Amy: *Who Killed Kirov?*, p.268; Orlov, Aleksandr: *Secret History of Stalin's Crimes*, 1953 p.13, 1954 p 26

[12] Chuev, Felix: *Molotov Remembers*, p.221

[13] Knight, Amy: *Who Killed Kirov?*, p.268

[14] Ibid. p.74; Conquest, Robert: *The Great Terror*, p.39; and Litvinov speeches concerning collectivisation and the Terror

[15] Orlov, Aleksandr: *Secret History of Stalin's Crimes*, 1953 p.17, 1954 p.31

[16] Conquest, Robert: *The Great Terror*, p.41; Orlov, Aleksandr: *Secret History of Stalin's Crimes*, 1953 p .21 1954 p.35; Montefiore, Simon: *Stalin, The Court of the Red Tsar*, p.132; Overy, Richard: *Hitler's Germany and Stalin's Russia*, p.52

Zaporozhets. Consequently, Nikolayev was silenced, removed and subsequently shot.[17] An order was issued by Stalin, although ostensibly it came from the Central Committee, to the effect that the investigation of all suspects be heard at an emergency rate without the participation of the parties. The order also prescribed that those found guilty would be executed without delay. Finally, no appeal would be allowed. This decree was compiled, in view of the shortness of time, by Stalin himself on 1 December, published in *Pravda* on 2 December and approved by the Politburo on 3 December.[18] Kirov's murder had given Stalin the opportunity to become an absolute dictator and he remained so for the rest of his life.

Borisov, who had been head of Kirov's guard, had apparently accompanied Kirov to the Smolny Palace, but Borisov did not accompany Kirov upstairs where he met his end. Borisov was arrested and two days later he was summoned under arrest to appear at the Smolny, but was killed on the way there. The official line was that he had been killed in a road accident, but apparently he had been murdered by those accompanying Borisov who were themselves subsequently murdered.[19] Kirov's coffin arrived in Moscow on 4 December, and a state funeral was held on 6 December. Stalin was a guard of honour along with Molotov, Voroshilov and Zhdanov.[20]

At the time of Kirov's murder, Litvinov was out of the country and, although the Soviet Union was enveloped in grief, Tanya states that her father said 'Fear.' Tanya is not aware of any other remark her father made about the murder. The implication is that Litvinov realised this event might be an excuse for Stalin to unleash a reign of terror.[21] History was to prove him correct. This view was confirmed by Mikoyan's son, who stated that the murder of Kirov had certain similarities to the burning of the Reichstag in 1933. Although it is not known whether the fire at the Reichstag was organised by the Nazis, it was used as a pretext for the persecution of the Communists and Social Democrats. The physical removal of Kirov meant the elimination of a future potential rival, but this was not the only goal. The principal objective, as with the fire at the Reichstag, was to manufacture a reign of terror.[22]

In 1956 Molotov claimed that Khrushchev initiated an enquiry into the assassination, but as its report was not published, Molotov assumed it had decided that Stalin was not implicated.[23] However, surprisingly, Molotov did not disclose he was the chairman of the

---

[17] Orlov, Aleksandre: *Secret History of Stalin's Crimes*, 1953 p.22, 1954 p.36 ; Conquest, Robert: *The Great Terror*, p.44; Overy, Richard: *The Dictators,* p.53

[18] Conquest, Robert: *The Great Terror*, p.41

[19] Orlov, Aleksandr: *Secret History of Stalin's Crimes*, 1953 pp. 23 &.24, 1954 p. 37   Montefiore, Simon: *Stalin, The Court of the Red Tsar*, p.134

[20] Montefiore, Simon: *Stalin, The Court of the Red Tsar*, p.136

[21] Tanya

[22] Mikoyan, Stepan: *Autobiography*, p.194

[23] Knight, Amy: *Who Killed Kirov?*, p.263; Chuev, Felix: *Molotov Remembers*, p.223

committee investigating the assassination. He was hardly likely to be an impartial chairman because, if Stalin was involved in the crime, then Molotov was surely an accessory to the crime. Not surprisingly, the enquiry found that Nikolayev had acted on his own.

Two members of a KGB working group who were interviewed by a journalist in *Pravda* in late 1990 insisted that they had scoured all the evidence and that there was nothing to suggest that Stalin murdered Kirov. On the contrary, they were the best of friends. However, this view was put in doubt when Yakovlev disclosed that, shortly after Kirov's murder, Orakhelashvili had been placed in charge of gathering together all of Kirov's papers, which included letters between Kirov and Stalin. These papers have never been located. Yakovlev asked whether they had been destroyed. Did they incriminate Stalin?[24]

Following Kirov's murder, the next significant although unpublicised event was Stalin's apparent rift with Molotov. On 19 March 1936 Molotov gave an interview with the editor of *Le Temps* concerning improved relations with Nazi Germany.[25] Although Litvinov had made similar statements in 1934, and even visited Berlin that year, this was before Germany's occupation of the Rhineland.[26] Watson believes Molotov's statement on foreign policy gave offence to Stalin. Molotov had made it clear that improved relations with Hitler's Germany could only develop if Germany's policy changed. Molotov then stated that one of the best ways for Germany to improve relations was by re-joining the League of Nations, but even that was not sufficient. Germany still had to give proof 'of its respect for international obligations in keeping with the real interests of peace in Europe and peace generally.'[27] As Litvinov during 1933 and 1934 had done his best to prevent the cordial relations created by Rapallo from declining, I do not think Litvinov would have disapproved of that statement; and if German policy had changed, Litvinov would have been delighted. However, Robert Conquest, unlike Watson, believed that the reason for Stalin's temporary rift with Molotov was not concerned with foreign policy but stemmed from the fact that Stalin was incensed with Molotov for attempting to try and dissuade Stalin from staging the famous trials against the old colleagues of Lenin.[28] Molotov, in the same interview, denied the continued existence of internal enemies except for a few isolated cases.[29] I think this is more likely to have given offence to Stalin.

Watson, Orlov and Conquest believe that there was a rift between Molotov and Stalin because Molotov's name was omitted from the list of those whom the conspirators were planning to kill, while all other prominent leaders were included. Then, in May 1936,

---

[24] Overy, Richard: *Hitler's Germany and Stalin's Russia*, p.51; Knight, Amy: *Who Killed Kirov?* p.266

[25] Stati I Rechi, 1935-1936, pp.231 and 232

[26] Ch.8, visit to Berlin No.148 and statement No 151

[27] Watson, Derek: *Molotov and the Sovnarkom 1930 to 1941*, p.161

[28] Conquest, Robert: *The Great Terror*, p.91

[29] Watson, Derek: *Molotov and the Sovnarkom 1930 to 1941*, p.161

Molotov went to the Black Sea on an extended holiday under careful NKVD supervision until the end of August, when apparently Stalin changed his mind and ordered Molotov's return.[30]

Rumours began to circulate that Litvinov might be removed because of differences between himself and Stalin. However, rather than remove his Foreign Commissar, Stalin heaped honours on Litvinov. First, on the 1936 anniversary of the Bolshevik Revolution, Litvinov stood beside Stalin at Lenin's tomb; and second, three days later, Litvinov received the Order of Lenin. Stalin did not speak and Kalinin's remarks at the event were not published. Litvinov took the opportunity to speak on his favourite theme of collective security. He criticised unnamed governments which did not stand up to aggression. Using skilful sarcasm, he stated that effecting a 'rebuff to openly planned aggression can be made only with the consent of and participation of the deliberate instigators of that aggression.'

Litvinov criticised governments that ignored the violation of international agreements and undisputed acts of aggression, that humoured those guilty of these acts, that flattered them in the hope they would be satiated with their success and would say: 'We sin no more.' However, 'History teaches us that aggression and expansion are insatiable. Every success, every concession that the aggressor gets is used by him for further attacks.'

Few would now disagree that the rise of Hitler on the international stage was caused by the fact that concessions were made to him, in response to his aggression, which encouraged further aggression. He was effectively rewarded for his attacks on the international order. Yet Hitler was not opposed when he was fairly weak.The trouble is that this example has been used since the Second World War to go to war against dictators such as Nasser and Saddam Hussein, with tragic results. The difference is that, unlike Germany, those countries were not capable of waging world war.

Litvinov then criticised the average-sized countries, which pursued the policy of so-called rapprochement with the aggressors – these countries included Belgium, Holland, and Denmark before the Second World War. Litvinov likened such policy to 'the rapprochement of a lobster with a shark in the hope that the shark will not gobble up' the lobster entirely, 'but will bite off only one claw for a beginning of course.' The only problem is that, like Churchill, Litvinov was quite prepared on occasion to appease aggression.[31]

Litvinov also then proceeded to try to distinguish between 'a politician who lies for the benefit of his fatherland and a Soviet politician who is one who tells the truth, not only for

---

[30] Watson Derek *Molotov and the Sovnarkon 1930-1941* p.162; Orlov, Aleksandr: *Secret History of Stalin's Crimes*, 1953 edition , pp. 69 & 151-156, 1954 edition pp. 81 & 162-165

[31] *Moscow News*, 18 November 1936, p.4 & 8. As to appeasement by Churchill, see Ch.12, No.97; as for Litvinov, see Ch.7, No.72

his own fatherland but for the benefit of all toilers [and] all mankind.' [32] This is entirely untrue. Throughout the history of the USSR Soviet politicians constantly lied when they thought it was expedient, including Litvinov when he complained about the British Government's action in taking a tough line over the arrest of the Metro Vickers employees when he himself did not believe the employees to be guilty.[33] Further, Litvinov praised the 1936 constitution as democratic, but this was not his real view. In fact, he had little faith in it and did not think the Soviet Constitution was democratic. Other Soviet representatives acted similarly. The Soviet witnesses lied at the Nuremberg War Crime Trials over the massacre of Poles in the Katyn forest but material in the Soviet archives released by Presidents Gorbachev and Yeltsin makes it clear that the murders were committed by the Soviet Union. Gromyko, in his memoirs in 1985, denied the existence of the secret protocol, which was agreed at the time of the Nazi-Soviet Pact; but it was found a few years later in the Soviet archives.[34]

In 1936, the Soviet Union said that it had adopted the most democratic constitution in the world. For the first time, deputies were elected directly to the Supreme Soviet, the highest legislative body in the USSR. Litvinov was among the privileged thirty who signed the document.[35] However, when he spoke about the constitution on 9 December 1936 at the All Union Congress of the Soviets, he was ambivalent. He said:

> Regarding the nature of democracy and the bourgeois liberties, we Marxists have always expressed our own opinions. This opinion was expressed by Comrade Stalin when in his report he compares the Soviet Constitution with the bourgeois liberties, which, while they bear the same name, are not equivalent.

However, Litvinov then gives a valid critique of liberal democracies, and refers to the press in America. He notes that:

> Most of the press was Republican which opposed President Roosevelt's re-election and such papers exercise tremendous influence on the internal and foreign policy of the country, paralysing the actions of the democratic government.

He then states that Roosevelt won a tremendous victory in the elections. This is rather contradictory, as this shows the strength of American Democracy.[36]

---

[32] *Moscow News,* 9 December 1936, p.5, Speech 28 November 1936
[33] See Ch.9, No.125
[34] Katyn Davies *N Europe A History;* Gromyko: *Memories* p.38 ; Secret protocol published in *Soviet Union Documentary History*, by Edward Acton and Tom Stableford p.7
[35] Fischer, Louis: *The Great Challenge*, p.232; Tanya.
[36] *Moscow News* 9 December 1936, p.5, Speech 26 November 1936

However, by 1943 Litvinov had changed his mind, comparing the US press favourably with the Moscow Press Bureau. When he had a long talk with Sulzberger in April 1943, he was one of very few Communist Ministers, if not the only one until Gorbachev, to criticise communist censorship. In complaining about the Moscow Press Bureau, Litvinov stated, 'I always liked to speak frankly to reporters'... and it was 'different when I was in Washington.'[37] Then he launched into a long and detailed attack on fascist states. However, privately, given what Litvinov stated to his family, he thought that there was little difference between the communism he saw in the Soviet Union and fascism. He said that the difference was that 'whereas communism had the right principles, fascism did not.'[38]

Litvinov went on to claim that the Soviet Union 'is the bulwark of democracy and freedom', although he then states that the Soviet Union is not concerned with the internal fascist regime of this and that country.

When Litvinov spoke on 23 November 1937, he publicly had no doubt that the Soviet Union was a complete democracy. He claimed:

> When we came to elect our representatives after the Revolution, they came to be elected in a democratic manner to the Party Congresses and the Congress of the Soviets. At one such Congress, I had the honour to be elected delegate of Leningrad. This year the toilers of the Union will elect their representatives to the highest legislative body under the conditions of a maximum of democratic forms by means of universal, secret, equal suffrage. I am proud of the fact that I shall too be a candidate voted upon and perhaps among those elected by the people.[39]

We now know from Tanya that when Litvinov stated that the Soviet Union was democratic because of the constitution, this was a lie. Tanya told me that her father had told Tanya's mother that he hoped that his policy of collective security would be successful and then Stalin would lose his obsession about capitalist encirclement and this would lead to a more liberal regime;[40] but was not Litvinov naïve? Meetings were called throughout Soviet Russia to denounce 'enemies of the people'[41], as Stalin needed enemies of the people to justify his oppressive policy.

Litvinov certainly had no confidence in the constitution, describing it to his wife as only a 'paper constitution.' Although in theory the 1936 Constitution was fully democratic, it failed to protect its citizens against arbitrary arrest and the courts were in no way

---

[37] *The New York Times*, 3 January 1952, p.9

[38] Tanya

[39] *Moscow News*, 8 December 1937 p.4 Speech 27 November 1937

[40] Tanya

[41] Sheinis, Zinovy: *Maxim Litvinov*, p.285

independent of the executive. However, as so often in his life, Litvinov correctly predicted future events, and said the Constitution would be of use later. In 1948, the USSR signed the Declaration of Human Rights. Article 19 states:

> Everyone has the right of freedom of opinion and expression. The right includes the freedom to hold opinions without interference and to seek, receive and import information and ideas through any media and regardless of frontiers.[42]

Stalin, having signed it, proceeded to break every provision of it, and the same was true of Brezhnev when he signed the Helsinki Treaty in 1976. This treaty stipulated that:

> Participating states recognise the significance of human rights and fundamental freedoms. The participating states will constantly respect these rights and freedoms in their mutual relations and will endeavour jointly and separately, including in co-operation with the United Nations, to promote the universal and effective respect for them.[43]

During the Brezhnev period the dissidents, of which Litvinov's own grandson would be one, constantly complained that all they were asking was for the authorities to abide by their own constitution, which was not happening.[44]

Kennan, a US diplomat, who, in the 50s, would become the US Ambassador to the Soviet Union, has argued that, in his speeches, Litvinov confined himself to the question of taking strong measures against Italy, Japan and Germany, and other matters interested him little.[45] Also, Hindus, an American journalist, described an incident when at a diplomatic reception Litvinov was asked who was a Menshevik, and he walked away in anger. Therefore, Hindus states, Litvinov avoided 'sacred cows, party politics, party doctrine' and 'subjects which were beyond the competence and authority of the Commissioner of Foreign Affairs'; but they were wrong.[46]

First, in 1931, Litvinov was appointed a member of Sovnarkom, a body originally chaired by Lenin, who was replaced in 1924 by Rykov. In 1930 Molotov replaced Rykov, but in 1941 he himself was replaced by Stalin, who assumed the office of Chairman of the People's Commissars. The role of Sovnarkom was ambiguous, but under the Chairmanship of Molotov its main activity was economic.[47] Litvinov was from time to time prepared to

---

[42] Applebaum, Ann: *Gulag: History of the Camps*, p.479
[43] Ibid.
[44] *The New York Times*, 27 August 1968, p.1
[45] Roberts, Henry: *Diplomats 1919-1939*, p.352
[46] Hindus, Maurice: *Crisis in the Kremlin*, p.52
[47] Rees, W A: *Decision-Making in Stalin's Command Economy*, p.17

enter into internal politics. Litvinov's 1936 speech and again his election speech of 1937 were remarkably similar to an election speech that a candidate in a democracy might make. In 1936, the speech was full of praise for the Soviet Union. He said:

> The Soviet Union is strong in record holders in all kinds of sports. It is strong in the boundless devotion of the state and in its ideals on the part of the large membership of the Young Communist League and the entire growing generation fired with enthusiasm. It is strong in its boundless natural riches, in the steady growth of its gigantic industry.[48]

Litvinov's speech on 27 November 1937 also praised the country's achievements, such as the colossal factories and power stations that had grown up, the successful completion of the Five Year Plan, the Baltic, White Sea and Moscow-Volga canals, the rise in both middle and higher education, the elimination of illiteracy and the success of Soviet musicians at international concerts. It could have been an election speech given in Britain by a supporter of the government in power seeking re-election.[49] The significant question is in how much of it did Litvinov believe?

It is extremely unlikely that Litvinov believed what he said in his 1936 speech when he stated that the Soviet Union 'was strong in its collective system of farming.'[50] I believe that Litvinov did not have faith in collective farming, because Sheinis informs us of a report that Litvinov received concerning a collective farm. Litvinov was appalled at the plight of the cows which had not been fed. They could not stand on their own and were kept from falling by a belt attached to the ceilings of the cowsheds. Without modern vehicles, the farm could not come out of the doldrums. Accordingly, Litvinov had a few of the Foreign Commissariat's vehicles transferred to the farm and extended other aid. The farmers showed their appreciation by calling the collective farm 'Litvinov Kolkhoz.'[51]

In August 1936 the first of the great treason trials opened against Kamenev and Zinoviev.[52] Having disposed of two likely rivals, Trotsky and Kirov, Stalin now decided to liquidate Bukharin who had been very prominent in the Soviet Communist Party since the Revolution and helped Stalin in his rise to power.

When Bukharin and his wife attended the 19th anniversary of the October Revolution on 7 November 1936, Stalin noticed Bukharin and sent a young army officer to invite Bukharin and his wife to come onto the platform reserved for Stalin's honoured guests.[53] However,

---

[48] *Moscow News*, 9 December 1936, p.5, Speech 28 November 1936
[49] Ibid. 8 December 1937, p.,4 Speech: 27 November 1937,
[49] Ibid. *Moscow News* 9 December 1936, p.5, Speeech 28 November 1936
[50] Sheinis, Zinovy: *Maxim Litvinov*, p.269
[51] Sheinis, Zinovy: *Maxim Litvinov*, p.269
[52] Getty, J Arch: *Road to Terror*, p.256
[53] Medvedev, Zhores: *Unknown Stalin*, p.276

within day, Bukharin was taken to a room in the Kremlin where he had to face a number of persons, including Radek, who confessed to criminal links with Bukharin. Radek was supposedly the head of another counter-revolutionary centre. Radek was in custody and on 30 January 1937 was convicted of treasonable activity, but his life was spared until 1939 when he was killed in prison.[54] Yefim Tseitlin declared that Bukharin had personally given Tseitlin a revolver, and had positioned him in the street in order to assassinate Stalin; but Stalin had taken a different route, and so the assassination did not take place.[55] As soon as Bukharin returned home, he intended to shoot himself, but could not manage to do so. Shortly afterwards, a group of strangers arrived at Bukharin's apartment and told him to vacate it. Bukharin rang Stalin to complain and was no doubt surprised when Stalin said, 'Tell them to go to the devil.' The uninvited guests beat a hasty retreat.[56] It is almost certain that Stalin had already decided that Bukharin must die. Did Stalin's act show certain nervousness on his part or was it sadistic? Did he aim to increase Bukharin's suffering by raising his expectations before dashing them?

On 23 February 1937 at the Central Committee, with Bukharin and Rykov in attendance, Yezhov accused Bukharin and Rykov of training various terrorist groups to carry out the assassination of Stalin and other members of the Central Committee. A plenum was established consisting of all the members of the Politburo plus a few prominent figures of the Central Committee, the most well-known being Litvinov.[57] Presumably, Litvinov was appointed to increase the credibility of the sub-committee, particularly among Left-wing sympathisers in non-communist countries. Bukharin's fate was placed in the hands of this Committee (not the Central Committee), of which the minutes are available. The Committee sat, according to the minutes, on 27 February 1937. Yezhov proposed, with the support of Budenny, Manuilsky, Shvernik, Kosarev and Yakir, that the cases of Bukharin and Rykov be transferred to the courts with an application for the death penalty; whereas Litvinov, Postyshev, Shkiriatov, Antipov, Khrushchev, Kosoir and Petrovsky voted for Bukharin and Rykov to be expelled and tried without application of the death penalty. Stalin proposed that they be handed over, not to the courts, but to the NKVD for investigation; which proposal, after having the support of Ulianova, Krupskaya, Vareikis, Voroshilov and Molotov, typically was carried unanimously.[58]

However, all the evidence is that Litvinov did not believe that Bukharin was guilty. Indeed, Tanya tells us that her father was surprised that, instead of confessing, Bukharin did not act in a more resolute manner. 'Why did Bukharin confess, because surely he must have realised that Stalin never kept his promises?'[59] However, it must have been a most

---

[54] Conquest, Robert: *The Great Terror*, 1990, p.165
[55] Medvedev, Zhores: *Unknown Stalin*, p.276
[56] Ibid. p.276
[57] Medvedev, Zhores: *Unknown Stalin*, p.280
[58] Getty, J Arch: *Road to Terror*, p.419
[59] Tanya

distressing experience for Bukharin, who had done so much to build up the Communist Party, and had now not only seen many old Bolshevik colleagues condemned, but also have accusations made against him, a factor that Litvinov appeared to have ignored. Senior Communist leaders did not always act without conscience. Mikoyan's son points to the anguish of his father as a member of the Politburo when the resolution to liquidate all the Polish officers was placed on the agenda. Mikoyan agreed as meekly as any other member because 'for him not to sign was impossible.'[60]

However, the support for the death penalty by six of the plenum indicates that had Stalin not had so much active support, the Terror would have been much less. If the motive of those who supported the death penalty was to win Stalin's praise for toughness, they did not achieve their object, because, among those who supported the death penalty, Kosarev and Yakir perished, whereas Litvinov continued to be Foreign Commissar for a further two years. Both Shkiriatov, who had not supported the death penalty, and Khrushchev, who eventually became one of Stalin's favourites, survived.[61] Perhaps a clue to Litvinov's survival is that, although Stalin was indeed a very cruel man, he did not necessarily respect cruelty in others. The compliance of Molotov, who supported Stalin in many of his cruel deeds, did not even protect Molotov's wife Polino, who was imprisoned; yet Litvinov survived, in spite of what Molotov considered treasonable interviews.

The Sub-Committee's decision was reported to a plenum of the Central Committee during the evening of 27 February 1937. Apart from Bukharin and Rykov, who attended, all other members of the Central Committee voted in favour of the Sub-Committee's recommendation that the cases of Bukharin and Rykov be transferred to the NKVD. On the same day that the verdict of the Central Committee was given, Bukharin and Rykov were arrested.[62] The interrogation is most fully described by Medvedev. Although Mikoyan told Medvedev there was no torture, this seems unlikely in view of what was happening at this time. Bukharin was concerned about the fate of his young wife. Bukharin knew that, when an important person was arrested, this led to other members of the family suffering. He was told that the other members of his family continued to live in the Kremlin, although his wife had been arrested, and sent to prison, while their children had gone to a children's home. Finally, no doubt moved by his desire to protect his family, Bukharin confessed.[63]

Bukharin's trial opened on 2 March 1938. The absurd accusations were made that:

> Bukharin had links with the internal and external enemies of the Soviet Union, was attempting to restore capitalism in the Soviet Union, was plotting the murder of the most important Soviet leaders and seeking to overthrow the Communist

---

[60] Mikoyan, Stepan: *Autobiography*, p.197
[61] Getty, J Arch: *Road to Terror*, p.417
[62] Getty, J Arch: *Road to Terror*, p.419
[63] Medvedev, Zhores: *Unknown Stalin*, p.283

regime in order to bring about the dismemberment of the Soviet State with the intention of turning Russia over to the fascist aggressor.[64]

On 12 March, Bukharin was found guilty and he was sentenced to be shot. On 14 March 1938, Bukharin made a contrite plea admitting he deserved to be shot ten times over for his crime:

> If I am granted physical life that life will be devoted to working for my Socialist fatherland in whatever condition I found myself, whether isolated in a prison cell, in a concentration camp at the North Pole, in Kolyma, wherever.

Bukharin's appeal for mercy was rejected and he was shot on 15 March. Just before he was was shot, he wrote a note to Stalin: 'Koba, why do you need me to die?'[65] However, in spite of Khrushchev's later criticism of Stalin, unlike Litvinov, Khrushchev actively participated in the Purges. Speaking at a party meeting on 22 August 1936, Khrushchev said:

> Just as Stalin with his sharp Leninist eye has always actively pointed out the path for our party as for the whole of the construction, so he has pointed out the corners the vermin can crawl out of. We have to shoot not only this scum but Trotsky should also be shot.[66]

Sheinis claims, and is probably correct, that Litvinov never attended any meeting to denounce 'enemies of the people', although in public speeches he did indicate that he approved of the Terror.[67]

On 11 June 1937, the Commander-in-Chief, Tukhachevskii, and eight other army officers were tried and sentenced to death on the same day. Later, on the same day, Stalin signed their death warrants and they were immediately shot.

The defector Orlov claimed, although only on the basis of second-hand testimony, that there was a planned *coup d'état* by Bukharin and Radek to arrest Stalin and either shoot him on the spot or expose his crimes to the Central Committee; but in the absence of any corroborative evidence, Overy does not believe there was any such plan.[68] An alleged plot was deliberately leaked by German counter-intelligence, which helped to increase Stalin's suspicion of the loyalty of the Army leadership. Schellenberg conspired to give to the Russians forged documents incriminating the Russian high command.[69] Overy claims that

---

[64] Ibid. p.293

[65] Ibid. p.295

[66] Volkogonov, Dmitri: *Rise and Fall of the Soviet Empire*, p.183

[67] Sheinis, Zinovy: *Maxim Litvinov*, p.285; see 77 *post*

[68] Overy, Richard: *The Dictators*, p.476, Orlov Alexandre *Secret History of Stalin's crimes* 1953 p.96, 1954 p.108

[69] Schellenberg, Walter: *Labyrinth*, p.46

the Soviet leadership was convinced of Tukhachevskii's disloyalty.[70] Stalin certainly was, as was Molotov, who in his conversations with Chuev justified Tukhachevskii's execution because Molotov was satisfied that Tukhachevskii was 'a dangerous conspirator in the military who was only caught at the last moment.'[71]

Whether the other leaders were convinced is more difficult to gauge. Certainly, Mikoyan did not believe it was right to slaughter all the Polish officers at Katyn, but nevertheless voted for their liquidation. Many of the others may have privately questioned whether it was either moral or sensible to execute the commander-in-chief in such circumstances. I think it is probable that some in the Politburo might have had doubts, but it was too risky to disagree with Stalin if you wanted to preserve your own life.

Tanya, Litvinov's daughter, tells us that her father did not believe in the generals' guilt.[72] This is consistent with Litvinov's reaction when Hilger asked him about the Great Purges (which were underway in Moscow) and the wholesale shooting of generals. Litvinov shrugged his shoulders and said he could not understand what was happening.[73] Certainly, Ivy Litvinov did not believe that many of the people who were accused were 'enemies of the people.'

Tanya remembers her brother discussing the show trials with a friend and repeating what each of the accused said. Ivy Litvinov was normally very careful about what she said, but on this occasion obviously felt she could not stand by without saying anything, and as she breezily passed through the room she said: 'It is all a pack of lies.' Tanya is confident that this was the opinion of her father.[74]

Sheinis tells of an incident that indicates Litvinov was very distressed at the Purges. When he once went to Paris to see his ambassador Potemkin, Litvinov said to a trusted colleague: 'What is happening? Lenin's trusted colleagues are being done away with.'[75]

The purges in the Foreign Commissariat were so devastating that Litvinov wrote to Stalin that the Soviet Union in nine capitals lacked an ambassador: Barcelona, Bucharest, Budapest, Copenhagen, Kovno, Tokyo, Sofia, Warsaw and Washington. The letter avoided any hint of criticism. It simply described the damage the Foreign Commissariat was causing to its efficient running and suggested a commission to solve the personnel problem, among whom the members would be Malenkov and himself.[76]

---

[70] Overy, Richard: *Hitler's Germany and Stalin's Russia*, p.476
[71] Chuev, Felix: *Molotov Remembers*, p.280
[72] Conversation with Tanya
[73] Hilger, Gustav: *Incompatible Allies*, p.113
[74] Tape of Tanya and conversation with Tanya
[75] Sheinis, Zinovy: *Maxim Litvinov*, p.286
[76] Resis, Albert: 'Fall of Litvinov', *Europe Asia Studies*, No.52, No.11, 200 pp. 33-56 @ p.33

Nevertheless, Litvinov publicly endorsed the Purges and the campaign against the alleged Trotskyites who were supposedly undermining Soviet society. He said:

> They know that the creation of arms dumps, strongholds, casemates and the organisation of internal armed detachments to serve and utilise these undertakings may be possible elsewhere, but not in the Soviet Union. They know that our People's Commissioner of Home Affairs will not give such plans a chance to mature and it is sufficiently vigilant and strong to nip the Trotskyite-Fascist spying and wrecking organisations in the bud.

The reason for joining in the condemnation was probably self-preservation. Litvinov, perhaps surprisingly, indicated to the US ambassador Davies that the Purges were justified. He did not say that Krestinsky, Bukharin and the rest were guilty, but indicated: 'He could not understand why men would confess to crimes that they must know were punishable by death unless they were really guilty.' He said 'He could not understand their final confessions, knowing them as he did, on any other basis than the theory that they were really guilty.' This is extremely naïve. Under torture, it is only the bravest of the brave like Gnedin who will not confess. Litvinov stated:

> It was regrettable, but the Government had to be certain and take no chances. It was fortunate that the country had a leadership strong enough to take the necessary protective measures.[77]

Davies' surprising comment was:

> The extraordinary testimony of Krestinsky, Bukharin and the rest would appear to indicate that Soviet fears were well justified, for it now seems that a plot existed at the beginning of November 1936 to project a *coup d'état* with Tukhachevskii at its head for May of the following year. It was touch and go whether it would be staged, but the government acted with great vigour and speed.[78]

Clearly if impartial outsiders were prepared to give credence to the allegations against Bukharin and the rest, it is not surprising that members of the Soviet elite should take the same attitude, at least, publicly.

If Litvinov's behaviour is open to criticism on this occasion, on another occasion the Litvinovs displayed considerable courage. When Boris Stomoniakov, who worked for Litvinov in the Foreign Commissariat, was about to be arrested, he tried to shoot himself, but only succeeded in injuring himself. The secret police rushed in and took Stomoniakov

---

[77] *Moscow News,* 8 December 1937 p.4, Speech 27 November 1937
[78] Davies, Joseph E: *Mission to Moscow*, p.172

to the prison hospital. Litvinov went to Stalin and said: 'This is a man you can trust.' Stalin replied: 'Max, you are too kind and trustful. I had a friend whom I thought I could trust with my head.' However, at Litvinov's request, Stomoniakov was transferred to the Kremlin hospital, but he was worse off because he suffered from migraine and, as they would not give him the required medicines, he died. The Litvinovs offered hospitality to Nyatov Stomoniakov, his wife. She was subsequently arrested, and then completely disappeared and was never heard of again. The Litvinovs showed considerable courage in this action, because some years later Polino Molotov's brother offered Polino hospitality after Stalin had told Molotov to divorce his wife. When Polino Molotov was subsequently arrested, her brother was also arrested. The same fate did not befall the Litvinovs.[79]

Tanya was warned by her father that the family could expect anything at any time, but Tanya never asked why. However, Tanya confirmed that her father slept with a pistol under his pillow and often when at home played bridge until three and four in the morning, as he did not want to be caught in his pyjamas. This story is verified by notes in Ivy's archives.[80]

The Litvinovs were on occasion at considerable risk. Ivy, who was very depressed because of the Terror, wrote to a friend in the West, but asked another friend in the Soviet Union to convey the letter to the friend in the West. The letter stated that Ivy had always sympathised with the Revolution, but the Soviet people still didn't know what was happening. She could not bear just disappearing and her children thinking she was 'an enemy of the people.' However, the friend, instead of conveying it to the USA, must have handed it over to the NKVD, because it ended up on Stalin's desk. When Stalin spoke to Litvinov, he told Litvinov to pacify his wife, but kept the letter in reserve in case he should want to move against Max or Ivy. In fact, Ivy was more afraid of her husband than Stalin.[81] By taking no action, Stalin showed leniency to the Litvinovs, which was not afforded to other Soviet citizens.

Ehrenburg states that there appeared no logic in how Stalin selected his victims. Why, for example, did he spare the novelist Pasternak, who took an independent line, but destroyed Koltsov, an editor of *Pravda*, who honourably carried out every task entrusted to him? Why did he do away with the biologist Vavilov, but spare the scientist Kapitsa? Why, having put to death all Litvinov's assistants, did he not have the obstreperous Maxim shot?[82] Litvinov thought that the reason for Koltsov's death was that he knew too much about Stalin's betrayal of the Republicans in Spain.[83]

---

[79] Tanya; and Sheinis, Zinovy: *Maxim Litvinov*, p.285
[80] Tanay; Archives
[81] Tanya; and Carswell, John: *The Exile*, pp.145 and 146
[82] Ehrenburg, Ilya: *Post-War Years*, p.277
[83] Tanya

1937 was not a happy year for Maxim and Ivy Litvinov. Following an association between Maxim and his adopted daughter, Ivy had turned her back on diplomatic duties and procured employment as a teacher of Basic English at one of the biggest engineering institutions in Sverdlovsk. This was an old mining centre 900 miles from Moscow but only a few hours by air, where some had enriched themselves in the 19th century. Ivy also taught music. However, whenever there was a holiday she flew home. Ivy said it was easy to speak to the children over the long-distance telephone, and the children often paid her long visits, indicating the privileged position of the Litvinov family.[84] An allegation was made that Ivy Litvinov had been seriously compromised, having had most intimate relations with many of those who had been imprisoned and executed, or were awaiting trial; but this has not been corroborated. This claim is not mentioned by Carswell, who had much closer knowledge of Ivy. It was the policy of Max and Ivy to keep out of Soviet factional politics. It seems more likely that these were rumours circulated by those who wanted to destroy the Litvinovs. Carswell was right that Ivy's departure to Sverdlovsk was the result of Maxim's association with their adopted daughter.[85] It is quite clear that Ivy was not exiled, as she returned to the family home during the holidays.

In January 1938 a surprising event occurred when Litvinov was criticised in public. The only other occasion this occurred was when, in 1941, the decision was made to dismiss Litvinov from the Central Committee. Zhdanov led the attack after first paying Litvinov a compliment:

> I think we have no difference of opinion that the Commissariat of Foreign Affairs, under the guidance of our Soviet Government, is carrying out a persistent policy of peace and that our esteemed People's Commissar has rendered great services in carrying out the peace policy of the Soviet State.

The reporter of the *Moscow News* stated that 'there was stormy applause and all the deputies rose.' Zhdanov then said:

> I have several questions with regard to the practical activity of the Commissariat of Foreign Affairs of which I would like an explanation.

> The first question on which I would like to receive an explanation is: that in Leningrad we have a large number of consuls of various foreign powers. Almost every foreign power has its consul. Here I might say that a number of foreign commissars exceed the limits of their authority and duties and behave in an impermissible fashion, engaging in disruptive activity against the people and the country to which they are accredited. It is also known that the USSR does not

---

[84] *Life*, 12 October 1942, p.123
[85] FRUS, 1937, vol.1, p.53; Carswell, John: *The Exile*, pp. 139-140

possess an equal number of consuls in these countries. The question arises as to why is this so? Because the People's Commissariat of Foreign Affairs permits such a situation, under which the number of consuls representing foreign states in the USSR is not equal but is greater than the number of consuls representing the USSR in foreign states. Does not the strength and might of our great Socialist power warrant equality in consular representation of our country in foreign states and of foreign states here?

One would have expected that most countries would be represented in a city the size of Leningrad, and presumably the reason why the Soviet Union decided not to appoint more Consuls abroad was because they chose not to do so. Obviously, the reason why Stalin wanted to close the foreign consulates in Leningrad rather than expand the consular service in foreign countries was because Stalin wanted to reduce contact between Soviet citizens and foreigners.

Litvinov was then criticised for not being firm enough in the Far East against Japan, but, presumably, the alternative was war.

Zhdanov also complained:

> France, with whom the Soviet Union maintains a close relationship and with whom rapprochement is taking place, permits on its territory the existence of organisations advocating and organising terrorism against the USSR. It is said that this is done on the basis of the law covering the right of asylum for foreigners. It seems that this is not so. It seems to me that the fact of the existence on French territory, on the territory of a state with which we maintain normal relations, with which we have the Mutual-Assistance Pact – the fact of the existence of such kind of organisations constitutes nothing else than a special and deliberate encouragement of active hostile doings by all kinds of scoundrels of Russian and non-Russian origin.

> And here we must ask: Does this Pact exist or does it not exist? Is there actually a pact or is there not? And I would like the Chairman of the Commissar of the Council of People's Commissars to turn his attention to these defects and take the necessary measures to remove them.

However, Zhdanov's criticism was rather negative, because he made no suggestions as to the measures he contemplated to deal with these so-called problems.

Zhdanov was in complaining mode because he also criticised the Commissar for Water Transport for inefficiency and the Committee for Arts for 'allowing a theatre to exist under their noses in Moscow, a theatre which by its grimaces and trickery tried to vulgarise plays of the classic repertoire, which did not create a single real Soviet play.'

Molotov also supported what Zhdanov stated about the Foreign Consulates, but made no direct criticism of the Foreign Commissariat, except to state: 'This matter deserves attention and of course the Foreign Commissar.' Molotov reported, 'The People's Commissars will take into account Comrade Zhdanov's remarks solidly supported by the entire Supreme Soviet and will take all appropriate steps in the near future.' He reported that two Japanese, two Polish and five German consulates had been closed. Molotov also criticised the hostile elements in France.[86]

After Zhdanov's speech, those present thought it was Litvinov's turn to be liquidated. Two friends of Litvinov, Voroshilov and Budenny, who visited the Litvinov dacha each year, were present and met Litvinov after the speech. Voroshilov said, 'You know how it is', rather implying that Zhdanov had received instructions from Stalin to make the speech. Litvinov replied, 'I know how it is.' However, Budenny, who was terrified at being seen with Litvinov, remarked, 'You know I am a terrible coward', and disappeared.[87]

It is almost certain that it was Stalin who authorised Zhdanov and Molotov to criticise Litvinov and his commissariat. At the time it was clearly believed by those attending the Supreme Soviet that these criticisms were the prelude to Litvinov's downfall. We can only speculate why Stalin authorised this public criticism at this time. However, these developments took place at a time when Stalin wanted more and more to isolate the population of the USSR from foreign influence and Stalin's fear that his objective might be undermined by contact with foreigners might well have been the rationale behind his action. Litvinov might well have been liquidated but for the Anschluss which took place within two months of these speeches[88] and Stalin's desire to have an experienced foreign commissar in the face of such a threat.

In 1937 the Soviet Union, not surprisingly, requested Poland, Italy, Germany and Japan – countries with which relations were deteriorating to limit their consulates to the number of Soviet consulates in those countries; but what was surprising was that in 1938 Czechoslovakia and Turkey were asked to reduce their consulates. These were two countries with which the Soviet Union enjoyed the best of relationships. The Soviet Union also decided to close the majority of its consulates in Turkey, Iraq and Afghanistan, which was done merely for the purpose of reducing the number of consulates of those countries in the Soviet Union. Schulenburg rightly reported to his Foreign Ministry that a reason for this policy was the Soviet Union's desire to be as completely isolated as possible from foreign countries. Schulenburg stated correctly: 'In my opinion, Britain was especially

---

[86] *Moscow News*, 26 January 1938, pp.8 and 9
[87] Conversation with Tanya
[88] Anschluss, Ch.13, Nos.54-56

pleased by this voluntary renouncement by her old opponent in power politics,'[89] because these changes reduced Soviet influence in the Near East. Britain and the Soviet Union in the past had often clashed in this area.

The only evidence of any discussion between Litvinov and his wife is a draft letter dated 11 June 1938 written by Max : 'I cannot think of taking a holiday this year. Last year I was the only one who took a holiday.'

A *New York Times* article on 3 January 1952, following Litvinov's death, asked: 'Why was he not purged?' By the Communist standards he deserved to be. He represented the policy that was being repudiated and a class − the old-guard Bolsheviks − that had been virtually liquidated. One answer is that Stalin obviously foresaw the possibility of using Litvinov again, which he did.

The second answer is that his original fall from grace came just after the tremendous purges of 1937/1939 and no more victims were needed. By the time the post-war purges came along he was too old and harmless.[90]

However, this does not appear correct if Stalin was deviously trying to liquidate Litvinov at the time of his death, [91] but it is correct if I am right that any such plot did not have Stalin's approval. Sheinis tries to answer this historical mystery by stating that abroad 'Litvinov was playing one of the leading roles in world politics.' At home, 'Litvinov enjoyed enormous prestige across the country'; but Stalin was not normally influenced by public opinion either in the Soviet Union or abroad. Sheinis also claims that Litvinov had not, unlike others, taken part in any factional group, and that Stalin 'kept him in reserve.'[92] A valid question is why did Stalin keep Litvinov in reserve if Stalin was confident that the German-Soviet pact would continue?

Gnedin, Litvinov's press officer, was arrested and imprisoned on 10 May 1939, shortly after Litvinov's dismissal.[93] Gnedin was subjected to torture to try to force him to provide evidence against Litvinov. Security investigator Voronovich testified that Beria and his deputy, Bogdan Kobulov, personally beat Gnedin for forty-five minutes, demanding Gnedin sign a statement about an espionage organisation that was headed by Litvinov.[94] Sheinis also states that such an incident took place.[95] I think Vaksberg is wrong when he stated that Gnedin signed a confession that Litvinov was part of a terrorist group. Vaksberg

---

[89] *Documents on German Foreign Policy*, 4th Series, Pt.1, pp. 904-906 @ .905

[90] *The New York Times* 3 January 1952 p.26

[91] Ibid; No.105 post

[92] Sheinis, Zinovy: *Maxim Litvinov*, p.300

[93] Vaksberg, Arkady *Stalin Against Jews*, p.84

[94] Nove, Alec: *Glasnost in Action*, p.99; Vaksberg, Arkady : *Stalin Against Jews*, p.84

[95] Sheinis, Zinovy: *Maxim Litvinov*, p.299

was influenced by his hatred for Stalin's anti-Semitism. Sheinis is right about the fact that Gnedin refused to sign a confession that he was part of a counter-revolutionary terrorist group. Tanya too does not believe Gnedin signed any confession;[96] but, if Gnedin did sign any confession, nothing happened to Litvinov.

Vaksberg claims that work on the case against Litvinov started in May 1939, but was terminated in October 1939.[97] However, nothing occurred in October 1939 (which, as far as the 1939-1945 war was concerned, was a very quiet month) that would be a reason for Stalin to terminate an investigation already begun. Vaksberg states that it was Stalin's friendship with Nazi Germany that saved Litvinov. 'Destroying the diplomat that Hitler hated would be too demonstrative a step.'

Vaksberg then said that Litvinov was removed from all power.[98] However, that did not happen for a further fifteen months. The reason for Litvinov's final removal was more likely to have been a desperate attempt to appease Hitler.[99] Vaksberg appeared sometimes to have allowed his justifiable hatred of Stalin's anti-Semitism to have clouded his judgment.

Further, Vaksberg claims a large trial of diplomats was being planned, including Maisky, Boris Stern, former ambassador to Finland and Italy, Suritz, ambassador to France, and Omansky, the ambassador to the USA; but this intended trial kept being postponed and once Barbarossa took place it was abandoned.[100] In spite of the problems caused by Barbarossa, surprisingly there was time to try Gnedin, who was sentenced to ten years in the camps.[101] Others were not so fortunate and were executed, such as Rozenberg, Khinchuk, Stark, and Davtyan.[102] Poor Gnedin would languish in prison until after Khrushchev came to power, and was finally released on 13 August 1955.[103]

However, by the autumn of 1941 any move against Litvinov would be out of the question, as his services were required as ambassador to the United States. The investigating officers told Gnedin: 'None of the questions regarding Litvinov have been asked of you.'[104] I wondered whether that meant the interrogation had not been approved by Stalin but ordered by Beria, and, should it be discovered, Beria was worried about Stalin's anger. Tanya never thought of that explanation and still believes the interrogation was ordered by Stalin. In that case, what was the motive for telling Gnedin to forget being asked any

---

[96] Tanya
[97] Vaksberg, Arkadiy, *Stalin Against Jews*, p.86
[98] Ibid.
[99] Ibid. Pope, Arthur: *Maxim Litvinov*, p.460; and Ch.14, No.119
[100] Vaksberg, Arkady: *Stalin Against Jews*, p.86
[101] Ibid.
[102] Ibid.
[103] Ibid.
[104] Tanya

questions about Litvinov? No concrete archival evidence has appeared on the question of whether it was Stalin's intention to bring a case against Litvinov. Tanya Litvinov is convinced, as was Khrushchev, there were plans to liquidate Litvinov, although Khrushchev believed this occurred in the post-war period.[105] However, the fact that Maxim and Ivy survived, despite being guilty of indiscretions, while many of his contemporaries were faultless in this respect, yet perished, surely indicates that the initiative to liquidate Litvinov was not approved by Stalin.

The reason for Litvinov's survival could have been Stalin's appreciation that Litvinov protected Stalin at the London Congress.[106] However, I believe the most important factor in Litvinov's survival was that Stalin never entirely trusted Molotov, who in 1936 was virtually under house arrest. Stalin was suspicious of Molotov because he had accepted hospitality while he was in the United States and had a brother living in the USA. Stalin thought that Molotov might have become a US spy.[107] Moreover, it was not inconceivable that Molotov might have been cajoled into leading a coup against Stalin. There was virtually no danger of Litvinov participating, as he was not within the inner circle of Stalin's advisors. Also, Litvinov, as Ivy describes him, 'was a misfit, not hunting as the other rulers did. He was very much a loner, wore elastic-sided ankle high boots, read the *New Statesman* and carried a mahogany walking stick.'[108]

No doubt Stalin was aware of the hostility between Litvinov and Molotov. Stalin probably thought this strengthened his position because, if he decided that he wanted to dismiss Molotov, he could do so easily, as Litvinov could replace Molotov in view of Litvinov's experience of foreign affairs.

Also, Litvinov, with his world-wide reputation, was useful in internal politics to give credence to Stalin's policies. There was, for example, Litvinov's membership of the committee that dealt with Bukharin, the fact he signed the constitution and Litvinov's open support for Stalin's Terror. These facts counter Hindus' traditional view that the reason Litvinov survived was because he abstained from subjects which were beyond the competence and authority of the Soviet Commissar of Foreign Affairs.[109] For the reasons given in this chapter, this is only partially correct. We indeed know that Litvinov privately spoke critically to Hilger about the Purges.[110]

However, we have an insight into what Litvinov actually thought of Stalin. When Litvinov met his old colleague Suritz in 1947, they both agreed that Stalin :

---

[105] Khrushchev, Nikita: *Khrushchev Remembers*, p.262; Ch 18 No.37
[106] See Ch.1, No.41
[107] Miner, Steven, in Craig:R. & Loewenheim. F. *Diplomats 1939-1979*, pp.66 and 88
[108] *Observer*, 25 July 1976, p.17; Washington Post 30th January 1977 H1
[109] Hindus, Maurice: *Crisis in the Kremlin*, p.52
[110] Hilger, Gustav: *Incompatible Allies*, p.113

was a great man in many ways, but he was unpredictable and he was stubborn, refusing to consider facts that did not correspond to his wishes, [in fact, suffering the same defect as Neville Chamberlain]. He (Stalin) thought he was serving the people, but did not want to know the people and did not wish to know them, preferring the abstract idea 'the people made to his own liking.'[111]

Khrushchev, in his Secret Speech, stated that 'his suspicion grew. His persecution mania reached unbelievable dimensions. Many workers were becoming enemies before his very eyes.'[112]

In Snow's interview with Litvinov in 1945, Snow asked Litvinov whether, as the Soviet population had shown considerable loyalty − would not the Party feel secure enough to tolerate genuine freedom of speech even within its own ranks ? Litvinov said, 'I think so', shrugging his shoulders, 'but what I think does not count. They do not think so. No there won't be any great improvement until the other powers give up the hope of destroying us by force.' However, I believe Litvinov is not correct. First many Soviet citizens fought in the German Army, probably mostly non Russians. For example about 300,000 Ukranians fought in the German Army. Secondly if Stalin had no enemies, he would find some. By his very nature it is impossible to believe he would participate in a democracy and if he gave up power, he would have been pursued relentlessly, as happened in Chile in respect of Pinochet. [113]

Was Litvinov in any way responsible for the Purges? Regretfully, the answer must be yes. Why was Stalin ever allowed to have the power he obtained? The time to stop him in his tracks was in the 1920s. By the 1930s, it was too late, by which time Stalin had been allowed to become an absolute dictator. Those who supported Stalin against Trotsky and thereby helped to bring about the eventual exile of the latter removed the one person who could mount a credible opposition to Stalin. Never has the saying 'evil happens because good people do nothing' been more true.

---

[111] Conquest, Robert: *The Great Terror*, p.57
[112] Khrushchev, Nikita: 'Anatomy of Terror' Secret Speech, p.53
[113] Snow, Edgar: *Journey from the Beginning* p. 317; Overy, Richard: *The Dictators* p.522

17: WAR

On 22 June 1941, the widely awaited invasion of the Soviet Union by Germany occurred (Barbarossa). The *Times* on 20 June stated: 'The only thing that is certain is that the German army stand ranged along the Soviet frontier';[1] in fact, the largest force ever assembled in the history of the world. Warnings were given by Cadogan, a senior British Foreign Office civil servant, to Maisky, the Soviet ambassador to Britain, who immediately informed Stalin and Molotov.[2] However, the Soviets did virtually nothing. Ivy tells us that her husband had followed with anxiety the steady advance of Hitler's armies across Europe and wondered how long Britain could hold out unsupported. Nevertheless, even to Litvinov, Barbarossa was a surprise, as he did not believe Hitler would risk embarking on a second front at this stage of the war. Litvinov told the Governor of Burma, when he was en route to the USA to take up his appointment as ambassador, that Litvinov had not expected Germany to attack the Soviet Union until Germany had dealt with Britain.[3]

The German invasion was certainly a surprise to Tanya, Litvinov's daughter. The first she heard of it was when she received a telephone call to the effect that Kiev was being bombed. She said, 'I do not like that sort of joke';[4] but of course it was true. However, it is my belief that, if Litvinov had possessed the information available, such as Maisky's report of his conversation with Cadogan, it would have been quite clear to Litvinov that there was a strong possibility that the invasion would occur. He would have been brave enough to warn Stalin and strongly advise him to take the appropriate measures.

The Soviet leaders, as well as Litvinov, were concerned that Britain might come to terms with Germany, a fear which now appears reasonable. Indeed, Litvinov was worried that Hess's flight meant that Britain was about to make peace with Germany. Litvinov stated all believed the British fleet steaming up the North Sea for a joint attack with Germany on Leningrad and Kronstadt.[5]

Unlike Beck, who allowed prejudice and public opinion to influence his decisions, Churchill showed his true statesmanship and, while Roosevelt dithered, Churchill immediately realised that this invasion might be the saviour of Britain. Time was to prove

---

[1] *Times*, 20 June 1941, p.1
[2] Maisky, Ivan: *Memoirs of a Soviet Ambassador*, p.149
[3] FO 954 31
[4] Tanya tape
[5] Bryant, Christopher: *Stafford Cripps*, p.241

him right. The same day as Barbarossa, Churchill broadcast Britain's intention to give full aid to the Soviet Union.[6] When Litvinov heard of Churchill's broadcast pledging such help, he was much relieved.[7] This is confirmed in the conversation Litvinov had with the Governor of Burma. Nevertheless, Litvinov was suspicious of the British aristocracy.

He said that Hess knew exactly where to go when he sought out the Duke of Hamilton.[8] Were Litvinov's suspicions so unreasonable, as there were some influential British people who favoured allowing Germany a free hand to attack the Soviet Union?[9]

However, was Britain's action so deplorable at that time in view of the Nazi-Soviet pact? There was much merit to the view that it was wise for the Soviet Union to have remained neutral in 1939 and that the acquisition of Eastern Poland and the Baltic States improved the Soviet Union's strategic position in 1941 to such a degree that Moscow was saved. Surely the Soviet Union's mistake was publicly siding with Germany? For example, the Soviets congratulated the German forces on the successful capture of Warsaw, and Stalin even told Hitler that if Germany was likely to be defeated, the Soviet Union would come to Germany's rescue; a policy that Litvinov would have opposed because, unlike Stalin and Molotov, he would have foreseen the danger to the Soviet Union if Britain was neutralised.[10]

Then Litvinov was installed in the Foreign Commissariat but, according to Ivy, was given no job so nobody knew what he was doing there. However two men appeared at the family dacha and plugged in the telephone. In any event, according to Sheinis, the instructions for Litvinov had been given by Stalin personally. Stalin said: 'You have come in your country clothes.' Litvinov replied: 'My clothes are moth-ridden.' Similar to Litvinov's action on the Beaverbrook visit, was this intended, to highlight to Stalin, Litvinov's displeasure that his services had not been required?[11]

On 9 July 1941 Litvinov broadcast in English – obviously with Stalin's approval. Litvinov condemned Germany's treacherous attack on the Soviet Union.

> No agreement or treaty, no document signed by Hitler and his henchmen, no promise or assurance on their part, no declaration of neutrality, no relations with them whatsoever can provide a guarantee against sudden and unprovoked attack. Hitler and his gang have considered themselves above all conception of peaceful co existence and international obligations. There is nothing that distinguishes their

---

[6] Churchill's broadcast: *Churchill's Complete Speeches*, vol.6, p.6427
[7] Cadogan, Alexander: *Diaries*, p.389
[8] FO 954 31
[9] Ch.13, No.132
[10] Laurence Rees BBC broadcast 2008 ; Bethell, Nicholas: *The War Hitler Won*, p.114
[11] Sheinis, Zinovy: *Maxim Litvinov*, p.303

society from the jungle.

Hitler has always ruled by the principle of divide and to attack. He uses the most insidious methods to prevent the intended victims from organising a common resistance, taking special pains to prevent war on two fronts against the most powerful European countries. His strategy is to mark down the victims and strike them one by one in an order prompted by circumstances.

Hitler intended first to deal with the Western States so as to be free to fall upon the Soviet Union.

However, Litvinov added,

Hitler had not the training of a Channel swimmer yet, so another plan matured in his brain. Believing that he had secured himself by a pact of truce in the West, he decided upon a Blitzkrieg, a lightning war in the East in order immediately after this war to fall with added strength upon Britain and finish her off. He worked at the same time to prevent simultaneous action against himself from the West and East by driving between them an ideological wedge.

Litvinov then proceeded to praise Churchill by describing his statement on the day of the attack as one delivered with that 'statesman-like promptness that is characteristic of him.' Churchill 'immediately informed the world he was not taken by surprise by Hitler's steps, declaring that a victory over the Soviet Union by Hitler would be a disaster and a catastrophe for the British Empire.'

Churchill was correct. He had previously ordered Cadogan to inform Maisky of what British intelligence had gathered concerning the threatening German troop movement.

Litvinov finally states: 'The people of the Soviet Union have responded with enthusiasm to the appeal of the Soviet Government and our beloved leader Stalin.'[12]

Fischer believes that the speech criticises Stalin because Litvinov considered Stalin was naïve in thinking both that he could avoid war by allowing Hitler to go West and that Stalin had to sign the Nazi-Soviet pact in order to prevent the Soviet Union being attacked by Germany. Fischer has always maintained that Stalin should not have gone to the defence of Poland, but should have defended France when she was attacked. It was in the Soviet interest to give maximum aid to France, as Roosevelt realised it was in the USA's interest to give maximum aid to Britain. By giving the obligatory praise to Stalin, Litvinov made it more difficult for criticisms to be made of his views.[13]

---

[12] Full text in *The New York Times,* 9 July 1941, p.6; Extract *Times* 9 July 1941 p. 3
[13] Fischer, Louis: *Great Challenge,* pp.31 and 55

Nevertheless, the broadcast could not be heard in the Soviet Union as it was broadcast after transmission ended. One might think this was because Stalin and or Molotov did not want to give Litvinov too much publicity, but this may not be so, as the broadcast was published in the Soviet press the next day. It was in fact only heard in Britain, and, although intended for the USA, could not be heard there owing to atmospheric conditions. The full text of the speech was published in *The New York Times*, the English *Times* publishing only a small extract.[14]

After Germany's attack on the Soviet Union, Litvinov wrote two letters, one to the Soviet blood transfusion service offering his blood – but the institution replied, stating that the blood of 65-year-olds was not so far needed. The other letter was to Molotov, offering Litvinov's services – but no reply was received. Litvinov remarked to his wife, 'I could hardly say I want his job.' Tanya, Litvinov's daughter, does not believe that her father actually told Molotov he wanted his job, as reported by Sheinis.[15]

Nevertheless, it does appear that, discreetly, Litvinov was being consulted, because we have a memorandum that he was seen by Stafford Cripps in the Kremlin, who reported: 'He looked very well and was enjoying a position of some importance in the Kremlin.'[16]

By the end of July 1941, German planes were attacking Moscow and Maxim insisted on sending his wife and family to Kuibyshev.[17]

Hopkins was sent by Roosevelt as his special representative to see Stalin, who met Hopkins on 31 July 1941. The interpreter was Maxim Litvinov, who was described on that occasion as not wearing old clothes but a garment 'similar to a morning coat which had been laid away in moth balls but which had now been brought out, dusted and aired as a symbol of completely changed conditions.'

Hopkins had two meetings with Stalin. On the first occasion Molotov also attended he meeting. On the second occasion he saw Stalin without any aides. Whether Molotov was there is not known. If he was there he said nothing. Stalin was most complimentary about President Roosevelt and the USA.

He asked Hopkins to send a personal message to the President which admitted that the might of Germany was so great that it would be difficult for Britain and Russia combined to crush the German military machine. He said that the one thing that could defeat Hitler, and without firing a shot, was the announcement that the United States was going to war with Germany; but Hopkins told Stalin his mission was entirely concerning the matter of

---

[14] No 12 ante; Cassidy, Henry Clarence: *Moscow Dateline*, p.64.
[15] Tanya; Sheinis Zinovy *Maxim Litvinov* p.303
[16] PRO microfilm, 26 July 1941; FO 954 24B, p.356
[17] Archives Box 7

supplies. Hopkins gave Stalin no cause for optimism, except that the question as to whether the USA entered the war would be decided by Hitler himself. American involvement depended on how far Hitler encroached on fundamental US interests.[18]

On 17 August 1941 Litvinov wrote an article for *Reynolds News*. He wrote that Hitler

> striving for domination over the whole world, has transformed nearly all of Europe and part of Asia and Africa into a huge battlefield covered with millions of corpses and heaps of ruins, but he will not be content until he has dragged into bloody war, for his own interests, those few countries that remain outside it.

> The Soviet Union is inspired by the consciousness and in the heroic and titanic fight which they are carrying on against the blood-thirsty Nazi hordes. There are centred [on the Soviet Union] the aspirations, the hopes and expectations of all peoples of Europe.

> Not only the Britons who are directly participating in the war and the Americans who have rendered aid to Britain and have promised the Soviet Union enormous material help, but all other nations as well can and must partake openly and secretly in this sacred war for freeing humanity from the nightmare of Nazism. It is especially important that the fight be waged by all participants simultaneously.

Then, reiterating his speech on 8 July 1941, Litvinov wrote:

> In all his calculations Hitler counted and counts on the possibility of smashing his enemies individually one after another. Only by withholding this possibility from Hitler can a swift victory over the enemy of mankind be achieved.[19]

In September 1941 Beaverbrook for Britain, together with Harriman for the USA, were sent by their respective governments to negotiate assistance for the Soviet Union. Prior to the proposed meeting, Beaverbrook thought it would be a friendly gesture to ask the Soviets to supply an interpreter, but Harriman had a low opinion of the one chosen.

Accordingly, only three hours before the meeting Beaverbrook asked for Litvinov; perhaps hardly surprising in view of Stalin having previously arranged for Litvinov to act as interpreter at the meeting with Hopkins on 30 July 1941. Litvinov was found and attended the whole meeting on 28 September. The meeting was extremely cordial. Litvinov was reported as cutting a pathetic figure. His clothes and shoes were shabby. Beaverbrook remembered that his waistcoat and trousers did not meet to cover the expanse of his shirt

---

[18] Sherwood, Robert: *White House Paper*, pp. 328-344
[19] *Reynolds News*, 17 August 1941, p.5

front.[20] This mode of dress contrasted with his appearance in formal clothes for the meeting of 30 July.[21]

Was the fact that Litvinov was under-dressed a protest that his talents were not being utilised? Beaverbrook frequently addressed his remarks to Litvinov. When Molotov spoke, Stalin brushed him aside, and Harriman, perhaps wrongly, interpreted this as a sign that Molotov was not in a secure position. Stalin seldom looked Harriman or Beaverbrook in the eye.

Stalin thought that Hitler had made a mistake by attacking on three fronts. If he had concentrated on Moscow, it would have undoubtedly fallen. Stalin nevertheless gave an assurance that if Moscow fell, the Soviet Union would fight a defensive war from behind the Urals; but, with the fall of Moscow, an offensive action would be more difficult in the future.

Stalin admitted that Germany had a superiority in the air of three to two. In tanks it was even greater. He needed 1100 tanks a month, but would settle for 500 a month from Britain and the USA. Stalin suggested that Britain might send troops to defend what was left of the Ukraine. This was a tall order given Britain was only one third of the size of the USSR and given all her commitments, although she could recruit help from her colonies and dominions.

Beaverbrook was nevertheless sympathetic. He replied that a build-up of British troops in Iran was under way. Harriman commented that, in the event of a breakthrough in the Middle East, if the Russian front collapsed, some of the troops might be sent to the Caucasus. Stalin observed that there was no war in the Caucasus (although there would soon be), but there was war in the Ukraine. When Beaverbrook suggested that the British and Soviet General Staffs might open up general discussions, Stalin made no reply, probably fearing too much fraternisation. Harriman referred to the lack of religious freedom in the USSR and asked for an assurance that Section 124 of the Soviet Constitution meant what it said in guaranteeing freedom of conscience and worship to all citizens. This intervention interrupted the extreme cordiality of the meeting.[22] The meeting was adjourned until the next day.

At the meeting the next day Stalin's attitude had changed. When Beaverbrook arrived, he handed a letter to Stalin from Churchill. This time Litvinov had rectified his appearance and he was smartly dressed. Beaverbrook noticed that the door was left open. Apparently, somebody was checking Litvinov's translation. At times Stalin seemed disinterested. He

---

[20] Harriman, Averell: *Special Envoy to Churchill and Stalin 1941-1946*, p.86
[21] See No. 18 *ante*
[22] Harriman, Averell: *Special Envoy to Churchill and Stalin 1941-1946*, p.87

turned to Harriman and asked why the USA could supply only 1000 tons of armour plate steel for tanks when US steel production was in excess of 50,000,000 tons. Harriman admitted that the USA had 60,000,000 tons, but pointed out that the USA's demand for steel was very great and that it would take time to increase capacity for this kind of steel. Stalin brushed aside the explanation and said: 'One only had to add alloys.' He complained that 'the paucity of the offer clearly shows you want to see the Soviet Union defeated.'[23]

Molotov was at these meetings, but he seemed to have played a minor role. When Harriman and Beaverbrook were leaving, Molotov reminded Stalin that he had not read the letter written by Churchill which Beaverbrook had handed to him. He ripped open the envelope, barely read it and thrust it back into the hands of his clerk.[24]

Stalin made three telephone calls during the meeting, dialling the number himself, and it appears likely that he was distracted by the declining situation on the front. As so little progress was made at the meeting, it was agreed that there should be another meeting the following evening.[25]

Next day the German newspapers announced that bitter quarrels had developed and that Britain and the USA would never find common ground with the Bolsheviks. At that stage it appeared that Goebbels might not have been far from the truth.[26]

At the third meeting Stalin was in a much better mood. This was perhaps on account of the German newspapers. Beaverbrook and Harriman went through a long list of materials which they all agreed were needed and could be supplied. At one stage Litvinov forgot his humble role and, bounding from his chair, cried, 'Now we shall win the war.'[27] Stalin mentioned the German propaganda with amusement and indicated it was for them to prove Goebbels a liar.[28]

Stalin was affable and in a jocular mood. At one moment he asked Beaverbrook if Maisky lectured him on communist doctrine. Beaverbrook said, 'I don't give him a chance.' Beaverbrook enquired, 'What about our fellow?' Stalin said that 'he was all right', with a lack of enthusiasm. Beaverbrook said, 'There was nothing wrong with him except he was a bore.' In that respect, Stalin said, 'Is he comparable to Maisky?' 'No,' said Beaverbrook, 'like Mrs Maisky.' Stalin liked the joke immensely.[29]

---

[23] Chisholm, Anne: *Beaverbrook*, p.414; Harriman, Averell: *Special Envoy*, p.89
[24] Sherwood, Robert E: *White House Papers of H L Hopkins*, p.390; Harriman, Averell: *Special Envoy*, p.89
[25] Sherwood, Robert E: *White House Papers of H L Hopkins*, p.390
[26] Sherwood Robert E: *White House Papers of H L Hopkins* p.391; Harriman, Averell: *Special Envoy*, p.90
[27] Chisholm, Anne: *Beaverbrook*, p.415
[28] Sherwood, Robert E: *White House Papers of H L Hopkins*, p.391
[29] Harriman, Averell: *Special Envoy to Churchill and Stalin*, p.94; Chisholm, Anne: *Beaverbrook*, p.416

In spite of the varied fortunes of the visit, the social entertainment for Beaverbrook and Harriman was not negected. On 30 September a big banquet took place in the best tradition of the Tsars. There were a hundred guests, including the whole of the Beaverbrook mission and the aircrew that had delivered part of the delegation to Moscow, and members of the British and US embassy staff. Hors d'oeuvres was served, followed by various varieties of caviar and fish, followed by cold suckling pig, chicken and a game bird. The banquet finished with ice cream and cakes. There were various fruits flown from the Crimea not available in the markets. Alcohol was not neglected. A number of bottles containing vodka, red and white wine and Russian brandy with champagne were supplied to accompany the dessert.[30]

When Molotov tried to speak, Stalin only brushed him aside. Litvinov, who addressed Stalin as Comrade Stalin, 'would get only brief and terse answers.'[31]

A Mr Laurence Cadbury was a member of the economic mission that travelled to the Soviet Union to advise and report on the help that the Soviet Union needed. He reported to the press that the greatest importance must be given to the three personal interviews with Stalin and referred to the emergence of Litvinov as a prominent figure in the Soviet conversations. This was an exaggeration, as his part in the meetings was mainly in the role of interpreter.[32]

Early in November 1941, Litvinov was summoned to see Stalin and told his services were required as ambassador to the United States. Japan was not yet at war, so it was safer to travel by the Far Eastern route. Litvinov arrived in San Francisco on 6 December, after travelling for 22 days.[33] Litvinov reached Washington on the day of Pearl Harbour. He was greeted by representatives from the Soviet Embassy, the State Department and the British Embassy, as well as Joseph Davies, the former ambassador to the Soviet Union, with whom the Litvinovs lunched.[34] Litvinov's arrival was noted by the Japanese press, who wrongly envisaged that this might increase the prospect of the Soviet Union's participation in US moves against Japan.[35]

On 8 December 1941 Litvinov presented his credentials to President Roosevelt. Litvinov told the President, 'The peoples of the Soviet Union are happy in the realisation that they are receiving from the American people not only their sympathy in the struggle, but also substantial material support, and it affords me great pleasure to bring the warm gratitude of my Government and my country for this generous support.'[36] President Roosevelt showed

---

[30] Chisholm, Anne: *Beaverbrook*, p.417

[31] Ibid. pp. 414 and 418

[32] *The New York Times,* 2 October 1941, p.2

[33] Sheinis, Zinovy: *Maxim Litvinov*, p.312

[34] *The New York Times,* 8 December 1941, p.8; Sheinis Zinovy: *Maxim Litvino, p.313*

[35] *The New York Times,* 7 December 1941, p.3

[36] Ibid.   9 December 1941, p.2; 10 December 1941, p.10

his enthusiasm for Litvinov's appointment by stating it is 'most fortunate that the Soviet Government have deemed it advisable to send as ambassador a statesman who has already held high office in his own country.'

Roosevelt also stated that Umansky: 'For more than two years has occupied and so ably performed the office you are now assuming.'[37] Upon Litvinov's arrival at the Soviet consulate in San Francisco, a member of staff suggested:'Umansky's leadership of the embassy had been immature.' Litvinov supported his predecessor by saying, 'Stalin told me that Umansky had acted correctly.'[38]

Soviet diplomats in the USA during the period of the Nazi-Soviet pact were obviously in a most difficult position because of the policy of their government, which was beyond the diplomat's control. Litvinov was right to give Umansky his support.

It should not be overlooked that Litvinov arrived in a country where the stiffening Soviet resistance to the German army, racing to take Moscow before the onset of the worst of the Russian winter, was winning the Soviet Union many American friends. *The Washington Post* reported:

> Both Mrs Cordell Hull, the Secretary of State's wife, and the Vice-President's wife, Mrs Wallace, had travelled to the Soviet Embassy for celebrations to mark the 24th anniversary of the Soviet Revolution in 1941, where they were greeted by Mr and Mrs Gromyko and Mrs Umansky. The Under Secretary of State, Sumner Welles, Jessie Jones, the Commercial Secretary, and Francis Biddle, the Attorney General, were also present. Most foreign countries except Spain and Finland were represented.[39]

Although some in the USA thought the Soviet Union should declare war on Japan, Litvinov's statement to the press on 14 December 1941 that the Soviet Union would not do so in view of the critical situation on the Eastern front brought little adverse comment.[40] Litvinov described Japan as one of the gangsters, but rightly stated that, although she had been massing troops along the border with Manchukuo for months, he did not think it would be in the interests of Japan to provoke the USSR at present.

In early December 1941 the Soviet Union's war relief organisation called a large meeting in Madison Square. The huge auditorium was filled to capacity. Litvinov, speaking in English, told of the terrible suffering in the Soviet Union. A woman in the front row ran up to the stage, unhooked her diamond necklace and flung it at his feet. Another waved a

---

[37] Ibid. 10 December 1942 p.10
[38] Sheinis, Zinovy: *Maxim Litvinov*, p.313
[39] *Washington Post*, 8 November 1941, p.3
[40] *The New York Times,* 14 December 1941, pp. 1 & 20; Sheinis Zinovy *Maxim Litvinov* p. 313

cheque for $15,000. However, at the end, Litvinov said quietly: 'What we need is a second front.'[41]

Litvinov wrote to his daughter: 'Despite the war, the press is interested in every step. Once Mummy had chilblains and limped. People began calling and giving advice. We had to be inoculated against smallpox. As a result, Mummy had a rash. The papers blew it up into a serious illness; a strange land and a strange people.'[42] The American press' interest is supported by Carswell.[43]

Carswell was right that Ivy was a most successful partner. She was 52 and extremely handsome, although she was worried about her weight. For the first time she was a real ambassador's wife.[44] Like Eleanor Roosevelt, she would map her own identity: writing, travelling, broadcasting and going to parties unaccompanied. However, Maxim had formed an association with his secretary which cast a shadow over his ambassadorship. Evidently, Ivy did not take this affair passively. Relations between Maxim and Ivy were very stormy.[45]

The first significant event which concerned Litvinov, following his appointment as ambassador, was the negotiations which led 30 of Britain and the USA's allies and the Soviet Union to subscribe to the Atlantic Charter. Roosevelt had been previously criticised for omitting religious freedom from the original treaty. In spite of Roosevelt inviting Litvinov to lunch, Roosevelt was disappointed that Churchill and he could not persuade Litvinov to accept the amendment without Stalin's instructions, which Stalin in due course gave. 32 nations signed up to the Charter. Another clause which Litvinov would not accept without reference to Stalin was that authorities as well as nations could subscribe to the charter, to enable the Free French and dissident organisations to participate.[46]

On 27 February 1942, at the annual dinner of a group of American journalists, Litvinov urged the Allies to take the offensive in Europe soon. He rightly stated that, only by simultaneous action on two fronts, separated by long distances, could Hitler's power be broken. He did not necessarily specify Western Europe. Presumably, Italy would suffice, although I cannot see how this could have been successfully accomplished without clearing the Axis from North Africa. In a warm gesture, Litvinov proposed a motion sending a message of appreciation to General MacArthur, that 'great soldier.'[47] In another key speech on 17 March 1942 he called on the Allies to take risks, as the Soviet Union had done. He said there might be greater risk in doing nothing rather than letting slip one opportunity

---

[41] Sheinis, Zinovy: *Maxim Litvinov*, p.317
[42] Ibid. p.319
[43] Carswell, John: *The Exile*, p.151
[44] Ibid.
[45] Ibid.
[46] Churchill, Winston: *The Second World War*, vol.3, 'The Grand Alliance', pp.605 and 607
[47] *Times*, 27 February 1942, p.4

after another. However, if Britain and the USA had mounted an invasion that failed, there would have been significant psychological damage to occupied Europe and a blow would have been dealt to the various resistance groups.

Evidence that Litvinov was winning the hearts of many Americans was illustrated by a report in *The New York Times* of 10 April 1942. A gala performance of music and ballet for the benefit of the Soviet Union's war relief was given to a capacity audience at the Metropolitan Opera House. $10,000 dollars was taken at the box office for assistance to the Soviet Union. As the Litvinovs took their seats at the beginning of the performance, Maxim acknowledged the applause from his box. A second round of applause commenced, which only ceased when Ivy Litvinov had risen and waved. Later in the performance, after the author Fanny Hurst, the evening's only speaker, made mention of the Litvinovs' presence, there was a further enthusiastic outburst.[48]

At the end of May 1942, Molotov joined his ambassador in Washington, having previously visited London and negotiated an Anglo-Soviet treaty of friendship. The meeting between the two men was not very cordial. At that time Litvinov did not, in his daughter's words, count for much, in spite of the fairly cordial relationship between Roosevelt and Litvinov.[49]

Roosevelt and Churchill realised that it was Molotov, not Litvinov, who had Stalin's ear. How far Roosevelt thought that Molotov wielded power in his own right is uncertain. Was Roosevelt influenced by Churchill's opinion of Molotov and Litvinov? In a letter to Roosevelt on 27 May 1942, Churchill stated: 'Molotov is a statesman; very different from what we saw of Litvinov.'[50] So obviously Churchill thought Molotov was more influential than I believe he was.

Molotov stated:

> I did not take him [Litvinov] along when I negotiated with Roosevelt and Hull. Hopkins was at Roosevelt's side. Pavlov accompanied me as my interpreter, even though Litvinov was the ambassador.[51]

Certainly, Molotov did not admit to Chuev that he himself was severely reprimanded on one occasion for his conduct while on his mission to the United States.[52] However, Litvinov, unlike his boss Molotov, was not hesitant in speaking his mind to Stalin. If the letters were not downright rude, Litvinov showed no hesitancy in giving his views. The old

---

[48] *The New York Times,* 10 April 1942, p.20

[49] Tanya

[50] Churchill, Winston: *The Second World War*, vol.4, 'Hinge of Fate', p.302

[51] Chuev, Felix: *Molotov Remembers*, p.68

[52] See Ch.19, Nos.74 and 75

man seemed to have gone mad, said the shocked Umansky. It appears unlikely that Gitlow is right in claiming that Litvinov's speeches had to be approved by Umansky.[53]

Two mass meetings, in Chicago on 19 July 1941 and in New York on 22 July 1941, called for a second front. The Chicago meeting was organised by the Slav Congress. It was inspired by pro-Russian sympathisers, but not dominated by communists. The meeting in New York heard a message in support from Wendell Willkie. Both meetings called for a rupture of relations with Vichy France and Spain, the latter an unwise move when Britain was doing everything to prevent Franco from being so dominated by Hitler that Franco gave the German Army a right of passage to Gibraltar.[54]

By 5 September Litvinov was very depressed with the Soviet Union's position. He was convinced Stalingrad would fall to the Germans. He took the view that an invasion of Europe would have been feasible during the winter of 1941/1942.[55] However, this appears unlikely. The idea of organising a second front in the autumn of 1942, when the British army was fully committed to the war in North Africa, was not a constructive suggestion.

This could have been a repeat of the winter of 1941. Britain diverted resources to defend Greece, but Britain lost Greece and was also thrown back in North Africa. Now the position in North Africa was far more critical with the German Army near the Egyptian border. The Dieppe raid was not a success, except to prove that any invader of the French coast would meet formidable German defences.

When, in October 1942, Litvinov was visiting Boston, he was asked whether he was going to speak publicly. Litvinov said 'No', because he would have to mention the Second Front, and he deemed it was expedient for him to say nothing on the subject. However, did not Litvinov do this to urge the Allies to take a more active role in the fighting?[56]

On 12 October 1942 Ivy Litvinov was asked by *Life* magazine to write an article about her husband and herself. *Life* stated: 'It is a personal triumph for Ivy Litvinov, whose wit and charm enliven the traditional dullness of Washington's social events.'[57]

Appreciating the human touch, Litvinov thought it would be a good idea if the Soviet Union could send a soldier from the front line. In October 1942 Ludmilla Pavlichenko arrived. She was very popular and, after receiving proposals of marriage passed on by Litvinov, Pavlichenko returned to the rigours of the Soviet Union.[58]

---

[53] Tanya; and Gitlow, Benjamin: *The Whole of Their Lives*, p.348

[54] Nicholas, George: *Washington Dispatches 1941 to 1945*, p.58; *Life*, 30 November 1942, p.12

[55] FO 954 25

[56] FRUS, 1942, vol.3, p.459

[57] *Life*, 12 October 1942, p.115

[58] Sheinis, Zinovy: *Maxim Litvinov*, p.335

Although Litvinov was ambassador from 1941 to 1943, only in 1942 was he in the US for the commemoration of the 1917 Russian Revolution. In that year Litvinov had the opportunity to prove what a good host he was. A lavish reception took place at the Soviet Embassy in Washington.

Life stated that, three years earlier, only the brave and the economist Leon Henderson dared attend the annual reception for the Russian Revolution, but it did not mention the enthusiasm displayed at the 1941 celebrations.[59] In 1942, 1200 guests, representing all the united nations, flowed up the carpet with a red star motif and through the regal reception hall to shake hands with the smiling, rotund Soviet Ambassador. Only the President and his staff at work on the African campaign were missing. Nobody was happier than the Russians that they had more serious affairs with which to attend. Vice-President Wallace, the Secretary of the Treasury Morgenthau, Under Secretary of State Sumner Welles and Mrs Woodrow Wilson, Edward Stettinius, the Lend-Lease administrator, and Tom Connolly, chairman of the Senate Foreign Relations Committee, were among the guests. In spite of the war, vodka from Moscow and Leningrad and a sturgeon from the Volga were supplied to the guests.[60]

Next day, the Litvinovs travelled to New York to attend celebrations in that city. Both *Life* and *The New York Times* on 9 November agreed that Madison Square was packed to overflowing with a wildly cheering crowd of 20,000 for the annual tribute to the Soviet Union in the presence of Maxim Litvinov. The dramatic spotlighting, the colourful pageantry, the collection and all the trappings were the same as in previous Novembers. However, the cheerleaders were not only the Soviet Union's old friends, but new friends like the Vice-President of the USA, General McNair, commanding general of Army Ground Forces, the capitalist Thomas Lamont and a Catholic professor, Francis McMahon, who said: 'Not speaking up for Russia would be disloyal to his religion and country.'

As this meeting neared its end, the massed flags of the thirty united nations fighting the Nazis were paraded on the platform in the centre of the auditorium. Then, Corliss Lamont presented to Litvinov four massive bound volumes, containing, it was said, a million signatures, with thousands more pouring in daily, from American citizens pledged to continued Soviet-American friendship. General McNair said:

> As the 1941 campaign had shown the strength of the Red Army, the enthusiasm of the US Army was unbounded. The campaign in 1942 has shown an even more skilful and determined Red Army and the US Army is looking forward to the day when it can fight beside the Red Army and bear our full share of the common burden and go forward with it to victory.

---

[59] No.39 *ante*
[60] *Washington Post*, 8 November 1942, p.12; *Life*, 30 November 1942, p.132

Mayor La Guardia sent his personal greetings to his colleague, the Mayor of Stalingrad. The Mayor sent what was then probably considered an optimistic but correct prediction that the only German soldiers who would enter Moscow would be an army of prisoners.

Litvinov, in his speech, asserted:

> Every act of international aggression beginning with 1931 could have been prevented by sincere co-operation between the Soviet Union and the other great powers.

> No one can fail to recognise the fatal mistake made in so long ignoring the Soviet Union as a powerful factor of peace. This mistake was undoubtedly one of the causes of the present war which has brought upon humanity greater suffering and hardships and caused greater destruction than the sum of all the wars in the preceding century, not excluding the Napoleonic Wars. Sincere and close co-operation between the great powers and the Soviet Union, on the other hand, would have destroyed the *raison d'être* of Hitlerism and upset all the calculations of the aggressive countries. It was not hard to prove that such co-operation could have prevented each and every act of international aggression since 1931, crowned by the present war.

This was a somewhat hypocritical remark, as Litvinov himself had refused international co-operation when Japan invaded Manchuria in 1931.[61]

Wallace, the Vice-President, gave a very optimistic address:

> Both the Soviet Union and the United States retreated into isolationism to preserve their peace. Both failed. Both have learnt their lesson. I am here this afternoon to say it is my belief that the American and Soviet people can and will throw their influence on the side of building a new democracy which will be the hope of all the world.[62]

However, there was no evidence that Stalin would continue to act other than as a ruthless dictator.

One Russian living in the United States who was prepared only to give qualified support to the Soviet Union was Kerensky, who was the Russian leader under the Provisional Government. He said:

---

[61] See Ch.7, No.72

[62] *The New York Times,* 9 November 1942, p.19; Dulles, Foster: *The Road to Teheran,* p.246; *Life,* 30 November 1942, p.132

I speak for all Russians residing in the United States, regardless of party, when I say that the victory of the Axis would mean the dismemberment of Russia and the enslavement of her people to Germany and Japan.

However, Kerensky only advocated helping the Soviet Union if Stalin abolished political commissars, restored Poland, liberated the OGPU slaves, ended the Terror and abolished collectivisation, which was unlikely. Kerensky wanted to see Litvinov, but Sheinis is correct in stating that Litvinov would not agree to this. However, Kerensky did see the British Ambassador, Lord Halifax, in spite of his role in appeasing Hitler.[63]

On 14 March 1943, at the request of Secretary of State, Cordell Hull, Litvinov called on him. Poland dominated the discussion. Cordell Hull warned Litvinov that the decision of the Soviet Government to break off diplomatic relations with the Polish Government in exile would have a profound effect in the United States. Litvinov then raised the question of the discovery of the Polish officers' bodies at Katyn and the controversy as to whether the murders had been committed by the Russians or the Germans. The ambassador defended his government by disagreeing with the proposal of the Polish Government in London that an investigation should be conducted by the International Red Cross on the grounds that it would be held on German territory and would obviously be completely controlled by the Germans. Litvinov then showed his anti-Polish sentiments by saying that Poles always behaved in this way. Certainly, Litvinov shared Stalin's hatred of the Polish Government in exile, saying:

> It was fantastic and dangerously unrealistic to revive Russia's fear by insisting on Churchill's absurd promise to return the London Poles to power in Warsaw. The old Beck crowd was through.[64]

Very soon the British Government realised that the murders had been committed by the Soviet Union, but chose to suppress it. Whether Litvinov suspected that the Russians had committed the atrocities was a fact that continued to be denied by the Soviet authorities until the Gorbachev era.[65] However, given Litvinov's anti-Polish bias, I suspect he did not doubt the official Soviet version of events although during the late 1920s and early 1930s Litvinov had been complimentary about the Poles.[66] Subsequently he became very antagonistic towards them because they sabotaged his proposed Eastern European Pact which Eden supported and Poland's treachery against Czechoslovakia at the time of Munich. In a conversation with a US journalist, Litvinov agreed with mainstream Soviet communist opinion when he said, 'Poland had got to be friendly towards the Soviet Union

---

[63] Abraham, Richard: *Alexander Kerensky*, p.371; Sheinis, Zinovy: *Maxim Litvinov*, p.337.

[64] FRUS, 1943, vol.3, p.389; Snow, Edgar: *Journey to the Beginning*, p.315.

[65] Katyn: A good summary of the event and subsequently is in Davies, Norman: *Europe: A History*, pp.1004 and 1005

[66] See Ch 8 No 58 and Ch 12 No 12-16

and must abandon the idea that she can be the springboard against us [the Soviet Union] and in that way get back her sixteenth-century Empire.'[67]

Litvinov, in March 1943, spoke at a luncheon to mark the second anniversary of Lend-Lease. Following previous complaints from William Standley, the US ambassador to the Soviet Union, that the Soviet people were kept in the dark about the help given by Lend-Lease, Litvinov stated:

> The supplies received through Lend-Lease had been an enormous help and as such are deeply appreciated by the people of the Soviet Union, who are fully aware of its extent.

Halifax and Soong expressed similar appreciation on behalf of Britain and China.[68] Litvinov's speech was reported in the Soviet press, as well as a speech by Sir Archibald Sinclair, the British Air Minister, in which he too pointed out that the bombing of Germany had kept many of their planes from the Russian Front. [69] Standley was well pleased with Litvinov's acknowledgment.[70]

However, Roosevelt himself had become annoyed with Litvinov's second-front zeal. Indeed, Roosevelt told Harriman : 'The US might ask for Litvinov's recall.' Harriman told Litvinov how upset the President was without actually saying what the President had said. All Harriman said was: 'If Litvinov continued that way, he would get into serious difficulties with the President. Litvinov, who had been ebullient, collapsed so completely.'[71] It must have been even more distressing because he must have realised that, not only did he not have Stalin's confidence, but that this was known among the principal allies.[72] Litvinov's ambassadorship was now experiencing a torrid time after it had started with such high hopes. Litvinov even stated that he had been forbidden by the Soviet Government from appearing in public or making any public speeches.[73] Sheinis' account of the ambassadorship, which portrays it as an unqualified success, is highly misleading.[74]

Life devoted a special edition to the Soviet Union on 29 March 1943. It especially praised Litvinov, who 'has interpreted Red Russia to the rest of the world and interpreted the Western democracies to Stalin and other leaders who have never been out of the Soviet ion.' In fact, Stalin had been out of the Soviet Union.[75] *Life* included an interview with

---

[67] Snow Edgar: *Journey to the Beginning*, pp.313 and 315; No 12 No 48 but see Ch 13 No 109

[68] Stettinius, Edward: *Lend-Lease: A Weapon for Victory*, p.327; *The New York Times,* 12 March 1943, p.1

[69] *The New York Times,* 14 March 1943, p.3

[70] Ibid. 15 March, p.4

[71] Harriman, Averell: *Special Envoy to Churchill and Stalin*, p.199

[72] Nicholas, Herbert George: *Washington Dispatches, 1941-1945*, p.167

[73] FRUS, 1943, vol.3, p.522

[74] Sheinis, Zinovy: *Maxim Litvinov*, pp.310-337

[75] See Ch.1, Nos.37-39

Joseph Davies, the former US ambassador to the Soviet Union. He was asked if the people of the USA could be assured that the rulers of the Soviet Union were people of goodwill towards other nations and that they required a peaceful, stable world. He answered:

> Their public statements of policy and their deeds in the past decade, both established when Litvinov was Foreign Minister, within or without the League, who was the outstanding advocate of collective security by non-aggressor nations in order to ensure a peaceful and stable world. War anywhere, Litvinov constantly urged, would engulf the rest of us, for peace was indivisible. Abyssinia, China, and agreeing to stand by Czechoslovakia with France against attack by Germany, all attested to the Soviet Union's sincerity "as men of goodwill." It is also in their practical best interest to have peace with and in the world.

Davies was then asked if the Soviet Union still used revolutionary activity as an instrument of Russian nationalism. He replied:

> The idea is being vigorously and assiduously preached by Goebbels and other Nazi propagandists in and out of Germany. The express oral assurances of Stalin, the commitment contained in the joint declaration of the United Nations and the treaty made with Britain have carefully killed the Hitler bugaboo which he [Hitler] had tried desperately and without success to sell to Europe these many years. The Soviet Union has an enviable record as a nation of keeping its obligations. Except as an instrument of military necessity, the Soviet Union will not promote dissension in the internal affairs of other nations.

Davies, when asked what would happen if the Russian economic system proved to be more efficient than the American system, stated:

> From what I have seen of both systems, I am firmly of the opinion we need not fear their competition. Our system of free enterprise, under rules of fair competition protected by the Government, contains springs of initiative and enterprise which under fair conditions surpass anything that a bureaucracy under Government administration can produce.[76]

What makes Davies' view distinct was that, although he often praised the Soviet Union, he did not believe, unlike many communist sympathisers, that the Soviet state had developed some superior form of economy.

On 7 May Litvinov informed Sumner Welles that he had asked for and been granted permission to return to Moscow. This is contrary to what Sheinis states, that he was recalled by the Soviet Government. Litvinov explained that the reason he wanted to return

---

[76] *Life*, 29 March 1943, p.49

to Moscow was to persuade Stalin that the policy Litvinov had in mind should be followed by the Soviet Union. Litvinov stated that he did not believe his messages were received by Stalin and criticised Molotov. In any event, none of Litvinov's recommendations had been adopted and he himself was entirely without influence on the policy or plans of his government.

Though Litvinov did not specifically mention the policy subject of his complaint, presumably it was to ensure that the Soviet Union pursued a policy of collaboration with the United States. Litvinov complained that Stalin was unaware of the importance of public opinion in the United States, which was the determining factor in the creation of US Government policy.[77] This is contrary to what Litvinov had said in his speech in February 1932 at the Disarmament Conference,[78] but a statesman should not be criticised purely because he changes his mind. Although Carswell says, 'Litvinov abstained from any criticism of Stalin's policies' (page155), this does not seem correct. This is also at variance with what Carswell says on p. 154, that Litvinov 'was beginning to talk to Americans about his old schemes of collective security and was unreceptive to thoughts of territorial security in terms of dependent states that charmed Stalin and Molotov.'[79] Sulzberger stated that Litvinov later bitterly complained about the behaviour of the Moscow Press Bureau and complimented the USA on their freedom of the Press by saying: 'How different it was when I was in Washington.'[80] The British ambassador, Lord Halifax, reported to the Foreign Office that Litvinov was saying he was fed up with the job here. Moscow gave no attention to his reports and told him nothing. He was going back to Moscow to have something of a showdown and did not know whether or not he would be returning.[81] Vaksberg also states that Litvinov warned Roosevelt when Litvinov called on him about a confidential letter that Stalin had initiated an anti-Semitic campaign in the country, but this has not been corroborated.[82]

Sheinis is right to state that Litvinov had been a good advertisement for his country. Diplomatic relations were established with Canada and Mexico in 1942, and in 1943 with Uruguay.[83]

It was hardly surprising that Litvinov was in fact contemplating disobedience. No doubt, given the royalties from his autobiography and lecturing, he would have had a secure income for life outside the USSR, rather than an uncertain existence in Soviet Russia. However, Ivy was against it. With the children in Russia, Ivy felt she could not do it. Tanya (Litvinov's daughter), agrees that it was the danger to her brother and herself that

---

[77] FRUS, 1943, vol.3, p.522
[78] See Ch.6, No.62
[79] Carswell, John: *The Exile*, pp.154 and 155
[80] *The New York Times,* 3 January 1952, p.9
[81] FO 954 26
[82] Vaksberg, Arkady: *Stalin Against Jews*, p.220
[83] Sheinis, Zinovy: *Maxim Litvinov*, p.336

prevented Max and Ivy from defecting, and Carswell is probably right that another reason was the discipline of long service and Litvinov's tendency to always put Russia's interests first.[84] However, Ivy temporarily remained in the USA.

Historians differ as to the reason for Litvinov's and Maisky's removal as they were recalled to Moscow about the same time. Although Ulam argues that they were removed because, following the Teheran conference, goodwill in the West was no longer thought to be of desperate importance and that, for the tough negotiations ahead, Stalin preferred people who were purely his tools. Further, Stalin felt more confident in dealing with Western leaders and less dependent on old-time professionals. However, at the time Litvinov and Maisky were removed, the Teheran conference had not taken place. Having listened in to Roosevelt's private conversation by bugging his bedroom,[85] Stalin was probably confident that Roosevelt had no underhand agenda against the Soviet Union.

Miner agrees with Ulam that, with the improved military position and the desire of the Kremlin to have 'Yes men' as ambassadors, it was no longer felt necessary to have Litvinov and Maisky as ambassadors, as a sop to Western sensibilities.[86]

Ehrenburg's view is that Stalin was annoyed at the postponement of the second front in France.[87] This view is supported by Maisky. He had no doubt that the cause of his departure was the letter Stalin received on 5 May 1943 informing him of the postponement of the second front until Spring 1944.[88] Maisky's wife agreed, as she told Jock Balfour's wife that her husband was recalled because Maisky failed to obtain a second front.[89]

However, Maisky may not be right. It might have been Stalin's displeasure at the fact that Churchill and Eden had flown to Washington to confer with Roosevelt, a conference to which the Soviet Union had not been invited. Moreover, in his 1976 article, Mastny expressed a completely different view that the removal of these two symbols of co-operation between the Allies signalled Stalin's willingness to consider a separate peace.[90]

I do not believe this was the reason. A German offer was made through the Japanese on 30 April which in any case was not accepted although Stalin might have agreed if the military situation had deteriorated. [91]

---

[84] Carswell, John: *The Exile*, p.155; Tanya

[85] Ulam, Adam B: *Stalin, The Man and the Era*, p.592; Beria, Sergo: *Beria My Father*, p.93

[86] Miner, Steven, in Craig's *Diplomats 1939-1979*, p.619

[87] Ehrenburg, Ilya: *The War Years*, p.119

[88] Maisky, Ivan: *10 Years an Ambassador*, p.362

[89] FO 954 26

[90] Mastny, Vojtech: *Russia's Road to the Cold War*, p.79; Cassandra: *Foreign Affairs*, January 1976, p.368; FRUS, 1943, vol.3, p.695

[91] FRUS 1943 vol.3 pp.694-696

On the contrary in July 1943 the German army was defeated at Kursk so why should Stalin accept a peace offer following the successful battle. In any case, why did Stalin need to indicate that the Soviet Union was prepared to consider a peace offer if one had already been made?

However, it is not necessarily a question of Stalin having a single reason for terminating Litvinov's and Maisky's ambassadorships. He may have come to his decision weighing up various factors and, except where I have indicated that the purported reason was not valid, any one or more of the other reasons may have influenced Stalin.

I believe Watson is wrong to be so confident that most of the reasons previously given were wrong and that the prime reason was that Litvinov and Maisky were needed in Moscow in connection with post-war planning.[92] However in support of Watson's views the US ambassador to the Soviet Union, Standley believed:

> The recall of Maisky and Litvinov indicates an intention on behalf of the Soviet Government to engage in post-war discussions and their presence here will be a help to the Allied cause.

Molotov, in making the announcement of the recall of Maisky and Litvinov, emphasised the fact that their recall was necessitated by the need for their advice in Moscow and there was a dearth in the Soviet headquarters of men who would have the breadth of knowledge and experience who would qualify them to advise Premier Stalin on his relations with the USA and Britain.

Molotov was absolutely correct. However the press and foreign representatives are still of the opinion and belief that this action on behalf of the Soviet Government was confirmation of the deterioration of Soviet-Anglo-American relations.[93]

The fact that Molotov stated that was the reason does not mean he was truthful. The Soviet leaders were inherent liars. [94]

Standley did not, of course, know Maisky's opinion was that the official version was not truthful and it was his failure to obtain the Second Front that was the real reason.

Gromyko was appointed ambassador to the USA. He was a man who would unquestionably follow orders and his lack of experience and flamboyancy and an almost martial loyalty was what Stalin and Molotov desired. However, both the USA and Britain realised that the dimly competent and taciturn economist was generally seen as a deliberate

---

[92] Watson Derek Molotov p.205
[93] FRUS, 1943, vol.3, p.568
[94] Ch.5, Nos.121-125; Gromyko *Andrei: Memories* p.38

advertisement of the Soviet Government's displeasure. [95]

After Litvinov returned to the Soviet Union, he wrote a final report at the request of Molotov on 2 June 1943.[96] It was perfectly polite, unlike some of the messages that, according to what Umansky told Tanya, Litvinov's daughter, Litvinov had sent from the US to Russia, which were downright rude. Litvinov's daughter believes the contents of the report were her father's genuine opinion rather than inserted to please his masters in the Kremlin.[97]

Litvinov stated that, although Roosevelt was less friendly to the USSR than when he met him in 1933: 'Roosevelt is more friendly than any other prominent American.' I wonder whether Litvinov appreciated the respect Roosevelt had for Litvinov because when, on 5 May 1943, Roosevelt decided to write to Stalin to suggest a face-to-face meeting between the two. Roosevelt stated that Litvinov 'was one of only two persons with whom he had discussed the subject.' Roosevelt was discontented because of Stalin's reluctance to discuss post-war problems.[98] Litvinov urged the appointment of a body to liaise with the USA.

> The benefits will be that it will permit us to influence in due time the strategic plans of the USA and Great Britain, ... and it will put an end to complaints and discontent in public opinion and in the ruling circle who say we are the only country among the United Nations that evade contact with the others in pursuit of our secret aims.[99]

Litvinov's understanding of US politics is shown when he reports that Roosevelt was not at all interested in the Baltic States and Poland, although he points out that Roosevelt could not say this openly for fear of alienating those voters who emigrated from Poland and the Baltic States. This suggests that Litvinov supported the incorporation of the Baltic States in the Soviet Union. [100]

Litvinov then made sarcastic remarks about Finland's obstinate disregard for the USA's request that Finland should drop out of the war and conclude a separate agreement with the USSR. He stated that Finland had adroitly used the fact that it was the only country that had supposedly paid its First World War debts; but, in fact, Finland had no debts, although the US was still ignorant of this situation.[101] In any event, Litvinov was wrong. Finland did have modest debts which she repaid.

---

[95] Nicholas Herbert George Washington Disptaches p.237; *The New York Times 1943* p.1

[96] Perlmutter, Amos: *FDR and Stalin*, p.231

[97] Tanya

[98] Perlmutter, Amos: *FDR and Stalin*, p.243; FRUS Conferences at Cairo and Teheran, p.3

[99] Perlmutter, Amos: *FDR and Stalin*, p.245

[100] Ibid. p.243

[101] Ibid.

Litvinov then considered the US position if there should be a change of President, but also warned that, like his predecessor, Democrat President Wilson, Roosevelt may be unable to execute his policy if the Democrats do not win control of the Senate.

Litvinov stated:

> [Although] under a Roosevelt Presidency dropping out of the war is impossible, in the event of a protracted war, without apparent chances of victory, the Senate may yield to the propaganda of the isolationists and try to cause a serious crisis by refusing credits. However, a premature cessation of hostilities is possible and could occur if an isolationist or semi-isolationist was elected as President.[102]

Litvinov realised that Roosevelt's motives were

> to get as much benefit for his country from the war as possible, and he plans to secure these benefits at the expense of the British Empire. In that regard he used to rely on a contribution from us, (USSR), but since there has been no response on our part, he has considerably softened his anti-British attitude. He has supposed it would be easier to come to an agreement with us than with Great Britain over the solution of post-war problems and I am inclined to attribute his persistent suggestion for a meeting with Stalin is to procure this intended agreement.[103]

Surely Litvinov's use of the words 'persistent suggestion for a meeting', to which Stalin refused to respond, was an indirect criticism of Stalin by Litvinov and therefore was a courageous thing to do.

In his remarks on the second front, Litvinov is very critical of the USA and Britain on account of the delay in its implementation. He states: 'The reason for the delay is that the policy of both countries was based on the goal of maximum exhaustion of the Soviet Union in order to diminish its role in the solution of post-war problems.'[104] What Litvinov stated was similar to Molotov's belief. Did Litvinov believe this was the Allies' motive? I am uncertain. Being ambitious, Litvinov realised that in Moscow his performance would be judged on whether he obtained a second front and how quickly it would be implemented. However, unlike other misdeeds of officials of the British Government, such as Henderson's attitude that Germany should be given a free hand if she wanted to attack the Soviet Union and the Katyn affair, no new archival evidence since the Second World War has come to light to support Litvinov's contention that the delay in implementation was other than for strategic reasons.

---

[102] Perlmutter, Amos: *FDR and Stalin*, p.244
[103] Ibid. p.240
[104] Ibid, p.233

Litvinov further states: 'There will be no hope of a second front being opened without serious pressure from us.'[105] No doubt, if Litvinov had been able to secure an invasion of Northern France in 1943, his reputation, with Stalin, would have risen and Litvinov may well have remained as ambassador. However, it does appear the Allies had badly misled Stalin by first stating that the second front could possibly take place in 1942, when it was never feasible. Until the Battle of the Atlantic was won, so much shipping was being lost that to transport an army's supplies was a very hazardous business. Troops could only be transported on the liners *Queen Mary* and *Queen Elizabeth*, which were too fast for U-boats to sink.[106] In March 1943, 514,744 tons of shipping were sunk for the loss of only twelve U-boats; but by June 1943 the monthly loss had declined to 21,729 tons, with the loss of seventeen U-boats.[107] The Battle of the Atlantic had finally been won by the Allies.

At the Casablanca conference in January 1943, it had been decided to commence Operation Overlord in September 1943.[108] If a plan for the invasion of Western Europe at this time had been implemented, Conrad Black, in his biography of Roosevelt, expressed the opinion that the war might have been shortened by six to nine months and that the final demarcation between Russian and Allied troops would have been considerably to the East.

Although the German army strength did not significantly change between September 1943 and June 1944, the Atlantic Wall was greatly strengthened.[109] The advance of the Allies from Sicily to Rome met unexpectedly strong German opposition, particularly at Monte Cassino, which blocked the Allied advance from 28 January 1944 to 18 May 1944,[110] so there was a strong argument for bypassing Italy and invading France.

Litvinov implies that he is in favour of a meeting between Stalin and Roosevelt, although presumably he thought it would be presumptuous of him to say so because he said : 'There is no hope of opening a second front without serious pressure from us, (The USSR).' He advocated pressure in a specific form without stating the form that such pressure should take.[111] Perhaps Litvinov did have more influence than that for which he has generally been given credit, because Stalin shortly afterwards agreed to a meeting with Churchill and Roosevelt in Teheran. However, Litvinov was wrong when he stated: 'Even an Anglo-American offensive from North Africa is unlikely' as a successful invasion of Sicily was mounted on 10 July 1943.[112]

---

[105] Ibid. p. 244

[106] Black, Conrad: *Roosevelt, Champion of Freedom*, p.798

[107] U-boats: Churchill, Winston: *The Second World War*, vol.5, 'Closing the Ring', p.10

[108] Casablanca Conference: Churchill, Winston: *The Second World War*, vol.4, 'Hinge of Fate', pp.604 to 662

[109] Black, Conrad: *Roosevelt, Champion of Freedom*, p.799

[110] Churchill, Winston: *The Second World War*, vol.5, 'Closing the Ring', pp.428 and 530

[111] Perlmutter, Amos: *FDR and Stalin*, p.244

[112] Sicily: Churchill, Winston: *The Second World War*, vol.5, 'Closing the Ring', p.31; and Perlmutter, Amos: *FDR and Stalin*, p.244

Litvinov's report futher stated:

> We must place our ambassador in a position where he can speak in front of the US public explaining our policy or various aspects of our policy present and in the future and to strengthen the information department at the embassy with a number of people who can speak English fluently. It is necessary to permit the embassy to admit some reliable Americans to work as translators and editors.[113]

After Maxim returned to the Soviet Union without Ivy, she described her time as happy. She started to write, spending much time in the New York Public Library. She brought her typewriter, which with her books she was allowed to leave at the library. Her decision to return was taken without enthusiasm.

Ivy's choice was partly to protect her family from any retaliation if she had defected, because she stated that she hated the idea of harming her family; but Ivy also affirmed that she did not like the idea of going round cap in hand in the USA. However, given her spirit of enterprise, it would have been extremely unlikely she would not have prospered, as many millions of US immigrants have prospered before and since. In November 1943 she set off to return to the Soviet Union via San Francisco. In a letter she wrote to a friend Bertha dated 18 November 1943 from San Francisco, a copy of which is with her papers, Ivy said:

> It seems incredible that I should have to give up my New York life prematurely with all that it meant, but on the other hand, once you are going, you feel you have got to go. In San Francisco I feel at least I am already half way there, with the uprooting already done.[114]

She had intended to go back to England where she had hoped to see her mother, who was still alive. Instead she flew across the North Pole to the Soviet Union.

Back in the Soviet Union, during that summer, Litvinov from time to time appeared at public gatherings such as when the US Government presented various decorations to certain personnel of the Red Army. However, as those to be decorated were on active service, Molotov accepted the medals for transmission to those receiving them.[115]

It was confirmed that Litvinov was appointed a vice commissar [116]although his seat on the Central Committee was not restored [117]

---

[113] Perlmutter, Amos: *FDR and Stalin*, p.246
[114] Archivs Boxes 1 & 3; *Carswell John: the Exile* p.157
[115] FRUS, 1943, vol.3, p.546
[116] The New York Times 23 August 1943 p.3
[117] Carswell, John: *The Exile*, p.157

It had been agreed that a conference of Foreign Ministers would take place after much argument about the venue.[118] The British delegation, headed by the Foreign Secretary, Anthony Eden, landed at Moscow airport on the morning of 18 October 1943. Litvinov was at the airport to meet the distinguished visitors and subsequently attended the luncheon.[119] The US delegation was lead by the Secretary of State, Cordell Hull.

The meetings of the Foreign Ministers took place every day and covered an immense amount of ground. The initial meeting took place on 19 October, and the Soviet Union immediately put forward the proposal that Britain and the USA take further measures to ensure the invasion of Northern France took place in the spring of 1944. In spite of Churchill writing to Eden expressing grave doubts as to the wisdom of the venture, it would have had a disastrous effect on the relationship of the USA and Britain with the USSR if the USA and Britain had gone back on their pledge. Eden believed that Lord Ismay had convinced the Russians that operation Overlord, the invasion of Northern France by Britain, the USA and their Allies would indeed be launched as soon as the USA and Britain could manage it in 1944.[120] Another matter successfully disposed of at the conference was that there would be one document governing the ultimate ceasefire.[121]

Litvinov was an official member of the Soviet delegation.[122] He attended the first meeting on 19 October,[123] but said little and attended very few meetings thereafter. His recorded remarks seem to have been concerning minor matters such as on 22 October, when the British representative Eden proposed a commission. Litvinov asked Cordell Hull, the US Secretary of State, whether he had in mind a special commission. Cordell Hull stated that he did not.[124] On 30 October Eden wanted it stated in the final conference declaration the right of peoples to choose their own governments and the repudiation by the great powers of any claim for areas of responsibility. Litvinov stated that he did not think the various declarations that Eden desired were necessary as they were contained in the Atlantic Charter. It seems that, as far as the Soviet Union was concerned, Litvinov's attendance was stage managed, so he made the occasional remark to show Britain and the USA he was not a deaf -mute.[125]

As always between the Soviet Union and her Allies, the most difficult problem to solve was Poland. Although Eden urged the Soviet Union to open up discussions with the Polish

---

[118] Foreign Ministers' Conference 1943: Eden, Anthony: *Memoirs*, vol.2, 'The Reckoning', p.405
[119] FRUS, 1943, vol.1, p.568
[120] Eden, Anthony: *Memoirs*, vol.2, 'The Reckoning', p.411
[121] Kettenacher, Lothar: 'The Anglo-Soviet Alliance and the Problem of Germany 1941-1945', in *Journal of Contemporary History*, July 1982, p.452
[122] FRUS, 1943, vol.1, p.560
[123] Ibid. p.577
[124] Ibid. p.608
[125] Ibid. p.680

Government in Exile in London, Hull failed to support him. Litvinov showed his extreme hostility to the Poles.[126]

The Foreign Ministers' Agreement was recorded in a secret protocol on 3 November 1943. It was agreed to form an advisory committee in London to begin work on the problems that would arise on the continent when Hitler's regime neared collapse. It was this body which achieved agreement on establishing zones.

Another committee in which the Soviet Union participated would consider the situation when the German army in Italy was defeated or overrun. The USA was anxious for a four-power declaration to include China, pledging themselves to a united conduct of the war. This was achieved on 30 October. Finally, a protocol agreeing on joint action between the Soviet Union and Great Britain was signed on 2 November 1943.[127]

Those who attended the conference sensed a far more friendly attitude than had existed before. For example, at a banquet for Eden and Harriman, Stalin proposed a toast to the US forces. General Deane responded by drinking to the day when advanced detachments of Soviet and US troops would meet in Berlin. Stalin paid him the high honour of walking around the table to General Deane's seat to click his glass and drink the toast to him personally.[128]

On 11 November 1943, presumably under orders, Litvinov called a meeting, attended by a number of ambassadors and chargés d'affaires, where he gave an unofficial summary of decisions made by the conference.

Litvinov dealt with three controversial matters:

First, in order to shorten the war, it was desired to try to persuade various neutral countries to enter the war. Anthony Eden had previously discussed with the Turkish Foreign Minister in Cairo the possibility of Turkey entering the war.

Litvinov then referred to Poland. He stated that Molotov had reaffirmed the desire of the Soviet Government to see an independent Poland established but, to his regret, he saw little possibility of securing a friendly relationship with the Polish Government in London.

Litvinov then concluded by saying that, despite press reports, no frontiers had been discussed, but on his own initiative he asserted that the Soviet frontiers were inviolable and would be defended by the Red Army.

---

[126] Harriman, Averell: *Special Envoy to Churchill and Stalin*, p.242
[127] Churchill, Winston: *The Second World War*, vol.5 '*Closing the Ring*', p.265
[128] FRUS, 1943, vol.1, p.690

Afterwards, Litvinov requested Clark-Kerr and Harriman, the British and US ambassadors to the Soviet Union, to stay behind and asked for their opinion on the talks. Clark-Kerr said he had grave doubts about the wisdom of being so specific about Turkey, as it would be all over Europe in no time; to which Litvinov replied: 'It would be a good thing if it was known.' Litvinov presumably thought the publicity might encourage Turkey to join the war. Harriman was displeased with Litvinov's remarks concerning the territorial claims, but thought it was unwise to embark on any discussion on this point. However, Harriman informed President Roosevelt that the reaction of the few United Nations to whom Harriman spoke was that it was well received as a friendly gesture to emphasise United Nations solidarity.[129]

During 1944 Litvinov sat as Chairman of the Special Commission on the Post-War Order, the other members being Maisky and Gromyko. There were three reports. The first was dated 15 November 1944 and looked at the prospect of Soviet-British co-operation. The second report on the Soviet relationship with the USA was dated 10 January 1945; and the final report, dated 11 January 1945, considered the questions of blocs and spheres of influence.[130] Although Pechatnov comments that this interesting episode escaped the attention of Phillips and Sheinis,[131] Phillips comments that the Commissions were a powerless sinecure.[132] Pechatnov agrees that it gave Litvinov little power. Also, Pechatnov comments that the idea of the commission and the involvement of Litvinov, Maisky and Gromyko was designed for Molotov to use the brains and experience of Litvinov and his colleagues without giving them real power.[133] Although Pechatnov feels this was extraordinary, normally a foreign minister in conjunction with the Prime Minister will use his subordinates' brains to feed information and advice while retaining real power. Nevertheless, Maisky claims that 'Litvinov played a part in the anti-Hitler coalition on Germany and other questions,'[134]so perhaps his influence was greater than has been assumed. However, Litvinov complained that nobody was listening to him.[135] At least we know Molotov did read Litvinov's report, because he wrote comments on it.[136] Litvinov was active with recommendations.

Litvinov, in his first report on relations with Britain, stated that it was very much in the interests of both Britain and the Soviet Union to prevent further German aggression. He saw Britain together with the Soviet Union as the only great continental powers in Europe following the defeat of Germany and the weakening of France and Italy. 'The very gravity of this question should strongly push Britain to reach an agreement with us [the USSR]

---

[129] FRUS, 1943, vol.1, p.700 to p.702

[130] Pechatnov, Vladimir: *The Big Three After the End of the Second World War*, p.10

[131] Pechatnov, Vladimir: *The Big Three After the End of the Second World War*, p.10

[132] Phillips, Hugh: *Between the Revolution and the West*, p.171

[133] Pechatnov, Vladimir: *The Big Three After the End of the Second World War,* p.10

[134] Maisky, Ivan: *Journey into the Past*, p. 271

[135] Sulzberger, Cyrus: *A Long Row of Candles*, p.248

[136] Pechatnov, Vladimir: *The Big Three After the End of the Second World War*, pp.11 and 12

which would be on a basis of an amicable separation of security spheres in Europe according to the principle of geographic proximity.'[137]

As for the second report concerning the USA, in the short term Lend-Lease, which the Soviet Union had no prospect of repaying, 'might become an irritant', although Litvinov warned that the USA might attempt to use Lend-Lease 'for extracting economic and political compensation unacceptable to us [the USSR].' Litvinov's report on US-Soviet relations concludes that 'there are no deep reasons for serious and long-term conflicts between the USA and USSR (with the possible exception of China). It is difficult to outline some concrete basis for co-operation apart from mutual interest in the preservation of world peace.'[138] However, in the longer term, mutual interests may be created 'by the USA's search for new markets coupled with the enormous reconstruction needs of the USSR. Further, there might be a basis of co-operation by supporting any anti-colonial aspirations of the USA.'[139]

In connection with the third report on the questions of blocs and spheres of influence, Litvinov was very ambitious regarding Soviet aspirations. He stated that their maximum spheres of security should include Finland, Sweden, Poland, Hungary, Czechoslovakia, and Turkey. Other countries in the Balkans except Greece, which, together with all the countries of Western Europe, should be in Britain's sphere of influence. Norway, Denmark, Germany, Austria and Italy should be in a neutral zone. Litvinov later amended his proposal to include Norway in the Soviet sphere of influence, while Sweden was placed within Britain's sphere of influence, although it was further away from Britain than Norway. Litvinov stated that Britain and the Soviet Union had a mutual interest in obtaining from the USA 'a fair settlement of Lend-Lease' and in the longer term 'opposing US expansion in the Far East.'[140]

Even more ambitious in Litvinov's final report was his recommendation that a trusteeship over Palestine would be desirable but hardly feasible. He sought to secure a foothold in the Middle East by gaining a trusteeship of Palestine. [141]

However, it is clear that Litvinov's conception of the spheres of influence was very different from that of Stalin and Molotov. Litvinov's conception was that this would prohibit any of the three victorious powers from entering into close relationships with a country in another sphere of influence against the will of that country or set up military bases in that country.[142] On the other hand, Litvinov appears to have envisaged that

---

[137] Pechatnov, Vladimir: *The Big Three After the End of the Second World War*, p.12
[138] Ibid. p.11
[139] Ibid.
[140] Ibid.
[141] Ibid. p.20
[142] Ibid. p.14

countries in the Soviet sphere of influence would be independently run on the model of post-war Finland. Litvinov further stated that there was likely to be a demand by Britain for guarantees regarding the nature of government and independence of countries. He did not suggest such behaviour should be resisted. However, Molotov angrily crossed out the suggestion.[143]

I think Litvinov underestimated the special relationship between Britain and the USA, although Stalin's confrontational attitude after the end of the Second World War did much to cement the US-British relationship. In spite of Litvinov's vast experience, I do not believe that we can maintain that Litvinov's report was superior to that of his colleagues. On the contrary, Maisky alone astutely foresaw that the greatest danger to the Soviet Union 'was a Chinese-US alliance. US technology plus Chinese human numbers spearheaded against the USSR.'[144] This was what in fact happened in the 1970s. Litvinov, Maisky and Gromyko made the mistake of disregarding the indigenous conditions and interests in those countries which were to become subject to Soviet power, like Lenin, who wrongly believed that the Polish workers would support the Red Army.[145] Nationalism would prove to be more powerful than Communist doctrine. The underlying assumption as to a docile and welcoming Europe can only be described as a combination of great power chauvinism and ideological romanticism which anticipated that liberated Europe would be far more hospitable to Soviet power than it actually was. The Soviets underestimated the traditional hatred on the part of the Polish people for the Soviet Union and misjudged other countries like Hungary, which just wanted to rule themselves.

Stalin was faced with three alternatives after the Second World War. Clearly, it was he and nobody else who would determine which of the alternatives would be pursued.[146]

First, with the prestige of the Soviet Union so high, Stalin could have pursued an insurrectionist policy by encouraging 'the communist parties in Western Europe and Asia to seize power', as in Czechoslovakia in 1948, by helping them where possible with the Red Army. There was some sentiment supporting that policy and some discussion as to its feasibility. This is not surprising. No prominent figure in the leadership advocated it, nor did Maisky, Gromyko or, of course, Litvinov support it. Holloway says that to have done so would have run the risk of creating a war with the West. In the key states of Italy and France, the Communists had their best opportunity to win a democratic election, but in spite of massive support failed to do so, but only after the USA had orchestrated a massive and subtle propaganda campaign in the West. Among various methods pursued was the fact that people of Italian descent in the USA were encouraged to write to their relatives in

---

[143] Ibid.
[144] Ibid. p.6
[145] See Ch.3, No.71
[146] Holloway, David: *Stalin and the Bomb*, p.176

Italy warning them of the dangers if the Communists were democratically elected.[147] In 1944 Litvinov no doubt was speaking the truth when he confirmed to an American diplomat: 'We do not want revolutions in the West, but if they happen we must approve.'[148] It is my belief that Stalin was in agreement with Litvinov on this.

The second alternative, which was the one Litvinov favoured as well as Maisky and Gromyko, was co-operation with the West. Initially, this seems to have been the course favoured by Stalin, such as when he agreed that the headquarters of the UN would be established in New York.[149]

The third option was for Stalin to pursue the policy which he deemed the best for the Soviet Union, and would keep him in power; and my view is that Stalin changed his mind in favour of the third course. The principal reason appears to be that the USA would not agree that the states occupied by the Red Army could not be democratic, partly because it would be detrimental to Roosevelt's electoral success, with so many immigrants from these countries among the US electorate. I consider Stalin genuinely believed that if he gave the USA and Britain a free hand in the areas which the victorious powers had agreed should be assigned to Britain and the USA, then Stalin should be given a similar free hand in Eastern Europe. Stalin had some grounds for believing this. Roosevelt, initially, had allowed Nazi Germany to take over ninety per cent of Europe, without taking any action; except financial assistance, to the allies of the US to fight the war.

At the beginning of July 1944 Litvinov drew the attention of Maxwell Hamilton, a counsellor at the USA Embassy, to an article which was about to be printed in a Leningrad literary magazine, *Zvesda*. Shortly afterwards, it was duly published in that magazine. Harriman, the American ambassador, believed it had been written or inspired by Litvinov and gives his ideas of the post-war order. The most significant aspect of the article is that it considered that any security organisation must be dominated by the big powers which proved in the present war to have real military power. They would normally supply the forces and decision-making must be unanimous. Thus, his opinion would appear to be in line with Molotov and Stalin. The role of small powers in such organisations would be limited to having bases on their territory and giving right of passage to troops, no doubt recollecting the difficulty of defending Czechoslovakia; although Litvinov accepted that at some point participation of their armed forces might be required. Also, he foresaw that small powers might be required to participate in economic sanctions.[150] Four weeks later Litvinov admitted he was the author of the above article.[151] On 22 August Litvinov told

---

[147] BBC programme: 'Cold War'
[148] FRUS, 1944, vol.3, p.1148 @ p. 1149
[149] Gromyko, Andrei : *Memoirs*, p.53
[150] FRUS, 1944, vol.1, p.694
[151] Mastny, Vojtech: *Russia's Road to the Cold War*, p.219

the Norwegian minister Andvord that he wished the views expressed in *Zvesda* were the the views of the Soviet Government.

In the 1946 interview with Hottelet, he spoke similarly, saying: 'If there is to be co-operation, it must be between the great powers. Obviously, Haiti or Denmark could not threaten world peace.' States showing fascist tendencies, and I am sure that Litvinov would include Spain in this category, should be excluded. However he accepted in due course enemies presumably would participate, providing they did not themselves have fascist tendencies.[152]

Notwithstanding the antagonism between Litvinov and Molotov, Litvinov was one of Molotov's guests at a small luncheon given by Molotov for the British ambassador. Harriman wrote: 'It was the most informal, natural and good humoured meeting with Soviet officials that I have attended.'[153] Litvinov was also present when Molotov gave a dinner on the visit to Moscow of General De Gaulle.[154]

Ivy however, was adopting by now a more cautious stance because, when the British Embassy in Moscow offered to send books, she begged that no books be sent nor people come to see her. 'It was better for both of us.'[155]

On 6 October 1944 Litvinov gave an extensive interview to the reporter Snow, who said: 'Many people think Maisky and you are being wasted, and that, as the two men in Russia who know most about USA and Britain, why are you not playing a more important role?' Litvinov said: 'We are on the shelf. This commissariat is run by three people: Molotov, Dekanozov and Vyshinsky.'[156]

Nevertheless, Litvinov was selected as a member of the delegation to agree armistice terms with Finland. This delegation travelled to Moscow on 7 September 1944. Litvinov's friend, Alexandra Kollontai, the ambassador to Sweden, worked with the Swedish Government to encourage Finland to end the war, for which aim she worked so tirelessly that she was even nominated for the Nobel Peace Prize.[157] The entire delegation was introduced to Harriman and Clark-Kerr (the American and British ambassadors). Neither Sheinis nor Phillips mentions this conference. The *Soviet War Weekly News* on 28 September 1944 carried a report which included a picture of the delegation that, between 14 September and 19 September 1944, was involved in negotiations. Agreement was reached between representatives of Great Britain, who on the one hand acted for the united nations (all

---

[152] Mastny, Vojtech: *Russia's Road to the Cold War*, p.220; *Washington Post*, 21 January 1952, p.4
[153] FRUS, 1944, vol.1V, p.828
[154] De Gaulle, Charles: *War Memoirs: Salvation*, p.66
[155] Lockhart, Robert: *Diaries*, 25 August 1944, p.349
[156] Snow, Edgar: *Journey to the Beginning*, p.314
[157] Clements, Barbara: *Bolshevik Feminist Life of Alexandra Kollontai*, pp.268 and 269

those countries actively fighting Nazi Germany) and the Finnish Government on the other hand. Great Britain was represented on the delegation by its ambassador, Sir Archibald Clark-Kerr, and Molotov led the Russian element of the delegation. He was accompanied by other high ranking Russian politicians such as Zhdanov and Dekanozov, as well as Litvinov. An armistice was achieved.[158]

Finland was cleverer than the other states in Eastern Europe such as Czechoslovakia, which failed to retain its freedom. It is rather ironical that, of all the states occupied by the USSR as a result of the Red Army advance, Finland, which was the only democracy to be an ally of Hitler's Germany, and had not only invaded the Soviet Union to recover territory lost in the Winter War, but had also occupied Soviet territory, received the best treatment. Finland agreed not only to imprison certain of their leaders who had agreed to participate in Operation Barbarossa, but also to pay reparations. Although Churchill condemned appeasement from weakness, Finland used it to good effect.

It seems unlikely that Molotov was enthusiastic about Litvinov's participation, so it would appear the decision was that of Stalin. Was the reason for Litvinov's participation because Stalin wanted as far as possible to prevent too much criticism from the USA at this stage of the war? He may have been concerned about the American public, whom Litvinov had described in his final report during his ambassadorship as being pro-Finnish.

However, Litvinov was still in sufficient favour to be a guest at one of the entertainments for Churchill when he visited Moscow in 1944. Litvinov was reported as asking General Deane whether Harriman had a fortune of $100 million. Deane confessed he did not know, to which Litvinov replied : 'How can a man with $100 million look so sad?'[159] This was an odd comment for one believing in communism to make.

Hindus, a US journalist, attended the 1944 celebration of the 27th anniversary of the Revolution, at which both Litvinov and Molotov were present. The invited guests, including Molotov, celebrated gaily and bibulously. It had just been decided that the Soviet foreign ministry should have a uniform.

> In his smart-looking uniform Molotov was unsmiling, but looking very pleased. He carried himself with a buoyant stateliness, whereas Litvinov seemed more embarrassed than pleased in his new uniform.

Sulzberger described Litvinov as looking less like a general than anybody I have ever seen. His grey uniform was rumpled and un-pressed, with food stains on the lapels.[160]

---

[158] FRUS, 1944, vol.3, p.618; *Soviet War Weekly News*, 28 September 1944, p.2
[159] Harriman, Averell: *Special Envoy to Churchill and Stalin*, p.362
[160] Sulzberger, Cyrus Leo: *A Long Row of Candles: Memoirs and Diaries 1933-1954*, pp.248 and 254; Hindus, Maurice: *Crisis in the Kremlin*, p.47

President Roosevelt's death on 12 April 1945 was met with genuine grief in the USSR. A memorial ceremony was held in the embassy on 15 April, attended by Molotov, as well as the other assistant commissars except Litvinov, who was ill. There is no reason to believe the illness was not genuine.

Pope claims in a letter to *The New York Times* that Stalin wanted to send Litvinov to the San Francisco conference, but Truman desired the foreign minister Molotov and evidently was pleased after the death of Roosevelt that Stalin decided to send his Foreign Minister in memory of President Roosevelt. However, there is no archival evidence to support Pope's assertion; nor do the surrounding circumstances suggest that, at that stage, Stalin ever envisaged sending Litvinov to San Francisco as alleged.[161]

Litvinov duly attended the Yalta conference involving Stalin, Roosevelt and Churchill. Lord Moran, Churchill's personal physician, stated that the Churchill delegation was met by Molotov, Litvinov, Vyshinsky and Pavlov.[162]

On 5 April 1945 Sulzberger had a long talk with Litvinov, who told Sulzberger: 'He [Litvinov] was working solely on post-war problems, with the exception of reparation. Also, nobody listens to him or pays any attention to him. He seemed utterly convinced that things were developing badly between the Allies and the USSR with negative implications for the world security organisation policy.' Litvinov was pessimistic about East-West relations. He stated: 'First the Allies make the mistake and rub us up the wrong way. Then the Russians make the mistake and rub the Allies the wrong way.'[163]

Sulzberger saw Litvinov at the May Day parade in Red Square. It was a glorious occasion. The Battle of Berlin had been won. When Litvinov appeared, he bowed to numerous acquaintances and then descended to the Square below. When Sulzberger asked Litvinov why he did not come up to the grandstand, he said he would prefer to be with the people. His pale and ugly face looked thoughtful and sad and expressed none of the exuberance of a magnificent triumph. He never once looked up at Stalin and his lieutenants standing atop Lenin's tomb. Litvinov just stared at the long rows of cannon and marching troops.[164]

---

[161] Harriman, Averell: *Special Envoy to Churchill and Stalin*, p.442; *The New York Times,* 6 January 1952, Part 4 p.8

[162] Moran, Lord: *Winston Churchill, Struggle for Survival*, p.218

[163] Sulzberger, Cyrus Leo: *A Long Row of Candles: Memoirs and Diaries 1933-1954*, p.248

[164] Ibid. p.254

18: RETIREMENT AT LAST

In the immediate period after the end of the war, Russian and US troops were fraternising in Berlin,[1] while in the Soviet Union the USA was so popular that on Moscow's VE Day a huge crowd assembled outside the American Embassy. When the US diplomats emerged, the Soviet people, to show their appreciation, carried the diplomats head high. However, this was not what Stalin wanted. If the Soviet Union had no enemies, there would be no need for repression. People would start asking questions. They would want to know whether the purges were justified and whether it was right to liquidate so many of the prominent Bolsheviks. However, the popularity of the USA was to be short lived, particularly among the intellectuals. Harriman spoke to Soviet intellectuals and writers, who asked him: 'Why the USA had to be so aggressive?' With much merit, they commented that, whereas the USA complained about Soviet behaviour in the independent states in the Balkans, she made no complaint about the previous fascist regimes.[2] This indicates how much the prestige of the USA had declined.

In the 1944 interview with Snow, Litvinov gave his views on the post-war order. When Snow asked Litvinov: 'Whether he saw the possibility of a united Germany after the Second World', Litvinov said: 'Why are you so interested in a united Germany?' Snow believed Litvinov's view on Germany was the same as most Soviet citizens, who favoured its division as the only guarantee of peace. According to Litvinov (the Allies) will not be able to agree 'on how to re-educate the Germans and how to make them harmless and peaceful people, so the alternative is the break up Germany into small states.' Litvinov had formerly 'hoped that the wartime Anglo-Soviet alliance could be transformed into an all-European defence pact. That hope was fading fast.'[3]

Litvinov stated: 'He had no faith in France [which] under De Gaulle was making a show of getting rid of the Fascist collaborators, but the worst are left untouched. The old crowd will survive and with them the corruption, intrigue and compromise.'[4] He was also highly critical that Franco had been allowed to stay in power.[5] Litvinov also fully discussed Poland with Snow,[6] and was highly critical of Britain:

---

[1] Sulzberger, Cyril: *A Long Row of Candles*, p.254
[2] FRUS, 1945, vol.5, p.921
[3] Snow Edgar *Journey to the Beginning* p.315
[4] Ibid. p.313
[5] Ibid. p.313
[6] Ibid. p.314; Ch.17, No.67, where Poland is fully discussed, in particular in relation to Katyn

She has never been willing to see a strong power on the continent and the idea of collaborating with a strong power for peace is too alien to her thinking. She is at work in France Italy and the Lowlands (Belgium and Holland) to undermine our alliance, presumably that already between the USA, Britain and the Soviet Union,.[7]

However, Litvinov agreed with Snow that the Soviet Union was acting in a similar way to Britain in undermining the alliance. Litvinov told Snow:

If each of us had made our purposes clear, the limits of their needs to each other, good diplomacy might have been able to avoid the conflict. Now it is too late. Suspicions are too rife.[8]

He also shared the view of mainstream Soviet politicians that the Soviet war-time allies 'have not given up the hope of destroying us [the Soviet Union] by force';[9] but I do not believe he was right. There was tremendous sympathy among the populations of Britain and the USA for the Soviet Union on account of the huge loss of life it had suffered in achieving victory over Germany, which Stalin did everything possible to squander by being unco-operative in small matters as well as large, such as creating difficulties when British and US servicemen wanted to marry Soviet women.

In June 1945 Snow returned to Moscow. Litvinov said:

Why did the USA wait until now to begin opposing us in the Balkans and Eastern Europe? You should have done it three years ago. Now it is too late. Your complaints only arouse suspicion here.[10]

However, in view of the critical remarks about Britain that Litvinov made to Snow in 1944, this remark is somewhat surprising.

In August 1945, after two atomic bombs were dropped by the USA on Japan, she surrendered. Litvinov told Snow his views on the atomic bomb. He was confident that if the Soviet Union and other powers had the bomb, 'nobody can use it' – another correct prediction by Litvinov – and then he said: 'It will be like poison gas and germ warfare.'[11]

When Litvinov met Harriman at the theatre in November 1945, Litvinov soon found another opportunity to convey his informed opinion about East-West relations who said he

---

[7] Snow, Edgar: *Journey to the Beginning*, p.315
[8] Ibid.
[9] Ibid. p.317
[10] Ibid. p.357
[11] Ibid. p.317

was disturbed by the international situation. He complained that neither side knew how to behave to each other and that this was why the London Conference broke down. Harriman wanted to know what the USA could do to 'satisfy Soviet opinion.' Litvinov said 'Nothing', which was really inconsistent in view of his previous criticism that neither the USA nor the USSR knew how to behave. I am sure Harriman would have been interested to know the answer. Litvinov then said: 'I believe I know what should be done, but I am powerless.' When Harriman told Litvinov 'he was extremely pessimistic.' Litvinov replied: 'Yes';[12] but it seems this was because Litvinov believed that negotiations between the Western powers and the Soviet Union had permanently broken down. However, when Harriman told Litvinov that the Foreign Ministers were going to meet in Moscow, Litvinov was 'almost jubilant.'[13]

In 1946 Litvinov was a successful candidate to the Supreme Soviet in the first post- war election in the town of Kondopog Karelia, rather than for the more prestigious constituency of Leningrad, which Litvinov had previously represented.

Litvinov's election biography, presumably published with official approval, contained many warm words:

> The enemies of the Soviet Union, enemies of peace and progress, have from time to time been exposed to the devastating power of Litvinov's logic, his sarcasm and wit. Comrade Litvinov is an outstanding personality and an old Bolshevik. He enjoys prestige all over the world and is working fruitfully to strengthen friendly relations with other countries and enhance the influence of the Soviet Union on post-war arrangements.

These were not the words that one would expect to hear in relation to someone in disgrace in a totalitarian state.

According to Sheinis, Litvinov did not go to Kondopog to meet his electorate on account of ill health, although there is no other evidence of his ill health at that time. Instead, Litvinov sent a message to his electorate which was published in a local newspaper. He thanked the populace for their trust in him and referred to the immense post-war task facing the country. Litvinov ended by promising

> to devote the rest of my life, as before, to the interests of our country and to carry out conscientiously to the full extent of my powers and skill all the work the Party and Government may entrust me.[14]

---

[12] FRUS, 1945 (Theatre), vol.5, p.921
[13] FRUS, 1945, vol.5, p.922
[14] Sheinis, Zinovy: *Maxim Litvinov*, p.342

On 23 May Litvinov told Smith, 'Before the end of the war and directly afterwards he had hoped for real co-operation, but wrong decisions had been chosen. I now feel that the best that can be hoped for is prolonged armed truce.'[15]

It was on a hot day in June 1946 that the *Washington Post* journalist Hottelet had an amazing interview with Litvinov. Hottelet had tried several Russians with whom he had previously had contact, but just received the brush off. It was suggested to Hottelet that he try Litvinov. Hottelet telephoned Litvinov's office and spoke to a female secretary who said she would consult the Deputy Foreign Secretary. She returned the call the next day to say it was in order. Hottelet still expected the interview not to take place, even when he set out to see Litvinov; but he was not to be disappointed.[16]

During the interview Litvinov indicated that the outlook was bad:

> There once seemed the chance that the two worlds would be allowed to exist side by side, but that is no longer the case and there has been a return in the Soviet Union of the outmoded concept of security in terms of territory. The more you have got, the safer you are.

He believed, 'The root cause is the ideological conception prevailing here that conflict between communist and capitalist worlds is inevitable.'[17] Litvinov said: 'He had some ideas', presumably to reduce the chasm between the Soviet Union and her former allies, but 'I will not give them unless the Kremlin calls; and they certainly will not call on me.' Hottelet reminded Litvinov that 'he had been on the shelf once before and was he sure that would not happen again?' But Litvinov replied, 'No, I am positive' and said, 'I am just an observer.'[18]

Hottelet asked himself not unnaturally why Litvinov risked his life and came to the conclusion it was a move against the Soviet machine's design to dominate the globe. Was it the case that the Soviet Union was seeking to rule the world? We do not know whether, at the time of the Hottelet interview, Litvinov knew of his pending dismissal. Hottelet believed Litvinov knew of his dismissal at that time and the reason why he gave the interview was because he believed he was not likely ever again to have a long conversation with a Westerner and was determined to be heard. Was it not motivated by the fear that the Soviet Union would be ignored? The sort of treatment she has received over Iraq. Was not Stalin's real fear internal rebellion caused by too many Soviet citizens having contact with the West and Stalin's need of enemies?

---

[15] Smith, FRUS, 1946, vol.6, p.763
[16] *Washington Post*, 21 January 1952, pp.1 and 4
[17] *Washington Post*, 21 January 1952, pp.1 and 4
[18] Ibid.

It is disappointing that Sheinis fails to mention this interview. It is assumed he knew of it, but he may have omitted it because it did not fit Sheinis's picture of Litvinov as a loyal Leninist.

After the interview, which lasted an hour, Hottelet, 'half expected to be arrested on the street.' Hottelet said: 'To have the story was uncomfortable enough: writing was out of the question. The censors would have killed it.'[19] Presumably, a journalist in a less honourable age could have taken the story out of the Soviet Union and then published it if he had not wanted to return, although his newspaper might have been banned from the Soviet Union. Next day Hottelet visited the American Embassy in Moscow and saw John Davies, the First Secretary, who agreed that the material was too risky to be published, but it was rushed to the Secretary of State.[20]

On 24 August 1946 the retirement of Maxim Litvinov was announced. *The New York Times* reported that Litvinov's removal was regarded as a symbol of Soviet intention 'to slam the Iron Curtain down thoroughly' and 'had a depressing effect on US officials who hope to achieve such an understanding some day.'[21] It coincided with the Soviet decision to reduce the USA's presence in the Soviet Union because of the Soviet Union's insistence that the naval attachés in Archangel and Vladivostok be removed. The personal high regard for Litvinov in the United States was shown by the remarks in a leading article in *The New York Times*: 'We could do with a little of the Litvinov spirit in Paris.'[22] This was a reference to the current Foreign Ministers' Conference then proceeding in Paris.

When Mastny asked Ivy about this interview in 1976, she denied that the Hottelet interview ever took place,[23] no doubt concerned about the fate of her children and grandchildren; but further evidence it did take place is revealed in a letter in the US archives which stated: 'The extent of the interview to a new arrived correspondent is simply amazing to us.'[24]

Hottelet prides himself on the fact that the contents of the interview were kept secret by himself, the State Office and people in whom Hottelet confided. It appears, however, that the conversation was bugged. Molotov refers to a bugged conversation with an American journalist in 1944, but probably Molotov had the date wrong.[25]

---

[19] Ibid. 23 January 1952, p.13
[20] Ibid.
[21] *The New York Times,* 25 August 1946, p.5
[22] *The New York Times,* 25 August 1946, Part 4, p.8
[23] Mastny, Vojtech: 'Reconsideration: The Cassandra in the Foreign Commissariat', *Foreign Affairs*, 1976, p.366
[24] FRUS, 1946, vol.VI, p.763
[25] Chuev, Felix: *Molotov Remembers*, p.68

About seven days later, Litvinov attended a session of the Supreme Soviet of the Russian Republic. When Litvinov came to the hall, he took no notice of the bustle but ambled down the rose-coloured carpets to his desk in the second row (middle), just in front of the speaker's chair. Litvinov carried a newspaper which he unfolded as he sat. For the rest of the evening, Hottelet never Litvinov lift his eyes from the newspaper, even when several times he prudently raised his hand to vote with the other deputies.

Whether Hottelet is right to regard this as a silent demonstration of dissent is debateable, although in favour of Hottelet's argument is the fact that *Pravda* and *Izvestiya* each consisted of only four pages and it would be difficult to spend such a long time reading them. Hottelet asked for an interview again about a week later, but was told that Litvinov was on vacation.[26]

Sheinis mentions that Litvinov would be told by Dekanozov of his dismissal on his birthday, 17 July 1946.[27]

In the British National Archives there is a record of a conversation on 5 June 1946 when Litvinov told Frank Roberts, head of the Soviet section of the British Foreign Office: 'As a result of decisions taken after the Second World War, Soviet foreign policy had taken the wrong course and it would be difficult to change it now.' He clearly meant to imply that the decision had been taken against friendly co-operation with Britain and the USA. When asked, 'What was the prospect for the resumed Paris Peace Conference?' Litvinov stated: 'The best that could be hoped for was an armed truce.'[28]

However, compared with Maxim, Ivy adopted a far more cautious attitude than she had done in 1944. This was because Ivy considered their position was far from safe. When Lavina Ponsonby saw Ivy in July 1946, Ivy told Lavina: 'I was allowed to see very few English people, being told by the Foreign Office whom she could see.' Lavina asked Ivy: 'Whether it was easier now.' She said, 'Not a bit.' Ivy stated :'I longed to see British and American films.' When Lavina asked Ivy whether 'I could lend her any books,' Ivy was obviously afraid that I would not be discreet. She did, however, say: 'It would be nice to see some magazines, but would I be careful.' When Lavina also said she 'would like to see Ivy again', Ivy said: 'Would I [Lavina] know who it was if Ivy rang up and did not give her name?'[29]

It was reported that Litvinov attended the Supreme Soviet on 17 February 1947. Others who attended included Marshal Zhukov and Marshal Rokossovsky.[30]

---

[26] *Washington Post*, 25 January 1952, p.21
[27] Sheinis, Zinovy: *Maxim Litvinov*, p.343
[28] FO 371 56833 15 June 1946 p.104
[29] FO 954, p.26
[30] *The New York Times,* 22 February 1947, p.5

In the winter of 1946/1947 Ambassador Smith saw Litvinov 'trudging along a country road wearing his old grey Foreign Office overcoat'; but it is not correct, as Hottelet stated: ' He was never again with an American or Englishman and possibly not with any Western foreigner.'[31]

Litvinov attended a reception on Red Army Day in 1947. He took Werth aside and told him:

> He was extremely unhappy about the way the Cold War was getting worse and worse every day. By the end of the war, he said, the Soviet Union had the choice of two policies: one was to cash in the goodwill she had accumulated during the war in Britain and the USA.

Stalin and Molotov had unfortunately chosen the other policy.

> Not believing that goodwill would constitute a lasting basis of any kind of policy, they had decided that security was what mattered most of all and had therefore grabbed what they could while the going was good, meaning the whole of Eastern and parts of central Europe.

At this point Vyshinsky walked past and gave the Litvinovs an extremely dirty look. Werth tells us that Litvinov was never to appear at a public reception again. Werth also mentions Ivy's indiscretion without telling us what Ivy had said.[32] It is rather surprising that she would commit such an indiscretion in view of the cautious attitude she had adopted to Lockhart, some three years earlier,[33] and the more recent encounter with Lavina Ponsonby.[34]

One of the most bizarre events concerning Maxim and Ivy's lives occurred when, on 4 November 1947, it was reported that the Hollywood Writers' Motion Picture Committee, which was alleged to be 100% communist-controlled, was criticised for having paid the hotel bill for Ivy Litvinov.[35] Should the critics not be reminded of the reception given to Maxim and Ivy Litvinov by American politicians and the public celebrating the 25th anniversary of the Bolshevik Revolution in Washington and New York in November 1942?[36] What would the politicians and public then said, if someone had been criticised for paying some bill for Maxim & Ivy?

---

[31] *Washington Post* , 25 January 1952, p.21; see No 32 post
[32] Werth, Alexander: *Russia at War*, p.839; Sheinis, Zinovy: *Maxim Litvinov*, pp. 343-.344
[33] Ch.17, No.155
[34] No.29 *ante*
[35] *The New York Times,* 4 November 1947, p.31
[36] Ch.17 (War), No. 60

No politician had tried harder than Litvinov, at considerable danger to his life, to do more to prevent the Cold War.

When Khrushchev, after his fall, wrote his memoirs, he revealed a plan to kill Maxim Litvinov by an arranged motor accident. Khrushchev implies that the plot was planned on Stalin's direct orders in a similar way to how he had arranged the murder of Mikhoels, described by Khrushchev as: 'One of the greatest actors of the Yiddish theatre, a man of culture.' It was announced that Mikhoels had fallen in front of a truck and had been buried with honours. In fact, the secret archives revealed he had been pushed, no doubt at Stalin's orders.[37]

However, I doubt whether the plot to kill Litvinov was initiated by Stalin. Otherwise, like Mikhoels the prominent actor, Litvinov would have perished. A more plausible explanation is suggested by Montefiore, who indicates that, although the murder was planned by Stalin, he changed his mind.[38]

It is probable that the instigators were either Beria or Molotov. They thought, in view of the disloyalty Litvinov had shown in respect of his unauthorised interviews to foreigners in which he had supposedly slandered the Soviet State, Stalin would approve Litvinov's liquidation. However, to their surprise, Stalin did not approve their plan. Nevertheless, Litvinov's daughter Tanya still believed it had been authorised by Stalin.[39]

On 6 April 1949 Salisbury wrote to Litvinov asking him to write a little memoir of President Roosevelt on the fifth anniversary of Roosevelt's death; but Litvinov declined on the grounds of indisposition. Otherwise, he said he would be pleased to have done so,[40] but presumably felt the task was too dangerous. In 1950 neither Litvinov nor Maisky stood for re-election to the Supreme Soviet.[41]

Ehrenburg tells us Litvinov occupied a considerable part of his retirement with daily visits to the Lenin Library and wrote a dictionary of synonyms which was never published. Litvinov regularly had lunch with his former ambassador, Suritz, in the Kremlin canteen.[42] Litvinov also visited the prominent feminist and retired Soviet ambassador to Sweden, Alexandra Kollontai.[43]

---

[37] Khrushchev, Nikita: *Khrushchev Remembers*, p.262; Overy, Richard: *Hitler's Germany and Stalin's Russia*, p.569
[38] Montefiore, Simon: *Young Stalin*, p.321
[39] Tanya
[40] Salisbury, Harrison: *The End of Stalin*, p.134
[41] Ibid. p.125
[42] Ehrenburg, Ilya: *Post-War Years*, p.279
[43] Clements, Barbara Evans: *Bolshevik Feminist Kollontai*, p.270; Farnsworth, Beatrice: *Alexandra Kollontai*, p.392

Correspondence between Kollontai and Litvinov has been located. One of these letters from Kollontai appears to be a veiled criticism of Stalin because she wrote to one of her friends. She called 'on the recipient of these letters for support for the heroic struggle of the Lenin party in order to leave something for posterity. In a hundred years time people will read everything avidly and will see our difficulties and struggles in a different light.' I believe the omission of any reference to Stalin is deliberate. However, letters written to Litvinov only mentioned such trivial matters as the weather.[44] Perhaps Kollontai thought Litvinov was more vulnerable.

At the new year of 1950, Maxim, as he often did, was listening to the BBC, in spite of the jamming of the radio by the Soviet authorities. There was a discussion as to who was the greatest genius of the first half of the 20th century. Tanya relates how she said Freud, Tanya's husband said Lenin; but, as her father revered Lenin, Tanya was surprised and pleased at what her father said. Maxim did not believe that a statesman could be a genius; only artists or scientists could. This surprised Tanya, as her father was very conservative. He had hated his daughter going into art.[45]

Sheinis states that on 16 November 1950 Litvinov declined an invitation to celebrate the fiftieth anniversary of the first issue of the paper which Lenin published – *Iskra.*[46] There was speculation that Litvinov might write his memoirs. However, he told both the British historian Andrew Rothstein and his friend Alexandra Kollontai that he was not writing his memoirs. Sheinis's wife said to Litvinov that she was sure he was writing his memoirs. He replied sarcastically: 'This is not the time to be writing memoirs', no doubt referring to the current repression in the Soviet Union.[47] Meanwhie Ivy had been far from idle. Besides giving willingly Maxim a certain amount of care, she carried out translation work.[48]

During Stalin's final years, he became violently anti-Semitic, which culminated in the arrest of the Jewish doctors after Maxim's death. Ivy, both on account of her being foreign and a Jew, would have been expected to have been a target, yet she was spared. There is every reason to believe that Maxim would have shared Ivy's opinion that 'the arrest of the doctors was patently absurd to any normal and intelligent person.'[49] However, not everybody thought that way. An acquaintance of Ivy, presumably Soviet, refused to take her sick child to the doctor because, she said, 'You never know what these doctors might do to these children. These doctors give them germs.'[50]

---

[44] Sheinis, Zinovy: *Alexandra Kollontai*, pp.318-320 and 323
[45] Ibid. pp.318-320
[46] Sheinis Zinovy: *Maxim Litvinov*, p.348
[47] Ibid.
[48] Carswll, John: *The Exile*, p160
[49] Ivy's archives, Box 6;
[50] Tanya.

Litvinov's last words to his wife were, 'English woman, go home', showing his sadness at the course the Revolution had taken and indicating his fear that she would be arrested. One of his wife's first statements following his death was: 'They did not get him.'[51] It was doubtful, as Stalin's reign was entering his final period of repression, whether Maxim and Ivy were in danger in so far as they both had previously both conducted themselves in a manner which invited Stalin's wrath and they survived; but Stalin was now more paranoid than ever.[52]

Pravda of 1 January 1952 contained an announcement by the Ministry of Foreign Affairs of the death of its former commissar, Maxim Litvinov. The obituary listed his achievements. It also stated that he had received the Order of Lenin, the Order of the Red Banner and the Medal for Valiant Labour during the Second World War.[53]

The New York Times describes how:

> For a few hours Litvinov's coffin lay in the ceremonial conference room at the Foreign Ministry. The pall-bearers were led by the Vice-Minister of Foreign Affairs, Andrei Gromyko, and deputy ministers Zorin and Gusev.[54]

It was a strange society where a person such as Gromyko, who had no respect for Litvinov and in fact wanted to blacken his character,[55] and for whom Litvinov had no respect, attended; while those who respected him, such as Alexandra Kollontai and Maisky, were not present because they thought it might not be safe for them to do so. However, Ehrenburg did attend, because he described Litvinov's dead face 'as looking inscrutably calm.' Also, Suritz's daughter was there, because Ehrenburg describes how she came up to him and said, 'Papa died today.'[56] Litvinov's wife Ivy was described as 'grief stricken but composed, in her trim grey coat and grey karakul hat.'[57] At the head of the funeral procession were three Foreign Office employees carrying the scarlet pillars of the Order of Lenin, the Order of the Red Banner of Labour, and the medal for valour which had been awarded to Litvinov for service to his country during the Second World War. The acting dean of the diplomatic corps, Chataigneau, sent a wreath; and a number of missions, including Albania, Mongolia, the East German Republic and Hungary, attended.

There was no wreath from the British embassy. Neither the British nor the US ambassador attended. This would appear to have been the personal decision of the ambassadors, a strange one with regard to a man who had been a good friend to the Western democracies.

---

[51] Carswell, John: *The Exile*, p.162
[52] Ivy Litvinov: Ch.16, No.32; *Maxim Litvinov*: Nos.16-21 and 32 *ante*
[53] FO 371 100915, NS 1851/ 1
[54] *The New York Times,* 2 January 1952, p1 &.4; Salisbury, Harrison: *End of Stalin*, p.235
[55] See Ch.19, No.88
[56] *The New York Times,* 3 January 1952, p.9; Ehrenburg, Ilya: *Post-War Years*, p.280
[57] Salisbury, Harrison: E *Moscow Journal* 'The End of Stalin' p.235

Following the funeral, Maxim Litvinov was buried at the Novodevichie Cemetery beside the icy Moskva river.[58] However, the British ambassador had at least sent a letter of condolence to Ivy Litvinov via the Deputy Foreign Commissar, Andrei Gromyko. A letter was received from Mr Gromyko thanking the ambassador for the expression of sympathy, but there was no indication that he had passed the letter to Ivy Litvinov.[59]

The same evening Narkomindel officials came, but with unusual consideration, after a superficial inspection they said that, as the hour was late, they would return the next day. They suggested that, if there were any personal papers, Ivy should remove them. The search next day was far more thorough and all Maxim's papers were removed, including two personal letters to Stalin which Maxim had written before his death. The first was a request to Stalin that his wife and children would not want. However, Tanya had written a note with the letter which stated that her brother and she did not need any help, as they were now adults and working. The other listed Molotov's mistakes. Tanya thought this was a tactful move, as Litvinov knew, of course, that Molotov would only carry out Stalin's policy. The mistakes to which he referred concerned the Soviet Union dragging its feet over peace with Austria and what Litvinov considered the unnecessary rift with Yugoslavia, as well as the occupation of East Germany.[60]

Khrushchev procured the treaty with Austria[61] as well as the reconciliation with Yugoslavia, both of which Litvinov had advocated and which Molotov continued to oppose.[62] Litvinov's forecast in respect of East Germany proved to be incorrect. As he wanted Germany to be broken up into small states, it is difficult to see why he was so opposed to the Soviet occupation of East Germany, which became a compliant ally of the Soviet Union and eventually its most prosperous satellite, until the Iron Curtain collapsed in 1989.[63]

Ivy later comforted herself that Papa died at the right time, as Stalin soon engineered the Doctors' Plot. Ivy stated Maxim

> would never have had all that attention, the round-the-clock nurses, the weekly consultations by the first-class heart specialists in the country, the antibiotics, the sedatives, and at last the oxygen tent. Two of the specialists who visited him were subsequently arrested, not to mention the fact that the further arrests and sackings of the employees were a serious drain on the minor medical and technical staff of the Kremlin hospital. There would not have been enough doctors and nurses to go

---

[58] *The New York Times,* 3 January 1952, p.9
[59] FO 371 100915   NS1851/2 NS1851/3
[60] Tanya
[61] Watson, Derek: *Molotov,* p.251
[62] Chuev, Felix: *Molotov Remembers,* p.83; Watson, Derek: *Molotov,* p.251
[63] Snow, Edgar: *The Journey to the Beginning,* p.315

round. Indeed, the therapeutist who came every day to take Papa's pulse and measure his blood pressure once confided in Tanya that if her father had been an ordinary citizen he would certainly have died after the first massive coronary.[64]

This is further evidence that Litvinov was not in disgrace.

Nevertheless, even after Maxim's death, Ivy, as she related in her private papers, continued to live in fear. She relates how:

> At night nothing but a wedge of grassland divided [my] dacha from a curve in the road from the station. Sometimes at dead of night a solitary car ground to a halt precisely at the point where two shafts of pale light landed on my pillow. Perhaps the driver had only stopped to consult his road map or rub a clot of snow and grit from his windshield. Anyhow, the lights invariably swung away after a few seconds, and the monster roared by, leaving the world to darkness and me. Not this time I told myself [and I need not] feel with the toe of my slipper for the small suitcase crammed with clothing and a warm blanket, always kept ready under each bed in case they took us away.[65]

There was a divergence of opinion among British Diplomats and the Foreign Office whether Litvinov was in disgrace Further evidence that Litvinov was not in disgrace was the generally favourable biography of Litvinov occupying 92 pages compared with Chicherin's 54 pages and Molotov's 292 pages which appeared in the 1950 edition of the Soviet Diplomatic Dictionary.[66]

---

[64] Ivy's archives, Box 9
[65] Ibid.
[66] Fo/371/100915 S 1851/1,Craig, Gordon: *Diplomats*, p.375

19: CONCLUSION

Maxim Litvinov was tremendously talented and a man of great ambition and drive.

His ambition is shown by the fact that he joined the army to free himself from the restrictions placed on Jews. Subsequently, in a Tsarist prison, he learned foreign languages and became fluent in French, English and German. Almost all his undertakings as a businessman in both Russia and England proved successful.

There is little doubt that, had he lived in a capitalist country and not gone into politics, he would have prospered. Socially his confidence is indicated by the fact that, though he was initially a poor émigré in England, he was quite comfortable in the company of Foreign Office diplomats who, particularly before 1914, were in the higher echelons of British society. However, the task of a biographer is to give praise where it is due and criticism where it is deserved, and Pope and Sheinis, by regarding Litvinov as one who could do no wrong, have done nothing to assist his reputation.

Fischer was one of many to portray Litvinov in glowing terms. Fischer describes Litvinov as 'full blooded, virile and tempestuous' and confirms his love of the cinema both in the USSR and abroad.[1] When Litvinov was appointed ambassador to the United States in 1941, the former British chargé d'affaires to the Soviet Union, Hodgson, in a letter to the *Times*, was generous in his praise of Litvinov. He wrote: 'Such an appointment should not be allowed to pass without comment by his friends' and Hodgson was 'happy to count himself as one of them.' While in Moscow, Hodgson stated: 'At no time did I find him lacking in helpfulness or in readiness within the measures of possibility, not only to seek a solution to the various problems but to put it promptly in effect.'

Hodgson's high opinion of Litvinov would be shared by his wartime successor Clark-Kerr, who described Litvinov as

> one of the ablest of Soviet public servants and indeed prominent among a handful of his compatriots who possess international status. He has a deep understanding of the psychology of English-speaking people who, with his quick-witted vitality, can be counted on to hold his own in any negotiations to the point of bullying his weaker opponent.[2]

---

[1] Fischer, Louis: *Men and Politics*, pp. 125 to 126
[2] *Times* 11 November 1941 p.5; FO 371 43416

Ehrenburg described Litvinov as

> the most peaceable sort of man, a portly, good natured paterfamilias, who devoted his leisure to the most innocent of pursuits abroad. When he had a couple of hours to spare, he went to the cinema. He took pleasure in good food and it was a joy to watch him eat; with such relish did he dip spring onions into sour cream, so appetisingly did he chew. He loved to pore over a large atlas, map-travelling in distant unknown lands.[3]

Also, Bullitt, in 1937, although by then very much disillusioned with the Soviet Union, nevertheless acknowledged that Litvinov was a good host. Litvinov gave parties which start 'at ten o'clock and go on far into the night, at which there was such a display of luxury as would put to shame the hospitality of London and Paris.'[4]

Litvinov certainly had a sense of humour. In 1918 Lockhart was informally appointed to meet Litvinov in a Lyons Corner House. At that time Britain had not recognised the Bolshevik regime, which caused the luncheon to close on a humorous note. When the two men came to order the dessert, there was pudding called diplomat on the menu. The waitress took the order and returned a minute later to say there was none left. Litvinov shrugged his shoulders, smiled and said, 'Not recognised even by Lyons!'[5]

Cyril Quinn, who served in the US hunger mission between 1921 and 1923, expressed great admiration

> of Litvinov's dexterity in negotiation, his unusual intelligence and persuasiveness. He found this first experience with a high-ranking Soviet official edifying, but disconcerting. If the rest of the Bolsheviks measured up to Litvinov in talent and determination, the USA faced formidable competition.[6]

When, in 1941, Litvinov was appointed ambassador to the United States, *The New York Times* commented:

> Stalin has decided to place his ablest and most forceful diplomat and one who enjoys greater prestige in this country. He is known as a man of exceptional ability, adroit as well as forceful. It is believed that Stalin, in designating him for the ambassadorship, felt Litvinov could exercise real influence in Washington.[7]

---

[3] Ehrenburg, Ilya: *Post-War Years*, p.277
[4] Jones, Thomas: *Diary with Letters*, p.211
[5] Lockhart, Robert: *Memoirs of a British Agent*, p.204
[6] Weissman, Benjamin: *Herbert Hoover and Famine Relief*, p.63
[7] *The New York Times,* 7 November 1941, p.1

Litvinov made a good impression on Eleanor Roosevelt. She stated that Litvinov, 'whose wife was English, was the most skilful in getting along with Western Government officials.'[8] Confirmation of this observation came from Sumner Welles, who referred to Litvinov 'as a man, who, in the years before Munich, had an opportunity to demonstrate the quality of his outstanding talents.'[9] Another American politician whom Litvinov impressed was Morgenthau, the US Financial Secretary, who depicted him as 'a warm, friendly man, sparkling in conversation, abundant in hospitality.'[10]

Litvinov's reputation quite possibly reached its zenith at the Disarmament Conference. Initially despised, Litvinov was able to win the respect of many of his fellow delegates. In 1933, Politis, the Greek delegate and chairman of the Security Committee,

> congratulated the Soviet delegation on the initiative it had taken, on the part it had played in the Security Committee and on the success it had finally achieved. It was with special pleasure he paid this tribute to the Soviet delegation since it demonstrated beyond doubt that when men rose above the contingences of day-to-day politics and allowed themselves to be guided by the more general ideas which should lead the civilised world, it was found that, whether a country was a member of the League or not, there was a community of ideals which was capable with a little goodwill of bringing to fruition the noblest and most difficult enterprises.[11]

Perhaps the most significant tribute was paid by President Roosevelt. When, after much contemplation, he decided to write to Stalin suggesting a meeting between them, he told Stalin the only people with whom he had discussed the letter were his old friend Joseph E Davies and Litvinov.[12]

Lord Cushendun used different language in the Preparatory Commission in 1929 saying:

> Unless we effect a good deal at the present session of the Commission, we shall very likely finally fail altogether and certainly make us the laughing stock of the world and no doubt that would be gratifying to the Soviet delegation.[13]

When Litvinov was appointed as ambassador to the USA, it came to be realised that he had little influence. Nevertheless, when Litvinov was first transferred back to Moscow the US Secretary of State, Cordell Hull, informed the Soviet chargé d'affaires that the USA had

---

[8] Roosevelt, Eleanor: *Autobiography*, p.242
[9] Welles, Sumner: *Time for Decision*, p.246
[10] Blum, John Morton: *Morgenthau Diaries*, p.57
[11] Disarmament Minutes, p.502
[12] FRUS, Papers for Cairo and Teheran, p.3
[13] Preparatory Minutes, Series 8, p.42

the highest regard for Litvinov and wanted to see him back in this country.'[14] *The New York Times* remarked on how:

> He worked shrewdly and with apparent sincerity for the Soviet Union and the communist cause. He merely happened to believe, as other communists did not, that communism and Western capitalism could exist in the same world. He seems now to have lost out, along with many Russians, caught in the current purges. We hope not. We could do with a little of the Litvinov spirit at Paris.[15]

Sumner Welles describes Litvinov 'as a blunt man. He is often brutal, but he never seemed to me devious.'[16] However, I do not believe this was entirely true. Particularly with regard to appeasement, he often criticised others for what he had practised himself. This lack of straightforwardness was tempered by a biting criticism which surfaced when Litvinov felt annoyed and the demands of prudence permitted its expression. In the last League of Nations session which Litvinov attended in 1938, he stated: 'Some of the delegates to the League of Nations had found it necessary to tremble before the wrath of the present dictators of Europe.'[17]

In spite of the rhetoric about communism promoting the equality of women, it was amazing how few women were ever appointed to the Politburo. In the West the wives of Churchill, Roosevelt and Attlee appeared with their husbands; whereas in the USSR, except for Polino Molotov, the rule among the Soviet leaders was that wives were not to be seen in public. Litvinov functioned independently from his wife and this may partly explain the fact that Litvinov from time to time was attracted to women other than his wife. However, Ivy had a love for Maxim that outlived him. Carswell suggested that Maxim's unfaithfulness might have been encouraged by the fact Ivy had cooled towards him at the time of his visit to the USA in 1933 for the recognition talks. I have no way of knowing how far these allegations are true. Nevertheless, Ivy's regard for Maxim was shown by her remarks after he died. 'They did not get him.' Ivy said later that She thus comforted herself that Litvinov died at the right time, as Stalin soon engineered the Doctors' Plot.[18] In my study of the Litvinovs, I could not fail to have an admiration for Ivy, a most versatile woman. In the early twenties she had to suffer the most hostile reception from her British acquaintances. In the 1930s and again in the 1950s she had to endure the appalling conditions of Stalin's Russia as well as her husband's unfaithfulness, but this left her with no bitterness.[19]

---

[14] FRUS, 1943, vol.3, p.540
[15] *The New York Times,* 25 August 1946, part IV, p.8
[16] Welles, Sumner: *Time for Decision,* p.29
[17] *The New York Times,* 30 September 1938, p.1
[18] Carswell, John: *The Exile,* pp.136-143; Archives Box 6
[19] Carswell, John: *The Exile,* p.162

Understandably, it was the one matter about which Tanya did not wish to talk. Ivy Litvinov was a very talented writer. Indeed, this was recognised by the American magazine *Life*, which asked her to write an article about herself, about her teaching of basic English in Russia, and of being an accomplished ambassador's wife.[20] The *Moscow News* published a photograph of her daughter Tanya and H G Wells at a sports ground, showing Litvinov to be a proud father.[21]

We have Eden's first-hand comments on his meeting with Stalin and Litvinov. Eden stated:

> I liked Litvinov. He was intelligent, shrewd and with a theme of foreign policy in which he believed sincerely. He knew Western Europe as one who had lived there and his outlook was more sophisticated than that of any other Soviet leader of the time.

Eden argues that Stalin was more pragmatic in his approach to Germany and more understanding of the German point of view. In that sense he was less scrupulous and had no prejudice against the Nazis as such, whereas Litvinov felt repugnance at the Nazi treatment of the Jews.[22] Litvinov, as a communist, did not practise his religion. I am not certain Eden is correct.[23]

Eden's opinion of Litvinov was shared by Seeds: 'I am sad at Litvinov's disappearance. I always found talks with him stimulating. We had got to understand each other well.'[24] Litvinov displayed the human touch. When Eden departed on the train, Litvinov said, in a loud voice that could be overheard, 'I wish you success. Your success will be our success.'[25] In the autumn of 1942, these sentiments were substantiated by Britain's success at El Alamein.

We have much evidence that Litvinov listened regularly to the BBC. Eden remarked that 'Litvinov was a communist and loyal Russian, of course, but he was also a good European. I found him fair and reliable as an international colleague.'[26]

Unlike Molotov's wife Polino, Litvinov seemed to have entirely severed all connections with his Jewish past and, like all of the communist elite, did not go near any place of religious worship. Litvinov agreed to the official Communist party policy of assimilating the Jewish

---

[20] *Life*, 12 October 1942, p.115

[21] *Moscow News*, 4 August 1934, p.1

[22] Eden, Anthony (Lord Avon): *Memoirs, Facing the Dictators*, p.162

[23] See No. 28-31 *post*

[24] Aster, Sidney: *The Making of the Second World War*, p.174

[25] Eden, Anthony: *Memoirs, Facing the Dictators*, p.162

[26] Eden, Anthony: *Memoirs, Facing the Dictators*, p.163

race. He was shocked when somebody referred to a Jew as 'a Yid.'[27] Unlike many Jews, he never showed any respect for other religions and appeared not to have demurred from the early Soviet policy of imprisoning and executing many clergy, particularly prelates. He did not oppose the policy of selling off the moveable church property.

Although passionate about such matters as disarmament, collective security, and the Second Front, I cannot find any particular condemnation by Litvinov of the abominable treatment of the Jews in occupied Europe both before and after the Holocaust was known about. In December 1942 Litvinov was summoned by Sumner Welles, who proposed that the Allies jointly set up a commission to collect and examine evidence of the persecution and barbarities taking place under Nazi rule. This was very much a US initiative in response to a deputation of their Jewry.[28]

Molotov's wife's (Polino Molotov) enthusiasm for the Soviet Jewry is shown by her support for the Anti-Fascist Committee, the proposed Jewish autonomous region in the Crimea and her interest in the appointment of Golda Meir as first ambassador to the Soviet Union. These facts showed she never lost her Jewish roots.[29] Even her husband, as Foreign Commissar, approved a statement from his office in December 1942 which highlighted Nazi atrocities against the Jews. The statement, which might to some have appeared exaggerated propaganda, proved to be in every way true. The article explained the Nazi plan was to

> concentrate nearly four million people in Eastern Europe for the purpose of putting them to death and described how Jews in Norway were rounded up. Old Jewish people were even removed from hospitals and homes for the elderly, separating wives from husbands, children from parents.[30]

However, perhaps Litvinov's motive in keeping quiet on the persecution of the Jews was concern for his own safety. If Stalin believed Litvinov, because he was a Jew, was too enthusiastic about the Jewish race, perhaps he might have been persecuted, like Molotov's wife.[31]

Litvinov faced much criticism from both his fellow communists, who suspected that he was not sufficiently committed to the cause, and capitalists, who felt that, because he often seemed so reasonable and understood the non-communist world, he was in fact a greater danger to the capitalist system. Gregory Bessedovsky, writing in the 1930s, acknowledged:

---

[27] Ivy Litvinov's tape; Tanya
[28] *The New York Times,* 13 December 1942, p.11
[29] Kostyrchenko, Gennadii: *Out of the Red Shadow*; p.55 ;Meir, Golda: *My Life*, pp.208 and 209
[30] *Moscow News*, 19 December 1942, pp.1 and 2
[31] See Ch.16, No.79

Litvinov had a good knowledge of men and affairs and is extremely cunning. Litvinov is extra-ordinarily short-sighted in his judgments. No one; could be less capable of a clear insight into problems of foreign policy. In his diplomatic conferences, Litvinov is just the same – he is coarse and imprudent.[32]

All the evidence I have produced indicates the exact opposite was the truth. Beck describes Litvinov as a 'petty tradesman who started off life in the suburbs of Warsaw (He is a Polish Jew and his real name is Wallach).' Unjustified hostility appears to have been engendered on account of Litvinov's Jewish origins. [33]   Henry Channon, in his diary, showed his anti-Soviet bias by describing Litvinov as 'the dread intriguer.[34]

Litvinov never had the rapport with Hodgson's successor, Esmond Ovey, as with Hodgson, Britain's first chargé d'affaires to the Soviet Union following resumption of diplomatic relations in 1929. In a letter to the British Foreign Secretary, Ovey stated that Maxim Litvinov very rarely dealt with internal affairs, but when he did, 'he has frequently shown himself to be singularly ignorant.'[35] Another severe critic of Litvinov was Reader Bullard, the British Consul, who was at the embassy during the time of the arrest and trial of the Metro-Vickers engineers. In Reader Bullard's diaries, Litvinov was described as: 'A shameless liar and exceedingly insolent' and Reader Bullard also labelled Litvinov 'this horrible little man being rude to the Ambassador and insisting that he could do what he liked with British subjects.' Reader Bullard would probably have been even more indignant if he had known that Litvinov did not believe in the engineers' guilt, providing Ivy Litvinov accurately recorded her husband's views.[36] Litvinov told the British ambassador Ovey: 'his methods of diplomacy might be successful in Mexico', which was Ovey's last post, 'but in the Soviet Union they were doomed to failure in advance.'[37] Arthur Henderson, the British Labour Foreign Secretary, was so annoyed that his ambassador had been treated so rudely that he recalled Ovey.

Beria described Litvinov as:

> a very bad organiser. Litvinov was rigid and obtuse and did not know how to use his wide range of relations so as to broaden his horizon and forms opinions of his own. He was overestimated by the Westerners. Personally, I regarded him as a mediocre opportunist, a pen-pusher who was jealous of people of talent.

---

[32] Bessedovsky, Grigory: *Revelations of a Soviet Diplomat*, pp.96 and 97
[33] Beck Joseph: *Final Report* ,p.190
34 Channon, Henry: *Diaries*, p.164
35 Carynnyk, Marco: *The Foreign Office and the Famine*, p.218
36 Bullard, Julian and Margaret: *Inside Stalin's Russia*, p.151; Tanya
37 DBFP, 2nd Series, vol.7, p.380, No.306; Bullard, Julian and Margaret: *Inside Soviet Russia* p.172

However, Beria esteemed Maisky and wanted him to replace Litvinov, rather than Molotov, as Foreign Commissar. Beria considered it important that the Western leaders thought that the Commissioner for Foreign Affairs and the Ambassadors were independent persons and in this respect he was probably right. Beria therefore regarded as an asset the fact that Maisky and Litvinov maintained outward appearances which led the Western Powers to view them as independent personalities who were obliged to follow a pro-Bolshevik policy.[38]

However, what is not disclosed is whether Litvinov and Beria were prepared to give advice to Stalin about what they believed rather than what they thought Stalin would like to hear. Beria gives no credit to the fact that Litvinov promoted Maisky to the key task of ambassador to Britain, an appointment which Molotov did not wish to change for over four years. Molotov, on taking over the Foreign Commissariat, failed to anticipate events as Litvinov had done. One example was German aggressiveness in pursuing a policy of dividing potential enemies. Litvinov would again prove he was right when he anticipated Pearl Harbour and gave a warning to the US military which they failed to take seriously.[39]

Maisky endeavoured to address as many British audiences as possible in order to break through the air of hostility towards the Soviet Union at the beginning of the 30s, a task which Litvinov 'encouraged' Maisky 'to undertake in every way possible.' Once Litvinov was dismissed this all changed. Maisky stated: 'Far from all the leading comrades' (including presumably Molotov) 'realised the value of such speeches.'[40] If Litvinov and Maisky could not make any impact, there was always the chance those less co-operative would replace them, and clearly this was a factor which the British Government should have considered.

The British Government ought to have realised that their repeated failure to respond to any of Litvinov's initiatives might result in his replacement by one not so favourably disposed to the democracies; or worse still, the Soviet Government might seek an accommodation with Hitler. Indeed, one result of the failure to even consult Litvinov over the Munich agreement was that Stalin reached the conclusion that Litvinov had little influence over France and Britain.[41]

In spite of Communist rhetoric about all their politicians being uninterested in personal ambition and only working for the good of the Communist state, rivalry and personality played as prominent a part as it does in capitalist societies. However, most of the Communist elite, although they lacked the vast capital resources of their capitalist counterparts, never spared themselves when it concerned their living expenses. They often

---

[38] Beria, Sergo: *Beria, My Father*, p.48
[39] Fischer, Louis: *Great Challenge*, p.42
[40] Maisky, Ivan: *Memoirs of a Soviet Ambassador*, p.211
[41] See Ch.13, No.80

entertained in the true Tsarist tradition even in wartime. The British monarchs, on the other hand, made sacrifices during wartime. When, in 1942, Stalingrad was in grave danger of capitulation and appeals were made to Soviet citizens to make supreme sacrifices, it was still possible for a sturgeon to be flown to the USA for the benefit of the guests at the 1942 annual celebrations of the anniversary of the Revolution. When Ivy was living in Sverdlovsk, she regularly returned the nine hundred miles to Moscow and often spoke on the long-distance telephone. Long-distance telephone calls and air travel were not cheap in the pre-war world and the majority of Soviet citizens could not afford such luxuries. However, Ivy Litvinov defended her husband from accusations of bribery.[42] In Litvinov's negotiations with foreigners, if the visitor left some gift on the desk: a box of Havanas, a gold-mounted fountain pen or a huge box of liqueur-filled chocolates. Ivy, who used to act as her husband's secretary, was instructed to catch the donor and return the items so there could be no suggestion of bribery. Litvinov said: 'Do you know I could be rolling in gold if I liked?'[43]

While Litvinov became unofficial ambassador to Britain during the First World War, most of his remarks on foreign policy were directed against the war. Although German troops were occupying France and Belgium, he thought that Britain and France should sue for peace.[44] Would not Germany have regarded such overtures as weakness and extracted the same humiliating terms to which Russia was forced to agree at Brest-Litovsk? Probably, Litvinov believed somehow a revolutionary war would start following a truce, although it is difficult to see his logic. This also seems rather at variance with his remark to Lockhart that he regarded 'English capitalism as less dangerous than German militarism.'[45] We do know that, as soon as the armistice of 1918 occurred, Litvinov was resigned to the fact that the prospects of world revolution were nil.[46]

On 24 March 1920, Litvinov summed up the Bolshevik programme in seven points,

1. Recognition of the republic of the Soviets.
2. Liberty to develop in peace and normality within its boundaries its social experiment.
3. Assurance given by the Soviets that they will not interfere in the internal affairs of other nations.
4. Mutual and serious guarantees to that effect.
5. Renewal of economic relations.
6. Disarmament of the Red Army as soon as possible.
7. Recognition of Russia's former debts and loans with interest.

---

42 Tape, Imperial War Museum

43 Ch.3, No.54; Ivy's papers, Box 9

44 Ch.2 No.16

45 Lockhart, Robert: *Memoirs of a British Agent*, p.203

46 Fisher, Louis: *Men and Politics*, p.124

There was no trace here of revolutionary zeal. Litvinov stated:
:

> We have triumphed over Yudenich, Denikin and Kolchak because they had the people against them. We do not wish either to avenge ourselves or attack anyone. We must be left in peace to work out among ourselves our social experiment. If the experiment succeeds, other people will follow it. If it fails, we will be obliged to try another method. In any case, none must interfere with us. That is all we ask. If we obtain this formal guarantee that there will be no foreign intervention, we will give on our side, the same guarantees not to seek to intervene in the internal affairs of other states. We make this offer in good faith. We do not wish any foreign alliances, but we do not wish to attack anyone. We are leaving our little Republics that have arisen around ourselves absolute freedom to adopt whatever regime they like.

This was a blatant lie. The Soviet Union never allowed these republics to act in any way contrary to Moscow's wishes. Litvinov continued:

> We respect the right of every country to dispose freely of its own affairs. We shall disarm as soon as we are freed from menace. We are convinced pacifists. We have had to fight because fight was forced upon us, but we are anxious to lay down our arms. We desire a renewal of normal commercial relations with other countries. Europe has need of Russian raw materials and we need manufactured goods in return.[47]

Before the Central Executive Committee on 14 April 1926 Litvinov reiterated the object of Soviet foreign policy, which was the conclusion of non-aggression treaties with all nations. Litvinov explained:

> We long ago proposed to all countries the conclusion with us of agreements which excluded the possibility of attacks on each other or participation in inimical action and would have secured reciprocal neutrality in respect of armed conflict with third parties. Our diplomacy will, as before, continue to follow carefully all the movements of our enemies, both open and secret, frustrating their crafty intentions and exposing their hostile machinations. In trying to strengthen the security of our state, we do not aim at injuring the interests of any other state with which we have normal and friendly relations. The basic factor of our diplomacy was and remains our desire to extend friendly connexions with other nations, to place them on a firm foundation and, together with this, to contribute to the general peace not in words but in deeds.[48]

---

[47] *The New York Times,* 24 March 1920, p.5
[48] Degras, Jane: *Documents on Soviet Foreign Policy*, vol.2, pp. 105 @ 106 and 117

On 4 December 1929, Litvinov admirably summed up the situation:

> The Union of the Socialist Republics from the first day of its existence has pursued a policy of peace, and, unlike other powers, have never resorted to military action except as a necessary step to defence due to a direct attack on the Soviet Union or armed intervention in its internal affairs. The Soviet Union has constantly pursued this policy and intends to pursue it independent of the Paris Pact for the abolition of war.

Once it was realised that workers in other states were not going to attempt to overthrow their capitalist economies by force, Litvinov pursued energetically the policy of establishing and maintaining diplomatic relations with all states and did not consider 'the refusal of relations to be a way of regulating international relations.'

The solution of national questions is on the basis of 'the utmost tolerance, and the respecting of national culture of nations.' In the short term, Litvinov's goal was to strive for the conditions of international peace.

> It would be madness to start this five-year plan demanding considerable extension of our resources if we were not at the same time determined, at whatever cost, not to allow any interruption of our peaceful conditions.[49]

Fischer sums up the principle of Litvinov's foreign policy before the Second World War: 'Litvinov wished to keep the Soviet Union at peace so it could develop internally and he sought to develop foreign trade.' Litvinov told Fischer that he, Litvinov, 'did not want to spend money on a Red fleet, but he wanted Russia to appear on the world stage.' These beliefs coincided with Stalin's views at the time.

Litvinov said that the revolution died in 1918. To him stands the credit of realising that the working class in Western Europe were not going to follow Russia in rising up against their capitalist overlords, preferring security to revolution. After all, the workers in the capitalist world were inestimably better off than their Russian counterparts and had more to lose in a revolution that might go horribly wrong. Lenin was reluctant to recognise that fact and stupidly thought that the Red Army would be welcomed rather than hated in Poland.[50] Very soon, Stalin too realised that a world-wide revolution was not going to occur and therefore the way forward was to build socialism in one country. In 1944 Litvinov stated: 'We do not want revolution in the West, but if that happens we must approve it.' This was consistent with Stalin's thinking in respect of not supporting the communists in Greece, as, unlike his Eastern European satellites, he did not consider there were significant strategic

---

[49] Documents, 1929, pp.189 and 190
[50] Fischer, Louis: *Men and Politics*, p.125; and see Ch.3, No.71

reasons involved in Greece. Therefore, he never formally recognised the insurgent government nor provided aid to match that coming from Britain and the USA.[51]

In a press statement on 12 December 1932 Litvinov stated:

> It is only when all states maintain relations with one another, we shall be able to speak seriously of international co-operation in the cause of peace, of international guarantees of the observation of pacts and agreements and the creation of authoritative international organisations.[52]

On 6 February 1933, at the Disarmament Conference, Litvinov made a powerful speech which must have inspired small states. He said:

> No consideration whatever of a political, strategic or economic nature, including the desire to exploit material riches or to obtain any sort of advantages or privileges on the territory of another State, no references to considerable capital investment or other special interests in a given state or the alleged absence of other attributes of state organisation in the case of a given country, shall be accepted as justification of aggression.

Although at that time Eden criticised the definition of aggression as a trap for the innocent and protection for the guilty, by 1946 the British were criticising the Soviet Government for not abiding by the Litvinov criteria. These high principles would apparently influence Litvinov throughout his life.[53] A few days before Litvinov died, Ivy asked Maxim whether he was thinking or just dozing, to which Maxim replied: 'I am visualising the map of the world.' Ehrenburg states that: 'Litvinov's cherished ambition was to fend off war, to bring nations and continents closer together and the map of the world was to him what tubes are to the artist.'[54]

Philip Mosely stated that 'Litvinov's outraged sarcasm was meant to sting and shame the Western nations into wars which at the last moment the Soviet Union would hold aloof but we certainly have no right to assume that this would have happened.'[55] Many in Britain considered that the Soviet Union might prove to be more faithful than her critics believed. She might have given effective help as part of an international force if the League of Nations had taken tough action in respect of Abyssinia in 1936 and Czechoslovakia in

[51] FRUS , 1944, vol.3, p.1148 @ p. 1149 ; Dunbabin, J P D: *The Cold War, the Great Powers and their Allies*, p.72

[52] Degras, Jane: *Documents on British Foreign Policy*, vol.2, p.551

[53] *Times*, 28 January 1946, p.4; Ch.6, No.85

[54] Ehrenburg, Ilya: *Post-War Years*, p.279

[55] Mosely, Philip: *Foreign Affairs Reader*, p.208

1938. In the Second World War, the Soviet Union proved a better ally to Britain than did France.[56]

Although, like Churchill and Roosevelt, Litvinov regarded himself as the champion of anti-appeasement, all three men constantly practised appeasement when it suited them. In respect of Churchill, it was his attitude to Japan in the 1930s and his response to the Italian invasion of Abyssinia. As for Roosevelt, it was his policy concerning Mussolini. In the case of Litvinov, in common with Churchill he wavered when it came to Japan.[57] As Foreign Minister when the international community wanted to take firm action against Japan over the invasion of Manchuria, Litvinov was very unreceptive. However, like Churchill, this stance did not stop Litvinov from listing Manchuria as a milestone on the road of appeasement. In 1941 Litvinov told Cripps that he thought the League of Nations could have been used to stop aggression, if it had been used properly in 1931.[58]

In spite of Litvinov's efforts, 'there was no return to the pre-war acceptance of the Soviet Union as a great power', although the Tsar had been a necessary part of the Concert of Europe. Instead, the Western powers foolishly tried to reconstitute Europe without the Soviet Union.[59] This was not a wise policy, as it created in Stalin's mind a suspicion towards the other great powers which found expression in 1944 and 1945. When he was able to exercise his muscle, he did so. If, especially after the Soviet Union entered the League of Nations in 1934, the other great powers, particularly Chamberlain in the late 1930s, had been prepared to treat the Soviet Union in the same way that the Tsar had been treated, Stalin might not have found it necessary to install the belt of satellite states in Eastern Europe. The evidence is that Stalin's motives for the creation of the satellite states were strategic rather than ideological, because he did not feel the need to control Finland and Greece, as in these cases he did not see a threat to the Soviet Union's security.

Roberts sums up Litvinov's acute perceptive skills: Litvinov's ability 'to detect major trends in the 1930s and to anticipate the course of events indicates his tremendous understanding of the decade.'[60] As Sumner Welles stated: 'No European statesman in the decade of the thirties spoke more clearly or spoke more truly. No responsible statesman of those years with the exception of Winston Churchill has proved more consistently right.'[61] It can be argued that Sumner Welles is not doing sufficient justice to Litvinov because, on the vital matter of the French army, Churchill was wrong to put his faith in that body of men, whereas Litvinov was less sanguine.

---

[56] Ch.14, Nos.76-78

[57] Churchill's appeasement discussed in Ch.12, No.97; Litvinov's appeasement discussed in Ch.7, No.72
Roosevelt's appeasement toward Japan ch, 15 No.103

[58] Estorick, Eric: *Stafford Cripps*, p.281; but see Ch,. 7 No 99-100

[59] Lederer, Ivo J: *British Foreign Policy Essays in Historical Perspective*, p.213

[60] Roberts, Henry, in *Diplomats*, edited by Gordon Craig and Felix Gilbert, p.376

[61] Welles, Sumner: *Time for Decision*, p.248

In February 1937 Litvinov complained to the USA's Ambassador about the blindness of the British Government to the threat Hitler presented and expressed the fear that the British and French Governments would try to reach an accommodation with Hitler.[62]

In March 1938 Litvinov told Hudson:

> He foresaw in the not too distant future a Europe entirely German from the Bay of Biscay to the Soviet frontier. Once this hegemony is firmly established in Europe and France neutralised, Hitler will be able to attack either Great Britain or the USSR. He will choose the first solution because it will offer greater advantages, with the substitution of the British Empire for the German Empire, and to succeed on this undertaking he will prefer to come to an understanding with the USSR.[63]

Litvinov stated that, in his opinion, despite the Anti-Comintern Pact, 'When the Germans are prepared to embark at last on their new adventure, these bandits will come to Moscow and ask for a pact.'[64]

Again, Litvinov foresaw that Japan would attack Pearl Harbour. Fischer states that, when Litvinov stopped at Honolulu two days before the assault on Pearl Harbour, he was entertained by the highest American Army and Naval officials. Litvinov told them about the unexpectedness of the Nazi blow against the Soviet Union. Litvinov said, 'A country at peace cannot get accustomed to the idea that it may soon be attacked and so it might be caught unawares. At this moment,' Litvinov stated, 'Japan may be planning a war on the United States. They might strike Honolulu.' Litvinov advised American officers 'to be vigilant night and day.' This is consistent with what Pope stated in a letter when he describes an incident which took place when Litvinov arrived in Honolulu on 5 December 1941 on his way to take up his post as ambassador to the USA. During a formal reception, at the Governor's house, attended by both General Short and Admiral Kimmel, Litvinov repeated what he had already said in Manila, that the Japanese 'will attack Pearl Harbour any moment now.' An unidentified American said they would be fools to attack the US then. 'They would be fools, but they will attack,' replied Litvinov.[65]

Steven Miner states:

> It was Molotov's very colourlessness that drew Molotov to Stalin. At least, until Stalin's final years, the two seemed ideally suited to one another. Molotov supplied the very talents that Stalin needed during his rise through the Bolshevik hierarchy

---

[62] Roberts, Henry: *Diplomats*, p.358; Davies, Joseph E: *Mission to Moscow*, p.60

[63] Roberts, Henry: *Diplomats*, p.363; Whittaker, John: *We Cannot Escape History*, p.268

[64] Roberts, Henry:*Diplomats*. p.359. as above; Seeds to Halifax, 3 April 1939 p.363; DBBP 3rd series vol 4 p.585

[65] *The New York Times*, 6 January 1952, Part 2 p.8; Fischer, Louis: *Great Challenge*, p.42

to supreme power, a legendary memory, huge capacity for work and organisation and a ruthlessness tempered by a dog-like loyalty towards his boss.[66]

Nevertheless, Litvinov, between 1930 and 1939, appears also to have formed a good working relationship with Stalin, but Litvinov had the advantage over Molotov of having travelled widely. He was a far more independently minded person. Whereas Hindus's *Crisis at the Kremlin* describes Molotov as 'a humourless man', Stalin 'enjoyed Litvinov's blunt and almost scorching wit during the time Stalin trusted Litvinov more than anybody else in the execution of the Kremlin's foreign policy.'[67] Stalin showed his confidence in Litvinov by continuing him in office as Deputy Commissar and then appointing him Commissar in 1930. Gromyko confirms that 'Stalin liked people with wit.'[68] I think those who state that Stalin liked Litvinov, such as Hindus and Miner, are more likely to be correct than those who state that Stalin disliked Litvinov, such as Astakhov. Tanya, Litvinov's daughter, is also of the opinion that Stalin liked her father.[69] Litvinov himself stated that 'the very confidential and apparently influential relationship he enjoyed with Stalin until 1939 was non-existent today.'[70] It therefore appears to Litvinov that his relationship with Stalin before Litvinov was dismissed in 1939 was good, notwithstanding the fact that many of Litvinov's colleagues had been liquidated in the purges. However, during the time Litvinov was the US ambassador, the relationship had obviously deteriorated, because Litvinov described it as 'non-existent today.'

There is some evidence that, although Stalin realised he needed Molotov, Stalin did not like him. Stalin's one-time bodyguard, Amba, stated: 'More general dislike for this statesman robot and for his position in the Kremlin could scarcely be wished and it was apparent that Stalin himself joined in this feeling.'[71] Amba asked the question:

> What then has made Stalin collaborate so closely with him? There are many more talented people in the Soviet Union and Stalin no doubt had the means to find them. Is he afraid of close collaboration with a more human and sympathetic assistant? With Molotov he is armoured against such temptation.[72]

Amba recalls an incident at a jolly party. Suddenly, Poskryobyshev whispered in Stalin's ear. When Stalin said:

---

[66] Miner, Steven, in *Diplomats 1939-1979*, edited by Gordon Craig and, p.66

[67] Hindus, Maurice: *Crisis in the Kremlin*, p.48

[68] Gromyko, Andrei: *Memoirs*, p.102

[69] Miner, Steven, in *Diplomats,1939-1979* edited by Gordon Craig and Francis Loewenheim, p.69; Hindus, Maurice: *Crisis in the Kremlin*, p.48; FRUS, 1943, vol.3, p.522; Tanya; Ch14 No 69

[70] FRUS, 1943, vol.3, p.522

[71] Amba, Achmed (Ahmad): *I Was Stalin's Bodyguard*, p.133

[72] Ibid. p.138

'Does it have to be right away.' Everybody realised at once that Molotov had telephoned. In about half an hour Stalin was informed of Molotov's arrival. Although the whispered conversation between Molotov and Stalin only lasted five minutes, the merriment of the gathering evaporated as everybody talked in hushed tones.

Amba stated: 'Then the blanket left. Instantly the gaiety returned.' Vareykis said that 'a gentle angel has flown past.' This is a Russian expression for when a sudden silence descends. Laurentyev exclaimed in a harsh Georgian accent, 'Go, friendly soul.' Stalin laughed the loudest at Laurentyev's joke.[73]

Stalin could be very rude to Molotov. In 1942 Stalin took Molotov to task for his handling of the negotiations with the Allies. He cabled Molotov on 3 June:

> [I am] dissatisfied with the terseness and reticence of all your communications. You convey to us from your talks with Roosevelt and Churchill only what you yourself consider is important, and omit all the rest. Meanwhile, the instance [Stalin] would like to know everything. What you consider important and what you think unimportant. This refers to the draft of the communiqué as well. You have not informed us whose draft it is, whether it has been agreed on with the British in full and why, after all, there could not be two communiqués, one concerning the talks in Britain and one concerning the talks in the USA. We are having to guess because of your reticence. We further consider it expedient that both communiqués should mention among other things the creation of a second front in Europe and that full understanding has been reached in this matter. We also consider that it is absolutely necessary both communiqués should mention the supply of war materials to the Soviet Union from Britain and the USA. In all the rest we agree with the contents of the draft communiqué you sent us.[74]

At the London conference in 1945, Molotov did not object to the attendance of China and France at discussions on the peace treaties. Stalin gave instructions that Molotov be sent a message alleging that,

> with Molotov's connivance, the Anglo-Saxons managed to bring in the Chinese and the French.[75]

Again, Stalin complained that Molotov had not properly exercised the censorship so articles were appearing reporting problems in the Soviet leadership. Stalin went so far as

---

[73] Ibid. p.133
[74] Rzheshevsky, Oleg: *War and Diplomacy*, p.210
[75] Foreign correspondence between Stalin, Molotov and other members of the Politburo, p.4

saying to Malenkov, Mikoyan and Beria: 'I can no longer consider such a comrade [Molotov] as my first deputy.'[76]

Tanya remembers her father saying to Molotov on the telephone, 'Only a fool like you would think such a thing' and he certainly regarded Molotov as a fool. Litvinov did not regard as an asset Molotov's willingness to do everything that his master Stalin wanted.[77]

The bad relationship between Molotov and Litvinov is corroborated by two independent sources. Hindus, in 1954, was perhaps the first person outside the Soviet Union to understand this hostility. In his book *Crisis in the Kremlin*, he states:

> It is well known in Moscow that Molotov always detested Litvinov. Molotov's detestation for Litvinov was purely of a personal nature. No Muscovite I have ever known, whether friend of Molotov or of Litvinov, has ever taken exception to this view. Molotov was always resentful of Litvinov's fluency in French, German and English, as he was distrustful of Litvinov's easy manner with foreigners. Never having lived abroad, Molotov always suspected there was something impure and sinful in Litvinov's broadmindedness and appreciation of Western civilisation.[78]

Although Litvinov never mentioned his relationship with Molotov in the Foreign Commissariat, Narkomindel, press officer Gnedin states:

> Even though Litvinov never referred to their relations [between Litvinov and Molotov], it was nevertheless well known that they were bad. Litvinov could have no respect for the small-minded intriguer and accomplice in terror like Molotov, and Molotov, for his part, had no love of Litvinov who, incidentally, was the one People's Commissar to have retained his independence.[79]

There is no doubt that relations between Molotov and Litvinov were stormy, although Molotov acknowledged to Chuev that Litvinov 'was not a bad diplomat – a good one.'[80] According to Sheinis, Litvinov stated: 'Molotov was not flexible enough as a diplomat.'[81] It seems likely that one of the reasons for Molotov's hostility to Litvinov was that Molotov did not receive from Litvinov the same respect which other party functionaries gave him.

In May 1939, at a meeting attended by Molotov and Stalin, Litvinov was informed of his

---

[76] Naimark, Norman: 'Cold War Studies and New Archive Material of Stalin', in *Russian Review*, January 2002, p.8
[77] Tanya
[78] Hindus, Maurice: *Crisis in the Kremlin*, p.48
[79] Medvedev, Zhores: *All Stalin's Men*, p.87
[80] Chuev, Felix: *Molotov Remembers*, p.68
[81] Sheinis, Zinovy: *Maxim Litvinov*, p.326

dismissal.   Molotov said: 'You [Litvinov] think we are all fools.' Although Read and Fisher, quoting from Litvinov's diaries, stated that the meeting was cordial, Louis Fischer adds that Molotov and Litvinov argued for an hour at that meeting, with Stalin present.[82] Hindus quite rightly states: 'Had Molotov possessed the power, he would have dismissed Litvinov from Foreign Commissar long before 3 May 1939.'[83] Presumably, Litvinov's further dismissal from the Central Committee in 1941 also pleased Molotov.[84]

In Molotov's speech justifying the Nazi-Soviet Pact, he stated: 'There were some short-sighted people in our country who, carried away with oversimplified anti-Fascist agitation, forget about the provocative work of our enemies.' Then Molotov said:

> In exposing the outcry raised in the British, French and North American press about German plans for seizure of the Southern Ukraine, it looks as if the object of this suspicious hullabaloo was to incense the Soviet Union against Germany, to poison the atmosphere and to provoke a conflict with Germany without any visible grounds.[85]

However, it would be Stalin and Molotov who was wrong and the democratic press right. In fact the seizure of the Ukraine and much more of the Soviet Union's territory was exactly what Germany intended to do, and in fact undertook.

Sheinis reports an incident shortly before Litvinov's appointment as ambassador to the USA in 1941. Litvinov discussed the question of the Nazi-Soviet pact. He gave qualified support to the Soviet Union's decision to enter into the pact, only adding, 'I would probably have concluded it, but in a different way'; which remark gained Molotov's anger. Sheinis states that Molotov withdrew permission for Litvinov to give unauthorised interviews to foreign journalists. However, Sheinis does not give the source, and Tanya, Litvinov's daughter, has never heard of this interview or the alleged restriction placed on her father.[86]

Although Molotov might have been angry, it does not seem that Stalin was, because, instead of censoring Litvinov, shortly afterwards Stalin appointed him ambassador to the USA. During the ambassadorship of Litvinov in the USA, when Molotov came for talks with President Roosevelt, Sheinis is no doubt right that there was considerable tension between the two men. We have an example related in Gromyko's memoirs of an argument about the Nazi-Soviet Pact when Litvinov and Molotov were travelling together in the Appalachian Mountains in 1942. Gromyko alleges that Litvinov defended the decision of Britain and France not to join the Soviet Union and give Hitler a firm rebuff, while

---

[82] See Ch.14, No.26
[83] Hindus, Maurice: *Crisis in the Kremlin*, p.48
[84] See Ch.14, No.115
[85] Degras, Jane: *Soviet Documents on Foreign Policy*, vol.3, p.366
[86] Sheinis, Zinovy: *Maxim Litvinov*, p.305; Tanya

Molotov took the official party line and criticised France and Britain, who were accused of pushing Hitler into a war against the Soviet Union. I think that Gromyko was not being truthful in reporting what Litvinov said, as this assertion is contrary to all of Litvinov's other utterances; but an alternative account is given by Haslam. According to him, Litvinov's view was that collective security with Britain and France was the right course of action, rather than the Nazi-Soviet Pact. However, the text does not support what Haslam states.[87] The tense relationship during Molotov's visit is further indicated by what Molotov stated to Chuev: 'We did not take him when we got down to brass tacks. Pavlov did the interpreting.'[88]

It is quite clear that the hostility between the two was mutual. Molotov complained to Chuev about an interview which Litvinov had with a foreign journalist. Although Molotov states that the interview was in 1944, in fact the interview referred to was with Hottelet in 1946. Molotov refers to that part of the interview where Hottelet asked Litvinov whether the Soviets will 'meet us half way.' Litvinov replied in the negative.[89]

Stalin drew ministers of defence, armaments and security as well as top-ranking intelligence officers into his decision-making circle. Molotov attended them all, although the other participants varied with the nature of the question to be decided.[90] Molotov's ubiquitous presence is supported by Zhukov, who states that Molotov was always present at the Supreme Command Stavka, where strategic and other important issues were discussed.[91]

Barmine shows emphatically that where Stalin had an interest in any subject there was no debate and his will was implemented.[92] We learn from Stalin's letters to Molotov that Stalin supervised many foreign policy decisions, such as the resumption of diplomatic relations with Britain following the election of the second Labour Government of 1929.[93]

Litvinov's suggested written response to Germany during the Kandelaki negotiations was amended by Stalin, Molotov, Ordzhonikidze and Voroshilov.[94] Further, the terms of the proposed pact between the Soviet Union, France and Britain as drafted by Litvinov was heavily amended by Molotov, Vorishilov and Kaganovich.[95]

---

[87] Gromyko, Andrei: *Memoirs*, p.312; Haslam, Jonathan: 'Soviet-German Relations and the Origins of the Second World War: The jury is still out', in *Journal of Modern History*, December 1997, p.785 @ p.788

[88] Chuev, Felix: *Molotov Remembers*, p.68

[89] Ibid. p.69; *Washington Post*, 25 January p.1

[90] Zubok Vladislav: *Inside Kremlin's Cold War*, p.84

[91] Zhukov, Georgii: *Reminiscences*, vol.1, p.371

[92] Barmine, Alexandre: *One Who Survived*, pp. 212 to 213

[93] *Stalin's Letters to Molotov*: (Letter 44), p.174; and (Letter 47), p.177; Ch 9 No 100

[94] Watson, Derek: 'Politburo and Foreign Policy in the 1930s', in *The Nature of Stalin's Dictatorship*, p.153

[95] Resis Albert: 'The Fall of Litvinov' in *Europe-Asia Studies* Vol 52 p.46

If Stalin felt he wanted advice before coming to a decision, he listened with great interest to his aides on matters in which he thought they had expertise. This applied to Litvinov on matters of foreign policy.[96] Stalin was prepared to change his mind following discussion. It is not correct to claim that he could never be made to change his mind. Originally, Stalin was very sceptical about reports that Britain and the USA were attempting to manufacture the atomic bomb.

Although by the autumn of 1941 Beria was receiving reports from various foreign sources concerning the USA and Britain's programme to invent and thereafter manufacture an atomic bomb, Beria waited until he had assembled comprehensive evidence before going to Stalin and presenting the facts. The result was that Stalin changed his views.[97]

Gnedin stated that the influence of Litvinov in the policy making was that of an expert:

> Responsible workers of Narkomindel presented the Commissar or his deputy with reports frequently interesting. The Commissar, it was understood, would always submit them with his proposals and notes to the Politburo. In this way the Commissar influenced decisions and even more by discussions. This can be said with confidence.[98]

The Soviet historian Trukhamovskii stated that, from time to time, the Politburo summoned Litvinov for advice. On one such occasion Litvinov stated that the international situation had changed dramatically with the rise of Hitler. Litvinov was asked how he thought Soviet policy should react. Litvinov recommended that the Soviet Union should enter the League of Nations and work for a defensive alliance with its ally Czechoslovakia.[99]

However, historians have tended to downgrade Litvinov's position in the Soviet hierarchy because of his lack of a seat on the Politburo, a body that in the period immediately before the Second World War met more and more rarely: it met six times in 1937, four times in 1938 and twice in 1939,[100] although in theory it was the supreme body exercising power. What did occur was that Litvinov had frequent contact with Stalin, such contacts being more influential than the process of voting in the Politburo, which in practice almost never functioned effectively.

---

[96] Orlov, Aleksandr: *Secret History of Stalin's Crimes*, 1953 Edition p.96, 1954 p.108

[97] Zaloga, Steven: *Target America*, p.13

[98] Watson, Derek: 'The Politburo and Foreign Policy in the 1930s', in *The Nature of Stalin's Dictatorship*, p.140

[99] Phillips, Hugh: *Between the Revolution and the West*, p.111

[100] Watson, Derek: 'The Politburo and Foreign Policy in the 1930s', in *The Nature of Stalin's Dictatorship*, p.152

Litvinov sat on various commissions, for example, in 1931, he sat with Stalin, Voroshilov and Molotov on a commission to reduce the military danger in the Far East, and in 1935, with Stalin in the chair, to consider a new constitution for the Soviet Union and among the other members were Molotov, Voroshilov and Mikoyan.[101] On occasions Litvinov attended important events with members of the Politburo and other VIPs; for example, Litvinov accompanied Stalin to the funeral of Voikov, following his assassination.[102] There are examples to show how ineffective was the voting in both the Central Committee and the Politburo. Once Stalin indicated his decision when attending either the Central Committee or Politburo, the result was a foregone conclusion. For example, there was no argument against the NKVD moving to investigate Bukharin[103] or the decision of the Politburo to liquidate all Polish officers.[104]

Another sign of Litvinov's status in the regime was the fact that he was frequently mentioned in the Soviet press in complimentary terms. An example is an article which reported:

> A number of organs of the European press comparing the speech of the British representative, Lord Cushendun, to that of Litvinov noted the defeat of Lord Cushendun in this historic tournament. Comrade Litvinov's speech was filled with consciousness of his own merit and at the same time filled with substance.[105]

Stalin, when he decided what he wanted to do, carefully supervised both Molotov and Litvinov. Tucker mentioned that the Foreign Commissar acted as Stalin's man and Litvinov's total subjugation was shown by the existence in a room adjoining the Narkomindel of a special line to the Kremlin. 'If a visiting foreign envoy raised a question requiring any kind of policy decision, Litvinov communicated with Stalin before replying.'[106] However, would not British Foreign Secretaries communicate with the Prime Minister before coming to significant decisions? Molotov was also very much under Stalin's control. Rab Butler, the Conservative politician, reported to the Foreign Affairs Committee that Molotov constantly left the room, no doubt to obtain instructions from Stalin. Whenever the ambassador attempted to maintain a sustained argument, Molotov interrupted by stating that the Soviet Government had given their decision and passed on to the next item on the agenda.[107]

Nowhere is the relationship between Molotov and Stalin better indicated than when Stalin grossly misinterpreted the name of the Agricultural Commissariat, referring to Narkomzyem instead of Narkomzem. Molotov who followed suit explained: 'If I had said

---

[101] Watson, Derek: *Molotov*, pp.113 and 124

[102] Gitlow, Benjamin: *I Confess*, p.433

[103] Purges, Bukharin: Ch.16, Nos.54-65

[104] Ch.17, Katyn, No.65

[105] Slusser, George and Eudin, Xenia: *Soviet Foreign Policy 1928 to 1934*, vol 1 Document 7, p.92

[106] Tucker, Robert: *Stalin in Power*, p.513

[107] CAB, 25, p.291

it correctly, Stalin would have felt I was correcting him and, being touchy and proud, he would have taken offence.'[108] Naimark made the point that, as between Molotov and Stalin: 'There was no question who was boss' and who was making Soviet policy, and 'Stalin watched Molotov like a hawk.'[109] Barmine asserts that Molotov acted purely as a rubber stamp for Stalin's decisions.[110]

I prefer the above interpretation as to the relationship between Molotov and Stalin than Zhukov's claim that Molotov did provide some debate. Zhukov states that after 'differences and serious argument erupted between them, it yielded a good solution in the end.'[111] That was an optimistic assessment. Certainly, the right decision was not reached over the failure to anticipate the German invasion, as , according to Zhukov the decision to rearm was taken too late[112] and the failure to withdraw, which resulted in the Russian armies being surrounded around Kiev and Kharkov. Further, by the late 40s Stalin no longer trusted Molotov, contrary to Zhukov's understanding. In his biography of Zhukov, Simonov suggests, as does Khrushchev, that Molotov stood up to Stalin.[113] However, Zhukov and Simonov's interpretation is not very convincing in view of what is stated above and the fact that, although we have considerable knowledge of the events preceding Barbarossa, Molotov never formed independent opinions. When Molotov became, in later life, very much subservient to his wife Polino, Stalin's daughter describes how Molotov 'yessed' his wife in the same way he had previously 'yessed' Stalin.[114]

General Bernard Montgomery on a visit to Stalin also confirms that all the Soviet Ministers seemed to be in awe of Stalin and shut up in his presence. Stalin would 'rag his politicians with great enjoyment' in Montgomery's presence. Stalin obviously regarded Montgomery as a soldier like himself and therefore capable of appreciating humour directed against politicians.[115]

In summary, there is no evidence that Molotov ever persuaded Stalin to pursue a different policy from that which he had already decided. Volkogonov could not find one case where any of the elite in government disagreed.[116] However, he is wrong concerning Litvinov. There are a significant number of instances where Stalin and Litvinov disagreed and Litvinov was not afraid to air his differences with Stalin.

---

[108] Tucker, Robert: *Stalin in Power*, p.586

[109] Naimark, Norman: 'Cold War Studies and New Archive Material of Stalin', in *Russian Review*, January 2002, p.7

[110] Barmine, Alexandre: *Memoirs of a Soviet Diplomat*, p.285

[111] Zhukov, Georgii: *Reflections and Reminiscences*, vol.1, p.371

[112] Gromyko, Andrea: *Memoirs*, p 187

[113] Khrushchev, Nikita: *Vospominaniya Ogenek*, No.376, September 1989; and Simonov N. Zhukov', in *Polkovodets I Chelovek*, No.2, Moscow 1988, pp.201 and 202

[114] Alliluyeva, : *Svetiana, Only one year* p.384

[115] Montgomery, Bernard: *Memoirs*, p.453

[116] Volkogonov, Dmitri: *Stalin*, p.220

Volkogonov stated that the only time Molotov disobeyed his leader was when Molotov and Malenkov, having debated the matter with their colleagues, decided to confer two honours as a mark of respect for Stalin's seventieth birthday: Hero of the Soviet Union and Generalissimo of the Soviet Union. However, they did not tell Stalin, who first heard of it when he opened his *Pravda* the next day. Stalin went to the Kremlin in a rage and summoned Molotov, Malenkov, Beria, Kalinin and Zhdanov. Stalin gave them a severe dressing down. Kalinin, whose office was nominally responsible, and Malenkov, who had failed to restrain the loyal impulse of his colleagues, were the most terrified. Molotov, as well as Beria and Zhdanov, knew Stalin's rage was a fake.[117] Although Stalin said he would not accept the medals, he did so just before the May Day celebrations.[118]

However, an occasion when Molotov did take an independent line which Volkogonov overlooked was when it had been decided to blow up the Cathedral of Christ the Redeemer, which stood on the proposed site for the Congress of the Soviets. Molotov thought the design was absurd because the structure was so huge that Lenin's head on the statue that surrounded it could not be seen from the entrance. Consequently, he would not authorise the work until forced to do so by Stalin and Voroshilov when they attended the commission.[119]

After Churchill made his Fulton speech, which included the famous statement 'From Stettin in the Baltic to Trieste … an Iron Curtain has descended across the continent', Stalin sent for Molotov and talked for a good hour.[120] There is, however, no reason to think that Molotov desired or would have pursued a different policy than the one followed by Stalin.

Churchill made the surprising remark in a letter to Roosevelt that 'Molotov was a statesman and had freedom of action very different from Litvinov.'[121] However, it appears that Churchill's diagnosis is wrong and Molotov did not have the freedom of action that Churchill believed.

Hindus describes Litvinov as 'an ideal man for Stalin's immediate purpose' of keeping the Soviet Union at peace so Stalin's plan of rapid industrialisation would not be hampered by external conflicts:

> His years of sojourn in the West, particularly his ten years he had spent in England, his marriage to a brilliant English woman, his studies of European and particularly

---

[117] Ibid. p.525
[118] Ibid.
[119] Watson, Derek: *Molotov*, p.106
[120] Volkogonov, Dmitri: *Stalin*, p.530
[121] Churchill, Winston: *The Second World War*, vol.4, 'The Hinge of Fate', p.280

British history and diplomacy, gave him a knowledge of the West which Stalin prized highly.[122]

Otherwise, surely Litvinov's indiscretions, especially in his later life, would not have gone unpunished. Why Stalin, if he trusted Litvinov, wanted to undermine his authority by imprisoning and executing many of his staff is a mystery. The same applies to why Stalin wanted to move against those in his commissariat such as Krestinsky, who was alleged to be pro-German, if eventually Stalin might move in such a direction. It shows the sadistic streak in Stalin. Fischer was basically correct when he stated: 'Soviet foreign policy followed the pattern of Litvinov's mind more than of his chief between 1929 and May 1939.'[123] I believe the answer is in the affirmative only because Stalin normally agreed with the policy that Litvinov was pursuing. The main exception was Spain. Stalin was more likely to give greater control to Litvinov if he, Stalin, was distracted by other matters. We have seen that, during the period of the Great Purges, internal repression took precedence over questions of foreign policy. This meant that no department of government would be excluded from the Purges, even if its effectiveness suffered.

To what extent did Litvinov believe he had a free hand in foreign policy? Unfortunately, Litvinov was not consistent. We have evidence as to what he thought of his power in his conversation with Norman Davis. At the time of the Brussels Conference on Japanese Aggression against China, Norman Davis stated that, when Litvinov used to attend international conferences before the autumn of 1937, he was accompanied by a few young men. At the 1937 Conference Norman Davis stated that the US embassy reported the following diplomatic gossip:

> Litvinov's position is not as strong as it once was. The younger men who are now surrounding Stalin have no knowledge of Europe, despise all foreigners and want to withdraw the Soviet Union into her own shell and concentrate on its [the Soviet Union's] own development, rather than foreign politics. Litvinov was accompanied by a high ranking official this time, Potemkin.

However, it appears that Davis might well be wrong, because Litvinov stated: 'As he was still given a pretty free hand in formulating Russian policy, he must take the rap for any failures.' Litvinov also implied that the decision as to whether to attend the Brussels Conference was his alone.[124] The reason why Litvinov's assistant Potemkin attended the Conference may have been for no other reason than that Litvinov had decided he might not want to attend the Conference for its full duration and had therefore decided to take his assistant with him. In fact, Litvinov left before the end of the conference. However, this is completely at variance with what Litvinov told Fischer in September 1938: 'I am a mere

---

[122] Hindus, Maurice: *Crisis in the Kremlin*, p 49
[123] Fischer, Louis: *Men and Politics*, p.124
[124] Moffat, Jay: *Moffat Papers*, p.174

messenger boy. I hand up the papers.'[125] Later, when Litvinov was ambassador to the United States, he told Hindus: 'I cannot be an errand boy any longer. Any clerk in my embassy can do the work I am supposed to do.'[126]

As one would normally expect in any state, all major decisions were taken by Stalin after he, as leader, consulted with whom he wished. However according to Zhukov, Molotov was always there and therefore he is responsible like Stalin for why the German invasion threat was not taken more seriously, supported by what Zhukov stated that the decision to rearm was taken too late.

In most states which are democracies, major decisions of foreign policy are taken by the executive. In the USA such decisions are taken by the President, after consulting the Secretary of State. In Great Britain, although there is a system of Cabinet government, dominant Prime Ministers, like Blair and Thatcher, with their enthusiasm to be seen on the world stage, exercise tremendous influence over foreign affairs. On the other hand, occasionally in Britain strong Foreign Ministers like Austen Chamberlain or Ernest Bevin, because of their dominant characters, determined many foreign policy issues themselves.[127]

A Foreign Secretary normally would not act independently of the Prime Minister or Cabinet, any more than in the USA the Secretary of State would not act independently of the President. It can be argued that Litvinov had no more opportunity to pursue an independent policy than Eden enjoyed under Baldwin and Halifax under Chamberlain. Although Baldwin was a rare example of a British Prime Minister who had little or no interest in foreign affairs and left it to his Foreign Minister, he limited Eden's authority by telling him that on no account must Britain go to war with the Soviet Union over Spain.[128] Similarly, Eden was told by Chamberlain that on no account would Chamberlain agree to sanctions against Japan,[129] as Hoover forbade his Secretary of State Stimson from agreeing to sanctions against Japan.[130]

The most difficult question to answer is how different Soviet foreign policy would have been if Molotov had been foreign minister in the 30s instead of Litvinov. The style would certainly have been different. Molotov would not have made the same friends and won the same respect from many non-communist democratic politicians. With Litvinov as Foreign Commissar, the Soviet Union enjoyed a much higher profile among many non-communist democratic politicians and the public in democratic countries than would have otherwise been the case. This profile would have been higher still had it not been for the purges. Another factor working against Soviet prestige and influence was Stalin's policy of

---

[125] Fischer, Louis: *Russia's Road From Peace to War*, p.290
[126] Hindus, Maurice: *Crisis in the Kremlin*, p.44
[127] Mackintosh, John: *The British Cabinet*, p.462
[128] See Ch.15, No.10
[129] Ibid. No.96
[130] See Ch.7, No.87

deliberately and constantly antagonising the Western democracies, such as imprisoning Soviet employees of the democracies' embassies in Moscow.

Litvinov probably had a certain amount of sympathy for Britain, although he was annoyed at the continued hostility of the Conservative Right towards the USSR. Nevertheless, Hochman is right to state that there is no evidence for the theory any such sympathies affected the way he conducted foreign policy or diminished his support of the Rapallo policy. Even after Hitler gained power in Germany, Litvinov was not enthusiastic about abandoning the Rapallo policy.[131]

Hochman refers to the different interpretations of Litvinov's power. Roberts is right to state that Litvinov did not pursue an independent course. Beloff, in agreement with Barmine, rightly affirms that if it was a matter in which Stalin was interested, there would be no debate.[132] Litvinov, as long as he was Foreign Commissar, did have a fairly free hand in the day-to-day running of foreign policy,[133] except when his views conflicted with Stalin's wishes. We now know that Litvinov sent reports almost daily to Stalin via Molotov, who was asking for approval of various foreign policy decisions. Stalin's office diary indicates that every time Stalin saw Litvinov in 1939, Molotov accompanied him;[134] but it seems that Litvinov had a hot line to Stalin personally.[135]

However, if it was not a matter in which Stalin was interested, the extent of Litvinov's powers is illustrated by Hindus's experiences. When Litvinov was Deputy Foreign Commissar, a parcel belonging to Hindus was impounded at the Soviet-Finnish border. The GPU border official stated it would be waiting at the Soviet Embassy in Helsinki. When it did not arrive, Litvinov intervened.

The very next day the parcel was located and the person who had found the parcel enquired where the Foreign Office wished it to be sent. When Hindus met Litvinov on the train, Litvinov told Hindus: 'The man who took away your sealed package was punished.'[136] In 1933, after an American journalist was threatened with expulsion by the censor for correctly describing the famine, Litvinov involved himself in the matter and prevented his expulsion.[137]

Litvinov's influence was still sufficient, during the period he was the Soviet ambassador to the USA, to obtain for Hindus a visa, although Hindus could not obtain it from Litvinov's

---

[131] Hochman, Jiri: *The Soviet Union and the Failure of Collective Security*, p.30 and see ch 8 No. 121

[132] Barmine, Alexandre: *One Who Survived*, p.212

[133] Hochman, Jiri: *The Soviet Union and the Failure of Collective Security*, p.30; Beloff, Max: *The Foreign Policy of Soviet Russia*, p.90; Roberts, Henry: *Diplomats*, pp.364 and 370

[134] Watson, Derek: 'The Politburo and Foreign Policy in the 1930s', in *The Nature of Stalin's Dictatorship*, p.141

[135] See No 106. *ante*

[136] Hindus, Maurice: *Crisis in the Kremlin*, p.50

[137] Ibid. p.51

predecessor.[138] After Litvinov had returned from Washington to Moscow, Hindus, who was at that time in Moscow, received two requests from New York editors for information on various aspects of wartime relations between the Soviet Union and the USA. Litvinov responded: 'I must tell you frankly I have no influence' with Stalin. Litvinov paused and then added, 'I know Stalin should honour this request.' He did not finish the sentence, but then said, 'I will see to it.' He finally stated: 'It had been brought to Stalin's attention.' However, Stalin did not reply.[139] When Hindus later made another request, Litvinov was not even prepared to help, and declared: 'There is really nothing I can do.'[140]

An example of when Litvinov's debating skills were successful was when he told the French ambassador 'he had to struggle against certain of his colleagues who desired the Soviet Government should demonstrate its desire for autocracy by renouncing the Franco-Soviet Pact, whose ratification had been awaited for nine months.'[141] This is an example where Litvinov's influence was sufficient to prevent the main focus of Soviet foreign policy of reaching an agreement with Germany, which many favoured, rather than Litvinov's preferred course of an agreement with Britain and France.

Roberts is one of the few historians to state that in many ways Litvinov's position was not unlike that of a British Foreign Secretary. Another person who clearly thought that Litvinov wielded some power and influence is Walters of the Secretariat of the League of Nations:

> It is not hard to see where a delegate is merely acting on instructions. Litvinov rarely asked for time to consult his government. He seemed always ready to decide on the spot whether to press his argument, to propose a compromise or to resign himself to accepting the majority.[142]

However, the difference between a British Foreign Secretary and Litvinov's office is that a British Foreign Secretary is equal to his other colleagues in coming to decisions on matters other than foreign policy, whereas Litvinov had no say whatever on matters other than foreign policy. A closer parallel is the US Secretary of State, whose duties are restricted to foreign affairs and other related matters.

Another fallacy subscribed to by many historians is that Litvinov kept aloof from the rivalry between Stalin and those to the Right and the Left. Litvinov undoubtedly, to a certain extent, supported Stalin in his rise to power.[143]

---

[138] Hindus, Maurice: *Crisis in the Kremlin*, p.43
[139] Ibid, p.44
[140] Ibid, p.46
[141] Watson, Derek: *Molotov*, p.151
[142] Roberts, Geoffrey: *Unholy Alliance*, p.49; Walters, Francis: *History of the League of Nations*, p.358
[143] Ch 9 No.4

Unlike Molotov, who did not say anything if he disagreed with Stalin, we have numerous instances of Litvinov openly disagreeing with Stalin, rather than maintaining silence as described below.

First, in 1921, Litvinov wanted to recognise Rumania's sovereignty over Bessarabia. Stalin and Chicherin disagreed.[144]

Second, Chicherin was enthusiastic about deepening the revolution in China. Litvinov advocated caution and argued that the Soviet Government should only play the trump card for the purpose of putting pressure on Britain. When Chicherin accused Litvinov of wanting to sell China down the river, Litvinov replied that it would be better to sell China down the river than miss the bus on concrete political opportunities.[145] Stalin on this occasion supported Chicherin against Litvinov and gave Litvinov a reprimand. Stalin complained to Litvinov:

> Reports have reached me that you speak of Karakhan and the policy he is carrying out in the sharpest terms. You do not hesitate to call this policy adventurous and Karakhan a rascal. Bear in mind Karakhan is carrying out in China, not his personal policy, but acts in accordance with the directives of the Politburo.[146]

Third, in 1929, Litvinov wanted to come to an agreement with Britain concerning Afghanistan, but Stalin did not. Litvinov argued that agreement was possible over Afghanistan and the East, but his Government (USSR) took a different view.[147]

Fourth, the Politburo, in the autumn of 1934, approved designation of a border zone along its western border in which nobody could enter without special permission. The result of this policy was the deportation of many Poles and Germans who were living there. By 1936 there were moves to implement such a policy in the Far East. The policy was courageously opposed by Maxim Litvinov, who considered it contrary to the Portsmouth Treaty, which forbade military measures on the Korean borders. Litvinov succeeded in preventing a change of policy until July 1937, but, after the intervention of Yezhov and Voroshilov, the ethnic cleansing of the border areas proceeded at full speed, in spite of Litvinov's opposition.[148]

A more frivolous occasion was at a social gathering in 1943 with Stalin, Litvinov and various foreign visitors, including Joseph Davies, former US ambassador who happened to

---

[144] Carr, Edward: *Bolshevik Revolution 1917-1923*, vol.3, p.346

[145] Hilger, Gustav: *Incompatible Allies*, p.112

[146] Dallin, David: *Rise of Russia in Asia*, p.241

[147] Fischer, Louis: *Men and Politics*, p.125

[148] Martin, Terry: *The Affirmative Action: Empire, Nations and Nationalism in the Soviet Union 1923-1939*, p.334

be a Soviet sympathiser. He showed a film about himself which included purge trials and put them in a favourable light. The foreign visitors were embarrassed as the film contained many inaccuracies, but Stalin kept a serious face. The Soviet viewers were quiet, although even they giggled at the historical absurdities, whereas Litvinov muttered 'Silly.'[149] On other occasions Litvinov criticised Stalin's policy to others.

First, he expressed his displeasure about the purges in the 1930s to Hilger.[150]

Second, in 1932 (when an émigré Socialist, Yu Denike, at a meeting in Geneva, complained of the disastrous policy of the German Communists who were attacking the Socialists rather than the Nazis), Litvinov expressed his full agreement with the Socialists in evaluating the Nazi danger, but said he could exert no influence on policy with which he was not in agreement. One of the participants told Yu Denike he was convinced of both Litvinov's sincerity and the fact that the disastrous policy of the German Communists was the result of a decision of the highest authorities in Moscow.[151]

This is confirmed by Hilger, who recalls during a stay in Lausanne in 1932 he received s delegation of of European Socialists .who pointed out the dangers of letting the Nazi's in Germany grow strong and who tried to convince him of common action by all states against Germany. Litvinov told them that he was not in agreement with his Government's policy towards National Socialism, but he was in no position to exert his influence in the suggested direction.[152]

Third, according to Litvinov's daughter, her father, as a staunch supporter of Republican Spain, was critical of the way Stalin intervened and then did not see it through.[153] Presumably, in the absence of determination to assist Republican Spain, Litvinov thought that the Non-Intervention Committee was the next best option because, if it could be rigorously enforced, it would have favoured the Spanish Government; but as it had not been enforced, it had favoured the rebels. Disagreements, if not known to the wider world, were rightly suspected. *The New York Times* reported in 1937 that Litvinov and Maisky wanted to co-operate with Britain and France in the Non-Intervention Committee in Spain, but Stalin was unyielding.[154]

Fourth, in 1939, the economic negotiations with Germany were opposed by Litvinov because of the possibility of German spies.[155]

---

[149] Eubank, Keith: *Summit at Teheran*, p.85
[150] Hilger, Gustav: *Incompatible Allies*, p.111
[151] Lederer, Ivo (editor): *Russian Foreign Policy Essays in Historical Perspective*, p.229
[152] Hilger, Gustav: *Incompatible Allies*, p.112
[153] Tanya
[154] *The New York Times*, 29 October 1937, p.4; Ch.15, No.62
[155] Carley, Michael: *1939*, p.91

Fifth, Litvinov criticised Soviet censorship of newspapers comparing the situation unfavourably with the USA.[156]

Sixth, in 1944, when Litvinov was interviewed by the American journalist Edgar Snow, Litvinov stated that the Foreign Commissariat was run by three men who did not understand Britain or the USA: Molotov, Vyshinsky and Dekanozov. Litvinov was especially critical of Dekanozov, 'who sat next to Ribbentrop for a year and that is all he knows about Europe.'[157] He deplored the low standard of diplomacy in the Foreign Commissariat, saying: 'If British diplomats were as bad as ours, the USA might fight Britain instead of the Soviet Union.'[158]

Finally, when he was the wartime ambassador to the USA he made known to White House officials his criticisms of his government in the following respects:

1. Notwithstanding his important post as ambassador to the USA, the Soviet Government 'neither sent him any instructions nor kept him informed of its policies.'[159]

2. Molotov, on becoming Foreign Commissar, had removed from the Foreign Commissariat 'every important official who had experience with the outside world and any personal knowledge of the United States or of the Western democracies.'[160]

3. Litvinov criticised Stalin because he was entirely unaware of the fact that 'public opinion in the USA was a determining factor in the creation of US Government policy.'[161]

4. The centralisation of power, because 'everything was centred on one individual – Stalin himself.'[162]

Litvinov's criticism of the Soviet Government also increased in the later years of the war and in the early part of the post-war period.[163]

Among historians in recent years there have been various revisionists' opinions to challenge the traditional favourable perception of Litvinov, but I believe they have little merit.

---

[156] See Ch.17, No.80
[157] Snow, Edgar: *Journey to the Beginning*, p.314
[158] Ibid.   p.316
[159] FRUS, 1943, vol.3, p.519
[160] FRUS, 1943, vol.3, p.522
[161] Ibid.
[162] Ibid.   p.523
[163] Ch.17, No.163; Ch.18, No.12; Hottelet interview, No.16

Initially, it was Roberts who tried to argue, against overwhelming evidence, that Litvinov was unenthusiastic about the proposed pact with Britain and France, while Molotov was more in favour.[164]

Second, Watson is probably correct that Litvinov was held in low esteem by various members of the Politburo, as he did not hunt and had a distinctive lifestyle;[165] but I do not believe that this was Stalin's opinion, who spared him and his wife from the purges in spite of conduct such as his wife writing to a US citizen criticising Stalin's Soviet Union.[166] and Litvinov's criticism of Stalin culminating in the Hottelet interview.[167] In 1936 Litvinov received the 'Order of Lenin' and later the Order of the Red Banner in the Second World War.

Third, although Watson tries to argue that Litvinov's low esteem is proved by the comparative few occasions Stalin's office diary shows Litvinov in attendance,[168] but I believe it is highly probable that Litvinov saw Stalin when it was not recorded in Stalin's office diary. Examples are when Stalin agreed to give Litvinov his dacha when Stalin called in Litvinov about the letter Litvinov's wife wrote and when Litvinov pleaded for Boris Stomoniakov.[169]

Fourth, Watson agreed that Litvinov was 'often summoned to and consulted by the Politburo;'[170] and he would not have been asked to attend unless his opinion was considered valuable.

Fifth, often very complimentary reports appeared in the Soviet press.[171]

Sixth, Litvinov was given a prestigious constituency in the elections.[172]

Finally, Litvinov was called upon to make key speeches such as those speeches to the Central Committee in 1928,[173] 1929[174] and 1933,[175] as well as an election speech in 1937.[176]

---

[164] Ch 14 No. 71

[165] Ch.3, No.121; Ch.16, No.108

[166] Ch.16, No.81

[167] Ch.18, No.12; Hottelet interview, Nos.16-20, 32

[168] See Watson, Derek: 'The Politburo and Foreign Policy in the 1930s', in *The Nature of Stalin's Dictatorship*, p.141

[169] See Ch.16, Nos.79 and 81

[170] Watson, Derek: 'The Politburo and Foreign Policy in the 1930s', in *The Nature of Stalin's Dictatorship*, p.141

[171] See 105 *ante*, where Litvinov was praised for a speech made at the Disarmament Conference

[172] See Ch.18, No.14

[173] Documents, 1928, p.169

[174] Documents, 1929, p.188

[175] Litvinov speech: *Moscow News*, 6 January 1934, pp.4 and 14

[176] Ibid, 8 December 1937, p.4; speech: 27 November 1937

Litvinov has attained a considerable reputation as an authority on such matters as disarmament and security, as well as on what amounts to aggression, being quoted by a Finish politician as well as Eden; and in November 1946 that effective disarmament cannot occur if there is no system of verification and inspection.[177]

An entirely different line of criticism levelled against Litvinov was that, in the negotiations with France and Britain prior to Litvinov's dismissal in May 1939, he was not harsh enough with Britain and France, while Stalin and Molotov was in favour of obtaining a better deal for the Soviet Union. That argument would be valid if they had managed to conclude an agreement with an adequate military protocol, so if the Soviet Union was attacked, Britain and France were committed to defend her militarily and they failed to do so.

Obviously, Litvinov was not so tough, because he was anxious to conclude the agreement with Britain and France as he thought that was the right policy and because he was afraid, as he was proved right, that, in his words, 'the bandits [Germany] would come to Moscow and conclude a pact with Hitler.'[178]

While Watson and Resis are highly critical of Litvinov, nowhere do they mention the disastrous policy which Stalin and Molotov were pursuing.[179] These two were wallowing in self-congratulation,[180] instead of concentrating their efforts on planning to defend their country against a probable attack. Molotov's argument that they did not want to provoke Germany was feeble.[181] While Stalin and Molotov thought they were clever, they were in fact stupid.

Perhaps the most important question has two sides to it. First, would Litvinov have ascertained German plans to invade the Soviet Union? Second, would he then have had the courage to tell Stalin? I believe the answers to both questions are in the affirmative. Litvinov's ability to foresee the invasion is indicated by Molotov's statement that the Soviets knew the invasion was coming. Molotov was proud that the USSR supposedly delayed it for a year and 10 months.[182]

My belief that Litvinov would have stood his ground on the crunch issue of the war is suggested by the fact that some soldiers were prepared to risk Stalin's wrath by disagreeing with him and even disobeying him. For example, on 21 June, Frolov asked to be allowed to move his rifle and armoured troops as a precaution against a possible German attack. The Defence Commissariat refused, but nevertheless in the afternoon Frolov began to move the

---

[177] Ch.6, No.85; *The New York Times*, 15 November 1946, p.3

[178] Roberts, Henry, in *Diplomats*, edited by Gordon Craig and Felix Gilbert, p.359

[179] Resis, Albert: 'Fall of Litvinov', in *Europe-Asia Studies*, vol.52, No.1, 2000, pp.45 and 46

[180] See Ch.14, No.111

[181] See Nos 182 & 191 post

[182] Chuev, Felix: *Molotov Remembers*, p.22

42nd and 52nd Rifles into position.[183] Again, Zhukov advised Stalin for good military reasons to give up Kiev. Stalin exploded, but Zhukov stood his ground. He said that, if Stalin thought he was talking rubbish, then Zhukov had better resign. He was replaced as Chief of Staff. With the encirclement of the Soviet army at Kiev, Zhukov was proved right.[184] Furthermore, in the spring of 1942 Vasilevsky insisted that, without reserves in the vicinity, the Kharkov offensive must be called off. Stalin talked to Timoshenko that night, who wrongly assured Stalin that the reserves were adequate. However, on 18 May Kleist tore a forty-mile gap in the 9th Army positions and laid bare the communications of Soviet soldiers in the bulge. Vasilevsky again approached Stalin to call off the offensive, but Stalin returned an obdurate refusal. Only on 19 May 1942 did Timoshenko order a halt to the offensive, but it was too late. The Germans took 200,000 prisoners.[185]

Military failures often caused the wrath of Stalin to descend on the commanders involved, who may not have felt confident enough and brave enough to defend themselves. However, when Stalin criticised Voroshilov for the failures in the Soviet-Finnish war, Voroshilov had the audacity to blame Stalin – with considerable justification. He said to Stalin: 'You are the one who annihilated the old guard of the Army. You had the best generals killed.' When Stalin rebuffed Voroshilov, he picked up his platter of roast suckling pig and smashed it on the table. Although he was relieved of his position as Commissar of Defence, neither his life nor his liberty were threatened.[186]

This incident reveals Stalin to be a cowardly bully. The best way to deal with Stalin was to stand up to him, as Voroshilov did on this occasion. Litvinov acted similarly. Meekness was not rewarded by Stalin, as Bukharin found out.

Molotov's views may not have been totally aligned with those of Stalin, but he was unwilling to act on them. Molotov disagreed with the Stalin policy of 'Socialism in One Country.' He felt it ran counter to Marxism-Leninism. Nevertheless, Molotov stated: 'I could not speak. How could I? I would be kicked out like a rag.'[187] This indicates that he was similar to most other people in dealing with Stalin. Rather than give Stalin their independent judgment, all they did was to anticipate what Stalin desired. Therefore, it was not likely that Molotov would be the one to try and persuade Stalin to alter his opinion in underestimating the German threat of invasion.

In 1941 Molotov, as Commissar for Foreign Affairs, was in charge of the apparatus which brought him intelligence from his foreign embassies relating to the planned invasion. Zubok stated that Molotov received dozens of ciphered cables from embassies all over the

---

[183] Erickson, John: *Road to Stalingrad*, p.103
[184] Ibid, p.178
[185] Ibid, p.347
[186] Khrushchev, Nikita: *Khrushchev Remembers*, p.154
[187] Chuev, Felix: *Molotov Remembers*, p.284

world, as well as reports from intelligence stations.[188] Shortly after the fall of France, reports came through from Soviet agents in Europe indicating that Hitler might turn East. Molotov had the advantage that the other Soviet leaders did not possess. He was able to go to see Hitler, and that is what he did. Unfortunately, Molotov entirely misunderstood Hitler. Molotov reported to Stalin, following his visit in November 1940: 'Hitler would not attack us.' It was the Foreign Commissar's duty to decide which information his department was receiving from various sources was reliable and this he failed to do. Molotov optimistically reported: 'The great interest of Hitler is to reach an agreement with us and strengthen his friendship with us over spheres of influence.' In a way, that was correct, in that Hitler wished the Soviet Union to move east against India and thus leave Hitler in sole control of Europe.[189] However, Molotov failed to understand what Litvinov had long understood: namely, the threat from Germany. Hitler's flattery would have made no impact on Litvinov, who fully appreciated the German menace.

The only error Molotov was prepared to admit was that the USSR should have perceived that, if Germany was going to attack the Soviet Union, June was the best month; and that the Soviet Union 'could have been 5% better prepared.'[190] This was not the private opinion of Zhukov. Gromyko states that Zhukov told him that before the war the political decision to arm fully was taken too late and that was the problem.[191] The trouble was that, before the Soviet Union overran Eastern Poland, a defence line − 'The Stalin Line' − had been constructed and then abandoned, against the advice of Zhukov, and there was no time to build an alternative.[192]

Pavlov, the Commander of the Western Front, had communicated to Stalin, Molotov and Timoshenko that it was urgent that the road-building programme on the Western Front, which was scheduled to take place over several years, should be completed during 1941. Further, the Command Centres proved to be totally inadequate for war-time duties.[193] Therefore, Molotov's explanation that they were 95% ready for the German attack seems totally inadequate.

What was far more serious was the loss of approximately 1200 planes at the main 66 airbases within hours of the war's beginning. Even the most elementary precautions were overlooked. Planes were lined up un-camouflaged in inviting rows.[194] If precautions had been taken even 24 hours before the German attack, many of these planes might well have been saved. France and Britain lost many planes in the German invasion of France because the planes were allowed to remain on the ground and so become sitting targets.

---

[188] Zubok, Vladislav: *Inside the Kremlin's Cold War*, p.84
[189] Haslam, Jonathan: 'Soviet-German Relations and the Origins of the Second World War: The jury is still out', in *Journal of Modern History*, December 1997, p.788
[190] Chuev, Felix: *Molotov Remembers*, p.27
[191] Gromyko, Andrei: *Memoirs*, p.187
[192] Overy, Richard: *Russia's War*, p.65
[193] Zhukov, Georgii: *Memoirs*, p. 200
[194] Overy, Richard: *Russia's War*, p.76

However, in the Battle of Britain, Germany's losses were greater than Britain's by a factor of two to one. This amounted to Germany losing some two thousand planes. Britain had learned the lessons of the French campaign. The defence of airfields against bombing was of prime importance. It was understood that planes in the sky were less vulnerable than if they were on the ground. However, these lessons were lost on the Soviets.

Litvinov felt he had a mission to prevent war. Military tactics were of no interest to him, so if he had been Commissar for Foreign Affairs and Stalin had sought his input he no doubt would have advised Stalin to rely on his military experts for advice.

Khrushchev, in his Secret Speech, revealed that on 22 May 1941 the Deputy Military Attaché cabled to say that the reported attack was scheduled for 1 June and the Soviet embassy in London cabled that Cripps, Britain's Left-wing ambassador, had been able to ascertain the attack was scheduled for the middle of June.[195]

Khrushchev did not disclose in his speech that, on 10 June 1941, Maisky was summoned to see Sir Alexander Cadogan, Permanent Secretary at the Ministry of Foreign Affairs. He was informed in great detail that German troops were moving towards the German-Soviet frontier. Maisky realised that it was in Britain's interests for war to break out between Germany and the Soviet Union. Nevertheless, in Maisky's words, 'the information was so precise and concrete that it should give Stalin serious thought to check the information and in any case give strict instructions to our Western Frontier to be on their guard.'

When Stalin and Molotov received Maisky's report of his meeting with Cadogan, not only warning of the attack but giving the actual details, Stalin and Molotov treated the information in a cavalier way. They published a Tass report stating: 'Relations with Germany were normal and Germany's intention to tear up the pact and undertake an attack on the USSR is devoid of any foundation.'[196] Molotov justified the action taken on the grounds that it was, supposedly, a highly responsible action and the move was aimed at depriving the Germans of any excuse for an attack.[197]

What is still not known is whether Molotov was confident that Germany would not attack, in which case, few can dispute that Litvinov was right to consider Molotov a fool; or whether for his own safety Molotov failed to warn Stalin, in which case Molotov should be considered a coward. Not everybody took this line. At least some of the Soviet generals were prepared to give Stalin advice which he did not want to receive. Would Litvinov as Foreign Commissar have done better than Molotov? He could hardly have done worse.

---

[195] 'Anatomy of Terror', Stalin's Secret Speech, p.45
[196] Maisky, Ivan: *Memoirs of a Soviet Ambassador*, p.149
[197] Chuev, Felix: *Molotov Remembers*, p.31

The warning that Sheinis alleges Litvinov gave to Stalin at the Central Committee is in doubt, [198] particularly as Litvinov did not think that Hitler would be foolish enough to attack the Soviet Union until Germany had defeated Britain.[199]

It is my view that Litvinov would not have been as complacent as Molotov. Even if the early warning by Great Britain was an attempt by Britain to sabotage the Nazi-Soviet pact,[200] if the reports from the Soviet spy in Tokyo, Sorge, were the result of deliberately erroneous information being fed to him and if the frequent invasions of Soviet airspace by Germany were all attempts to provoke the Soviet Union to retaliate, surely the most elementary step Molotov should have taken was to have sent one of his trusted officials to physically investigate the border territory. No doubt he would have observed what a Japanese general saw on 18 June 1941 when travelling from Berlin to Moscow by train: the ceaseless activity of Wehrmacht units moving up to the Soviet frontier.[201] Litvinov, also, unlike Molotov, would have taken seriously Maisky's warning, as Litvinov had great respect for his ambassador to Britain. By 1941, Maisky was an ambassador of great experience and he also enjoyed many contacts with influential figures in the British establishment who had opposed Chamberlain's foreign policy and others on the Left who sympathised with Russia but were not communists. Would not Litvinov have considered Maisky to be the best judge as to whether the information provided by Cadogan was true or false? Maisky certainly thought it was more likely to be true than false.

Litvinov correctly predicted that the whole of Europe would fall under German domination before it occurred. Stalin's action in dismissing Litvinov was in my view the most costly mistake that any Russian politician had ever committed. It cost twenty million Soviet lives and by 1945 had produced a country which was left in ruins, from Moscow to Leningrad and Stalingrad to the Polish border!

---

[198] Ch.14 no 116
[199] Archives Box 7
[200] See Ch.17, No.2
[201] Tolstoy, Nikolai: *Secret War*, p.223

EXPLANATIONS

'Tanya' refers to conversations with the author between 2002 and 2004

'Archives' refers to Ivy Litvinov's papers lodged with the Stanford University, California

'Tanya's tape' refers to the taped conversation with a representative of the Imperial

War Museum, London

Details of the following items referred to in the footnotes are included in the bibliography

Primary Sources:

DBFP *Documents on British Foreign Policy*

DGFP *Documents on German Foreign Policy*

FRUS *Documents on the Foreign Relations of the United States*

Preparatory Minutes

Disarmament Minutes

Secondary Sources:

Survey of International Relations

The following words, when used in quotations, have been changed to reflect what the person intended to convey:

'England' for Britain

Since the formation of the Soviet Union in 1922, 'Russia' for the Soviet Union

'America' for the USA

PRIMARY SOURCES

Details of the following items referred to in the footnotes are included in the bibliography

Documents: *Documents on International Affairs*, London, Oxford University Press

DBFP: *Documents on British Foreign Policy 1939*, Her Majesty's Stationery Office

DGFP: *Documents on German Foreign Policy*, London: HMSO (1957)

FRUS: *Documents on the Foreign Relations of the United States*, United States Government Printing Office

Preparatory Minutes: *Preparatory Minutes of the Disarmament Conference of the League of Nations 1925-1931*

Disarmament Minutes: *Minutes of the Disarmament Conference of the League of Nations 1932-1934*

'Archives' refers to Ivy Litvinov's papers lodged with Stanford University, California

'Tanya's tape' refers to the taped conversation with a representative of the Imperial

War Museum, London

Acton, E and Stableford, T: *The Soviet Union: A Documentary History*, Exeter: University of Exeter Press (2007)

Amery, Leo: *Amery Diaries, 1929-1945, The Empire at Bay* (edited by John Barnes and David Nicholson), London: Hutchinson (1988)

Blum, A: *From the Morgenthau Diaries: Years of Crisis 1928-1938*, Boston: Houghton Mifflin Company (1959)

Bruce Lockhart, R: *Diaries* (edited by Kenneth Young), London: Macmillan (1973)

Bullard, J and M: *Inside Stalin's Russia: The Diaries of Reader Bullard*, Charlbury: Day (2000)

Cadogan, Sir A: *The Diaries of Alexander Cadogan, 1938-1945* (edited by David Dilks), London: Cassell (1971)

Channon, Sir H: *Diaries of Sir Henry Channon*, London: Weidenfeld & Nicholson (1967)

Churchill, W: *Complete Speeches* (edited by R James), London and New York: Chelsea House in association with R R Bowker Co (1974)

Degras, J: *Royal Institute of International of Affairs Soviet Documents on Foreign Policy*, London: Oxford University Press (1951)

Eden, A: *Foreign Affairs* (speeches), London: Faber & Faber (1939)

Eudin, X and Slusser, R: *Soviet Foreign Policy 1928-1934*, Pennsylvania: Pennsylvania University Press (1967)

Gromyko, A: *Soviet Peace Efforts on the Eve of World War 2*, Moscow: Progress Publishers (1976)

Jones, T: *Diary with Letters 1931-1950*, London: Oxford University Press (1964)

Khrushchev, N: *Anatomy of Terror* (Stalin's Speech, 1956; introduction by Nathaniel Weyl), Washington DC: Public Affairs Press (1956)

Lih, Lars T, Naumov, Oleg, and Khlevniuk, Oleg V: *Stalin's Letters to Molotov 1925-1936* (trans. by Catherine A Fitzpatrick), New Haven and London: Yale University Press (1995)

Lockhart Diaries (edited by Kenneth Young, 1973), London: Macmillan (1980)

Moffat, J: *Moffat Papers*, Cambridge, Mass: Harvard University Press (1956)

Molotov's Speech: 2nd session of the Central Executive Committee

Molotov Statement of the Supreme Court Ratification of the Pact of Non-Aggression, August 1939, London: Modern Book

Molotov, Litvinov and Stalin: German Attack on the Soviet Union, London: Anglo-Russian Parliamentary Committee

Nicholas, H: *Washington Dispatches. 1941-1945*, London: Weidenfeld & Nicolson (1981)

Pownall, H: *Diaries*, vol.1 1933-1949, edited by Brian Bond, London: Leo Cooper (1972)

Sherwood, R: *The White House Papers of Harry Hopkins*, London: Eyre & Spottiswood (1948)

Sontag, R: 'Nazi-Soviet Relations 1939-1941', *Documents from the Archives of the German Foreign Office*, Washington DC: US Government Printing Office for the Secretary of State (1948)

SECONDARY SOURCES

Abraham R, *Alexander Kerensky*, London: Sidgwick & Jackson (1987)

Alliluyeva S, *Only One Year*, London: Hutchinson (1969)

Alliluyeva S, *Twenty Letters to a Friend* (tr. by Priscilla Johnson), Harmondsworth: Penguin (1968)

Amba A, *I was Stalin's Bodyguard* (tr. by Richard & Clara Winston), London: Frederick Muller (1952)

Andrews E, *The Writing on the Wall*, London, Sydney and Boston: Allen & Unwin (1987)

Applebaum A, *Gulag: History of Soviet Camps*, Allen Lane, an imprint of Penguin Books (2003)

Aster S, *Making of the Second World War*, London: Deutsch (1973)

Avrich P, *Kronstadt*, Princeton NJ: Princeton University Press (1921)

Bailey T, *Diplomatic History of the American People*, New York: Appleton

Century Crofts (1969)

Barmine A, *Memoirs of a Soviet Diplomat*, London: Lovat Dickson (1938)

Barmine A, *The One Who Survived*, New York: Putman (1945)

Beck J, *Final Report*, New York: Robert Spellers & Sons (1957)

Beckett F, *Stalin's British Victims*, Stroud: Sutton (2004)

Bedell-Smith W, *Moscow Mission 1946-1949*, London: William Heinemann (1950)

Beloff M, *Foreign Policy of Soviet Russia 1929-1941*, 2 Volumes, London: Oxford University Press (1947)

Beria S, *Beria My Father*, London: Duckworth (2001)

Besedovsky G, *Revelations of a Soviet Diplomat*, London: Williams & Norgate (1931)

Bethell N, *The War Hitler Won*, London: Allen Lane Penguin Press (1972)

Bettington C, *Cultural Walks 1 & 2, Exploring the Vanishing East End: Tower Hamlets.*

Bilainkin M, *Ten Years Ambassador*, Woking: George Allen and Unwin (1944)

Black C, *Franklin Delano Roosevelt, Champion of Freedom*, London: Weidenfeld & Nicolson (2003)

Bolloten B, *Spanish Civil War: Revolution and Counter Revolution*, New York: Harvester, Wheatsheaf (1991)

Boyd A, *Soviet Air Force Since 1918*, London: Macdonald & Jane's (1977)

Brovkin V, *Bolsheviks in Russian Society: The Revolution and the Civil Wars*, New Haven, London: Yale University Press (1977)

Browder R, *Origins of Soviet-American Diplomacy*, Princeton, NJ: Princeton Press (1958)

Bruce Lockhart R, *Memoirs of a British Agent*, London & New York: Putman (1941)

Bryant C, *Stafford Cripps: The First Modern Chancellor*, London: Hodder & Stoughton (1997)

Buchanan G, *My Mission to Moscow*, London: Cassell (1923)

Buchanan T, *The Spanish Civil War and the British Labour Movement*, Cambridge: Cambridge University Press (1991)

Budurowycz B, *Polish-Soviet Relations 1932-1939*, New York & London: Columbia University Press (1963)

Bullard W, *The Camels Must Go: An Autobiography*,

Bullitt W, *For the President, Personal and Secret: Correspondence between Franklin D Roosevelt and William C Bullitt*, Houghton Mifflin (1972)

Bullock A, *Hitler and Stalin, Parallel Lives*, London: Harper Collins (1991)

Butler R, *The Art of the Possible*, London: Hamish Hamilton (1971)

Carley M, *1939*, Chicago: Ivan R. Dee (1991)

Carr E, *The Bolshevik Revolution 1917-1923*, London: Macmillan & Co Ltd (1950)

Carr E, *Interregnum*, London: Macmillan Press (1954)

Carr E, *Socialism in One Country*, Macmillan & Co Ltd (1964)

Carr E, *Foundations of a Planned Economy*, London: Macmillan Press (1976)

Carr E, *German-Soviet Relations Between the Two World Wars 1919-1939*, London: Oxford University Press (1958)

Carr E, *Russian Revolution from Lenin to Stalin*, Basingstoke: Palgrave Macmillan (1979)

Carr E, *Twilight of the Comintern*, Basingstoke: Macmillan (1982)

Carswell J, *The Exile*, London: Faber & Faber (1983)

Carynnyk M, *The Foreign Office and the Famine*, Kingston, Ontario: Limestone Press (1988)

Cassidy H, *Moscow Dateline 1941-1943*, Boston: Houghton Mifflin Co (1943)

Chamberlain W, *Russian Revolution 1917-1921*, London: Macmillan & Co (1935)

Chisholm A and Davie M, *Beaverbrook: A Life*, London: Hutchinson (1992)

Chuev F, *Molotov Remembers*, Chicago: Ivan R. Dee (1993)

Churchill W, Vol.1: *The Gathering Storm*; Vol.2: *Their Finest Hour*; Vol.3: *Grand Alliance*; Vol.4: *Hinge of Fate*; Vol.5: *Closing the Ring*; Vol.6: *Triumph and Tragedy*. London: Cassell & Co (1948-1954)

Clark R, *Fall of the German Republic*, London: Allen and Unwin (1935)

Clements B, *Bolshevik Feminist: The Life of Aleksandra Kollontai*, Bloomington and London: Indiana University Press (1979)

Coates W & Z, *A History of Anglo-Soviet Relations*, London: Lawrence & Wishart (1943)

Conquest R, *Stalin and the Kirov Murder*, London: Hutchinson (1989)

Conquest R, *The Great Terror: A Reassessment*, London: Oxford University Press (1990)

Coogan T, *De Valera: Long Fellow, Long Shadow*, London: Hutchinson (1993)

Craig G, *Diplomats 1919-1939*, Princeton: Princeton University Press (1953)

Craig G. & Loewenheim F, *The Diplomats 1939 to 1979*, Princeton, NJ: Princeton University Press (1994)

Dallin D, *Rise of Russia in Asia*, London: Yale University Press (1949)

Dalton H, *Fateful Years*, London: Frederick Muller (1957)

Davies J, *Mission to Moscow*, London: Victor Gollancz (1942)

Davies N, *Europe: A History*, Oxford University Press (1996)

Debo R, *Revolution and Survival*: *The Foreign Policy of Soviet Russia 1918-1919*, Liverpool: Liverpool University Press (1979)

Debo R, *Survival and Consolidation*: *The Foreign Policy of Soviet Russia 1918-1921*, London: McGill-Queens University Press (1992)

De Gaulle C, *War Memoirs Salvation 1944-1946* (tr. by R Howard), London: Weidenfeld & Nicolson (1960)

Deutscher I, *The Prophet Armed: Trotsky 1879-1921*, London: Oxford University Press (1954)

Deutscher I, *The Prophet Unarmed 1921-1929: Trotsky*, London: Oxford University Press (1970)

Domarus M, *Hitler's Speeches and Proclamations 1932-1945*, London: Taurus (1992)

Dulles F, *The Road to Teheran*, Princeton: Princeton University Press (1944)

Dunbabin J P D, *The Great War, the Great Powers and their Allies*,

London & New York: Longmans (1994)

Dyck H, *Weimar Germany and Soviet Russia*, London: Chatto & Windus (1966)

Eden A, *The Eden Memoirs*: Vol.1 *Facing the Dictators*; Vol.2 *The Reckoning*, London: Cassell (1960-1965)

Ehrenburg I, *The War 1941-1945* (tr. by Tatiana Shebunina, in collaboration with Yvonne Kopp), London: MacGibbon & Kee (1964)

Ehrenburg I, *Post War Years 1945-1954* (tr. by Tatiana Shebunina), London: MacGibbon & Kee (1966)

Encyclopaedia American, New York: American Corporation New York (1977)

Englander D, *A Documentary History of Jewish Immigration in Britain 1840-1920*, Leicester: Leicester University Press (1994)

Erickson J, *Road to Stalingrad*, London: Weidenfeld & Nicolson (1975)

Estorick E, *Stafford Cripps, A Biography*, Melbourne: William Heinemann (1949)

Ettinger E, *Rosa Luxemburg's Letters to Leo Jogiche*, London: Pluto (1981)

Eubank K, *Munich*, Norman: University of Oklahoma Press (1963)

Eubank K, *Summit Conferences 1919-1960*, Norman: University of Oklahoma Press (1960)

Eubank K, *Summit at Teheran*, New York: William Morrow & Co (1985)

Farnsworth B, *Kollontai Socialism, Feminism and the Bolshevik Revolution*, Stanford: Stanford University Press (1980)

Fenby J, *Generalissimo Chiang Kai-Shek and the Nation He Lost*, London: Carroll & Grant (2004)

Figes O, *People's Tragedy*, London: Jonathan Cape (1997)

Fink C, *Genoa Conference*, Chapel Hill: London (1985)

Fischer L, *Life of Lenin,* London: Weidenfeld & Nicolson (1965)

Fischer L, *The Soviets in World Affairs*, London: Jonathan Cape (1930)

Fischer L, *Russia's Road From Peace to War*, London: Harper (1969)

Fischer L, *Great Challenge*, London: Jonathan Cape (1947)

Fischer L, *Life and Death of Stalin*, London: Jonathan Cape (1953)

Fischer L, *Men and Politics: Autobiography*, Westport, Conn: Greenwood Press (1941)

Fisher H, *Famine in Soviet Russia*, Freeport, NY: Book for Libraries Press (1927)

Fitzpatrick S (ed. by Alexander Rabinowitch and Richard Stites), *Russia in the Era of NEP: Explorations in Russian Society and Culture*, Bloomington: Indiana University Press (1991)

Furuya K, *Chang Kai-Shek, His Life and Times* (abridged English edition by Chung Ming Chan), New York: St John's University (1981)

Gaddis J, *Russia, The Soviet Union and the United States: An Interpretive History*, London and New York McGraw-Hill (1990)

Gafencu G, *The Last Days of Europe: A Diplomatic Journey in 1939*, London: Frederick Muller Ltd (1947)

London and New York: McGraw-Hill (1990)

Getty J, *Origins of the Great Purges: The Soviet Communist Party Reconsidered*, Cambridge: Cambridge University Press (1985)

Gilbert M, *Israel: A History*, London: Doubleday (1998)

Gitlow B, *The Whole of Their Lives*, Boston: Western Islands (1965)

Gitlow B, *I Confess: The Truth About American Communism*, New York: E P Dutton & Co (1940)

Gorodetsky G, *Precarious Truth: Anglo-Soviet Relations 1924-1927*, Cambridge: Cambridge University Press (1977)

Grayson R, *Austen Chamberlain and the Commitment to Europe*, London: Frank Cass (1997)

Grey I, *First Fifty Years in Soviet Russia 1917-1967*, London: Hodder & Stoughton (1967)

Gromyko A, *Pamiatnoe*, Moska Politizdat (1990)

Gromyko A, *Memoirs*, London: Hutchinson (1989)

Gunther J, *Roosevelt in Retrospect*, London: Hamish Hamilton (1950)

Hamilton M, *Arthur Henderson: A Biography*, London: William Heinemann (1938)

Harriman W, *Special Envoy to Churchill and Stalin 1941-1946*,

New York: Random House (1975)

Harvey O, *Diplomatic Diaries of Oliver Harvey*, London: Collins (1970)

Haslam J, *Soviet Union and the Threat From the East*, Basingstoke: Macmillan Press (1992)

Haslam J, *The Soviet Union and the Struggle for Collective Security in Europe 1938-1939*, London: Macmillan, in association with Russian and Eastern European Studies: University of Birmingham (1984)

Heineman J, *Hitler's First Foreign Minister: Constanin Freiherr von Neurath, Diplomat and Statesman*, Berkeley: University of California Press (1979)

Hilger G & Meyer A, *The Incompatible Allies*, New York: Macmillan & Co (1953)

Hindus M, *Crisis in the Kremlin*, New York: Doubleday & Company (1953)

Hoare S, *Nine Troubled Years*, London: Collins (1954)

Hochman J, *Soviet Union & Failure of Collective Security 1934-1938*, London: Cornell University Press (1984)

Holloway D, *Stalin & The Bomb*, New Haven and London: Yale University Press (1994)

Hosking G, *History of the Soviet Union*, London: Fontana Press (1985)

Hosking G, *Russia and the Russians*, Belknap Press of Harvard University Press (2003)

Hull C, *Memoirs of Cordell Hull*, London: Hodder & Stoughton (1948)

Jacobs D, *Borodin: Stalin's Man in China*, Cambridge, Mass, London & Harvard University Press (1981)

Jackson G, *The Spanish Republic and the Civil War 1931-1939*, Princeton, NJ: Princeton Press (1965)

Johnson C, *Borah of Idaho*, New York & Toronto: Longman & Co (1936)

Jukes G, *Russo-Japanese War 1904-1905*, Oxford: Osprey (2002)

Karnow S, *Mao: Inside China's Cultural Revolution*, Harmondsworth: Penguin (1984)

Kennan G, *Russia and the West Under Lenin and Stalin*, Boston: Little Brown (1960)

Khrushchev N, *Anatomy of Terror* (Stalin's Speech, 1956; introduction by Nathaniel Weyl), Washington, DC: Public Affairs Press (1956)

Khrushchev N, *Khrushchev Remembers*, Boston: Little Brown (1970)

Khrushchev N, *Khrushchev Remembers Glasnost Tapes*, Boston: Little Brown (1990)

Kiaupa Z, *History of Lithuania*, Vilnius: Baltos Lankos (2002)

Kissinger H, *Diplomacy*, New York, London: Simon & Schuster (1984)

Kleist P, *European Tragedy*, Times: P Gibbs & Phillips (1965)

Knei-Paz B, *The Social and Political Thoughts of Leon Trotsky*, Oxford: Clarendon Press (1978)

Knight A, *Kirov: the Kremlin's Greatest Mystery*, New York: Hill Wang (1990)

Konovalov S, *Russo-Polish Relations: A Historical Survey*, London: Cresset Press (1945)

Kostyrchenko G, *Out of the Red Shadows: Anti-Semitism in Soviet Russia*,

Amherst, NY: Prometheus Books (1995)

Krivitsky W, *I Was Stalin's Agent*, London: Hamilton (1939)

Lansbury G, *Miracle of Fleet Street*, London: Victoria House Printing Co (1925)

Lederer I, *Russian Foreign Policy: Essays in Historical Prospective*, New Haven, London: Yale University Press (1962)

Leventhal F M, *Arthur Henderson*, Manchester: Manchester University Press (1989)

Librach J, *Rise of the Soviet Empire*, Washington and New York: A Praeger (1964)

Litvinov M, *The Bolshevik Revolution: Its Rise and Meaning*, British Socialist Party, second edition (1918), third and enlarged edition with foreword by Ivy Litvinov (1919)

Lockhart R, *Memoirs of a British Agent*, London & New York: Putman (1934)

Machray R, *Poland 1914-1931*, London: G Allen & Unwin (1932)

Mackintosh J, *British Cabinet*, London: Stevens (1977)

Macleod I, *Neville Chamberlain*, London: Frederick Muller Ltd (1961)

Mahaney Wilbur Lee *The Soviet Union, the League of Nations and Disarmament* Philadelphia University Press, Pennsyvania (1940)

Mamatey V, *History of Czechoslovak Republic*, Princeton, NJ: Princeton University Press (1973)

McCormack G, *Chang Tso Lin in North East China 1911-1928*, Folkestone: Dawson (1978)

Maisky I, *Memoirs of a Soviet Ambassador: The War 1939-1943* (tr. by Andrew Rothstein), London: Hutchinson (1967)

Maisky I, *Journey into the Past*, (tr. by Frederick Holt), London: Hutchinson (1962)

Maisky I, *Who Helped Hitler?* (tr. by Andrew Rothstein), London: Hutchinson (1964)

Mango A, *Ataturk*, London: John Murray (1999)

Marquand D, *Ramsay Macdonald*, London: Cape (1977)

Martin T, *Nations and Nationalism in the Soviet Union 1923-1939*, Ithaca, London: Cornell University Press (2001)

Mastny Vojtech, *Russia's Road to the Cold War*, New York, Guildford: Columbia University Press (1979)

Medlicott W, *British Foreign Policy Since Versailles*, London: Methuen & Co (1940)
Medvedev R, *Let History Judge*, London: Macmillan (1971)

Medvedev Zhores & Roy, *The Unknown Stalin* (tr. by Ellen Dahrendorf), London:

I B Taurus (2003)

Meir G, *My Life*, London: Weidenfeld & Nicolson (1975)

Middlemas K & Barnes J, *Baldwin: A Biography*, London: Weidenfeld & Nicolson (1969)

Mikoyan S, *Autobiography* (tr. by Ashen Mikoyan), Shrewsbury: Airlife (1999)

Modin *Y. My Five Cambridge Friends* (tr. by Andrew Roberts)), London: Headline (1994)

Moise E, *Modern China*, London: Longman (1995)

Montefiore S, *Stalin: The Court of the Red Tsar*, London: Weidenfeld & Nicolson (2003)

Montefiore S, *Young Stalin*, London: Weidenfeld & Nicolson (2007)

Montgomery of Alamein, *Memoirs*, London: Collins (1960)

Moore H, *Soviet Far Eastern Policy 1931-1945*, Princeton, NJ: Princeton University Press (1945)

Moran Lord, *Winston Churchill: The Struggle for Survival*, London: Constable (1966)

Moseley G, *China: Empire to People's Republic*, London: B T Batsford (1958)

Mosely, P. (editor), *Soviet Union 1922-1962: A Foreign Affairs Reader* (Council on Foreign Relations), London, New York: Frederick A Praeger (1963)

Murray N, *I Spied for Stalin*, London: Odhams Press (1950)

Nabokoff C, *The Ordeal of a Diplomat*, London: Duckworth & Co (1921)

Nicolson H, *George V: His Life and Reign*, London: Constable & Co (1952)

Northedge F and Wells A, *Britain and Soviet Communism: The Impact of Revolution*, London: Macmillan (1982)

Nove A, *An Economic History of the USSR*, Harmondsworth: Penguin Books (1972)

Nove A, *Glasnost in Action*, London: Unwin Hyman (1989)

O'Connor T, *Diplomacy and Revolution*, Ames: Iowa State University (1988)

Orlov S, *The Secret History of Stalin's Crimes*, New York: Random House (1953)

Overy R, *Russia's War*, London: Allen Lane (1998)

Overy R, *Hitler's Germany and Stalin's Russia*, London: Allen Lane (2004)

Payne R, *The Life and Death of Lenin*, London: W H Allen (1964)

Pechatnov V (tr. by V M Zubok), *Big Three After World War 2 working Paper 13*, Woodrow Wilson Center for Scholars (1995)

Pechatnov V (tr. by V M Zubok),*The Allies are Pressing on You to Break your will*

Correspondence Between Stalin, Molotov and Other Members of the Politburo,

Working Paper 26 September 1945 to December 1946, Woodrow Wilson Center for Scholars (1999)

Perlmutter A, *FDR and Stalin, 1943-1945*, Columbia, Mo, & London: University of Missouri Press (1993)

Phillips H, *Between the Revolution and the West*, Boulder, Co, & Oxford: Westview Press (1992)

Pipes R *Russia Under the Bolshevik Regime*, London: Harvill Press (1997)

Pope A, *Maxim Litvinov*, New York: L B Fischer (1943)

Possony S, *Lenin: the Compulsive Revolutionary*, London: George Allen & Unwin (1994)

Postgate R, *The Life of George Lansbury*, London: Longmans, Green & Co (1951)

Prazmowska A, *Eastern Europe and the Origins of the Second World War*, Basingstoke: Macmillan (2000)

Preston P, *Franco*, London: Harper Collins (1993)

Rathbone E, *War Can Be Averted*, London: Victor Gollancz (1938)

Read A & Fisher D, *The Deadly Embrace: Hitler, Stalin and Nazi Soviet Pact 1939-1941*, New York: W W Norton & Co (1988)

Rees E (editor), *The Nature of Stalin's Dictatorship*, Basingstoke: Palgrave Macmillan (2003)

Rees E A, *Decision-making in Stalinist Command Economy*, Basingstoke: Palgrave Macmillan (1997)

Reiman M, *The Birth of Stalinism* (tr. by George Saunders), Bloomington: Indiana University Press (1987)

Resis A, *Fall of Litvinov* Harbinger of the German Soviet Non-Aggression Pact Europe Asia Studies, vol.52 Issue 1 (2000)

Reynaud P, *In the Thick of the Fight* (tr. by James Lambert), London: Cassell & Co (1955)

Roberts G, *The Soviet Union and the Origins of the Second World War:*

Russian-German Relations and Road to War 1933/1939, Basingstoke: Macmillan (1995)

Roberts G, *Unholy Alliance*, London: Taurus (1996)

Roberts G, article in *Historical Journal*, 'Infamous encounter ? The Merekalov Weizsacker meeting 17th April 1939 ', vol.35 Issue 4, December (1992)

Roberts G, article in *Soviet Studies*, 'Soviet-Nazi Pact', The Soviet Decision for a Pact with Germany Vol 44 Vol 1January (1992)

Roberts J, *General History of Europe 1880-1945*, London & New York: Longmans (1967)

Rose K, *George V*, London: Weidenfeld & Nicolson (1983)

Roskill S, *Hankey: Man of Secrets*, Vol.3 3 1931-1963, London: Collins (1963)

Rowland P, *Lloyd George*, London: Barrie & Jenkins (1975)

Salisbury H, *Moscow Journal: The End of Stalin*, Chicago: University of Chicago Press (1961)

Schellenberg W, *Schellenberg Memoirs* (ed. and tr. by Louis Hagan), London: Andre Deutsch (1956)

Schuman F, *Europe on the Eve*: *The Crisis of Diplomacy 1933-1939*, London: Robert Hale (1939)

Schuman F, *Night Over Europe: The Diplomacy of Nemesis 1933-1940*, London: Robert Hale (1941)

Scott W, *Alliance Against Hitler: Origins of the Franco- Soviet Pact*,

Durham, NC: Duke University Press (1962)

Serge V, *Memoirs of a Revolutionary* (ed. and tr. by Peter Sedgwick), London: Oxford University Press (1963)

Service R, *Lenin: A Biography*, London: Macmillan (1985)

Service R, *Stalin*, Basingstoke: Macmillan (2004)

Sheinis Z, *Alexandra Kollontai*, Frankfurt am Main: Verlag Marxistische Blatter (1984)

Sheinis Z, *Maxim Litvinov* (tr. by Vic Schneireson), Moscow: Progress Publishers (1988)

Shepherd J, *George Lansbury at the Heart of Old Labour*, Oxford: Oxford University Press (2002)

Shirer W, *Rise and Fall of the Third Reich*, Secker & Warburg (1961)

Snow E, *Journey to the Beginning*, London: Victor Gollancz (1959)

Stettinius E, *Lend-Lease: A Weapon for Victory*, Harmondsworth & New York: Eyre & Spottiswoode (1944)

Stimson H, *Far-Eastern Crisis: Recollections and Observations*, New York & London: Harper & Brothers Publishers (1936)

Taylor A.J.P., English History 1914-1945 Oxford Clarendon Press (1965)

Tolstoy N, *Stalin's Secret War*, London: Cape (1981)

Toynbee A, *Survey of International Affairs*, London: Oxford University Press (1925-1977)

Traina R, *American Diplomacy and the Spanish Civil War*, Bloomington & London: Indiana University Press (1968)

Trotsky L, *Stalin: An Appraisal of the Man and his Influence* (ed. and tr. by Charles Malamuth), London: Hollis & Carter (1947)

Tucker R, *Stalin in Power*, New York: Norton (1990)

Tucker R, *Stalin as Revolutionary*, London: Chatto & Windus (1974)

Ulam A, *Stalin: The Man and his Era*, London: Taurus (1973)

Ullman R, *Anglo-Soviet Relations 1917-1921*, Princeton, NJ: Princeton University Press; London: Oxford University Press.

Vaksberg A, *Stalin Against the Jews* (tr. by Antonina W Bouis), New York: Knopf (1994)

Volkogonov D, *Lenin* (tr. by Harold Shukman), London: Weidenfeld & Nicolson (1994)

Volkogonov D, *Rise and Fall of the Soviet Empire* (tr. by Harold Shukman), London: Harper Collins (2008)

Volkogonov D, *Stalin: Triumph and Tragedy* (tr. by Harold Shukman), London: Weidenfeld & Nicolson (1991)

Walker-Smith D, *Neville Chamberlain: Man of Peace*, London: Robert Hale (1940)

Walters F, *History of the League of Nations*, London: Oxford University Press (1952)

Ward C, *Stalin's Russia*, London: Edward Arnold (1993)

Watson D, *Molotov: A Biography*, Basingstoke: Palgrave Macmillan (2005)

Watson D, *Molotov and Soviet Government 1939-1941*, Basingstoke: The Centre for Russian and Eastern European Studies, University of Birmingham

Weissman B, *Hoover and Famine Relief to Soviet Russia 1921-1923*, Stanford: Hoover Institution Press (1974)

Weizsacker E von, *Memories of Ernst Von Weizsacker* (tr. by John L Andrews) London: Victor Gollancz (1951)

Welles S, *Time for Decision*, London: Hamish Hamilton (1945)

Werth A, *Russia at War 1941-1945*, London: Barrie & Rockliff (1964

Wheeler-Bennett J, *Munich: Prologue to Tragedy*, London: Macmillan (1963)

White S, *Origins of Detente*, Cambridge: Cambridge University Press (1985)

Zaloga S, *Target America*, Novato, CA: Presidio (1993)

Zhukov G, *Reminiscences and Reflections* (tr. by Alexander Smirnov), Moscow: Progress Publishers (1985)

Zhukov G, *Memoirs of Marshal Zhukov*, London: Jonathan Cape (1971)

Zimmern A, *The League of Nations & the Rule of Law*, London: Macmillan & Co (1936)

Zubok V, *Inside the Kremlin's Cold War*, Cambridge, Mass: Harvard University Press (1996)

INDEX

References to photographs are shown in **bold**.

A

Abyssinia 158, 294–9, 316, 318, 384, 389, 391, 484

Addison, Christopher (British Minister of Agriculture) 247

Afghanistan 98, 175, 202, 422, 499

aggression, Litvinov's definition 128–30, 175, 254, 288, 469–70, 483, 503

Albania 345, 368, 389, 469

Alexandrovsky, Sergei (Berlin Soviet Embassy counsellor) 189

Alliluyeva, Svetlana (Stalin's daughter) 405

Amba, Achmed (Stalin's bodyguard) 486–7

American Relief Association 53, 57–8

Amery, Leopold (British politician and journalist) 298

Anderson, William Crawford (British socialist politician) 24

Andreasian, Napoleon (Soviet party official) 405–6

Andvord, Rolf (Norwegian ambassador to Soviet Union) 457

Antipov, Nikolai (Soviet politician) 414

appeasement policies
    Abyssinia 298
    and Churchill 92, 298, 403, 458, 484
    Czechoslovakia 329–30
    and Litvinov 409, 484
    and Neville Chamberlain 160, 335, 337, 338, 507
    and Roosevelt 484
    Sino-Japanese war 398
    Soviet leaders in Far East 149, 160, 161, 162–3
    see also Munich agreement (1938)

ARCOS affair (1927) 84, 90, 146, 151, 214–17

Ardashev, Viktor (Lenin's cousin) 19

Asquith, Herbert Henry 48, 120, 209

Astakhov, Georgy (Soviet diplomat) 345, 349, 364, 369, 486

Ataturk, Mustafa Kemal 308

Atlantic Charter (1941) 436, 451

Attlee, Clement 288, 323, 377–8

Austen, Jane, Litvinov's appreciation of 14

Australia, Patterson Scheme 248

Austria
    Anschluss 318–19
    post-WWII Soviet-Austrian relations 470
    social-democrats 11

B

Bacon, Arthur (British Russian-speaking cobbler) 5–6

Bakmeteff, Boris (Russian ambassador to USA) 261–2, 269

balance of power concept 122

Baldwin, Stanley 167, 214, 217, 287–8, 303, 378, 496

Balfour, Arthur (British Prime Minister) 17, 38

Baltic States
    and the Bolshevik government 46–7
    and Britain 211, 212, 291
    Eastern Locarno 281, 287
    and Germany 186, 193–4, 290
    and Poland 112, 172–3, 276, 290
    Soviet acquisition of 428, 447
    and tripartite agreement proposals 347, 349
    and the US 260, 447

Barmine, Alexandre (Soviet defector) 78, 86, 96, 372, 490, 493, 497

Barthou, Louis (French Foreign Minister) 63–4, 230, 281–2, 283–4, 287

Bartlett, Vernon (British journalist) 336–7, 338

Beaverbrook, Max Aitken, Lord (British minister) 373, 428, 431–4

Beck, Józef (Polish Foreign Minister)
    Danzig 346
    Eastern Locarno 281, 287
    lack of statesmanship 427

on Litvinov 358–9
Litvinov on 441
Polish capture of Vilnius (1923) 173
Polish-German non-aggression pact (1934)
   279–80, 290
Soviet admission to the League of Nations
   282–3
Soviet infringement of Polish airspace
   (1938) 326
visit to UK (1939) 344
Bedell-Smith, Walter (US ambassador to
   Soviet Union) 466
Belgium, 1940 surrender 366
Beloff, Max (historian) 402–3, 497
Benes, Edvard 124–6, 329–30
Berdichevsky, Arcadi and Freda (victims of
   Soviet purges) 101
Beria, Lavrenty
   22nd anniversary of Russian Revolution 374
   brutal interrogation of Gnedin 423
   Czechoslovakia's surrender 325
   influence on Stalin 491
   on Litvinov 478–9
   Litvinov's dismissal 354, 358
   and Maisky 478–9
   plot to kill Litvinov 467
   Stalin's faked rage at honours 494
Berlin, Treaty of (1926) 182, 184
Bernstorff, Johann Heinrich von (German
   delegate) 106, 116, 117, 218
Bessarabia 72, 93, 168, 169–70, 174–5, 499
Bessedovsky, Grigory (Soviet diplomat) 89,
   96, 477–8
Bessonov, Sergei (Soviet Embassy counsellor)
   308, 309
Bevin, Ernest 78, 496
Billings, Noel (British MP) 31
Black, Conrad (newspaper magnate and
   biographer) 449
Blair, Tony 109, 496
Blum, Léon 315, 380
Bolsheviks
   1905 3rd Congress of the Russian Social
      Democratic Labour Party 4
   1907 5th Congress of the Russian Social
      Democratic Labour Party 5
   1915 Socialist parties conference 10, 12

British Foreign Office on 198
Daily Mail on 45
Hitler on 305, 310
Kerensky on 33
Litvinov on 18–19, 80
Lockhart on 18, 37
and the Mensheviks 3, 4, 19, 26
Woodrow Wilson on 39
Bonch-Bruyevich, Vladimir D. (Soviet
   politician and historian) 3
Bonnet, Georges-Étienne (French Foreign
   Minister) 323, 335, 350
Boothby, Robert (British MP) 211, 338
Borah, William (US Senator) 271
Borisov, Mikhail (Kirov's guard) 407
Borodin, Mikhail (Soviet Comintern agent) 99,
   142, 146–7, 151, 152
Borsig, Ernst von (German industrialist) 181
Bowerman, Charles William (British trade
   unionist and politician) 24
Brest-Litovsk, Treaty of (1918) 23–4, 27–30,
   49, 64–5, 97, 257, 480
Brezhnev, Leonid 286, 412
Briand, Aristide 109, 111, 154, 167, 217, 240–
   1
   see also Kellogg–Briand Pact (1928)
Britain see United Kingdom
Brockdorff-Rantzau, Ulrich von (German
   ambassador to Soviet Union) 82, 178, 180
Bromage, Bernard (author) 356
Browder, Earl (US Communist leader) 359
Browder, Robert Paul (historian) 269, 273
Brown, John (British army officer) 402
Brown, W. F. (US official) 54, 55–6
Bruning, Heinrich (German Chancellor) 184
Brussels Conference (1937) 315, 397–401, 495
Buchanan, George William (British
   ambassador to Russia) 17, 24–5
Budenny, Semyon (Soviet military
   commander) 40, 414, 422
Budurowycz, Bohdan (historian) 280
Bukharin, Nikolai
   British-Soviet relations 224
   Chicherin's criticism of 97
   Kellogg-Briand Pact 112
   trial of 384, 413–16, 418, 492, 504

Bullard, Reader (British diplomat) 91, 228, 269, 478

Bullitt, William Christian (US ambassador to Soviet Union) 44–5, 137–8, 258, 272, 273–4, 473

Bullock, Alan (historian) 319

Bundists 5

Butler, R. A. (British politician) 326–7, 492

C

Caballero, Francisco Largo (Spanish Prime Minister) 382–3

Cadogan, Alexander (British diplomat) 131, 337, 343, 349, 427, 429, 506–7

Campbell, John Ross (*Communist Weekly* editor) 208

Cannes Conference (1922) 61, 63

Carr, Edward (historian) 76–7, 179, 180, 186, 266, 286, 401–2

Carswell, John (historian)
  angry Dockers' attack of Stalin story 6
  Ivy and Maxim Litvinov's decision not to defect 444–5
  Ivy and Maxim Litvinov's life in the US 436
  Ivy Litvinov's life in Sverdlovsk 420
  Litvinov and Beria 358
  Litvinov and Stalin 444
  Litvinov's disappointment in the Bolsheviks 80
  Litvinov's dismissal 365
  Litvinov's marital unfaithfulness 475
  Litvinov's prison escape 2

Casablanca Conference (1943) 449

Cassidy, Henry (US journalist) 372

Cave, Sir G. (British Home Office Minister) 25

Cecil, Robert (British Politician) 49, 74, 116–17, 155, 218, 246

Chamberlain, Austen
(British Foreign Secretary)
ARCOS affair 215
  Attlee and rearmament 288
  British foreign policy, influence on 496
  France and Franco-Soviet relations 167
  Geneva Conference (1927) 85
  Litvinov, meeting with (1927) 218, 222
  Litvinov's definition of aggression 130
  Locarno Treaty (1922) 83
  Soviet defaming of UK 84

Soviet government and 1926 General Strike 212–13
  'Soviet problem' secret meeting (1927) 217
  Soviet-British relations, opposed to severance of 211, 215
  Zinoviev Letter affair 209–10

Chamberlain, Joseph 197

Chamberlain, Neville
  appeasement policy 160, 335, 337, 338, 507
  avoidability of war 352
  British failure to re-arm 329
  Czechoslovakia 322, 323, 326, 341–2
  Franco-Soviet Pact (1935) 315
  Germany and the Soviet Union fighting each other 367
  and his foreign secretaries 496
  and Hitler 345
  and the League of Nations 289, 317
  Litvinov's dismissal 364, 365
  and Lloyd George 42, 335, 343–4, 347
  Maisky on 339
  Munich agreement 325, 328, 329, 332–3
  and Poland 343–4
  Sino-Japanese war 398
  Soviet tripartite agreement proposals 350, 361
  and the Soviet Union 339, 343–5, 347–8, 349, 402
  Spanish Civil War 378, 392
  and Stalin 372

Chang Hsueh-Liang (Chinese General)16-165

Chang Hsueh-liang (Manchurian leader) 147, 148, 149–50, 154

Chang Tso-lin (Manchurian leader) 145–6, 147–8

Channon, Henry (British MP) 198, 341, 345, 478

Chataigneau, Yves (French diplomat) 469

Cheka 19, 38, 53, 56, 78, 79

Chiang Kai-shek 144–5, 147, 151–2, 164–5, 395–6, 400, 403

Chicherin, Georgy (Soviet foreign minister) **232**
  assessment of 94–101
  assessment of by Gromyko 97, 98, 100
  personal details

Chicherin, Georgy (cont.)
  capable of lying 101
  ill health 85, 89, 99
  London arrest and release (1917) 16, 17
  obituaries 99–100
  suspicious of international meetings 86
  political career
    Asia 98
    Bessarabia 93, 499
    Brest-Litovsk Treaty 97
    British recognition of the Soviet Union 76

    British-Soviet relations 97–8, 198–9, 201,
      205–6, 207–8, 210, 213–14
    China 98–9, 142, 151, 499
    Daily Herald affair 200, 201
    Disarmament Commission (1925) 102
    dismissal 99
    Franco-Soviet relations 167–8
    Geneva Conference (1927) 85
    Genoa Conference (1922) 62–5, 67–8,
      400
    German-Soviet relations 97, 98, 179, 180–
      1, 182
    Kellogg-Briand Pact (1928) 98, 111–12
    London Committee for the Repatriation of
      Émigrés 15
    peace proposals to Allies (1919) 44–5
    Polish-Soviet relations 172, 173
    prisoner exchange agreement (1920) 199
    Rapallo Treaty, architect of 62–3, 68, 96
    Russian-Polish War (1920) 93
    Shakhty case 182
    US-Russian relations 258, 259, 260
    US-Soviet relations 262, 263, 264, 266,
      267
    Washington Conference (1921-22) 61
    see also Rapallo, Treaty of (1922)
  relationship with Stalin 68, 85, 88–9, 98, 99,
    100
  relationships with
    Brockdorff-Rantzau 178
    Karakhan 99
    Lenin 68, 77
    Litvinov 9, 81, 85, 89, 94–6, 97–8
    Stalin 68, 85, 89, 98
  views on

    League of Nations 86, 95, 276–7, 278
    Locarno Treaty 82–3, 181, 182
    Red Terror 19–20, 100
    relaxation of foreign trade monopoly (late
      1920s) 88–9
    US famine relief effort 57
    world revolution 93–4
Chilston, Aretas Akers-Douglas, 2nd Viscount
  (British ambassador to Soviet Union) 101,
  292, 378
China
  Abyssinia 391
  Chiang Kai-shek 144–5, 147, 151–2, 164–5,
    395–6, 400, 403
  Chicherin and Litvinov on 98–9, 499
  Kuomintang 141, 142, 143–4, 146–7
  Lend-Lease 442
  Long March 164
  Manchuria 152–63
  Mao Zedong 147, 164, 396
  Mongolia 141–2, 143
  Moscow foreign ministers meetings protocol
    452
  Russian-Chinese railway affair 140–1, 147–
    50, 161–3, 164
  Sino-British relations 403
  Sino-Japanese conflict over Chinese railway
    119, 140–1, 161–2, 164
  Sino-Japanese war (1937) 164, 165, 387,
    395–401
  Sino-Soviet non-aggression pact 396
  Sino-Soviet relations 396, 402–4
    1927 raiding of Soviet Embassy 84, 145–
      6, 197
    diplomatic relations restored 143, 161,
      163
    diplomatic relations severed 89–90, 150,
      161
  Sino-US relations 396, 403–4
Chossudovsky, Evgeny (United Nations
  official and author) 96
Chuev, Felix (biographer) 239, 417, 437, 488,
  490
Churchill, Winston
  Abyssinia 298, 29Anschluss 319
  anti-Bolshevik feelings 42–3

Churchill Winston (cont)
   appeasement 92, 298, 484
   appeasement from weakness 403, 458
   Atlantic Charter 436
   Belgium and evacuation of Dunkirk 366
   British failure to re-arm 329
   Czechoslovakia 323, 324, 325
   Fulton speech 494
   Germany's reoccupation of the Rhineland
     307
   on Hilter's dictatorship 189
   and the League of Nations 289
   letter to Stalin via Beaverbrook 432–3
   on Litvinov's importance as US ambassador
     437
   and Lloyd George 42–3, 64
   on the Macdonald disarmament plan 133
   and Maisky 226
   on Molotov 494
   Moscow visit (1944) 458
   Munich agreement 328
   on the Nazi persecution of the Jews 189
   Operation Barbarossa (1941) 427–8, 429
   Operation Overlord (1944) 451
   Roosevelt, meeting with 445
   Sino-British relations 403
   Soviet complaint about speech 211
   on the Soviet government 214
   Soviet tripartite agreement proposals (1939)
     349
   on Stalin and collectivisation 239
   Stalin and the Eastern Front 367
   Sudetenland 320
   Sumner Welles on 484
   Teheran Conference 449
   and the USA 109, 138
   Versailles Treaty, opposed to revision of 228
   Yalta Conference 459
Clark-Kerr, Archibald, Sir (British ambassador
  to Soviet Union) 226, 453, 457–8, 472
Clemenceau, Georges 38, 45
Clive, R. H. (British Chargé d'Affaires) 42
Clynes, J. R. (British trade unionist and
  politician) 41–2
co-existence, policy of 62, 63
Colby, Braintree (US Secretary of State) 260
Collier, Laurence (British diplomat) 364

Comintern (or Third International)
   agents in Soviet embassies 146, 197
   and Borodin 99, 142
   and China 142, 163
   creation of 45–6
   'Curzon Ultimatum' 204
   denunciation of the Versailles Treaty 178–9
   dissolution of 196
   and German Communist uprisings 177, 179
   and Lenin 195, 196
   and Litvinov 264
   and the Soviet government 101, 196–7
   and the UK 85, 92, 195–6, 224
   and the US 264–5, 273–4
   Zinoviev Letter affair 208–10
Connally, Tom (US senator) 439
Conquest, Robert (historian) 405, 408
Cremer, William Randall (British MP) 6
Cripps, Stafford (British ambassador to Soviet
  Union) 319, 322, 333, 370, 430, 484, 506
Croft, Henry Page (British MP) 27–8
Cromie, Francis (British sub-mariner) 42
Crooks, Will (British MP) 6
Curtius, Julius (German Foreign Minister) 183,
  245, 246, 247
Curzon, George (British Foreign Secretary) 38,
  199, 203, 204–6, 213
Cushendun, Ronald McNeill, 1st Baron of
  (British minister) 105, 114, 206, 474, 492
Czechoslovakia 44, 68, 319, 320–30, 341–2,
  458
   see also Munich agreement (1938)

D

Daily Herald, The 50, 200–1
   see also Herald, The
Daladier, Édouard (French Prime Minister)
  322–3
Dallin, David (historian) 142
Dalton, Hugh (British Cabinet Minister) 378,
  395
Davies, John (US diplomat) 464
Davies, Joseph E. (US ambassador to Soviet
  Union) 362, 418, 442–3, 474, 500
Davis, Norman H. (US diplomat) 361, 398, 400
de Gaulle, General 457, 460

De La Warr, Herbrand Sackville, Earl (British Lord Privy Seal) 315, 325

De Valera, Éamon (Irish statesman) 283, 284

Deane, John R. (US general) 452, 458

Debo, Richard (historian) 78

Declaration of Human Rights 412

DeConde, Alexander (historian) 157

Dekanozov, Vladimir (Soviet Foreign Affairs Deputy Commissioner) 354, 358, 457, 458, 465, 501

Delbos, Yvon (French Foreign Affairs Minister) 385

Denike, Yu. (émigré Socialist) 500

Denikin, Anton (Russian White general) 37, 40, 42, 46

depression see Great Depression (1929)

Dimitrov, Georgi (Comintern General Secretary) 374

Dirksen, Herbert (German diplomat) 190, 247

disarmament
    Disarmament Commission of the League of Nations (1925) 102
    Disarmament Preparatory Commission (1927-30) 102–8, 113–19
    Geneva Conference (1927) 85
    Geneva Disarmament Conference (1932-34) 119–39
        Benes plan 124–6
        British (Macdonald) plan 131–5, 139
        French plan 130–1, 134
        Germany's withdrawal from 135–6
        Litvinov' definition of aggression 128–30, 175
        Litvinov's call for permanent peace commission 136–8
        Litvinov's overall contribution 139
        Maisky on British-Soviet relations 226–7
        US (Hoover) plan 122–5, 130, 139
    Lausanne Conference (1922-23) 72–4, 102
    Litvinov authority on 502
    London Conference (1930) 116, 123
    Moscow Conference (1922) 74
    vs. security 121–2, 127
    Soviet general disarmament proposals 74, 105, 107–8, 113–14, 121, 122, 139
    Soviet partial disarmament proposals 106, 114, 121, 138–9

Washington Conference (1921-22) 61, 115
    see also League of Nations

Doctors' Plot 468, 470, 475

Dovgalevsky, V. S. (Soviet Ambassador to UK) 219, 221–3

Drummond, Eric Franklin (Secretary of League of Nations) 159

Dubrowsky, David Efimovitch (Soviet Red Cross director) 273

Duff-Cooper, Alfred (British diplomat and MP) 303, 349

Duranty, Walter (US journalist) 74, 25527

dumping 247–8, 2

E

Eastern Locarno 193, 281–2, 287, 288

Eberlein, Hugo (German socialist) 46

Eden, Anthony(Lord Avon) British Foreign Secretary and Prime Minister)
    Belgium and 1940 evacuation of Dunkirk 366
    Disarmament Conference (1932-34) 116, 126, 131
    Eastern Locarno 287
    Germany's reoccupation of the Rhineland 307
    Halifax's visit to Germany 300
    on Hitler 292–3
    influence on British foreign policy 194, 496
    and the League of Nations 317
    and Litvinov 303, 476
    Litvinov's definition of aggression 130, 483, 502
    and Macdonald 135
    Moscow foreign ministers meetings 451–3
    and Mussolini 296, 383–4
    Nyon Conference (1937) 386–8
    on Poland 292
    political ambitions 81
    Roosevelt, meeting with 445
    Sino-Japanese war 397–8, 399, 401
    Soviet admission to League of Nations 230, 282–3
    Spanish Civil War 378–9, 383, 385
    on Stalin 292–3, 476
    Sudetenland 320

527

visit to Berlin 289
visit to Moscow 287, 289–93
Edward VIII, King of United Kingdom 303, 315
Ehrenburg, Ilya (Soviet poet and author)
    on the Great Purges 419
    on Lenin and Litvinov 77, 79
    on Litvinov and culture 375
    on Litvinov and the Nazi-Soviet Pact 370
    on Litvinov's ambition to fend off war 483
    on Litvinov's dismissal as US ambassador 445
    on Litvinov's dismissal from the Party Central Committee 375–6
    on Litvinov's funeral 469
    on Litvinov's personality 473
    on Litvinov's retirement years 467
    on Stalin and the Nazi-Soviet Pact 372
Einstein, Albert, support for Soviet entry into League of Nations 284
Erkko, Eljas (Finish Foreign Minister) 352–3
Estonia
    customs preference agreement 249
    debts to the USA 255
    Dorpat Treaty 46, 47
    Eastern Locarno 281
    Geneva Disarmament Conference (1932-34) 175
    Kellogg-Briand Pact 174
    Litvinov's appointment as envoy to 50–1, 59, 77
    Moscow Conference (1922) 74
    Soviet-Estonian relations (1920s) 172, 173
Eubank, Keith (historian) 322, 323

F

Fabian Society 8
Fabro, Mr (French Procurator General) 7
Fairburn, M. S. (British *Daily Herald* journalist) 33
Figes, Orlando (historian) 3, 39
Finland
    debts to the US 259, 447
    declaration of independence 40
    foreign policy 330
    Geneva Disarmament Conference (1932-34) 175

Lausanne conference (1922-23) 73
Maisky Helsinki airport incident 352–4
Moscow Conference (1922) 74
recognition of the Soviet Union 50
Soviet-Finnish relations 130, 172
Soviet-Finnish Winter War (1939) 4, 324, 457–8, 504
Soviet peace proposals to Allies (1919) 44–5
Soviet tripartite agreement proposals (1939) 347, 349
Tsarist oppression of 12, 14
Fischer, Louis (US journalist)
    assessment of his portrayal of Litvinov 472
    on Chicherin and Asian countries 98
    on Chicherin and the Genoa Conference/League of Nations 86
    on Chicherin's funeral 100
    on Litvinov and Czechoslovakia 321–2, 323–4
    on Litvinov and Operation Barbarossa 429
    on Litvinov and the Anschluss 319
    on Litvinov and the Japanese threat 485
    on Litvinov and the Nazi-Soviet Pact 369
    on Litvinov and the prisoner exchange talks 47
    on Litvinov and world revolution 92
    on Litvinov's and Chicherin's areas of agreement 95
    on Litvinov's dismissal 355, 356, 358, 363
    on Litvinov's foreign policy principles 482
    on Litvinov's influence on Soviet foreign policy 495–6
    on the Nazi-Soviet Pact 348, 370
    on Polish-Soviet relations 173
    on the Russian/Chinese railway affair 148, 150
    on Soviet anti-foreigners campaigns 274–5
    on Stalin and the Kellogg-Briand Pact 112
    on US-Soviet relations 266
    on Wilson and Bolshevism 39
Fisher, David (historian) 356, 358, 488–9
Foch, Ferdinand (French general) 45, 205
France
    1940 defeat 366–7
    Abyssinia 296–7, 298, 391
    Allies' intervention in Russia 38–9
    Anschluss 319

France (cont)
  Atlantic Charter 436
  Bessarabia 168, 169–70
  Czechoslovakia 322–6, 328
  Disarmament Preparatory Commission (1927) 104–5, 106
  Franco-Polish relations (1939) 366
  Franco-Soviet Non-aggression Pact (1932) 169–71, 194
  Franco-Soviet Pact (1935) 295–6, 305, 314–15
  Franco-Soviet relations 166–71, 372
  Franco-US relations 109–10
  French Socialists and WWI 9
  Geneva Disarmament Conference, French plan 130–1, 134
  Geneva Disarmament Conference, Hoover's plan 123–4
  Hitler and rearmament of Germany 169
  Hitler and Vichy France 393
  Kellogg-Briand Pact 110–11
  Munich agreement 331–2
  Rhineland 75, 307, 314
  Rhur, occupation of 178
  Sino-Japanese war 400
  Soviet tripartite agreement proposals (1939) 347–50, 363, 365
  Soviet Union, recognition of 76, 96, 166–7, 170
  Spanish Civil War 378, 380, 383, 385–9, 390
  Stalin on France 'the most aggressive of nations' 169, 240
  Treaty of Locarno (1925) 81–2, 83
  Treaty with Russia (1920) 47, 49
Franco, Francisco
  belligerent rights 391, 393
  departure of volunteers 391
  and Hitler 393–4
  Litvinov on 394–5, 460
  and Mussolini 377, 392, 394
  nature of regime 377
  see also Spain
François-Poncet, André (French diplomat) 244–6
Friedrikson, L. Kh. (Soviet official) 311, 313

G

Gamelin, Maurice (French general) 323
Gaus, Friedrich Wilhelm (German Under State Secretary) **235**
Gedye, G. E. R. (US journalist) 357
Geneva conferences *see* disarmament; League of Nations
Genoa Conference (1922) 59, 61–8, 72, 74, 86, 276, 400
George V, King of United Kingdom 48, 158, 200, 208, 225, 293, 303
George VI, King of United Kingdom 315–16, 401
Germany
  Abyssinia 299
  Anschluss 318–19
  Beaverbrook-Harriman-Stalin talks 433
  burning of the Reichstag 407
  and Chicherin 97, 98
  Communist uprisings (1921-23) 92, 176–7, 179
  Czechoslovakia, invasion of (1939) 341–2
  Disarmament Conference (1932-34) 123, 125–6
  Disarmament Preparatory Commission (1927) 104, 106
  Eastern Locarno 281
  German Communists 185–6, 191, 194, 500
  German Social Democrats 7, 9, 175–6, 184–6, 191, 382, 500
  Italo-German relations after Spanish Civil War 394
  Japanese-German relations 402
  Kapp Putsch 176
  Katyn massacre 410, 415, 417, 441, 448
  Kellogg-Briand Pact 112
  League of Nations 135–6, 168
  Litvinov on post-war Germany 460
  Litvinov's definition of aggression 130
  Locarno Treaty 81–4, 181
  Marshall Plan 135
  Molotov on 368
  Munich agreement 160, 287, 320, 322, 325, 327–33, 334, 338–9
  National Socialists 117, 184, 185, 186, 188
  Nuremberg War Crime Trials 410

Germany (Cont)
  Polish-German non-aggression pact (1934)
    279–80, 290
  Rhineland 75, 299, 302, 305–7, 310, 314
  Rhur, French occupation of 178
  Shakhty case 95, 182
  Sino-Japanese war 398
  Soviet agents trials 181

  Soviet-German economic agreement (1936)
    308, 309
  Soviet-German military collaboration 177–8
  Soviet-German relations (1914-32) 77, 166,
    170, 175–86
  Soviet-German relations (1932-38) 186–94,
    299–306, 308–14, 351, 408, 490
  Soviet-German relations (post-Munich) 334–
    7, 345, 348–9, 352
  Spanish Civil War 378–9, 380–1, 382, 383,
    385–9, 390, 393
  Spanish-German relations after Spanish
    Civil War 393–4
  WWII
    Battle of Britain 505
    invasion of the Soviet Union 430, 503–7
    Kursk defeat 445–6
    Operation Barbarossa 375, 376, 424, 427–
      30, 458
  see also Hitler, Adolf; Nazi-Soviet Pact
    (1939); Rapallo, Treaty of (1922);
    Sudetenland; Versailles, Treaty of (1919)
Gibson, Hugh (US diplomat) 117–18, 122, 123,
  124
Gilbert, Martin (historian) 121
Gilbert, Prentiss (US diplomat) 154
Gitlow, Benjamin (US Communist Party) 273,
  438
Gnedin, Yevgeny (Soviet diplomat)
  interrogation and Litvinov's dismissal 355
  on Litvinov 's influence as an expert 491
  on Litvinov's relationship with Molotov 488
  Soviet-Nazi rapprochement 299, 301, 308
  trial and imprisonment of 418, 423–4
Goering, Herbert L. (German official) 309
Goering, Hermann 185, 309, 311, 393, 433,
  443
Gompers, Samuel (American Federation of
Labor) 262
Gorbachev, Mikhail 44, 77, 165, 225, 411
Gorky, Maxim 4, 8, 53, 54
Great Britain see United Kingdom
Great Depression (1929) 237–8, 242–4, 248,
  251–4, 259, 261, 267
Great Purges (1930s)
  impact on foreign policy 313, 417, 495
  and Khrushchev 416
  and Litvinov 100, 313, 351, 417–18, 423–4,
    426, 502
  victims of
    Berdichevsky (Arcadi and Freda)
    Borodin 147
    Bukharin 384, 413–16, 418
    Gnedin 418, 423–4
    Kirov 405–8
    Mikhoels 467
    Red army generals 416–17
    Stomoniakov 419
    Trotsky 90–1, 416, 426
    Yurenev 313
Greenwood, Hamar (British minister) 47
Gromyko, Andrei
  ambassadorship to US 435, 446
  on Chicherin 97, 98, 100
  on Litvinov, Molotov and the Nazi-Soviet
    Pact 489–90
  Litvinov's funeral 469–70
  on Nazi-Soviet Pact secret protocol 410
  post-WWII co-operation with the West 456
  Special Commission on the post-war order
    (1944-45) 453–5
  on Zhukov and lack of adequate Soviet
    defences 505
Grzybowski, Waclaw (Polish ambassador to
  Soviet Union) 333, 345
Guesde, Jules (French socialist politician) 10
Gunther, John (US journalist and author) 377

H
Hague Conference (1922) 68–72, 276
Halifax, E. F. L. Wood, Earl of (British Foreign
  Secretary)
  Bolshevism, hatred of 365
  British assistance to Poland and Rumania
    343, 344, 345–6

Halifax E.P.L(cont)
  British foreign policy, influence on 496
  British inertia in face of German threat 350
  Hitler, erroneous view of his thinking 372
  Kerensky, meeting with (1943) 441
  Lend-Lease 442
  on Litvinov's disappointment with
    ambassadorship to US 444
  Litvinov's remark on German hegemony
    333,
  on Neville Chamberlain's policy towards the
    Soviet Union 339
  visit to Germany (1937) 300
Hankey, Maurice (British diplomat) 156
Harding, Warren G. 54, 58, 261
Hardinge, Charles (British diplomat) 26
Harriman, William Averell (US ambassador to
  Soviet Union)
  Finland delegation (1944) 457
  foreign ministers meeting (1943) 452, 453
  Litvinov on 458
  Litvinov on post-war order 461–2
  Litvinov's relationship with Molotov 457
  Moscow meeting with Beaverbrook (1941)
    431–4
  restoration of the Chiaturi mine by US firm
    263
  Roosevelt's dissatisfaction with Litvinov 442
  Soviet intellectuals' view of the US 460
  Zvesda post-war order article 456
Harvey, Oliver (British diplomat) 331–2, 342,
  361
Haskell, Col. William N. (US Director of
  Russian famine relief) 57
Haslam, Jonathan (historian) 308, 309, 311,
  312–13, 403, 490
Helsinki, Treaty of (1976) 412
Hemming, Francis (British diplomat) 391
Hencke, Andor (German official) 309
Henderson, Arthur (British Foreign Secretary)
  Geneva Disarmament Conference (1932-34)
    134, 136
  and Kerensky 31–2, 34
  recall of Ambassador Ovey 228, 478
  resumption of British-Soviet relations 219–
    24

  and Second International 196
Henderson, Leon (US official and economist)
  439
Henderson, Nevile (British ambassador to
  Germany) 339–40, 448
Herald, The 33, 34, 43
  see also Daily Herald, The
Herbette, Jean (French diplomat) 112, 167
Herriot, Édouard (French Prime Minister) 76,
  166–7, 169–71, 284
Hess, Rudolf 338, 427, 428
Hilger, Gustav (German diplomat)
  on Chicherin and Litvinov 95–6, 99
  on German-Soviet military collaboration
    177–8
  on German students incident 181
  on Kandelaki's mission 300
  on Litvinov and China 151
  on Litvinov and the Great Purges 417, 425,
    500
  on Litvinov's dismissal 359
  on post-Munich German-Soviet relations
    334
  on Soviet ambivalence towards National
    Socialism 186–7
  on Soviet export policy 248
Hindenburg, Paul von 184–5
Hindus, Maurice (US journalist)
  on Litvinov and Molotov in foreign ministry
    uniforms 458
  on Litvinov's avoiding party politics
    discussions 412, 425
  on Litvinov's dismissal 356
  on Litvinov's influence 496, 497–8
  on Litvinov's relationship with Molotov 488,
    489
  on Litvinov's relationship with Stalin 486,
    494–5
Hitler, Adolf
  1939 speeches 352, 360
  Abyssinia 299
  anti-Soviet campaign (1936-37) 310
  appointed Chancellor 185–6
  on Bolshevism 305, 310
  and British disarmament plan 133
  Churchill on 189
  on Eastern Locarno 281

Hitler Adolf (Cont)
   Eden on 289–90, 292–3
   and Franco 393–4
   German presidential elections (1932) 184
   Germany's rearmament 136, 169, 288, 289
   greater Germany 158–9
   Halifax's erroneous view of 372
   the 'Jewish question' 300
   Joseph Davies on 443
   Kandelaki's mission 300
   League of Nations, withdrawal from 135–6
   Litvinov on 185, 192
   Litvinov's definition of aggression 130
   Litvinov's dismissal 359, 360
   on Locarno Treaty 305
   loss of armies in the East 45
   and Merekalov 335
   Molotov, meeting with (1940) 504–5
   Nazi-Soviet Pact 369
   and Neville Chamberlain 345
   on Rappalo Treaty 194
   rewarded for his aggression 409
   Roosevelt, attack on 352
   Soviet-German relations 188–9, 190, 194, 336
   Spanish Civil War 392, 393
   Suritz on 300
   and the Versailles Treaty 133, 135, 192, 288, 305
   and Vichy France 393
   and Yurenev 313
Hoare-Laval pact 296–7, 298
Hoare, Samuel (British Foreign Secretary) 296–7, 298
Hochman, Jiri (historian) 313, 497
Hodgson, Robert McLeod (British ambassador to Soviet Union)
   on arbitrary arrest in the Soviet Union 62
   ARCOS affair (1927) 214
   on the Comintern 195
   'Curzon Ultimatum' affair 203–5
   on Litvinov 472
   need for Soviet markets 114, 212
   recognition of the Soviet Union 206–7, 208
   Spain and Franco 378
   worsening of British-Soviet relations 211–12
Holloway, David (historian) 455

Hollywood Writers' Motion Picture Committee 466
Holocaust 284, 286, 329, 359, 477
Hoover, Herbert
   American famine relief 53, 54, 55, 56, 57–8
   debts moratorium 254–5
   disarmament 'Hoover plan' 122–5, 130, 139
   Japanese invasion of Manchuria 155, 157–8, 161
   on Litvinov and Soviet-US relations 273
   and Stimson 155, 496
Hopkins, Harry L. (Roosevelt's adviser) 430–1
Hottelet, Richard (US journalist) 355, 457, 463–5, 466, 490, 502
Hudson, Austin (British Trade Minister) 337–8, 343
Hugenberg, Alfred (German Economics Minister) 190
   Hugenberg Memorandum 290
Hughes, Charles Edward (US Secretary of State) 261, 278
Hughes, William M. (Australian Prime Minister) 42–3
Hull, Cordell (US Secretary of State)
   and the Anschluss 319
   on Italy and the Neutrality Act 297
   on Litvinov 474
   on Litvinov's Peace Commission proposal 138
   meeting with Litvinov 441
   meeting with Molotov 437
   Moscow foreign ministers meetings 451–3
   Russian Revolution anniversary celebrations 435
   and Sino-Japanese war 396, 400–1
   US recognition of the Soviet Union 254, 268, 275
Hurst, Fannie (US novelist) 437
Hussein, Saddam 409

I

Inskip, Thomas (British Cabinet Minister) 323, 330, 331
International Committee of Women 286
Ioffe, Adolph 67, 79
Iskra (newspaper) 2–3, 468

Italy
  Abyssinia, invasion of 158, 294–9, 316, 318, 384, 389, 391, 484
  Albania, occupation of 345, 368
  Italy (cont)
  Italo-German relations after Spanish Civil War 394
  Italo-Soviet relations, restoration of 76
  Spanish Civil War 378–9, 380–1, 382, 383–4, 385–9, 390–1, 393
  see also Mussolini, Benito

J

Japan
  aggressive intervention in Eastern Siberia 401–2
  and Chiang Kai-shek 147
  German-Japanese relations 402
  Manchuria 152–63
  Pearl Harbour 401, 403, 434, 479, 485
  Russo-Japanese war 4, 141
  Sino-Japanese conflict over Chinese railway 119, 140–1, 161–2, 164
  Sino-Japanese war (1937) 164, 165, 387, 395–401
  Soviet-Japanese neutrality pact (1941) 403
  Soviet leaders' differing views on 151
  Soviet Union, recognition of 152–3
  Stalin on 163–4
  US-Japanese relations 403
Jews
  Churchill on persecution of 189
  conscription of Russian Jewish émigrés in British Army 27
  Doctors' Plot 468, 470, 475
  Hitler and the 'Jewish question' 300
  Litvinov and Judaism 270
  Litvinov and the Nazi persecution of the Jews 476–7
  Litvinov's Jewish background 1, 472
  Litvinov's Jewish background and antisemitism 218, 356, 357, 358, 375, 477–8
  Maisky's Jewish background 375
  Polish Jewish population 287, 329, 359
  Tsarist oppression of 14
  Vilnius 172

see also Holocaust
Joffe, Adolph Abramovich (Soviet diplomat) 47
Jones, Tom (British civil servant) 378
Jouhaux, Léon (French trade unionist) 87
Joynson-Hicks, William, Bt (British Cabinet Minister) 211, 215

K

Kaganovich, Lazar 352, 374, 405, 490
Kalinin, Mikhail 272, 409, 494
Kamenev, Lev 201, 207, 413
Kandelaki, David (Soviet trade representative) 299–300, 302-303, 308–9, 311–13, 351, 490
Kapitsa, Pyotr (Soviet physicist) 419
Kapp, Wolfgang (Kapp-Lüttwitz Putsch) 176
Karakhan, Lev (Soviet diplomat)
  China 143, 152, 499
  dismissed by Litvinov 96
  Litvinov on 99
  and Lockhart 36, 40
  and Stalin 96
  on Trotsky's attack of the Czechs 258
  on US intervention in the Russian Civil War 258
Katyn massacre 410, 415, 417, 441, 448
Kautsky, Karl (Czech-German Social Democrat) 8
Kellogg–Briand Pact (1928)
  and Bessarabia 175
  Litvinov's misgivings about 120, 128
  and Manchuria 150, 154, 157, 159, 396
  nature of pact and debate 109–11
  Soviet support for the Pact 86, 98, 111–12, 174, 266
  Stalin on France and the Pact 240
Kellogg, Frank B. (US Secretary of State) 278
Kennan, George (US ambassador to Soviet Union) 329, 380–1, 384, 385, 412
Kerensky, Alexander 18–19, 30–5, 141, 171, 259, 269, 440–1
Kettle, Michael (historian) 209
Khinchuk, Lev (Soviet ambassador to Germany) 189, 190, 424
Khrushchev, Nikita
  Austria and Yugoslavia 470
  Bukharin's trial 414, 415

Khushchev Nikita (cont)
    on German invasion of the Soviet Union 506
    Great Purges 416
    Kirov's murder 405, 407
    on Molotov and Stalin 493
    on plot to kill Litvinov 424–5, 467
    on Stalin 426
    on Trotsky 416
Kimmel, Husband E. (US admiral) 485
Kindermann, Carl (German student) 181
King, Joseph (British MP) 25
Kirov, Sergei 289, 405–8, 413
Kissinger, Henry 367–8
Kleist, Peter (German diplomat) 345
Knight, Amy (historian) 406
Kobulov, Bogdan (Beria's deputy) 423
Kolchak, Admiral Alexander (Russian White
    general) 46, 259, 269
Kollontai, Alexandra (Soviet ambassador and
    author) 264–5, 286, 293, 457, 467–8, 469
Koltsov, Mikhail (*Pravda* editor) 419
Kopp, Viktor (Soviet diplomat) 99, 499
Kosarev, Aleksandr (Komsomol leader) 414,
    415
Krassin, Leonid (Soviet diplomat) 47, 67, 167,
    178, 200, 201, 206
Krestinsky, Nikolai (Soviet diplomat)
    Chicherin's funeral service 100
    first Soviet ambassador to Germany 178
    Germany's reoccupation of the Rhineland
      310
    On Nazi Germany 189, 190–1
    Rapallo Treaty 187
    Soviet agents trials 181
    and Stalin 495
    trial of 418
Krivitsky, Walter (Soviet intelligence officer
    and defector) 381
Krupskaya, Nadezhda 414

L

La Guardia, Fiorello (Mayor of New York) 440
Lamont, Corliss (US socialist philosopher) 439
Lamont, Thomas W., Jr. (US banker) 439
Lansbury, George (British Labour Party leader)
    200–1, 207
Lansing, Robert (US Secretary of State) 259

Latvia
    customs preference agreement 249
    Eastern Locarno 281
    Kellogg-Briand Pact 174
    Moscow Conference (1922) 74
    recognition of Soviet Russia 50
    Soviet-Latvian relations 172, 173
Lausanne Conference (1922-23) 72–4, 102
Lausanne, Treaty of (1923) 308
Laval, Pierre (French Foreign Minister) 287,
    294, 295, 296, 319
    see also Hoare-Laval pact
Law, Andrew Bonar (British Prime Minister)
    199
Law, Richard (British government minister)
    338
League of Nations
    Abyssinia 296–9, 316, 318, 391
    Anschluss 319
    Chicherin on 86, 95, 276–7, 278
    and Churchill 289
    Czechoslovakia 326
    Eastern Locarno 287
    and Eden 317
    European Union idea 240–1
    Genevan Pan-European conference (1931-
      32) 241–50
    German-Soviet Berlin Treaty 182
    Germany's attempt to be admitted 168
    Germany's rearmament and Eden's visit to
      League of Nations (cont)
    Germany's reoccupation of the Rhineland
      305–6
    Germany's threat and deterioration of
      German-Soviet relations 299–304
    Germany's withdrawal from 135–6
    Henderson on re-establishing British-Soviet
      relations 219
    Japanese invasion of Manchuria 153–4, 156,
      158–60
    Lausanne conference (1922) 72, 73, 74
    Litvinov on 75, 86, 95, 127, 137–8, 240,
      316–18
    Negrín's request 388–9
    and Neville Chamberlain 289, 317
    Polish capture of Memel 75
    Polish capture of Vilnius 172

League of Nations (cont)
  Polish invasion of Lithuania 276
  Security Committee 103–4
  Sino-Japanese war 396–7
  Soviet application and admission to 171,
    194, 230, 269, 275, 279, 282–6, 484
  Soviet disenchantment with 334
  Soviet initial opposition to 276–8
  Soviet-Polish relations 279–81
  Spanish Civil War 381–2, 391–2
  and Stalin 102, 278, 279
  Stresa Conference (1932) 249–51, 293–5
  US relationship with 277–8,
  women's equality petition 286
  Woodrow Wilson's support for 259
  World Economic Conference (1927) 86–8,
    278
  see also disarmament; Nyon Conference
    (1937); Walters, Francis P. (Secretariat of
    League of Nations and historian)
League of Russian Revolutionary Socialist
  Democracy Abroad 2
Leeper, Sir Reginald (British diplomat) 14–15,
  17–18, 35
Lena Goldfields affair (1930) 210, 224
Lenin, Vladimir **231**, **232**, **233**
  1901 League of Russian Revolutionary
    Socialist Democracy Abroad 2
  1903 Second Russian Socialist Congress 2–3
  1907 5th Congress of the Russian Social
  Democratic Labour Party 5
  1913 International Socialist Bureau meeting
  8
  1914 Second International Conference 9
  1915 Socialist parties conference 14
  1918 Brest-Litovsk Treaty 24, 28–30
  1918 plot against 35
  1919 peace proposals to Allies 44
  1921-23 famine 53–4, 55, 56
  1922 Genoa Conference 62, 67
  1922 Hague Conference 72
  1922 Rapallo Treaty 92
  autocratic leadership 33, 225
  and Chicherin 68, 77
  and the Comintern 195, 196
  death 77
  on the defence of Petrograd 40–1

execution of cousin 19
  on the failure of the Polish Revolution 50
  ill health 68–9
  Iskra 2–3
  Ivy Litvinov on 80
  and Litvinov 2–3, 7, 14, 38, 60, 77, 79–80,
    468
  Marxism-Leninism 77–80, 504
  on the NEP 52
  praised by Ramsay Macdonald 41
  Sovnarkom chairman 412
  on surveillance of foreigners 56
  Trotsky on 90–1
  US-Russian relations 258
  US-Soviet relations 262–4, 267
  on world revolution 45–6, 177, 482
Liddell-Hart, Basil Henry (historian) 160–1
Liebknecht, Karl 12
Life magazine 15, 438, 439, 442–3, 476
Lithuania
  customs preference agreement 249
  Eastern Locarno 281
  Kellogg-Briand Pact 174
  Polish-Lithuanian relations 73, 75, 172, 173–
    4, 276
  recognition of Soviet Russia 50
Litvinov, Ivy (Litvinov's wife), **235**
  her life
    connection with Carswell 6
    dinner in Eden's honour 292
    editing a Russian/English dictionary 468
    funeral of George V 303
    Great Purges years 417, 419
    incident with Potemkin's wife 373
    joins Maxim in Estonia 51
    joins Maxim in Moscow 59
    Kuibyshev 430
    life after Maxim's dismissal 372, 375
    life in the US 436, 437, 450
    Life magazine article 15, 438
    living in fear of arrest 471
    marriage and children 14, 15, 47, 51,
      350,420
    Maxim's death 468–70, 483
    Maxim's unfaithfulness 475
    New York Times interview 464
    precautionary measures 457, 465, 466

Litvinov (Ivy) Cont
  reasons for not defecting 444–5
  religion 270
  secretary of UK ' People's Embassy 27
  Stalin and her letter to a friend in the West
  419
  standard of living 479–80
  Sverdlovsk job 419–20
  talented writer 475
  on Litvinov
    accusations of bribery 479–80
    Copenhagen and 'plutocratic' husband 47
    his dismissal 354, 357
    his happiest time 81
    and the Metro-Vickers incident 228, 478
    'misfit' description 425
    and the Nazi-Soviet Pact 369
    and the NEP 52–3, 80
    and news of the Russian Revolution 15
    and Vyshinsky 376
  views on
    Doctors' Plot 468
    Lenin 80
    Russian Revolution 19, 419
    Stalin's Soviet Union 502
    Trotsky 80
    US famine relief 55
Litvinov, Maxim **231, 232, 234, 235**
  personal details
    ambition and drive 81, 472
    background 1, 472
    BBC listener 468, 476
    capable of lying 101, 410
    death 468–70, 483
    dictionary of synonyms compiler 467
    Jewish background and antisemitism 218,
      356, 357, 358, 375, 477–8
    liking for English literature 14
    liking for international meetings 86, 88
    London jobs (up to 1917) 8, 9, 14
    marital unfaithfulness 419, 420, 436, 475
    marriage and children 14, 15, 47, 51
    medals 309, 409, 469, 502
    no interest in military tactics 506
    plot to kill him 424–5, 467
    political status and influence 491–2, 495–
      8, 502

    pseudonyms 1, 7, 27–8
    reputation and testimonies 472–5, 476,
      477–8, 484, 494–5, 501–3
    retirement and last years 465–71
    sense of humour and wit 473, 486
    Soviet Diplomatic Dictionary biography
      471
    standard of living 55, 59, 79, 444, 479–80
    style as Foreign Commissar 140
    systematic working methods 95
    thoughts of defecting 444–5
  political career (1899-1917)
    1903 Second Russian Socialist Congress
      2–3
    1905 3rd Congress of the Russian Social
      Democratic Labour Party 4
    1907 5th Congress of the Russian Social
      Democratic Labour Party 5–6
    1907 12th International Socialist
      Conference 7
    1913 International Socialist Bureau
      meeting 8
    1914 Second International Conference 9
    1915 Socialist parties conference 10–12,
      14
    1917 London Committee for the
      Repatriation of Émigrés 15
    early revolutionary activity and prison 1–
      2
    escape to Bulgaria 5
    escape to Switzerland 2
    first meeting with Chicherin 9
    first meeting with Lenin 2
    first meeting with Stalin 5
    involvement with revolutionary
      newspapers 2–3, 4, 468
    and the Mensheviks 7
    news of the Russian Revolution 15
    Paris and London 7–8
    provision of arms to revolutionaries 4–5
    Rosa Luxemburg on 8
  political career (1917-22)
    1918 Allies' intervention 40, 41
    1918 Brest-Litovsk Treaty 28–30
    1919 peace proposals to Allies 42–3, 44–5
    1919 peace talks with Baltic States 46

Litvinov Maxim (cont)
1919 Press Statement propaganda outside Russia 43
1920 Copenhagen trade talks 47
1920 prisoner exchange agreement 46–7, 60, 198–9
1920 Russian-Polish War 93
1920 treaty with France 47
1921 British-Soviet trade talks 47),
1921 British-Soviet trade talks 47
1921 appointment as Deputy Foreign Commissioner 59, 60
1921 appointment as envoy to Estonia 50–1
1921 British-Soviet trade talks 47
1921 famine relief agreement with the US 53–7, 58, 60
1922 Genoa Conference 62–5, 67, 72, 400
1922 Hague Conference 68–72
1922 Lausanne Conference 72–4
1922 Rapallo Treaty 91, 497
1922 treaty with Czechoslovakia 68
Bolshevik ambassador 17–18, 20
British-Soviet relations 198–203
Chicherin's release 17
Comintern 196
criticism of Kerensky 34–5
Daily Herald affair 200–1
eviction from London Embassy premises 30–1
first diplomatic bag 27
Foreign Collegiate appointment 38
Labour Leader 1918 article 20–2
Labour Party Conference (1918) 32
Labour Party Conference address (1918) 22–5
on Lockhart 18
Lockhart/Litvinov arrests 35–7
meeting with Mersey Russian mutiny sailors 26
protest against Russian émigrés' conscription in British Army 27, 28
recognition of the Soviet Union 76
return to Moscow 36
revolutionary activities in UK 27–8
supervision of foreign currency 51
US-Russian relations 35, 38, 257–8, 261, 264–5
WWI and advocacy of unilateral peace 9, 23–4

political career (1922-39)

1925 Locarno Treaty 82–4
1927-30 Disarmament Preparatory Commission 102–8, 113–18
1927 Geneva Conference 85
1927 World Economic Conference 86–7
1928 Kellogg-Briand Pact 86, 98, 111–12, 120, 128
1929 speech to Central Committee 90
1930 London Conference 116
1931-32 Genevan Pan-European conference 241–7, 250
1932-34 Geneva Disarmament Conference 119–21, 124–5, 127–9, 134, 136–9
1932 Stresa Conference 250–1
1933 World Economic Conference 251–6
1935 Franco-Soviet Pact 295–6
1936 Council of the League of Nations meeting 305–6
1937 Brussels Conference 495
1939 tripartite agreement proposal 347–8, 349–50
Anschluss 318, 319
appointed member of Sovnarkom 412
appointment as Foreign Commissar 90, 95, 96, 140
British-Soviet relations (1922-37) 84, 180–1, 198, 203–18, 220–9, 303, 315–16
British-Soviet relations (1938-39) 338–9, 345–6, 349
Bukharin's trial 414–15
Comintern 196–7
Czechoslovakia 320–9, 341, 342
Eastern Locarno 287, 288
Eden's visit to Moscow 289–93
Franco-Soviet relations 166, 169, 171, 305
German invasion of the Soviet Union 506–7
German-Soviet relations (1922-32) 176, 180, 181, 182–5

Litvinov (Maxim) (Cont)
German-Soviet relations (1932-38) 186–94, 299–303, 304, 305–6, 309–10, 311–14, 408
German-Soviet relations (post-Munich) 337
Great Purges 313, 416, 417–19, 423, 424–5, 426
159-163
Japanese invasion of Manchuria
Japanese-Soviet relations 151, 153, 164, 401–2
Kirov's murder 407
League of Nations 277, 278–9, 284–5, 286, 289, 294–5, 334
League of Nations and Abyssinia 296–9, 316, 318
League of Nations and Czechoslovakia 326
League of Nations and the Rhineland issue 307
Litvinov protocol 89, 112, 288
Munich agreement 328, 332–3, 334
Polish-Soviet relations 173–5, 180, 279–81, 333, 345–6
Rumanian-Soviet relations 169–70
Sino-Japanese war 165, 398–400, 401
Sino-Soviet relations 84, 144–6, 148, 149–52, 161–3, 402, 404
Soviet economy 89, 237–8
Spanish Civil War 377, 379–82, 384–9, 390, 391–2
US-Soviet relations 266, 267–75
Zhdanov's public criticism of 420–3
political career (1939-46)
ambassadorship to US 373, 424, 434–42, 443–50, 496, 501
Atlantic Charter negotiations 436
back at the Foreign Commissariat 430
Beaverbrook-Harriman-Stalin talks 431–4
disagreement with US and UK on Second Front 442, 448–9
dismissal as Foreign Commissar 350, 351–65
dismissal from the Party Central Committee 375–6
final dismissal 463, 464–5
Finland delegation 457–8
Hottelet interview 355, 464
Katyn massacre 441
Lend-Lease 442
Moscow foreign ministers meetings 451, 452–3
Nazi-Soviet Pact 356, 368–71, 373
on Nazi world domination ambitions 431
Operation Barbarossa 427–30
plot to kill him 424–5, 467
post-dismissal duties and life 372–5
post-US ambassadorship duties 450–1, 453, 457–9
post-war duties 462
Special Commission on the post-war order (1944-45) 453–5
Yalta Conference (1945) 459
relationship with Stalin
alleged defence of Stalin against angry Dockers 6
anticipating Stalin's desires 406
areas of disagreements 498–501
assessment of Stalin's character 425–6
aversion to Stalin's communism 187
comparison with Lenin 79–80
criticism of Stalin's power 501
enjoying Stalin's support 89, 90, 98, 255, 309, 409, 486
first meeting with 5
'hot line' to Stalin 497, 502
losing Stalin's support 355, 376, 437, 444, 448, 486
posthumous letters to Stalin 470
spared from the purges 423, 424–6, 502
special relationship 355
Stalin and Ivy's letter to a friend in the West 419
Stalin and Zhdanov's public criticism of Litvinov 422
Stalin's and Litvinov's pragmatism 293
Stalin's gift of a dacha to Litvinov 59
standing up to Stalin 493, 504
supporting Stalin against Trotsky 91
relationships with other Soviet politicians
Borodin 99, 151
Bukharin 414
Chicherin 9, 17, 81, 85, 89, 94–6, 97–8

Litvinov (Maxim) (Cont)
   Dekanozov 501
   Kirov 407
   Kollontai 467–8
   Lenin 2–3, 7, 14, 38, 60, 77, 79–80, 468
   Maisky 226
   Molotov 355, 371, 373, 376, 437, 457, 488–90, 501
   Potemkin 315, 373
   Trotsky 80, 91, 92, 93, 100, 240
   Vyshinsky, 501
  relationships with/views on other personalities
   Chamberlain (Neville) 319, 343
   Edward VIII 303
   Franco 394–5, 460
   Harriman 458
   Herriot 171
   Laval 319
   Lloyd George 200
   Ribbentrop 369–70
   Roosevelt 368, 437, 447–8, 467, 474
   Simon 319
   Sumner Welles 286, 443, 474, 475, 484
  views on
   Afghanistan 98
   aggression vs. defence 128–30, 364
   appeasement 409, 484
   atomic bomb 461
   attracting foreign capital 102
   avoidability of war 351–2
   balance of power concept 122
   British aristocracy 428
   capitalism and wars 136
   China 98–9
   collectivisation 240, 413
   communism 36, 45–6, 411
   culture 375
   economics 242–4
   freedom of the press 44
   friendship between nations 274
   geniuses 468
   German Communists 500
   German Socialists 7
   Great Purges 417–18
   individual freedom 95
   Japan and Pearl Harbour 485
   League of Nations 75, 86, 95, 127, 137–8, 240, 284, 316–18
   Locarno Treaty 180, 181, 306, 314
   National Socialism 187, 189, 500
   azi Germany's expansionism 431, 485
   Nazi persecution of the Jews 286, 476–7
   Nazi-Soviet Pact 370, 489–90
   NEP 52–3, 80, 89
   Poland and the Poles 441–2, 452
   post-war order 456–7, 459, 460–2, 463, 465, 466, 470
   public opinion 120, 288
   Rapallo Treaty 96, 183, 187, 192, 290, 408
   religion 51, 476–7
   Rumania's right to Bessarabia 93
   Russian Civil War and Red Army 46
   Russian Revolution 18–19, 20–3
   Soviet achievements 413
   Soviet army officers' trials 417
   Soviet Constitution 410, 411–12
   Soviet foreign policy principles 481–2, 483–4
   Spanish War 384–5, 390, 393, 500
   US press 410–11, 444, 500
   women's equality 286
   world revolution 92, 93, 177, 456, 480–2
   writing his memoirs 468
Litvinov, Mikhail (Litvinov's son) 15
Litvinov, Pavel (Litvinov's grandson) 412
Litvinov protocol 89, 112, 288
Litvinov, Tanya (Litvinov's daughter) **236**
  birth in Britain 14
  on Gnedin's interrogation 424
  on her parents' thoughts of defecting 444
  on Litvinov and avoidability of war 351–2
  on Litvinov and Czechoslovakia 320
  on Litvinov and Molotov 488
  on Litvinov and Potemkin 373
  on Litvinov and the Spanish Civil War 384–5, 390, 393, 500
  on Litvinov being liked by Stalin 486
  on Litvinov during the Purges 419
  on Litvinov not being authorised to talk to foreign journalists 489
  on Litvinov wanting Molotov's job 430

Litvinov Tanya (cont)
   on Litvinov writing for academic journals 374
   Litvinov's ambassadorship to the US 437, 447
   on Litvinov's appreciation of the Nazi threat 185
Litvinov, Tanya (Litvinov's daughter)
   on Litvinov's comparison between Lenin and Stalin 79–80
   on Litvinov's dismissal 351, 356–7, 358, 364, 365
   on Litvinov's opinion of Bukharin 414
   on Litvinov's reaction to Kirov's murder 407
   on Litvinov's remark on geniuses 468
   on Litvinov's views on culture 375
   on Litvinov's views on the Soviet army officers' trials 41
   On Litvinov's views on the Soviet constitution 411
   on Molotov and his wife 493
   on Molotov's alleged attack on Litvinov 354
   note with Litvinov's letter to Stalin 470
   photographed with H.G. Wells 476
   on plans to liquidate Litvinov 424, 467
   on Sheinis' Litvinov-Ribbentrop story 369
   support for the Spanish Republican cause 377
   sympathy for Austrians after Anschluss 318–19
Lloyd George, David
   1918 Allies' intervention 42
   1919 Russian peace proposals to Allies 45
   1920 prisoner exchange agreement 199
   1922 Genoa Conference 63–5, 67–8
   and Churchill 42–3, 64
   Daily Herald affair 201
   on Joseph Chamberlain and British-Russian relations 197
   Litvinov on 200
   negotiations with the Bolsheviks 17, 38
   and Neville Chamberlain 42, 335, 343–4, 347
   on Russia and private property/compensation 70
Lloyd-Greame, Philip (British diplomat)70
Locarno Treaty of (1925)

and 1932 Stresa conference 293–4
and 1935 Franco-Soviet Pact 295
Chicherin's views on 82–3, 181, 182
France's criticism of 130–1
and Franco-Soviet relations 167–8
Hitler's views on 305
Litvinov's views on 180, 181, 306, 314
Soviet government's views on 81–4, 181, 210
Stalin's views on 83
see also Eastern Locarno

Lockhart, R. H. Bruce (British diplomat) 17–18, 20, 35–7, 40, 97, 466, 473, 480
Lodygensky, Georges (Russian Red Cross) 51
London Committee for the Repatriation of Émigrés (LCRE) 15
London Conference (1930) 116, 123
Lunacharsky, Anatoly **234**
Lüttwitz, Walther von (Kapp-Lüttwitz Putsch) 176
Luxemburg, Rosa 8, 176
Lytton Report 156, 159–60,400

M

MacArthur, Douglas (US general) 436
Macdonald, Ramsay
   Brest-Litovsk Treaty 30
   Geneva Disarmament Conference (1932-34) 131–5, 139
   Herriot's visit 166
   Hoover and the Japanese capture of Shanghai 158
   on Lenin 41
   quoted by Austen Chamberlain 212
   recognition of the Soviet Union 167, 206
   World Economic Conference (1933) 254
   Zinoviev Letter affair 209
Macleod, Iain (British government minister) 299
McMahon, Francis (US Catholic professor) 439
McNair, Lesley J. (US general) 439

McNeill, Ronald *see* Cushendum Ronald 1st Baron (British Minister)

Ivan Maisky, (Soviet Ambassador to UK)
  appointed ambassador to UK 226–7
  and Beaverbrook 433
  and Beria 478–9
  Channon on 345
  Maisky Ivan,(Cont)
  China and the US 396
  Churchill 226
  dismissal 445–6
  Eden's visit to Moscow 287
  German invasion of the Soviet Union 506, 507
  German-Soviet rapprochement 336–7
  Halifax and British assistance to Poland and Rumania 345–6
  on Litvinov and Czechoslovakia 325
  on Litvinov and the Nazi threat 185
  on Litvinov ready to return to Russia (1918) 17
  on Litvinov's ambassadorship to UK 20, 30–1
  Litvinov's direct instructions to 315, 351
  and Litvinov's dismissal 362
  Litvinov's friendship 226
  and Litvinov's funeral 469
  on Litvinov's style as Foreign Commissar 140
  London Committee for the Repatriation of Émigrés 15
  membership of the Party Central Committee 375
  Metro-Vickers incident 228
  Munich agreement 327, 328, 332
  Munich agreement and British-Soviet relations 338–9
  on Neville Chamberlain 339
  Neville Chamberlain and Poland 343
  Operation Barbarossa 427, 429
  Spanish Civil War 381, 390–1
  Special Commission on the post-war order (1944-45) 453–6
  Stalin and Czechoslovakia 324
  Stalin and Spain 500
  Stalin and the Finland airport incident 352–4
  Supreme Soviet elections 467

Malenkov, Georgy (Soviet Politician) 354, 358, 417, 494
Manchuria 152–63, 396
Mantel, J. J. (US railway expert) 150
Manuilsky, Dmitry (Soviet politician) 414
Mao Zedong 147, 164, 396
Marriner, Theodore (US diplomat) 109–10, 275
Marshall Plan 135, 330
Martov, Julius (Russian Menshevik) 4, 5
Marx, Karl (Marxism) 78, 79, 292, 329, 398, 410
Marxism-Leninism 77–80, 504
Masaryk, Tomáš 324, 329
Mastny, Vojtech (historian) 445, 464
Medlicott, William (historian) 347
Medved, Feodor (Leningrad NKVD chief) 406
Medvedev, Roy (Soviet historian and dissident) 6
Medvedev, Zhores (Soviet biologist, historian and dissident) 415
Meir, Golda (Israeli ambassador to Soviet Union) 477
Mensheviks
  1907 5th Congress of the Russian Social Democratic Labour Party 5
  and the Bolsheviks 3, 4, 19, 26
  and Litvinov 7
Merekalov, Alexei (Soviet ambassador to Germany) 313, 334–5, 348, 352, 369
Metro Vickers incident (1933) 129, 227–8, 254, 410, 478
Meyerowitz, Siegfried (Latvian Premier) 56
Meynell, Francis (*Daily Herald* director) 200
Mikhail, Grand Duke *see* Romanov, Grand Duke Mikhail Aleksandrovich
Mikhoels, Solomon (Soviet actor and theatre director) 467
Mikoyan, Anastas (Soviet Commissar of Trade)
  22nd anniversary of the Russian Revolution 374
  Bukharin's trial 415
  credit negotiations with Germany 334
  and Karakhan 96
  Katyn massacre 415, 417
  meeting with Stalin about Germany's intentions 352

Mikoyan Anastas (cont)
  New Economic Policy (NEP) 75
  US-Soviet trade 266
Mikoyan, Stepan (Mikoyan's son) 405–6, 407,
  415
Miner, Steven (historian) 364, 445, 485, 486
Modin, Yuri (KGB agent) 384
Moffat, Jay (US diplomat) 495

Molotov, Polino (Molotov's wife) 415, 419,
  475, 493
Molotov–Ribbentrop Pact *see* Nazi-Soviet Pact
  (1939)
Molotov, Vyacheslav **235**
  biographical details
    early revolutionary activity and betrayal 1
    imprisonment of his wife 415
    knowledge of foreign countries 360
    sense of humour 78
    working style 496
  British-Soviet relations 220–1, 349, 363,
    365, 372
  Churchill on 494
  Finland delegation 458
  Franco-Soviet relations 169
  Germany (up to 1941 invasion)
    German-Soviet relations 192, 349, 408
    on Germany's territorial ambitions 368
    Kandelaki mission 312, 490
    meeting with Hitler (1940) 504–5
    meeting with Stalin about Germany's
      intentions 352
    Munich agreement 328, 332
    Nazi atrocities against the Jews 477
    Nazi-Soviet Pact 371, 373
    see also Nazi-Soviet Pact (1939)
  League of Nations, Soviet entry into 279,
    285–6
  Litvinov
    antagonism between the two men 355,
      371, 373, 376, 437, 457, 488–90, 501
    bugging of Hottelet interview of Litvinov
      464
    Litvinov's and Maisky's recall to Moscow
      446
    Litvinov's dismissal 353, 354, 355–6,
      357–8, 362, 363

    Litvinov's posthumous letter to Stalin re.
      Molotov's mistakes 470
    plot to kill Litvinov 467
    Zhdanov's public criticism of Litvinov
      422
  Poland 359, 452
  and Roosevelt 368, 458–9
  Sino-Soviet relations 403
  Soviet politics
    17th Party Congress 405–6

    22nd anniversary of Russian Revolution
      374
    appointed Foreign Commissar 96
    Bukharin's trial 414
    collectivisation 239
    foreign ministry uniforms 458
    Kirov's murder 406, 407–8
    New Economic Policy (NEP) 75
    and Potemkin 315
    receiving direct reports from diplomats
      351
    removal of Foreign Commissariat officials
      501
    Sovnarkom 412
    and Stalin 353, 408–9, 425, 485–8, 490,
      492–4, 496, 504
    surveillance of US nationals 56
    on Tukhachevskii 417
  US recognition of the Soviet Union 272
  WWII
    Beaverbrook-Harriman-Stalin talks 432,
      433, 434
    German invasion of the Soviet Union
      503–7
    Hopkins-Stalin meetings 430–1
    Operation Barbarossa 427
    Second Front issue 448
    Special Commission on the post-war
      order (1944-45) 453, 455, 456
    Yalta Conference 459
Mongolia 141–2, 143
Montefiore, Simon (historian) 5, 405, 467
Montgomery, Bernard (British general) 493
Monzie, Anatole de (French diplomat) 166–7
Morel, E. D. (British socialist politician) 207

Morgenthau, Henry, Jr. (US Treasury Secretary) 439, 474

Morley, Raymond (advisor to F. D. Roosevelt) 254

Moscow Conference (1922) 74

Mosely, Philip (historian) 483

Mosley, Oswald (Britsh Fascist Leader) 237

Motta, Giuseppe (Swiss politician) 246, 283

Munich agreement (1938) 160, 287, 320, 322, 325, 327–36, 338–9, 341–2

Munzenberg, Willi (German communist) 315

Mussolini, Benito
    Abyssinia 296, 299, 391, 484
    Eden on appeasing Mussolini 383–4
    and Franco 377, 392, 394
    Nyon Conference 387–8
    restoration of Soviet-Italian relations 76
    Stresa Conference 294

N

Nabokov, Konstantin D. (Russian ambassador to UK) 18, 26, 27

Nadolny, Rudolf (German ambassador to Soviet Union) 131, 134, 186, 290, 334

Naimark, Norman (historian) 493

Napoleon 37, 45, 164, 440

Nasser, Gamal Abdel 409

Nazi-Soviet Pact (1939)
    Gromyko on Litvinov's and Molotov's disagreement 489–90
    impact on Poland 359
    impact on Soviet prestige 329
    impact on US-Soviet relations 324
    Litvinov's and Maisky's warnings 339
    and Litvinov's dismissal 348–9, 356, 363, 368–72, 373
    secret protocol 410
    signing of **235**
    Soviet justification (Falsification of History) 360
    vs. tripartite agreement proposals (France, UK and Soviet Union) 347

Negrín, Juan (Spanish Prime Minister) 383, 388–9, 391–2

Neurath, Konstantin von (German Foreign Secretary)
    Berlin Treaty 183–4

Geneva Disarmament Conference (1932-34) 126

German-Soviet relations under National Socialism 187–8, 194, 289, 300, 309, 312–13
    Nazi-Soviet Pact 369

Nikolayev, Leonid (Kirov's assassin) 406–7, 408

Nine Power Treaty (1922) 396, 397–8, 400

Nixon, Richard 367–8

Noel-Baker, Philip (British Cabinet Minister) 155

Northledge, F. S. (historian) 215–16

Novaya Zhizn' (newspaper) 4

Nove, Alec (historian) 238, 371

Nuorteva, Santeri (Comintern Director of Propaganda) 195–6

Nuremberg War Crime Trials 410

Nyon Conference (1937) 385–8

O

O'Connor, Timothy E. (historian) 85, 94

O'Grady, James (British MP) 46–7, 94, 95, 198

Orakhelashvili, Mikhail (Kirov's colleague) 408

Ordzhonikidze, Grigory (Sergo) 96, 490

Orlov, Aleksandr (Soviet defector) 384, 405, 406, 408, 416

Ossinski, Nikolai (Soviet diplomat) 87–8, 278

Overy, Richard (historian) 186, 405, 416

Ovey, Esmond (British ambassador to Soviet Union) 184, 225, 227–8, 478

P

Painlevé, Paul (French Prime Minister) 167

Papen, Franz von (German Chancellor) 290

Paris Peace Conference (1919) 38, 44, 46, 48

Pasternak, Boris 419

Patterson Scheme 248

Paul-Boncour, Joseph (French Prime Minister) 102–3, 121, 124

Pavlichenko, Ludmilla (Soviet female soldier) 438

Pavlov, Dmitry (Soviet general) 505

Pavlov, Vladimir (Soviet diplomat and interpreter) 459

Payne, Robert (author and historian) 45, 54
Pechatnov, Vladimir (historian) 453
Pétain, Maréchal Philippe 367
Petrescu-Comnen, Nicolae (Rumanian Foreign Minister) 323
Petrovsky, Grigory (Soviet politician) 414
Phillips, Hugh (historian)
    on Chicherin and Rapallo 68, 96
    on Chicherin's release 17

    Phillips, Hugh (Cont)
    on Litvinov and the Disarmament Preparatory Commission 104–5
    on Litvinov and the Finland delegation 457
    on Litvinov's escape to Bulgaria 5
    on Litvinov's relationship with the Mensheviks 7
    on Poland and the Soviet admission to the League of Nations 282
    on the Special Commission on the post-war order (1944-45) 453
Phillips, William (US Under Secretary of State) 268
Piatnitsky (or Pyatnitsky), Osip (Soviet Comintern leader) 191
Pilsudski, Józef Klemens (Polish Dictator)48, 49, 50, 93, 173, 200
Plekhanov, Georgy 4
Plymouth, Ivor Windsor-Clive, Earl of (British Under-Secretary of State for Foreign Affairs) 331
Poincaré, Raymond (French Prime Minister) 168
Poland
    and the Baltic states 112, 172–3, 276, 290
    Bessarabia 175
    British-Polish relations 343–4
    Czechoslovakia 323, 328
    Danzig 345
    Eastern Locarno 288
    Eden on 292
    Franco-Polish relations 366
    German-Polish non-aggression pact (1934) 279–80, 290
    Jewish population 287, 329, 359
    Katyn massacres 410, 415, 417, 441, 448
    Kellogg-Briand Pact 174
    Lausanne conference (1922) 72–3, 74
    Lenin on the failure of the Polish Revolution 50
    Lithuanian-Polish relations 73, 75, 172, 173–4, 276
    Litvinov's attitude towards 441–2, 452
    Moscow foreign ministers meetings 451–2
    Munich agreement 330
    Nazi-Soviet Pact, impact on 359
    Russian-Polish War (1920) 48–50, 93, 120, 171–2, 176, 200
    Soviet acquisition of Eastern Poland 428
    Soviet-Polish Non-aggression pact (1932) 175
    Soviet-Polish relations 166, 171–5, 180, 279–81, 282–3, 333, 345–7
    Teschen, annexation of 323, 333
    Versailles Treaty and Polish Western border 180
    WWII casualties 329
Politis, Nicholas (Greek delegate) 130, 474
Ponsonby, Lavina (friend of Ivy Litvinov) 465, 466

Pope, Arthur (biographer of Litvinov)
    assessment of his biography of Litvinov 472
    on Austen Chamberlain and the 'Soviet problem' 217
    on Bukharin and the Kellogg-Briand Pact 112
    on Litvinov and the Japanese threat 485
    on Litvinov and the San Francisco conference 459
    on Litvinov and the US recognition of the Soviet Union 256
    on Litvinov as a new kind of diplomat 97
    Litvinov's alleged defence of Stalin against angry dockers 6
    on Litvinov's criticism of German socialists 7
    On Litvinov's Dismissal as Foreign Affairs Commissar357
    on Litvinov's dismissal from the Party Central Committee 375
    on Litvinov's experience of prison 1
    on Litvinov's first meeting with Ivy 14
    on Litvinov's job with London publisher 9

Portsmouth, Treaty of (1905) 499

Portugal, and Spanish Civil War 380, 383, 389, 392

Possony, Stefan (economist and military strategy specialist) 50

Postyshev, Pavel (Soviet politician) 414

Potemkin, Vladimir (Soviet First Deputy Foreign Affairs Commissar) 301, 315, 333, 351, 362–3, 369, 373, 495

Potresov, Alexander (Russian Menshevik) 4

Pownall, Sir Henry (British general) 298

Preston, Paul (historian) 390, 393, 394

Priestley, J. B. 338

Purcell, A. A. (British Labour Party politician) 207

Pyatakov, Georgy (Bolshevik revolutionary) 75

Pyatnitsky (or Piatnitsky), Osip (Soviet Comintern leader) 191

Q
Quinn, Cyril (US famine relief mission) 473

R
Radek, Karl (Russian Communist Dissident) 68, 142, 188, 414, 416

Radziwill, Prince Janusz (Polish diplomat) 73

Rakovsky, Christian (Soviet ambassador to UK and France) 167, 206–7, 208–9, 210, 213, 276

Ransome, Arthur (British author and *Manchester Guardian* correspondent) 92

Rapallo, Treaty of (1922)
  Allies' reactions to 65–8
  Chicherin, architect of 62–3, 68, 96
  Hitler on 194
  importance of for German-Soviet relations 177–8
  and Litvinov 96, 183, 187, 192, 290, 408
  and the Locarno Treaty 82–4
  and National Socialism 187
  ratification of prolongation 184
  and recognition of the Soviet Union 72
  and Soviet financial commitments 70
  and Stalin 92
  and Trotsky 68, 92, 94

Rathbone, Eleanor (British MP) 320, 389–90

Rathenau, Walter (German Foreign Minister) 65, 178

Rayski, Ludomil (Polish army commander) 280

Read, Anthony (historian) 356, 358, 488–9

Reilly, Sydney (British spy) 209

Resis, Albert (historian) 347, 354, 503

Reynaud, Paul (French politician) 367

Rhineland 75, 299, 305–7, 310, 314

Rhur 178

Ribbentrop, Joachim von **235**, 345, 359, 369–70, 371, 501

Ribbentrop–Molotov Pact *see* Nazi-Soviet Pact (1939)

Riga, Peace Treaty of (1921) 171, 283

Roberts, Andrew (historian) 78

Roberts, Frank (British Foreign Office) 465

Roberts, Geoffrey (historian) 301, 312, 365, 498, 501

Roberts, Henry L. (historian) 357, 484, 497

Roberts, John Morris (historian) 176, 377

Rokossovsky, Konstantin (Soviet general) 465

Romanov, Grand Duke Mikhail Aleksandrovich 15

Rommel, Erwin 344–5

Roosevelt, Eleanor 474

Roosevelt, Franklin D.
  and the Anschluss 319
  and appeasement 484
  Atlantic Charter 436
  debts moratorium 255–6
  Hitler's attack on 352
  Hopkins-Stalin meetings 430–1
  on Litvinov 368, 437, 447, 474
  Litvinov on 447–8, 467
  Macdonald disarmament plan 134–5
  meeting with ambassador Litvinov 434–5
  meeting with Churchill and Eden 445
  Molotov on 368
  Mussolini's invasion of Abyssinia 297
  New Deal 237
  Operation Barbarossa 427
  post-WWII Eastern Europe 456
  reception of his death in Soviet Union 458–9
  recognition of the Soviet Union 268–74
  Second-Front disagreement with Litvinov 442

Roosevelt (Franklin D) (cont)
  Sino-Japanese war 396, 397, 398, 400, 401
  Soviet bugging of his bedroom 445
  and Stalin 445, 447
  Teheran Conference 274, 445, 449
  World Economic Conference (1933) 254
  Yalta Conference 459
Rosenberg, Alfred (Nazi Party) 190, 278, 290, 336
Roskill, Stephen (historian) 156
Rothstein, Andrew (historian) 468
Rothstein, Theodore (British communist) 17–18
Rouchdy Bey, Dr (Turkish statesman) 105
Rubinshtein, N. (historian) 58
Rumania
  Bessarabia 72, 93, 168, 169–70, 174–5, 499
  Czechoslovakia 323–4
  Kellogg-Briand Pact 174
  Lausanne conference (1922) 72
Russia
  1905 Revolution 3–5
  1917 Revolution 18–23
  Civil War 38–42, 258, 259
  Kronstadt mutiny 53, 94
  oppression of Finland 12, 14
  oppression of Jews 14
  Provisional Government 17–18, 29
  Russo-Japanese war 4, 141
  see also Brest-Litovsk, Treaty of (1918);
    Rapallo, Treaty of (1922); Soviet
    Russia/Soviet Union
Russian Orthodox Church 51, 53, 54, 79
Russian Red Cross 51, 56
Rykov, Alexei 69, 224, 412, 414, 415

S

Salisbury, Harrison (US journalist) 467
San Francisco Conference (1945) 459
Schacht, Hjalmar (German Minister of Economics) 300, 301, 302, 308, 311–13
Schellenberg, Walter (German counter-intelligence chief) 416
Schnurre, Karl (German diplomat) 335, 337
Schulenburg, Friedrich-Werner von der (German ambassador to Soviet Union) 313, 321, 334, 359, 422
Schuman, Frederick (historian) 364

Scott, William Evans (author) 95, 187
Second International 9, 26, 196
security, vs. disarmament 121–2, 127
Seeckt, Hans von (German general) 177–8, 181
Seeds, William (British ambassador to Soviet Union) 226, 337–8, 343, 347, 355, 362–4, 476
Selassie, Haile 391
Sembat, Michel (French socialist) 10
Serge, Victor 238–9
Shakhty case (1928) 95, 182
Shaw, Bernard, and the Soviet admission to the League of Nations 284
Sheinis, Zinovy (Litvinov's biographer)
  assessment of his biography of Litvinov 472
  events omitted in biography 453, 457, 464
on France and the UK on Czechoslovakia 326
on the Hague Conference 69
on the Japanese invasion of Manchuria 160
on the Kronstadt mutiny 53
on Litvinov
  and Chicherin's release 17
  and collective farming 413
  and Czechoslovakia 321
  and 'enemies of the people' 416
  and Gnedin's interrogation 423–4
  and the Great Purges 417
  his alleged defence of Stalin against angry Dockers 6
  his alleged warning of a German attack 506
  his ambassadorship to the US 442, 443, 444
  his declining an invitation to Iskra celebrations 468
  his definition of aggression 364
  his dismissal as Foreign Commissar 351, 357–8
  his dismissal from the Party Central Committee 375, 376–7
  his eight years of 'tranquillity' 81
  his escape to Bulgaria 5
  his eviction from his London Embassy premises 30–1
  his final dismissal 465
  his hearing the news of the Russian Revolution 15

Sheinis Zinovy (Cont)
  his Kondopog election 462
  his meeting Ivy 14
  his wanting Molotov's job 430
  and *Iskra* 3
  and Kerensky at the 1918 Labour Party
    Conference 32
  and the League of Nations 284
  and Molotov 488, 489
  and the Nazi-Soviet Pact 370
  and the Nyon Conference 387
  and Potemkin 315
  and Ribbentrop 369–70
  Sheinis, Zinovy
    and the Socialist parties of the Entente
      conference 10, 12
    spared by Stalin 423
  on Maisky and the Finland airport incident
    352–4
  on Russia 'without gendarmes' 38
  on the St Petersburg 1905 massacre 3
  on Western powers and Asia 401
Shirer, William (US journalist and historian)
  394
Shkiriatov, Matvei (Soviet Communist leader)
  414, 415
Short, Walter (US general) 485
Shostakovich, Dmitri (Soviet composer) 375
Shtein, Boris (Soviet diplomat) 76, 352
Shvernik, Nikolai (Soviet politician) 414
Simon, John (British Foreign Secretary)
  British-Soviet trade agreement 227, 249
  Eastern Europe 281
  Japanese invasion of Manchuria 155, 156, 160
  Macdonald disarmament plan 131
  Military conversations with Soviet union
    363
  meeting Hitler in Berlin with Eden 287, 289
  Metro Vickers incident and lifting of
    embargo on Soviet purchases 254
  Stresa agreement and League of Nations 295
Sinclair, Archibald, Bt (British Air Minister)
  442
Skoblevsky, Pyotr Aleksandrovich (Soviet
  general) 181
Smith, Derek (author) 372
Smith, Walter Bedell (US ambassador to Soviet

Union) 463, 466
Snell, Harry (British Peer) 331
Snow, Edgar (US journalist and author) 394–5,
  426, 457, 460–1, 501
Socialist parties of the Entente countries 10–14,
  25
Sokolnikov, Grigory (Soviet ambassador to
  UK) 86–7, 96, 225–6, 246–7
Soong, T. V. (Chinese Minister of Foreign
  Affairs) 442
Soviet Russia/Soviet Union
  Abyssinia 391
  Atlantic Charter 436
  Austrian-Soviet relations 470
  Baltic countries 46–7, 428, 447
  Berlin, Treaty of 182, 184
Soviet Russia/Soviet Union (Cont)
Bessarabia 169–70, 174–5
British-Soviet relations
  1921 British-Soviet Trade Agreement
    178, 202, 227, 249
  1924 British-Soviet commercial treaty
    207
  1927 ARCOS affair 84, 90, 146, 151,
    214–17
  1930 Lena Goldfields affair 210, 224
  1933 Metro-Vickers incident 129, 227–8,
    254, 410, 478
  1943 British-Soviet protocol 452
  British-Soviet relations (1919-22) 27–8,
    97–8, 166, 168, 195–203
  British-Soviet relations (1922-27) 203–17
  British-Soviet relations (1928-37) 89,
    217–30, 289–93, 303, 315–16, 337–9
  British-Soviet relations (1938-41) 343–7,
    349, 352, 355, 362–3, 365, 372, 430–1
  and the Comintern 85, 92, 195–6, 224
  recognition of the Soviet Union 76, 96,
    167, 206–8
  Soviet tripartite agreement proposals 347,
    349–50, 363, 365
China
  Chiang Kai-shek's anti-Soviet campaign
    144
  Kuomintang 142, 146–7
  Mongolia question 143

Soviet Russia (Cont)
 Russian-Chinese railway affair 140–1,
  147–50, 161–3, 164
 Sino-Japanese war 387, 397, 398–400,
  401
 Sino-Soviet relations 89–90, 143, 150,
  161, 163, 396, 402–4
 Sino-Soviet relations and raiding of
  Soviet Embassy 84, 145–6, 197
 Czechoslovakia 320–30
 domestic affairs
  1917 Revolution 18–23
  1936 Constitution 410, 411–12
  Cheka 19, 38, 53, 56, 78, 79

  Civil War 38–42, 258, 259
  collectivisation 238–40
  Communist elite's privileges 79, 479–80
  Doctors' Plot 468, 470, 475
  famine and US relief effort 51–2, 53–8,
   93, 140
  Five Year Plan 88–9, 114, 121, 240, 248,
   252, 302, 413
  foreign trade and dumping 247–8, 249
  foreign trade monopoly, relaxation of 88–
   9
  freedom of the press 44
  Great Depression and Soviet economy
   251–3
  human rights 412
  Kirov's murder 405–8
  Kronstadt mutiny 53, 94
  New Economic Policy (NEP) 52–3, 75,
   80, 89, 91–2
  scissors crisis 74–5
  Sovnarkom 412
  trials of army officers 416–17
  War Communism 52, 80, 91
  women's equality 286, 475
  see also Great Purges (1930s)
Estonia
 Estonian-Soviet relations 46, 47, 172, 173
 Litvinov's appointment as envoy to 50–1,
  59, 77
 Finish-Soviet relations 44–5, 50, 130, 172
  Finnish-Soviet Winter war (1939) 4, 324,
   457–8, 504

Franco-Soviet relations
 1932 Franco-Soviet Non-aggression Pact
  169–71, 194
 1935 Franco-Soviet Pact 295–6, 305,
  314–15
 Franco-Soviet relations 166–71, 372
 Soviet tripartite agreement proposals 347,
  349–50, 363, 365
German-Soviet relations
 ambivalence towards National Socialism
  186–9
 German-Soviet economic agreement
  (1936) 308, 309
 German-Soviet military collaboration
  177–8
 German-Soviet relations (1914-32) 77,
  166, 170, 175–86
 German-Soviet relations (1932-34) 186–
  94, 299–306, 308–14, 351, 408
 German-Soviet relations (post-Munich)
  334–7, 345, 348–9, 352
 Katyn massacre 410, 415, 417, 441, 448
 Shakhty case 95, 182
 Soviet agents trials 181
 Soviet support for German Communist
  uprisings 179
Japan
 Japanese aggression in Siberia 401–2
 Manchuria 152–4, 158–61, 162–3
 political recognition of the Soviet Union
  152–3
 Soviet-Japanese neutrality pact (1941)
  403
 Soviet leaders' differing views on Soviet-
  Japanese relations 151, 163–4
League of Nations
 admission to 171, 194, 230, 269, 275,
  279, 282–6, 484
 disenchantment with 334
 initial opposition to 276–8
Mongolia 142
Munich agreement 328, 332, 334
Polish-Soviet relations
 Katyn massacre 410, 415, 417, 441, 448
 Polish-Russian war (1920) 48–50, 93,
  120, 171–2, 176, 200
 Polish-Soviet Non-aggression (1932) 175

Soviet Russia (cont)

    Polish-Soviet relations 166, 171180,279–81, 282–3, 333, 345–7

    Soviet acquisition of Eastern Poland 428

Spanish Civil War 378–93

Teschen and Soviet-Polish relations 333

Turkish-Soviet relations 308

US-Soviet relations

    Lend-Lease 442, 454

    popularity of the US in the Soviet Union 140, 435–6, 439–40, 460

    US recognition of the Soviet Union 76–7, 96, 121, 123, 254, 256, 259–60, 267–75

    US Russian famine relief programme 53–8, 140

    US-Soviet relations (1917-22) 38–9, 257–62

    US-Soviet relations (1922-37) 262–75

    US-Soviet relations (1939-41) 352, 430–1

    US-Soviet relations (1941-43) and Litvinov's ambassadorship 373, 424, 434–42, 443–50, 464, 496, 501

WWI

    1918 Allies' intervention 38–40, 41–2, 52

    1919 peace proposals to Allies 42–3, 44–5

    1920 lifting of Europe's and US blockade 46

WWII

    German invasion of the Soviet Union 430, 445–6, 503–7

    Harriaman-Beaverbrook-Stalin talks 431–4

    Operation Barbarossa 375, 376, 424, 427–30, 458

    post-war alternatives 455–6

    Second Front issue 367, 448–9

    Special Commission on the post-war order (1944-45) 453–5

see also Kellogg–Briand Pact (1928); Locarno, Treaty of (1925); Nazi-Soviet Pact (1939); Rapallo, Treaty of (1922); Russia; Russian Orthodox Church

Soviet Union *see* Soviet Russia/Soviet Union

Spain

    belligerent rights 390, 391, 393

    Civil War 377–93

    disagreement between Litvinov and Stalin 500

    Nyon Conference (1937) 385–8

    post-Civil War relations with Germany and Italy 393–4

    POUM 382–3, 384–5

    withdrawal of volunteers 391–2, 393

    see also Franco, Francisco

Special Commission on the post-war order (1944-45) 453–6

Stalin, Joseph **232**, **235**

    and 5th Congress of the Russian Social Democratic Labour Party 5–6

    and China 144, 145, 146, 147, 149, 151–2, 396

    and the Comintern 196

    and Czechoslovakia 324

    domestic affairs

        17th Party Congress 405–6

        22nd anniversary of Russian Revolution 374

        1936 Soviet Constitution 410

        antisemitism and the Doctors' Plot 468

        Bukharin's trial 413–16

        Collectivisation 238, 239

        Declaration of Human Rights 412

        Five Year Plan 89

        foreign trade and dumping 248

        foreign trade monopoly, relaxation of 88–9

        Gnedin's interrogation 424

        Great Purges 313, 419, 426

        Industrial/military might and respect 146

        Kirov's murder 405–8

        Mikhoels' murder 467

        plot to kill Litvinov 467

        Shakhty case 95, 182

        Socialism in one country 482–3

        Sovnarkom 412

        Stomoniakov's arrest 419

        trials of army officers 416–17

        trials of German citizens 166

        Trotsky's downfall 90–1

    and Eastern European satellite states 484

    and France

        France 'the most aggressive of nations' 169, 240

Stalin Joseph Cont)
   Soviet tripartite agreement proposals 347–8, 350
   and Germany
      German Communist uprisings 179
      German invasion of the Soviet Union 503–7
      German offer of extended credit 302–3
      German Social Democrat-Communist alliance 186
      German Social Democrats 382
      German-Soviet relations 192–3, 194, 352
      Kandelaki's mission 312, 490
      Nazi-Soviet Pact 356, 370–1, 372, 373
   Stalin's March 1939 speech 340–1
   and Japan 151, 154–5, 163–4
   and the Kellogg-Briand Pact 112
   Khrushchev on 426, 493
   and the League of Nations 102, 278, 279
   and Litvinov's dismissals 354, 355, 360–1, 364–5, 445
      see also Litvinov, Maxim, relationship with Stalin
   and the Locarno Treaty 83
   and the Munich agreement 332, 334, 336

   Stalin Joseph (cont)
   Personal Traits
   capable of changing his mind 491
   cowardly bully 504
   faked rage at honours 494
   sadistic streak 495
   and the Rapallo Treaty 92
   relationships with
      Borodin 147
      Chicherin 68, 85, 88–9, 98, 99, 100
      Karakhan 96
      Krestinsky 495
      Maisky (Finland airport incident) 352–4
      Molotov 353, 408–9, 425, 485–8, 490, 492–4, 496, 504

      Roosevelt 445, 447
      see also Litvinov, Maxim, relationship with Stalin
   and Spain

Spanish Civil War 380, 389–90, 500
Spanish Civil War and POUM 382–3, 384–5
and the UK
   accusations of sabotage against British companies 166
   British-Soviet relations 198, 221, 223–4, 229–230, 347, 349, 372
   Eden on Stalin 292–3
   Eden on Stalin's approach to Germany 476
   Metro Vickers incident 129
   relations with the Labour Party 225
   Soviet tripartite agreement proposals 347–8, 350
and the US
   US recognition of the Soviet Union 272–3
   US-Soviet relations 266, 267, 275
WWII
   Beaverbrook-Harriman-Stalin talks 431–4
   German invasion of the Soviet Union 503–7
   Hopkins-Stalin meetings 430–1
   Moscow foreign ministers meetings banquet 452
   Operation Barbarossa 427
   post-WWII alternatives 455–6
   Stalin and Churchill on the Eastern Front 367
   Teheran Conference 274, 445, 449
   Yalta Conference 459
Stalinism 78
Standley, William (US ambassador to Soviet Union) 442, 446
Stark, Leonid (Soviet diplomat) 59, 424
Stein, Boris (Soviet diplomat) 104, 132–3, 182
Stettinius, Edward, Jr. (Lend-Lease administrator) 439
Stimson, Henry (US Secretary of State) 150, 154, 155, 156, 157–8, 496
Stinnes, Hugo (German industrialist) 181
Stomoniakov, Boris (Litvinov's colleague) 100, 418–19, 502
Stresa Conference (1932) 249–51,
Stresa Conference (1936) 293–5
Stresemann, Gustav (German Foreign Minister) 82, 179–80, 181, 183

Sudetenland 320–1, 324, 330, 331
  see also Munich agreement (1938)
Sulzberger, Cyrus Leo (US journalist and
  author) 411, 444, 459
Sumner Welles, Benjamin (US Under
  Secretary of State)
    on Churchill 484
    commission into Nazi atrocities 477
    Japanese invasion of Manchuria 157–8
    on Litvinov 286, 443, 474, 475, 484
    Soviet Embassy celebrations of the
      anniversary of the Russian Revolution 435,
      439
Sun Yat-sen (leader of Kuomintang) 141, 143

Suritz, Jacob (Soviet ambassador to Germany
  and France)
    ambassadorship to France 350
    ambassadorship to Germany 300–2, 309,
      310, 311, 312–13
    death 469
    Litvinov's dismissal 362
    lunches with retired Litvinov 467
    on Stalin 425–6
Symons, Julian (poet) 377

T

Taylor, A. J. P. (historian) 155, 208
Teheran Conference (1943) 274, 445, 449
Teschen, Polish annexation of 323, 333
Thatcher, Margaret 109, 496
Third International *see* Comintern (or Third
  International)
Thomson, Basil (British police officer) 26
Thorne, Christopher (historian) 156
Thorne, Will (British MP) 6
Timoshenko, Semyon (Soviet Defence
  Commissar) 374, 504, 505
Tippelskirch, Werner von (German diplomat)
  360
Tito, Marshal Josip Broz 330
Titulescu, Nicolae (Rumanian ambassador to
  UK) 169
Tompson, Basil (British police officer) 26
Toynbee, Arnold (historian) 160, 320
Trollope, Anthony, Litvinov's appreciation of
  14

Trotsky, Leon
    5th Congress of the Russian Social
      Democratic Labour Party 5
    assessment of 91–4
    Brest-Litovsk Treaty 28–30
    on British-Soviet relations 205
    Buchanan on 24
    Chicherin's London arrest and release 16
    collectivisation 240
    confiscation of Church property 51
    on the defence of Petrograd (1919) 41, 91
    downfall 90–1, 413
    exile 426
    industrial efficiency drive 74–5
    Ivy Litvinov's view of 80
    Karakhan on his attack of the Czechs 258
    Khrushchev on 416
    on Lenin 90–1777
    and Litvinov 80, 91, 92, 93, 100, 240
    Litvinov's letter re. Lockhart 18, 20
    and the Mensheviks 4
    Rapallo Treaty 68, 92, 94
    Russian-Polish War (1920) 48–9, 93
    on Stalin 91
    US-Soviet relations 257, 262, 263–4, 267
    on world revolution 177
Troyanovsky, Alexander (Soviet ambassador to
  USA) 78, 272
Trukhamovskii (Soviet Historian) 491
Truman, Harry 459
Tucker, Robert (historian) 492
Tukhachevskii, Mikhail (Soviet Commander-
  in-Chief) 303, 416–17, 418
Turkey 308, 452–3
Twardowski, Fritz von (German diplomat) 302

U

Ukraine
    famine relief 55
    Germany's territorial ambitions 190, 193,
      278, 310–11
    Polish invasion of (1920) 48
    WWI and Civil War 30, 39, 45
    WWII 432, 489
Ulam, Adam B. (historian) 444–5
Umansky, Konstantin (Soviet ambassador to
  US) 435, 438, 447

United Kingdom
Abyssinia 296–7, 298, 391
and the Anschluss 319
Atlantic Charter 436
British-Russian relations 17–18
British-Soviet relations
    1921 British-Soviet Trade Agreement
      178, 202, 227, 249
    1924 British-Soviet commercial treaty
      207
    1927 ARCOS affair 84, 90, 146, 151,
      214–17
    1930 Lena Goldfields affair 210, 224
    1933 Metro-Vickers incident 129, 227–8,
      254, 410, 478
    1943 British-Soviet protocol 452
    British-Soviet relations (1919-22) 27–8,
      97–8, 166, 168, 195–203
    British-Soviet relations (1922-27) 203–17
    British-Soviet relations (1928-37) 89,
      217–30, 289–93, 303, 315–16, 337–9
    British-Soviet relations (1938-41) 343–7,
      349, 352, 355, 362–3, 365, 372, 430–1
    and the Comintern 85, 92, 195–6, 224
    recognition of the Soviet Union 76, 96,
      167, 206–8
    Soviet tripartite agreement proposals 347–
      50, 363, 365
Czechoslovakia 322–8
disarmament
    Disarmament Preparatory Commission
      (1927-28) 104–5
    Ramsay Macdonald's disarmament plan
      131–5, 139
General Strike (1926) 84, 97, 210–11, 212–
  13, 217
Independent Labour Party 8, 10, 12
Japanese invasion of Manchuria 155–8, 160–
  1
Kellogg-Briand Pact 110–11
Labour Leader 9, 10, 20–2
Labour Party and Stalin 225
Labour Party Conference (1918) and
  Kerensky's address 31–4
Labour Party Conference (1918) and
  Litvinov's address 22–5

Lend-Lease 442
on Litvinov's definition of aggression 130
Litvinov's funeral 469–70
Locarno Treaty 81–4
Munich agreement 325, 327, 328, 329, 331–
  2, 341–2
Mussolini 383–4
and Nazi Germany 302
Polish-British relations 343–4
Rapallo Treaty 83–4
Sino-British relations 403
Sino-Japanese war 397–8, 399–400, 401
Spanish Civil War 377–9, 380, 383, 385–9,
  390–1
US and debts moratorium 255
US-UK special relationship 109
WWII
    Battle of Britain 505
    Beaverbrook-Harriman-Stalin talks 431–4
    Second Front issue 448–9
    see also Teheran Conference (1943);
      Yalta Conference (1945)
United States of America
Abyssinia 297
Atlantic Charter 436
British-US relations 109, 138
debts moratorium 254–5, 259
disarmament
    Disarmament Preparatory Commission
      (1927) 118
    Hoover's partial disarmament proposals
      122–4, 125
    Litvinov's call for permanent peace
      commission 138
Franco-US relations 109–10
Hague Conference (1922) 73
Japanese invasion of Manchuria 154, 155,
  156–8, 161
Japanese-US relations 403
Kellogg-Briand Pact 109
League of Nations 277–8
Lend-Lease 397, 403, 439, 442, 454
Marshall Plan 135, 330
Russian/Chinese railway affair 141, 150
Sino-Japanese war 397–8, 400–1
Sino-US relations 396, 403–4
Soviet-US relations

United States of America (cont)
  Lend-Lease 442, 454
  Litvinov on Roosevelt and American
    politics 447–8
  Litvinov's funeral 469
  popularity of the US in the Soviet Union
    140, 435–6, 439–40, 460
  US recognition of the Soviet Union 76–7,
    96, 121, 123, 254, 256, 259–60, 267–75
  US Russian famine relief programme 53–
    8, 140
  US-Soviet relations (1917-22) 38–9, 257–
    62
  US-Soviet relations (1922-37) 262–75
  US-Soviet relations (1939-41) 352, 430–1
  US-Soviet relations (1941-43) and
  Litvinov's ambassadorship 373, 424, 434–
    42, 443–50, 464, 496, 501
  US Communists 196–7
  US press, Litvinov on 410–11, 444
  WWII
    Beaverbrook-Harriman-Stalin talks 431–4
    Madison Square war relief meetings 435–
      6, 439–41
    Pearl Harbour 401, 403, 434, 479, 485
    Second Front issue 438, 448–9
    see also Teheran Conference (1943);
      Yalta Conference (1945)
USSR see Soviet Russia/Soviet Union

V

Vaksberg, Arkady (historian) 423–4, 444
Vandervelde, Émile (Belgian socialist
  politician) 10, 25, 196
Vareikis, Iosif (Soviet politician) 414
Vasilevsky, Aleksandr (Soviet general) 504
Vavilov, Nikolai (Soviet biologist) 419
Versailles, Treaty of (1919)
  British views on 126, 133, 183, 228, 314
  and the Comintern 178–9
  German views on 106, 116
  and Hitler 133, 135, 192, 288, 305
  Litvinov on 183, 314
  and Poland's Western border 180
  and the Rapallo Treaty 177
  Soviet views on 75, 104, 125
  US views on 118, 124, 157, 259

Voikov, Pyotr (Soviet diplomat) 173, 492
Volkogonov, Dmitry (Soviet army officer and
  historian) 78, 79, 371, 493–4
Voroshilov, Kliment (Soviet Commissar for
Defence)
  Bukharin's trial 414
  cleansing of Soviet border areas 499
  destruction of Cathedral of Christ the
    Redeemer 494
  dinner for Bullitt 272
  Kandelaki negotiations 490
  irov's murder 407
  meeting with Stalin on German intentions
    352
  Rapallo Treaty 187
Voroshilov, Kliment (Soviet Commissar for
Defence) (cont)
  Soviet-Finnish war and annihilation of the
    Red Army old guard 504
  Soviet Ukraine 310–11
  Weimar Republic 98
  Zhdanov's public criticism of Litvinov 422
Vorovsky, Vatslav (Soviet diplomat) 43, 85,
  102, 106
Vpered (newspaper) 3
Vyshinsky, Andrei 375, 376, 457, 459, 466,
  501

W

Wallace, Henry A. (US Vice President) 439,
  440
Wallach, Moses (Litvinov's father) 1
Wallhead, Richard Collingham (British MP)
  207
Walters, Francis P. (Secretariat of League of
  Nations and historian)
    on Hitler and the British disarmament plan
      133–4
    Lausanne conference (1922) 73
    on Litvinov and the League of Nations 286
    on Litvinov's power and influence 498
    on the Russo-Polish war (1920) 120
    on the Soviet Unions' change of attitude
      towards the League of Nations 278
    on the Soviet Union's disenchantment with
      the League of Nations 334

Walters Francis P (cont)
   on the Soviet Union's will to fight fascist
     aggression 328
   Spanish Civil War and the withdrawal of
     foreign volunteers 392
   see also League of Nations
Washington Conference (1921-22) 61, 115
Watson, Derek (historian) 315, 351, 408, 446,
   502, 503
Weinstein, Gregory (Soviet diplomat) 203–5
Weissman, Benjamin (author) 58
Weizsacker, Ernst von (German diplomat) 104,
   182, 345, 369
Wells, Audrey (historian) 215–16
Wells, H. G., photographed with Tanya
   Litvinov 476
Werth, Alexander (British journalist and
   author) 466
Wheeler-Bennett, John (historian) 327
Wiehl, Emile (German official) 334–5
Williams, J. H. (British trade unionist) 35
Willkie, Wendell (US presidential candidate)
   438
Willm, Madam (French barrister) 7
Wilson, Hugh (US diplomat) 138
Wilson, Woodrow 39, 44, 257–9, 261, 448
Winterton, Edward Turnour, Earl (British
   Cabinet Minister) 327–8
Wirth, Joseph (German politician and writer)
   65
Wolkoff, Admiral Nikolai (Russian Provisional
   Government naval attaché) 26
Wolscht, Theodor (German student) 181
World Economic Conference (1927) 86–8, 278
World Economic Conference (1933) 190, 251–
   6
Wrangel, Pyotr (Russian White general) 41
WWI
   Allies' intervention in Russia 38–9
   Paris Peace Conference (1919) 38, 44, 46, 48
   prisoner exchange agreement 198–9
   Russia's peace proposals 42–3, 44–5
   and the socialist movement 9, 175–6
   Socialist parties of the Entente countries
     conference (1915) 10–14
   Treaty of Brest-Litovsk (1918) 23–4, 27–30,
     49, 64–5, 97, 257, 480

   see also Genoa Conference (1922); Hague
     Conference (1922); Rapallo, Treaty of
     (1922); Versailles, Treaty of (1919);
     Washington Conference (1921-22)
WWII
   Allies' invasion of Sicily 449
   Atlantic Charter 436, 451
   Battle of Berlin 459
   Battle of Britain 505
   Battle of the Atlantic 449
   Beaverbrook-Harriman-Stalin talks 431–4
   Casablanca Conference (1943) 449
   France's defeat 366–7
   German attack on Moscow 430
   German defeat at Kursk 445–6
   German invasion of the Soviet Union 503–7
   Hopkins-Stalin meetings 430–1
WWII
   Lend-Lease 397, 403, 439, 442, 454
   Moscow foreign ministers meetings 451–3
   Nuremberg War Crime Trials 410
   Operation Barbarossa (1941) 375, 376, 424,
     427–30, 458
   Operation Overlord (1944) 449, 451
   Pearl Harbour 401, 403, 434, 479, 485
   Polish casualties 329
   San Francisco Conference (1945) 459
   Second Front issue 344–5, 367, 438, 448–9
   Special Commission on the post-war order
     (1944-45) 453–6
   Teheran Conference (1943) 274, 445, 449
   Yalta Conference (1945) 459
   see also Munich agreement; Nazi-Soviet
     Pact

Y

Yagoda, Genrikh (NKVD chief) 406
Yakir, Iona (Soviet general) 414, 415
Yakovlev, Aleksandr (Soviet politician and
   historian) 408
Yalta Conference (1945) 459
Yezhov, Nikolai (NKVD chief))406, 414, 499
Yudenich, Nikolai (Russian White general) 46
Yugoslavia 249, 470

Yurenev, Konstantin (Soviet ambassador to
   Germany) 313

Z

Zaporozhets, Ivan (Leningrad NKVD deputy head) 406–7

Zhdanov, Andrei (Chairman of the Supreme Soviet)375, 401–2, 407, 420–3, 458, 494

Zhukov, Georgy (Soviet army commander) 402, 465, 490, 493, 496, 503, 505

Zimmern, Alfred (historian) 158

Zinoviev, Grigory 90, 208–10, 213, 215, 382, 413

Zubok, Vladislav (historian) 504